CLASSICAL INDIAN PHILOSOPHY

PETER ADAMSON AND
JONARDON GANERI

CLASSICAL INDIAN PHILOSOPHY

a history of philosophy without any gaps, volume 5

OXFORD
UNIVERSITY PRESS

OXFORD
UNIVERSITY PRESS

Great Clarendon Street, Oxford, OX2 6DP,
United Kingdom

Oxford University Press is a department of the University of Oxford.
It furthers the University's objective of excellence in research, scholarship,
and education by publishing worldwide. Oxford is a registered trade mark of
Oxford University Press in the UK and in certain other countries

First Edition published in 2020

Impression: 1

Published in the United States of America by Oxford University Press
198 Madison Avenue, New York, NY 10016, United States of America

British Library Cataloguing in Publication Data
Data available

Library of Congress Control Number: 2019945432

ISBN 978–0–19–885176–9

Printed and bound in Great Britain by
Clays Ltd, Elcograf S.p.A.

CONTENTS

PART II THE AGE OF THE *SŪTRA*

PART III BUDDHISTS AND JAINAS

NOTE ON PRONUNCIATION

This note follows M. Coulson, *Sanskrit: An Introduction to the Classical Language* (London: 1976), 4–19, where a very detailed explanation can be found.

Vowel sounds. The short "a" in Sanskrit (written "a" with no diacritical mark), sounds like the English vowel "u" in "but" or "duck," which is why we have English renderings of words like "pundit" and "Punjab." The long "a" (written "ā") is completely open, as in "father." There are long and short versions of the other vowels, with "i" as in "pin" and "ī" as in "fee," "u" as in "put" but "ū" as in "boo," "e" as in "made" and "ai" as in "bite," and finally "o" as in "rope" but "au" as in "found." There is also a vowel "ṛ", usually pronounced as if "ri," thus *Ṛg-veda* is pronounced "*Rigveda.*"

Consonant sounds. Consonants are classified as voiceless or voiced, unaspirated or aspirated, and there are five types, velar, palatal, retroflex, dental, and labial (see the excellent interactive chart at https://ubcsanskrit.ca/lesson1/devanāgarī.html). The voiceless stops are "k," "c," "ṭ," "t," and "p," pronounced as in "kill," "chill," "try," French "tout," and "pill." The retroflex "ṭ" is made with the tongue against the front of the roof of the mouth rather than against the teeth. The aspirated versions of these stops are written as "kh," "ch," "ṭh," "th," and "ph." Note that the "h" indicates aspiration only, and so they are not pronounced as in "thin" or "physics," but simply as before but now with an outbreath. The unaspirated voiced stops (voiced because pronounced with a vibration of the vocal chord) are "g," "j," "ḍ," "d," and "b," and they closely resemble their English equivalents. These too have aspirated versions, "gh," "jh," "ḍh," "dh," and "bh," pronounced with both vibrating vocal chord and outbreath.

Nasals. There are five nasal sounds in Sanskrit, one for each of the five consonant groups mentioned before. They are transliterated as "ṅ," "ñ," "ṇ," "n," and "m." Thus "aṅga" sounds like English "hunger" without the "h," while "pañca" sounds like "puncher."

There are four unaspirated semi-vowels, "ya," "ra," "la," and "va." Of these, "va" is somewhere between English "v" and "w."

There are three sibilants, palatal "śa," retroflex "ṣa," and dental "sa." The dental "sa" is most similar to English "s," palatal "śa" sounds like "sh" as in "ship," and the retroflex "ṣa" is, as before, made with the tongue against the front of the roof of the mouth.

The last pure sound we will mention here is the voiced version of unvoiced English aspirant "h." So in "hata," meaning "killed," the "h" involves both outbreath and voicing. When unvoiced, it is written with a special sign called a visarga (which in Devanāgarī looks like a colon) and occurs only at the end of a syllable.

Finally, the common conjunct sound "jña" is usually pronounced "gya" (as in "jñāna," "knowledge").

PREFACE

This book wasn't supposed to exist. When the *History of Philosophy Without Any Gaps* was launched as a podcast series, which became the basis of this series of books, the intention was to begin with ancient Greek thought and cover its reception in later European history as well as the Islamic world. This is the project embodied by the four books published so far, on *Classical Philosophy*, *Philosophy in the Hellenistic and Roman Worlds*, *Philosophy in the Islamic World*, and *Medieval Philosophy*. But as a number of listeners to the podcast rightly pointed out, this version of the project was too narrow. How can a series claim to cover philosophy "without any gaps" without dealing with India and China? The book you are holding in your hands (or the "book" you are reading on a screen) represents a step towards a more genuinely comprehensive history of philosophy. The aim is now to cover philosophy in all historical periods and in all cultures. It's an ambition that will presumably never be realized fully. But in hopes of coming as close as possible the series' original author, Peter Adamson, is joining forces with several collaborators who will bring expertise on philosophical traditions from around the world.

Writing a truly global history of philosophy means dealing with a wide range of cultures that did not use the originally Greek word "philosophy" or produce texts that can easily be categorized as "philosophical works." To include, say, African oral traditions[1] or Native American belief systems in a history of philosophy means being open to the idea that unusual bodies of evidence may be of interest to the historian of philosophy, for instance reports of traditional sayings or tales rather than discursive, argumentative treatises. In truth, ancient India does not really present us with that sort of challenge. You could have a very narrow, restrictive definition of philosophy and still find that there is plenty of material from India that satisfies this definition. There is no lack of written sources to consult, stretching back indeed to some of the earliest texts from any culture in the form of the Vedas. And as you can see by merely skimming through this volume or even just perusing the table of contents, all the main areas of philosophy were explicitly addressed and made the subject of detailed dialectical debate. Particularly prominent are issues within epistemology, philosophy of language, and the philosophy of mind, but we'll also be looking at texts devoted to ethics, metaphysics, and more.

Not infrequently, we'll be coming across ideas within these various departments of philosophy that resonate with European thought. This is rather reassuring. The fact that thinkers of India wound up independently exploring some of the same options that emerged in Europe suggests that philosophical reflection tends to converge on a certain range of questions and answers, regardless of cultural motivation and background.[2] Then again, it would be somewhat disappointing if Indian philosophy were just a duplicate of European philosophy, but in other languages. In that case we could save ourselves the trouble of dealing with texts in Sanskrit, Pāli, and other Indian tongues. (Or alternatively, we could just study Indian philosophy and forget about the Greeks and their legacy. After all, learning ancient Greek, Arabic, Latin, and so on is no picnic either.) Happily, we will also find that India offers many distinctive ideas, exploring problems that may seem unfamiliar to students of "Western" philosophy and offering different answers to familiar questions.

Before moving on to the rest of the book, we owe you a few warnings. Despite the "without any gaps" slogan, it will not offer exactly the same kind of coverage found in other installments of the series. For instance, the recently published volume devoted to medieval philosophy looks at a larger number of figures and texts, and more or less in chronological order. Here, we instead organize the discussion mostly in terms of schools, not as a thinker-by-thinker or generation-by-generation narrative. This makes sense given the nature of the material, and not only because dating figures and texts is often difficult. Authors often felt strong allegiance to one movement and opposed others, and foundational texts typically need to be read together with later commentaries to make them comprehensible. In this respect our approach is more like the one taken with Hellenistic philosophy in an earlier volume.

We also need to be modest about the extent to which our discussion in this book really does avoid gaps. We are covering a vast chronological and intellectual terrain here, and aim to provide readers with a philosophically informed guide to that terrain, rather than something on the order of an encyclopedia, where every known thinker gets a mention. It must also be said that the state of scholarship on ancient Indian thought is not comparable to, say, ancient Greek philosophy, where nearly all texts are well edited and reliably translated, and have been made the object of extensive secondary literature. In comparison, the study of Indian philosophy is only at its beginning. Still, one should not be too pessimistic. Though much remains to be done, there is plenty of good work on Indian philosophy, and this book will hopefully offer readers a way into that body of literature.[3]

As in other volumes of the series, we do adhere to the "without any gaps" approach by touching on a broader range of topics and treatises than you'll find in other introductions to the topic. Thus we will be tackling such diverse themes as Sanskrit grammar, attitudes towards gender, Āyurvedic medicine, cosmological conceptions of time, Tantric ritual, and classical Indian theater. (In pursuing the last two themes, we venture into chronologically later figures than those covered in the rest of the book, which is why these two chapters have been placed in the final section.) In part we cast a wider net simply in order to take up issues of intrinsic philosophical interest, but these chapters are also intended to show how ideas found in more strictly philosophical texts penetrated throughout Indian society. More generally, we hope that readers will come away from the book with an appreciation of the place of philosophy within Indian history, as well as the place of Indian culture within the history of philosophy.

ACKNOWLEDGEMENTS

We would firstly like to thank the experts who agreed to appear as interview guests on the podcast series: Brian Black, Amber Carpenter, Monima Chadha, Francis Clooney, Jessica Frazier, Elisa Freschi, Rupert Gethin, Marie-Hélène Gorisse, Ujjwala Jha, V.N. Jha, Philipp Maas, Kit Patrick, Graham Priest, and Jan Westerhoff. These scholars were also generous with their suggestions and feedback for the book; we are also grateful for advice offered by several other colleagues mentioned in the notes to the chapters below, and for useful feedback from two anonymous referees who read the manuscript for the press. For the production of the podcast series on India, we are thankful to Andreas Lammer and Bethany Somma, as well as to Julian Rimmer for maintaining the website. We also thank Peter Momtchiloff from Oxford University Press for his continued shepherding of this book series.

Finally, Peter Adamson would as always like to record his gratitude to his family for their love and support: his parents, brother Glenn, wife Ursula, and children Sophia and Johanna. Jonardon Ganeri would like to thank all the students who bravely took his Indian Philosophy classes at King's College London over many years.

TIMELINE

Author	Date	Best-Known Work
Origins: Philosophies of Path and Purpose		
Uddālaka, Yājñavalkya, Śāṇḍilya, et al.	*circa* (hereafter *c.*) 7th–6th cent. BCE	*Views Recorded in Bṛhadāraṇyaka and Chāndogya Upaniṣad*
Mahāvīra Jina	*c.*599–527 BCE	*Views Recorded in the Āgama*
The Buddha	566–486/480–400 BCE	*Views Recorded in the Nikāya*
Payāsi, Makkali Gosāla, Ajita Kesakambala, et al.	*c.*5th–4th cent. BCE	*Views Recorded in the Nikāya*
	5th–1st cent. BCE	*Later Upaniṣads*
Kauṭilya	*c.*370–283 BCE	*Arthaśāstra*
Moggalaputra Tissa	*c.*240 BCE	*Kathāvatthu*
"Vyāsa"	200 BCE–200 CE	*Mahābhārata*
Patañjali	*c.*150 BCE	*Mahābhāṣya*
	within (hereafter w.) 100 BCE–50 CE	*Milinda-pañhā*
The Age of the Sūtra: Philosophy Before Dignāga		
Jaimini	w.250 BCE–50 CE	*Mīmāṃsā-sūtra*
Bādarāyaṇa	w.250 BCE–50 CE	*Brahma-sūtra*
Kaṇāda/Ulūka	w.0–250	*Vaiśeṣika-sūtra*
Gautama/Akṣapāda	w.150–250	*Nyāya-sūtra*
Nāgārjuna	w.100–250	*Mūlamadhyamaka-kārikā*
"Manu"	w.100–300	*Mānava-dharma-śāstra*
Āryadeva	w.180–280	*Catuḥśataka*
"Kundakunda"	w.200–400	[many attributed]
Śabara	w.200–400	*Mīmāṃsāsūtra-bhāṣya*
Patañjali	w.325–425	*Pātañjala-yoga-śāstra*
Īśvarakṛṣṇa	*c.*400	*Sāṃkhya-kārikā*
Asaṅga	*c.*340–420	*Yogācārabhūmi*

(continued)

Author	Date	Best-Known Work
Vasubandhu	c.350–430	*Abhidharmakośa-bhāṣya*
Umāsvati	c.400	*Tattvārthādhigama-bhāṣya*
Buddhaghosa	w.400–500	*Visuddhi-magga*
"Tiruvaḷḷuvar"	w.400–600	*Tirukkuṟaḷ*
Vātsyāyana	c.450	*Nyāya-bhāṣya*
Bhartṛhari	w.400–500	*Vākyapadīya*
The Age of Dialogue: A Sanskrit Cosmopolis		
Dignāga	480–540	*Pramāṇa-samuccaya*
Praśastapāda	530	*Padārthadharmasaṃgraha*
Cīttalai Cāttaṉār	w.500–600	*Maṇimēkalai*
Bhāviveka	c.500–570	*Madhyamakahṛdaya*
Sthiramati	c.500–570	commentaries on Asaṅga and Vasubandhu
Samantabhadra	530–590	*Āpta-mīmāṃsā*
Candrakīrti	600?	*Prasannapadā*
Uddyotakara	540–600	*Nyāya-vārttika*
Kumārila Bhaṭṭa	540–600	*Śloka-vārttika*
Dharmakīrti	550–610	*Pramāṇa-vārttika*
Prabhākara ("Guru")	c.600	*Bṛhatī*
Śāntideva	w.690–790	*Bodhicaryāvatāra; Śikṣāsamuccaya*
Maṇḍana Miśra	c.700	*Brahmasiddhi; Bhāvanāviveka; Sphoṭasiddhi*
Siddhasena Mahāmati	710–770	*Nyāyāvatāra*
"Bṛhaspati" (Purandara?)	w.700–800	*Cārvāka-sūtra*
Śaṅkara (-ācārya)	flourished (hereafter fl.) 710	*Brahma-sūtra-bhāṣya;* commentaries on the Upaniṣads
Akalaṅka	c.720–780	*Laghīyastraya*
Śāntarakṣita	725–788	*Tattvasaṃgraha*
Haribhadra Sūri	fl. 770	*Ṣaḍdarśana-samuccaya*
Uṃveka	730–790	*Tātparyaṭīkā*
Dharmottara	740–800	commentaries on Dharmakīrti
Kamalaśīla	740–795	*Tattvasaṃgraha-pañjikā; Bhāvanākrama*

The Age of Disquiet		
Jayarāśi	c.800–840	*Tattvopaplavasiṃha*
Bhaṭṭa Udbhaṭa	c.850	comm. on *Cārvāka-sūtra*
Jayanta Bhaṭṭa	fl. 880–890	*Nyāya-mañjarī*
Utpaladeva	c.925–975	*Īśvarapratyabhijñākārikā-vivṛtti*
Bhāsarvajña	c.950	*Nyāya-bhūṣaṇa*
	c.925–975	*Mokṣopāyaśāstra*
Vācaspati Miśra	fl. 960	polymath
Anuruddha	10th cent.?	*Abhidhammatthasaṅgaha*
Bhaṭṭa Rāmakaṇṭha	c.950–1000	commentaries on Sadyojyotiḥ
Śrīdhara	fl. 990	*Nyāyakaṇḍalī*
Jñānaśrīmitra	c.975–1025	*Apohaprakaraṇa*; *Īśvaradūṣaṇa*
Abhinavagupta	950–1020	*Tantrāloka*; *Vivṛtivimarśinī*
Udayana (-ācārya)	c.1000	*Kiraṇāvali*; *Ātmatattvaviveka*
Ratnakīrti	990–1050	*Kṣaṇabhaṅgasiddhi*; *Santānāntaradūṣaṇa*
Prabhācandra	980–1065	*Prameyakamalamārtaṇḍa*
Pārthasārathi Miśra	1050–1120	*Nyāyaratnamālā*; *Śāstradīpikā*
Rāmānuja	w.1017–1137	*Śrībhāṣya*
Hemacandra	1088–1173	*Pramāṇa-mīmāṃsā*
Vijñāneśvara	w.1100–1200	*Mitākṣarā*
Śrīharṣa	w.1100–1200	*Khaṇḍaṇakhaṇḍakhādya*
Vasiṣṭha	1200	*Yogavāsiṣṭha*
Citsukha	1225–1284	*Tattvapradīpikā*
Madhva (-ācārya)	1238–1317	[many]
Veṅkaṭanātha ["Vedānta Deśika"]	1269–1370	commentaries on Rāmānuja, etc.
Philosophy from Gaṅgeśa		
Gaṅgeśa (-upādhyāya)	c.1325	*Tattvacintāmaṇi*
Vardhamāna	c.1350	commentaries. on Udayana
Mādhava Vidyāraṇya	1297–1388	*Jaiminīyanyāyamālā*; *Jīvanmukiviveka*
Ceṇṇibhaṭṭa	c.1350	*Sarvadarśanasaṃgraha*
Jayatīrtha	1343–1388	commentaries on Madhva; *Pramāṇapaddhati*

(continued)

Author	Date	Best-Known Work
"Kapila"	w.1300–1500	*Sāṃkhya-sūtra*
Śaṃkara Miśra	1430	*Bhedaratna; Vādavinoda*
Vācaspati Miśra II	1440	*Khaṇḍanoddhāra; Tattvāloka*
Pragalbha	1470	commentaries on Śrīharṣa, Gaṅgeśa, etc.
Jayadeva/Pakṣadhara Miśra	1470	commentaries on Gaṅgeśa etc.
Early Modernity: New Philosophy in India		
Raghunātha Śiromaṇi	c.1460–1540	*-dīdhiti* commentaries; *vādas*
Vyāsatīrtha	1460–1539	*Nyāyāmṛta*
Rūpa Gosvāmin	1470–1550	[many]
Jīva Gosvāmin	1560	[many]
Appayya Dīkṣita	1520–1593	[many]
Madhusūdana Sarasvatī	w.1540–1640	*Gūḍhārthadīpikā; Advaitasiddhi*
Kṛṣṇadāsa Sārvabhauma	c.1550	*Bhāṣā-pariccheda*
Vijñānabhikṣu	c.1550–1600	*Vijñānāmṛtabhāṣya; Sāṃkhyapravacanabhāṣya; Yogavārttika*
Bhaṭṭoji Dīkṣita	1590?	*Śabdakaustubha*
Nīlakaṇṭha Caturdhara	c.1600–1650	*Bhāratabhāvadīpa [on MBh.]*
Rāmabhadra Sārvabhauma	fl. 1610s	commentaries on Raghunātha, etc.
Muḥibballāh Illāhābādī	1587–1648	*al-Tawiya bayna al-ifāda wa'l-qabūl*
Jagadīśa Tarkālaṃkāra	fl. 1600–1620	commentaries on Raghunātha, etc. *Sūkti*
Mullā Maḥmūd al-Jawnpūrī	died (hereafter d.) 1652	*al-Ḥikmat/Shams al-bāligha*
Dārā Śikūh	1615–1659	*Majmaʿ al-baḥrayn*
Khwāja Khwurd	d. 1663	
Jayarāma Nyāyapañcānana	fl. 1650s	*Padārthamālā*
Gadādhara Bhaṭṭācārya	c.1604–1709	commentaries on Raghunātha, etc.; *vādas*
Raghudeva Nyāyālaṃkāra	fl. 1650s	*vādas; vicāras; Dravyasārasaṃgraha*; comm. on Śrīharṣa; etc.

Yaśovijaya Gaṇi	1624–1688	[many]
Muḥibballāh al-Bihārī	d. 1707	*Sullam al-ʿulūm*
Mahādeva Puṇatāmakara	fl. 1670–96	*Nyāyakaustubha*
Ḥabīb Allāh Patnah-ī	d. 1728	
Kamāluddīn Sihālwī	d. 1760	*al-ʿUrwā al-wuṯqā*
Abd Alī Baḥr al-Ulūm	d. 1810	*al-ʿUjāla al-nāfiʿ*
Rāmamohana Raya	1772–1833	*Tuḥfat al-muwaḥḥidīn*
Freedom and Identity on the Eve of Independence		
Hiralal Haldar	1865–1942	*Neo-Hegelianism*
Mohandas Karamchand Gandhi	1869–1948	*Hind Svarāj*
Krishnachandra Bhattacharyya	1875–1949	*The Subject as Freedom; Svarāj in Ideas*
Ramachandra Dattatrya Ranade	1886–1957	*A Constructive Survey of Upaniṣadic Philosophy*
Bhimrao Ramji Ambedkar	1891–1956	*The Buddha and His Dharma*
Jawaharlal Nehru	1889–1964	*The Discovery of India*
Anukulchandra Mukerji	1888–1968	*The Nature of Self*
Mian Mohammed Sharif	1893–1965	*In Search of Truth*
Ghanshamdas Rattanmal Malkani	1892–1977	*Philosophy of the Self*
Ras Vihari Das	1897–1976	*Philosophical Essays; Kanter Darśana*

Source: Reprinted from Jonardon Ganeri (ed.), *The Oxford Handbook of Indian Philosophy*, 'Timeline: Indian Philosophy in a Hundred Thinkers', pp. xix–xxviii, doi: 10.1093/oxfordhb/9780199314621.001.0001.

Abbreviations:

c. = *circa* ("approximately")

w. = probably lived within the interval

fl. = flourished

d. = died

MAP OF INDIA

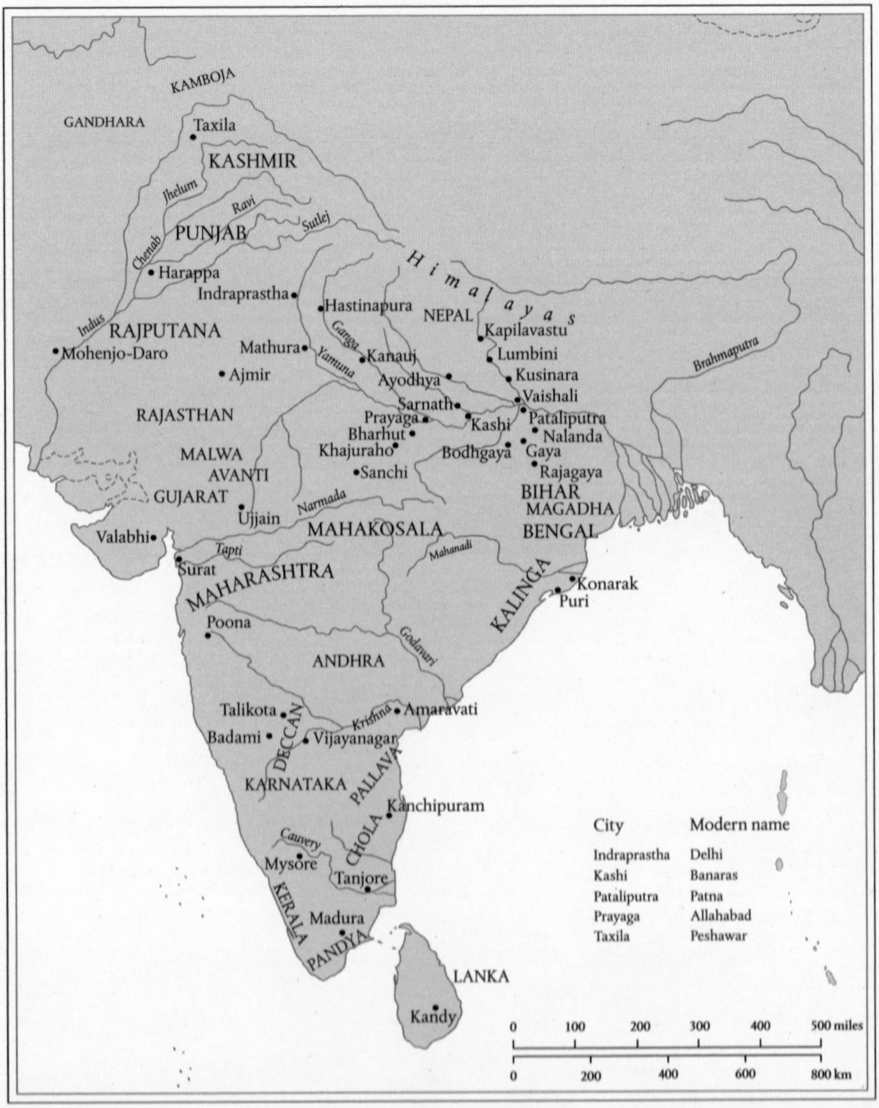

Source: Reprinted from Stanley Wolpert, *A New History of India*, 8th edition, 'Pre-Muslim India, ca. 1200', p. 105. Copyright © 2009, reproduced by permission of Oxford University Press.

PART I

ORIGINS

1

BEGIN AT THE END

AN INTRODUCTION TO PHILOSOPHY IN INDIA

"It is one's self which one should see and hear, and on which one should reflect and concentrate. For by seeing and hearing one's self, and by reflecting and concentrating on oneself, one gains the knowledge of this whole world."[1] In these lines of the *Bṛhadāraṇyaka*, or *Great Forest Upaniṣad*, we are invited, even exhorted, to philosophize. We are promised that an examination of the self (*ātman*) will lead ultimately to an understanding of all things. Neither here nor anywhere else in the Upaniṣads do we find the word "philosophy." No surprise there, as the word *philosophia* is ancient Greek. Accordingly, historians of philosophy mostly restrict their attention to the intellectual traditions that can be traced back to the Greeks. Philosophy was born with the Pre-Socratics, reached maturity with Plato and Aristotle, and was then inherited by the Romans, medievals, and moderns. It has been pursued more or less without interruption for the past two and half millennia in Europe. This is what people mean when they talk about "Western philosophy." Yet the word "philosophy" was known also to the Islamic world, where the so-called *falāsifa* thought of themselves as engaging in the enterprise begun by the Greeks. They presented themselves as successors of Plato and Aristotle, even when they lived far from Europe. The greatest philosopher of the Islamic world was Avicenna, and he hailed from modern-day Afghanistan, which hardly makes him a "Western" philosopher.

It is this broader story, the story of philosophy among cultures that used the word "philosophy,"[2] that has been explored so far in this book series. In the four volumes that have appeared so far, the ideas of thinkers from ancient Greece, the Roman Empire, the Islamic world, and medieval Christendom have been explored "without any gaps." And that story is continuing. But in this book, we'll be looking at a tradition of philosophy that arose in India, and independently of the Greeks' *philosophia*. You might already be wondering, though, whether it really makes sense to speak of "philosophy" in a culture not inspired by the Greek tradition of *philosophia*. To this, our answer would be that India has produced literature bearing all the hallmarks of philosophy as it is standardly understood. We'll be discussing material of philosophical interest in texts as early as the Vedic writings, especially in the Upaniṣads. But it's easier to make the point with works that come along somewhat later. Consider the case of the *Dispeller of Disputes* (*Vigrahavyāvartanī*), written by the radical Buddhist thinker Nāgārjuna in the second century AD (on which see Chapters 36–7). The title promises arguments, and arguments are what you get. Nāgārjuna wants to defend his trademark view that nothing has *svabhāva,* meaning "independent reality." Rather, all things are dependent and relative, or as he would put it, "empty." In a technique as fundamental to Indian philosophy as to the procedures of Aristotle's Lyceum and the medieval universities of Europe, Nāgārjuna sets out criticisms of his own position and then responds to them.

His imagined opponent tries one of the oldest tricks in the philosopher's book, which is to show that Nāgārjuna will refute his theory simply by trying to state it.[3] When Nāgārjuna says "nothing has independent reality," the opponent asks what status this very statement has. After all, if *nothing* has independent reality, then neither can this statement, so the statement itself is "empty." But if it is "empty" then it makes no positive assertion at all. The opponent anticipates that Nāgārjuna may say that the statement is purely negative, since it is a mere denial of existence. But this will not work, since even a denial of existence must itself be something existent. To all this, Nāgārjuna responds by insisting that his statement is not a thesis or proposal of any kind, whether negative or positive. He compares the situation to that of an unreal, magical being trying to block the action of another unreal, magical being. Later we'll get into the question of what sense, if any, Nāgārjuna's response might make. For now, the point is that this is all indisputably philosophy, and of a broadly familiar kind. We have a realist pitted against a skeptic; we have accusations of self-refutation from the realist side; we have the skeptic making careful distinctions between different kinds of speech act, and even inventing creative analogies to bolster his case.

More generally, we find that Indian thought investigates pretty well all the areas and problems central to the history of philosophy as the Greeks conceived it. There are attempts to articulate the foundations of knowledge, and to reduce metaphysical reality to a few fundamental kinds of entity (or, in Nāgārjuna's case, to no entity at all). We find arguments for atomism and for conceptions of time and space. Indian thinkers make developments in logic, and present theories of ethics and political legitimacy. The upshot is that, far from wondering whether there is anything in Indian thought that corresponds to so-called "Western" philosophy, it is often tempting to draw detailed comparisons between individual Indian thinkers and specific philosophers of Greece or later traditions. Again, Nāgārjuna would provide a striking example. As we'll also mention below, he's reminiscent of the equally radical and methodologically scrupulous Sextus Empiricus, a Greek thinker who also lived in the second century AD. Another obvious parallel, and one frequently drawn by scholars, compares the pleasure-loving, materialist Cārvāka school to the Epicureans (see Chapter 32).

Such resonances may, of course, be no coincidence. Didn't Alexander the Great bring his army as far as India? And aren't we told that Greek philosophers like Pyrrho, the original Greek skeptic and inspiration for Sextus Empiricus, traveled east in search of wisdom? The prospect of mutual interaction and influence is an alluring one, to which we will also be devoting some attention (Chapters 47–8). But for the most part, we're going to avoid making constant allusions to philosophy in Europe. Instead, we'll focus on Indian thought as an object of study in its own right, with only occasional comparisons or contrasts to the figures and ideas from the "Western" tradition. Even if its themes and even some of its specific arguments would be at home in philosophy as it is familiar to us from European thought, we should also be open to the idea that India may challenge and expand our notion of what philosophy is, and could be. Think again about that Upaniṣadic exhortation to reflect on the self, in order to know the world. What conception of the self and the world does that imply, what conception of philosophy and its potential? The Upaniṣads do not recommend idle theoretical speculation or technical virtuosity for its own sake. Nor were such abstract goals the driving force in later periods. Even Nāgārjuna's radical skepticism was offered as a means to achieve the core Buddhist goal of avoiding suffering. For Buddhists, the good life is one of detachment from worldly things, and what could lead to detachment from things better than coming to see them as unreal?

That there is a highest good, that this good is a way of living, a kind of human flourishing, and that practicing philosophy is a constitutive part of it, something embedded in the good life—this is not what students are typically told when they show up to study philosophy at modern universities. Yet this tendency may bring Indian philosophy closer to the roots of European philosophy, not further away. Ancient philosophy begins at the end, or at least with a conception of what our end might be. Aristotle called it our *telos*, meaning final end, goal, or purpose of life itself. The French scholar Pierre Hadot has proposed that the Greeks saw philosophy itself as a "way of life," built around what Hadot has called "spiritual exercises."[4] Just as the athlete embarks on a training regime or an invalid takes medicine in hopes of returning to bodily health, so the person in search of wisdom undertakes philosophy, his or her goal being the health of the soul, or the self.

Our opening quote from the Upaniṣads suggests that this idea had some currency in ancient India. If you want to achieve wisdom, it tells us, then begin by reflecting upon your own self. And there is plenty of confirmation in other Indian philosophical literature. For now we'll discuss just one example in more detail: a discussion of the ends of human life, which is found tucked away in four chapters of the *Book of Peace* (*Śānti-parvan*).[5] This is a voluminous work of philosophical reflection found within the even more voluminous Hindu epic, the *Mahābhārata*. The *Book of Peace* attempts to integrate general ethical insights into the moral framework of the epic, so there is good reason to think that it reflects values that were widely shared in ancient Indian culture.

At one point the *Book of Peace* poses the question, what is the "highest good (*niḥśreyasa*)"? Its answer is direct and unequivocal: the highest good is the taming of the self. We must subdue and pacify the self's inclination to reach out to things that are "external" to it, where "external" means both physically exterior and also outside of one's influence. So the taming in question is a pulling back, a drawing in, a restraint. Here one might think of a metaphor found in the *Bhagavad-gītā*, or *Song of the Lord*, another part of the *Mahābhārata*, which tells us to withdraw one's senses as a tortoise withdraws its limbs. Taming the self is a form of self-control. It means replacing fear, anger, and envy with a profound steadiness of mind, with imperturbability in the face of either pain or pleasure (see further Chapter 12). When we "reach out" to things outside the self, we are motivated by greed, by a wish to obtain things that are in fact beyond our control. Thwarted desire and anger are the inevitable results. But with one's greed in check, one lives the life of wise conduct, fearless in the face of death, greeting both pleasure and pain with equanimity, delighting in no acquisition and pained by no loss. To ask what would be the point of such a life is itself pointless. There is no further goal for such a life, such as wealth or fame, because living well is its own reward.

Isn't this ethics of restraint opposed to the sentiment we found in the Upaniṣads? There, we were told to seek knowledge of the self; in the *Book of Peace*, the goal is instead taming or restraining the self. But the clash is only apparent. For the *Book of Peace*, greed goes hand in hand with ignorance. Greed is a failure to understand that none of the things one seeks to obtain is going to last. The greedy person is also ignorant of the nature of his own malady. He always expects to be gratified by that one more bit of wealth or pleasure, not realizing that greed is, of its nature, insatiable. Anger, too, is the result of ignorance, for it is the offspring of greed and the vexation that comes with noticing the faults of others. With knowledge comes forbearance, and tolerance of others.

The *Book of Peace* calls the state of soul recommended here *tapas*, which makes it sound as though enlightenment is available at any good Spanish restaurant. But in fact *tapas* means something like "spiritual austerity." A beautiful metaphor is offered to illustrate it. One who lives wisely and with self-control treads softly upon the earth: "Just as the passage of birds in the sky or of fish in the water leaves no visible trail, he leaves no trail behind him."[6] Admittedly, such a life has the drawback that such a person is regarded by others as weak and simple. Good thing, then, that with self-control and self-knowledge comes tolerance, so that our wise person will forgive the others who look down upon him. Even this downside is no downside at all, or at least not one that will bother the "tamed" one (*dānta*): his state is one of perfect tranquillity (*praśama*).

Appealing though the results may sound, should we be so easily convinced to give up on our desires, our hopes, and our fears? This advice threatens to lead, not just to taming the self, but to extinguishing it altogether. No wonder, we may begin to think, that for some philosophers of India there is only one thing you need to know to understand the self: that there isn't one. Following in the wake of this suspicion is something closer to an accusation. The Indian philosophers, we are told, may have agreed with the Greeks about the existence and uniqueness of a highest good. But where the Greeks located this good in a life of worldly flourishing and virtue, the Indians thought of it as something that lies "outside" of life. Indian thinkers are the "holy naysayers" mocked by Nietzsche in *Thus Spoke Zarathustra*. They believed that mundane living is a condition from which we should flee, and that philosophy is little more than an elaborate escape kit, a mere instrument that helps us to reach this otherwordly end but does not after all form an essential part of it.

But things have changed since Nietzsche. Nowadays, when we hear someone talking about the "distinctively Western" or the "distinctively Indian," we immediately realize—or should realize—that we are in the territory of invention rather than discovery. Contrasts such as the one between the life-affirmers and the world-deniers are just too tidy to have any basis in historical fact. And as we look more closely at the Indian philosophers, we will see that they are not the nihilists and "naysayers" of Nietzsche's imagination. True, a great deal is said about such transcendental spiritual goals as *mokṣa*, *mukti*, and *nirvāṇa*, and these goals are represented as an ultimate, idealized aspiration for all. In practice though, it is the chosen few who have such ends as these. The vast majority of human beings aspire to something less remote. There is no sharp division here between the philosophical traditions of India, China, and Greece. The Chinese and the Greeks (especially the Stoics) likewise thought of the "sage" as having goals of a higher order, remote from anything appropriate to ordinary human beings. Human beings do not aspire actually to become sages. Instead, the otherworldly sage is an ideal to steer by as we pursue goals within this world. Buddhists are not necessarily really trying to become a Buddha, even if thinking of themselves as "trying to become a Buddha" might be a good and effective way to achieve their real goal, which is to lead a good Buddhist life. Striving for a transcendent ideal might itself be a "spiritual exercise," a practice that forms a part of the good for a human being.

In which case it would be a mistake to read the descriptions of the transcendental states and the means to reach them as if they were literal expressions of a path from the world of men to the world of the gods. This helps to explain the fact that the ideal states of Indian thought are often described in negative, even unappealing terms. We are promised a life free from pain, free from suffering, free from anger and desire, and often free from pleasure too. European readers have frequently struggled with the idea of aiming for an existence that is so colorless, a life little better than that of an amoeba. Perhaps the very fact that the ideal states are described in such unappealing terms shows us that these are not really intended as descriptions of the good for human beings. We should instead ask: how does the idea of striving to achieve such a state help one make progress? And what exactly is the attainable goal toward which one progresses, as one pursues this frankly unattainable goal? Might it be that reflecting on a life entirely devoid of both pleasure and pain will help us to re-examine pleasure and pain themselves? One might be led to be wary of pleasures, rather than to avoid them altogether, so that one builds one's life around something other than the pursuit of pleasure. If I genuinely believe that the ideal state involves no pleasure at all, I am apt to allow myself to be nourished by the pleasures I do have without being distracted from my other goals by the need to seek out new pleasures. In other words, I may come to lead a life of restraint and self-control.

2

SCRIPTURES, SCHOOLS, AND SYSTEMS

A HISTORICAL OVERVIEW

The fact that philosophy was pursued as a "way of life" in ancient India, just as in classical Greece, makes it tempting to treat the two intellectual cultures in parallel. But when you consider the geographical size of India, its population, and the fact that Indian culture outlived that of the ancient Greeks and Romans, a different comparison may seem more legitimate. Try thinking of the history of philosophy in India as analogous to the *entire* history of philosophy in Europe. European philosophy has featured a bewildering range of periods and sub-periods, long-running debates and sudden paradigm shifts, dozens of major figures and countless minor figures, many of whom remain poorly studied—and in approaching philosophy in India, we should set our expectations to a similar scale. Then, too, just as in European philosophy, the relevant texts have been composed in many languages, including Pāli, Prakrit, Sanskrit, Malayalam, Gujarati, Tamil, Telugu, Marathi, Persian, Arabic, Urdu, Bengali, Kannada, Punjabi, Hindi, Tibetan, and Assamese. From the time of the British colonial occupation, it has also been written in English. Indian philosophy spans religious divides, with Hinduism, Buddhism, Jainism, and Islam being only the most dominant faiths.

To cover all of this material "without any gaps" would be a daunting task indeed. It would call for an ecumenical approach, drawing from different languages, regions, and religious cultures, inclusive of dissenters, heretics, and skeptics, of philosophical ideas in thinkers not themselves primarily philosophers. It would look past India's northwestern borders with the Arabic and Persianate world, its northeastern boundaries with Tibet and China, or the southern and eastern shores that link it with lands of Theravāda Buddhism today. And it would begin with the earliest texts of the Indian tradition, and carry on the story down to the twentieth century. We are not going to attempt all of that in the present book, though. Apart from a few forays into later developments as we pursue specific themes (for instance in chapters on aesthetics and on Tantra, both of which will feature the tenth-century Śaivite philosopher Abhinavagupta), we will press on only as far as the revolutionary Buddhist thinker Dignāga, who died in the middle of the sixth century AD. Since we'll be beginning with the Upaniṣads and other developments from the middle of the first millennium BC, this means we will cover at least the first thousand years or so of the history of Indian philosophy.

One might be tempted to label that timespan as the "ancient" period of Indian thought. Actually, this would go along with the first temptation, since speaking of a "ancient" period would underline the parallel between India and Greece. But the term "ancient" is problematic with respect to the Indian tradition, because of the exceptional longevity and continuity of that tradition when contrasted with other classical civilizations. So unlike Oscar Wilde, who could resist everything except temptation, we're going to insist on a different way of dividing up India's intellectual past, one that isn't borrowed from a history of Western civilization.[1] We'll take our cue from the ideas already sketched in the opening chapter, by devoting the first part of the book to texts and ideas that emerged roundabout the eighth century BC up to the second century AD. This was a time for philosophies of path and purpose, when philosophy was seen as a way of life and a vehicle through which one could achieve liberation or release from suffering.

Our story will begin with the ancient wisdom of the Vedas, which were actually set down well before even our earliest period began. Apparently the embodiment of the beliefs of a group of people who called themselves the Āryans, the Vedas offer prescriptions for ritual practice. They are seen as the ultimate source of the religion we call Hinduism.[2] As we'll see, the Vedas contain passages that reward philosophical reflection. Such reflection began early on, with the Upaniṣads, beautiful and majestic works that comment on and extrapolate from the Vedic texts in the process articulating the unity of humanity, ritual, and cosmos. And speaking of majestic, this was also the period which gave us the grand Hindu epic, the *Mahābhārata*, some ten times as long as the *Iliad* and the *Odyssey* combined. It contains, as a sort of inserted interlude, a famous discourse between two of its characters known as the *Song of the Lord*, or *Bhagavad-gītā*. The *Gītā* has justly been the subject of a great deal of attention, but we shouldn't overlook the interesting philosophy to be found elsewhere in the epic.

Indian philosophical culture was not monolithic, but marked by disagreement and diversity—again, just like European philosophy. This is already illustrated by our early period, as two schools of thought arose to challenge the values and beliefs of the Vedas and the literature that grew up around them. One of these two schools was Buddhism. The Buddha himself probably lived after the earliest of the Upaniṣads had already been written. Our phrase "philosophies of path and purpose" is in part inspired by him. The last of his four Noble Truths is called the "truth of the path," with the path leading from suffering to *nirvāṇa*, a state of health in which one is free from spiritual as well as physical pain. This goal of liberation was shared by the Jaina school, famous for its ethic of absolute non-violence. Though these two schools already feature in the early period, they will be with us throughout our story, as both Buddhism and Jainism divide into various sub-traditions and produce ever more sophisticated and disputatious texts, displaying the rivalry that existed both within and between schools of thought.

Before moving on to the next stage in the development of Indian thought, we should warn you that this whole narrative has more uncertain dates than a junior high school dance. Precise chronology for specific thinkers and texts is rarely, if ever, available. Usually the best one can hope for is a firm relative chronology: if one text directly cites another, we know it is later than the text from which it quotes. But often not even relative chronologies are possible. Compounding this difficulty is the fact that attaching an author's name to a text is tricky business. Many of the writings we'll discuss are compilations that were edited and re-edited over a long period of time, and the authors traditionally assigned to them may be no more than literary fictions. Then, too, a text may be attributed to a famous philosopher as a way to give it extra clout.

Even the date of the Buddha is controversial.[3] Tradition teaches that he died in 486 BC at the age of 80. Modern scholarship is pushing his date forward, though, perhaps to somewhere around 400 BC or even later. On the other hand a recent excavation of the Mahā Devī temple at his historical birthplace, Lumbini, has unearthed evidence suggesting that the traditional date may be correct after all. Only time will tell; or maybe it won't. Whenever it was that he lived, it was an interesting time from a philosophical point of view, and the records of his life contain colorful reports of a whole host of unusual and unconventional thinkers. One of them was the founder of Jainism, Mahāvīra, who lived perhaps a little earlier, and who like the Buddha espoused values alternative to those of the typical householder.

We see attempts to meet that challenge in a second period, which we will call the "Age of the Sūtra." With the aforementioned caveats in mind, and mostly for the sake of giving you some dates to bear in mind, we'll say that this period runs from about 100 BC until AD 350. If you've read the other books in this series, you may find it helpful to notice that our first period, the time of the Upaniṣads, *Mahābhārata*, and the emergence of Buddhism and Jainism, is contemporaneous with the Pre-Socratics, Plato, and Aristotle, and the rise of the Hellenistic schools. Our second period, the Age of the Sūtra, would be roughly contemporary with the revival of

Platonism and Aristotelianism and carry on through the lifetimes of men like Plotinus and Augustine. For those who are not so steeped in ancient European philosophy, it may be more useful if we say that the first period overlaps with classical Greece and the Roman Republic, while the Age of the Sūtra would be contemporary with the Roman Empire up to the time of Christianization under Constantine.

The term *sūtra* means "thread," and a *sūtra* is both a single philosophical aphorism and a text comprising an entire collection of such aphorisms. While such texts may at first glance seem rather disparate and lacking in unity—more tangle than tapestry—the Age of the Sūtra was in fact a period of system-building. We see this not so much with the *sūtras* themselves as with the commentaries written upon them. Such a commentary, called a *bhāṣya,* would set out to construct a systematic body of concepts, weaving the threads into a single cloth. Those who composed the first *bhāṣyas*—like Śabara, Vātsyāyana, and Śaṅkara, to name but three of the commentators—became the founders and in some cases even namesakes of long-lived philosophical traditions. It's right about here that people usually speak of the "six systems of Indian philosophy" that emerged from literature devoted to the *sūtras.* These six systems are Sāṃkhya, Yoga, Nyāya, Vaiśeṣika, Mīmāṃsā, and Vedānta. We can see these as the fruit born of the blossoming *sūtra* literature. For instance, the last two of these six schools take their names from the *Mīmāṃsā-sūtra* and *Vedānta-sūtra,* works which attempted to explain the meaning of the earlier Vedic literature.

Of course, we will be paying attention to these six traditions, but it's another case where we don't particularly like the way that the terrain is usually mapped. The six-system classification is an anachronistic way of organizing this material, and one that has a strong bias toward mainstream Hinduism's commitment to the veracity of the Vedas, and ignores less mainstream movements as well as all the dissenters, especially the Buddhists and the Jainas. To say nothing of thinkers like Bṛhaspati, author of yet another *sūtra* that gave its name to an intellectual tradition: the *Cārvāka-sūtra.* Yet all these divergent movements belong to a more general trend, in which philosophers attempted to crystallize their wisdom in the form of systematic treatises. This is not to say that they dropped the idea that learning philosophy is a way to the highest good, and thus a path with a purpose. But now the primary task was to describe humankind, the world in which humans find themselves, and the capacities with which humans can know about that world. To use the language of the tradition, the earlier preoccupation with the self is thus joined to an interest in *pramāṇas,* the sources of human knowledge, and the *prameyas,* the world as it is known.

This period saw change not just in the way philosophy was written, but also the very language in which it was written. Until the second century AD, works of Buddhist and Jaina philosophy were typically composed in Pāli and Prakrit, languages which, while not dissimilar to Sanskrit, were not destined to become the main vehicle for intellectual discussion. When thinkers of these schools switched to Sanskrit, the implications were far-reaching. Now confronted on their own linguistic ground, the system builders of the Vedic tradition found themselves having to defend their ideas as never before. They did so by exploring and adapting the ideas of their antique texts, while also borrowing and appropriating Buddhist and Jaina ideas. The result was a third period which completes the first millennium of Indian philosophy. This age runs from, let's say, AD 150 to 550—an era of Buddhist analysis and Jaina synthesis.

Among the most notable Buddhist philosophers in this period were Nāgārjuna and his immediate disciple Āryadeva. Buddhism is not a single, monolithic tradition any more than is Indian philosophy as a whole, and one of its four main schools was initiated by Nāgārjuna. It was known as the Madhyamaka or "Middle Way" school. Another of the Buddhist schools, Sarvāstivāda, was systematized in the period by Vasubandhu. Before Vasubandhu, we have Buddhaghosa, a central figure of Theravāda Buddhism, who went to Sri Lanka to study the founding texts of Buddhism in their original Pāli versions. A fourth school was Yogācāra, which found a major exponent in Dignāga, who lived at the end of our period, dying in about AD 540. He studied and taught in the great Buddhist center of scholarship and education, Nālandā, founded in that same century and destined to become one of the world's leading educational centers five centuries before the first medieval university was founded in Bologna in 1088. Dignāga's disciple Dharmakīrti, would go on to reinvent Dignāga's system, and adapt it to the needs of new Buddhist communities in ways that might not have found approval with Dignāga himself. Dharmakīrti's massive treatise, called *Commentary on the Methods of Knowing*, was decisive in shaping the next period of Indian philosophy. This was a further, cosmopolitan age of dialogue in Sanskrit that runs until, let us say, the transitioning of Buddhists like Kamalaśīla to Tibet in the ninth century.

You don't need to worry about remembering all these names just yet—we'll look at them in more detail later. Our point for now is just that, around the time of the fall of the Roman Empire in Europe, Buddhism was developing in philosophical sophistication and proliferating into various branches. Much the same happened in the Jaina tradition. The most important Jaina thinkers in this period are Kundakunda and Umāsvati. Umāsvati's treatise, the *Sūtra on What Is* (*Tattvārthādhigama-sūtra*), became the common philosophical heritage of two Jaina sub-traditions, the

Digambara and the Śvetāmbara. As the ambitious name of the treatise implies, it is a systematizing work in Jaina metaphysics, epistemology, and philosophy of mind. Key Jaina ideas were more fully developed in a slightly later thinker, Siddhasena Divākara, who lived in the fifth century AD. Important later Jaina philosophers include Haribhadra Sūri and Akalaṅka both of whom lived in the eighth century, Prabhācandra, who lived from 980–1065, and in the next generation Hemacandra. Their belief in the principles of tolerance and harmony led them to a philosophy of pluralism in metaphysics and ethics, and to a kind of relativism or perspectivism in epistemology and semantics.[4]

Having now surveyed this terrain, even if only briefly, we can now return to the question of what it means to speak of "philosophy" in India. Given that the Greek word *philosophia* did not exist in Sanskrit or the other languages of ancient India, scholars have often highlighted the Sanskrit term *darśana* as an equivalent, or at least as a way to refer to an Indian philosophical system.[5] But this may be misleading. Derived from a verb meaning to "to see" (*dṛś*), it can certainly mean a point of view, a perspective, or a doctrine. Yet it can also mean "vision," which could suggest that Indian philosophical systems are based on insight rather than argument. We would therefore prefer to point to an earlier Sanskrit term, *ānvīkṣikī*. This means something like "critical inquiry" or "investigation." And this word, unlike *darśana*, was in fact adopted and used by the classical Indian philosophers themselves.[6] One of the earliest known texts in which the term *ānvīkṣikī* is discussed is the *Arthaśāstra* or *Treatise on Advantage*, a work on government, politics, and economics dating perhaps from the fourth century BC (see Chapter 10). Its author, Kauṭilya, a royal minister in the Magadha Empire, is said to have written it to educate princes in the skills necessary for successful and prosperous rule. Kauṭilya states that there are four branches of learning in which young princes should be trained.[7] These are *ānvīkṣikī*, the method of rational investigation; *trayī*, the religious canon made up of the three Vedas; *vārttā*, the science of material acquisition, such as trade and agriculture; and *daṇḍanīti*, meaning literally "rule by stick"—in other words, political administration and government. Kauṭilya then explains the meaning of the first method, *ānvīkṣikī*. He writes: "distinguishing with proper reasons, between good and evil in the Vedic religion, between profit and loss in the domain of wealth-generation, and between right policy and wrong policy in political administration, and determining the comparative validity and invalidity of all these disciplines in special circumstances, *ānvīkṣikī* renders help to people, keeps their minds steady in woe and weal, and produces adroitness of understanding, speech and action."

For Kauṭilya, *ānvīkṣikī* is not just one branch of knowledge among many, but rather a means of studying the proper aims and methods of knowledge as such. So he adds, "investigation has always been considered as a lamp for all branches of study, the means for all activities, [and] the support for all religious and social duties." Kauṭilya also lists the different sorts of "investigation" known to him, namely *sāṃkhya*, *yoga*, and *lokāyata*. These are also the names of early Indian philosophical systems, but Kauṭilya more likely means to refer to different methods for approaching a philosophical inquiry: by listing and enumeration, by dividing and reconnecting, or by empirical experimentation. Early though this work is, it lays out an agenda that will be followed by many centuries of Indian thinkers. The three methods of Kauṭilya will continue to be used, but also supplemented by two more: *nyāya* and *mīṃāṃsā*. These may ring a bell, since they also became the names of two schools of thought that will arise in what we are calling the Age of the Sūtra. *Nyāya*, which will unsurprisingly enough become a hallmark of the Nyāya system, refers to a procedure of observation and deduction. It was developed in the context of medical diagnosis and prognosis. *Mīṃāṃsā*, meanwhile, is a technique for interpreting texts. Like the three methods listed by Kauṭilya, *nyāya* and *mīṃāṃsā* are thus in the first instance nothing more nor less than techniques of reasoning. Such techniques will come to characterize philosophy in India just as much as, or rather even more than, any body of doctrines. In the Age of the Sūtra, inquiry will come to be seen as an end in itself. But in the earliest period, such systematic concerns remain mostly implicit, as philosophers search above all for the path to liberation.

3

KINGDOM FOR A HORSE

INDIA IN THE VEDIC PERIOD

When you consider that they can't talk, animals have played a surprisingly prominent role in the history of philosophy. The Cynics were named after the dog (*kuon* in Greek), the medievals wondered what a donkey would do if faced with two equally appealing bales of hay, and in more recent times giraffes have appeared prominently in a series of books about the history of philosophy. Since we are discussing India, you may be expecting a mention of cows, sacred or otherwise. But it turns out that the animal with the strongest claim for spurring on Indian philosophy is the horse. It is not indigenous to the subcontinent, but migrated into India along with a people who called themselves the Āryans, referring to their cultural and linguistic identity and not, of course, to some notion of a shared race. With the Āryans and their horses came the Indo-European language that would develop into Sanskrit, as well as the religious beliefs that would make their way into the sacred texts to which so much of Indian philosophy responds, the Vedas.

The Āryans were not the first people to live in India. There is extensive archeological evidence of earlier civilizations, who established cities in the Indus valley as early as the third millennium BC. Which raises the question of where, exactly, the Indus valley is. Well, you can imagine the subcontinent as a diamond which is blunt and broad at the northern end, tapering to a point at the southern end where it juts into the Indian Ocean (see also the map at the start of this book). At the northern join between the subcontinent and the rest of Asia, the terrain is mountainous. Actually that's putting it mildly, since we're talking about the Himalayas and Hindu Kush. From these higher elevations, waters flow down into a plain dominated by two rivers, the Indus in the northeast and the Ganges at more or less due north. Further ranges of mountains divide this Indo-Gangetic plain from a large plateau in the center of India: the Deccan. (Though it forms the northern part of the actual peninsula, the word "Deccan" actually comes from the word for "south," since it lies to the south of the Indo-Gangetic region.) Much of our story is going to play out in the northern plain and in the Deccan, though we'll need to consider a wider range of locales and cultures to understand the full history of Indian philosophy.

But it is along the Indus River that our story, or rather backstory, begins. This was the site of Harappa and Mohenjo-daro, two ancient cities that existed before the coming of the Āryans. This was no primitive society. The Harappan cities were well laid out and traded with people as far away as Mesopotamia. It unfortunately has not been possible to decipher the Harappan script. In fact we don't even know to which language group it belonged; possibly Dravidian, a group which includes Tamil and some other languages. Certainly there were numerous languages spoken in the subcontinent prior to the coming of the Āryans, and influence from these languages can be detected in the Sanskrit of the Vedic literature. The story of the Āryans' arrival to India has provoked a good deal of speculation, indeed wild speculation, indeed ideologically inspired fantasy dressed up as sober scholarship. It used to be thought that the Āryans swept into the region as conquerors, unstoppable on their horse-drawn chariots, only to be slowly corrupted by the inferior races of India as they mingled with them over the generations. Now, scholars not only reject such racist descriptions of the process, but also lean toward thinking that the Āryans gradually migrated into India rather than overwhelming the region militarily.[1]

But they did really have horse-drawn chariots. Archeologists have found seals made by the Harappan people whom the Āryans supplanted, and these feature images of various animals, including even the hippopotamus, which of course means "river horse." But we never find actual horses on them.[2] This makes for a striking contrast to the revelatory texts that preserve the Āryans' religious traditions: the Vedas. They mention horses with great regularity and even put it at the center of one of the most important rituals. In the famous "horse sacrifice," a stallion would be allowed to roam free for a year before being killed and dismembered, the parts offered up to the gods. This was a ritual that could only be carried out by a king with the assistance of priests, intermediaries to the gods who were also handy with a knife. The oldest of the Vedas is the *Ṛg-veda*, dated on linguistic grounds to around 1200 BC. It contains a description of the horse sacrifice, which includes instructions aimed at the priest: "The axe converges on the thirty-four ribs of the prize-winning horse, who has connection with the gods. Arrange his legs, undamaged, into patterns, and carve them up joint by joint, having called them out in order."[3]

While the horse sacrifice was a particularly elaborate and exalted ceremony, it nonetheless captures the social dynamic of Vedic religious practice fairly well. Animals, dairy products, vegetable offerings, and most famously a hallucinogenic plant called *soma* were sacrificed by being offered into flames. The sacrifices were a collaboration between the two elite classes of society, the priests or *brahmins*, and the aristocratic warriors or *kṣatriya*. The systematization of caste would then be completed with the addition of two more groups: the tradesmen and farmers of the "commoner" or *vaiśya* class, and finally the serfs or laborers, known as the *śūdra*. This last group was entirely excluded from the Vedic rituals and would have had its own separate religious practices. The *Ṛg-veda* refers to the four classes and even explains them through a kind of cosmology, which centers on the word *puruṣa*—a word worth remembering, as we'll be encountering it often. It can mean "the self" or simply "person," but the *Ṛg-veda* here characterizes *puruṣa* as "all that yet has been and all that is yet to be," thus drawing a parallel between a single being and the whole cosmos. The gods are said to have sacrificed *puruṣa*, dividing it just as the priests would cut up an animal. From *puruṣa* were extracted various species of animals, including goats, cattle, and, yes, horses, as well as the four classes of humankind: "When they apportioned *puruṣa* into how many parts did they arrange him? What was his mouth? What his two arms? What are said to be his two thighs, his two feet? The *brahmin* was his mouth, the ruler (*rājanya*, i.e. *kṣatriya*) was made his two arms. As to his thighs—that is what the freeman (*vaiśya*) was. From his two feet the servant (*śūdra*) was born" (10.90.11–12).

With all this talk of archeology, migrations, economic stratification, religion, and horses, you may have the mounting feeling that you're reading a history book and not a history of philosophy book. But with this passage we have arrived at central themes of Vedic thought, themes with far-reaching philosophical implications. The beginning of the passage equates *puruṣa* with all things. The later texts known as the Upaniṣads will build on this and similar suggestions in the Vedas to argue that a knowledge of the self—*puruṣa* or *ātman*—is tantamount to a knowledge of the whole world. But the *Ṛg-veda* isn't simply saying that there is an ultimate unity between the self and the universe. It suggests that reality can be divided into natural parts, much like a skillfully butchered sacrificial animal. On the basis of the passage just quoted above, this becomes a kind of justification for the class system. Obviously this looks to our eyes like a self-serving account, representing as it does the interests of the *brahmin* and *kṣatriya* classes, the very people who carried out and benefitted from the sacrifices described in Vedic literature.

But there's more going on here than the cynical rationalization of an elitist culture. If we look ahead to the Upaniṣads, we see them also drawing systematic parallels between the parts of human or animal bodies and the parts of the universe. At the risk of beating a dead horse, let's consider another example featuring the Āryans' favorite animal. The very beginning of the *Great Forest* (*Bṛhadāraṇyaka*) *Upaniṣad* (1.1) consists of an extended analogy, or even identification, between the parts of a sacrificial horse and the parts of the cosmos. The head of the horse is the dawn, its body (*ātman*) is the year, its back the sky, its feet the days and nights, its bones the stars, its flesh the clouds, and so on. The passage concludes, "When it yawns, lightning flashes; when it shakes itself, it thunders; and when it urinates, it rains. Its neighing is speech itself."[4] The Upaniṣads tell us that, when we understand the parts and powers of horses and humans, we travel a path from microcosm to macrocosm. Studying the structure of animals and humans is a way, even *the* way, to uncover the hidden structure of all things. The priest himself is a paradigm case. We read somewhat later in the first section of the *Great Forest Upaniṣad* that he is *brahman* personified, a whole world in himself (1.4).

This holistic philosophical understanding was the stock in trade of the *brahmin* class. It was they, and only they, who had expertise in the fine points of ritual and insight into the nature of the gods, which is why their assistance was needed by the warrior aristocrats of the *kṣatriya* class. Thanks to the rituals carried out by the *brahmins*, the *kṣatriya* could hope for divine favor, which might bring insurance against calamity, large and healthy families, and ever-increasing wealth. More ambitiously, they could turn to the *brahmins* for an explanation of the origin of all things, as suggested in a verse of the *Ṛg-veda*: "Unperceptive, I ask also the perceptive poets about this in order to know, since I am unknowing: what also is the One in the form of the Unborn that has propped apart these six realms?"[5] And what did the know-it-all *brahmins* get of out the deal? It's here that the cows finally come in. Many times in the Upaniṣads, a sage is promised head of cattle in return for their wisdom. This can even be the occasion for gentle comedy: a *brahmin* comes to court and the king asks him whether he is "after cows or subtle disquisitions." "Both, your majesty," replies the sage (4.1).

The Upaniṣads show that within the symbiotic relationship between rulers and priests, the knowledge claims of the *brahmins* did not go unchallenged. Another remarkable passage of the *Great Forest Upaniṣad* describes a dialogue between a king named Ajātaśatru and a priest named Dṛipta-Bālāki (2.1). The priest offers to give an account of *brahman*, or "fundamental reality." Naturally, he's offered a thousand cows if his statement is deemed convincing. The priest begins by suggesting that *brahman* resides in the sun, a proposal instantly rejected by the king. The sun may be the greatest of all beings, but it is not to be identified with *brahman* itself. A long chain of further ideas follow: *brahman* is in the moon, in space itself, in wind, water, sound, or body (*ātman*). The king slaps down every suggestion, using almost the same words each time. Finally Dṛipta-Bālāki admits defeat, and asks to learn from the king instead of the other way around. The king agrees to enlighten him, even though it is, as he says, "a reversal of the norm for a *brahmin* to become the pupil of a *kṣatriya*."

If this seems a rather heavy-handed way of hinting that the *brahmins* might have something to learn from the *kṣatriyas*, it was as nothing compared to the challenges that emerged around the fifth century BC. This was the age of the Buddha and of Mahāvīra—the tradition of thought he founded, "Jainism," takes its name from Mahāvīra's epithet *Jina*, meaning "conqueror." It's significant that both Buddha and Mahāvīra were members of the *kṣatriya* aristocracy, rather than the priestly *brahmin* class. Both abandoned their wealth to lead lives of ascetic restraint, already an implicit criticism of the literal and spiritual economy that lay at the heart of the Brahmanical tradition. Sometimes the criticism was more explicit. Buddhists and Jainas increasingly raised doubts about the efficacy of Vedic rituals, and the very possibility of attaining the kind of understanding claimed by the *brahmins*. It's no wonder that Indian philosophy early on developed an obsession with the methods that might lead to knowledge, since knowledge was the commodity that earned the *brahmins* their very livelihood. In these debates an elite way of life, and not just epistemology, was at stake.

But Buddhism and Jainism offered more than mere criticism of the Brahmanical system of thought. Indeed, they promised their followers something that could not be achieved through any ritual: liberation. The classic texts of Brahmanical culture allude to one of the beliefs we associate most readily with the Indian tradition: the cycle of reincarnation. In an oft-quoted passage of the *Bhagavad-gītā*, we read, "As a man casts off his worn-out clothes and takes on new ones, so does the self cast off its worn-out bodies and enter new ones" (2.22).[6] Rather than being relieved at the prospect of returning again and again to bodily existence instead of dying outright, Indian thinkers often set as their goal "liberation," escape from the relentless cycle. Consistently with the exaltation of knowledge so typical of the Upaniṣads, one of the later Upaniṣads states: "when a man has understanding, is mindful and always pure, he reaches that final step, from which he is not reborn again" (*Kaṭha Upaniṣad* 1.3). The Buddhists and Jainas duly offered their own versions of liberation, with the Buddhists subjecting to a radical critique the very idea of a self or soul that could pass from one body to another.

From what's been said so far, you may have the impression that these dissenting schools were insurgents against the elite, a kind of living rebuke to the religious beliefs and power structures of ancient India. But of course Buddhism would itself develop into a major world religion, and this process already began in antiquity. The Buddhists may have been dismissive of the rituals outlined in the Vedas, but they had their own alternate forms of religious observance, such as burial practices different from those used in the Vedic tradition. As for the social position of the Buddhists and Jainas, we should not necessarily assume that these were teachings for the economically weak. After all, the Buddha himself came from a royal family, and in the longer term both movements would receive their fair share of political support. We see this with the rulers of the powerful Mauryan Empire, which held much of the territory of the subcontinent in the period around the third century BC. It was founded in 321 BC by Candragupta Maurya, who expanded his initial territory in part by taking advantage of the power vacuum that resulted when the conquering armies of Alexander the Great pulled out of northwestern India.[7] King Candragupta had a *brahmin* advisor named Kauṭilya, who is said to be the author of a political treatise called the *Arthaśāstra*—we mentioned it in the last chapter and will be considering it more fully in Chapter 10.

With this dynasty, we see that the dissenters' ideas too could appeal to the ruling class that had sought wisdom from the *brahmins* for so many generations. It is said that Candragupta himself abdicated his kingship after becoming an adherent of Jainism. We have much more evidence concerning the intellectual allegiance of Candragupta's grandson Aśoka. Appalled by the violence he witnessed in a military campaign against the region of Kāliṅga (the eastern coast), Aśoka sought to wield his royal power in a fashion consistent with Buddhist teachings. His armies would not make war, except in self-defense, and as ruler he would look to the welfare of all his subjects. Aśoka had inscriptions erected around his empire in a variety of languages; his edicts were even translated into Greek and Aramaic for the northwestern regions. This is just one example of the interpenetration of Greek and Indian culture in the generations following Alexander's conquests. During the Hellenistic period the Bactrian ruler Demetrius extended his rule into the Punjab and Indus valley. Tradition records that another Greek king, Milinda or Menander, converted to Buddhism. A supposed dialogue between this king and a Buddhist teacher named Nāgasena survives as the so-called *Questions of Milinda*; again, we'll return to this text later.

But before getting into the Buddhist and Jaina traditions and their critique of Brahmanical culture, we need first to understand better what they were criticizing. That means, first and foremost, understanding the Upaniṣads, works that set out to expound the meaning of the Vedic texts and the rituals they described. Devised over the course of many generations, they are monuments of world literature and foundational texts of the Hindu religion. And of course they are full of philosophical material, which is sometimes suggestive and metaphorical, sometimes frankly argumentative and disputatious, and always well worth careful attention.

4

HIDE AND SEEK

THE UPANIṢADS

What is the most central philosophical activity? Well, perhaps the most *common* philosophical activity is writing an essay for a philosophy class late at night after lengthy procrastination. Then there is publishing books and articles on the topic, which professional academics tend to do after considerably more procrastination than they'd let their students get away with. But the core practice of philosophy does not need to involve writing at all. It is dialogue: a calm and frank exchange of ideas, arguments, examples, and counterexamples. To be a philosopher is to be willing and even eager to test your view against rival views, to subject your theories to refutation and meet such refutation with well-considered defense, or indeed by changing your mind. In ancient philosophical literature, it is of course Plato who leaps to mind as the greatest exponent of the philosophical dialogue. But a second place of honor should be reserved for the Upaniṣads.

The texts traditionally labeled as Upaniṣads react to and elaborate upon the ideas, and sometimes specific passages, of the Vedas.[1] There are four Vedic texts, also called *saṃhitās*, which form a substantial body of literature. The oldest one, the *Ṛg-veda*, has ten books, each of which contains on average about 100 hymns. This and the other *saṃhitās* are dense and difficult works which call out for exegesis and exposition, and that is what they got, in the form of a multi-layered tradition of writings, with the Upaniṣads forming only one layer. (In Sanskrit tradition by the way, the words "Veda" or "Vedic" are used to refer to all of this literature collectively: the earliest revelatory texts plus the layers of commentary.) A given Upaniṣad will be associated with a specific *saṃhitā* which inspired it but without providing close, line-by-line commentary. Instead the Upaniṣads are heterogeneous collections that mix scenes of dialogue with anecdotes, parables, poetic metaphors, and advice.

The earliest of the the Upaniṣads date from around or before the sixth century BC, but more were written for many centuries afterwards.[2] The two oldest, the *Great Forest* and *Chāndogya* Upaniṣads, were both composed before the time of the Buddha. We say "composed" rather than "written" because, like the *saṃhitās*, the Upaniṣads were transmitted orally over many generations. Numerous hints of this are preserved in the written versions, for instance the use of repetition to aid memorization, and even turns of phrase that make it clear that a certain gesture is intended to go along with the recitation. The Upaniṣads are symbolic, evocative, and inspirational, plastic in meaning, and just as open to interpretation as the sacred texts of other religious traditions. What they offer the philosopher is not so much close conceptual analysis or system-building as the setting down of broad themes. The most fundamental of these themes is the uncovering of hidden connections between things. Indeed, the very term *upaniṣad* means a "hidden connection," or possibly a "secret teaching," a meaning it acquires through its etymology as "sitting near to" one's teacher.[3]

That, and the fact that these works respond to revelatory religious texts, may lead us to expect the Upaniṣads simply to declaim their esoteric wisdom for our benefit, if only we can understand it ourselves. But more often claims of knowledge are put into the mouths of various characters who are then challenged by others. We just saw an example in the last chapter, in the passage where a king rejected a series of attempts to explain the concept of *brahman*. Here and elsewhere students and would-be teachers are said to "fall silent" because they find themselves unable to answer a question, or to improve upon the answers others are giving. The listener or reader is thus invited to consider the basis and reliability of the claims being made. At the same time, we get a vivid impression of the ancient social context. We see our protagonists in courtly settings, with the elite scholars of the day strutting their stuff for rich benefactors and striving against one another to claim admiration and material rewards, like those cows we mentioned.

This is well illustrated by the third section of the *Great Forest Upaniṣad*, which dramatizes not so much a debate as a competition. We are at the court of a king named Janaka, who plans to lavish gifts upon a group of priests who will carry out a sacrifice. When he announces his intention to discover who among them is "most learned," a *brahmin* named Yājñavalkya steps forward (3.1). He is questioned by a series of rivals, and reduces each of them to silence. He bests them over the function of religious rituals, but also when it comes to such philosophical issues as the means by which we grasp the world around us (3.2) and that core concern of the Upaniṣads, the self (*ātman*; 3.4, 3.7). Interestingly, a woman is also allowed to join the debate, one of several female characters who appear in the Upaniṣads and take full part in the debate (see further Chapter 14). Her name is Gārgī Vācaknavī. She has two goes at questioning Yājñavalkya, first when she pursues him along a cosmological regress: people say that the world is "woven upon" or supported by water, but what supports water? Air, comes the reply. But then what supports air? And so on, via the sun and the stars, and the realm of the gods, until Yājñavalkya tells her to stop asking questions, lest her "head shatter apart" (3.6). But Gārgī is apparently impressed. Shortly thereafter, she declares that if Yājñavalkya can answer a further difficult line of questioning, he should be deemed invincible in debate (3.8). Her second inquiry is similar to the first, and elicits another regress of explanatory cosmic principles. But this time the buck is stopped. He satisfies Gārgī by telling her that all things are "woven upon" space, and space upon that which can never perish. She pronounces him the victor, and before long the other *brahmins* agree, or at least give up trying to get the better of him (3.9).

This dialogical setting for philosophy is going to be a long-running feature of Indian thought. It will especially characterize the texts written in the Age of the Sūtra, which will feature abundant mutual refutation by members of the various schools. We're not going to see many interlocutors in that period who are willing to "fall silent." But in that later context, philosophers are themselves engaged directly in intellectual disputes. The Upaniṣads are more like the Platonic dialogues: they depict named individuals having discussions with one another. One result is that the same questions don't always get the same answers, even in a single Upaniṣad, never mind in different works of the genre. More consistent is the range of themes that appear throughout these texts, such as the aforementioned idea that there are unseen connections between things, which will yield themselves up to those who seek what is hidden.

We see this with the beginning of the *Great Forest Upaniṣad*, already mentioned above (Chapter 3), where the parts of a sacrificial horse are compared to aspects of the universe. The idea here is that the world as a whole shares the same arrangement as the sacrificial object. This is in fact supposed to explain the very efficacy of sacrificial rites. By means of ritual, human beings can effect a reordering and even a repair of the world. The parts of the cosmos stand in a one to one relation with the objects that are in the ritual domain: the dawn is the head of the horse, the sky is its back, and so on. A similar claim is made about the human body, which is presented as a sort of cosmological "map." The same Upaniṣad contains the following extended analogy (2.5):

speech	fire
sight	the sun
breath	the wind
mind	the moon
hearing	the heaven
body	earth
self	space
hair	plants
blood, semen	water

Sometimes a physical theory seems to underlie the alignment of microcosm and macrocosm. Shortly after the passage on the sacrificial horse, the *Great Forest Upaniṣad* describes a conflict between demons and gods (1.3). We are told how the demons introduced evil into the speech, smell, sight, hearing, and minds of the gods. But they are unable to corrupt the "breath of the mouth," which is said to be the most fundamental aspect or essence of the body. Breath also plays a role in the natural world: wind is simply breath that is "freed from death." Finally and most importantly, breath is also the foundation of speech.

This provides a connection to the ritualistic concerns of the Vedas. The chapter concludes by pointing out that a ritual prayer is itself a form of speech. The chanting of the priest is "held up by breath," as is the whole world. As one reads further, one finds the *Upaniṣad* concluding with some rather frank advice on sexual practices. You'd think this would be a rather jarring shift, but true to form, there are subtle connections to what has gone before. The text posits an intimate relation between the male seed and breath. In fact pregnancy can supposedly be prevented if the man exhales into his partner's mouth and then inhales his breath again, thus extracting the power that was first given up into the woman (6.4). Our advice would be that couples do not try this at home.

The *Great Forest Upaniṣad*, from which we've been quoting, is the oldest of the Upaniṣads. It sets the tone for those that would follow, using the familiar as a map or template to understand what is unfamiliar and unknown. As another of the oldest texts, the *Chāndogya Upaniṣad*, puts it: "You must surely have asked about that rule of substitution by which one hears what has not been heard before, thinks of what has not been thought of before, and perceives what has not been perceived before" (6.1). What we are learning to perceive from such "substitutions" is an underlying grid of correspondences, which match bodily parts and vital functions to the primary elements and celestial bodies. The ultimate ground for the correspondences is called *brahman*. It is a unifying cosmic principle, whose role is described in the *Kena* ("*By Whom*") *Upaniṣad*:

> By whom impelled, by whom compelled, does the mind soar forth?
> By whom enjoined does the breath march on as the first?
> By whom is this speech impelled, with which people speak?
> And who is the god that joins the sight and hearing? (1.1)
>
> That which is the hearing behind hearing,
> the thinking behind thinking,
> the speech behind speech,
> the sight behind sight.
> It is also the breathing behind breathing.

> Freed completely from these,
> the wise become immortal,
> when they depart from this world. (1.2)
>
> What one cannot see with one's sight,
> by which one sees the sight itself.
> Learn that that alone is *brahman*,
> and not what they here venerate. (1.6)

You may notice that these passages use the same taxonomy we've seen above, featuring breath, speech, hearing, sight, and thought. But notice too that *brahman* is more than just one element in the net of correspondences. It is something more fundamental, a "breathing behind breathing," unseen because it is that "by which one sees." We can learn something about both humans and the cosmos by seeing the links between them, but *brahman* remains more elusive. It is inexpressible because it is that in virtue of which we speak, and unthinkable because it is that in virtue of which we think. This may sound like a dead end, an ancient Indian version of negative theology. Would you really hand over a thousand cows for this?

But the Upaniṣads make one final, dramatic move, by identifying *brahman* with the *ātman*. To quote the *Chāndogya Upaniṣad*: "This self of mine that lies deep within my heart—it contains all actions, all desires, all smells, and all tastes; it has captured this whole world. It is *brahman*. On departing from here after death, I will become that" (43.14.4). Perhaps then we should understand the Upaniṣads to teach that the order of things, the division of things into classifications, is itself in a correspondence with the order of our minds. If self and world are organized along fundamentally analogous lines, then self-control and self-understanding become methods for controlling and understanding the world. This idea is supported by a remark in the *Kena Upaniṣad*: "we have taught you the hidden connection relating to *brahman* itself. Of this hidden connection, austerity, self-control and rites are the foundation, the Vedas are all the limbs, and truth is the abode" (4.7). Or, to quote a modern scholar of the Upaniṣads, "each Upaniṣadic teaching creates an integrative vision, a view of the whole which draws together the separate elements of the world and of human experience and compresses them into a single form."[4]

Of course, this ancient Indian literature is not unique in holding out the prospect of a unified explanation of the world and of our experience. The peculiar twist is that the single reality behind the multiple aspects of the world is also the reality of the individual self or subject. The Upaniṣads seem to tell us that there is no hope of forming a unified conception of the world while leaving out the self, that a conception of the nature of the self is the key to a conception of the nature of the world.[5] Much later Śaṅkara, a philosopher who lived around AD 700 and systematized Advaita Vedānta, interpreted the idea as a denial of the reality of difference (see Chapter 20). That's a rather technical and metaphysical, and also contentious, way to capture the idea the Upaniṣads express with metaphors, with the connections it draws between animal or human and world, and with its cyclical cosmology.

Take for instance the idea that the world emerges from a single unity, only to resolve eventually back into it. The *Muṇḍaka Upaniṣad* offers a powerful image to express this: "As a spider spins out threads, then draws them into itself . . . So from the imperishable all things here spring" (1.1). David Hume was apparently aware of this verse, and asked how the Indian philosopher could compare God with anything so contemptible as a spider. But it is poetry, not philosophy, that sustains the metaphor. It expresses the grand integrative vision, in which the whole world is spun out and drawn back in to a single imperishable thing. The same point is made when God is compared to a magician, or to a potter, fashioning the eternal atoms into new forms.[6]

The path to wisdom charted here looks like a short trip: we want to understand the world, then realize that the world conforms to the self and vice versa. The rest should be easy. We need only understand ourselves in order to understand all things, and what lies closer to hand than our own selves? The catch is that the self is elusive, for the very reason that *brahman* was found to be elusive. As Gārgī knew, the wisest are those who persevere in the search for that which is most fundamental, that upon which "all things are woven." One of the other sages who tests Yājñavalkya in that debate is named Uddālaka. He reappears in the *Chāndogya Upaniṣad*, where he is depicted promising his son Śvetaketu the knowledge that will account for everything, the knowledge of the totality. Uddālaka tells his son to fetch the fruit of a banyan tree, to cut it open and find the seed, and then to cut open the seed (6.12). Śvetaketu finds nothing inside, but Uddālaka tells him that within the seed is the finest essence, on account of which the banyan tree has grown. It is, he adds, the essence "that constitutes the self of this whole world; that is the truth; that is the self." A single essence, an essence within an essence, unifies, integrates and explains the whole—but this essence is also invisible. Thus seeing the correspondence, and perhaps even identity, between self and world is only the first step of a longer journey. For the self is not the sort of thing that just offers itself up for our understanding.

Another recurrent theme of the Upaniṣads is that the self has five "sheaths," namely food, breath, mind, intellect, and bliss. Thus the *Taittirīya Upaniṣad* declares: "Now, a man here is formed from the essence of food . . . Different from and lying within this man formed from the essence of food is the self consisting of lifebreath . . . Different from and lying within this self consisting of breath is the self consisting of mind . . . Different from and lying within this self consisting of mind is the self consisting of intellect . . . Different from and lying within this self consisting of intellect is the self consisting of bliss, which suffuses this other self completely" (2.1–5). This suggests that breath is not fundamental after all, even if directing our attention toward it is a crucial part of coming to understand the underlying essence of the self. Our task as self-knowers is to get past superficial appearances to progressively deeper notions of the person. You are what you eat! No, you are your breath. Or more fundamentally still, your mind. And so on.

Notice that the procedure is the same as the one applied to the cosmos as a whole in the dialogue between Gārgī and Yājñavalkya. When the world is reduced to water, water to air, air to the stars, and the stars to the divine, or when we identify the self with food, then breath, then mind, we are not just following an indefinite regress. And contrary to what it may seem, we are making progress, reaching a more profound level of understanding with each step. It's an encouraging thought, which comes along with an equally discouraging warning: *brahman* or the self may be so fundamental that it cannot be understood. There is no trace of egotism or individual character here. Since it is that which underlies and explains other things, it cannot be understood in light of anything else. Does the journey toward grasping the self ever reach its destination?

5

INDRA'S SEARCH

THE SELF IN THE UPANIṢADS

One traditional way to think about the distinctiveness of Indian, as opposed to European, philosophy, has been that it first emerged and was always pursued in a religious context. After all, we think of Buddhism, Jainism, and Hinduism primarily as religions, not schools of philosophy, even if these traditions produced many philosophical arguments and texts. But this contrast between philosophy in India and in Europe can be challenged. Religious ideas were rarely far from the concerns of European thinkers, from the pagans in antiquity to the theologians of the medieval period and beyond. And of course it's notoriously difficult to say whether, or in what sense, Buddhism constitutes a "religion." We are exploring the history of philosophy, not the history of religion, so we don't necessarily need to decide that issue. We do, however, need to notice, and understand, the undeniably religious elements in the ancient Indian texts we are approaching from a philosophical angle. Among these elements, probably the most striking is the presence of gods, who routinely appear as characters in the Upaniṣads and the *Mahābhārata*. Despite rejecting much of the ritual practice and intellectual content of Brahmanical culture, the Buddhists also continued to recognize and talk about the gods. What philosophical relevance did the gods have for these traditions? Can we even speak of a "natural theology" in Buddhism or the sacred texts of Hinduism?[1]

If we can, it is only by dropping some of the expectations we might associate with that phrase. While the gods are a striking presence in these texts, a striking absence is any interest in creation of the world, if by "creation" we mean bringing the universe to exist out of nothing and at a distinct point in time. Instead, we standardly find a picture of world-cycles, each cycle lasting for a vast period and being followed by another, equally lengthy period (see Chapter 31). On the other hand, we already saw that in the *Ṛg-veda* the gods are said to have extracted the species of animals from *puruṣa*. And one particular god, Prajāpati, is briefly described as a creator. He appears again in this guise in the *Mahābhārata*, where he is said first to fashion a body for himself, and then the matter (*pradhāna*) underlying the whole universe, from which he makes all other things. The Upaniṣads also occasionally convey the idea that all things are caused by, or depend on, Something, since in these texts *brahman* is a fundamental support for all reality—indeed the word *brahman* means that which "bears up" all things. Still, if *brahman* is divine it is a rather impersonal divinity. It is rarely said to create, reward, or punish. Already in the earlier Vedas, the universe is portrayed as having a moral order independent of any theological force. That continues to be the case with the development of ideas about *karma*, where God's involvement often consists only in a kind of cosmic bookkeeping, since He is invoked to explain how it is that our good and bad deeds are guaranteed to affect our future fates.

For these reasons, the great scholar of Indian philosophy Bimal Krishna Matilal has written that in this tradition, the gods are seen "as window-dressing and more a part of the cultural heritage of India than anything else."[2] Still, though we may not find creation from nothing or a divine command theory of ethics in our philosophical texts, we do find gods. Indeed we even find them *taking part* in philosophical discussions. The teacher at the center of the *Bhagavad-gītā* is Kṛṣṇa, an avatar or incarnation of the god Viṣṇu. And they appear as sage-like interlocutors in the Upaniṣads, which may be understood as a strategy for lending authority to the teachings being unfolded. One of the most famous of all stories in the Upaniṣads has as its main character Indra. He is a familiar divinity for anyone who has paged through the *Ṛg-veda*, though certainly not the only god acknowledged in that text.[3] Natural phenomena like wind, sun, heaven, and dawn are recognized as deities, and elements in the Vedic ritual—like Agni, the ritual fire, and Soma, the sacrificial plant—are also seen as divine. But since the *Ṛg-veda* centers on the sacrifice of Soma, and since this plant is offered up to Indra, he is the most prominent god in the text, far more so for example than Viṣṇu, who plays only a minor role.

By the time of the *Chāndogya Upaniṣad* (at 8.7.1–8.12.6) Indra is assigned a far lesser role. He is presented not as an almighty creator or even a priestly king—as sometimes in the *Ṛg-veda*—but instead as searching after wisdom. Here he is a figure who takes to heart the ubiquitous Upaniṣadic exhortation to go in search of your true self. As we saw in the last chapter, this search ends with the realization that there is a hidden correspondence between one's self and the cosmos, and that both in turn correspond to the space in which the Vedic ritual is carried out. You'd think that as a god, Indra would be explaining this to a human. Instead, he is the one on a journey of self-discovery. The gods and demons, we are told, have heard that Prajāpati speaks of a self "by discovering which one obtains all the worlds, and all one's desires are fulfilled" (8.7.2). This fits with the presentation of Prajāpati in the *Ṛg-veda*, which in addition to exalting him as a creator, says that he possesses a knowledge beyond that of the other gods. Along with one of the demons, Virocana,

Indra goes to live as a celibate in Prajāpati's ashram, in hope of learning the secret of this self. The first thing they learn is patience. It takes thirty-two years before Prajāpati finally speaks, and that only to ask Indra and Virocana what they want.

Up until this point, the story will be familiar to anyone who has tried to get their driver's license renewed. But the ensuing conversation is one you wouldn't get out of any government bureaucrat. When Prajāpati learns of their quest to discover the self, he fobs them off with an answer he knows to be false:

> "Look at yourselves in a pan of water. And let me know if there is anything you do not perceive about yourselves." So they looked into a pan of water. Prajāpati asked them: "What do you see?" And they replied: "Sir, we see here our entire body (*ātman*), a perfect likeness down to the very hairs of the body, down to the very nails." Prajāpati told them then: "Adorn yourself beautifully, dress well, and spruce yourself up, and then look into a pan of water." So they adorned themselves beautifully, dressed well, and spruced themselves up, and then looked into a pan of water. Prajāpati asked them: "What do you see?" And they replied: "Sir, as the two of us here are beautifully adorned, well dressed, and all spruced up, in exactly the same way are these, sir, beautifully adorned, well dressed, and all spruced up." "That is the self; that is the immortal; that is the one free from fear; that is brahman," Prajāpati told them. And the two of them left with contented hearts. Seeing the two depart, Prajāpati observed: "There they go, without learning about the self, without discovering the self!" (8.8.1–4)

But Indra isn't so easily fooled. He quickly realizes that the reflected self cannot be that for which he seeks. For if the body can be made beautiful, so too can it become lame and crippled. He returns for further instruction.

Prajāpati makes him wait another thirty-two years, but his reward is only to be fobbed off again, this time with the following answer: "the one who goes happily about in a dream: that is the self; that is the immortal; that is the one free from fear; that is *brahman*." Indra falls for the lie at first but is unconvinced upon reflection. The self as it appears in dreams can still suffer anxiety and disappointment. He goes back for a better response and is told to—you'll never guess—wait thirty-two more years. Still he doesn't get the real answer, but is told, "When one is fast asleep, totally collected and serene, and sees no dreams: that is the self; that is the immortal, that is the one free from fear; that is *brahman*" (8.11.1). Yet again Indra goes away happy; yet again he starts to have doubts and returns to Prajāpati. This time, he needs to wait only five more years, making a total of one hundred and one (8.11.3).

At this point, Indra is finally given the true answer. You'll be glad to hear that you only have to wait briefly to learn what it is. First though we want to dwell on the nature of this story, and the way it is told. Prajāpati displays an astonishing reluctance to share his wisdom, as well as the willingness to deceive not just the demon Virocana but even a god. He also insists on long periods of harsh living as a condition for receiving his instruction. It's noteworthy too that Indra only seems to improve his understanding by going away, content with the answer he's received, and then beginning to question that answer. Indra is forced to go step by step through numerous proposals, each an improvement on its predecessor. There's an implied idea here about how knowledge and learning work—if not in general, then at least when it comes to the central upaniṣadic concern of the self. One cannot simply leap to a final, adequate grasp of the self without first having other, preparatory understandings. Before moving on to each new stage of understanding, Indra needs to understand what was inadequate about the previous stage.

Indeed, one must see why each idea of the self is false if one is even to speculate upon the truth or falsity of the next proposal. If Indra did not first come to see that his self cannot be a reflected image, he could not appreciate the less obvious doctrine that the true self is the one he encounters in dreams. Notice too that Prajāpati lets Indra figure out for himself what is wrong with each inadequate understanding. Indra must do more than merely understand that he is not a reflection or the one who enjoys a dreamless sleep. He must also come to see the flaws in these accounts as the result of his own personal investigation and discovery. So Prajāpati could not simply have told Indra the final doctrine straight away, nor could he have told him that any of the preceding doctrines were false. He could only "feed" Indra each doctrine and wait to see if Indra will discover it to be false.

Why is the self so hard to find, and why does its discovery demand this "do it yourself" approach? It takes Indra, who is himself a god, more than a century to find out, even with Prajāpati prodding him along. The answer may be that the self is, ironically, so close that it is nearly impossible to find. Things that are outside us are usually possible objects of sensation: if you want to perceive the Eiffel Tower you just need to go to Paris, but no plane ticket will bring you to a vantage point from which you can behold the self. Nor is the self something that can be grasped by some process of deduction or through the testimony of another person. There is, as the later Indian philosophers would say, no *pramāṇa* leading to this knowledge. As we suggested in the previous chapter, *brahman* and the self make knowledge possible without themselves being knowable. Our natural instinct when looking for the self is to seek it among the objects of consciousness, since this is the strategy that works with all other things. But in this one case, that strategy is ill-conceived.

Other passages in the Upaniṣads confirm that the self is not within the purview of the senses and mind, precisely because it is what makes sensing and thinking possible, so that it is "too close" to be seen. In the *Great Forest Upaniṣad*, this idea is expressed by the sage Yājñavalkya, shown in conversation with his wife Maitreyī:

> When there is a duality of some kind, then the one can smell the other, the one can see the other, the one can hear the other, the one can greet the other, the one can think of the other, and the one can perceive the other. When, however, the Whole has become one's very self (*ātman*), then who is there for one to smell and by what means? Who is there for one to see and by what means? Who is there for one to hear and by what means? Who is there for one to greet and by what means? Who is there for one to think and by what means? Who is there for one to perceive and by what means? By what means can one perceive him by means of whom one perceives this whole world? Look—by what means can one perceive the perceiver? About this self (*ātman*), one can only say "not—, not—." He is ungraspable, for he cannot be grasped. He is undecaying, for he is not subject to decay. He has nothing sticking to him, for he does not stick to anything. He is not bound; yet he neither trembles in fear nor suffers injury. (2.4.14)

Again, the point is that the self is not an object of thought. In fact, it is not even a possible target of language, which is why Yājñavalkya says that one can only say of it "not— not—." As the same sage says elsewhere, "you can't see the seer who does the seeing; you can't hear the hearer who does the hearing; you can't think of the thinker who does the thinking; and you can't perceive the perceiver who does the perceiving. The self within all is this self of yours" (*Great Forest Upaniṣad* 3.5.2).

All of this helps us to make sense of the stages in Indra's education. Of the three bogus accounts he is offered, the first two attempt to represent the self as a possible object of consciousness. Perhaps it is an object of sensory awareness, the reflected image in a pool of water? Surely not, for it is the subject of sensation, not something that is sensed. Perhaps then it is instead an object of dream consciousness? Indra again sees through the ruse, and is ready to move on to the idea that the self is no object of consciousness at all, but simply whatever undergoes dreamless, contentless sleep. But Indra realizes that this is not the self, because it is in fact nothing at all. As he observes, "this self does not even know any of these beings here. It has become completely annihilated" (8.11.2).

Once Indra has diagnosed the shortcomings of all these ideas of the self, and shown himself to be a waiter more expert than you'll find in any restaurant, he is ready to hear the truth from Prajāpati. Here it is:

> The one who is aware: "Let me smell this"—that is the self; the faculty of smell enables him to smell. The one who is aware: "Let me say this"—that is the self; the faculty of speech enables him to speak. The one who is aware: "Let me listen to this"—that is the self; the faculty of hearing enables him to hear. The one who is aware: "Let me think about this"—that is the self; the mind is his divine faculty of sight.

Is this answer worth the wait? Well, the conception of self found here can certainly claim to improve on those that have come before. Prajāpati presents the self as that which underlies thought, speech, and sensation.[4] Another of the Upaniṣads uses the analogy of a chariot: the intellect is the charioteer, the mind the reins, the body the chariot itself, while senses are the horses that pull the whole thing along (*Kaṭha Upaniṣad* 3.3–4). But that might suggest a more active understanding of the self than the one Prajāpati puts forth. Strictly speaking, the self is the source of neither action nor will. It stands still, observing itself as it watches, as it hears and thinks. It is not merely the one who sees, nor the one who decides to look, but the one who is aware of seeing, of looking. Yet neither is it a detached or impassive self, disengaged from its own desires and actions, because it is aware of itself even as it pursues them.

Again, the self is that in virtue of which the subject of consciousness is self-conscious, but is not itself an object of consciousness. In what, then, can self-discovery consist, if the self is not something we can discover? A helpful hint can be found in the *Great Forest Upaniṣad*, where Yājñavalkya tells his wife: "when a drum is being beaten, you cannot catch the external sounds; you catch them only by getting hold of the drum or the man beating that drum" (2.4.7). His proposal is, then, that, when we experience sensation, we can catch the sensing self only by getting hold of the sensing; when thinking goes on, even the thinker can catch his or her self only by getting hold of the thinking. We reach the self not directly, but by catching it in its activity of sensing and thinking. Thus is the self discovered, in the shadowy edges of experience. Philosophers nowadays might put the point by saying that the self is known only through the phenomenological quality of thinking, in the flavor of the experience of "what it is like" to think. There is something that it feels like, from within, to be thinking, and in focusing upon this instead of the thought one is thinking, one comes to be obliquely aware of the self. We should abandon our instinctive assumption that the self is some kind of core or center of consciousness. Instead, the self pervades all of consciousness, and can be extracted (*pra-jñāna*) from it. With all due respect to Prajāpati, we again find it most helpful to quote Yājñavalkya for this point:

> As a mass of salt has no distinctive core and surface—the whole thing is a single mass of flavour—so indeed, my dear, this self has no distinctive core and surface; the whole thing is a compact mass (*ghana*) of cognition (*prajñāna*). (*Great Forest Upaniṣad* 4.5.13)

This brings us back to the point that the self is so hard to find precisely because it is always present to us. The phenomenal character of experience itself is barely noticeable, hidden as it is behind the "false desires" that come with our worldly concerns.

Even if this message was delivered by one god to another, it is not necessarily religious in character. Admittedly the self-knowledge we've been talking about has something in common with a mystic's awareness of God, because it can be grasped only indirectly and not easily put into words, if at all. But it is a further step, and one taken only in the more theistic later Upaniṣads, to identify this experience with a mystical awareness of the divine. On the other hand, when you think of religion and the Upaniṣads, it is probably not self-knowledge that first springs to mind anyway. Your thoughts are more likely to turn to the cycle of rebirth, and above all to the law of *karma*, which governs the fate of each individual in the next life. Happily you won't have to wait for the next life to find out more about this, though; only for the next chapter.[5]

6

YOU ARE WHAT YOU DO

KARMA IN THE UPANIṢADS

It's the rare philosophical concept that inspires dance music. You won't find meditations on determinism in the back catalogue of Kool and the Gang, or Madonna setting reductionist theory of mind to a disco beat. Every rule has an exception, though, and in this case we find one in the shape of Culture Club's 1983 hit "Karma Chameleon." Actually, this may be the exception that *proves* the rule, since a close reading of the lyrics betrays a somewhat shaky understanding of the philosophical concept in question. The singer Boy George complains to his beloved, "when you go, you're gone forever." Which is very much missing the point. The ancient Indian notion of *karma* turns precisely on the idea that when we go, we are *not* gone forever. We will be reborn, and the actions we performed in this life will affect our fate in the next. Unlike Boy George's wardrobe, the consequences of this idea for Indian philosophy and religion can hardly be exaggerated. In this chapter, we'll start to see why.

The rebirth theory sounds like an optimistic one. Surely we all fear death, and would all welcome the chance to live forever, even if in another form. Well, that's not how many ancient Indians saw things. Their goal was rather to escape from the cycle of rebirth, which is after all just as much a cycle of redeath. Since *karma* was the factor that would tie them to their next incarnation, it seemed that the only way to achieve liberation was to eliminate all *karma* from oneself. Extreme measures were taken in pursuit of this goal. The early Jainas devised a practice that has been called "immobility asceticism."[1] After years of training, they would attempt to stay completely still until they died from thirst, hunger, or exposure. The point of this was to avoid engaging in any action whatsoever, since all actions, whether good or bad, result in *karma*. The suffering undergone during the agonizing process of death would cleanse the *karma* acquired in earlier stages of life. Another group that dissented from the Brahmanical worldview, the Ājīvikas, were more pessimistic and thought that the cycle of rebirth was impossible to escape, and that there was no point trying to affect one's *karma*.[2] To achieve liberation, each individual just has to wait until the cycle of incarnations comes to an end—which the Ājīvikas expected to take millions of years.. And you thought Indra showed patience!

This whole idea of *karma* and rebirth can be found in the earliest Upaniṣads, so we may naturally associate it with the Brahmanical tradition rather than these dissident groups. However, there's some debate over the origins of the theory. We don't find it in the Vedas themselves, which as you'll remember are the even earlier texts to which the Upaniṣads are reacting. Some scholars nonetheless assume a Vedic background for the doctrine, while others see it as a kind of interloper into Brahmanical culture. According to this view, the notion of *karma* had already existed in the northeastern region of India in the valley of the River Ganges.[3] When the upholders of Brahmanism migrated into this area from their homelands in the Indus valley, they fell under the influence of this older tradition and incorporated *karma* into their teachings. The debate has turned on some surprising details, for instance the prevalence of metaphors involving rice to express the cycle of rebirth, and use of rice in rituals aimed at manipulating *karma*. It's been pointed out that this is not a crop local to the Indus region, where farmers instead used wheat, while rice is characteristic of agriculture in the Ganges.[4] This fine-grained historical analysis suggests that *karma* is not really a Brahmanical idea but was instead part of the indigenous culture further east.

Wherever it was first born, *karma* was at the very least (and fittingly enough) reborn in the Upaniṣads. Let's quote again from the *Great Forest Upaniṣad* (3.3.2):

> "Yājñavalkya, tell me—when a man dies, and his speech disappears into fire, his breath into the wind, his sight into the sun, his mind into the moon, his hearing into the quarters, his physical body into the earth, his soul (*ātman*) into space, the hair of his body into plants, the hair of his head into trees, and his blood and semen into water—what happens to that person?" Yājñavalkya replied: "My friend, we cannot talk about this in public. Take my hand; let's go and discuss this in private." So they left and talked about it. And what did they talk about? They talked about nothing but *karma*. And what did they praise? They praised nothing but *karma*. Yājñavalkya told him: "A man turns into something good by good action and into something bad by bad action."

Here we have one of the "hidden teachings" that give the Upaniṣads their name. In this case, the secret doctrine not fit for public consumption was the doctrine of *karma*: that we are made into what we are by what we do. In particular, it is the moral quality of what we do that will shape the life we are going to enjoy or suffer.

So here in an early Upaniṣad, we have the core idea that most people (though not Boy George) associate with *karma*: be good, or else. Your moral decisions in the here and now will bring you reward or punishment down the line, in the next life if not in this one. But is the theory of *karma* simply an account of moral retribution? That doesn't sound very appealing, or for that matter very philosophical. And it gets worse. It's tempting to see the *karma* theory as a way to justify the inequality of Brahmanical culture, with the *brahmins* being rewarded for their good deeds in a former life, while male members of the lower castes (and all women!) are being punished for the crimes they must have committed in their own former lives. Thus we find in the *Chāndogya Upaniṣad* the idea that those who engage in pleasant conduct will "enter a pleasant womb," like that of a *brahmin*, *kṣatriya*, or *vaiśya*, whereas those who are of "foul behavior" will enter the foul womb of a dog, pig, or an outcast (5.10.7).

But this would be a reductive and inadequate understanding of *karma*. The doctrine is in fact a way to affirm human freedom, and to give us a motivation for trying to act well. To see why, it will help to consider two alternative and rival theories. One was held by the unorthodox ascetic Gośāla, the leader of the aforementioned Ājīvikas, who denied that the cycle of rebirth can be escaped. Gośāla held that everything happens exactly as it is predestined to happen by "fate (*niyati*)," so that human action is ineffective and inconsequential. The Ājīvika tradition did not live on past antiquity, as did the other schools of thought we've been discussing, but Gośāla's views are described in the recorded dialogues of the Buddha, as follows:

> There is no power in humans, no strength or force, no vigour or exertion. All that lives is without control, without power or strength, they experience the fixed course of pleasure and pain through the six kinds of rebirth . . . Because pleasure and pain have been measured out with a measure limited by the round of birth-and-death, and there is neither increase nor decrease, neither excellence nor inferiority. Just as a ball of string when thrown runs till it is all unravelled, so fools and wise run on and circle round till they make an end of suffering.[5]

So the Ājīvikas denied that we have any responsibility for our actions. In fact, they could be understood to deny that "action" is possible at all, if to act involves making rational choices. How then should one live, if the idea that reason can be the guide of human action is a myth? Gośāla thought the answer lies in asceticism. One should withdraw as far as possible from the pretense of action at all, and instead live as a renunciate and forest-dweller. This ascetic lifestyle was embraced especially by those Ājīvikas who claimed that their eons of waiting were finally over, and that in their present lives they were experiencing the last of their many incarnations.

Precisely the opposite conclusion was drawn by another group, the materialist philosophers known as the Cārvākas. Again, their ideas are reported in the Buddhist canon, where they are represented as insisting that there is no good or evil in the world, and that a human is nothing more than flesh and blood:

> This human being is composed of the four great elements, and when one dies the earth part reverts to earth, the water part to water, the fire part to fire, the air part to air, and the faculties pass away into space. They accompany the dead man with four bearers and the bier as fifth, their footsteps are heard as far as the cremation-ground. There the bones whiten, the sacrifice ends in ashes. It is the idea of a fool to give this gift: the talk of those who preach a doctrine of survival is vain and false. Fools and wise, at the breaking-up of the body, are destroyed and perish, they do not exist after death.

So for a Cārvāka there are no reasons to act morally because there are no moral reasons for action. As we'll see later (Chapters 32–3), this attitude lent itself to a hedonist ethic, which allowed that deliberative action is possible but claimed that only one thing can guide our deliberations. Like Madonna, they were living in a material world, and they set their heights on no goal more exalted than leading a pleasurable life.

What is the alternative to Ājīvika fatalism and Cārvāka moral skepticism? It is to think, first of all, that there is such a thing as deliberative action, action governed by reason and reflection. And second, it is to believe that moral considerations should play a role in such deliberation. If one is to counter the doctrines of fate and chance, one needs to show that there are moral motivations for action. That is why the doctrine of *karma* was taught, as a simple and effective solution to a tricky problem. The doctrine "requires that a man's own 'character' be his own 'destiny,'"[6] and that each action has its appropriate consequences. Those actions that are good, springing from a clear-sighted mind and a virtuous disposition, result in future happiness and well-being (*sukha*); actions that are bad, deriving from ignorance, greed, and malice, produce only suffering (*duḥkha*).

Of course, if these consequences are actually to make a difference to my choices, I must believe that the results of good and bad actions will affect me and not someone else. The agent (*kartṛ*) of the action (*karma*) must be the same person as the enjoyer (*bhoktṛ*) of the result (*phala*). So the *karma* doctrine implies, or perhaps assumes, that the world is governed by justice, with each person guaranteed to reap what he or she sows. This may seem to bring the *karma* theory closer to a religious conviction. But as we saw in the last chapter, it was only gradually that divine oversight was invoked in this sort of cosmic context. In the Upaniṣads it appears to be just a brute fact that there is a moral order built into the universe. Only as the tradition develops are divinities made responsible for overseeing the dispensation of justice in light of karmic merit and demerit. In the earlier period, the world is simply presented as a just place, with each person's long-term happiness in proportion to their virtue. The "law of *karma*" is one that needs no lawgiver.

But is this really a way to place morality on firm foundations? It looks more like a naked appeal to self-interest. Each of us is told: "You had better behave well, since you and you alone will suffer the consequences of your misbehavior," or more optimistically, "If you want to flourish and be happy, you must behave well." The goal I'm being told to pursue is my own overall happiness in the long run, with virtue a mere instrument for achieving that objective. Of course it's welcome news that the world is just set up in such a way as to reward the good and punish the bad, with the vicious winding up as dogs and pigs while the virtuous get, if you will, a womb with a view, one with an outlook on happiness. But the doctrine appears to give us no reason to exercise genuine altruism, to have moral concern for the interests of others. If I am only trying to optimize my own future well-being, it seems that I am making no effort to further the well-being of others. The Buddha had a simple and brilliant answer to this challenge: he denied that there is any metaphysical distinction between self and others. Concern for others and concern for oneself are thus one and the same. We'll be looking at this Buddhist theory of "no-self (*anatta*)" in more detail shortly (see Chapter 8). For now, we just want to note that it reconciles *karma* with altruism, by extending the scope of what can properly be called "self-interest."

Another objection to the *karma* doctrine is even more straightforward: it just isn't true that good conduct is the best route to attain happiness. To the contrary, we see regularly that the good suffer and the wicked flourish. It's all too obvious that I can further my own interests by cheating and lying. Of course things would not turn out well for me if everyone acted that way all the time. But in a world where people generally behave well, the clever and wicked will prosper at the expense of the morally upright. It's here that we can see the ethical relevance of an aspect of the doctrine that may seem more at home in religious belief: the doctrine of rebirth or transmigration. If I am worried about not only this life but also the next, that may change my calculations as to what is truly advantageous. It's hardly a winning strategy to secure riches and pleasure through devious actions now, if it means I'll be born as a dog next time around.

But that does not really solve the problem so much as postpone it. How can we be sure that justice will be meted out in the next life for the sins we commit now? We need a guaranteed connection between good action and what is good for the individual. Such a connection is forged in one of the most famous writings of ancient India: the *Bhagavad-gītā*, the dialogue between Arjuna and Kṛṣṇa embedded within the *Mahābhārata*.[7] On the eve of a mighty battle, the warrior prince Arjuna is wracked with doubt. Facing him on the battlefield are not some unknown and nameless enemies, but his own kinsfolk and elders. They are guilty of heinous crimes, and Arjuna has both caste duty and social convention on his side. Yet he cannot persuade himself that it is right to kill his own family members, preferring, as he says, the life of a beggar and a mendicant. Kṛṣṇa intervenes, and tries to convince him that he must fight the battle. His advice rejects the kind of instrumental reasoning bound up with the *karma* theory.

Kṛṣṇa tells Arjuna that any action undertaken out of desire for some result will only lead to further desires. Whatever the outcome of each action, this way of thinking about our choices can end only in suffering. For one can never satisfy all one's desires, and the more one acts with the hope of getting rewards, the more one is liable to disappointment and frustration. As Kṛṣṇa puts it, "From attachment springs desire, from desire is anger born" (2.62). The goal of the *karma* theory was to guide one's deliberations and actions by moral considerations, in order to achieve long-term benefit. Now Kṛṣṇa argues that none of this matters. For no matter what goal you choose to desire, you will find only further discontent. How then ought one motivate oneself to act, if not from a desire for the results of the action? Kṛṣṇa claims that the truly virtuous action is not one that aims at some objective, whether in this life or another, but instead an action free from desire for any result (*niṣkāmakarma*). "Action alone is thy proper business," he says, "never the fruits [it may produce]; let not your motive be the fruit of action" (2.47).

But how do I know which action to perform, if not by looking to a cosmic system of just reward and punishment? Simple: one must do that which is natural or proper to oneself, one's *svadharma*. Kṛṣṇa says, "hear just how a man perfects himself by [doing and] rejoicing in his proper work" (18.45). Thus the *Gītā* tells us that we must act, but without formulating a desire that would be fulfilled by acting. Kṛṣṇa's advice to Arjuna is instead to act according to his duty and nature, but remain detached from any self-interest in the results of his actions. To act in a way that is true to one's character is to act well. It may still turn out that the consequences, as prescribed by the principle of *karma*, will also be good, but one should not be motivated to act by those consequences.[8]

7

CASE WORKER

PĀṆINI'S GRAMMAR

The power wielded by the *brahmins* of ancient India stemmed not from armies or wealth, but from knowledge. That power was duly expressed, not in wars or lavish building projects, but in words and ritual deeds—the sacrifice of animals and plants, the uttering of chants and formulas. It's a testament to the intimate relation between Brahmanical authority and language that they produced some of the world's oldest literature. That literature frequently refers to language, especially spoken language—remember that the Vedas and Upaniṣads were transmitted orally for many generations before being written down. "Speech" is duly a running theme in the Upaniṣads, as when the self (*ātman*) is said to consist of speech, mind, and breath (*Great Forest Upaniṣad* 1.5.3), or the purifying sacrifice to be enacted through two things, mind and speech. The ritual can succeed only when both are correct, as a cart cannot roll on only one wheel (*Chāndogya Upaniṣad* 1.16.1–2).

No wonder then that ancient India was also home to one of the most impressive figures in the history of linguistics: Pāṇini, who seems to have lived from the sixth to the fifth centuries BC. His fame rests upon the *Aṣṭādhyāyī*, or *Book in Eight Chapters*, a dense and technical work describing the grammatical structure of Sanskrit by means of thousands of aphoristic remarks. It's an astounding achievement, even if it draws on the work of earlier grammarians. The composition and subsequent reception of the *Eight Chapters* and other texts ascribed to Pāṇini illustrate more general features of the Indian literary tradition. For one thing, the whole endeavor presupposes a religious context. It is the sacredness of the Sanskrit language that makes it worth analyzing in such minute detail, and the most obvious precursor to Pāṇini's grammar can be found in works that discuss Vedic verses on a word-by-word basis.[1] But you don't have to be a historian of religion to appreciate the results. Indeed, most of the scholarship devoted to Pāṇini is by specialists in linguistics, and says nothing at all about his cultural or religious setting. Instead, he is taken seriously as a figure whose ideas can be compared with those of modern-day linguists like Noam Chomsky.

For another thing, the reception of Pāṇini's work followed a pattern we'll be seeing often in the rest of this book.[2] Like the philosophers of the various schools, the Pāṇinian grammarians produced layers of commentary on their authoritative source text, which in their case was the *Eight Chapters*. The aphorisms in which Pāṇini set down his grammar were called *sūtras*, brief remarks that were meant to be memorized. Later grammarians added comments called *vārtikka*, intended to supplement Pāṇini, for instance by making additional points deemed to be absent in the original *sūtras*. There was also the detailed form of exegesis known as *bhāṣya*, which unfolded the teaching, and often added illustrative examples. The most important such text in the grammatical tradition was the *Mahābhāṣya* (*Great Commentary*) of Patañjali, written in the second century BC. Generally speaking such exegesis was intended to explain and expand on the founder's remarks, but it was also possible in a *bhāṣya* to challenge or correct those remarks.

Patañjali confirms the point we were just making about the religious imperative of Pāṇini's grammar, since he writes at the beginning of his commentary that "grammar should be studied for the sake of the preservation of the Vedas."[3] Yet Pāṇini's grammar is no Vedic commentary. It is a study of the entire Sanskrit language. The grammarians do not necessarily analyze Vedic verses, but devote their attention to quotidian examples of language like "Devadatta is cooking rice." In coming to this text, then, the philosophically minded reader should not expect to find a vision of the universe and its relation to the individual, as in the Upaniṣads. Instead, grammar constituted a reflection on the structure and implicitly the nature of language. Patañjali says that grammar offers "instruction about words," but of course it isn't the sort of instruction that children receive from their parents when they are learning to talk, or for that matter the sort that you'd receive if you took a class on Sanskrit.[4]

The ancient grammarians did explain the formation of individual words, but obviously they could not proceed by considering each word in the language individually. That would be a never-ending task, as captured in the nice story that the god Bṛhaspati taught our patient friend Indra about language for 1,000 years one word at a time, at which point they still hadn't finished the subject.[5] Instead, grammar must deploy generalization and abstraction. One of Pāṇini's most important breakthroughs is to use abbreviations to stand in for a range of possible cases, something we might compare to the way logicians use variables to expose the form of a logical argument. (In fact Aristotle invented this convention in ancient Greece not much later.) Thus he can quickly state a rule that applies to an indefinite number of linguistic expressions. One can imagine doing the same thing in English, like this: "let 'V' stand for a verb; then 'V' followed by '-ed' is the past tense of that verb." This rule would allow you to derive "walked" from "walk," or "cooked" from "cook." And this is in fact pretty much how Pāṇini's grammar works. He builds words out of basic roots with add-ons to show features like the case of a noun. The basic procedure will be familiar to you if you've ever studied a language with declinable nouns, such as Greek or Latin, which are by the way related to Sanskrit and have many of the same grammatical features.

But even if you have studied Greek, Latin, or (even better) both, you may find some of Pāṇini's proposals surprising. We are usually taught that the basic components of a sentence are subject and predicate. Pāṇini instead makes *action* the core notion of his grammar. That is why the *Eight Chapters* are supplemented with a list of all the verbal roots in Sanskrit, with these providing the core or basis of the whole language. What we would think of as the subject of a sentence is for him the agent of the action described in that sentence.[6] Alongside the agent and the action, the other key part of a sentence is what he calls the "patient" of an action. (For those of you who know that "declining a noun" doesn't mean refusing to look something up in a dictionary, we'll mention that this "patient" is going to be put in the accusative case.) In the sentence "Devadatta is cooking rice," the rice—we would call it the "object" of the verb—is the "patient" of the action of cooking. Then additional components of the sentence can be added to indicate the place where the action is happening, the instrument that is being used to perform it, and so on, as when we say "Devadatta is cooking rice in the pot with fire." As Pāṇini explains, in Sanskrit one simply indicates the function of each noun using case endings. In English, by contrast, we tend to use prepositions such as "in" and "with."

Insofar as they play different functions in a sentence, nouns become what Pāṇini calls *kārakas* or "contributory factors for some action." Patañjali puts it like this: "a thing becomes a *kāraka* with respect to the accomplishment of an action in which it participates."[7] In our example, Devadatta plays the role of the *kāraka* of "agent," which is primary and presupposed by all the other *kārakas* since no action can be performed without an agent. Pāṇini says that there are six such thematic case-roles: agent, patient or recipient, instrument, donor, target, and locus. If one were to say "the leaf falls from the tree to the ground," the leaf would be the agent because it functions independently; the tree is the donor; and the ground is the locus, or where the leaf falls. If one says "the king gives wealth to the *brahmin* by his own hand," then the king is the agent, wealth is the object given, and we also have the *brahmin* as recipient and the hand as the instrument by which the act of giving takes place. The importance of action in the theory is indicated by the fact that the relationship we express with the preposition "of," but expressed using a case marker in Sanskrit, is not considered by Pāṇini to denote a *kāraka*. The reason is that "of" just denotes a relationship between two nouns, as in "the greed of the *brahmin*," rather than a relationship between the verb and a contributory factor. Thus Pāṇini's *kārakas* are not in fact the same as the grammatical cases of Greek or Latin, but more like "thematic roles" that words can play.[8] Indeed, the same grammatical role might be marked with different endings in different contexts, not always by the same linguistic marker.

Of course, sentences can get much more complicated than the ones we've been considering. What if the verb is passive, as when we say "the rice is being cooked?" Or what if we have a word which doesn't take case markers (what grammarians call "indeclinable")? What if we are using compound words? This is why Pāṇini gives us so many rules. His guidelines tell you what to do in these and many other circumstances. In a feature of his grammar much commented upon by linguists, Pāṇini sees that some rules constitute exceptions to other rules. There are most general rules that cover all words, something that the grammarians compare to the rain that falls on all alike. Then sometimes a more specific rule will trump a general rule. Consider the fact that in English, a verb that already ends in –e doesn't in fact get –ed added to show past tense, but only –d, as with "liked" or "shared," words without which no one could describe what they've been doing on social media. To capture this, Pāṇini even takes care to put the more general rules earlier in his list of *sūtras*, and specifies that a later entry will overrule an earlier entry with which it conflicts.

So far, we've been talking about Pāṇini and his followers as if they were simply describing the way that Sanskrit works. But that isn't the only way to think about grammar. Imagine that a friend says, "do you want to come with?" or, even worse, "do you want to come with Jonardon, Peter and I?" If you are a bit of a pedant, you wouldn't simply add these to your list of the grammatical constructions used in English, even though your friend was speaking English and even though these solecisms are actually quite frequent. Instead you would correct your friend: "you have to say 'come with *me*,' not just 'come with,' because the word 'with' takes an object." The ancient Indian grammarians were also sticklers on such points, and thought of their rules as marking the difference between correct and incorrect language. Their mission was not merely descriptive, but prescriptive, or as philosophers might say, "normative." In other words, they were not so much telling us how we talk, but how we *ought* to talk.

Yet neither, of course, were they at liberty to decide arbitrarily what counts as correct Sanskrit. As Patañjali said, "if you want pots, go to a potter, but if you want words, don't go to a grammarian,"[9] meaning that you should instead go find some actual language users and see how they form their sentences. What's called for is a kind of compromise between the descriptive and normative conceptions of grammar. The Pāṇinians do want to describe how people speak, but only when they speak correctly. Hence they demarcated a group of people called the *śiṣṭa*, the "well-educated" or "learned." Grammar describes the speech of these people, not that of the riff-raff on the street. The Pāṇinians went so far as to say that such elite language users are distinguished by their upright moral character, and not only their class or levels of education, the underlying assumption being that speaking correctly means thinking correctly.[10]

Here's an example of how this worked in practice.[11] We've seen that Pāṇini made agents and actions central to his analysis of language. But what about a sentence like "the pot cooks the rice"? One option would be to rule this out as simply incorrect, as it is Devadatta who is cooking the rice *in* the pot. But this is not what the grammarians say. Sanskrit users routinely referred to inanimate things as if they were agents, and were happy to say that pots cook rice. (We do the same, of course: if you were told to get the "rice-cooker" out of the cupboard, you wouldn't think Devadatta was stashed in there, but an inanimate appliance.) The grammarians were prepared to allow this usage, and laid down no rule forbidding us to treat a pot as having the *kāraka* of agent. This led to a difference of opinion between the grammarians and the "Naiyāyikas," or logicians, who insisted that only a living thing can be dignified with the word "agent (*kartṛ*)." (Notice that this is the same word used for "agent" in the theory of *karma*, discussed in the previous chapter.) Pāṇini's approach was more pragmatic, and gave due weight to actual language use. It is perfectly correct to say either that Devadatta is cutting the tree or that the axe is cutting the tree. So it must be allowed that the axe is an "agent" even though we know that it is really the "instrument" of cutting.

Here we've come to what may be the deepest philosophical question raised by the work of Pāṇini and his successors: does the study of grammar expose the structure of the underlying reality to which language refers? Or is it merely the study of linguistic usage, which may or may not tell us anything about the world? This is not a question Pāṇini addresses. He restricts himself to devising the many rules needed to form sentences properly. But some scholars have thought that he presupposes something deeper below the surface grammar of sentences. This would be what philosophers call the "semantic" level, as opposed to the level of syntax. At the semantic level we deal with meaning, rather than mere grammatical form. With this distinction in hand, we may suspect that with the disagreement as to whether a pot can be an agent, the logicians and grammarians were talking past one another. It is proper to use the word "pot" to play the *syntactic* role of an agent, and this is what interested the grammarians. It is a different matter whether the word "pot" actually *means* an agent.

But scholars don't agree about the importance of semantics in Pāṇinian grammar. According to one reading, Pāṇini asks us to look at the semantic role of a word to determine what syntactic role it should receive.[12] For instance, you don't generate passive verbs in his system just by mechanically modifying an active verb form. Rather, you go back to square one and see that what is wanted in a given sentence is a passive meaning. Only then do you look at your grammatical rulebook and find out what the correct ending will be. Against this, it's been argued that Pāṇini is really only interested in the construction of words, and out of words, sentences, so that he has no interest in semantics at all. After all, grammatical syntax can be thought of as indifferent to meaning, as shown by the fact that you can form grammatically correct sentences that don't have any sensible meaning. The Indian grammarians gave the wonderful example, "There goes the son of a barren woman with his hair-top bedecked with sky-flower, bathed with the milk of a tortoise carrying a bow made of the horn of a rabbit."[13]

Yet later grammarians definitely paid attention to the question of how words relate to meanings, if only in the process of staking out the proper boundaries of grammar as a science. Patañjali gave the example of a cow, and asked whether the grammarian is interested in the actual animal with a tail and hooves. No: it is the *word* that is discussed in grammar. And the word is, he says, "that which when uttered causes one to think of the cow," or "the sound by which meaning (*artha*) is understood."[14] This meaning is permanently linked to the word "cow," and what is meant by it could be either cows in general or some particular cow. There are difficult philosophical issues lurking here. If the meaning of "cow" is a general one, then do we have to posit some universal nature of "cow-ness" for the word to latch on to? European philosophers did not have a monopoly on the so-called "problem of universals." That problem was obliquely raised through consideration of the function of words, and it is going to be tackled head-on by other philosophers among the Buddhists, Mīmāṃsā, and the Nyāya school who even use the same example of the cow and milk it for all it's worth.

While we can't credit the earliest grammarians with similarly elaborate philosophical reflections on this problem, they did forge a number of conceptual instruments that went into the Indian philosopher's toolbox. One that is closely connected to what we've just been discussing is the use–mention distinction. It's one thing to refer to the word "cow," and another actually to use this word to refer to cows. It's the difference between a statement like "'cow' has three letters" or "'cow' is a noun," and one like "I see a cow in the field." We nowadays mark this distinction using quotation marks for words that are being mentioned instead of used. The ancient Indian grammarians had no such orthographical device, but

Pāṇini has nonetheless been credited with making the distinction between use and mention.[15]

Nor does the contrast we've been drawing between grammarians and logicians mean that the grammarians were blind to logical issues. Patañjali formulated two of the most basic laws of reasoning: that double negation is equivalent to affirmation (if something is "not not a cow" then it is a cow), and that there is no third option between an assertion and its denial (the "law of the excluded middle").[16] The fact that they were able to disagree on certain points, as with the question of the agency of pots, shows that Indian grammarians and logicians were at least operating in closely adjacent fields, even if they were plowing different furrows. All this gives the historian of philosophy good reason to take an interest in the Pāṇinians. Beyond the philosophical relevance and interest of their own ideas, we can also see them as foreshadowing developments in philosophical schools yet to come. The activities of the Mīmāṃsā school will be predicated on the idea that the sacred language of Sanskrit is fixed for all time. This is a reminder of the religious context that originally gave rise to Pāṇini's project, and a reassertion of the value of the grammatical tradition which will continue to go hand in hand with devotion to the rituals and culture of brahmanism.[17] But as we've already indicated, the earliest phase of Indian thought was not marked by a monolithic agreement as to the value of that culture. Appropriately enough, we've sandwiched Pāṇini between the Upaniṣads and the critics of brahmanism. And next, we'll turn to the greatest of those critics: the Buddha.

8

SUFFERING AND SMILING

THE BUDDHA

"The first step is admitting you have a problem." This advice is, famously, aimed at those who may be suffering from addiction. But according to the Buddha it applies to us all. His teaching centers on the "Four Noble Truths," the first of which is that all of us have a problem so pervasive and so difficult to escape that we usually fail to perceive it as a problem at all. The problem is that we are alive, and life is suffering. If that's the bad news, the worse news is that death is no escape. For, in keeping with the doctrine of rebirth and karmic retribution, death will free us from only our current portion of suffering, and deliver us directly to another. How can we possibly free ourselves from our predicament? Only by attaining a better understanding of that predicament, which includes coming to understand that we have no selves that need to be set free in the first place.

With this teaching, the Buddha signaled his disagreement with the Brahmanical tradition represented by the Upaniṣads, which made *ātman* (the self) a central preoccupation. But then, the Buddha was no *brahmin*. According to the elaborate legend of his former lives and final incarnation,[1] he chose to be born into the *kṣatriya* class, as a royal prince. After his mother dreamed of a white elephant which entered into the side of her body, she conceived the child who would become the Buddha. When he was born, he could already speak and walk. His first deed was to take seven steps and proclaim that life is full of sorrow, and that he had come after innumerable life cycles to help free both gods and men from this misery. Despite this precocious declaration, he would spend his youth and early adulthood oblivious of his mission. He grew up in comfort and luxury before he was set on the path to enlightenment when, as a young man, he ventured forth from the palace and was confronted for the first time by old age, sickness, and death. He retreated to the forest and took up the extreme ascetic practices associated with the Ājīvakas, only to find them ineffective. Rejecting this path, the Buddha sat beneath a tree and began to meditate. When enlightenment came, he did not keep his newly found wisdom to himself, but gathered students to him—the first Buddhists, and certainly not the last.

These details, and far more besides, are contained in the earliest writings about the Buddha and his teachings, sometimes called the "Pāli canon" because they were written in the Pāli language. As with the Upaniṣads and other ancient Indian texts, we're dealing with an originally oral tradition here, which was set down in writing only centuries after the Buddha's lifetime, which was probably in the fifth century. His sayings and conversations are collected in the works called *nikāyas*, which are in turn only one of three bodies of early Buddhist literature, known as the "three baskets (*tipiṭaka*)." The other two baskets are the *vinaya piṭaka*, which give instruction for Buddhist monks, and the most philosophical of the texts, the *abhidhamma* (Sanskrit: *abhidharma*) or "higher teaching." The Pāli canon is the most obvious source for early Buddhist religion and philosophy, but not the only one. We also have biographies of the Buddha written in Chinese, from the second to fourth centuries AD. Nor should we overlook the importance of architectural and iconographical material, notably the ancient burial mounds called *stūpas*, surrounded by decorative railings and statues.[2] We're going to draw freely on such later material in this and the next chapter, so as to present the fundamentals of early Buddhism as a tradition. It would be far more ambitious, and perhaps even impossible, to separate the Buddha's own teachings from the history of its reception.

Probably you don't need an archeologist's help to conjure up an image of the Buddha: sitting cross-legged, eyes half-shut, smiling beatifically. And you might wonder, what's with the smiling? Why look so serene, when your message to humankind is that life consists of suffering? Well, it turns out there's some good news after all. There are three more Noble Truths, which concern the cause of suffering, what it would mean to escape suffering, and the path toward that escape. But before we look at the solution to our problem, let's think more about the problem itself. Is the Buddha's rather bleak assessment of our situation plausible? Sure, life does involve disease and—if you're lucky—old age, with death providing the inevitable conclusion. But in the meantime there is plenty of opportunity to enjoy life: the silent films of Buster Keaton, the occasional almond croissant, and of course books about the history of philosophy. True, the Buddha had no access to any of these, but presumably there were equally worthwhile things available to enjoy in antique India (well, almost equally worthwhile).

Perhaps then it would help to set the Buddha's first Truth in its historical setting. Life in premodern societies, and of course in less affluent places today, is a precarious and often unpleasant affair. The story of how the Buddha leaves the palace and is shocked by the conditions beyond its walls is telling here. Nor should we forget that other spiritual and philosophical movements of his time were taking a rather critical attitude toward life on earth. The Jainas and Ājīvakas sought to escape the cycle of rebirth entirely, rather than seeking the best rebirth possible. These points could help to explain the Buddha's dramatic conclusion about the pervasiveness of suffering. Then too, some propose a different understanding of this central term "suffering," or *dukkha* (Sanskrit: *duḥkha*). Might the correct translation be something less dramatic and more obviously inevitable, like "dissatisfaction"? Unfortunately, this wouldn't really make the teaching more plausible. The problem to which the Buddha is pointing must be not only inevitable, but severe. After all, "into each life some rain must fall" doesn't mean we should think of nothing but finding an umbrella. We need an interpretation that makes "suffering" an all-pervasive and dire phenomenon, such that we have reason to restructure our entire lives in order to follow the Buddhist path.

Some light may be shed by turning to the second Noble Truth, which reveals the cause of suffering. In a word, it is desire: lusting for pleasure, coveting possessions, and wanting to avoid death. Both our longing for certain things and our aversion to other things fall under the heading of what the Buddhist texts call *taṇhā* (Sanskrit: *tṛṣṇā*) a general term for attached desire or "craving."[3] The counterproductive goals mentioned by the Buddha included the very goods that Brahmanical ritual was intended to achieve, such as a large family. For the Buddhist, the pursuit of these things guarantees *dukkha*. When you do not yet have them you suffer from your unfulfilled craving, and the stronger your desire grows the more you will suffer. When you do have them that brings suffering too, as you fear their loss. In the longer term, a life guided by desire keeps us stuck in the never-ending cycle of reincarnation, with rebirth offering nothing but further opportunity to suffer.

This is why the Buddha gave up his life as a royal prince, and more importantly the values that it entailed. However cosseted he might be, he would still have to fear those universal perils of illness, age, and death. Following his example many Buddhists have abandoned the "life of the householder," a life devoted to family and material prosperity. They became "renouncers," who withdrew from society to live a monastic lifestyle, though of course Buddhism is also followed by laypeople who support the monks and try to live by the Buddha's teachings. But we should not be misled by the term "renouncers." Remember that the Buddha tried a lifestyle of extreme asceticism and found that it did not bring him to enlightenment. Instead he taught a "middle way" between the householding life and the self-abnegation of some anti-brahmanic traditions. This is highlighted at the very beginning of what has come down to us as his "first sermon," which encourages students to avoid the "two extremes," on the one side a life devoted to passion, on the other deliberate self-torment and pain. Both are, according to the Buddha, "ignoble" and "useless."[4]

Though the Buddha was rejecting the ideas and values of the *brahmins* and their patrons, he did have at least one thing in common with some of them: he believed that salvation would come through knowledge. The cause of suffering is desire, but desire itself has a further cause, which is ignorance. Another chapter of the same *niyāka* that transmits the first sermon explains that ignorance gives rise to *kamma* (Sanskrit: *karma*), and *kamma* to consciousness, which leads to sensation and therefore to desire. Desire, in turn, leads to rebirth, and once you are born you are, of course, subject to the familiar dangers of death, age, grief, and so on.[5] The only way to get off this train of tears is to avoid boarding at the first station, by replacing your ignorance with understanding.

For the Buddhists the Vedic sacrifices are no more effective than the rigorous asceticism practiced by the Ājīvakas and Jainas. Though the Buddhists accepted the reality of the gods, they too were seen as subject to the cycle of rebirth. So even the gods are in need of liberation. And there was another difference between the Buddha's teaching and the Brahmanical tradition. Instead of exposing the hidden truth and correspondences that underlie everyday reality, as the Upaniṣads claimed to do, early Buddhism seeks to unmask that reality as merely conventional. It's here that we move into the territory of the third and fourth Noble Truths, as we come to see how our life would need to be if we were to escape suffering, and how to attain that goal. The Buddha's recommendation is as simple as it is radical: you can avoid being attached to the things that falsely seem to benefit you now and in the future, if you give up on the idea that you have a self that can be benefitted. It is through embracing and acting in accordance with this theory of "no-self (*anatta*; Sanskrit: *anātman*)" that we reach *nibbāna* (Sanskrit: *nirvāṇa*) which is liberation from all suffering.

Here there may seem to be a contradiction within the Buddha's teaching. We've been encouraged to give up on all desire. But what about desire for liberation? Couldn't that too constitute a kind of longing or unsatisfied craving? In that case the Buddha's teaching would just replace one sort of desire for another, as if he told us we could stay dry by coming in out of the rain to take a shower. But the project need not be a self-defeating one.[6] After all, the whole teaching is predicated on the desire to avoid suffering. When we learn that suffering comes from cravings and fears, our initial desire to avoid suffering should be transformed into a more useful desire. We should desire to lose all desire. This new desire is vital if we are to reach our goal, and it may fall away once all other desires have been eliminated. When enlightenment and liberation come, the desire for liberation will no longer serve any purpose. One Buddhism scholar has proposed that "craving [is] a stepping stone to getting rid of craving altogether."[7] Alternatively the Buddhist can simply distinguish between the self-centered desires described as *taṇhā* and the enlightened pursuit of escaping the cycle of rebirth that is characterized by such self-centered desires.

Certainly the Buddha is not advising us to conceive, and follow, a "desire" to eliminate or annihilate our selves. True, like contemporary Jainas and Ājīvakas, he is trying to help us escape from the karmic cycle. In his first sermon the Buddha lists, among the desires that lead to suffering, the longing to continue existing—but also the longing to cease existing.[8] The Buddhist way is instead to come to the realization that there *is* no self to annihilate. We've already said that this is diametrically opposed to Brahmanical thought, but it's worth restating the point. The Buddhists reject the idea that there is some unseen, unchanging center of identity that underlies all cognition, all awareness. That leaves a lot of room for them to accept less metaphysically ambitious notions of the self, of course. You don't need to accept the reality of a permanent self to believe that there is *some* sense in which you are the same person who started reading this chapter a few minutes ago or that, while reading, you can be aware of yourself reading.

Yet it seems clear that the Buddhists did want to critique and revise our everyday assumptions about the reality of persons, and other things. One classic text on the issue appears in the *Milinda-pañhā*, the aforementioned Buddhist text which depicts a sage called Nāgasena in conversation with the Hellenistic king Menander or Milinda.[9] Though the setting is reminiscent of the Upaniṣads, the doctrine is not. At one point in the discussion, Nāgasena tries to persuade the king that the familiar objects around us are considered to be whole substances only by convention. His example is a chariot. There is nothing more to it than its parts: the axle, the yoke, the wheels, the reins, and so on. Yet this does not mean that there is no sense in which we can truly say, "here is a chariot." It just means that the word "chariot" is a conventional one, a term we find convenient to apply to the whole aggregate of parts. Another nice example given in the Buddhist literature is a fist, which is evidently nothing more than the hand and fingers temporarily clenched together.[10] And so it is with people, too. We are aggregates that can lose and gain parts over time.

One can imagine a critic responding that every aggregate is made up of constituents. These constituents may be made up of still further constituents, as this paragraph is made up of sentences, which are in turn made up of words. But in the end we must come to fundamental parts, like the letters of the words.[11] So if we are looking for fundamental realities that make up each person, why not identify the self as such a reality? Because the Buddhist has a rival answer to the same question. The Buddhists applied the name *dhamma* (Sanskrit: *dharma*) to the simple components of any aggregate. In the case we are most interested in, there are five types of *dhamma* that go to make up the person. To emphasize their merely aggregative nature, these are called *khandhas* (Sanskrit: *skandha*), which means "heaps." The *khandhas* include all aspects of our being: physical form, bodily feelings, emotions, perceptions and thinking, and consciousness itself. That list may look vaguely familiar, since in the Upaniṣads these phenomena are the ones that conceal the more fundamental self hidden within. But for the Buddhists, there is nothing to a person over and above the conglomeration of momentary *khandhas*. You are nothing other than your bodily states, your feelings and perceptions, all of which are present only momentarily, existing for a fleeting moment only to be replaced by other *khandhas* of the same kind. Not that it would be right to identify yourself with any of these *khandhas*, individually or in aggregate. That would again represent attachment to the self.[12] There are just the *khandhas*, and that is it.

So here we have arrived at what may be the most notorious philosophical doctrine of Buddhism, that we are nothing more than flowing streams with no firm identity from time to time. This idea is going to be defended, and the Brahmanical theory of the unchanging self attacked, with great virtuosity by later Buddhists like Nāgārjuna. But we already see it emerging in the Pāli canon, often in the context of discussing reincarnation. Given that the Buddhists rejected the conception of an enduring self, you might expect that they would simply have given up on the whole idea of a cycle of rebirth. But there was no chance of that. It was a core teaching of the Buddha that actions have consequences, and the theory of *karma* we explained in an earlier chapter is a pan-Indian one. This requires a commitment to rebirth, since the consequences evidently do not always materialize within the lifespan of the one who performs the action. The key point is that causal continuity replaces identity as the relationship that holds across lives, and is sufficient to maintain fidelity to the ethics of *kamma*.

According to one of the *Nikāyas* the Buddha compared the person going through the cycle of reincarnation to a dog tied to a stake, fruitlessly running around in circles.[13] Even the idea that caste membership is based on one's deeds in former lives can be found in early Buddhist literature; the Brahmanical tradition did not have a monopoly on this idea. Unlike the Brahmanical authors, though, the Buddhists with their "no-self" doctrine had an obvious difficulty in explaining the possibility of reincarnation. Their solution seems paradoxical, or even no answer at all. Reflecting on the widespread belief that we will be requited for our actions in the next life, they denied that "he who experiences the fruit of the deed is the same as the one who performed the deed," but also denied that the two stand in no relationship whatsoever.[14]

We can see this by thinking more carefully about the nature of an aggregate which is changing over time. Take a giraffe. Every day it loses and takes in matter thanks to its digestive cycle. So if we were very strict about it, we might say that it is not exactly the same from day to day. Today it consists of different parts than the ones that made it up yesterday. On the other hand it seems equally obvious that today's giraffe is not completely different from yesterday's. It retains some parts that it had before, which is why we can truthfully say that this giraffe gamboling through the field now is "the same" as the one that was sleeping in her stable last night. And remember, the Buddhists are out to reject the Brahmanical idea that the self is *completely* the same across time, an unchanging foundation of identity which endures through changes in our perceptions, and even from one life cycle to the next. If a person is nothing but an aggregate of changing *khandhas*, then it obviously fails to have complete sameness across time. Still it might be "the same" in some weaker sense, for example because the stream of *khandhas* is causally interconnected in some way.

Buddhist philosophy was itself a changing agglomeration, with different thinkers holding rival views at one time and across the centuries. So it was when it came to this question we've just raised: what, if any, weaker sense of persistence might take a person from one incarnation to another? A minimal view, suggested by Nāgasena's discussion of the chariot, would be that talking about one person as being the same across time would be merely a useful convention. At the other end of the spectrum, some Buddhists will later endorse the idea of an underlying subject that overlies or emerges from the *khandhas* and that can undergo rebirth. They called this subject the *puggala* (Sanskrit: *pudgala*), and their school was accordingly called the Puggala-vāda.[15] Other Buddhists, unsurprisingly, felt that this was tantamount to conceding the Brahmanical view of self. There are similar tensions in early Buddhist literature about how, exactly, our actions determine our fate in the next life. Sometimes the Buddha is quoted as mocking the Jaina idea that actions cause *kamma* to adhere to us from one life to another. At other times we find him insisting—like the Ājīvakas—that the right course is to avoid action entirely, precisely because it brings *kamma*.[16] Perhaps the inevitability of such tensions explains why once, when the Buddha was asked whether there is really a self, he simply refused to answer.[17] This strategy was a favorite of the Buddha's. Like many great thinkers, he had not only innovative and original proposals to make, touching on questions in metaphysics, epistemology, and ethics—as we'll see next, he also had an interesting view about the status of these very proposals.

9

CROSSOVER APPEAL

THE NATURE OF THE BUDDHA'S TEACHING

With his doctrine of no-self, the Buddha rejected the Upaniṣadic idea of a search for the self as misguided. The century and more that the god Indra devoted to that search was a waste of time, since what he was looking for never existed. Yet with the four Noble Truths, the Buddha implicitly affirmed the Upaniṣadic conception of philosophy as being about "path and purpose": there may be no journey of *self*-discovery, but there is a journey nonetheless. For the Buddha the destination is *nibbāna,* the extinction of attachment and desire. This means that the function of his teaching is much like that of the Upaniṣads: to help the student along a path of inner conceptual development. The Buddha was at pains to ensure that his disciples understood this, and offered two analogies to capture the nature of his own philosophy: he compared it to a raft, and to a poisonous snake.

Imagine, the Buddha says, that a man builds a raft in order to get across a river from a dangerous place to a place of safety. He then thinks to himself, "This raft has been very helpful to me. Suppose I were to hoist it on my head or load it on my shoulder, and then go wherever I want."[1] That would be silly, and the *dhamma*—the Buddha's teaching—is similar to the raft. It is for the purpose of crossing over, not something to hold on to after you are on the other side. After explaining this, the Buddha tells his students: "when you know the *dhamma* to be similar to a raft, you should abandon even the teachings, how much more so things contrary to the teachings." What should we make of this? Rafts are just the thing when you are trying to cross a river. When that condition is no longer met, the value disappears. Indeed the raft becomes an encumbrance. Likewise, the teachings of the Buddha help the student to "cross over," to leave behind the world of craving and attachment and reach the state of enlightened life. But when their purpose is finished, the simile seems to imply, the Buddha's teachings are of no further use, even an encumbrance. Attachment in any shape or form is a cause of suffering, and that applies even to being attached to the truth.

Charming as it is, the analogy brings with it a problem: it appears to say that the Buddha's teachings are only instrumentally valuable. They are useful because they get us where we want to go, but only for that reason. This means that it makes no difference whether they are even true. After all, beliefs don't have to be true in order to be useful, which is why it is the rare parent who doesn't occasionally mislead, if not outright lie, to their children (from "Santa will put coal in your stocking if you don't behave" to "don't worry, everything will be all right," when sadly, it won't). On this account of the Buddha's message, it could even be that the Brahmanical theory of the unchanging self is true after all. It's just that believing in this truth brings suffering with it, so that it is better for us to be convinced that the theory is false. Worse still, we must ask ourselves whether the Buddha *knows* that his teachings could be untrue. In that case he wouldn't merely be embroidering a useful story, he would be telling a lie, albeit a helpful one. Surely, this is not the lesson we should draw from the analogy of the raft?

Here we should turn to another passage in which the Buddha explains the status of his teachings.[2] We are in the midst of a dialogue between the Buddha and the prince Abhaya, who asks whether it is proper to "utter such speech as would be unwelcome or disagreeable to others." The Buddha replies that he can give no straightforward answer. To explain why, he asks Abhaya what he would do if he saw a child put a pebble in its mouth. The prince replies that he would remove it, even if it meant hurting the child. The Buddha then responds with a list of the different possibilities of speech: for instance he would not say that which is untrue, unbeneficial, and unpleasant to others; nor would he say what is true but not beneficial. But out of his famous compassion, he would speak truthfully, beneficially, and agreeably—and he would know the right time to do it.

In the Buddha's list of types of speech, there is a glaring omission: he simply ignores the possibility of speech that is beneficial without being true. This is no oversight, for the case is clearly an awkward one. Apparently he does not think that lying is always wrong; otherwise, why mention the unbeneficial lie but fail to mention the beneficial one? The Sri Lankan Buddhist scholar K.N. Jayatilleke speculates that, for the Buddha, there simply are no such cases. He suggests that the Pāli term "beneficial" (*attha*) means "what is morally good in the sense of being useful for the attainment of the goal of *nibbāna*." And "since falsehood or the assertion of a statement which is false (*musāvāda*) was considered a moral evil, it would have been held to be logically or causally impossible for what is false, i.e. what is morally evil to result in what was useful in the sense of being morally advantageous or good (*attha-saṃhitam*)."[3] If this is right, then it turns out that there are no "white lies," no beneficial untruths. And indeed, the Buddha is said to have discouraged his disciples from lying, without making exceptions for situations where it would be expedient or helpful to do so. Nonetheless, the later Buddhist tradition continued to flirt with the idea of compassionate lying. In a famous Mahāyāna Buddhist text, the *Lotus Sūtra*, we have the parable of a father who gets his children to leave a burning house by promising that there are toys outside. After telling this story, the Buddha says to his interlocutor Śāriputra, "what do you think . . . was [the father] guilty of falsehood or not?" Śāriputra responds:

> No, this rich man simply made it possible for his sons to escape the peril of fire and preserve their lives. He did not commit a falsehood . . . because if they were able to preserve their lives, then they had already obtained a plaything of sorts. And how much more so when, through an expedient means, they are rescued from the burning house![4]

And the Buddha agrees. So, in yet another sign of the diversity of the Buddhist tradition, we find conflicting messages about the usefulness of misleading statements.[5]

There's yet another issue raised by the raft analogy. So far, we've been talking about the status of the teachings for someone who is in the midst of "crossing over" to enlightenment—does it matter whether they are true or not? But one can pose the same question from the point of view of someone who has *already* crossed over, from the point of view of enlightenment. In the last chapter we talked about the idea that the paradoxical desire to lose all desire could be resolved, if we suppose that this desire drops away once *nibbāna* is reached. Similarly, the raft analogy seems to say that the Buddha's teaching itself can be left aside after it has served its purpose. This may put some readers in mind of Wittgenstein, who encouraged us to see the proposals of his *Tractatus Logico-Philosophicus* as a ladder that can be thrown away once one has achieved a full understanding of his philosophy. To use another analogy that appears in Mahāyāna Buddhist writings, philosophical instruction could be like a medicine that "purges" us of our ignorance, but is then expelled along with whatever is purged.[6]

This way of conceiving the role of philosophy may seem inevitable, once we accept that the purpose of philosophical reflection is to bring us along the path to happiness or, what may amount to the same thing, to release us from suffering. After all, what guarantee is there that the beliefs that will make you happy just happen to be the ones that are true? We should not forget, though, that the Buddha traces suffering to attachment, attachment to desire, and desire to *ignorance*. He seems to presuppose that we will be freed from our worldly predicament precisely by understanding that predicament more fully. To this extent at least, we can see the Buddha as a bringer of truth, if not as a bringer of straightforward doctrine. The process of enlightenment is a therapeutic one, and brings us to a vantage point that may in some sense render the Buddha's teaching otiose. Still, there is no denying that it begins by dispelling falsehood.

So the Buddha may after all believe that truth will set you free, but that doesn't mean that it will set you free all at once. Just consider: you know now about the four Noble Truths. Perhaps deeper reading would deepen your grip on the Buddha's teaching, but it looks like our modest book should already have put you in touching distance of enlightenment. Yet we know that things are not that easy. It requires lengthy, perhaps lifelong, commitment and training to give up on desire and attachment. Understanding the four Truths is the easy part (otherwise we could hardly have explained them in a single chapter). The difficult thing is to live accordingly. The Buddha presented another analogy intended to express this point. He said that his teachings are like a poisonous snake. Just as if you want to catch a snake, you have to be careful to take it by the head and not the tail, so one must be careful to take the Buddha's words in the right way. This is a philosophy that bites.

It's worth quoting the relevant passage, since it tells us a lot about the way the Buddha wants us to understand and use his message. He tells us that some "misguided men" learn the *dhamma*, or teaching of the Buddha, but do not inquire into its meaning:

> Instead they learn the *dhamma* only for the sake of criticising others and for winning in debates, and they do not experience the good for the sake of which they learned the *dhamma*. Those teachings, being wrongly grasped by them, conduce to their harm and suffering for a long time. Why is that? Because of the wrong grasp of those teachings. Suppose a man needing a snake, seeking a snake, wandering in search of a snake, saw a large snake and grasped its coils or its tail. It would turn back on him and bite his hand or his arm or one of his limbs, and because of that he would come to death or deadly suffering. Why is that? Because of his wrong grasp of the snake.[7]

The Buddha's warning to misguided students is the same given by Jack Nicholson in the movie *A Few Good Men*: "you can't handle the truth!" They expect the wrong thing from the Buddha's teaching, supposing that learning is there to make you seem learned, that knowledge is something you display by winning arguments. With the analogy of the raft, we saw that the teaching may in some sense have a merely instrumental value. These misguided students see it that way too. But they are using it as an instrument to reach the wrong goal, hoping that it will help them to satisfy the desires for victory and esteem, which ironically are the very sort of desire that the teaching instructs them to abandon. To approach the Buddha's teaching the right way, we need to be open to its power to change our goals and desires, rather than hoping that it will allow us to satisfy the goals and desires we already have.

What should a good teacher do when confronted with students like these, who are not ready to learn? Lying is a strategy we've already considered and found problematic. But there's another option, often chosen by the Buddha: remain silent. This was not, of course, because he was bested in argument, as happens in the Upaniṣads, which often depict a character "falling silent" in defeat at the end of a dialectical inquiry. Rather, it is because he knows when speaking the truth will be beneficial, and when it will not. In the aforementioned early Buddhist dialogue, the *Milinda-pañhā*, the king Menander points to an apparent contradiction in reports about the Buddha. On the one hand, it is said that he kept nothing hidden, unlike other teachers who kept things "hidden in their fists." On the other hand, we know that he was in the habit of refusing to answer questions. So which is it: did he teach the truth openly or not?[8]

Nāgasena responds that there are *four* sorts of question. Some call for a straightforward response, some for further clarification, others should elicit a question in reply, and some should just be met with silence. And this makes sense. If someone asks you whether the color blue is heavier than the number four, you couldn't reasonably be expected to give a simple answer. That might be a situation where you should instead respond with another question, such as, "what makes you think that colors and numbers have weight?" But when would it be right to refuse to respond at all? Nāgasena says, "there is no utterance or speech of the Buddha's that is without reason, without cause." This suggests that it is up to the Buddha's interlocutor to *deserve* an answer, or to be in a position where some answer or other would be productive. If he is confronted by someone who only wants to win debates or boast of his enlightenment, then the Buddha will confront him with stony silence rather than pearls of wisdom.

This carefully calibrated teaching strategy may seem like a rather extreme form of tough love. But it is love nonetheless. One might say that compassion is not just a part of the Buddha's teaching; it is his hallmark, and according to Buddhist tradition distinguishes him from others who have achieved enlightenment. Not content to be liberated himself, he set down a teaching by which all of humankind could be freed from suffering. Here we reach another puzzle, though. The Buddha tells us that we can escape suffering by giving up attachment to things. But why should that lead to, or indeed have anything to do with, compassion? It's clear that a person who abandons desire would refrain from many sorts of wrongdoing. Why kill someone if you have no thirst for vengeance, or cheat and steal if you care nothing for wealth?

But compassion doesn't mean simply avoiding misdeeds, it means actively pursuing the welfare of others. Is the Buddhist like someone who has confused the first rule of medicine, "do no harm," with the whole of the medical enterprise?

Certainly not. Buddhist ethical teaching in fact lays great emphasis on what is called "skillful action (*kusala*)," the sort of action born out of a proper understanding of things, and claims that this will include action that is morally upright and compassionate.[9] This is enshrined in the "eightfold path" laid down by the Buddha. It begins with right understanding, but does not end there. Rather, one must pursue right speech, right action, and so on up to the level of right mindfulness and concentration. The Buddhist should of course take the right view upon things, by rejecting the reality of a stable, unchanging self and seeing that attachment leads to suffering. But that is only the first step. It takes long training and practice to *live* in accordance with the right view, which is why monasticism plays such a fundamental role, and includes such practices as searching self-criticism and obedience to strict rules of discipline.

So good behavior is a crucial part of the Buddhist path. But why, exactly? In what way does it free us from suffering? One answer that is prominent in Buddhist literature is that bad deeds will doom you to a worse life in your next reincarnation. Great stress is placed upon action that is *puñña*, or "karmically fruitful." A good next life, rather than total liberation, is the goal that is pursued by ordinary Buddhists. It is a feasible goal that gives the Buddhist a reason to behave well. But, we might object, it is surely the wrong sort of reason. I should not show compassion to others for my own sake or the sake of my own future self—and not just because I don't really have a self, but because compassion should be altruistic. It should be directed toward the good of those for whom I am compassionate. Indeed, the Buddha warns that a truly good action must be performed out of the right motive. That motive should not be desire for a favorable reincarnation. Like any other desire, such a motive would inevitably lead to suffering. If promises and threats concerning the next life do play a role, it may again be like that of the raft, useful for those who are making progress but not for those who have arrived.

Might compassion itself be like a raft or ladder that we discard upon arrival? That would be a disquieting thought. Surely benevolence and morality in general should characterize the perfect sage, not be something that the perfect sage has left behind. Yet the Buddhist texts sometimes suggest that this is indeed the case, as when they state that the *arahat*, meaning someone who has achieved full enlightenment, has "moved beyond *puñña*" and is no longer concerned with virtue. On the face of it this seems to clash with the depictions of the Buddha's zeal to help others. But it may be that such passages simply mean that the *arahat* is no longer concerned with action insofar as it bears on favorable reincarnation, having given up desire for this or anything else. Or perhaps the idea is that he need not actively deliberate about his actions, since he has reached the state where he just naturally acts well, because his actions are not attached to desire.[10] Or again, maybe we should understand that virtues like compassion take a different shape depending how far one has gotten along the path.

To see why the *arahat* would in fact act well, we need to go back to the idea of giving up attachment. So far we've been thinking of this in a purely negative fashion. To abandon greed, for instance, would mean never acting out of greed or even having greedy thoughts. But the opposite of greed is not the mere absence of greed. It is generosity. The Buddhist rejection of such things as envy, hostility, and greed is meant to bring about positive states of mind that are opposed to these sources of suffering. If you have no desires and are not even committed to the permanence of your own self, you will be much more inclined to share whatever you have. This is the moral counterpart of Buddhism's claim to provide a more adequate understanding of the world. When the Buddha helps us to banish ignorance, this is not only a matter of giving up false beliefs but replacing those false beliefs with positive beliefs that are true. Just as the *arahat* is ultimately freed even from the exertion that the rest of us devote to being good, so what significance or value the Buddha's teachings have depend on what stage on the path you have reached.[11]

10

CARRY A BIG STICK

ANCIENT INDIAN POLITICAL THOUGHT

What would your life have been like if you'd been born (or reborn) in ancient India? Going on what we've discussed so far, you're likely to imagine yourself as a sophisticated *brahmin*, well-schooled in the Vedas and in ritual sacrifice, as a noble *kṣatriya* warrior, perhaps as a Buddhist monk or nun, or if that life seems too easy, a radical renouncer of the Ājīvika or Jaina school. But of course it's far more likely you would have been a farmer or a cowherd. Texts like the Upaniṣads or the Buddhist canon give us, at best, only occasional and indirect insight into the quotidian reality of such people. Good thing, then, for the *Arthaśāstra*. This lengthy and elaborate treatise on affairs of state lays down detailed regulations governing the lives of all ancient Indians, from the king to the slave, from the *brahmin* to the ascetic. The reader who is interested in the dairy industry can learn from the *Arthaśāstra* that ancient Indian cows wore bells on their necks so that they might be easily located; that cattle were in danger of being attacked by crocodiles and tigers; that buffalo milk produces slightly more butter when churned than cow's milk; and that a cowherd who milked his animals twice a day in the dry season would have his thumb cut off (§2.19).[1]

Of course, it is not only issues of milk and butter that are clarified by the *Arthaśāstra*. It covers such topics as warfare, law, gender relations, slavery, and economics. It is a useful source for understanding the political context of Indian philosophy, packed with information about the four classes of society and the attitude of kings toward their subjects and toward rival kings. So there is no doubting its interest for the historian. What about its interest for the historian of philosophy? Should the *Arthaśāstra* be considered an early, pioneering work of political thought? Is its philosophical significance real but implicit, like the contribution of Pāṇini's *Book in Eight Chapters* to the philosophy of language? Or does the practical orientation of the *Arthaśāstra* mean that we would be mistaken to approach it from a philosophical point of view? After all, the Indian philosophical tradition is known especially for its philosophy of the self, its metaphysics, its epistemology—not for its political thought. No less an observer than Max Weber, the founder of modern sociology, claimed that Buddhism in particular was too otherworldly to bother with politics, and one might easily assume that the same goes for ancient Indian philosophy as a whole.[2]

That assumption is, however, overturned by the opening sections of the *Arthaśāstra*. From the very start, it's clear that however much this text may tell us about the lives of cowherds and farmers, it is written for the ruling elite. Part of its goal is to instruct rulers, and presumably would-be rulers, in the basic principles of governance. The reader of the *Arthaśāstra* will learn, for instance, about the seven elements (*prakṛti*) of a well-run state: the ruler himself, his officials, the territory over which he rules, the fortification, the treasury, allied states, and—last but certainly not least—*daṇḍa*, which literally means "stick" and is used here to refer to the army and to punishments imposed by the state. According to the opening lines of the *Arthaśāstra*, the "stick" is the subject of a whole branch of knowledge, called *daṇḍanīti*, which has been variously translated as "government," "science of punishment," and "rule of law" (§1.1). Future kings should be educated in this art, among others, from a young age (§1.5). *Daṇḍanīti* may even have been the original title of the work we now call the *Arthaśāstra*.[3] But the latter title is perhaps more appropriate. *Artha* means "advantage" or "success," so *Arthaśāstra* might be translated as "the art of the advantageous." That title fits the ambitions of the treatise, whose fifteen books tell you how the ruler should wield the "stick" of legal punishment and the military to best advantage.

You might be wondering when we are going to tell you who wrote the *Arthaśāstra*. If only it were that easy! The treatise presents itself as the work of Kauṭilya, who was the chief minister under Candragupta, founder of the Mauryan Empire in the northwest of the Indian subcontinent. Candragupta lived in the later fourth century BC, making him a contemporary of Alexander the Great; according to legend, the two mighty rulers even met face-to-face. At first glance, then, the *Arthaśāstra* would seem to be the advice of a powerful official for his even more powerful monarch. The problems start with the second and third glances. Ever since the manuscript preserving the treatise came to light in the early twentieth century, there has been disagreement over its dating and the role of the historical Kauṭilya in its composition. Worse still, the text seems to have gone through a subsequent process of reorganization, so that we are reading a much different work than the one that was originally composed.[4]

As if all that weren't complicated enough, the original version of the *Arthaśāstra* itself drew on earlier writings. Like Pāṇini compiling and building on the work of earlier grammarians, "Kauṭilya" (as we may as well call the author) reports on the political ideas of others even as he sets forward his own. This is most clear in the numerous passages that juxtapose a range of opinions on some question. Kauṭilya's own view appears as the final and correct word on the subject, often because it adopts a reasonable middle ground in comparison to the extreme views of others. To give just one example, a question is raised about how a good ruler should seek advice (§1.15). One idea is that the king should keep his own counsel, another that he should be open to ideas from absolutely everyone—even a child might offer a good suggestion—and still another that he should get input from a circle of experts. Kauṭilya adopts a compromise position. The king should discuss each matter with a small handful of ministers, like Kauṭilya himself in fact, though Kauṭilya is tactful enough not to say so. He adds a similarly pragmatic view on the membership of the king's council. Where others have insisted that some precise number of ministers is ideal, Kauṭilya says that it depends on circumstances.

Rival opinions are sometimes ascribed to specific, named individuals, making these passages in the *Arthaśāstra* reminiscent of the dialogues described in the Upaniṣads. These reports may even reflect actual debates at court.[5] Certainly, the impression is that there was lively discussion about political matters among ancient Indian intellectuals. This is confirmed by the existence of other writings from roughly the same period, collectively called the *Dharmaśāstras*, including the so-called *Laws of Manu* (*Manu-smṛti*).[6] These treatises will be an important inspiration in the Brahmanical tradition, and themselves draw on ideas found in other parts of that tradition, for instance early Mīmāṃsā. For the moment, we can just note on the historical front that there are often resonances between the *Dharmaśāstras* and the *Arthaśāstra*, on whose basis scholars have tried to determine lines of historical influence.

The word *dharma* that gives the *Dharmaśāstras* their name is not to be confused with *dharma* as it appeared in our discussion of the Buddhist doctrine of no-self, where it meant a part of an aggregate. Here *dharma* means something like "upright conduct" or "duty" in the widest sense—moral, social, and religious. How much should we read into the contrasting titles, *Dharmaśāstras* and *Arthaśāstra*? Is the *Arthaśāstra* really about expediency instead of morality, about taking advantage rather than taking heed of one's duty? That's certainly not the impression given at the start of the work. In a chapter that describes the stratified society of ancient India, the *Arthaśāstra* defines the four classes—*brahmin*, *kṣatriya*, *vaiśya*, and *śūdra*—in terms of their various duties, and likewise for such social groups as "householders" and "ascetics" (§1.3). The state will flourish so long as each group carries out its distinctive duties. As for the ruler, great emphasis is placed on his character, with warnings about kings of the past who came to grief because of their wrathfulness, susceptibility to pleasure, vanity, and so on (§1.6). Later, we are told that the king's happiness is bound up with that of his subjects (§1.19; see also §6.2).

A similarly moralistic take on political life is found in the sections of the *Arthaśāstra* that deal with law. Kauṭilya states that the imposition of justice is a crucial responsibility of the king (§3.1). Many of the detailed legal provisions also seem to consider not simply which laws will be expedient, but which are most just. Kauṭilya has much to say about which punishments should be meted out for which crimes, and adopts the fundamental principle that the punishment should indeed fit the crime. This manifests itself in attractive ways, as when Kauṭilya lays down that people should be excused from blame for an accident if they took reasonable precautions, and in not so attractive ways, as when he says that the fine to be paid for violating the rights of a slave is smaller than the one paid for wronging a free citizen (§3.13).[7]

Yet for long stretches of his *Arthaśāstra*, Kauṭilya takes a purely pragmatic, if not cynical, approach to his subject. Religion in particular features chiefly as a social phenomenon which the king should use to manage his subjects. This has led some readers to see the *Arthaśāstra* as an early example of the kind of materialist, even atheistic attitude more explicitly espoused by the philosophical school known as Cārvāka.[8] Kauṭilya has good reason for this hard-headed approach. He conceives political life largely as a struggle against various threats to stability and prosperity. He calls internal and natural threats to the community "thorns" and explains how the ruler may best remove them, by taking precautions against floods and other natural calamities, to say nothing of attacks by tigers and demons (§4.3). Of even greater interest to him is the external threat posed by enemy kings. He offers ample advice on how to defeat enemies in war, and also on manipulating and deceiving them. The moralist tone of other passages is nowhere in evidence as he speaks of how best to use spies, how to encourage subversive factions within a rival state (§1.14), or how an enemy king can be tricked into letting himself be captured (§5.6). When it comes to financial matters, Kauṭilya is not above suggesting some rather underhanded techniques for filling the royal treasury, such as planting counterfeit money on an enemy of the state as a pretext for confiscating his property (§5.2). If Kauṭilya's emphasis on the need for each group within society to carry out its role may have reminded us of Plato's *Republic*, this aspect of his teaching comes closer to evoking Machiavelli.[9]

The apparent tension between the moralistic and Machiavellian approaches in the *Arthaśāstra* could be explained in light of the composite nature of the work: it combines ideas from different authors with different mindsets. Alternatively, one might see Kauṭilya as a moralist who is realistic enough to know that building a just society will require the ruler to get his hands dirty now and again. Or one could argue in the other direction. Perhaps the talk of *dharma*, of the king's admirable character, and of legal justice is to be explained in light of Kauṭilya's practical aims. The king should impose moderate punishments and hold his subjects to their duties, not as ends in themselves, but as factors that contribute to the stability of the community and his continued rule.

The oscillation between the king as stick-wielding enforcer and the king as moral paragon was embodied by Candragupta, the monarch served by the historical Kauṭilya. His empire was built on conquest, perhaps aided by the power vacuum that Alexander the Great left behind when he departed from northwestern India.[10] Yet at the end of his life, he supposedly became devoted to the spiritual path of the Jainas. His death is even reported as the consequence of radically ascetic practices, though it is also said that he was poisoned by none other than Kauṭilya, whose *Arthaśāstra* just happens to mention a debate over whether a king's minister should seize power on the demise of the monarch (§5.6). In the absence of an heir, the Indian tradition did recognize the possibility of having the aristocracy elect a new leader. This custom is reported by the Greek historian Megasthenes and perhaps represented in a story that has Indra being chosen as king by the other gods.[11] But when a son was available, power would pass to him, and this was the case with the Mauryan dynasty.

Which brings us to the most famous political ruler of ancient India: Aśoka. He was Candragupta's grandson, and thus inherited dominion over the empire, which he went on to expand through further conquest. Aśoka gives us another, and even more acute, case of the paradigmatic choice that faces the ruler—whether to pursue brutal pragmatism or pious virtue. The many legends told about Aśoka have him making the former choice early in his reign.[12] He was known as Caṇḍāśoka, or "Aśoka the cruel": he had ninety-nine of his brothers killed to eliminate challengers for the throne; when he learned the 500 women of his harem were mocking his ugliness, he had them all burnt alive; he built a horrific prison and torture house known as Aśoka's Hell. But then, he underwent a dramatic transformation, from merciless tyrant to a moral exemplar who despised violence so much that he disliked even the killing and eating of animals—a conversion, if you will, from stick to carrot.

What could account for such an about-face? In a word, Buddhism. It was especially the Buddhist tradition that transmitted and elaborated the legends of Aśoka. Unfortunately, it was chronologically implausible that the mighty king could actually have met the Buddha. So the biographers settled for claiming that in his previous life, Aśoka was a humble child who offered the passing Buddha the only gift he could manage, a handful of dirt. After being reincarnated as a king and indulging in the aforementioned cruelties, Aśoka mended his ways thanks to the influence of a Buddhist monk named Samudra. He took to the teaching with the same enthusiasm and commitment he had previously reserved for sadistic tyranny, building 84,000 *stūpas*, or burial mounds, in honor of the Buddha. (The number may reflect a traditional figure for the number of atoms in the human body.[13]) Over the protests of his ministers, he gave away all his wealth and on his deathbed had only half a piece of fruit left to donate to the monks. There are also tales of his showing humility by physically serving the *sangha*, or Buddhist monastic community. Of course, such stories encouraged the generosity of later monarchs and aristocrats, who were invited to follow Aśoka's example. But there was a deeper point. Buddhists retained the Brahmanical conviction that political rulers should not only respect wise sages but even defer to them, for instance by prostrating themselves at their feet, as Aśoka supposedly did in honor of a Buddhist *arahat* named Upagupta.[14]

In more recent times the picture of Aśoka preserved in Buddhist narratives has been complemented, and challenged, by a series of inscriptions scattered around the former Mauryan Empire. These ancient inscriptions were written during the reign of Aśoka as a means of promulgating his edicts. Written in Prakrit, they were set down in a script that was incomprehensible to future generations, and were deciphered only in the nineteenth century. To some extent the edicts confirm the presentation of Aśoka in the legends. Some of the inscriptions lay down rules to be followed by Buddhist monks, and in general it is clear that Aśoka did identify himself as a Buddhist. Yet he is far more ecumenical in his approach than the legends would have us believe. In several edicts he insists on harmony between different schools, rather than encouraging all simply to adopt Buddhism. Sometimes it even seems that he is beyond sectarian divisions entirely, at least in his role as king (for instance at Rock Edict 4, Pillar Edict 6). Furthermore, it looks as though his personal conversion to Buddhism may have been rather gradual.[15] There is, nonetheless, a kind of "road to Damascus" conversion moment implied in the edicts, too, in the form of an inscription recording Aśoka's shock and remorse over the slaughter involved in his war against the Kalinga kingdom, the very conflict which expanded his empire to cover most of the Indian subcontinent (Rock Edict 13).

The Aśoka of the edicts does present himself as a moral paragon, but not as the humble ascetic of the Buddhist tradition. Instead he is a teacher who exhorts and instructs his subjects to observe *dharma*. Or he is the wise father, responsible for the moral education of his children, namely all those who fall under his rule (Kalinga Edict 2; see also Rock Edict 1). He encourages *dharma* by appointing special ministers to travel through the realm as moral educators. Note that these ministers are not Buddhist monks but government officials, which again suggests that Aśoka was adopting a lofty position of moral authority beyond all sectarian divisions.[16] The actual ethical doctrines espoused in the inscriptions are nothing too spectacular: honor your parents, respect life, speak the truth, show kindness toward animals and slaves (see e.g. Rock Edicts 2, 3, 11). More interesting is the implication that political authority should be wielded with an ethical purpose in view. To underscore the point, Aśoka innovates by introducing a moral dimension to traditional kingly practices. He styles himself as one who still seeks conquest, but now through *dharma* rather than war, and records how he has toured his lands in an effort to promote *dharma* rather than to enjoy the pleasures of the realm (Rock Edict 8).

In all this we may see a comparison between Aśoka and the Buddha himself, who we should remember was likewise from the *kṣatriya* ruling class, and who was not content to achieve enlightenment and liberation for himself but sought to liberate others. Aśoka pursues a similar goal within political life, rather than abandoning that life as the Buddha did. Aśoka is the king whose merit and *dharma* consist in the encouragement of merit and *dharma* among his subjects. This echoes the most idealistic passages of Kauṭilya's *Arthaśāstra*, such as the one that makes the king's happiness inextricably bound up with that of his subjects. Naturally one could take a more cynical view of the edicts. Aśoka was one of the first world emperors to use moral teaching to secure unity and obedience among his people, but he certainly was not the last. We might think of the program of public morality in ancient Rome during the reign of Caesar Augustus. But even the most jaundiced eye must see that Aśoka at least based his rule on the consent of the people, rather than violent coercion. As he put it in an edict placed, significantly enough, in the conquered land of Kalinga (Kalinga Edict 2), Aśoka wished to rule by persuasion, not fear.

11

BETTER HALF

WOMEN IN ANCIENT INDIA

At the start of the last chapter we asked you to imagine yourself in ancient India, and considered some of the roles that society might have offered you: *brahmin*, warrior, monk, or farmer. But let's not forget the approximately 50 percent chance that you would have been a woman. As in other pre-modern literary traditions, ancient Indian writings were composed mostly by men and mostly for men. Women made up half the population, but from the point of view of these authors they were not the better half. A classic statement of misogynism can be found in the *Laws of Manu*: a wife "should do nothing independently, even in her own house . . . Though [her husband] be uncouth and prone to pleasure, though he has no good points at all, the virtuous wife should ever worship her lord as a god" (§5.147–8). Many of the other texts we've been discussing so far seem to express the same attitude. Discussions of reincarnation took it for granted that it would be worse to be reborn as a woman than as a man; political treatises excluded women from leadership of the state; and philosophical wisdom was usually represented as the privilege of men. It was men who taught other men to achieve liberation through renunciation, knowledge, and self-discipline, even when the men in question were gods, like Indra or Kṛṣṇa.

Yet the life of renunciation was open to women as well as men. There were nuns in both the Buddhist and Jaina communities, though as we'll see this was not uncontroversial and nuns did not enjoy the same status as monks. On occasion, we find both Hindu and dissident literature acknowledging that women can reach *mokṣa*. More remarkable still are the female thinkers and sages who turn up in the Upaniṣads and the *Mahābhārata*. We find depictions of women holding their own with men, even defeating men, in philosophical argument. Still, these texts rarely if ever challenge the assumption that women are generally inferior to men. Allowed to participate in philosophical debates, the female thinkers of Indian literature are not separate, but neither are they equal.

To get some sense of the status of women more generally, we can turn again to Kauṭilya's *Arthaśāstra*. Especially its third book has a lot to say about women, and it makes for rather grim reading. It lays out rules concerning the beating of wives, the fines to be levied for women who flirt, and a scale of punishment for rapists, with those who rape slaves treated more leniently than those who assault free women (§§3.3, 3.9). Kauṭilya recognizes a type of marriage that is effectively just the result of abduction, though he does at least discourage this practice by stipulating that in such a case the wife's property will not be transferred to the new husband. It is mostly husbands who can initiate divorce, even if there are cases where a wife can leave her husband, for instance if he goes abroad for a prolonged period (§§3.2, 3.4). In general, the *Arthaśāstra*'s interest in women is largely confined to regulation of sexual activity and the transfer of property within families.

What of the more religious aspects of Brahmanical culture? An important role was reserved in Vedic practices for the wife of a sacrificer. Though only men could sacrifice, the ritual could be effective only if the wife was present.[1] As one text puts it, "A full half of one's self is one's wife. As long as one does not obtain a wife, therefore, one can never be reborn, for he then remains incomplete."[2] But again, the wife is certainly not the husband's *better* half. The wife's role is above all to enable the husband to achieve his sacrificial purposes. When women feature in the symbolism attached to rituals, it is usually in the form of comparisons between ritual objects and her sexual organs. Sex itself is also laden with ritual overtones, as when we read in the Upaniṣads that a man can use knowledge to acquire the merits of a woman through intercourse. Women can acquire the merit of men too, but without the knowledge (*Great Forest Upaniṣad* §6.4). The virtue of women is all important, not because we should care so much about women being virtuous, but because the virtue of a man's wife will have karmic benefits for him.[3]

Along similar lines, the Upaniṣads present marriage as having above all the purpose of providing a man with children, or rather, with sons. Through the wife, the husband quite literally reproduces himself, so that when he sees his son it is like seeing his own face in a mirror. "The father is the same as the son," as one text puts it, "and the son is the same as the father."[4] This father–son relationship finds its ultimate expression in the "rite of transfer" (mentioned e.g. at *Great Forest Upaniṣad* §2.5). In this ritual a man and his son would lie one atop the other, so as to pass on *karma* and vital functions from one generation to the next. In fact, the Vedic tradition often seems to assume that the self that belongs to each of us, the *ātman*, has a gender—and you'll never guess which one. The self is associated with male gods like Puruṣa and Prajāpati, and we hear of the *ātman* producing a female body from his own, and then immediately engaging in sexual intercourse with her.[5] Of course, the Upaniṣads recognize that women, and for that matter animals and perhaps even plants, have an inner self too. But one might easily infer that at core, we are all male, even those of us unfortunate enough to be living our current life in female bodies.

Here, incidentally, we have one of the reasons why asceticism was such a radical development within Indian culture.[6] Renouncing the householder life, as did Buddhist and Jaina monks, meant among other things renouncing sex and procreation. Their vow of chastity was not just a form of self-discipline, but a departure from deeply held ideas about the transference of *karma*, and even of the self, from parent to child. But if chastity was a dramatic gesture on the part of men who became monks, it was downright shocking when women renounced family life and with it their *dharma*.[7] The task of the *kṣatriya* warrior is to fight, the duty of the humble *śūdra* to serve his betters. Likewise, woman has a special kind of *dharma*: her role is to be a devoted wife and to bear children. Monasticism offered an escape from these expectations. Much as ancient Christian women turned to asceticism to avoid the constrictions of family life,[8] so Buddhist and Jaina nuns may have taken their vows in order to live a life that was in a sense *less* cloistered, and certainly held out greater prospects of individual fulfillment.

This was unsurprisingly seen as problematic, even within the Buddhist and Jaina movements.[9] Within Jainism, there was controversy concerning the appropriateness of a monastic life for women. This renouncer movement split into two branches, Śvetāmbara and Digambara, meaning respectively "white clad" and "sky clad." This refers to the white clothing of the Śvetāmbara and the nudity of the Digambaras, which they adopted as part of their asceticism and withdrawal from wider society. Since it was thought that women could not decently, or safely, follow the lead of their "sky clad" brethren, for the Digambaras they were effectively barred from the perfect renunciation that would lead to liberation. The Śvetāmbara Jainas, by contrast, believed that women can achieve this goal. They have even claimed that one of the "ford-makers" was a woman. As for the Buddha, he was no stranger to radical ideas. But according to some stories, even he had a hard time accepting the notion that women should join his community of renouncers. Nuns were admitted to the Buddhist *saṅgha* only a few years after the Buddha began to accept men as monks. When he relented by ordaining his own aunt, it was with misgivings. He is quoted as stating that a monastic community that includes women is like a field afflicted by mildew, and that with this rule change the future lifespan of his teaching (*dhamma*) would be halved from 1,000 to 500 years. Even once the nuns were admitted, they were made subservient to the monks and required to submit to their authority.[10]

But this could still seem preferable to staying at home as a wife. One Buddhist nun rejoiced in her freedom from "three things: mortar, pestle and my crooked husband."[11] This is a quote from a work included in the Buddhist Pāli canon and devoted entirely to women, an anthology of poems called the *Therīgāthā*.[12] Though the women it describes have refused to live as the consorts of men, the text itself is a companion to a second work about Buddhist monks, the *Theragāthā*. Some passages are found in both texts, with fairly small changes from one to the other. For example, both include a story with a chaste hero who rebuffs a seduction. In the female version of the story, a nun is approached by a sexual predator and tries to dissuade him by discoursing on the decaying nature of bodily things. She describes her own body as a corpse, and as a "painted puppet." When this doesn't work she removes one of her eyes and hands it to her would-be seducer, which does the trick.[13] (Note to Oedipus: it's better to tear out your eyes *before* getting into an unwise sexual relationship.) The passage is typical of the *Therīgāthā*, which is full of meditations on decay, illness, and death, all in aid of the suppression of bodily desires. Indeed, this theme is more prominent in the *Therīgāthā* than in its partner text for male Buddhist monks. This may suggest that the authors, or compilers, believed that women are more prone to the lure of bodily pleasure than men. These possibly sexist assumptions notwithstanding, the *Therīgāthā* is remarkable for its assumption that women can indeed achieve liberation.

What about Brahmanical literature? We've seen that the Upaniṣads and *Laws of Manu* can easily be mined for evidence of appalling attitudes toward women. But that isn't the whole story. As so often with these ancient texts, the *Laws of Manu* contain passages that lean in the other direction, including one that allows women to pursue the life of a wandering ascetic (*yati*, §8.363). As for the Upaniṣads, we've already seen them giving women a significant role in ritual practices, and the same goes for philosophical debate. We saw that in the *Great Forest Upaniṣad* a female sage named Gārgī Vācaknavī goes toe to toe with the philosophical hero Yājñavalkya (see Chapter 4).[14] Admittedly, she is silenced by him in debate. She's told that she is "going too far" when she repeatedly asks what underlies each of a successive series of cosmic principles. Keep this up, Yājñavalkya warns her, and your head will explode! Still, Gārgī outdoes the other male brahmins who are in attendance. She acknowledges Yājñavalkya's pre-eminence when they do not, and threats about shattering heads notwithstanding, she is ready and able to question him a second time after being left unsatisfied by his first series of answers.

Nor is that the only scene featuring Yājñavalkya and a female interlocutor. We also mentioned above a passage in the *Great Forest Upaniṣad* where he has a discussion about the self with his wife Maitreyī (see Chapter 5). This scene begins with Maitreyī asking her husband how she can attain immortality (§4.5). Notice that she's not asking how she can help Yājñavalkya to live forever. It is Maitreyī who wants to achieve this for herself.[15] Given the historical and religious context, this might seem presumptuous, but Yājñavalkya is far from affronted. To the contrary, he favors Maitreyī over his second wife precisely because of her philosophical keenness, which is contrasted to the other wife's interest in nothing but "womanly matters (*strīprajñā*)." Furthermore, Yājñavalkya seems to see the relation between two spouses in unusually equal terms. It's par for the course when he says, "it is out of love for oneself (*ātman*) that one holds a wife dear," but remarkable that he adds, "it is out of love for oneself that one holds a *husband* dear."

In keeping with its promise that it contains all things, the *Mahābhārata* also features several interesting and powerful female characters. The most obvious example is Draupadī, the wife of all five Pāṇḍava brothers and thus a major character in the epic.[16] Like Arjuna and other male heroes, Draupadī is honored with portentous predictions upon her birth: she will "lead the *kṣatriyas* to their doom" (§1.155). And she does indeed go on to urge warlike behavior, castigating one of her husbands, Yudhiṣṭhira, for his failure to follow the warrior *dharma* (§3.33). She has good reason for her stance, having been put up as a gambling stake and treated with great disrespect at the fateful dice game that triggered the conflict between the two branches of the family. Draupadī also gives us a counterexample to the notion that ancient Indian texts were aimed solely at men. Within the narrative framing devices of the epic, Draupadī and other women often play the role of an audience for various stories and lessons. These women make claims to knowledge and are seen as potential learners of the teachings that the *Mahābhārata* seeks to impart.[17]

This fits with a tradition related about the entirety of the *Mahābhārata*, which is that it was written by Vyāsa for women and *śūdras*. If it is a "fifth Veda," it is a Veda for everyone, whereas the other Vedas are for the priestly and ruling classes. That doesn't sit so well with the *Mahābhārata*'s obsessive interest in warrior *dharma*, but it does find an echo in the *Bhagavad-gītā*. Kṛṣṇa teaches that even women and *śūdras* can attain liberation through devotion to him (§9.107). And another section of the *Mahābhārata* (§12.308) offers what may be the most astonishing example of a female philosopher in antique India: Sulabhā.[18] Her story is found in a part of the epic in which Bhīṣma, lying on his deathbed, is explaining techniques of liberation to Yudhiṣṭhira. He tells of a king named Janaka, who claims that he has managed to achieve liberation even while carrying out his royal duties. Word of this reaches Sulabhā. She has achieved liberation the old-fashioned way—by rejecting the life of a householder and wandering as a rootless ascetic—and she finds it hard to believe that Janaka has really attained spiritual freedom while living as a king (§9).

So Sulabhā does the obvious thing: uses her Yoga power to transform her appearance into that of a stunningly beautiful woman, teleport to the king's court, and implant her mind into his body so that the two of them can have an internal dialogue within Janaka's soul (§§16–17). Janaka is the first to speak, and does so in arrogant and disdainful terms. He boasts that he has reached freedom without asceticism but only through knowledge (§29), which has enabled him to resist all forms of attachment. To him it is the same whether someone anoints his right arm or cuts off his left (§36). This ethic of unattached action is, of course, the very teaching offered by Kṛṣṇa in the *Gītā*, so we may be expecting his claims of liberation to be ratified. But Janaka begins to seem a less appealing figure as he rails against Sulabhā (§§57–65). Who is this upstart young woman, he wants to know, who has dared to enter his royal presence, and for that matter his very body?

Now it is Sulabhā's turn to respond. She first instructs him on the qualities of a good speech, and promises to exemplify those qualities with her own remarks. These will be pleasing, neither too long nor too short, adapted to her audience, and free of emotion (§86). It's a characteristic feature of ancient Indian writings: the form of speech is inextricably bound up with the truth that it teaches. Once Sulabhā begins her perfect discourse, she exposes the king's hypocrisy. Using ideas reminiscent of the Sāṃkhya philosophical tradition, she argues that the true self is more fundamental than, and underlies, all other features of a person. Janaka's demand to know who she is, and his interest in her gender and class, show that he does not understand this basic truth (§127). Furthermore, the life of a king is indeed incompatible with liberation. He must constantly cope with the demands of other political actors and follow the *dharma* of the *kṣatriya* (§§153–8), instead of devoting himself solely to spiritual concerns as Sulabhā herself has done.

In conclusion, our narrator praises Sulabhā for her appropriate and convincing words. She does better even than the remarkable Gārgī from the Upaniṣads, besting her rival philosophically and successfully challenging ideas that are defended elsewhere in the *Mahābhārata*. Along the way she defies and undermines traditional ideas about gender. According to her, the true self is not in fact male. It has no gender at all, but is the underlying source of this and all other differences. Of course, the very depiction of Sulabhā itself constitutes an affront to those same traditional ideas. It was often believed that women could not attain liberation, either because of their fundamental inferiority or because it was impossible for them to undertake rigorous ascetic practices. They would be too vulnerable without men to protect them. Yet Sulabhā wanders free. She has refused to act as a woman is expected to act, and she knows exactly what she is *not* doing.

Does the story of Sulabhā, and the depictions of such figures as Gārgī and Maitreyī in the Upaniṣads, prove that there really were female Hindu sages in antiquity? It's hard to say. In this chapter, we've mostly been asking what these texts tell us about the way women were seen and assuming that they reflect historical reality, at least to some extent. But perhaps this is backwards. We could instead ask what the inclusion of such women tells us about the texts. It's striking that the strong female philosophers of the *Great Forest Upaniṣad* are both associated with the even stronger male philosopher Yājñavalkya. His willingness to debate with women on a more or less equal footing is unusual, if not unique. The point of this may be to mark him as an innovative and idiosyncratic figure, rather than to insist that women can do philosophy too, never mind tell us that there really were female philosophers.[19] It's also worth noting that characters like Gārgī and Sulabhā are presented in various ways as being masculine. Gārgī refers to herself as a warrior, using a word with male gender, and Yājñavalkya's philosophically minded wife Maitreyī is pointedly contrasted to his other, more feminine wife.[20] Meanwhile Sulabhā delivers her speech from within the body of a man. It's a reminder of the fact that when these ancient women, whether fictional or real, speak to us, this speech is always filtered through the agency of men.

12

GRAND ILLUSION

DHARMA AND DECEPTION IN THE *MAHĀBHĀRATA*

Suppose you're minding your own business one day, when suddenly a group of strangers rushes up to you. "You have to help us," they gasp. "We're being pursued by a group of murderous thieves, who want to rob and kill us! Don't tell them which way we ran!" Sure enough, shortly after they sprint away, a group of cruel looking men arrive, and ask which way the first group has gone. You're now in a dilemma. You could say nothing, in which case the robbers seem likely to torture the information out of you; you could lie and send them the wrong way; or you could tell the truth and send the murderers after their victims. If you've ever been a philosophy student, or are tolerant enough to spend your time hanging out with philosophers, you may already have been asked to consider this puzzle. It was raised by Immanuel Kant as a challenge to his own teaching that no one should ever lie. But the example appears earlier than Kant, in fact much, much earlier. It features in the eighth of the eighteen books of the *Mahābhārata*, in the form of a story told by none other than God himself, incarnated as the charioteer Kṛṣṇa. In this version the dilemma is confronted by a priest who has vowed always to tell the truth. He duly informs the murderers which way they should go to find their victims. Good though his intentions are, the priest is later sent to hell for his decision.[1]

The *Mahābhārata* has plenty to teach us about ethics, though it does not pursue this subject abstractly, as for instance Kant's *Critique of Practical Reason* does. This is, rather, ethics investigated through the telling of stories. The product of generations' worth of orally transmitted narratives, it is a monument in the landscape of Indian literature, which holds within it a whole culture and has since antiquity had religious meaning for its readers.[2] As just mentioned, the *Mahābhārata* refers to itself as a "fifth Veda" (§§1.57, 12.327). It is one of a pair of ancient epics, the other being the *Rāmāyaṇa*, which makes it almost irresistible to draw comparisons to the *Iliad* and *Odyssey* of Greek antiquity. All four epics feature superhuman heroes who endure warfare while being manipulated by the gods, and like Homer's *Iliad* and *Odyssey* the *Mahābhārata* is ascribed to a single bard, named Vyāsa. But the *Mahābhārata* is a more capacious work, and of more obvious importance for the historian of philosophy than the Greek epics. Embedded within the *Mahābhārata* is a section called the *Song of the Lord*, or *Bhagavad-gītā*—which, like the *Iliad*, centers on the reluctance of a great warrior to fight—and it is among the greatest texts of ancient Indian philosophy.

We'll be looking at the *Gītā* in the next chapter. First, we want to look at a few scenes from the rest of the epic that address this question, which also came up in our discussion of the Buddha, of whether deception can ever be morally justified. It is only one of the many philosophically redolent themes we could have picked out of the *Mahābhārata*, which makes a point of its own comprehensiveness, boasting "what is not here does not exist anywhere" (§§1.56, 18.5). But it is a particularly apt theme given that the *Mahābhārata* also makes a point of its own status as a narrative, a story whose telling is brought constantly to the reader's attention. This is highlighted by the multiple frames within which the epic is presented. The entirety is purportedly the work of the bard Vyāsa, but we hear it at several removes. He recited it first to his son and several disciples, one of whom recited it again from memory, with this then being repeated by yet another bard whose recitation is supposedly the basis of the full version that has come down to us.[3]

This version is in fact not just full but stuffed to bursting, often with material that may seem rather extraneous: stories and digressions that have been called "subtales." These probably show that the epic narrative was treated as a framework, with many generations of storytellers adding new material that would have been relevant to the concerns of their own time. The result is a text that is invented and reinvented, and makes us constantly aware of that inventedness. Vyāsa, Kṛṣṇa, and other figures both act within the narrative and tell various stories. This literary device, which allows the myth-maker to enter the plot of his own myth, reveals what the *Mahābhārata* is about: the elusiveness of truth and the ambiguity of moral rightness. Within the narrative too, the heroes engage in all manner of deception, with the plot often driven forward by lies, tricks, and subterfuge. This is epic as grand illusion, featuring characters who are themselves illusionists.

Even a brief summary of the central story will get the point across. It tells of two families within the same lineage, whose line is known as the Bhārata, which is also the name of the geographical territory of India. Hence the title: *Mahābhārata* can be translated as "great tale of the Bhārata," with "great" referring to its enormous scope. The text itself tells us that the narrative circulates in longer and shorter forms, with our text of course being very much the long form (§1.1), a point underscored by a further story that relates how it was literally weighed in scales against the four Vedas and found to be heavier. Pitted against each other in the epic tale are two sets of brothers, the Pāṇḍavas and Kauravas. The Pāṇḍavas are the heroes of the tale, led with some reluctance by their oldest brother Yudhiṣṭhira, famed for always telling the truth. This side also includes the great archer Arjuna, whose reluctance to fight against his kin provokes Kṛṣṇa to preach the *Gītā* to him in order to persuade him to enter the battle. On the other side, the Kauravas are a hundred brothers led by the anti-hero Duryodhana, who cheats the Pāṇḍavas of their birthright by duping Yudhiṣṭhira in two games of dice. The rest of the story tells of the wanderings of the Pāṇḍavas and their ultimate return and victorious eighteen-day war against the Kauravas, at the cost of massive bloodshed on both sides. As in the *Iliad* and *Odyssey*, there are set pieces detailing the deeds and deaths of central heroes, with some of the most prominent deaths again involving deception and lies.

To understand the significance of these scenes, we need to think about the nature of the moral code that is potentially being violated in such acts of treachery. And that means thinking again about *dharma*. We've already encountered this word, and its Pāli equivalent *dhamma*. It was used in early Buddhism for the "teaching" of the Buddha, and appears repeatedly in the moralizing inscriptions of the Buddhist king Aśoka. You'll see it translated in ways that suggest a disconcertingly wide range of application, from "law" to "morality" to "religion." In modern India, it is indeed sometimes used to mean simply "religion," for instance when the enterprise we call "philosophy of religion" is rendered *dharma-darśana*.[4] But in the ancient context, *dharma* captures only part of what we might mean by "religion," roughly the part where religion bears on moral conduct. It was sometimes noted that living in accordance with *dharma* was not sufficient to secure liberation from the cycle of reincarnation, even if it might be necessary for attaining that highest religious goal.[5] In general terms, one's *dharma* consists in all the various sorts of duties one has, as a particular individual, as a member of a family and of a society, and simply as a human being.

In our earliest surviving literature, though, *dharma* does not really have this meaning of a general moral code or law. Instead, it is used in a way that is closer to its etymological basis in a verb root meaning "preserve" or "support." The first Vedas thus use *dharma* to speak of supporting the cosmos, or when Indra "holds apart" the rivers from the plants. This same usage is found in ancient Iran. Zoroastrian texts employ a word with the same linguistic origin to talk about God holding the heavens so that they do not fall.[6] The word *dharma* does not, however, play much of a role in subsequent Vedic literature. When it does appear, it is especially in social and legal contexts, where *dharma* has to do with the king's role of upholding order and justice. It is contrasted to the so-called "law of the fish" where, in the absence of the protective shelter of royal law, the smaller would be left to the mercy of the bigger.[7] This suggests a rather down-to-earth answer to the question of which actions accord with *dharma*. Just look at existing social practice. When a certain behavior is accepted as praiseworthy, that is *dharma*, while a behavior that earns rebuke is its opposite, *adharma*.[8] Here we might see a parallel between *dharma* and linguistic correctness as envisioned by the Sanskrit grammarians. We mentioned Patañjali's advice: if you want words, don't go to a grammarian but to a competent language user. Likewise, if you want ethics, don't ask a philosopher but find people who are agreed to be ethical.

This does get us closer to the distinctively ethical meaning of *dharma*, and in fact it recalls the socially embedded idea of virtue set out in Aristotle's *Nicomachean Ethics*. But *dharma* ultimately took on the more ambitious sense of an abstract, general set of moral requirements. It seems that this happened especially, and perhaps specifically, with the advent of Buddhism.[9] The Buddha's *dharma*, or teaching, was aimed at everyone regardless of their social role or caste, and the same universalism was expressed in Aśoka's inscriptions.[10] This sense then becomes pervasive in subsequent Indian literature, not least in the *Dharmasūtras* that we contrasted to Kauṭilya's *Arthaśāstra*. At this stage *dharma* could be articulated as one of the main goals of life, alongside *artha* or "practical advantage" and *kāma* or "pleasure." (Movements like the Buddhists and Jainas added a fourth, greater goal: *mokṣa*, or "liberation."[11]) Of course this more ambitious conception of *dharma* as an absolute code or law that applies to all alike makes it much harder to know exactly how one might obey its strictures. As one of the *Dharmasūtras* puts it, "*Dharma* and *adharma* do not go about saying 'Here we are!'"[12]

And this brings us back to the *Mahābhārata*. Passages like the parable of the truth-telling priest and murdering thieves show us that it is no easy matter to say where *dharma* leads. Even those who sincerely strive to live well may go astray, and this is especially clear in the case of moral dilemmas, where every choice seems to be wrong. It is no accident that Kṛṣṇa's tale focuses specifically on the case of truth-telling, since this is a recurrent theme in the epic. The leader of the Pāṇḍavas is the morally upright Yudhiṣṭhira, whose commitment to honesty is symbolized by the fact that his chariot floats a little above the ground as he rides. He comes crashing back to earth, quite literally, when he finally indulges in a falsehood (§7.164–5). He does so out of desperation, since there is no other way for him to slay the Kaurava hero Droṇa. Rather astonishingly, it is the divine Kṛṣṇa himself who suggests the base stratagem by which Droṇa may be defeated:

> He cannot in any way be defeated by force in battle. Casting aside virtue, O Pāṇḍavas, resort to a method fit for victory, so that Droṇa might not kill everyone in battle. I think that he will not fight if [his son] were killed. Let some man say that he has been slain in battle.

This proposal meets with mixed reactions among the Pāṇḍavas. Arjuna immediately disagrees with the advice, whereas his warlike brother Bhīma thinks it's a splendid idea. Truth-telling Yudhiṣṭhira is torn. He absolutely wants to win—indeed, it's said that he is "addicted to victory"—but is reluctant to spoil his spotless moral record.

In the end the Pāṇḍavas hit upon the following subterfuge: they will kill an elephant whose name just happens to be the same as Droṇa's son. Then they can tell Droṇa of the death, thinking of the elephant but letting Droṇa assume the son is meant. As Arjuna puts it, this covers a lie with a truth, as if with armor. At first it is Bhīma who, with no compunctions, tells Droṇa the misleading news. But Droṇa is suspicious and asks for confirmation from Yudhiṣṭhira, who confirms the fateful lie, though he mutters under his breath that it is only an elephant that has died, so that Droṇa will not hear him.[13] The ruse works. Droṇa drops his weapons, ready himself to die in his grief, and is killed. But the success is short-lived. Droṇa's son will wreak great destruction on the Pāṇḍavas, and poor Yudhiṣṭhira has lost his spotless reputation. He is later forced to witness his brothers suffering in hell, a vision that is then revealed to be an illusion in return for his part in deceiving Droṇa.

Despite the bitter fruits reaped by Yudhiṣṭhira, the *Mahābhārata* actually has a rather ambivalent attitude towards such deceptions. In a similar passage, Kṛṣṇa warns the Pāṇḍavas that the Kaurava leader Duryodhana can only be killed by tricking him (§9.57). And in this case, he is given a speech indicating how such conduct can be justified, or perhaps the right word would be "rationalized" (§9.60):

> When enemies become too numerous and powerful, they should be slain by deceit and stratagems. This is the path formerly trodden by the gods to slay the demons; and a path trodden by the virtuous may be trodden by all.

This advice seems to reverse a slogan found elsewhere: "where *dharma* is, there is Kṛṣṇa" (§6.41). To put it another way, if it's good enough for the gods then it's good enough for us. Perhaps the idea here is that a good end justifies whatever means are necessary. In the passages just mentioned, Kṛṣṇa insists that it is *only* by deception that the Pāṇḍavas can be victorious, and as he himself remarks, "where *dharma* is, there is victory" (§9.62). On this reading, the tricks played by the Pāṇḍavas are excused because they bring about the correct result, namely the defeat of their enemies, who are themselves tricksters. Don't forget that the whole war can be traced to Duryodhana's double dealing in the dice game that deprives the Pāṇḍavas of their kingdom.

But if the end justifies the means, what accounts for the passages that seem to pass disapproving judgment on the Pāṇḍavas, and especially Yudhiṣṭhira, for their ignoble tactics? A banal answer could be to refer to the protracted and many-handed writing of the *Mahābhārata*. As we suggested with the *Arthaśāstra*, it is no surprise that a lengthy work composed by numerous authors of different generations would contain the occasional self-contradiction. But perhaps the *Mahābhārata* does not want us to think that things are so simple, that the way of *dharma* is either to tell the truth and lose or win by lying, and that we just need to figure out which answer is the right one. It's been aptly remarked that "the *Mahābhārata* never wants to resolve itself,"[14] and so it is here, for there are multiple ethical imperatives at work. Certainly it's good to tell the truth, but it's also good to defeat wicked enemies and secure victory for your clan, especially if a god is encouraging you to do so. As Bimal Matilal has argued, the role of Kṛṣṇa in these passages could be that of a moral innovator who teaches the Pāṇḍavas to shake off the "rigid code of conduct" previously cherished by Yudhiṣṭhira, that one should tell the truth in all circumstances. It's the same code followed by the priest who led murderers to their victims. Matilal suggests that Kṛṣṇa is here "a moral agent [who] gave up moral integrity to avoid a total miscarriage of justice in the end."[15]

But even if the duty to tell the truth is somehow trumped by other concerns, it may remain as a duty nonetheless. This is why it makes sense for the *Mahābhārata* to show the consequences of Yudhiṣṭhira's actions, with the dramatic devices of the grounded chariot and vision of hell. For him, and for all of us from time to time, the best thing to do may involve doing something wrong, something against *dharma*. To this we may add that the *Mahābhārata* recognizes that the *dharma* of one group or person may differ from that of another. Veracity is Yudhiṣṭhira's calling card, and it is in the most fundamental sense "out of character" for him to collude in a lie. He thus violates what may be called his *svadharma*, the duty or code that is relevant to him specifically.[16] For a different man like Bhīma, whose character revolves solely around the *kṣatriya* code of victory, the dilemma we've been discussing would hardly arise, or not arise at all. No wonder that Yudhiṣṭhira tried to have it both ways by muttering under his breath in response to Droṇa. His *dharma* as a truth-teller was clashing with his *dharma* as a *kṣatriya* leader. In other passages, he tries to escape by questioning the very validity of that *dharma*. The code of the warrior is actually no better than the law of the fish, where the strong prevail. Better to give up that code, even if it means retreating from the life of the *kṣatriya* and becoming an ascetic. As Yudhiṣṭhira observes, "The peaceful man sleeps happily, as he has given up both victory and defeat" (§5.70).

Here we have the central insight that emerges from the moral dilemmas of the *Mahābhārata*. The epic recognizes that such dilemmas may be genuinely tragic, and that not all duties can be satisfied. This does not mean that there is no right response at all. It seems clear that in Kṛṣṇa's story of the priest and the murderers, the priest should not have told the truth. What it means is that we as moral agents are complex beings, with different sorts of duty and responsibility: Yudhiṣṭhira is a truth-teller by character and inclination, a warrior by circumstance. This leads him into a conflict that can only be resolved by betraying himself or his responsibilities. The same sort of dilemma is the catalyst for the most famous section of the *Mahābhārata*: the *Bhagavad-gītā*.

13

WORLD ON A STRING

THE *BHAGAVAD-GĪTĀ*

"Everyone should read two couplets (*ślokas*) of *Gītā* every day. It is a scripture of 700 couplets and it can be finished in a year. Read it again and continue this till the end. After reading it three to four times, you will discover a path to lead a life, the way I discovered." These are the words of the BJP minister for external affairs, Sushma Swaraj, who proposed having the *Bhagavad-gītā* declared India's national book.[1] It was not an entirely innocuous suggestion, as officially enshrining this Hindu classic would send a none too subtle message to non-Hindus in India. But you don't have to be a Hindu nationalist to admire the *Gītā*.[2] Mahatma Gandhi memorized parts of the work and took from it inspiration for his campaign of non-violent resistance. Aldous Huxley sought in it a source for what he termed a "perennial philosophy," and the early American writers Henry David Thoreau and Ralph Waldo Emerson both admired it greatly. At the other end of the spectrum, Nazi-era Indologists in Germany found in the *Gītā* evidence of a pure monotheism untainted by supposedly "Semitic" ideas. Looking back on the same troubled period of the twentieth century, Robert Oppenheimer is even said to have quoted its line "now I am become death, the destroyer of worlds," with regard to his work on the atomic bomb. When it comes to furnishing a sentiment for any occasion, no greeting card company can compete with the *Gītā*.

This widespread feeling that the *Bhagavad-gītā* is a text for all time and all people is rather surprising, given how few of us have ever had to decide whether to unleash devastating war against several dozen siblings. That is the difficult choice facing the hero Arjuna at this stage of the *Mahābhārata*. As the action opens in the section known as the *Bhagavad-gītā*, we are on the brink of a final battle between the Pāṇḍavas and Kauravas. Or perhaps we should say that this is where the inaction opens. Arjuna, the greatest warrior among the Pāṇḍavas, brings both his chariot and the narrative of the whole epic to a grinding halt, because he is beset by doubt. His dilemma fits into the pattern we were just discussing: it is a conflict rooted in conflicting demands of *dharma*. On the one hand Arjuna is an outstanding example of a *kṣatriya*, or elite warrior. He is a prince and a son of the god Indra, a fabled archer whose bow boasts its own name, the sort of guy whose birth was celebrated not with cigars and cuddly toys, but instead with the prediction: "Through the might of his arm the fire god will be fully sated with the fat of all the creatures in the Khāṇḍava forest" (*Mahābhārata* §1.114, trans. Smith). On the other hand, Arjuna is reluctant to kill his own family members. He feels the pull of two responsibilities, to the law of the warrior or *kṣatriya-dharma*, and the law of kinship or *kula-dharma* (*Gītā* 1, 73).[3] What is he to do?

Perhaps nothing. Arjuna proclaims that, before killing his own kinsmen, he would be better off giving up the life of a warrior entirely and becoming a renouncer, the same temptation we just saw being voiced by his older brother Yudhiṣṭhira. Arjuna's problem is a distinctively philosophical one. It is not that he knows the right thing to do and lacks strength or courage to do it, but that he is genuinely puzzled about his duty, his *dharma* (2, 73). Fortunately Arjuna has a resource that is unavailable to your average moral philosopher: God is quite literally his co-pilot. It turns out that his charioteer Kṛṣṇa is an incarnation of the highest of all divinities, the Creator of the entire universe, and the speaker of most of what is to follow. Hence the title *Bhagavad-gītā*, which means *Song of the Lord*. Kṛṣṇa sets out a detailed argument intended to inspire Arjuna to follow his true path, his *svadharma*, that is, the *dharma* that is uniquely appropriate to him. It is even better to carry out one's own path badly than another's well (3, 85), and he was born for this occasion. As Bimal Matilal puts it, "The entire Bhārata war was for Arjuna. It was his game and he should play."[4]

So is the *Bhagavad-gītā* just a plot device, intended to push the narrative forward after giving Arjuna a chance to air his moral scruples? Hardly. The authors of the *Gītā* take this opportunity to explore the deeper question of why any of us should ever undertake any action at all. We say "authors," and not "author," because scholars believe that the *Gītā*, like the whole of the *Mahābhārata*, was composed by numerous writers who had various agendas. While these authors do not forget the dramatic context of Arjuna's choice, they situate that choice within what seem to be several different philosophical and religious contexts. The not displeasing result is that Kṛṣṇa becomes a kind of chorus, his single voice expressing numerous viewpoints that may or may not ultimately fit together to offer a single, unified basis for Arjuna's action.

Kṛṣṇa begins with the most obvious tactic: he tells Arjuna to stop being a wimp, or actually to stop "acting like a eunuch" (2, 73). If he refuses to fight, he will earn only shame (2, 77). This is a direct appeal to Arjuna's sense of *kṣatriya-dharma*, his code of honor as a warrior. As such it can hardly suffice, since it does nothing to answer his concerns about *kula-dharma*, the responsibilities he bears towards his kinsmen. So in this opening speech Kṛṣṇa also appeals to traditional ideas about reincarnation. The relatives that Arjuna may kill, and Arjuna himself should he be slain, will all be reborn. Discarding our bodies in this way is no more dramatic than changing our clothes. The true self, by contrast, is invulnerable: "Swords do not cut him, fire does not burn him, water does not wet him, wind does not parch him" (2, 75–7). Having lowered the stakes in this way, Kṛṣṇa adds that the consequences of fighting should in any case be irrelevant to a true *kṣatriya*, who ought to fight bravely regardless of the outcome. Here he plants the seeds of a deeper thought, which will blossom fully over the rest of the *Gītā*. No one, whether warrior or peasant, should act with an eye to the fruits of their action.[5]

We already touched on this idea of "unattached" action when we were talking about *karma* (see Chapter 6). But it's worth a closer look, because as Arjuna himself points out (3, 81), it isn't so clear why there is any point in acting at all without striving to achieve some purpose. If the fruits of action are nothing to me, why not disengage entirely and become a "renouncer," as Arjuna has already threatened to do? This solution was adopted in spectacular style by ascetics like Gośāla and his Ājīvika movement, and by the early Jainas. But here in the *Gītā* Kṛṣṇa gives it short shrift, stating that complete inaction is simply an impossibility: "no one lives even a moment without doing some act, for the forces of nature cause everyone to act" (3, 81), and later on, "no one who has a body can renounce all acts completely; he is the true renouncer who renounces the fruits of his acts" (18, 139). To this idea that nature forces us to engage in at least some actions, Kṛṣṇa adds that inaction too can have fruits (4, 87). Here we might think of our phrase "sins of omission." If you see that a child is about to be hit by a truck and do nothing but watch as the tragedy unfolds, it will be no good telling the child's parents that her death wasn't your fault because you're in the action-renouncing business.

While these passages seem quite dismissive of inaction, others concede that a life of deliberate inaction is at least a stage upon the right path (5, 91). It is just a less advanced stage than the life of unattached action. At one point Kṛṣṇa distinguishes the more simpleminded strategy, which he calls mere "relinquishment (*saṃnyāsa*)," from the genuine "renunciation (*tyāga*)" that consists in acting without regard to results (18, 137). Here the *Gītā* offers a real innovation, even if it is one that can also be found in other ancient Indian texts, like certain Upaniṣads. And like the Upaniṣads, it devises memorable and striking metaphors for its teachings, as when it describes the true renouncer as being like a tortoise. Just as the tortoise draws in its limbs, so the renouncer withdraws even from his senses and focuses on his interior insight (2, 79). But if you were Arjuna, you might still feel unsatisfied. He's been told that he should *not* act with a view to the fruits of action, but he hasn't been told what he *should* look to when he is acting—if anything. Toward what should interior insight be directed?

Kṛṣṇa's answer is simple: think of me. "I am the origin of this entire universe and its dissolution," he proclaims, "all this is strung on me as strands of pearls are strung on a string" (7, 99; for this image, see also 9, 105 and 11, 119). Here we have the core teaching of the *Gītā*, or at least the core teaching of one or more of its authors. It justifies action in terms of a devotional theism, which does not outright abandon a plurality of gods but insists that one highest God is the true object of all proper worship. Again, the *Gītā*'s concerns echo those of some later Upaniṣads, such as the *Śvetāśvatara Upaniṣad* which likewise makes a single God the cause of all things.[6] Also characteristically Upaniṣadic is the *Gītā*'s interest in sacrifice, which it frequently mentions and approves, saying things like, "The world is not of him who fails to sacrifice" (4, 89; see also 3, 83; 6, 93; 18, 139). And you can see why the authors might have been nervous. The *brahmins* of Vedic culture offered more fruits than a greengrocer, promising that correctly performed sacrifices would bring wealth, a large family, cattle, and a propitious rebirth. Like the Buddhists and other dissident groups, the *Gītā* distances itself from this cash cow view of ritual. Yet it encourages us to keep sacrificing anyway. Ritual sacrifice even becomes the paradigmatic approved action, since it is one action that we must surely undertake with our minds set upon God.

Kṛṣṇa's exhortation to Arjuna is then to wage war as a kind of sacrifice, to perform this action out of nothing but devotion to him. Perhaps it is this idea of "devotion (*bhakti*)" that has made the text so meaningful to so many readers down the centuries. You don't have to be a mighty warrior to devote your life to God, as the *Gītā* explicitly recognizes. The stratifications of Vedic culture are upended, as Kṛṣṇa promises that even women and the low-born *śūdras* can be liberated through sincere devotion to him (9, 107). The point here is not just that we should direct our thoughts to Kṛṣṇa as we act. Just as he created the world and continues to support it and "hold it together" (3, 83), we should act so as to maintain cosmic harmony, or as the *Gītā* says, "keep the wheel rolling." It is this, rather than any fruits that may accrue to us thanks to our action, that provides the motive for the true renouncer.

Of course, you couldn't blame Arjuna for being puzzled by this. How is his going to war going to help hold the world together? Here the narrative context of the whole epic merges with the philosophical thrust of the *Gītā*. Arjuna is simply *supposed* to fight. This is what he is there to do, and the narrative can only resume once he makes up his mind to do so. The war, however destructive it may turn out to be (spoiler alert: very), is destined to take place and Arjuna is fated to take his place in it. In this respect, the *Gītā* fits well into the rest of the *Mahābhārata*, which often suggests that the events it narrates were foreordained.[7] The theistic setting of the *Gītā* adds a further dimension to this fatalist outlook, though. Part of Kṛṣṇa's divine role is to ensure that things unfold as they should. From his lofty vantage point, the future events in the narrative are already present. He knows that they will and indeed must occur. This is perhaps the meaning of Kṛṣṇa's saying that he is "time, grown old to destroy the world" (11, 117),[8] which is an alternative translation of the passage Oppenheimer supposedly quoted when he was musing on the atomic bomb. One might go so far as to say that as Kṛṣṇa speaks to Arjuna, he is not so much trying to persuade him to fight as informing him that he is in fact going to fight, so he may as well get on with it. Kṛṣṇa puts it like this: "Fettered by your own task, which springs from your nature, you will inevitably do what you in your folly do not want to do" (18, 143).

The religious teachings of the *Gītā*, its emphasis on a divine plan and on such issues as sacrifice, may make it seem like an Upaniṣad inserted into the epic of the *Mahābhārata*.[9] But scholars have detected another strand on which its pearls of wisdom are strung: Sāṃkhya philosophy. There's no general agreement about when exactly the *Gītā* was written, with educated guesses having it written in stages anywhere between the fourth century BC and the fourth century AD. But it must predate the composition of the central text of Sāṃkhya thought, Īśvarakṛṣṇa's *Sāṃkhya-kārikā*, and that was written some time before the sixth century AD, when it was translated into Chinese.[10] We'll be returning to Īśvarakṛṣṇa's ideas later (in Chapter 22). For now, we just want to show how some of those ideas already appear in the *Gītā*, which is itself evidently drawing on older strands of Sāṃkhya thought.

The most obvious is a fundamental contrast between two principles, *prakṛti* and *puruṣa*, which we might roughly translate as "nature" and "observer mind." We can restate the doctrine of non-attached action in these terms. Like a tortoise pulling in its limbs, the renouncer "withdraws" from *prakṛti*, and focuses on his true self, which is his *puruṣa*. The *Gītā* also contains more general descriptions of the way that the two principles interrelate. It says, "*Prakṛti* and *puruṣa* are both beginningless . . . *Prakṛti* is stated to be a cause inasmuch as it is the agency in the production of products, while *puruṣa* is stated to be a cause in that he experiences happiness and unhappiness" (13, 125). The *puruṣa* is the true, purely observing, self and remains unchanging despite its connection with body, and via the body with the whole realm of nature and the natural aspects of the mental. So here we might see the *Gītā* as responding to Buddhism by reasserting the idea of an enduring self, some notion of which we already find in earlier Upaniṣads.[11]

Yet, like all-seeing Kṛṣṇa, the *Gītā* looks forward and not just backward. The future Sāṃkhya philosophical movement is going to be intertwined with the tradition called Yoga, and that intertwining is already found here in the *Gītā* and in fact also in other parts of the *Mahābhārata*.[12] The *Gītā* frequently talks about *yoga* as a path toward enlightenment, which suggests that the would-be sage needs to undergo training and spiritual discipline, rather than just learning about the contrast between nature and the self. *Yoga* thus becomes another word for the path of unattached action and the practitioner of *yoga* (the *yogin*) is synonymous with the true renouncer that Kṛṣṇa is describing, better than those who merely embrace asceticism and refuse to engage in action (6, 93 and 97). Through the insight of *sāṃkhya*, Arjuna can learn about his *puruṣa* or *brahman*, a true self who transcends nature; through the practice of *yoga*, he can learn to see the world solely from the vantage point of this true self. Since actions and their consequences unfold in the world, in the realm of nature or *prakṛti*, they cannot touch him (5, 93).

Before leaving the *Gītā*, we should notice one final implication of the text, one which would not have been lost on its original readers. We've said that Kṛṣṇa's song is not just for mighty warriors like Arjuna. It is a message we can all take to heart. But that doesn't change the fact that Arjuna is indeed a mighty warrior, a *kṣatriya* prince. The *Gītā* has a special message for such elite readers, and Kṛṣṇa makes sure they don't miss it by saying that the teaching he reveals is a *rājavidyā*, meaning "royal wisdom" or "knowledge of kings" (9, 105). The king is in a uniquely appropriate position to do as we are being taught, by imitating the divine king through his actions.[13] Arjuna emerges from this part of the epic as an ideal ruler, who does as he should because he ought to, and out of devotion to the highest Lord rather than in pursuit of his own advantage. One can easily imagine King Aśoka nodding with approval. Just to hammer the point home, the *Mahābhārata* offers us a negative example too, the Kaurava leader Duryodhana. For all his duplicity and wickedness towards the Pāṇḍavas, his most heinous sin is that he puts himself and his own interests above all else, rather than submitting to the divine rule of Kṛṣṇa.[14]

We've said that few people face the sorts of situation confronting Arjuna and, for that matter, Duryodhana. But in a broader sense, we all do, whether we are princes or paupers. Warfare is a common human experience, and even more common is the opportunity to do violence to other humans, and to animals. Violence is an abiding theme of the *Mahābhārata*, which depicts not only Arjuna's hesitation on the eve of a great battle, but the horrendous devastation wrought by that battle. It may seem strange that Kṛṣṇa should urge Arjuna on toward this end. But just consider that he also endorses the practice of animal sacrifice. Apparently, he thinks that some blood must be spilled if the wheel of the world is to keep turning as it ought to. Yet other movements and texts of ancient India were adamantly opposed to such sacrifice. Some, notably the Jainas, sought to avoid doing any violence at all, intentional or unintentional. This commitment to an ideal of non-violence is a legacy that has come down from antiquity to modern times, not only in India with Gandhi's tactics, but across the world. Many non-Indian vegetarians take inspiration, to say nothing of recipes, from Indian culture. So let's now turn to this notion of non-violence, which cuts across the intellectual divides of ancient India.

14

MOSTLY HARMLESS

NON-VIOLENCE

Of all the academic disciplines taught and studied at university, philosophy may be the one that is hardest to avoid in real life. You can decline to read literature; very few people ever get around to doing any physics or geology; and if you play your cards right, you can probably even get away without doing much math (though not if you actually play cards). Philosophy, though, is inevitable. We all wrestle with philosophical problems, even if we don't think of them that way. This is especially true when it comes to ethical dilemmas. One of the most obvious is the question of whether it is morally defensible to eat animals. Whether you are rich or poor, it is certainly possible to live as a vegetarian. So the decision to eat meat or abstain from it is one that faces everyone. If you do it, then it is either because you think there's nothing wrong with doing so, or because its wrongness doesn't weigh heavily enough with you to stop you from tucking into a nice, juicy steak now and again.

Even though the ethics of killing animals for food is a prominent example of philosophy in everyday life, it has only recently become a topic that is much debated among philosophers. Nowadays there are figures like the utilitarian Peter Singer, who is well known for his arguments in favor of vegetarianism. This contrasts sharply with ancient and medieval philosophy in Europe. Apart from a few exceptions, notably the late ancient thinkers Plutarch and Porphyry, philosophers in those periods rarely bothered to argue at length for or against meat consumption.[1] In ancient India, by contrast, non-violence was one of the key themes of religious and philosophical culture. Buddhists and especially Jainas defined themselves in part by their reluctance or refusal to eat meat. Animal sacrifice was of course central to the Vedic culture that the Buddhists and Jainas sought to criticize. Yet the texts that grew out of that culture often encourage us to avoid harming animals. Exhortations to avoid violence can also be found in such works as the *Laws of Manu* and the *Mahābhārata*, despite the fact that its most famous section, the *Bhagavad-gītā*, consists of a dialogue recommending participation in war. Nor is this a matter of purely historical interest. Still today, one of the most famous aspects of Indian society is widespread vegetarianism.

So this topic really gives us something to sink our teeth into. The first point that needs to be made, though, is that the topic is actually not vegetarianism. What we really need to discuss is what the traditions refer to as *ahiṃsā*, meaning "non-violence" or "non-injury."[2] While it may seem that avoiding violence implies never killing animals, this is denied in some Vedic texts, which claim that sacrifice of animals could be consistent with *ahiṃsā*. Conversely, those who did think that non-violence implied benevolence toward animals (including vegetarianism) never thought that it meant only this. *Ahiṃsā* obviously includes avoiding violence toward humans too, and as we'll see, Jainas believe that one can inflict *himṣā* on plants, and even commit acts of violence by lighting a fire or drinking water straight from a well.

It is a matter of controversy how and why ancient Indians began to think in terms of *ahiṃsā*, but scholars have most often explained it by alluding to religious practices.[3] Its origins may lie in the fear that ritualized violence could lead to retribution. This could then have led to ritual taboos and practices designed to deflect the blame for violence away from the sacrificer engaged in the ritual. For instance, one might recite a formula to secure expiation for slaying an animal, or place a blade of dry, and thus already dead, grass between an axe and a tree being chopped down to make a post for the sacrifice. (Notice that in this second case, it is a plant and not an animal that is seen as the potentially injured party.) On this reckoning, the doctrine of *ahiṃsā* was not an external critique of Brahmanical culture, with Buddhists and Jainas accusing the priests of violence. Rather, those accusations from the outside mirrored anxiety or "embarrassment" about sacrificial violence within the Vedic tradition.

A related controversy, which bears on the philosophical relevance of *ahiṃsā*, is whether non-violence was pursued for moral as well as religious reasons. If the concern is really to avoid retribution, then eschewing violence may seem unrelated to moral concerns. The sacrificer would be worried about himself, not the animal he is killing. As the *Laws of Manu* explain, with what sounds like a tone of wistful regret, we can't eat meat without injuring the living, and doing this hinders us from a blessed afterlife, so we have to do without meat (§5.48). On the other hand, a fear of vengeance implies that the animal (or plant) being harmed does have interests of its own, the ones that the sacrificer is in danger of violating.[4] Besides, *ahiṃsā* was not only justified in terms of pure self-interest. One Buddhist work contains the following reflection, which is strikingly reminiscent of the Biblical "golden rule":

> Since I want to live, it would not be agreeable and pleasant to me if somebody were to take my life. For another person, too, it would be disagreeable and unpleasant if I were to take his life, since he wants to live. Precisely that which is disagreeable and

> unpleasant to me is disagreeable and unpleasant also to the other. How then could I inflict upon the other that which I find disagreeable and unpleasant to myself?[5]

And we can find similar ideas in Hindu texts, including the *Mahābhārata*.[6]

But more than Buddhism or Hinduism, it was Jainism that was characterized by an unswerving devotion to *ahiṃsā*. Indeed it has been called a "religion of non-violence."[7] If you know only a little about Jaina beliefs and practices, then what you know probably concerns the extreme measures taken to avoid harming other creatures: Jaina monks wearing masks to avoid inhaling insects, and gently sweeping the ground in front of them as they walk, to avoid treading on any unseen life forms. Jainism takes its name from the honorific *jina*, or "conqueror," bestowed upon Mahāvīra. Roughly contemporary with the Buddha, Mahāvīra is often called the "founder" of Jainism, but this is incorrect, at least according to the belief of the Jainas themselves. Rather, he was the last in the line of twenty-four so-called "ford-makers (*tīrthāṅkara*)," whose name refers to their role of providing a "ford" or way out of the unending flow of reincarnation. The Jainas see Mahāvīra and his predecessors as divine saviors. All of the ford-makers taught the same lessons about how we escape the cycle of rebirth (*saṃsāra*).

We saw briefly in Chapter 6 that the Jainas believed this could be achieved only through the total elimination of *karma*.[8] Even good *karma* has the effect of tying you to rebirth, though such *karma* at least helps you secure a relatively favorable rebirth. The Jaina teaching on *karma* presupposes a dualist understanding of the human person, according to which the soul (*jīva*) is an immaterial entity that enters into a relation with the physical world (*ajīva*) and, in particular, a series of individual bodies. *Karma*, too, is described as if it were a physical substance. It is compared to "dust" which gets stuck to the soul more easily when we give in to passion or bad intention. The Jaina texts nicely express this by calling passion *kaṣāya*, which literally means "glue" or "resin." And of course, according to the Jainas it isn't only barbecue ribs that will make you sticky. The consumption of any meat builds up bad *karma*, since it inevitably involves the death of another being that desires to live.

But for the Jainas asceticism is more than observing *ahiṃsā*, and observing *ahiṃsā* is more than abstaining from meat. It has been remarked that Jainism "is the most ascetic among the world's organised religions today, if not in world history."[9] Renouncers and laypersons alike look to the example of the ford-makers and especially Mahāvīra, whose self-restraint reached superhuman levels. Never mind eating meat—he and the other ford-makers are said to have gone for weeks or even a year at a time without eating anything at all. Through extreme practices, the Jaina ascetic can divest himself or herself of all *karma*, and attain the status of a *kevalin*, meaning someone who is "alone," that is, without the accretion of *karma*. The notorious practice of *sallekhanā*, in which a renouncer adopts total immobility until he succumbs to death through thirst, exposure, and hunger, has been criticized as a form of religiously inspired suicide. But the Jainas are firm in insisting that those who take this path do not desire death (according to legend, that would include Candragupta, the king who founded the Mauryan dynasty and the grandfather of Aśoka). Rather, they are simply trying to avoid the acquisition of new *karma* that could compromise their hard-won status as a *kevalin*, and doom them to yet another rebirth.

As for the requirements of *ahiṃsā*, vegetarianism is only the beginning. A delightful story from the Jaina tradition brings home what might be expected of the perfectly non-violent renouncer.[10] One day a forest fire erupted in a wood, and all the animals gathered around a lake to avoid the flames. They were packed together tightly, rubbing shoulder to shoulder in the limited space. An elephant lifted its foot briefly, and just then a rabbit darted to the spot on which it had been standing. Rather than putting its foot down and crushing the rabbit, the elephant stood with his foot held aloft for three days, before finally collapsing and dying from fatigue. The happy end to the tale is that the elephant is reborn as a human, and later reincarnated as an associate of Mahāvīra himself.

You might argue that in their pursuit of absolute non-violence, the Jainas likewise don't have a leg to stand on. You cannot get through life without ever harming a living thing. After all, we need to eat, and plants, too, are alive. As a leading scholar of Jainism has written: "The desire for food is the prime cause for all forms of *hiṃsā*, since food cannot be consumed without destroying another life form."[11] So far from denying this, the Jainas avoid consuming many types of fruits and vegetables, such as those they believe to be "aggregates" of a large number of life forms. The dietary restrictions extend even to water, which should be drunk by a Jaina ascetic only when it is strained so as to remove small life forms. But even with these measures, avoiding all violence is still going to be difficult or impossible for the Jaina renouncer, at least without assistance. Fortunately, help is at hand in the shape of the Jaina layperson. As in Buddhism, the Jaina monastic lifestyle is facilitated by the support of other followers, who content themselves with living in accordance with less rigorous precepts. For instance, the renouncer is forbidden to handle fire, since that would obviously result in the death of small creatures who might get caught up in the flames. So instead he may take water that has been boiled by the layperson to free it of microscopic living things. Similarly monks subsist on alms of food, donated by laypeople. Similar practices are followed in the Buddhist community.

Is this really a coherent way of handling the ethical dilemma? Consider the following analogy. Suppose I need a lot of money in a hurry and the only way

I can think to get it is by robbing my rich uncle. But there's a catch: my moral scruples forbid me to do so. So I resort to the expedient of getting my less fastidious friend to rob my uncle's house, and splitting the cash with him. I may not have committed the robbery myself, but surely I would be morally culpable. In the same way, it would seem the Jaina renouncer must shoulder the burden of *hiṃsā* inflicted in the preparation of any food or water he consumes, even if he didn't do the preparing himself. But let's not leap to conclusions, because there's more to the Jaina story. The renouncer is only allowed to take food and drink that was prepared without him in mind, and he will verify that this is the case before accepting it. In other words, the renouncer should live on leftovers, food and drink that just happen to be available and on offer from the laypersons. So to go back to our analogy, what the renouncer is doing is more like taking a charitable donation from a thief, after ensuring to his satisfaction that the money was not stolen for his sake.

A critic of Jaina renunciation will probably not be satisfied. If you knowingly benefit from a morally dubious act, doesn't that by itself put you in a morally dubious situation? One possible response would be to invoke another aspect of the Jaina understanding of non-violence, which is the centrality of intention. We said before that it is passion, desire, or intention that causes *karma* to stick to the soul. By religiously avoiding violence, and by eating only food that was originally intended for others, the renouncer avoids intending violence, and does not benefit from an intention to do violence *on his behalf*. He is, quite literally, an innocent bystander. The same point will apply in a case like unintentionally killing an insect or plant by stepping on it. A renouncer's conscience in such a circumstance is clean, but only so long as he has taken every precaution to avoid its occurrence. Good examples of such precautions, apart from the ones we've already mentioned, are the practice of avoiding travel during the rainy season—when more vegetation and life forms are in harm's way—and refusing to eat at night. Before electricity, eating after sundown ran a significantly greater risk of accidentally consuming a bug. (In fact, when you put it that way, maybe no one should eat after dark.)

The importance of intention to the Jaina code is shown by the story of Yaśodhara.[12] He is a king who has caused blood to be shed in war; but death was never his goal, so he has remained pure. Then, for complicated reasons, he decides to perform an animal sacrifice. To avoid killing a real living thing, he has a fake rooster made up out of flour, a practice also recorded in other texts. Even though no real rooster is slain, King Yaśodhara is elaborately punished in the afterlife, simply because his *intention* was violent. Notice, too, how the narrative implies that a Jaina king could pursue military aims. Similarly Jaina laypersons have frequently served as soldiers. It has even been proposed that the "heroic" ethic of Jaina asceticism was seen as continuous with the warrior heroism celebrated in texts like the great Hindu epics.[13] Having said that, only Jaina laypersons will engage in warfare. The way of the Jaina renouncer would be to die rather than do violence.

How does the Jaina understanding of non-violence stack up against modern-day ideas about violence? It's easy to see a contrast with the utilitarian approach, which tries to minimize the amount of harm and suffering in the world, including the harm and suffering inflicted on animals. The Jainas do have a tradition of trying to persuade others to adopt non-violent ways. But the ancient Jaina approach to *ahiṃsā* seems to be directed toward a different, more individualist goal. The idea is not simply to reduce the overall amount of violence, though that result is certainly going to be achieved too. Rather the Jaina wants to avoid being *personally* implicated in any act of violence. It's sometimes been complained that the Jaina renouncer is actually inflicting violence on himself, so severe is his ascetic practice. But we might rather have the opposite worry, that the renouncer seems to be concentrating only on his own self-interest. This is why the radical renouncer needn't worry that his lifestyle depends on a degree of *hiṃsā* being committed by lay believers. Like other ancient ethical traditions within and beyond India, Jainism is about shaping and perfecting the self. The renouncer will indeed leave the world a better place than he found it, but the main thing is to leave the world and not come back, by purifying his soul and becoming a *kevalin* unencumbered by *karma*.

The Jaina teaching was also challenged by the rival belief systems of its own time and place. The Buddhists complained that Jaina asceticism was excessive. Remember that the Buddha himself began his spiritual quest by engaging in extreme discipline and self-denial, including a starvation diet, but he came to adopt a less punishing "middle way" between the extreme asceticism of a Mahāvīra and the plush life of a householder. We are told that he parted ways with a follower named Devadatta, who wanted the Buddhist community to adopt more rigorous practices including strict vegetarianism.[14] Instead, the Buddhist writings suggest that meat might be allowed for the Buddhist monk, on the same basis used by the Jainas for their vegetarian diet: consumption is licit provided the meat was not actually prepared with the monk in mind. It may even be that this rule was absorbed into Buddhism from Jaina practices.[15] Hindu authors, too, could exploit the idea of intention to legitimate that most un-Jaina of practices, the animal sacrifice. We see this in texts composed at various times and places: the *Laws of Manu* say that slaying animals in a ritual context is in fact *ahiṃsā*, and does not count as real killing (5.39, 5.44), while the *Bhagavad-gītā* suggests that sacrifice is needed to "hold the world together."[16] This was also the basis on which Arjuna was encouraged to go into battle, so long as the fight would be undertaken with Kṛṣṇa in mind and not the intention of achieving any result for himself.

The upshot is that there was a shared philosophical rationale for *ahiṃsā* across these ancient traditions, despite the wide variation in the practices deemed consistent with non-violence. Given the competition between the rival groups, more emphasis was inevitably placed on the disagreement than on the agreement. For centuries to come, the Hindus will sneer at the squalid lifestyle of the dissident sects, Buddhists will snipe at Jainas for their absurdly excessive self-punishment, and Jainas will proudly claim to be the only ones who really take non-violence seriously. One Jaina text mocks the Buddhists' willingness to eat animals that died of old age. This, the author remarks, is like seducing a widow after her husband has died. The underlying desires are the same as those of a man who would slaughter an animal to get meat, or murder a husband to steal his wife.[17]

Disagreements over the demands of *ahiṃsā* and asceticism also erupted within the Jaina community itself. We mentioned earlier (in Chapter 11) the split between Śvetāmbara and Digambara Jainas, the latter being those whose monks included nudity within their rigorously ascetic lifestyle. And their stringent interpretation of Jaina principles also emerged in disputes about diet. They insisted that a perfect *kevalin*, like Mahāvīra or any other renouncer who has attained liberation, would no longer need to eat at all, thus freeing them from even indirect contact with *hiṃsā*. The Śvetāmbaras, by contrast, endorsed the more commonsense view that the need for food, unlike the need for sex and material comfort, is an inevitable, if regrettable, part of embodied life.

A common question posed about the traditions we've been examining in the book so far is whether they are really philosophical, or rather religious. You may have noticed that along the way, we've occasionally distinguished the philosophical and religious aspects of the texts. But the issue of non-violence shows that the line is, at best, a blurry one. The concept of *ahiṃsā* may seem simple: it boils down to doing no harm. Yet it has taken the form of both a religious taboo and an ethical precept, and its interpretation has been advanced through a wide variety of means, ranging from doctrinaire assertion, to subtle debate, to crude insult. That's a feature of Indian intellectual life that is going to stay with us as we go forward—especially the bit about subtle debate, though we'll also be seeing the occasional crude insult. Nothing typifies philosophy in our next period, which we're calling the "Age of the Sūtra," so much as disagreement and debate—both between rival schools and within single schools. Traditions will split apart, as did the Jainas. The highly disputatious context will lead to new reflections on argumentative method. And some groups, including the Jainas, will be led to question whether any viewpoint is really better off than its rivals.[18]

PART II

THE AGE OF THE *SŪTRA*

15

A TANGLED WEB

THE AGE OF THE *SŪTRA*

It's at this point in our story that things get complicated. Indian intellectual life in the period we've already covered was lively, to say the least. But now we're going to see such a proliferation of philosophical texts, movements, schools, and rivalries that it may be hard to keep track of them all. Historians have stepped forward to offer ways of organizing all this material. They have made a basic distinction between so-called "orthodox" and "heterodox" movements, with the orthodox movements growing out of the Brahmanical culture of the Vedas. On this side, historians have spoken of six "systems" or "schools" that take on the ideas we find in works like the Upaniṣads, certain passages of the epics, the *dharma-sūtras*, and the *Laws of Manu*.[1] These six schools are Sāṃkhya, Yoga, Nyāya, Vaiśeṣika, Mīmāṃsā, and Vedānta. Collectively, they would represent the "Hindu" perspective, which will be challenged by skeptical and relativist attitudes among "heterodox" thinkers, meaning basically Buddhists and Jainas, who opposed orthodox theories concerning ritual, metaphysics, and epistemology.

But we have already expressed our dissatisfaction with this relatively neat account (see Chapter 2). The most obvious problem is that it very much reflects the so-called "Hindu" point of view. "Orthodox" literally means "right-believing," so framing things in this way is almost like saying "there were two kinds of Indian philosophers, the good guys and the other guys." While we're at it, it's also problematic to refer to the six "orthodox" schools as "Hindu." We've occasionally applied the term "Hindu" to works that express traditional Brahmanical and *kṣatrīya* values, as when we called the *Mahābhārata* a "Hindu epic." But in fact the application of the name "Hindu" to such early texts is a rather contentious bit of retrospective labeling.[2]

The label of "orthodoxy" also suggests an unrealistic degree of agreement between the six schools, or some central authority that is the arbiter of correct teaching. Neither suggestion would be accurate. Admittedly, some of these philosophical movements do eventually grow together. In the eleventh or twelfth century, the Vaiśeṣika and Nyāya systems effectively merged to form a single school, so that scholars feel free to speak of a single "Nyāya-Vaiśeṣika philosophy." We also see an intimate association between Sāṃkhya and Yoga. But it would hardly be worth distinguishing the systems into six if they all ultimately coalesced into a single, "Hindu" outlook. In fact, there are prolonged disputes between these so-called "orthodox" schools, and for that matter within individual schools. These often split apart into sub-traditions, much as we saw with the Jainas dividing into the "white-clad" and "sky-clad" factions. Also omitted in this doxography are other "Hindu" movements, such as Śaiva philosophy.

So we want to suggest a different and more ideologically neutral contrast, based on the way that philosophical texts were *composed*. In this second section of the book, we are going to look at what we will call the "Age of the *Sūtra*." This is a period stretching over the first several centuries AD, when philosophy centered on the interpretation of compressed, lapidary statements called *sūtras*, literally meaning "threads." So pregnant with meaning were these *sūtras* that commentary was needed to deliver their meaning fully. These further, explanatory texts are called *bhāṣyas*. It's something we have already seen with the Sanskrit grammar of Pāṇini, which was also written in the form of *sūtras* and received an influential *bhāṣya* from the second century AD grammarian Patañjali (Chapter 7). The "Age of the *Sūtra*" is also the age in which Sanskrit, the language of the Vedas, becomes dominant across the spectrum of philosophical writing. So it's apt, and perhaps no coincidence, that Pāṇini's *Eight Chapters* provided a model for the way texts would be written. Each school traced its ideas to a founding text produced in the form of *sūtras*, which were made the subject of authoritative commentary in *bhāṣyas*. In fact the habit of pairing *sūtra* with *bhāṣya* was so deeply ingrained that, in some cases, a single author might write both the aphoristic remarks and a commentary of his own on those remarks.

It may seem perverse to put so much emphasis on the *sūtra* format. Isn't the content more important than the form in which the content is presented? But we shouldn't underestimate the way that the form of a text shapes its content, and shapes the way a text is understood by readers. Philosophy in this period was moving away from the exhortations and evocations of the earlier period—when "philosophies of path and purpose" were dominant—and toward systematic inquiry. This went hand in hand with the writing of *bhāṣya* commentaries. A good *bhāṣya* was one that uncovered the philosophical principles and arguments implicit in the *sūtras* being commented upon, exposing the coherence and completeness of the ideas and showing how those ideas could be justified and defended from the criticisms of rivals. It is the job of the commentator to weave the "threads" into a unified conceptual web, which commentators called a *tantra*, literally meaning "warp" (think weaving, not Star Trek).

Vātsyāyana, the author of a major commentary on the *Nyāya-sūtra*, explained that "a tantra is a system (*śāstra*) consisting in the statement of a collection of interrelated ideas."[3] We also see commentators characterizing their task as the amplification or "expansion (*prapañcaka*)" of what is said in the *sūtra*. So (to use a metaphor that would be somewhat more at home in Star Trek), a *sūtra* is like a compressed data file that needs to be "decompressed," its meaning unfolded by the commentator who adds the *bhāṣya*.[4] This was no easy task. From Pāṇini's *Eight Chapters* onwards, *sūtras* typically seemed to be nothing more than lists, offered to the reader as a series of isolated statements with no organizing structure or principle. It was the commentator's job to impose (or, he would say, reveal) an intelligible structure on this material. He would begin by identifying the chief overall theme of the text at hand, and then dividing the *sūtras* by sub-theme into groups (*prakaraṇa*), thus turning what was a mere list into something more like a network of ideas and arguments with mutual connections (*saṅgati*). The goal was not to provide an alternative version of the text that would be easier to follow, as if the *bhāṣya* could simply replace the *sūtra*. It was to guide the reader through the original text. Like the Greek commentaries devoted to Plato and Aristotle in the same historical period, the *bhāṣyas* have a fundamentally pedagogical purpose.

The six so-called "systems" all used the *sūtra-bhāṣya* style of composition. So, too, did the Buddhists, but they gave it a new and distinctive twist. The term *sūtra*, or *sutta* in Pāli, is here reserved for the recorded word of the Buddha himself in its entirety. They instead only use the term *kārikā* for compressed epigrammatic statements, on which commentaries are written. And there were other *sūtra*-based philosophical movements outside the supposedly orthodox, "Hindu" mainstream. In particular, we will need to look at Cārvāka philosophy. This is not one of the "six systems," but it does have its own foundational document in the shape of Bṛhaspati's *Cārvāka-sūtra*. Another warning is needed here, by the way. As we'll see, Bṛhaspati did not emerge from nowhere with his *sūtra*; he was not boldly going where no one had gone before. Rather, he continued an older tradition of naturalism that had begun already with Payāsi, who was probably a contemporary of the Buddha. And that's typical. Each founding text is ascribed to a founding father, so that we have Gautama initiating Nyāya philosophy with his *Nyāya-sūtra*, Patañjali beginning Yoga philosophy with his *Yoga-sūtra*, and so on. But we need to reckon with the possibility that these supposed foundations were themselves built out of found materials.

Usually people think of the *sūtras* as canonical texts that initiated the various traditions. But it would be safer to think of them as the oldest *surviving* texts that came to be *recognized* as canonical in each tradition, and to remember that *sūtras* may in part be compilations based on still older, otherwise lost literature. This helps to explain another feature of the *sūtras* that doesn't fit very well with the usual antithesis between orthodox and heterodox philosophies: the agenda and terminology of the supposedly "unorthdox" traditions frequently turn up in "orthodox" literature. If you turn to the *Yoga-sūtra* you'll find the idea that we can escape the cycle of rebirth by eliminating all desire, which is obviously reminiscent of Buddhism. This is not entirely surprising. In the earlier period, we saw a gap opening between Brahmanical culture and the *śramaṇa* movements, the groups who emphasized renunciation and an ascetic path to liberation: the Buddhists, Jainas, and Ājīvikas. But as in a good history of philosophy, we also saw this gap being closed. Non-attached action and non-violence, for example, were motifs that appeared on both sides of the divide between Brahmanical and *śramaṇa* philosophy. At the political level, we also saw how rulers might pay due respect to sages of both persuasions. The standout example is Aśoka, who is best known for his attraction to Buddhism but in fact seems to have seen himself as transcending sectarian divisions. Aśoka was exceptional, but in this case he was an exception that became the rule. Later rulers would continue to bestow favor on both Brahmanical and dissident groups. Toward the end of the age of the *sūtra*, we find a southern dynasty called the Ikṣvākus whose female members gave gifts to the Buddhists, while the male kings carried out Vedic sacrifices.[5]

Archeologists are grateful that later rulers followed Aśoka in another respect. As he had done, they occasionally put up stone inscriptions to communicate with their subjects. In fact there are even cases where a king added inscriptions of his own alongside the words of Aśoka. This was done around AD 150 on behalf of the king Rudradaman, and what he had carved into the rock is quite telling. For one thing, it shows a continued alliance between royalty and philosophy: Rudradaman boasts that in addition to his martial prowess and good looks, he has "knowledge and practice of grammar, music, logic, and other great sciences."[6] But even more interesting than what he has to say is the language in which he says it, namely Sanskrit (whereas Aśoka's inscriptions are mostly in Prakrit). It's really at this stage that Sanskrit is beginning to establish itself as the main language you need to learn if you want to read the primary sources of Indian philosophy. The Buddha himself would have spoken Prakrit, and as we saw the Buddhist canon was composed in Pāli. But as we move forward almost all philosophical literature is written in Sanskrit. For Brahmanical authors Sanskrit, the language of scripture and of Pāṇini's grammar, has a unique status: it alone is without beginning.[7] Buddhists are never going to accept that Sanskrit has such an exceptional status (if anything, they would make similar claims concerning Pāli), yet they, too, begin to write in the same language as their Brahmanical adversaries.

And adversarial relationships are indeed crucial to philosophy in the age of the *sūtra*. From our earlier description of the *sūtra* and accompanying *bhāṣya* as a web of interconnected ideas, you might have gotten the impression that the resulting text is a self-contained, systematic presentation of ideas—more reminiscent of the *Elements* of Euclid than the dialectical exchange of Plato's dialogues or the treatises of Aristotle. In fact, though, the systems emerged only gradually, and in response to intellectual rivals. As Johannes Bronkhorst has written, "under pressure from competitors, the Indian thinkers of the early classical period were forced to do more than just preserve the teachings they had received; they had to improve and refine them—perhaps in order to avoid becoming the laughing stock of those they might have to confront at a royal court or at some other occasion. In doing so, they created systems of philosophy that might deviate considerably from the pre-systematic teachings which they had inherited."[8] Precisely because the authors of these works are sensitive to challenges from other schools, they constantly allude to potential objections (*pūrva-pakṣa*) and seek to supply well-reasoned answers to those objections (*siddhānta*).[9] In this respect, philosophical literature in the age of the *sūtra* holds on to something of the "dialogue" structure that was such a hallmark of the Upaniṣads and the more philosophical sections of the *Mahābhārata*, to say nothing of many stories told about the Buddha in the Pāli canon.

One final cautionary note about the classification into six "systems" is that these traditions are not equally "systematic." The idea applies pretty well to Nyāya and Vaiśeṣika, but less well to Yoga, which was not so much a philosophical system as a philosophical method. As such, it recalls the "philosophies of path and purpose" we have seen in the earlier period. Also the canonical *sūtras* of a school may in fact be composed retrospectively, in an attempt to provide these traditions of thought with the same sort of authority and historical lineage that other schools were claiming to have. The *Sāṃkhya-sūtra*, in fact, dates from as late as the fourteenth century!

So what are the main topics of debate being pursued in the *sūtras* and their commentaries? Here, too, we see a degree of continuity with the earlier period. One dominant question is whether there is or is not a "self" that underlies all cognition and experience. As we know, the Buddhists deny this while the Brahmanical culture asserts the reality of the self. But we should beware of oversimplification. Within Buddhism there are disagreements in this period about how we can account for the apparent survival of one and the same person across time, and even across incarnations. On the Brahmanical side, meanwhile, there are major differences of opinion, with the Mīmāṃsā school developing the self as an empirically engaged agent, where other traditions hold on to the idea of the self as a pure consciousness that remains in itself aloof from cognition and agency. The means by which the self (if there is one) comes to know the world around it, and its own nature, was also much debated in this period, with the Nyāya school making especially powerful contributions in epistemology. Against such positive accounts of knowledge, a more skeptical note is struck within Buddhism and also Jainism. The Jainas develop the remarkable idea that truth depends inevitably on one's own standpoint, what we would now call a "perspectivist" or "pluralist" approach to epistemology.

In metaphysics too, there are fundamental disagreements in this period: the Vaiśeṣika philosophical school tries to establish six fundamental categories of reality, and again there are very different rival views, including the aforementioned naturalism of the Cārvākas. While much of the philosophical action thus relates to issues in philosophy of mind, epistemology, and metaphysics, thinkers in this period do not simply drop the earlier concern with ethics and salvation. The brilliant philosopher Nāgārjuna, founder of the Madhyamaka school within Buddhism, is a good example. He is best known for his radical doctrine of "emptiness," but he never loses sight of the fact that the goal of accepting this doctrine (or perhaps we should say "non-doctrine") is freedom from suffering.

Let's now finish this introductory chapter with a quick run-down of the various schools. This will probably be too much for you to take in all at once, but it may be helpful as a first glimpse, and you might want to stick a bookmark in here so you can refer back later (unless you're reading on an electronic device, in which case you can stick in a "bookmark"). Let's begin with Nyāya, not for chronological reasons but because it will allow us to look at fundamental issues concerning the nature of knowledge and the means by which it may be achieved. Its foundational treatise, the *Nyāya-sūtra*, was probably compiled somewhere in the first or second century AD. The traditional name of the compiler is Gautama, sometimes called Akṣapāda, "One whose eyes are in his feet," apparently in reference to the foundationalism and empiricism of his system. He forcefully advocates the so-called *pramāṇa* method as a method for rational inquiry, a *pramāṇa* being a way of gaining knowledge or a principle of justification. For him all knowledge is based on three main sources—perception, inference, and testimony—though he adds a fourth source called "comparison," whose exact meaning is somewhat unclear. The first and fifth chapters of the *Nyāya-sūtra* concentrate on techniques for conducting debates, and it has been speculated that they originally formed a separate text of their own. So the main issues in Nyāya philosophy are the nature of philosophical inquiry, the epistemology of the sources of knowledge (*pramāṇa*), and the theory of debate. As we have already mentioned, there is an allied philosophical system called Vaiśeṣika. Its canonical text is Kaṇāda's *Vaiśeṣika-sūtra*, which may already have been composed around 100 BC. Vaiśeṣika's main claim to fame is something we have also already mentioned: a six-category metaphysics that influenced thinkers across the spectrum of Indian philosophy.

A third system, Mīmāṃsā, was in the first instance a system of Vedic hermeneutics. In other words it was concerned with the interpretation and clarification of the Vedas, the defense of Vedic authority, and the analysis of the meaning of Vedic ritual injunctions. As you might guess, the foundational text for this tradition is called the *Mīmāṃsā-sūtra*. It is difficult to date this *sūtra* with any accuracy. Perhaps in some form it already existed in about 400 BC, and its compilation as the version we have now took place in the following few centuries. The *Mīmāṃsā-sūtra* is traditionally attributed to Jaimini, while the *bhāṣya* was written by Śabara in about AD 400. Though Mīmāṃsā continued to focus on Vedic interpretation, this endeavor led them to consider a much wider range of philosophical issues. They shared with Nyāya a broadly "realist" epistemology, and contributed in particular to the theory of perception. In the seventh century, the school divided into two sub-schools, one following Kumārila Bhaṭṭa and the other Prabhākara. Jaimini's *Mīmāṃsā-sūtra* has traditionally been juxtaposed with Bādarāyaṇa's *Vedānta-sūtra* (also known as *Brahma-sūtra*).

We can sum up the division of labor as follows. Jaimini, in the *Mīmāṃsā-sūtra*, is focused on the ritual formulations of the Vedas, and on the concept of *dharma* or duty, the actions one ought to perform. Hence the name of the school. *Mīmāṃsā* means "investigation," and for Jaimini the investigation that matters is the one that helps him to understand the ritual prescriptions of the Vedas. In the case of Bādarāyaṇa's *Vedānta-sūtra*, the clue to its motivation is again in the name. *Vedānta* means "what is at the end of the Veda," that is, the Upaniṣads. So the philosophical themes of the Upaniṣads are also the themes of Bādarāyaṇa and the Vedānta school that follows in his wake: cosmic unity, *brahman*, and the quest to discover *brahman* within one's own self. The *Vedānta-sūtra* illustrates our point about interschool rivalry. Its four chapters defend the view that *brahman* is the central concern of the scriptures, and that there is only one consistent interpretation of them. These claims are set out in opposition to the ideas of the Vaiśeṣikas, not to mention the Buddhists and Jainas, who are all subjected to refutation. In the *Vedānta-sūtra* we also have an extended description of the spiritual exercises that will lead an individual to comprehend his or her identity with *brahman*.

This reference to spiritual exercises leads us naturally on to the *Yoga-sūtra*, whose commentary is attributed to the mythical Vyāsa. More likely, though, both the *sūtra* and the *bhāṣya* were written by someone called Patañjali—the same name, but probably not the same man, as the grammarian who commented on Pāṇini. This Patañjali itemizes the elements needed to subdue or arrest mental disturbance. Most important are restraint (*yama*) and observance (*niyama*), restraint from injuring others, from stealing, from lying, and from greed, observance of habits of cleanliness, purification, and study. Then there are posture, regulation of breathing, abstraction of the senses, concentration, meditation, and trance. Backing up this account of spiritual discipline is a detailed theory of the nature of the mind, in which the unchanging self is distinguished from the states that constitute a mental life. The Yoga school became more emphatically theistic, God being treated as a self of this sort, one unaffected by suffering or actions.

Providing further theoretical backbone to spiritual discipline, and yet without any obvious initial acceptance of theism, is Sāṃkhya philosophy. We mentioned that in this case the *sūtra* of the school came only much later. Its foundational document is instead Īśvarakṛṣṇa's *Sāṃkhya-kārikā*, meaning "verses on Sāṃkhya." Īśvarakṛṣṇa insists on a strict dualism between the self (*puruṣa*) on the one hand, and nature or matter (*prakṛti*) on the other. It is out of original matter that the material world evolves, according to the law that an effect pre-exists in its cause. Strikingly though, what evolve first are the mental phenomena: intellect (*buddhi*), then sense of self (*ahaṃkāra*), then mind (*manas*), then the five domains of sense-experience and the senses, and only then the five material elements, air, light, water, earth, and aether. All this is essentially a part of nature, with the true self transcending all processes of natural evolution.

And there you have it! Along with the Cārvāka naturalists, these six schools are going to be occupying our attention in this section of the book. So all these unfamiliar names will become familiar in due course, as we get to know Nyāya epistemology, interpret Mīmāṃsā hermeneutics, and tackle some of the positions taken up in Yoga. After we've looked at all these schools, it will be time to turn to the critical voices among the Buddhists and Jainas. But since skeptical worries form such an important part of the context for this whole period, we're going to begin by exploring the emergence of nagging philosophical doubts, concerning the efficacy of action—especially Vedic ritual—and the possibility of knowledge.

16

WHEN IN DOUBT

THE RISE OF SKEPTICISM

The contrast we'll be pursuing through the rest of this book, then, is one between schools who set forth their thought in the *sūtra* and *bhāṣya* form, and the rival traditions of Buddhist and Jaina philosophy. The clash had political consequences, as we can see from stories about persecution of Buddhists by rulers who sought to uphold the Brahmanical teachings. For us of course, the clash is more significant for its philosophical implications. The rift can in general terms be viewed as a contrast between realist movements and skeptical ones. Buddhist and Jaina thinkers raised objections against the core philosophical notions of other schools, on topics like language, the mind and self, practical action, and the efficacy of ritual. They also expressed doubts when it came to the very possibility of systematic inquiry. This challenge was often on the mind of commentators who expounded the meaning of the various *sūtras*.

It's clear that the schools' foundational texts do indeed presuppose the possibility of knowledge, and promise that it can be achieved through philosophical inquiry. To see this, you only have to read as far as the first sentence of each *sūtra*. We mentioned just now that the *Mīmāṃsā-sūtra* and the *Brahma-sūtra* (aka. *Vedānta-sūtra*), respectively the founding documents of the Mīmāṃsā and Vedānta schools, are complementary texts, with the former aiming at the duties of Vedic ritual, the other at knowledge of the unifying cosmic principle of *brahman*. The two works even have nearly identical beginnings. The first sentence of the *Mīmāṃsā-sūtra* is, "Now, then, an inquiry into *dharma* (*athāto dharma-jijñāsā*)." And the first sentence of the *Brahma-sūtra* is, "Now, then, an inquiry into *brahman* (*athāto brahma-jijñāsā*)." Undergraduates, take note: when you're writing philosophy essays, follow the example of these *sūtras* and just cut to the chase.

Something similar goes for the *Vaiśeṣika-sūtra* and the *Yoga-sūtra*. They do not begin with promises of "inquiry" but launch into what they term an "explanation" or "exposition." Thus the *Yoga-sūtra* begins with another admirably straightforward line: "Now, an exposition of *yoga*" (*atha yogānuśāsanam*)."[1] As in a well-run modern-day yoga class, you know where you stand. You're about to hear what *yoga*, meaning psycho-physical discipline, means and involves. Apparently the lost founding text of the naturalist Cārvāka school began with even greater confidence, starting with the line: "Now, then, we will explain reality (*tattva*)." Of course, if a skeptic were to convince us that inquiry and philosophical explanation were in fact impossible, we could save ourselves a lot of time and stop reading all these *sūtras* right there.

Knowing this, and knowing that the best defense is a good offense, early commentators openly raise worries about the very possibility of inquiry. Expounding the *Mīmāṃsā-sūtra*, Śabara says on behalf of a hypothetical critic that "It must either be commonly known what *dharma* is, or else not commonly known. If it is commonly known, then there will be no inquiry. If, however, it is not commonly known, then all the more so. So this work of inquiry into duty is quite pointless."[2] The word for "inquiry" is *jijñāsā*, which literally means "desire to know." Śabara's point, then, is that a desire to obtain something—in this case *dharma*—presupposes that one knows what one wants to obtain. To desire knowledge of something, then, means you must already know it; a paradox. The same point is made by a later Mīmāṃsā writer, Kumārila Bhaṭṭa: "It is possible to know that which is commonly known, but being commonly known there is no desire [to know it]. On the other hand, that which is not commonly known, being impossible [to know], is all the more not [a possible object of a desire to know]."[3] In another sign of the relation between the Mīmāṃsā and Vedānta schools, commentators on the *Brahma-sūtra* expressed the same worry. We find it in the eighth-century thinker Śaṅkara. Since the *Brahma-sūtra* begins with that promise to inquire into *brahman*, Śaṅkara begins his commentary by raising the same skeptical challenge: if we don't know what *brahman* is, how can we go in search of it? But if we do, then there is nothing to discover.

Curiously, the realist thinkers who were most interested in epistemology were also the ones who failed to confront this problem directly. These were the proponents of Nyāya, who early on at least seem simply to take for granted that there is a way to investigate, to inquire, to achieve knowledge. They are keenly interested in establishing a method by which to answer the sort of questions you probably ask yourself all the time, like "is yonder entity a man or a tree-stump?" They are less interested in the more abstract question whether there could even be such a method. For the Nyāya, doubt is not a state of epistemological paralysis. It is a state in which one already has partially grasped an object, so that it can be the target for further questioning. Thus the puzzle of inquiry does not even arise.

Another ancient thinker who did raise the puzzle that worried Śabara, Kumārila Bhaṭṭa, and Śaṅkara was Plato. In his dialogue the *Meno*, he has Socrates confront an identical puzzle, to the effect that one would need to have knowledge of something in order to inquire into it.[4] Plato has Socrates suggest a fairly radical solution to this puzzle, namely that we all already know everything that it is possible for us to know, having learned these things before we were born. We have merely forgotten these things, and need to be reminded. But this isn't the only, or even most obvious, way to resolve the paradox. It does seem fruitless to inquire into something about which one already has perfect knowledge. Likewise, if one hasn't the foggiest notion or clue about something, inquiry into that thing is impossible—how would you get started, or even formulate a plan to inquire into it? The natural thought is that our situation must, at the outset, lie somewhere in the middle ground. Inquiry begins not from a cognitive blank state or from complete mastery, but from partial understanding or uncertain belief.

This in fact is exactly what Śabara says in his response to the skeptical challenge. He assumes that the inquiry into *dharma* arises because we in fact have *too many* beliefs about it. There is conflict between different conceptions of duty, the sort of conflict we saw being depicted in the *Mahābhārata*. It is in order to decide between these rival beliefs that we undertake an investigation. This does seem a good explanation of how we avoid "starting from scratch" in moral philosophy. But it doesn't give us any reason to think that two people who disagree about *dharma*, or for that matter *brahman*, are really disagreeing about the same thing. Can the clash between a Vedānta philosopher and a Buddhist critic really be resolved on the basis of commonly held assumptions? Or are they just talking past one another, using the same words in very different ways?

Śaṅkara's commentary on the *Brahma-sūtra* anticipates and answers this question. He admits that people disagree about the qualities of *brahman* but insists that we all have a common idea of it, which gives us only "partial" knowledge. As proof, Śaṅkara offers an etymology of the word *brahman* itself: "its very nature (*svabhāva*) is said to consist in what is eternal, pure and consciousness; bound up with the omniscient and the omnipotent. For the meanings such as 'being eternal' and 'being pure' are derived from semantic analysis of the word *brahman*, these meanings following from the verbal root *bṛh*."[5] Here we have another reminder of the importance of Sanskrit grammar for philosophers. It was commonly held that linguistic analysis (called *vyutpatti* or *nirvacana*) can explain why we use certain words for certain things. On the basis of its verbal root, the word *dharma* was claimed to mean "that which upholds." Likewise here, Śaṅkara conjectures that the term *brahman* is derived from the verbal root *bṛh*, meaning "to grow." This shows that *brahman* is in some way maximally great. It is, so to speak, all grown up.

This might seem a rather flimsy response to the skeptic, but Śaṅkara has a second and more formidable move to make, one that will again remind us of European philosophy. He argues that the paradox of inquiry poses no threat to an investigation about *brahman*, because this is a case where we have direct knowledge. As he says, "Every one knows of the existence of his own self, and does not think 'I am not.' If the existence of one's own self were not perfectly well known, any one of us could think 'I am not.'"[6] The parallel with European thinkers like Augustine and Descartes is almost too obvious to need emphasizing. But unlike Descartes, with his famous "I think, therefore I am," Śaṅkara does not use immediate knowledge of one's own existence to refute global skepticism. He just wants to show that the inquiry into *brahman* promised at the beginning of the *sūtra* is indeed possible. He alludes to the Upaniṣadic statement, "You are that (*tat tvam asi*)," which he interprets as meaning "This self is *brahman*." Since it cannot be doubted that there is a self, and since the self is *brahman*, neither can there be doubt concerning *brahman*. There is, in other words, something for us to investigate.

But if we have immediate knowledge of the self, or *brahman*, why do we need to inquire into it? Because our intimate awareness of *brahman* does not include an understanding of its true nature. As Śaṅkara observes, there are intense disagreements about the self, with the materialists and "common folk" assuming that the self is the body, the Buddhists thinking it is just the flow of our cognitions, the Nyāya thinking it is an agent and subject of experience distinct from the body, the Sāṃkhya agreeing that it differs from the body but denying that it is an agent, and so on. We'll get into these disputes in the coming chapters. For now our point, and Śaṅkara's point, is that there is indeed plenty of dispute on this topic, and hence plenty of reason to engage in the philosophical investigation undertaken in the *sūtra*.

So far, we've been looking at hypothetical skeptical challenges raised and answered by non-skeptical authors. But such objections weren't merely hypothetical. The history of skepticism in India is at least as old, if not older, than the history of philosophy in India. The *Hymn of Creation* included in the ancient *Ṛg-veda* includes the verses:

> Who really knows? Who shall here proclaim it?—from where it was born, from where this creation?
>
> The gods are on the side of the creation of this (world). So then who does know from where it came to be?
>
> This creation—from where it came to be, if it was produced or if not—he who is the overseer of this (world) in the furthest heaven, he surely knows. Or if he does not know. . . ?[7]

Here, the *Ṛg-veda* suggests that the secrets of creation may elude even the gods. Obviously, mere humans aren't going to do better. There are skeptical thoughts, too, in some of the Upaniṣads, which occasionally propose the idea that mystical insight is the only way to overcome the limitations on human knowledge. Thus we read in the *Kena Upaniṣad*:

> If you think "I know it well"—perhaps you do know ever so little the visible appearance of *brahman*. There is that part of it you know and there is that part which is among the gods. And so I think what you must do is to reflect on it, on that unknown part of it:
>
> I do not think that I know it well;
> But I know not
> that I do not know.
> Who of us knows that,
> he does know that;
> But he knows not,
> that he does not know.[8]

But the skeptical challenges that really worried the Mīmāṃsā and Vedānta thinkers were not the ones they found in their own sacred texts. They needed to respond to the dissident *śramaṇa* movements, who from the very beginning used philosophical arguments to undermine the claims of Vedic authority. Even the authors of epic literature were unsettled enough to respond. So in the *Mahābhārata*, the god Indra in the guise of a jackal ruefully remarks:

> I used to be a learned skeptic who scorned the Vedas; I was devoted to logic and the science of debate, both of which are pointless. I formulated arguments based on reason and proffered rational statements in assemblies, abusing and denouncing brahmins over their sacred words. The heretic doubts everything—he is a fool who fancies himself learned. As a result of his *karma*, brahmin, he will become a jackal just like me.[9]

Though the Buddhists are frequently going to adopt the skeptic's role in coming centuries, the Buddhist canon also contains passages condemning skeptical thinkers. The Buddhist *Nikāya* mentions such a skeptic, named Sañjaya Belaṭṭhaputta, and has this to say about him:

> Sañjaya Belaṭṭhaputta said: "If you ask me: 'Is there another world?' if I thought so, I would say so. But I don't think so. I don't say it is so, and I don't say otherwise. I don't say it is not, and I don't not say it is not. If you ask: 'Isn't there another world?' . . . 'Both?' . . . 'Neither?' . . . 'Is there a fruit and result of good and bad deeds?' 'Isn't there?' . . . 'Both?' . . . 'Neither?' . . . 'Does the Tathāgata exist after death?'

> 'Does he not?' . . . 'Both?' . . . 'Neither?' . . . I don't not say it is not." Thus, Lord, Sañjaya Belaṭṭhaputta, on being asked about the fruits of the homeless life, replied by evasion. Just as if on being asked about a mango he were to describe a breadfruit-tree . . . And I thought: "Of all these ascetics and brahmins, Sañjaya Belaṭṭhaputta is the most stupid and confused." So I neither applauded nor rejected his words, but got up and left.[10]

Skepticism doesn't get much more extreme than this. Sañjaya went further than Nancy Reagan, whose slogan was "just say no," by disavowing even disavowal.

Together with the development of systematic philosophy in the age of the *sūtra*, we see the rise of rival forms of skepticism. Three great critical thinkers of this and later periods are Nāgārjuna, who lived in the second century AD, the ninth-century thinker Jayarāśi, and in the twelfth-century Śrīharṣa. Of these three only Jayarāśi can be called a skeptic in the sense of completely withholding all belief. For Nāgārjuna was a Buddhist, indeed the founder of a branch of Buddhism known as Madhyamaka, while Śrīharṣa seems to have had underlying metaphysical commitments too. But all three used skeptical arguments against an idea cherished by other thinkers of their times: we can know things, and also know that we know them.

It may seem simply obvious that knowledge is "reflective" in this way. If I know there is a giraffe in the room, then I must also know that I know there is a giraffe in the room. But as our three skeptics pointed out, it is far from obvious. Suppose I ask you how you know there is a giraffe in the room. You might say, "well, I haven't gone into the room myself, but I have it on good authority that there is a giraffe in there. I was told by my friend who is a zookeeper, and he ought to know." But if pressed, you would probably admit that testimony is sometimes misleading or outright fallacious. So, even while still thinking you know there is a giraffe in there, you might now be willing to concede that you aren't actually *sure* that you know there is a giraffe in there. But let's say you go in and look for yourself. Now you've directly witnessed the giraffe, and the only remaining puzzle is how they got it in through the front door.

But not so fast. I might ask you how you know that your sense-experience of the giraffe gives you knowledge. If you were an Indian philosopher you might explain that eyesight, and sense-experience in general, is what you and other such philosophers call a *pramāṇa*, in other words a way of knowing. There are other *pramāṇas*, like inferences based on evidence and perhaps in the right circumstances, even testimony. Your view on which things count as *pramāṇas* will depend on which school you follow. But to make a long story short, there are indeed some ways of knowing, and you are using one of them to know that there's a giraffe in the room. And here we come to the elephant in the room: the viability of this whole idea of a *pramāṇa*. The skeptic will ask how any supposed *pramāṇa* can be trusted if we do not first establish that the *pramāṇa* is truly reliable. As Nāgārjuna puts it:

> If just such objects are established for you by way of a means of knowing (*pramāṇa*), tell me how you establish those means of knowing [themselves]. If the means of knowing are established through other means of knowing, then there is an infinite regress.[11]

In our example, you need to justify and confirm your conviction that sense-experience can give you knowledge no less than you need to justify your conviction about the giraffe in the room.

You might say, "well I'm looking at a giraffe, and my eyes work, and I am not dreaming or hallucinating, and so on. That's good enough for me." Maybe, but it won't be good enough for Nāgārjuna. He'll point out that you don't *know* your eyes are working, you don't *know* that you aren't hallucinating, and so on. How could you? Obviously, sense-perception cannot ratify its own trustworthiness. Perhaps you are instead making an inference of some kind: when you trusted your eyes in the past things went well, so you know they are dependable. You are thus appealing to another *pramāṇa*, the *pramāṇa* of inference. But the skeptical reply is obvious, and Nāgārjuna doesn't hesitate to give it. How can you know that this inference is reliable, any more than you know that your eyes are working? You can already see why skeptics in India were regarded as very irritating people.

And it gets worse. Jayarāśi stages a further attack on realist epistemologists.[12] He challenges them to define knowledge itself, and argues that it cannot be done. He reasons as follows:

> The system of sources of knowledge is based on correct definitions, and the position of knowables is dependent on the sources of knowledge. In the absence of a correct definition, how can the sources of knowledge be themselves taken as objects of correct expression and practical behaviour? If you say that even without a correct definition we can resort to usage, we reply that we can just as well resort to usage to the effect that "the soul has colour," "the pot experiences pleasure," and so on.[13]

Here, the point isn't exactly that you can't know that you are knowing. It is the even more fundamental worry that you can't even know what knowledge *is*. Before you can take yourself to know anything, you must first define knowledge; but how can you be satisfied that any definition constitutes knowledge, if you don't already know what knowledge is? Like Nāgārjuna, Jayarāśi is directing his fire at a rather abstract, highly philosophical target. He is attacking epistemologists, not the person with pressing practical concerns, like whether she needs to clear her front room of giraffes. Jayarāśi is happy to admit, in fact, that normal people have an ordinary kind of "knowledge" that makes their lives possible. As he puts it: "even those who know the true state of affairs say 'The ways of the world should be followed . . . as far as worldly practice is concerned, the fool and the learned are similar.'"[14]

A few more centuries down the line, we come to our third skeptic, Śrīharṣa. He's responding to a new proposal about how knowledge is acquired, which came from the eleventh-century thinker Udayana. Udayana's suggestion was that knowledge could be reached through what philosophers nowadays call "counterfactual" reasoning. Suppose I am in doubt whether there is a giraffe in the next room. I might reason as follows: if there were a giraffe in there, I would smell it. Yet no fragrance of giraffe hangs in the air. I conclude that the room is giraffe-free. This sort of inference looks eminently reasonable; indeed, it looks to be a big part of what reasoning *is*. But, as you will by now be expecting, Śrīharṣa points out that counterfactual inferences themselves stand in need of justification.[15] In our example, I am only able to rule out the presence of the giraffe in the next room by invoking the rule, "if there were a giraffe there, I would smell it." But what makes me so certain about that? Again, the threat of a regress looms, as every inference I make seems to call for some further inference to ground it, a new inference that will be no more secure than the first.

It's a familiar fact that these sorts of paralyzing skeptical challenges are, in real life, not paralyzing at all. We just saw that Jayarāśi believed his skeptical arguments would leave ordinary, everyday knowledge standing. In the European tradition too, skeptics have cheerfully gotten on with their business, acting for all the world as if they have the sorts of beliefs their arguments seem to undermine. This was true of ancient skeptics like Sextus Empiricus,[16] and David Hume famously jettisoned his skeptical worries when he left his study. But ancient Indian thinkers of the *śramaṇa* traditions posed further skeptical challenges that had more practical implications. They questioned the efficacy of Vedic ritual, and the reality of the supernatural entities such rituals seemed to presuppose. This was no abstract musing on the possibility of knowledge in general, but a gauntlet thrown down against the elite of the Brahmanical tradition. Thinkers of the Mīmāṃsā and Nyāya schools rose to the challenge. The thinkers of Mīmāṃsā, especially, insisted that the Vedas are an indispensable source of vital truths that could be attained in no other way.[17]

17

MASTER OF CEREMONIES

JAIMINI'S *MĪMĀṂSĀ-SŪTRA*

In the Brahmanical culture which spawned the philosophical schools we'll be looking at in the coming chapters, nothing was more central than the practice of ritual. From the spectacular expenditure of a king in the year-long horse ritual to more everyday offerings of plants or milk into a fire, rituals were the way for householders to propitiate the gods. They were also the key to the high status of brahmin priests. So it was inevitable that the validity of ritual, and the authority of the Vedic texts on which ritual practices were based, would be a central point of dispute between the Brahmanical tradition and its critics. For the Buddhists, rituals were nothing special, just another set of actions undertaken in the pursuit of desires that we would be better off without. Adherents to the Veda, though, called the authoritative texts *śruti*, meaning "what is heard," and considered them a source of knowledge about the duties laid upon humanity.[1]

As we've just seen, texts of the Brahmanical tradition often allude to the challenges posed by Buddhists and other skeptics. In the *Nyāya-sūtra*, the enemy critique of ritual is summed up as follows: "the Vedas cannot command assent, because they suffer from the following epistemological defects: falsity, inconsistency, and repetition" (2.1.57). The first charge of falsity derives from the fact that the promises of Vedic ritual are not always fulfilled. A householder seeking wealth might, for instance, adapt a ritual involving boiled rice by instead putting one hundred gold coins in the boiling water. (You might think that someone with a hundred gold coins is already doing pretty well, but let's leave that aside.) In carrying out this ritual, the sacrificer follows a kind of rule: "if you want to be rich, then boil gold coins and then offer them in sacrifice." The charge is that this is false in the sense that someone may well undertake the ritual without gaining wealth. Or one may perform a different ritual aiming at the growth of one's family, yet remain childless.

Perhaps the defender of the Veda could take a leaf from the Buddhists and other *śramaṇa* movements, and direct attention away from such concrete goals. Don't worry about family and riches. Focus on spiritual matters, where the rituals can reliably deliver, or at least, where it is harder to tell whether the ritual delivers or not. We find such an injunction in the *Maitrāyaṇīya Upaniṣad*: "one who desires heaven should perform the fire (*agnihotra*) ritual" (§6.36). But Vātsyāyana, a commentator on the *Nyāya-sūtra*, had to admit that this shift of focus from material to spiritual goods might not be enough. A skeptic could still reply that if *any* of the ritual injunctions in the Vedas are "false," then that brings Vedic authority as a whole into disrepute. If you can't rely on these rituals to get kids and gold, why think they will get you into heaven?

The other two objections seem less damning: the Vedas are "inconsistent" and "repetitive." But they are a cause of equal worry to the Naiyāyikas. The Veda tells us both "after sunrise, perform the sacrifice," and also "the sacrifice performed after sunrise goes to the dogs." Then there are cases where the same thing is said again and again, something the critic compares to the rambling of a drunkard (*pramatta-vākya*). Implicitly, the critic is saying that there are rules of rational, trustworthy discourse, and that the Vedas violate these rules. An adequate account would fit with empirical reality, be consistent, and say what is needed and no more. It's telling that this line of attack appears most clearly in the logic- and rationality-obsessed Nyāya tradition, when they are considering objections against their own position. Actual Buddhist critique of ritual tended to focus more on the violence of rituals involving animals. In fact, the Nyāya may even have imagined the objection themselves: before getting up to perform the sacrifice after sunrise, these potential defects in the Veda were keeping them up at night. They leapt to defend the rationality of their sacred text. Admittedly, rituals sometimes fail, but that is always because of faulty execution by the sacrificer, not a defect in the rules governing the ritual. As for apparently inconsistent rules, these simply apply to different situations. The sacrifice after sunrise "goes to the dogs" only if you had previously resolved to perform it before sunrise. As for repetition, it is sometimes useful. Fathers seem to be convinced that once a fertility ritual works, then when the mother is giving birth later on it will make sense to remind her repeatedly that she should breathe and push (readers who have given birth will have to be the judge of how helpful this really is).

But even the staunchest defender of the Vedas would have to admit that they are problematic texts. In addition to the three difficulties raised and then defused in the *Nyāya-sūtra*, rituals are often described in insufficient detail. Some kind of rational method was needed to systematize the Vedic injunctions and to understand how we should proceed in the face of incomplete information. This was the ambition of the Mīmāṃsā school, whose mission was to expound and interpret the Veda in the hopes of establishing consistent ritual conduct. This is of philosophical interest, because their ideas can be generalized from the ritual context so as to offer a general theory of practical action.[2] They deal with gaps in the Veda by reasoning from one case to other, analogous cases. If a ritual is described with insufficient precision, this can be remedied through the procedures they called "transfer (*atideśa*), adaptation (*ūha*), and annulment (*bādha*) of details." To complete the instructions for one ritual, one might look to another, similar ritual, which serves us as a "model (*prakṛti*)." The details of the model are borrowed for the ritual we need to carry out. It's like when you are replacing the battery in your car for the first time. You know what to do because you've replaced batteries in other cars, and can adapt the procedure to the different design of this one.

The logicians called this golden rule of Vedic interpretation "rice-in-the-pan" reasoning, since it is like when you are cooking rice and taste just one grain to see if all the others are cooked. In that case, you unthinkingly transfer a property from one thing (the grain that you tasted) to others (the rest of the rice). It's particularly striking that Mīmāṃsā apply rice-in-the-pan reasoning to the context of duties, or what they would have called *dharma* in the context of ritual. As we know, *dharma* has broader, moral connotations too.[3] So we could extrapolate from Mīmāṃsā exegesis to an idea about ethical reasoning as a whole: we know the right thing to do in one situation because, despite its specificity and complexity, it is similar to other situations where we knew what to do. And the *Mīmāṃsā-sūtra* itself encourages us to extrapolate in this way: "*Dharma* depends upon the Veda, so whatever is not Veda is not to be trusted" (1.3.1).[4]

But how can this be, given that the Veda is at best an incomplete guide to our ritual and moral duties? Well, it may be incomplete, but it is the only guide we have. Most of our knowledge comes, directly or indirectly, from sense-experience. But our senses tell us nothing about morality and ritual. Here the Veda is our only source of knowledge. Jaimini highlights this in the aforementioned opening sentence of his *Mīmāṃsā-sūtra*, by framing the inquiry into Vedic exegesis as an inquiry into *dharma*. To this fundamental conviction of the Mīmāṃsā, we can add another, namely that the world has always been as we see it now. The Veda has always been here and has always governed ritual practices. We can therefore feel confident that the rituals as handed down to us have a basis in the Veda even if that basis is obscure to us. And by the way, these are not claims that apply only to a certain community or region. The Veda's authority in matters of *dharma* is not just unchallenged but also universal in scope. The *Mīmāṃsā-sūtra* at one point wonders whether ritual practices described as applying in one geographical region should be restricted to that region. No, comes the response: by its very nature *dharma* applies in all places and times (1.3.15–23).

This is typical of the structure of the *Mīmāṃsā-sūtra*, which becomes a model for many later texts. The *sūtra* often reads as a kind of dialogue between two characters.

One voice speaks for an apparent, or prima facie view; he is the *pūrva-pakṣin*. Having weighed up the pros and cons, this voice is then typically overruled by another one that delivers the decisive, considered position; he is the *siddhāntin*. The position of the *siddhāntin* thus coincides with that of the *Mīmāṃsā-sūtra* itself. It's tempting to say that the *siddhāntin* is effectively the voice of Jaimini, but as usual there are historical uncertainties about the authorship of the *sūtra*. The date of its composition is already problematic. It may have been written around the fourth to second century BC, and (again, as usual) we have to reckon with the possibility that it was composed in stages and not by only one author. It also explicitly refers to earlier and contemporary thinkers, including someone named Bādarāyaṇa (1.1.5), which is also the name of the author of the *Vedānta-sūtra*. So right at the outset of the two traditions, we see a suggestion that the Mīmāṃsā and Vedānta schools are intertwined.[5] In fact they are sometimes referred to as two branches of Mīmāṃsā. Jaimini's *sūtra* is the foundational text of "prior," or *pūrva mīmāṃsā*, whereas the Vedānta pioneered by Bādarāyaṇa can also be called "posterior," or *uttara mīmāṃsā*. The point of this is that Jaimini and his followers are focusing on the original Vedas and their ritual prescriptions. "Vedānta" meanwhile, as we mentioned in Chapter 15, means "at the end of the Veda," an allusion to the more obviously philosophical material in the Upaniṣads. In both cases, the school is staging an inquiry into the underlying principles of the relevant texts. Indeed, this is what the word *mīmāṃsā* means, an "inquiry" into doubtful or difficult aspects of the Vedic tradition.

The *Mīmāṃsā-sūtra* is the longest of the collections to emerge in the age of the *sūtra*, with a massive 2,745 *sūtras* compared to, for instance, only 555 in the *Vedānta-sūtra*.[6] And it's not only its size that makes the text so formidable. If you crack open the *Mīmāṃsā-sūtra* and start reading, you'll immediately feel that you need help. As with other *sūtra* collections, this is a difficult and obscure text, perhaps not even meant to be read without an accompanying commentary. Thank goodness then for Śabara, who lived several centuries after the composition of the *Mīmāṃsā-sūtra*. His commentary is considered authoritative by all Mīmāṃsakas, but around the seventh century AD the school split into two rival factions named after two further interpreters, Kumārila Bhaṭṭa and Prabhākara Miśra. As we go through these layers of text and commentary, things get increasingly sophisticated and philosophical, in part because of the need to respond to rival schools.[7] But there is plenty of philosophically interesting material already in Jaimini himself, which we can better understand with the help of Śabara.[8]

Unlike earlier works offering exegesis of the Veda, Jaimini operates at a rather abstract and general level. He is interested in the rules governing rituals, but expresses that interest above all by considering the rules governing those rules.

We've already seen this with his proposal to transfer rules from one ritual context to another. Indeed, when he mentions specific ritual practices it is usually only to provide an example to illustrate his overall theory. At the heart of that theory is an analysis of human action. Rituals are of course very special actions, but they are actions nonetheless, so to understand them we need to explore the mechanisms of action more generally.[9] Whenever you do something, you are at least implicitly following a kind of rule or injunction, which applies to you because of some desire you have. You might be in the mood for a nice bowl of risotto. Having conceived this desire, you apply the rule "if you want to have rice for dinner, cook the rice in boiling water."[10] In general, the causal situation (*bhāvanā*) involves an agent who has a desire, the object or advantage that is desired, the instrument by which it is achieved, and the procedure. In our example the agent would be you, the object would be the rice you want to eat, the instrument would be cooking, and the procedure would be the whole sequence of steps involved: gathering firewood, getting water from the well, and so on. In the cases Jaimini is interested in, like "one who desires riches should boil gold coins," we instead have the sacrificer and his desired goal of wealth, while the instrument is the ritual sacrifice and the procedure is the steps needed to carry out the sacrifice.

This may all seem quite straightforward. But if you think back to our discussions of Buddhism and the *Bhagavad-gītā* you'll see that Jaimini's account is far from philosophically uncontroversial. He's claiming that any action presupposes the presence of desire in the one who performs the action (6.3.8). Instead of giving up all desire or detaching yourself from the outcome of what you do, you should act by following the rules that apply to you in virtue of your desires. It may seem surprising that Jaimini makes participation in Vedic ritual so contingent on the sacrificer's goals. Don't we all have a standing obligation to perform the religious rites? As it turns out, the answer is no. There is no "pure duty" to perform the Vedic rites, for without desire the injunction (*codanā*) to perform a ritual simply does not apply. To a counterargument that some rituals in the Veda specify no intended outcome (*artha*) at all, Jaimini responds that in such instances heaven serves as the default object of desire, for heaven is happiness, and happiness is "desired by all" (4.3.15). Another interesting consequence is that women are invited to participate in the ritual, and not merely because their husbands need to use them as living instruments. Rather their involvement is justified on the basis that they too have desires (6.1.20).

This might give you the impression that ritual is being subordinated to human whims and projects. But just the reverse is the case. For Jaimini, what has ultimate and intrinsic value is the ritual itself. One might say that the ritual uses the human agent rather than the other way around. The sacrificer and his desire provide the occasion for the ritual. Without human goals no ritual would occur. But that doesn't mean that the ritual has no value beyond the fulfillment of those goals. Instead the ritual exists "for its own sake (*sva-artha*)." In a particularly dramatic illustration of this, it was laid down that if a sacrificer dies partway through a ritual, his bones could be placed within an antelope skin, and this posthumous puppet would then be made to carry out the remaining steps of the ceremony.[11] Francis Clooney has summed up Jaimini's view as follows: "By seeing himself as only one element in the web of relationships, [the sacrificer] transcends his self-centeredness, even as he admits it, and lets it lead him to the sacrifice... he learns to play his part without worrying about ridding himself of the desires which integrate him into the larger whole."[12]

The Mīmāṃsā viewpoint is diametrically opposed to Buddhism in its total commitment to the value of ritual and the authority of the Veda, and also in its endorsement of human desire. Yet it also captures something of the spirit of Buddhism, and may be responding to the Buddhist challenge by incorporating some of its ideas.[13] We have a subtle shift away from concrete goals like money and family, and toward "heaven (*svarga*)" as a universal aim. We do not have the elimination of desire, obviously, but we do see a humbling of the individual's desire as a mere contributing factor in the ritual. And most strikingly, we have an elimination of the supernatural. The *Mīmāṃsā-sūtra* does not tell us to sacrifice to please the gods, or to perform rituals out of an absolute religious obligation. Instead ritual is understood as being parallel to humdrum, everyday actions. If you want to get such-and-such a goal, then you need to follow the prescribed procedure. If the goal in question is risotto, then consult a cookbook (or note 10 of this chapter); if the goal has to do with *dharma*, then consult the Veda.

Indeed, though scholars sometimes describe the Veda as a "revealed" or "revelatory" text, Mīmāṃsā is adamant that it was not revealed by anyone in particular. The Veda has no author and the "seers" (*ṛṣis*) who expounded it were not like the prophets of the Old Testament. They simply transmitted the authoritative Veda, which existed before them and indeed has always existed. Again, we can see here how human agency is being sidelined to some extent, subordinated to the intrinsic value of the Veda just as human agency is subordinated to ritual. The forefathers who passed on wisdom and also reliable practices to us may have been admirable and trustworthy, but they did not invent or compose the venerable teaching. The most a human can do is to serve as a conduit from the past to the future. He is never a conduit between the divine and the rest of humanity, like the prophets of the Hebrew Bible or Muḥammad in Islam. This is because no such conduit is needed. The Veda has always been here, an eternal source of knowledge set down by neither God nor man.[14]

18

INNOCENT UNTIL PROVEN GUILTY

MĪMĀṂSĀ ON KNOWLEDGE AND LANGUAGE

In the Islamic religion, it is believed that God sends different revelations to different peoples: the Torah for the Jews, the Gospel for the Christians, and finally and definitively, the Quran for the Muslims. This idea was extended to the traditions of India. Buddhists and Hindus, too, were seen as "peoples of the book," and the Muslim prince Dārā Shikūh, who lived in India in the seventeenth century, even detected an allusion to the Upaniṣads in the Quran itself.[1] But the Mīmāṃsā school would have rejected this well-meaning analogy. Where the Torah, Gospels, and Quran are thought to be sent to humankind from God through divine revelation, Mīmāṃsakas held that their holy books, the Vedas, are without any author at all. The Veda did not come from the gods or from any prophet, and it was not sent. It is permanent (*nitya*), as is language itself.

This idea obviously forms part of the Mīmāṃsā attempt to establish unimpeachable authority for the Veda. But why depend on such a radical proposal, one rejected even by other Brahmanical schools, like the Nyāya? For starters, we can note that if the Veda is permanent and has no author, then it cannot contain any errors. After all, errors only arise when there is someone, like an author, who is in a position to make a mistake. If the Veda has no author, it must be entirely trustworthy. But there is more to the teaching than that. The Mīmāṃsakas ground their account of the Veda in an empiricist and naturalist account of human knowledge. Roughly speaking, their reasons for acknowledging the truth of the Veda are the same as your reasons for acknowledging that you are reading a book right now, and that the objects in your immediate environment are what they seem to be.

The roots of this epistemology lie in a passage of the *Mīmāṃsā-sūtra*, where Jaimini writes: "perception is the knowledge which one has by the senses coming in contact with something existent" (1.1.4). He's straightforwardly endorsing the idea that sense-perception can give us accurate information about things. To put it in the terms of later philosophical developments, sensation is a *pramāṇa*, a source of knowledge. But we know from our discussion of skepticism in ancient India that such claims were not going to go unchallenged, and it looks as though a skeptic would have a particularly easy time casting doubt on this particular *pramāṇa*. She need only point out that sensation is often misleading. That stuff cooking in the pan looks like rice but it's actually tapioca; that guy looks like Jim Rice, who used to play baseball for the Red Sox, but it's actually his twin brother. Of course the empiricist can insist that sensation is very rarely misleading, so we can depend on it generally speaking. But the Mīmāṃsakas do not seem to be ideally placed to make that response, because they are happy to use so-called "rice-in-the-pan" reasoning in other contexts, as when they explain why the detailed prescriptions of one ritual can be transferred to another. How then can they stop the skeptic from arguing from the misleading nature of one sense-experience to the doubtfulness of sensation as a whole?

The Mīmāṃsā answer is that sensations are innocent until proven guilty.[2] The idea comes into the commentary tradition quite early, already before Śabara's authoritative commentary on Jaimini: we should take every cognition to be true unless it is trumped by another cognition that overturns it.[3] The commentators, including Śabara, do readily admit that a variety of factors can undermine sensation in this way. You might taste the stuff in the pan and realize it is too sweet to be rice, or you might be drunk or deranged, which would undermine your sensations and beliefs more generally. Nowadays philosophers call such things "defeaters." We can say then that in the absence of anything that "defeats" a sense-perception, the perception should be taken as true. In a further development of this idea, Kumārila Bhaṭṭa states in his commentary on Śabara's *bhāṣya* that sensations possess what he calls "intrinsic validity (*svataḥ prāmāṇya*)."[4]

What does this mean? Later Mīmāṃsakas couldn't agree. A minority view understood Kumārila to be saying that a sensation is valid so long as it arose in a reliable way. So long as you are not in fact deranged, drunk, and so on, your cognitions are reliable. It is up to each of us to check whether our cognitions arose in a trustworthy fashion. If so, we may and indeed should put our trust in them. Others thought Kumārila's point was that valid sensations actually present themselves to us as true. If you see rice in a bowl in front of you in normal conditions, you have no hesitation in taking yourself to know there is rice in front of you. Only if there is some warning sign, like a strange taste to the rice or an awareness that you're drunk, would you even consider doubting the perception you are having. As Kumārila puts it, "that cognition which is unshaken and does not conflict with cognitions [occurring] at other times and places is a *pramāṇa*."[5] In normal conditions, we should not bother fretting about the possible falsehood of our cognitions, and for sure we should not give in to the worries raised by the skeptic that *all* cognitions may be unreliable.

But doesn't this just amount to an unjustified leap of faith? It is no good for Kumārila to insist dogmatically that we can trust our perceptions. This is precisely what the skeptic denies, and she has good reason for this, namely that perceptions are at least occasionally misleading. The Mīmāṃsakas can make another move here, though, by borrowing a weapon from the skeptic's own arsenal. If we demand some sort of confirmation or justification for every one of our cognitions, then a regress looms: each cognition will need another cognition that confirms it. If I double-check whether the stuff in the bowl is rice by tasting it, how do I know that I am tasting accurately? I might test this further sensation by asking you to taste the food too, but your agreement that the rice really is rice is also open to skeptical challenge. The moral that a skeptic draws from this, as we know, is that no *pramāṇa* is reliable. Mīmāṃsā draws the reverse conclusion: there must be some kinds of foundational cognitions, since otherwise we could never be confident of knowing anything at all; but of course we are confident in having knowledge.

Now let's go back to the idea that the Veda has no author.[6] Though this eventually became a distinctive claim of Mīmāṃsā, it does not appear explicitly in Jaimini himself. What he says is that words are always prior to their speakers (1.1.29–30), which can be taken to imply that the Veda (and language in general) are permanent. Again, the perfect and absolute authority of the Veda can only be challenged on the basis of some defeater. If it had been authored, then we could always fear that the author, even a divine author, may have made some mistake. We should trust in sensation unless we have reason to think that the sensation came about in some kind of defective manner. We should trust in the Veda in exactly the same way, except that in this case there can be no worry that it came about in a defective manner, because it did not "come about" at all!

It may seem that this purchases the authority of the Veda too cheaply. Its validity is claimed to be supreme simply because it has no competition, so it wins by default.[7] But put yourself in the position of Jaimini or Kumārila. Certainly the Vedic tradition was coming under fire from Buddhists, Jainas, and others, so it's not as if the Mīmāṃsakas were oblivious to the phenomenon of religious pluralism. Yet Kumārila was confident that the alternatives could easily be exposed as invalid. The critics of Vedic ritual, meanwhile, had provided no good reasons to doubt the efficacy of the ritual, or at least no reasons that the Mīmāṃsakas thought were any good. Finally, if there were good reasons to doubt, we would know about them. Kumārila is so confident in the sources of human knowledge that for him, the absence of a cognition supporting something is a good reason to reject that thing, as long as the conditions are favorable.[8] If you are in a position to know about the contents of a pan, yet have no evidence that there is rice in the pan, that in itself would be reason to believe there is no rice in the pan. Likewise there is no cognition, nor even the possibility of any cognition, that could overturn Vedic authority. With no defeaters in sight, Mīmāṃsā declares victory.

Their stance on these issues has various other implications. One takes them into conflict yet again with the Buddhists. Where Buddhism denies the existence of an enduring self, Mīmāṃsā insists upon it. We recognize automatically that there is an "I" who was experiencing the things we remember experiencing, and feel that this is who we still are. Just as I see that there is a dirty pan in the sink waiting to be washed, so I remember *myself* eating the rice that was prepared in that pan. Making short shrift of the nuanced critique offered by the Buddhists, Mīmāṃsā thinkers simply assume that we are right in taking ourselves to be enduring subjects of experience, since there is nothing to defeat that impression.[9] (And again, one might add that nothing *could* overturn the impression that one has a self.) But the most far-reaching and celebrated aspect of the Mīmāṃsā view on the permanent authority of the Veda is their inference that language itself must be permanent.

The Mīmāṃsakas offer a whole battery of arguments to support this surprising claim. For one thing, they say, children learn language by watching adults use language. We have no evidence that things have ever been otherwise. So, basing ourselves as always on our experiences of the world, we may assume that language has always been passed down from generation to generation. Furthermore, there is good reason to think that things *cannot* be otherwise. Take a word like "cow," or in Sanskrit *go*.[10] It refers to cows universally, not any particular cow, and when I say it on numerous different occasions I am using one and the same word over and over, not a new word each time. Or we might say, appealing to Mīmāṃsā epistemology, that it certainly *seems* I am using the same word over and over, and there is no reason to doubt this, so we can take it to be true.[11]

The Mīmāṃsā argument here may seem rather unconvincing, insofar as it assumes that the word "cow" has either *always* been with us, or is actually a new word every time it is uttered. There would seem to be another possibility, namely that each word is introduced at some point and thereafter comes to be used with a stable meaning, thanks to convention and agreement among the users of the relevant language. Against this Mīmāṃsā argues that even if one can learn the meaning of individual new words, there is no way to introduce language *as such*. It is impossible to learn to speak or understand speech without engaging in, and observing, linguistic activity. Children who are learning to talk have to discover the meaning of each word by seeing how their elders talk.[12] Once we are competent language users, we can learn new words by hearing them explained with other words. It's inconceivable that this process could ever have begun from a situation where there was no language at all.

A critic might point out that if I say to the person assisting me in a ritual, "Bring the cow" (a standard example in the Mīmāṃsā texts), then I am referring to some specific cow, not cows in general. How can this be, if the word "cow" is universal in its reference? The answer given by Mīmāṃsā is that a word on its own cannot refer to anything in particular. For this you need context, which at least includes the context provided by the rest of the sentence, and typically also other sentences and the circumstances in which they are spoken.[13] By putting the words "bring the" in front of the word "cow" as I'm erecting a post, I can get my assistant to understand that he should fetch the particular cow that is about to be tied to the post and sacrificed.

Even if this answer satisfies the critic, it will not satisfy the Mīmāṃsakas themselves. As the tradition developed, a dispute emerged concerning the relation between words and sentences.[14] This was one aspect of a split within Mīmāṃsā, with two rival factions following the lead of the commentators Kumārila and Prabhākara. Kumārila accepts that words have a general meaning when standing by themselves. The simple utterance "cow" does signify something. But that meaning is affected by putting the words into a complete sentence, connecting them so as to produce a new, composite meaning. This is why Kumārila's idea was called the "theory of the connection of what has been expressed (*abhihitānvaya-vāda*)." By contrast, Prabhākara teaches that words must appear within a sentence in order to have any meaning at all. This view is called the "theory of expression through what has been connected (*anvitābhidhāna-vāda*)."

And it may seem rather implausible. Surely, if I just say the word "cow," it does call some meaning to mind for you. But Prabhākara's view should not be dismissed so easily. Certainly many words do seem to lack fixed meaning apart from context. Consider a word like "at" and its different meanings in the phrases "the cow is *at* the sacrificial post," "we will sacrifice her *at* sunrise," "the cow looked *at* me with her big brown eyes," and "all *at* once, I decided I couldn't go through with it." What Prabhākara is saying also makes particular sense given the overall aim of Mīmāṃsā, which is an inquiry into ritual injunctions like the aforementioned "one who desires heaven should perform the fire ritual." Injunction (*codanā*) is the most important of the four kinds of statement found in the Veda, the other three being the formula (*mantra*) spoken during the ritual, the statement that indicates a name, and the commendation of a goal to be pursued in a ritual context.[15] Jaimini states that a ritual injunction is a meaningful unity composed out of the words it contains (*Mīmāṃsā-sūtra* 1.1.25). And of course not just any string of words will do. Here we see that Mīmāṃsā and Sanskrit grammar are closely intertwined, as Mīmāṃsā too embraces the idea we found in Pāṇini, that the action expressed by the verb is central to the meaning of a sentence. The distinctions drawn here can be quite subtle, as when it is pointed out that verbs may be put in the middle voice when the action in question is performed by the sacrificer rather than the attending priest. The middle voice indicates that one is performing an action *for oneself*, and not for somebody else.[16]

A more basic point about ritual injunctions takes us back once more to the core mission of Mīmāṃsā, which is to inquire into Vedic language. Whereas normal, everyday language typically describes the world we see around us, an injunction inevitably makes reference to the goal sought in the ritual. The fact that ritual injunctions are directed to such a goal shows that their validity is not grounded in sense-perception (*Mīmāṃsā-sūtra* 7.2).[17] When the Veda tells you how to sacrifice so as to have children, get rich, or for that matter get to heaven, it is looking to an unobservable reward: about what ought to be, not what already is. This is distinctive, even definitive, of the language that reveals *dharma*. Here, by the way, we have another reason why the Veda cannot be trumped or overturned. How could sensation come into conflict with the Veda, since sensation tells us nothing about the questions that are at stake in Vedic ritual, namely questions of *dharma*?

Despite this, Mīmāṃsā is adamant that the words used by the Veda are being employed in their normal sense. If the Veda tells us to tie a cow to a post, it is not using the words "cow" and "post" in some allegorical, extended, or unfamiliar sense. It's simply calling a cow a cow and a post a post. Still it is a unique source of knowledge, and one that could only have been delivered in the form of language. We need language to describe and articulate goals that are not yet present, and to explain how those goals are to be achieved. This is typical of Mīmāṃsā, a theory devoted to interpreting the sacred Veda, but offering an epistemology grounded in sense-experience and an analysis of language that can apply just as well to sentences uttered by cowherds (assuming, that is, that the cowherds in question speak Sanskrit). Mīmāṃsā makes no appeal to supernatural forms of knowledge, and in fact impatiently rejects such claims when they are made by other schools. The claim that the Buddha was omniscient is brusquely dismissed, as is the notion that Yoga can confer a special form of insight on its practitioners. Such supposed forms of cognition simply have no basis in our normal experience. And it is normal experience we should follow, along with testimony in the form of language—unless of course we have good reason not to.[18]

19

SOURCE CODE

BĀDARĀYAṆA'S *VEDĀNTA-SŪTRA*

Our look at the Mīmāṃsā school may not have persuaded you that Vedic ritual can really bring its promised fruits. But given the abundant intellectual harvest we've gathered in Jaimini and his successors, you're hopefully now convinced that a tradition devoted to the exegesis of sacred texts can at least be philosophically fruitful. Perhaps, though, you're the stubborn type. If so, we still have hope of getting you to see things our way, because we aren't yet done with Mīmāṃsā in the broader sense. As we mentioned, Jaimini, Śabara, Kumārila, and Prabhākara are representatives of what is called Pūrva ("prior") Mīmāṃsā. But it was Uttara ("posterior") Mīmāṃsā that gave rise to one of the most famous branches of Indian philosophy. It is also called Vedānta, and like Mīmāṃsā as a whole it eventually subdivided into different groups with their own approaches. The most famous approach is that of the eighth-century thinker Śaṅkara. That approach is called "non-dualist," or "Advaita" Vedānta, a name you may well have come across before reading this book.

We found that it was difficult to grasp the founding text of Pūrva Mīmāṃsā without the help of its commentator Śabara. So it is with Śaṅkara's understanding of Uttara Mīmāṃsā. The popularity of Śaṅkara's philosophy makes it tempting to equate Vedānta with his thought. But just as we tried to understand the *Mīmāṃsā-sūtra* in its own right rather than looking immediately at later commentary, so we now want to discuss the founding text of Vedānta. In its current form it was composed in the fifth century AD, several centuries before Śaṅkara.[1] Predictably it is known as the *Vedānta-sūtra* or *Uttara-mīmāṃsā-sūtra*. Its primary subject, as announced in the very first line, is *brahman*, so naturally enough it is sometimes called the *Brahma-sūtra* (as in Ch.16 above). Then, too, because it speaks of the nature of a self that possesses a bodily form (*śārīraka*), it has been called the *Śārīraka-sūtra*.

This confusing welter of titles for a single book could hardly be more appropriate. For the core mission of the *Vedānta-sūtra* is to investigate a single source of all things, which presents itself in many guises. That source is, of course, *brahman*. The *sūtra* also explores the relationship between our individual selves and this transcendent principle; it tells us how we can come to know *brahman*; and it promises us liberation from the snares and karmic consequences of bodily existence if we attain this knowledge. Described in this way the *Vedānta-sūtra* may sound like a systematic work of philosophical cosmology. But if so, the system is not easy to extract. Like the *sūtra* texts that stand at the origin of other philosophical traditions, the *Vedānta-sūtra* is compressed and difficult to understand. If Śaṅkara's authority looms over the text, this is in part because we need his help and that of other commentators to decode it.

Though the *sūtra* form is to some extent to blame for the difficulty of the work, another reason is that the *Vedānta-sūtra* is a philosophical treatise that doubles as a work of exegesis devoted to the Upaniṣads. (Remember "Vedānta" probably refers to these works, which were "at the end of the Veda."[2]) Actually, we should be more specific here. Texts honored with the name of the Upaniṣads continued to be produced concurrently with, and long after, the composition of the *Vedānta-sūtra*. We might even say that later Upaniṣads are themselves an expression of the Vedānta tradition. The *Vedānta-sūtra* is devoted to the interpretation of a more select group of early Upaniṣads, especially the *Chāndogya Upaniṣad* but also the *Great Forest Upaniṣad* and others. Thus it refers to several of the Upaniṣadic passages we discussed earlier, like the scenes of dialogue featuring Yājñavalkya. Key passages like these came to be known as "great sayings (*mahāvākya*)," and to receive especially focused treatment from later Vedāntins.[3]

The reason this makes the *sūtra* difficult to read is that it rarely identifies the passages it is interpreting. We need to know the Upaniṣads so well that even a single keyword will be enough to tell us which text is at stake, or failing that we need the help of the commentators. To give just one example of this very frequent feature of the text, there is a *sūtra* that says simply, "because of abiding and eating" (§1.3.7: *sthity-adanābhyāṃ ca*). The context shows that this is supposed to help convince us that *brahman* holds up all things. But the remark remains incomprehensible until you realize that the *sūtra* is alluding to a passage about two birds, one of which is eating while the other just sits quietly (*Māṇḍūkya Upaniṣad* §1.1.3). The idea then is that the bird who is eating symbolizes the individual soul engaged in worldly action, while *brahman* simply abides unchanging.

This is a good example of the interpretive project that dominates the *Vedānta-sūtra*. It reads the sacred texts as putting forward a single, coherent doctrine centering on the concept of *brahman* (§1.1.4). The same goes for later Vedāntins, except that for them the *sūtra* itself, and for good measure the *Bhagavad-gītā*, joined the Upaniṣads as fundamental sources of wisdom and insight into the nature of *brahman* (thus Śaṅkara commented on the *Gītā* as well as the *Vedānta-sūtra* and several early

Upaniṣads). This *brahman*-centric approach was rejected by other Brahmanical schools. When the *Vedānta-sūtra* confronts and refutes the teachings of those schools, it typically concentrates on showing that the Vedānta way of looking at things is better grounded in sacred texts. This is not faith triumphing over reason, but a sign of the dialectical context: the opponents being targeted are themselves committed to the truth of the Upaniṣads. Exegesis is thus the ground on which the *sūtra* chooses to wage its philosophical battles.[4]

Although the *Vedānta-sūtra* shares the interpretive aims of the *Mīmāṃsā-sūtra*, it is not just a second installment of that *sūtra* that moves on to looking at the Upaniṣads.[5] This can best be illustrated by talking about the men who are credited with writing the two *sūtras*. The *Mīmāṃsā-sūtra* was supposedly written, or at least compiled, by Jaimini. Yet he is mentioned there in the third person. The same happens in the *Vedānta-sūtra*, which names and reports the ideas of its own putative author, Bādarāyaṇa.[6] At several points Bādarāyaṇa's ideas are contrasted to those of Jaimini. In the *Mīmāṃsā-sūtra* it's Jaimini who usually gets the last, decisive word in any given debate. Here, in the *Vedānta-sūtra*, it is instead Bādarāyaṇa whose view is allowed to triumph over those of Jaimini and other interpreters. This is presumably why the later tradition credits Bādarāyaṇa with having authored the text. But it might be safer to use the technical terms of *sūtra* literature and say that Jaimini's opinion is treated as an "initial" or prima facie view (*pūrva-pakṣa*), only to be corrected by the more adequate view (*siddhānta*) of Bādarāyaṇa.

The authoritative position, if not authorship, of Bādarāyaṇa has important consequences for the *Vedānta-sūtra*. Where Jaimini placed all his focus on Vedic ritual, Bādarāyaṇa is more interested in the prospect of liberation through the knowledge of *brahman* (§§1.1.7, 1.3.2, and 3.4.19 for the contrast with Jaimini). At one point, we are told that a person with such knowledge can dispense with such things as lighting ritual fires (§3.4.25). In keeping with this, Bādarāyaṇa is less wedded than Jaimini to the life of the householder and tends to emphasize the superiority of the ascetic life led by renouncers. The knowledge of *brahman* imparted in the Upaniṣads is valued for its own sake, and not, as Jaimini would have it, as a supplement that helps us grasp the purpose of ritual (§3.4.8). While this is the most significant disagreement between the two, there are several others. Bādarāyaṇa thinks that even the gods can achieve liberation by knowing *brahman* whereas Jaimini restricts this to humans (§1.3.31 and 33) and even denies the existence of gods. One of the core doctrines of Mīmāṃsā is that the Veda had no origin, and though this idea can be found in the *Vedānta-sūtra* (§1.3.28–9), so also can the idea that the Veda has its source in *brahman*.

It's typical of the age of the *sūtra* that the Vedānta theory is developed through this sort of argumentation. Bādarāyaṇa—or whoever was ultimately responsible for the

Vedānta-sūtra as we now read it—constantly raises objections against himself and goes on to refute those objections. Some of the most important objections have to do with the nature of *brahman* as a cause. How can we believe that all things were produced by *brahman*, given that *brahman* is transcendent above those things? It seems impossible that a cause could give rise to things that are utterly unlike it. To this Bādarāyaṇa replies simply that such things are known to happen (§2.1.4–5). He doesn't condescend to provide an example, but the commentators suggest what he may have in mind. Śaṅkara's remark on this passage mentions cases where the living can emerge from the dead, as when a scorpion is spontaneously generated from a pile of manure, and conversely, where something inanimate comes from what is living, as when we grow hair and fingernails.

But why, the objector persists, would *brahman* even bother to produce the world? For no real reason, suggests Bādarāyaṇa. It's out of mere "sport" or "play" (*līlā*) that *brahman* does so (§2.1.32–3). But wouldn't *brahman* have had good reason *not* to cause the world as we see it? After all, it is full of suffering and unjust inequality. True, concedes Bādarāyaṇa, but this is not the fault of *brahman*. All suffering is a punishment for wicked deeds, which may have been committed in past lives (§2.1.34–6). Since the cycle of rebirth (*saṃsāra*) has been going on endlessly, any particular case of suffering can always be referred back to earlier actions that justify this suffering. This, notice, is a point of agreement between Mīmāṃsā and Vedānta. Both accept that the world has always existed much as it does now, even if Bādarāyaṇa insists that our eternal world has a source in *brahman*, whereas this notion is foreign to Jaimini.

The world caused by *brahman* may be permanent, but it does have a kind of conceptual sequence. Not coincidentally, this sequence is going to remind you of things we saw in the Upaniṣads. You might remember that when Yājñavalkya was challenged by Gārgī to provide the fundamental principle upon which "all things are woven," he eventually satisfied her by saying that this principle might be "space" (see Chapter 4). Naturally, Bādarāyaṇa accepts this idea and infers that space is the very first effect of *brahman* (§2.3.1–7), or at another point, that space is even identical to *brahman* (§1.1.22). From space emerge other principles, which will probably remind you of something else: the elements of ancient Greek cosmology. Here, we get the sequence air, fire, water, and earth, produced one after another with *brahman* as their ultimate source. They will eventually return to *brahman*, dissolving into it in the reverse order of their generation, when the world-cycle finally ends (§2.3.8–15).

From this passage, we can see that the universe is like an effective stand-up comedian: it has great material. The best material possible in fact, namely *brahman* itself, which is both the moving cause that gives rise to all things, and in some way the "stuff" out of which things are made. As long as we're referring to Greek philosophy, we could take a leaf from Aristotle and say that *brahman* is both the efficient and material cause of the world. Both ideas, Bādarāyaṇa would say, are captured in the dictum that *brahman* is "the support of heaven, earth, and all other things" (§1.3.1). Though it takes on the forms of other things, *brahman* is in itself formless (§3.2.11, 14, 24). It is characterized in various ways throughout the Upaniṣads, something freely admitted in the *Vedānta-sūtra*. But many of these characterizations are metaphors, a favorite one being that *brahman* is like the sun or light whose rays fall on and illuminate many things (§3.2.15, 18 and 28; see also §1.1.22 and 29, §1.3.22 and 40). The sacred text may occasionally be misleading in its attempt to describe *brahman* in a way we can appreciate, as when it suggests that *brahman* has size (§3.2.33). In fact this is not so, because nothing other than it exists, so it is everywhere, pervading all things rather than occupying any particular dimensions (§3.2.36–7).

This brings us to a fine example of something we mentioned when we first started describing the age of the *sūtra*, namely that the different so-called "Hindu schools" in fact entered into heated disputes with one another. Bādarāyaṇa's insistence that *brahman* is the "material cause" of all things brings him into direct conflict with the Sāṃkhya school, which is mentioned explicitly and made the target of a sustained critique (§§1.4, 2.2). We'll be looking at Sāṃkhya soon (Chapter 22). For now, all we need to tell you is that this school sees the world as evolving naturally from an underlying material stuff called *pradhāna or prakṛti*. Though Sāṃkhya, too, positions itself within the Brahmanical tradition, on this score it would seem to be diametrically opposed to Vedānta. Far from recognizing an intelligent, divine, creator mind that manifests itself as all things, Sāṃkhya has all things being generated from *pradhāna*, an unintelligent stuff.

Against that notion, Bādarāyaṇa invokes that most familiar proof that a guiding intelligence produced the universe: its striking, apparently providential order. He appeals not so much to a stock example, as a livestock example. Trying to get the world we see out of *pradhāna* without the intervention of *brahman* would be like trying to get milk out of grass without the involvement of a living cause, namely a cow (§2.2.5). As usual, this philosophical dispute is bound up with an exegetical dispute. Bādarāyaṇa wants us to see not just that the Sāṃkhya theory makes no sense, but that it cannot make sense of key Upaniṣadic texts. This emerges especially clearly in the tradition of commentary on the *Vedānta-sūtra*, with Śaṅkara delving into extensive exegesis of background passages to show that the Sāṃkhya school isn't understanding those passages properly (as in his commentary on §1.4.1, discussing *Kaṭha Upaniṣad* 1.3.10 and 11). Of course the *Vedānta-sūtra* sets its face against more radical forms of materialism and naturalism too. Not only do the Vedas clearly reject such attitudes, but if we were to rely on sensation and material causes, it's clear that we could never attain the goal of liberation that is so dear to Bādarāyaṇa (§1.1.5–11). Materialist explanations fail for the world as a whole, and also for the human individual, because the self is in fact independent of the body (§3.3.53–4).

Here we come to what may be the single most famous teaching of the *Vedānta-sūtra*, famous in part because it plays such a central role in Śaṅkara's version of Vedānta. This is the idea that *brahman* has a very intimate relationship to the individual self. What sort of relationship, exactly? Well, that's not an easy question to answer. Śaṅkara's school of Advaita Vedānta insists that nothing is real apart from *brahman*. This of course includes every individual self. So the apparent fact that each of us is distinct from other things, and from the ground of all existence, is actually an illusion. Śaṅkara can draw on compelling evidence in the *Vedānta-sūtra* to support this interpretation. We find Bādarāyaṇa suggesting that there is ultimately no difference between *brahman* as cause and the things that it creates (2.1.14). When it comes to the self, meanwhile, he tells us that *brahman* is identical with our vital breath (2.4.8–9), and instructs us to grasp *brahman* by meditating on it as being our own self (4.1.3). Other passages, though, seem to draw a firm distinction between the individual self and the highest self that is *brahman* (e.g. 1.2.21–2).

We can glimpse here signs of a debate that was in fact already raging before the time of the writing of the *Vedānta-sūtra*. We know (in part thanks to the *sūtra* itself) that earlier scholars prepared the way for Bādarāyaṇa by commenting on the Upaniṣads and that they had different ideas about the self and its relation to *brahman*. It was suggested that *brahman* is simply the material constituent for the individual self, or that the individual self is distinct from *brahman* yet becomes identical to *brahman* once it is liberated from the body.[7] Perhaps the best we can conclude, on the basis of the *Vedānta-sūtra* itself, is that the relation between *brahman* and individual self is held in tension between identity and difference. Certain passages want to have it both ways, as when we are told that *brahman* relates to individual selves like a snake to its coils (3.2.27). But as we turn to Śaṅkara we find a more radical (or perhaps, more explicitly radical) version of Vedānta, which resolves the tension in favor of outright monism.

20

NO TWO WAYS ABOUT IT

ŚAṄKARA AND ADVAITA VEDĀNTA

Some philosophers want to leave the world pretty much as they find it. They seek a deeper understanding of reality as it seems to be, putting their trust in everyday experience. Other philosophers want to overturn common sense. They believe that reality is actually very different from the way it may seem. These two approaches are often ascribed to the ancient Greek thinkers Aristotle and Plato, but the contrast could be applied with at least as much accuracy to the ancient Indian thinkers Śabara and Śaṅkara, who were pivotal commentators of Pūrva Mīmāṃsā and Vedānta. On the face of it the two commentators belong to a single tradition, devoted to the interpretation of the earlier and later parts of the Veda. But Śabara and the Mīmāṃsakas who followed him were implacable defenders of common sense. For them, the world is as we see it and has always been so. Śaṅkara couldn't agree less. For him the world is an illusion, which masks the single underlying reality of *brahman*. To accept the reality of the everyday world is ignorance (*avidyā*), while to know the sole reality of *brahman*, and the identity of the self (*ātman*) with *brahman*, is to achieve liberation.

As Śaṅkara never tires of insisting, this astonishing doctrine is stated quite clearly in numerous Upaniṣadic passages. He points to such texts as: "*brahman* is without a before and an after, without an inner and an outer. *Brahman* is this self here which perceives everything"; "the finest essence here, that constitutes the self of this whole world; that is the truth, that is the self"; and "it is *brahman* alone that extends over this whole universe, up to its widest extent."[1] Of course, other thinkers committed to the authority of the Vedas were well aware of these passages too, but it was Śaṅkara who put them at the heart of his understanding of Vedānta. Before him and after him, other Vedāntins accepted that *brahman* is the true, single source of all things, while maintaining that the world we see around us is real. For them, everyday reality emerges as a modification of *brahman*, which has taken on the forms of the things we see around us. But Śaṅkara denied that there could be two levels of reality, one more apparent and one more fundamental. *Brahman* is not two. It is single and supreme, unchanging and ineffable. Hence the name of the tradition founded by Śaṅkara: Advaita ("non-dual") Vedānta.

His philosophical theory may be unprecedented and radical, but there's at least one thing about Śaṅkara that could hardly be more familiar: we don't know exactly when he lived. The traditional date of his birth is AD 788, which is probably a bit too late, but it's safe to assume he was active in the eighth century.[2] This could make him a younger contemporary of Kumārila, the great exponent of Pūrva Mīmāṃsā. Śaṅkara's activity as an exegete was unprecedented in its scope and set a new standard for later commentators. He commented on several Upaniṣads and on the *Bhagavad-gītā* which, according to him, "encapsulates the essence of the meaning of the whole Veda."[3] The most celebrated work of Śaṅkara, though, is without doubt his lengthy commentary (*bhāṣya*) on the *Vedānta-sūtra* ascribed to Bādarāyaṇa. You may feel it a bit unfair that we should have to wade through so much material only to find out that all of it, along with everything else apart from *brahman*, is unreal. If so, then a shortcut is offered by a far briefer introductory work called the *Upadeśa-sāhasrī*, which encapsulates his teaching.[4]

On the other hand, Śaṅkara is well worth perusing at any length because he makes for great philosophical reading. Unlike the compressed and elliptical *Vedānta-sūtra*, his commentary mounts elaborate arguments, often in the course of refuting other schools of thought. Śaṅkara also has a good line in analogies. He explains his fundamental idea that the apparent reality of everyday life is an illusion (*māyā*) by comparing it to the foam on the surface of the sea, to the way that a sea shell may seem to be made of silver, and to the snake that upon further inspection turns out to be a coil of rope (*Upad.* 19, 51, 109). To those who wonder how a single *brahman* can make itself manifest itself as an illusory world, he responds that the single moon can appear as two moons to someone suffering from double vision (*Bhāṣya* §2.1.27). The individual soul that finally gives up its ignorance and accepts the true reality of *brahman* is like a weary carpenter who lays down his tools, or a tired falcon that finally alights to rest (*Bhāṣya* §2.3.40).

Four major centers of Hindu worship also honor Śaṅkara as their founder, which may remind us of Buddhist monastic practices. The most famous of them is at Śṛṅgeri, where a beautiful temple was later built and still stands today. All of this has earned Śaṅkara a leading place in the history of Indian religion and philosophy. Still, we should bear in mind that Advaita has been only one of many sub-schools within the larger tradition of Vedānta. Centuries later, there would emerge a rival approach pointedly called Dvaita ("dual" as opposed to "non-dual") Vedānta,[5] a realist alternative to Śaṅkara's Advaita in the shape of Rāmānuja's Viṣiśṭādvaita "qualified non-dualism," and a variety of other interpretations of Vedānta. Already within a generation or two of his own life, Śaṅkara was being heavily criticized by other Vedāntins, including another major commentator on the *Vedānta-sūtra* named Bhāskara.[6] He was appalled by Śaṅkara's tendency to abandon the ritualistic aspects of the Vedic tradition, which seemed to Bhāskara to be the inevitable consequence of deeming the world of actions and fruits to be a mere illusion. Modern-day scholars have discovered that, despite Bhāskara's disdain for Śaṅkara and his Advaita approach, their two commentaries share a lot of common material, which suggests that both were drawing on a rich earlier tradition of Vedānta.[7] Unfortunately that tradition is otherwise largely lost, but we do know something about a precursor of Śaṅkara named Gauḍapāda.[8] Though we've been describing Śaṅkara as a pivotal figure in the development of Vedānta, in fact many of his key ideas (and some of those nice analogies) are already found in Gauḍapāda. Śaṅkara speaks of him with admiration, calling him by a title (*paramaguru*) that could mean he was the teacher of Śaṅkara's teacher.[9]

But we don't need to get into the question of how much of the credit for Advaita should go to Gauḍapāda, and how much to Śaṅkara. For us the questions are rather what this doctrine amounts to and whether there is any reason to believe it. On the latter question Śaṅkara is very clear. Just as Pūrva Mīmāṃsā taught that matters of *dharma* are taught only by the Veda, so Śaṅkara says that we could never come to know the truth of *brahman* if left to our own devices. Advaita is grounded in interpretation of the sacred texts (*śruti*), not in philosophical arguments. Since many of Śaṅkara's rivals, like the Sāṃkhya school, also accept the authority of Vedic literature, he frequently tries to refute them simply by quoting scriptures that fit better with his own view than with theirs. He even complains that Sāṃkhya makes inferences from experiences of the world around us, when it should be appealing to *śruti* (*Bhāṣya* §1.1.4). For him their empirical approach is wrongheaded. We cannot learn about *brahman* from observation of the world, because the world is precisely an illusion that masks *brahman*. In itself *brahman* is formless, so even with the resources of *śruti* it eludes both thought and speech (*Bhāṣya* §2.1.4). The closest we can come to an experience of *brahman* would be an experience that is empty, utterly devoid of form. This is what happens in moments of deep sleep, when we aren't even dreaming (*Bhāṣya* §§1.3.8–9 and 42, 1.4.18, 2.1.6 and 9, 3.2.7, 3.3.17).

While this may sound rather mystical and anti-rationalist, in another sense Śaṅkara is a philosopher's philosopher. Most ancient Indian thinkers, both within and outside the Brahmanical tradition, believed that even the deepest understanding needed to be combined with long practice. For Śaṅkara such things as meditation and ritual may be useful as steps along the path to liberation. But ultimately liberation is secured through knowledge (*Bhāṣya* §1.1.3; *Upad.* 2). If you really come to understand that your individual self is identical to *brahman*, you will immediately be freed from all suffering, and for that matter from all pleasure. This is because *brahman* is unchanging and remains unaffected by the processes and experiences that the individual self undergoes as a result of its ignorance (*Bhāṣya* §1.2.8). We reach liberation by being slowly weaned away from this individual self, giving up on such identifying features as caste, family affiliations, and even the desire to engage in ritual (*Upad.* 19–20, 30–2), since *brahman* can of course never acquire the fruits of such rituals (*Bhāṣya* §4.1.13).[10]

Though it's evident why a Vedic traditionalist such as Bhāskara was so annoyed by Śaṅkara, we may have a rather different worry. Doesn't Advaita amount to a kind of nihilism? After all, *brahman* is formless and ineffable. So when Śaṅkara says that *brahman* alone is real, he may seem to be saying that the only reality is nothing at all. But this isn't quite right. Though *brahman* is not to be confused with the individual self (the *jīva*), *brahman* is still recognizably a kind of self. It is, for lack of better terms, consciousness or awareness.[11] However, it is a special, pure kind of consciousness that is not aware of anything in particular. Consider again Śaṅkara's example of deep sleep. According to him, when we are asleep like this there is not just pure emptiness. Rather it is like an act of seeing without any visible object. Consciousness is evident to itself even when there is nothing of which it is conscious, the way the sun is in itself luminous before it illuminates other things (*Upad.* 93).[12]

This may seem a rather fine distinction. Does it make so much difference whether there is nothing at all or nothing but a conscious self that is conscious of nothing in particular? To Śaṅkara, it makes all the difference. This emerges from a remarkable critique of Buddhist thought found in his commentary on the *Vedānta-sūtra*.[13] The critique is remarkable, in part because Śaṅkara seems to be deeply influenced by Buddhism, or more precisely, to have absorbed Buddhist ideas indirectly from his predecessor Gauḍapāda. The Advaita rejection of everyday reality looks very Buddhist, as do its faith that liberation will ensue upon a proper understanding of the self and its admission that Vedic ritual becomes irrelevant for the liberated person. With his dismissal of caste and family as aspects of the illusory self, Śaṅkara also seems to think that all people can potentially be liberated, just as the Buddhists did. This is problematic when it comes to the lowest class, the *śūdras*, since the *Vedānta-sūtra* seems to exclude them from the path to liberation (1.3.34–8). Śaṅkara admits that they cannot study the Vedas, but holds out the prospect of other forms of learning (*Bhāṣya* §1.3.38). As an aside, it's worth mentioning that in one of the many legends that surround the life of Śaṅkara, it is told how he once shied away from touching a man of no caste (a *cāṇḍāla*) because such people are impure. The man castigated him, reminding him that Śaṅkara's own Advaita teaching implies that such distinctions are irrelevant to the true self.[14]

In any case, these possible borrowings from the Buddhists didn't stop him from attacking them on philosophical grounds. He complains that the Buddha taught several inconsistent theories, all of them false, perhaps because he was such a spiteful character that he deliberately wanted to confuse people (*Bhāṣya* §2.2.32). This breathtakingly rude remark suggests that Śaṅkara felt no sympathy for the Buddhist tradition, and that he didn't realize (or didn't care) that the supposedly inconsistent teachings he was attacking were in fact put forward by different, rival strands within Buddhism. But if his critique lacks historical nuance, it does manage to be philosophically astute. In a particularly interesting part of his commentary, Śaṅkara aims his fire at the Buddhist view that there is no enduring self. Instead, according to the Buddhists, there are the only momentary features and acts of consciousness called *skandhas*. These cause one another across time and aggregate to create the illusion of a coherent, enduring individual (see Chapter 8).

Śaṅkara offers several arguments to refute this theory. For one thing it is hard to see how a *skandha* that exists only fleetingly at one moment can cause another *skandha* to exist at the next moment. For at the time it should be causing the new *skandha* to arise, it is already gone (*Bhāṣya* §2.2.20). Here Śaṅkara is invoking a plausible assumption of his own, namely that effects cannot depend on non-existent causes (*Bhāṣya* §2.1.15). Furthermore, the phenomenon of memory shows that the same individual does survive over time (*Bhāṣya* §2.2.20).[15] For part of what I remember when I look back at a past experience is that it was *me* who had that experience. When I fondly remember eating an almond croissant this morning, I am in no doubt that the person who enjoyed the taste of that croissant is the same person I am now. This argument about memory doesn't seem sufficient by itself, since the Buddhist has an alternative explanation to offer: it only seems that the former aggregate of *skandhas* is identical with the present aggregate because of the causal links between the two. But Śaṅkara has already blocked this response, when he insisted that the momentary nature of the aggregates prevents them from forming such causal chains.

A more surprising diatribe against the Buddhists comes next. Śaṅkara takes up a teaching of the Mahāyāna school of Buddhism, which we'll be discussing later (Chapters 36–8). This teaching, called *vijñānavāda*, rejects everyday reality as an illusion. Śaṅkara dismisses this scornfully: it is futile to deny that external things do cause our experiences, since this is patently obvious (*Bhāṣya* §2.2.28). Experience clearly involves both a subject and object, yet the various Buddhists being attacked here have managed to deny both, doubting both the existence of an enduring self and of real things for us to perceive. But hang on a minute: how can Śaṅkara, of all people, be insisting on the reality of the world around us? Doesn't he, just like his Mahāyāna Buddhist opponent, take that world to be mere illusion? This is precisely the response made by Śaṅkara's own opponent and critic, the rival Vedānta commentator Bhāskara. He accuses Śaṅkara of rank hypocrisy, insisting on realism when responding to the Buddhists only to fall into anti-realism when setting out his own Advaita teaching.[16]

The suspicion of inconsistency deepens when we look at other sections of his commentary on the *Vedānta-sūtra*. For every passage emphasizing the illusory nature of all things other than *brahman*, we can find another passage suggesting that *brahman* does really produce the world we see around us by taking on form. We find Śaṅkara emphasizing that *brahman* can make the elements of things without using any instrument or pre-existing material, like the spider produces its web from nothing but itself (*Bhāṣya* §2.1.25). Or, he insists that *brahman* is the stuff out of which things are made, as well as being the agent that makes those things (*Bhāṣya* §1.4.24). Or, he distinguishes between a higher and lower *brahman*, the first devoid of form, the second a version of *brahman* in which it takes on forms that make it available to our experience, or allow it to play the role of the individual, embodied self (*Bhāṣya* §4.3.14). What is the point of all these assertions if the supposed things made by *brahman*, and also the individual self, are nothing but illusions?

A more sympathetic reader than Bhāskara might take refuge in historical explanations. Perhaps Śaṅkara includes contradictory materials in his own commentary simply because he is reproducing ideas from previous commentators, many of whom were more realist than Gauḍapāda and than Śaṅkara himself. On this reading his *Bhāṣya* would be like a microcosm of the Vedānta tradition as a whole. One historian has written that "since the Vedānta school itself split up . . . and adopted ideas from the other schools, the history of Vedānta philosophy is really something like a miniature copy or reflection of the entire history of Indian philosophy."[17] But is Śaṅkara really so thoughtless as to compile disparate materials like this, without even attempting to be consistent? That would be pretty disappointing, especially since it's in this same section that he insults the Buddha for putting forth inconsistent teachings! So let's consider other possibilities.

Some scholars believe that Śaṅkara's own ideas developed throughout his career, moving away from the radical teaching of Gauḍapāda and toward a more realist understanding of things.[18] But a really satisfying solution needs to extract a philosophically defensible position from the commentary. And this is by no means impossible. Remember that for Śaṅkara, we cannot just reason our way to the unique reality of *brahman*. This is a truth found only in *śruti*, sacred literature that is rejected by the Buddhists. So it's entirely consistent for him to say that the Buddhist has no basis for rejecting the deliverances of everyday experience. Furthermore, even once the authority of *śruti* is accepted, Śaṅkara does not believe that we should just immediately abandon everyday experience. This isn't the first move in his philosophy, it's the last move. Before we get that far, it is a useful step on the path of liberation to think of *brahman* as a fundamental underlying cause of real things. We should then realize that effects are somehow implicitly present in their causes. The effect is not wholly non-existent before it manifests itself, like "the son of a barren woman," Śaṅkara's nicely chosen example of a thing that cannot exist at all (*Bhāṣya* §2.1.18). If effects were not somehow prepared or contained in their causes, anything could be produced from anything, like clay pots made out of milk.

While this account of causation already improves on the Buddhist account, we need to make the further realization that effects are really nothing other than their causes. Pots are really just clay organized in a certain way (*Bhāṣya* §2.1.14). It is on this basis that we can understand the forms imposed on the underlying cause as in fact unreal. Śaṅkara speaks here of "superimposition." The guise under which *brahman* presents itself is a kind of mask, and it is sheer ignorance to mistake the mask for what lies beneath. Or to put it in more philosophical language, it is ignorance to confuse a real thing with a property that is falsely ascribed to that thing. Again this can be illustrated with the false appearance of a sea shell, which looks like it is made of silver (*Upad.* 51). Only after following this fairly arduous and challenging philosophical chain of thought will we be ready for the radical conclusions of Advaita Vedānta. And without the prompting of *śruti*, we would have no reason or warrant to follow the argument to its conclusion. For all his philosophical sophistication, Śaṅkara looks ultimately to the Upaniṣads, the sole source for our knowledge of the unchanging consciousness that is *brahman*.

21

COMMUNICATION BREAKDOWN

BHARTṚHARI ON LANGUAGE

Have you ever noticed how intellectuals tend to think that their own chosen discipline happens to be the most important of all? Historians are quick to remind us that those who forget the past are doomed to repeat it, mathematicians that their proofs attain to the highest degree of certainty. And of course philosophers boast of pursuing the "queen of sciences," with the other disciplines being mere subjects. So it's par for the course when Bhartṛhari, one of the greatest figures in classical Sanskrit grammar, tells us that the study of language constitutes the "door to liberation" (§1.4; cf. §§1.11 and 1.132).[1] Bhartṛhari is, however, modest enough to give others the credit for opening up that door. He looks back to the work of the great Pāṇini (see Chapter 7), but is responding directly to the later Patañjali, whose *Great Commentary* (*Mahābhāṣya*) on Pāṇini is the inspiration for Bhartṛhari's own treatises.[2]

Bhartṛhari is thus heir to a long tradition. Pāṇini worked in the sixth or fifth centuries BC, Patañjali in the second century BC, with both drawing on further, more shadowy authors. Bhartṛhari then comes along in the fifth century AD, a full millennium after Pāṇini. He was apparently the first to write a super-commentary (called *Ṭīkā* or *Dīpikā*) on the commentary of Patañjali. But his fame rests especially on another work, the *Treatise on Words and Sentences* (*Vākyapadīya*). Bhartṛhari lays down his thoughts in compressed verses, often presupposing knowledge of the texts to which he is alluding. Of course Indian intellectuals didn't hesitate to provide such exegetical works with their own further commentaries, and the *Vākyapadīya* is no exception. An accompanying explanatory work, called a *Vṛtti*, may even have been written by Bhartṛhari himself.[3] Whether or not this is so, the *Vṛtti* is a helpful guide to the argument of the much more compressed *Vākyapadīya*.

Even more than Pāṇini or Patañjali, Bhartṛhari really shows us the philosophical importance of the Sanskrit grammatical tradition. Indeed, his boast that grammar is the "door to liberation" suggests that for him, the study of language just *is* philosophy. Where other Indian thinkers saw meditation or ethical discipline as the route to liberation, Bhartṛhari takes a far more intellectualist stance: it is knowledge that sets us free.[4] Not knowledge of grammatical details like case endings or the difference between singular and plural, though we can read about these things at length in the *Vākyapadīya*. The analysis of language is, rather, a step along the path to a higher form of understanding in which we grasp the reality that underlies and gives rise to language. This reality is *brahman*. It's for this reason that we are covering Bhartṛhari now, having just looked at the Vedānta tradition.[5] Like the Vedāntins, he is convinced that *brahman* is the single, fundamental principle of all things, which is known to us only because of the Veda (§§1.5, 1.16).

Bhartṛhari offers a distinctively linguistic version of this idea. Grammar is, of course, worth studying simply in order to interpret the Sanskrit texts of the Veda correctly. More fundamentally, though, it is language that accounts for the division or differentiation of the single *brahman* into the multiple reality we experience. To understand why, we must ask what exactly Bhartṛhari understands language to be. It's not an easy question to answer, although he says a lot about it. On this and other topics, the *Vākyapadīya* includes summaries and refutations of various other views, with Bhartṛhari's own position occasionally remaining unclear. He also uses technical terms whose significance is not immediately obvious. In this case, the most important such terms are *sphoṭa* and *śabda*. Roughly, *sphoṭa* is the implicit meaning of language, while the language used to represent this meaning is *śabda* (§1.20). That sounds pretty straightforward, except that *śabda* can occur either in the mind or in actual verbal speech. Bhartṛhari says that language in the mind gives rise to expressed language like one fire kindling another (§1.46). When you hear an utterance you also depend on your mental representations in order to understand what you are hearing (§1.53). You thereby get access to the meaning, or *sphoṭa*, that the speaker was trying to express.[6]

Bhartṛhari's view thus far sounds pretty commonsensical. Suppose I want to warn you that there's a giraffe in your kitchen. I may formulate a sentence to this effect in my mind and then utter it aloud. This will trigger comprehension in your mind, along with the hope that the giraffe will clean up last night's dishes. The verbal utterance and the two mental acts all point towards a single, shared meaning: that there is a giraffe in the kitchen. It's right about here that things get more controversial. The meaning or *sphoṭa* is in a sense the core of language, since capturing meaning is the whole point of the linguistic enterprise. According to Bhartṛhari meaning in itself has no parts (§1.74), and is not subject to time. Only actual verbal utterances are affected by time, since we need to speak one word after another, whereas a meaning can be represented in the mind all at once (§2.22).

Bhartṛhari's analysis is diametrically opposed to a rival view, which he associates with the Mīmāṃsā school (see Chapter 17). According to the Mīmāṃsakas known to Bhartṛhari, meaning is not prior to linguistic expression. Rather, they say, it is actually the result of a verbal utterance, whose parts work together to express and give rise to the intended meaning (§2.4). So in our example, individual words like "giraffe" and "kitchen" are fitted together in a suitable grammatical structure, which results in a meaningful sentence. For Bhartṛhari, this gets things backward. Individual words have no meaning in their own right, but only come to signify in the context of a sentence, just as the sounds that make up a word, like "gir-" and "-affe," are not in themselves meaningful (§§1.73, 2.52–6, 2.206). He asks us to consider the fact that the individual words of a sentence pass away as they are uttered. When one says "there is a giraffe in the kitchen," the word "giraffe" has already come and gone by the time I get to the word "kitchen." That means that the words cannot come together to give rise to a united meaning, because they do not all exist at the same time (§2.15). Consider also the fact that we sometimes use individual words that have no referent. If I utter the less alarming sentence, "there is *not* a giraffe in the kitchen," the word "giraffe" is clearly not signifying any actual giraffe. It is therefore meaningful not just by itself, but only as part of a whole sentence (§2.241). In fact, Bhartṛhari concludes, the words and the sentence as a whole make an inner meaning "manifest," without actually constituting the meaning (§2.409).

Something analogous happens from the listener's point of view. Rather than grasping the meaning of each individual word as one listens, one comprehends the meaning of the whole sentence all at once in a "flash of understanding" (*pratibhā*, §2.143) that occurs when the sentence reaches its conclusion (§1.84).[7] Here Bhartṛhari anticipates a possible objection from the proponent of the Mīmāṃsā theory. This opponent may say that part-by-part composition of meaning would account better for logical relations between sentences, such as contradiction (§2.75–6). Take our two example sentences again: "there is a giraffe in the kitchen" and "there is not a giraffe in the kitchen." The second sentence sure looks like the first sentence with one part added, namely the word "not," which generates a new and contradictory meaning. To this Bhartṛhari simply replies that relations between sentences, including contradiction, have to do with the degree of overall "resemblance" between the indivisible meanings of the sentences in question (§2.93).

Despite his holistic approach Bhartṛhari also has much to say about the grammatical features of individual words, like the case and gender of nouns. Ultimately, though, grammar is the study of the way communication breaks meaning down. The grammarian analyzes the parts of speech that allow us to express meaning, but in so doing he should realize that the meaning is unified and prior to linguistic expression. The Mīmāṃsā approach to language, for him, would be like trying to understand a pot by starting from broken shards rather than the whole vessel (cf. §2.249). Here we may have our own flash of understanding, as we note the affinity between Bhartṛhari's theory of language and the Advaita Vedānta theory of reality. Much as Advaita encourages us to see the multiplicity of phenomenal experience as an expression of the single source that is *brahman*, so Bhartṛhari thinks that divisible speech expresses indivisible meaning.

Actually there's more here than just an affinity. Bhartṛhari probably influenced the development of Advaita Vedānta. And his theory does not postulate a mere analogy between language and phenomenal experience. Rather, language is the very means by which we have experience and come to know the world. Even in the most rudimentary perceptions, such as those had by small children, there is what he calls a latent "seed (*bīja*)" of language, which cannot be communicated.[8] Full-blown cognition, though, is always linguistic, so that our knowledge is "permeated by words" (§1.131; cf. §§1.118 and 3.474). This may seem to be fairly commonsensical. It's quite plausible to say that we can only grasp things around us by filing them under certain descriptions or concepts, so that we are able to put our experiences into words. When I perceive that alarmingly tall animal in the kitchen as a giraffe, my ability to do so arguably depends on my having the word "giraffe" in my vocabulary.

Let's look more closely at these concepts by which we classify the things that we perceive. Philosophers nowadays would call them "universals," and Bhartṛhari does the same—the Sanskrit term he uses is *jāti*. He is very interested in universals, in part because they are so critical in the study of grammar. Some grammarians thought that language refers in the first instance to individual things, like the particular giraffe in your kitchen. For Bhartṛhari, though, meanings are primarily universal, and the universal is what we really mean by *sphoṭa*. This is shown by the way that words work, especially in languages like Sanskrit, where you can start with a basic noun and then add endings to indicate gender and number to apply that noun to a particular object or objects (§§1.66, 3.315); for an example in English consider the four words "actor," "actors," "actress," and "actresses." The universal meaning is what licenses us to apply the same word to these many objects, as in all those cases we are talking about someone who acts on stage. Bhartṛhari again uses here the notion of "resemblance" (§3.400). We apply the word "giraffe" to all giraffes because they resemble one another in the relevant way, while differing in other respects (this giraffe is in the kitchen doing dishes, that one in the study reading about philosophy). Even the same individual bears a relation of resemblance to itself at other times. This is why we are allowed to say "you are like yourself" (§3.565), which sounds a bit odd, though one might imagine saying it to an old classmate at a school reunion.

Most Indian thinkers believed that language reveals the structure of reality,[9] and as an expert in language Bhartṛhari was hardly going to disagree. So for him, the primacy of the universal at the level of meaning shows that reality itself is in the first instance universal and only then particular. Individual things reveal the universal, just as individual words reveal the meaning of a whole sentence (§1.95). We might be reluctant to move so quickly from the level of language or its meaning to the level of reality. What guarantee do we have that language captures the way things are? But Bhartṛhari has good reason to assume that it does, because he adheres to a belief we first encountered in Mīmāṃsā: the Veda and language itself are permanent (*nitya*, §1.28). Bhartṛhari takes this to imply that there is a primordial classification of reality in terms of universals, which are the meanings eternally revealed in the language of sacred texts.

That makes him sound a bit like Plato. Universals, like Platonic Forms, would give significance to our words and also be the fundamental principles of all things. But remember that for Bhartṛhari, the truly fundamental principle of all things is *brahman*. How then do his universals relate to this single source? Scholars don't agree on this point.[10] One suggestion has been that *brahman* is effectively the most general universal, identical with "being," or to put it another way, with the class of all things that exist. Other universals add further differentiation, progressively narrowing down this most general universal. Apart from *brahman*, nothing is just a being. Rather, some beings are alive, some living things are animals, some animals are giraffes, and some giraffes, though not many, are in kitchens. On this reading Bhartṛhari would sound less like Plato and more like a Neoplatonist making use of Aristotelian logic. (To be specific, he would sound like Porphyry, whose famous "Porphyrian tree" consisted in just such a hierarchy of genera containing lower species.) But this reading of Bhartṛhari has been challenged fairly persuasively. What we really find in the *Vākyapadīya* is the idea that universals are all identical with *brahman* and constitute various means of expressing its fundamental reality. In favor of this interpretation is the nice parallel that would result between the relation of the universals to *brahman* on the one hand, and the relation of individuals to the universal on the other hand. Just as the universals divide *brahman* while being identical with it, so individual giraffes both divide and yet are somehow identical with the universal *giraffe* (§3.338, 341 and 346).

Whichever interpretation we adopt, it's clear that for Bhartṛhari universals form a second layer of principles which manifest and differentiate the most fundamental reality that is *brahman*. In a further step, the universals are themselves made manifest, on the metaphysical side by individuals, on the linguistic side by mental representation and speech. Less clear is whether all this amounts to the sort of radical proposal we found in Śaṅkara's "non-dual" version of Vedānta.[11] Is Bhartṛhari saying that the language to which he has devoted himself so assiduously is actually, in the end, a kind of falsification or misrepresentation of the single reality of *brahman*? Is our world of experience, structured as it is by language, just an illusion? If so, then grammar would seem to be less a door to liberation and more a ladder to be thrown away once liberation is achieved through the grasp of *brahman*.

Much as with the *Brahma-sūtra* (aka. *Vedānta-sūtra*), one can find passages in the *Vākyapadīya* to support both dualism and non-dualism. In favor of dualism, in other words the idea that the world of experience is indeed real, though a secondary, lesser reality than *brahman*, we have the fact that *brahman* is said to possess "powers" for the production of other things (§1.2), and to take on "forms" when these things are produced (§1.115). One of Bhartṛhari's most celebrated images would fit well here. He says that *brahman* is like a peacock's egg, which reveals a welter of brilliant colors once it hatches and produces the bird and its plumage (§1.51).[12] In favor of non-dualism, though, we have passages that connect language with unreality. In at least some cases words can express non-existent things, something Bhartṛhari compares to the circle we see when looking at a whirling firebrand (§1.130). Elsewhere he remarks that the study of language is a path to truth even though it deals with what is unreal (§2.238). Comments on the beginning of the *Vākyapadīya* found in the explanatory *Vṛtti* also tend in a non-dualist direction.[13]

This side of Bhartṛhari brings him close not only to the later Śaṅkara, but also to contemporary Buddhists who were more forthright in condemning the world of experience as an illusion.[14] In fact one thinker who reacted to Bhartṛhari was the great Buddhist thinker Dignāga, and he was quick to point out the skeptical implications lurking in Bhartṛhari's theory. Language may distort reality by dividing it, pulling it apart into an infinity of fragments.[15] Whether this counts as a criticism of Bhartṛhari or just an insightful remark revealing what Bhartṛhari himself wanted to say, depends on how we interpret the words of this most philosophical of grammarians.

22

THE THEORY OF EVOLUTION

ĪŚVARAKṚṢṆA'S *SĀṂKHYA-KĀRIKĀ*

We have now come far enough in our examination of Indian philosophy to ask a pivotal question: what would the Muppets make of it? Like the Indian thinkers themselves, different Muppets would probably have differing opinions. Miss Piggy, famously outraged by the mere mention of words like "bacon" and "porkchop," would admire the Jaina ban on non-violence toward animals. The self-abnegating Scooter is practically a Buddhist already. Sam the Eagle would no doubt endorse the strict political line taken in Kauṭilya's *Arthaśāstra*, while the Swedish Chef might feel kinship with the *sūtra* texts, since you usually can't tell what the heck they are saying either. Over on *Sesame Street*, we can guess at the favorite school of the Count (or to give him his full name, Count von Count), the Muppet vampire who has taught generations of children basic arithmetic. He would want to get his teeth into Sāṃkhya, the tradition whose name literally means "counting" or "enumeration."

It's a name no less appropriate than that of the number-loving Count. Sāṃkhya, too, loves numbers, and offers a whole system of itemizing lists. These catalogue, among other things, the twenty-five principles (*tattvas*) that constitute the self and the cosmos, the eight tendencies (*bhāvas*) that guide human behavior within the cosmos, and the fifty types of result for humans, ranging from five basic misunderstandings of the world to nine kinds of contentment.[1] The lists are mentioned, though usually not spelled out in full detail, in the oldest surviving treatise of the school, namely the *Sāṃkhya-kārikā* ascribed to Īśvarakṛṣṇa (it is called a *kārikā* rather than a *sūtra* because of its verse form).[2] It is thought that he lived between AD 350 and 450. This sounds very ancient, and it is. Yet like other supposed founding fathers we've met in other Indian traditions, Īśvarakṛṣṇa was himself heir to an even more ancient tradition. In fact you can make a case that Sāṃkhya is the oldest of the Vedic "schools," especially if you add the caveat that it existed long before being a school. At the end of the *Sāṃkhya-kārikā* (§59–62), Īśvarakṛṣṇa is revealed to be a fairly late entry in the list of Sāṃkhya thinkers. The real founder, here called simply the "great sage," is identified by ancient commentators as Kapila. He was followed by two more teachers, by the names of Āsuri and Pañcaśikha, with Īśvarakṛṣṇa coming some unspecified number of generations later.

Whatever the accuracy of this lineage, there's no doubt that Sāṃkhya reaches back far into the past. Its characteristic ideas have been traced back to the earliest Vedas, and there are passages in the Upaniṣads and the *Mahābhārata* that have unmistakable similarities to the teaching of Īśvarakṛṣṇa, with the enumeration of principles anticipated already in the *Chāndogya Upaniṣad* (§6.2–5). The historical figures we just mentioned pop up in earlier texts, as when the *Mahābhārata* describes how Pañcaśikha defeated 100 other sages in debate (§12.211–12). As we'll be seeing, Sāṃkhya develops in concert with the tradition of Yoga, which provides a kind of practical complement to Sāṃkhya's enumerative system-mongering, and this link, too, figures in the earlier texts. The *Mahābhārata* says that Yoga and Sāṃkhya share a single teaching, though we also read there that different teachers identify themselves as followers of one or the other school (§§12.295.42–3 and 289.2).[3]

It would seem that in the *Sāṃkhya-kārikā*, Īśvarakṛṣṇa, too, was reaching into the past, retrenching to a more conservative presentation of the system to challenge more recent innovations. As so often, our oldest text ushers us into the middle of an ongoing conversation. We shouldn't assume that Īśvarakṛṣṇa's ideas are definitive of Sāṃkhya just because it is his work that has survived and not those of his rivals.[4] On the other hand, Īśvarakṛṣṇa's ideas did come to dominate the conversation as it continued on from his time. We have another opportunity to do some counting here, since there are no fewer than eight early commentaries on the *Sāṃkhya-kārikā*. Two of them are by authors with familiar names: Gauḍapāda and Patañjali. The latter is not to be confused with the grammarian Patañjali, who wrote the most authoritative commentary on Pāṇini, but it's possible that the Gauḍapāda who commented on the *Sāṃkhya-kārikā* is the same as the Vedāntin who anticipated Śaṅkara's ideas. What is certain is that Śaṅkara himself really had it in for Sāṃkhya. As we mentioned earlier (see Chapter 20), he sternly criticized the whole approach taken by Īśvarakṛṣṇa and his heirs, taking exception to their cosmology, their conception of the self, and their epistemology.

As Count von Count might say, the reason is as clear as the difference between one and two. In Śaṅkara's "non-dual" version of Vedānta there is only one principle, *brahman*, and it is the only thing that is real. Sāṃkhya, by contrast, is dualist. The Bert and Ernie of the Sāṃkhya system, two very different characters that together form a close partnership, are called *puruṣa* and *prakṛti*. We first met the word *puruṣa* back when discussing the cosmology of the *Ṛg-veda* (see Chapter 3). The gods cut up *puruṣa* in a world-forming sacrifice, fashioning its limbs into the different groups of

Indian society. In that context *puruṣa* seemed to be something like an originary human, complete with body. In the *Sāṃkhya-kārikā*, though, *puruṣa* means something far more abstract. It is that which witnesses all, yet remains inactive (§19). This description suggests that we are talking about pure consciousness, the subject underlying all objects of awareness. Of course that is a thoroughly Upaniṣadic idea, which is here being used as a foundation for the whole Sāṃkhya system.

Thus far the Vedāntins could agree. But they would have to reject the next move made in Sāṃkhya, which is to identify pure consciousness as only one of two fundamental principles. You'll see the name of the other one, *prakṛti*, translated as "nature" or "primordial matter." It is the principle of things in a somewhat more familiar sense: that which gives rise to all other things by undergoing a complex, step-by-step process of transformation. As it does so *puruṣa* remains inactive, maintaining an unending silent vigil as it observes the development of *prakṛti*. So this is not dualism as we may think of it from other traditions, like Gnosticism. Sāṃkhya does share the idea of two independent principles, neither of which is the cause of the other. But we don't have God acting on matter here, or a good principle coming into conflict with a counterbalancing source of evil. Instead nature or *prakṛti* spontaneously turns itself into all things while consciousness or *puruṣa* just bears witness. Yet there is a role for *puruṣa* in explaining the phenomena that result. Īśvarakṛṣṇa says that though *prakṛti* is productive, it is also unintelligent (§10). Without *puruṣa* there could be no awareness within the products of nature (§17). The two principles are thus compared to a blind man cooperating with a lame man (§21). Nature is blind, since on its own it would lack the consciousness that is the core of mental life; consciousness is lame, since without nature it would remain inert.

So far we've only managed to count up to two. We have a lot of work to do if we're going to get up to twenty-five principles. The remaining twenty-three are of course not as fundamental as *puruṣa* and *prakṛti*. They are in fact going to be the phenomena that emerge from *prakṛti*, as it undergoes what Īśvarakṛṣṇa calls "modification" (§56). In scholarly literature on Sāṃkhya these twenty-three results are sometimes called "the evolutes," which sounds more like a 1950s singing group than anything else. But the term makes sense, since they "evolve" out of *prakṛti* in a gradual process. Īśvarakṛṣṇa appeals to the idea that effects "pre-exist" in their causes (§9), an assumption that appears in Vedānta, as when Śaṅkara argues that all things are virtually present in *brahman* like pots are already somehow in the clay from which they will be made. This makes a certain amount of sense. It shows how pots do not just emerge from complete non-being when they are made, and also why you can produce only certain things using a given material. You can put a chicken in every pot, but you can't make a chicken out of a pot, though it would be a great act for the Amazing Gonzo to try on the *Muppet Show*.

Before we go on to talk about the effects that are produced out of *prakṛti*, let's look a bit more closely at this principle and the forces that cause it to change into them. Unfortunately, taking a closer look at *prakṛti* will be difficult. The *Sāṃkhya-kārikā* speaks of it as "unmanifest (*avyakta*)," and as too subtle for us to perceive (§8). Though it contains all other things implicitly, in itself it is actually none of these things. As a result we cannot grasp it directly, only as a kind of postulate or hypothesis. Īśvarakṛṣṇa has the resources to justify this maneuver. He touches briefly on a theme we'll be exploring in much greater depth when we get to the Nyāya school: the sources of knowledge. In Sāṃkhya there are three such sources, namely direct perception, inference, and valid testimony (§4). In the case of the underlying nature that is *prakṛti*, we use "inference." We reason that it must be real without being able to grasp it directly, on the basis that there must be a single principle to explain how there is order and limit in things (§§15–16).

As for the mechanism of change, this is one of the most intriguing yet elusive aspects of Īśvarakṛṣṇa's presentation of Sāṃkhya. He speaks of three *guṇas*, which literally means "cords" or "threads." So, staying at the level of metaphor, we might think of a rope made of three intertwined strands. At a more philosophical level, the *guṇas* are the "functional modes"[5] by which nature transforms. In other words, they are interacting tendencies that are inherent in *prakṛti*. The three *guṇas* are called *sattva*, *rajas*, and *tamas*. We've already seen some words in this chapter that are hard to translate, but like the Cookie Monster, these really take the cake. They go back deep into the literary history of Vedic culture.[6] Originally they may have alluded to sun, sky, and earth, which come together to make it possible to grow food. They are also associated with white, red, and black, perhaps an evocation of some traditional color scheme for clothing.

Here in the *Sāṃkhya-kārikā*, though, they are the three forces of change responsible for the evolution of things from *prakṛti* (§§12–13). The first of the *guṇas* is *sattva*, connected to lightness and pleasure; the second, *rajas*, has to do with change and the upheaval that causes suffering; the third is *tamas*, which is "heavy" and has to do with resistance and despondency. Thus we have a striking combination of cosmological and psychological traits associated with each, which is going to be a hallmark of the whole Sāṃkhya system.[7] Within the cosmos, we are told, there are different realms dominated by the three different forces. This apparently is meant to explain the difference between the divine heavenly realm, humanity, and animals and plants, so that the *guṇas* govern all things "from *Brahmā* down [to] a blade of grass," as Īśvarakṛṣṇa puts it (§§53–4). Psychologically, *sattva* was historically linked to liberation, and here in the *Sāṃkhya-kārikā* we are told that individual selves may be dominated by *sattva* or by *tamas*, that is, lead their lives wisely or not (§23).

In both the cosmos and the person, the really central point is that the three *guṇas* operate together dynamically, somehow causing each stage of the evolution to proceed from the last. The metaphor of the rope may be of help here, if we imagine nature extending strands out from itself and developing in ever-increasing complexity. Or we may look back to the *Mahābhārata*, which already spoke of how the *guṇas* are "created in regular order and dissolve in reverse order, like the waves of the sea."[8] Not to be outdone, Īśvarakṛṣṇa offers his own analogy, comparing the three forces to a lamp (§13). The commentators helpfully explain that he means the oil, fire, and wick that together allow for illumination.

Given that *prakṛti* is often understood in material terms, it may be tempting to understand all this as a purely physical process. But a look at the first results that emerge from the activity of the *guṇas* throws some doubt on this (§22). The immediate product of *prakṛti* is *buddhi*, also called "the great one (*mahat*)." It is the first thing that is "manifest," so that we can have some direct grasp of it. Yet again, the translation of *buddhi* is open to debate, but a possible rendering would be "intellect," since we are apparently dealing with a kind of impersonal, undirected thought or striving to create further stages. Next our emerging subject acquires a sense of its own identity, in a stage literally called "I-making (*ahaṃkāra*)."[9] Here we are apparently talking about self-awareness, the ability to take a first-person view on things. Only at the next stage does Īśvarakṛṣṇa introduce "mind (*manas*)," which is responsible for actual thinking and perceiving inner sensations, including pleasure and pain. Collectively these three powers—*buddhi*, *ahaṃkāra*, and *manas*—are called the "interior organ," as opposed to the external organs of sense (§33). Just as we said that the cosmic dualism of Sāṃkhya is not like that of Gnosticism, so here we should note that Īśvarakṛṣṇa's dualism is not the same as we find in, say, Plato or Descartes, where a mental principle is contrasted to a physical principle.[10] Admittedly, one of the two principles of Sāṃkhya is pure consciousness, which might remind us of the Cartesian mind. But all other aspects of mental life are placed squarely on the side of the other principle, *prakṛti*. The capacities needed for thinking are even the first things to be generated, though we should bear in mind the caveat that none of these capacities could be "aware" at all if not for the lurking presence of consciousness, in the form of *prakṛti*'s unoriginated partner *puruṣa*.

We're still only up to five items: these two fundamental principles plus the three aspects of the interior organ. But now things get going more quickly. The mind generates the five sense faculties—vision, hearing, and so on—plus five anatomical powers to match, like speaking and moving. With this "exterior organ" we seem to have a well-rounded person who has a mental life, the capacity for sensation, and further abilities for interacting with the world. The catch is that there isn't really a world yet, only a person. So these fifteen principles have to be complemented by the five sensible features of the world, which generate five bodily elements, the four that would be familiar from Greek philosophy—air, earth, fire, and water—plus something called *ākāśa,* which might mean empty space or some kind of "aether" that pervades the universe. This finally gets us up to twenty-five.

Obviously there are a lot of philosophical issues one could raise here, but we will follow the example of Īśvarakṛṣṇa and pass over most of them. We do want to mention two things, one a point of relative detail and then a more general puzzle. The detail has to do with those sensible features generated toward the end of the evolutionary process. They are presented very generically. It seems that we're talking about the whole phenomena of taste, smell, sound, and so on, not particular flavors, scents, or noises. Supposedly the generic sensibles actually give rise to the elements, and particular qualities like a given color can come about only once we have these physical elements and the compounds made from them. Some authors, including our favorite philosophizing grammarian Bhartṛhari, claim that for Sāṃkhya everyday bodies are actually *made* of sensible qualities. If this were right then there would be nothing more to a pot than its color, hardness, the metallic sound made when it falls on the Swedish Chef's head, and so on. But it seems likely that in the earlier tradition represented by Īśvarakṛṣṇa the qualities were assumed to belong to an underlying subject. This subject is of course *prakṛti,* the quasi-material principle that has ultimately transformed itself into the things of everyday experience.[11]

As for the broader puzzle, we've already mentioned it: the rather disconcerting way that the twenty-five principles cut across the cosmological and human realms. These principles take in sensation and the sensible, the mental and the material, the private and the public. Does this really make sense? In the initial stages of the evolution we have a description of human psychological powers. Before long, though, these powers are somehow producing physical entities like the elements. One suspicion might be that the physical aspects of the evolution are really just a kind of illusion, a kind of show that the mind puts on for itself when it is bound to nature. In fact a passage late in the *Sāṃkhya-kārikā* says that the phenomenal world is like a dance watched by the audience that is *puruṣa* (§59). This reading could head in a direction taken by some later commentators who came after Śaṅkara. They sought to reconcile Sāṃkhya with Advaita Vedānta's conviction that the phenomenal world is an illusion. But there might be other reasons that the world out there is so closely connected with the world of the mind. We know that Vedic literature frequently compared the cosmos with an individual animal, person, or God. The theory of the three *guṇas* lends support to this boundary-crossing idea: the same forces that yield a person's mind and body also give rise to a physical universe.[12]

And, in fact, there are major obstacles to any reconciliation between Sāṃkhya and Vedānta. Not only does Sāṃkhya embrace two fundamental principles where Vedānta has only one, it also resists the Vedāntic notion that there is ultimately only one true self, namely *brahman*. The fact that there are different courses of life and experiences proves, says Īśvarakṛṣṇa, that *puruṣa* itself is many (§18). Apparently you have one pure consciousness, and I have another. Yet there is a point of deep agreement between these two Vedic schools as well. Both are convinced that knowledge of their teaching will bring liberation. In the very first sentence of the *Sāṃkhya-kārikā*, we are told that the purpose of the teaching to come is to release us from suffering. And supposedly the early Sāṃkhya thinker Pañcaśikha held out this as a prospect for all, and not just the priestly caste. "A knower of the 25 principles," he said, "in whatever order of life he may be and whether he wears braided hair, a top-knot only, or is shaven, is liberated from existence."[13]

But why would counting up to twenty-five principles, or going through the other enumerative lists offered by Sāṃkhya, help us to achieve this goal? One might suspect that Īśvarakṛṣṇa is just trying to keep up with the Buddhists, who built their whole teaching around the pervasiveness of suffering and the path that leads to escape. But Sāṃkhya, too, is built from its very foundations to pursue the goal of liberation. Postulating the *puruṣa* does address the philosophy of mind, by making pure consciousness prior to all experience. But Īśvarakṛṣṇa also insists that without *puruṣa* there can be no liberation. Only a pure, contentless consciousness can stand outside the turmoil and suffering of the world that emerges from *prakṛti*. Consciousness can declare itself satisfied now that it has seen the evolved world, while nature can be satisfied at having shown itself and been seen.

So now we know what we have to give up if we want to be liberated: everything. We must let go of all physical action, all sensation, all mental activity, even any sense of individual self, saying, "I do not exist, nothing is mine, I am not" (§64). This is what it means to identify with the passive witness that is *puruṣa*. Īśvarakṛṣṇa calls this an escape from ignorance. Ignorance is not the reason why the world evolved from *prakṛti*; that was a spontaneous, natural process. Ignorance is instead what keeps us bound to the world once it has evolved.[14] This bondage is unnecessary, because we can just choose to cast ourselves in the role of audience instead of performer. To take oneself to be *puruṣa* is already to be liberated, simply because *puruṣa* stands outside the evolutionary process. It was never unfree in the first place.

23

WHO WANTS TO LIVE FOREVER?

EARLY ĀYURVEDIC MEDICINE

At the beginning of his *Sāṃkhya-kārikā*, Īśvarakṛṣṇa speaks of a threefold suffering that his teaching aims to dispel. Like any self-respecting author of a foundational text in Indian philosophy, he doesn't bother to tell us exactly what he means. Fortunately, like any self-respecting commentator, Gauḍapāda hastens to explain. Suffering is threefold because its cause may be internal, external, or divine. Internal suffering in turn has two forms: bodily and mental. After our discussion of Sāṃkhya, we have a pretty good idea of where mental suffering comes from. It is the inevitable anguish arising from ignorance about the nature of the true self. But what about bodily suffering? This, says Gauḍapāda, is caused by the disordering of three substances within the body, namely wind, bile, and phlegm. So, here we have a threefold enumeration, illustrating the first of two aspects of the first item by means of another threefold enumeration? Yes, this is Sāṃkhya all right. But the idea that bodily disease is caused by wind, bile, and phlegm would have been familiar to Gauḍapāda's readers from another Indian tradition: Āyurveda.

Unlike "Sāṃkhya," "Āyurveda" is still a name to conjure with. It is practiced across the English-speaking world as a kind of "alternative" medicine. It also continues to play a role in India itself, where ancient ideas are combined with more recent medical theories to form what is sometimes called "Modern Āyurveda." But in this chapter we'll be looking at a version of Āyurveda that is anything but modern. The medical texts of the tradition go back to the early centuries AD. The oldest complete surviving treatise is called the *Caraka-saṃhitā*, the name alluding to its author or rather compiler, a man named Caraka. According to the testimony of the text itself, he is passing on wisdom first handed down by the gods to the mythical Aśvins, who are also mentioned in the *Mahābhārata*.[1] Their medical teaching eventually passed to Ātreya, a sage who is often quoted in the *Caraka-saṃhitā*. It's thought that Caraka himself wrote around AD 300, with the surviving redaction of his text produced around AD 500. Apart from the *Caraka-saṃhitā*, we have some other very old medical treatises, including one that focuses especially on surgical techniques called the *Suśruta-saṃhitā*.[2]

After all the talk we've had of fulfilling one's *dharma*, of achieving liberation from suffering and worldly existence, of trying to grasp one's identity with *brahman*, it's somewhat refreshing to find that Āyurveda has the more straightforward goal of prolonging your life. Indeed this is what "Āyurveda" means: "knowledge of longevity." Caraka makes no apologies for this relatively modest aim. He freely admits that a long life is not the only worthwhile thing. One may also seek wealth and seek to secure a good fate after death. But to pursue these goals, one first needs to remain healthy for as long as possible in this present life. As Caraka puts it, "when life is lost, everything is lost" (60). Yet Āyurveda also recognizes that each person has a proper, limited lifespan. This explains why even the best doctor cannot prolong the life of some patients, and why it may be pointless even to try.[3]

We might be surprised that lifespan was ever thought to be a matter for human intervention. The doctrine of *karma* suggested that everyone's lifespan is preordained at the moment of birth.[4] It's a familiar problem, one that obviously confronts any fatalist worldview. Just think of the ancient Greek Stoics, who were thoroughgoing determinists. They had to answer the so-called "Lazy Argument," namely that a determinist would have no reason to go to the doctor, since if he is fated to die from his illness then he will surely die, whether or not he gets medical treatment, but if he is fated to live, then such treatment will be unnecessary. Confronting his own version of the problem, Caraka quotes the sage Ātreya saying that lifespan is not simply fated by *karma*, but rather determined by several factors (86–8). For starters, there is more than one kind of *karma*, since our fate is affected by what we did in previous lives but also what we do now. And even the combined karma has only a "weak" influence, so that our actions can change the outcome. Clearly our lifespan cannot be entirely predetermined. If it were, then never mind not going to the doctor, you wouldn't even bother to avoid stepping off cliffs! Still, the good physician is not out to prolong your life indefinitely. He just wants to get you to the "right time" for death, much as the axle of a chariot is meant to wear out after a certain time.

This issue illustrates a running theme in early Āyurveda, namely a tension between its naturalist and scientific outlook and older cultural beliefs that are retained in the texts. Examples are littered throughout both the *Caraka-saṃhitā* and the *Suśruta-saṃhitā*: invasive diseases are caused by poor judgment and bad hygiene, including those diseases brought on by demons (57); wind or breath is both a fundamental constituent of the body and a divine force that causes all things (161); differences between twins are caused by both karma and an unequal distribution of blood and generative seed.[5] It's tempting to praise the medical authors for their more naturalist, "scientific" proposals while deploring their inability, or unwillingness, to abandon religious ways of thought. But we should do them the courtesy of realizing that there could be a well thought out synthesis here, not only a tension between the old fashioned and the newfangled.

In favor of this more generous interpretation we offer a passage from early in the *Caraka-saṃhitā*, which entertains a skeptical objection to the third of Caraka's goals, the favorable afterlife. To someone who doubts that we do in fact live on after death, Caraka invokes the sort of epistemological theory we often find in Indian philosophical literature. He recognizes four sources of knowledge, or *pramāṇas*: authority, perception, inference, and reasoning (63). All four testify that we may be reborn after past lives. Most obviously, Vedic authority says so. But perception too confirms it, by noting that people don't always take after their parents and must therefore have some other source. The same ways of knowing are used in medicine itself. Great weight is placed on authoritative testimony, given that the Āyurvedic teaching is supposed to have come ultimately from the gods themselves. Caraka also works with theoretical premises that are clearly the result of inference and reasoning, as we'll see below. But of the four *pramāṇas* the most important may be perception. Āyurveda stresses the use of the senses, especially in diagnostics. According to Suśruta, we should examine a patient by using all five senses, and also by asking questions, what would nowadays be called taking a medical history (130–2).

The *Suśruta-saṃhitā* also has plenty of concrete advice for trainee surgeons. Before cutting up human bodies, first learn the technique by practicing with melons, gourds, hunks of meat, and other items similar to the various parts of the body (128). Practical experience also allows physicians to proceed despite the infinite variety in the conditions of patients (75). No one can teach you what to do in every case; you must learn by doing. Yet Āyurveda combines this sort of hands on approach with speculative reasoning about the human body. Neither theory nor practical experience suffices on its own. To use only one would be like a bird trying to fly with one wing.[6] A good doctor must understand the principles that give rise to the human body, and that influence the constitution and health of each individual body.

As they unfold this theoretical basis for medicine, the Āyurvedic texts allude to something like the cosmological theory we saw in Sāṃkhya. There are five elements, namely aether, wind, earth, fire, and water, and our bodies are ultimately composed from these elements, as is our food. In a manner also reminiscent of Sāṃkhya, different foods are classified in accordance with six flavors, namely sweet, sour, salty, bitter, pungent, and astringent. The doctor needs to know the characteristics of foods, since a buildup of harmful humors in the body can be combatted by eating something with an opposing nature.[7] Suffering from an excess of wind? Then eat a sweet, sour, or salty dish, or perhaps something that has all three flavors, like dill pickles with caramel coating (well, perhaps not that, but you get the idea). Once food is digested it is transformed into so called "nutritive juice (*rasa*)," which passes into the heart and is then circulated around the body (154).

Alongside these ideas about elemental composition, there is the notion that wind or breath is a fundamental principle of the body.[8] This is another point of agreement between our Āyurvedic texts and older works like the Upaniṣads. If you look at summaries of the ancient medical theory, you'll often see wind listed as simply one among three bodily "humors," alongside the aforementioned bile and phlegm. But this is somewhat misleading, and in numerous ways. In fact, taking our inspiration from Sāṃkhya, let us count the ways. First, bile and phlegm are opposed to each other, with wind playing a more fundamental and leading role, perhaps because of its prominence in Vedic literature.[9] Second, in some passages blood is treated as if it were another of the humors. It is a chief product of nutrition and, when processed in the body over the course of a month, turns into menstrual blood in women and semen in men. Blood can also cause disease when it is corrupted or in excess, which is why doctors should practice bloodletting. Suśruta goes so far as to remark that "blood is life" (160), a maxim still endorsed today by cardiologists and vampires.

Third, and most importantly, it isn't clear that wind, bile, and phlegm are really "humors," as we would understand that term in the context of ancient European medicine.[10] There the four humors were said to be blood, black bile, yellow bile, and phlegm, which certainly looks like a similar list. However, authors like Galen understood the humors as constitutive substances that need to be in qualitative balance. Our language today actually preserves the theory, as when we speak of someone being "melancholic," literally meaning characterized by "black bile" (in Greek *melaina chole*).[11] In the Indian context, by contrast, these three substances—called *doṣas*—are initially conceived solely as sources of disease. In the earliest references to the theory, which comes long before the two Āyurvedic *Saṃhitās*, there is no talk of getting them to be in balance, only of eliminating them or at least keeping them from being "riled," because it is when they are stirred up that they cause illness. If you want to understand how the *doṣas* were understood in early India, a better parallel than the science of ancient Greece might be the folk medicine of modern-day Italy. There you may be afflicted by a *colpo d'aria*, the dreaded "blast of air" that will likely lead to a sick day off work, assuming you aren't already on strike.

Which leads us naturally on to the working conditions of the ancient Indian doctor. Though this topic isn't addressed head on by Caraka or Suśruta, they do give us quite a bit of information in passing remarks. It would seem that high-born doctors, those of the *brahmin* or *kṣatriya* castes, may have practiced medicine on a charitable basis, whereas *vaiśya* doctors presumably received payment.[12] There was a formalized process by which students would attach themselves to masters, and once trained they would adopt a distinctive outfit. Suśruta says that the physician should dress in white, and carry an umbrella and a stick (130). Both he and Caraka emphasize that moral probity is of the utmost importance in practicing medicine. The patient must trust the doctor and the doctor must earn this trust, though he need not be above the occasional deception, as when he withholds the news that a patient doesn't have long to live or hides the fact that a medicine involves the meat of animals that aren't usually on the menu.

Yes, the medical texts do prescribe the consumption of meat, and even the drinking of blood, as a form of treatment. The oldest texts treat this as a matter of course, but later commentators are made nervous by the departure from the strictures of non-violence. One offers the excuse that in medicine we are pursuing health, not *dharma*.[13] Nor is this the only place where Caraka and Suśruta seem remarkably uninterested by what we might call medical ethics. Caraka provides a list of patients that a wise doctor will not attempt to cure (90–1). We have already seen that this will include those who have an incurable terminal illness (he does accept that a doctor can manage an incurable chronic ailment). The list also mentions that poor people shouldn't be treated, which is rather shocking until you realize that he may mean the patient cannot afford to buy the medicines needed for the treatment, as could have been customary.[14] More admirably, Suśruta suggests that doctors who collect fees should waive them for a poor patient.

Finally, one shouldn't bother trying to treat very wicked patients, like those who actively enjoy wrongdoing. This isn't a form of punishment, but is more like the injunction against treating the untreatable. The undertaking would be doomed to failure, which will harm the doctor's reputation. Why though should a patient's wickedness make any difference to his or her prognosis? Because diseases are actually *caused* by bad character and bad judgment. We saw Caraka claiming that all diseases caused by external factors, including demons, are brought on by ethical failings. An apparent exception would be epidemics, such as a plague. Caraka himself, or his sources, noticed the difficulty. He includes a passage in which the wise medical man Ātreya explains the causes of epidemics (79–82). Given the emphasis on individual constitution in Āyurveda, it seems strange that a huge number of people may be struck by the same illness all at once. But this can be explained by other factors, like corruption of the air or water in the place where the victims live. This doesn't seem to fit with a moralist medical outlook, which would link health to good character and disease to bad. Are we really meant to believe that everyone in a plague-ridden city ate the wrong foods and indulged in debauched behavior? Not quite. Ātreya instead says that epidemics are brought on by wicked political rulers. It is their evil deeds that cause their lands to be abandoned by the gods and thus afflicted by adverse weather conditions (83).

By now it should be clear that ancient Āyurvedic texts are remarkably sophisticated. We have dealt only with the oldest preserved literature, yet we've seen explorations of good medical practice, explanations of disease at the moral, physical, and religious levels, and a theory of knowledge that explains how medical understanding can be acquired in the first place. Of course all this did not come out of the blue. It's evident from the *Saṃhitās* themselves that they are drawing on and quoting earlier authorities. But can we trace the story back even further? Caraka and Suśruta are at pains to associate themselves with Vedic authority.[15] There is that story about their medical art being passed down from the gods, and they make liberal use of terminology and ideas from Vedic culture. Even the word *āyurveda* itself is found for the first time in the *Mahābhārata*. But is that culture really the ultimate source of their thought? The Vedas do not develop medical theory with anything like the complexity of Caraka and Suśruta. To take one example, Suśruta's discussions of surgery display a formidable understanding of anatomy, whereas the scattered references to anatomy in the Vedas seem more like chance observations made in the context of animal sacrifice. More generally, Vedic prescriptions for curing illness tend to involve magic and religious ritual, not diet, drugs, or surgery.[16]

Instead, it has been suggested that Āyurveda grew out of a very different part of Indian culture. It may have emerged from the ascetic *śramaṇa* movements that dissented from the Vedic mainstream, and from Buddhism in particular.[17] One reason to suspect this is that in classical Brahmanical culture, physicians were likely seen as impure because of the physical contact they had with a wide range of people. As a result medical men were likely to be itinerant healers rather than the respected and nattily dressed aristocrats portrayed by Suśruta and Caraka. (An interesting hint in this direction is that the name "Caraka" actually means "someone who wanders.") It's also mentioned that medical students should roam freely offering medical services following their training. So perhaps early doctors had a touch of the vagabond about them. This would have made them natural bedfellows of the supreme social outsiders of the *śramaṇa* movements.

This is pretty speculative, but might be confirmed by allusions to medicine in the Buddhist texts themselves. The Pāli canon tells us that the Buddha instructed monks to nurse one another and allowed them to keep medicine. In one passage he is quoted to the effect that illnesses are caused by excess of wind, phlegm, or bile, and in some cases by *sannipātika*, a harmful combination of several humors. This is in fact a highly technical term of medical art; a contemporary expert has said it would be as if the Buddha blamed illness on "hemoglobin levels."[18] And it makes sense that the Buddhists could have been medical pioneers, even leaving aside the idea that doctors would have been disdained by the *brahmin* elite. Buddhism is all about the avoidance of suffering. Just as the Buddha's "Middle Way" discouraged extreme asceticism, it would have encouraged the elimination of painful illnesses. Then, too, the Buddhists were exhorted to reflect on the transience of physical existence and to contemplate dying bodies. In one passage that makes the point nicely, the Buddha enumerates the parts that make up the human body: "hair, nails, teeth, skin, flesh, sinews, bones, bone marrow, kidney, heart, liver, pleura, spleen, lungs, bowels, intestines, stomach, excrement, bile, phlegm, pus, blood, sweat, fat, tears, grease, saliva, mucus, and urine."[19]

Of course, the Āyurvedic authors themselves give no sign of Buddhist allegiance. To the contrary, we've seen them emphasizing the Vedic lineage of their art. This may, however, be a Hindu "veneer" laid over an originally non-Vedic body of thought.[20] On the other hand, as long as we're contemplating non-Vedic sources, what about the Greek ideas we mentioned above? It's almost irresistible to make comparisons, and perhaps draw historical connections, between Greek and Indian medical theories.[21] Most obviously there is the theory of humors. Admittedly, the Indians had three humors and not four, which aren't even three of the four Greek humors, since they didn't include wind. And maybe they aren't really conceived as humors but rather as pathogens. So perhaps this is not such an obvious parallel after all.

What about the centrality of breath in Āyurveda, then? This sounds like an idea also found in Greek medical literature, including the Hippocratic text *On Breaths*. The Hippocratics also appealed to local conditions ("airs, waters, and places") to explain illnesses, including epidemics. Much later in the Greek tradition we have Galen, some of whose ideas would meet with Caraka's approval. The good doctor must assess the condition of each individual patient, and master both theory and practice. Here too, though, there is room for doubt. The Sanskrit terminology of the *Saṃhitās* is innocent of Greek loan words, and no scholar has been able to find a smoking gun to prove Greek influence on Indian medicine or vice versa (appropriately enough, given that smoking and guns are both bad for your health). The parallels are suggestive and intriguing, but that's about all we can say with the current state of research.

24

PRACTICE MAKES PERFECT

PATAÑJALI'S *YOGA-SŪTRA*

If you enrolled in a yoga class, what would you expect to learn? Stretching techniques and better posture; an intense awareness of your body and your breath; an improved ability to focus; and perhaps even the art of meditation. But not the power to levitate, read minds, or foresee the future. For that you would presumably need to consult a Jedi master; the change of only one letter, from Yoga to Yoda, would make all the difference. Or would it? Just open the foundational text of the grand tradition of Yoga, and page down to the third chapter.[1] It promises that the adept *yogin* does indeed wield the magical powers just mentioned, and other powers besides: recall of previous lives, the ability to speak other languages, heightened senses, and supernatural stealth (3.16–40). This rather occult portion of the text is rarely highlighted in scholarly discussions of early Yoga, perhaps because interpreters find it embarrassing, or just irrelevant to the philosophical teaching of the *sūtras*. But it should not be discounted. The talk of supernatural powers fits with the overall message of Yoga, which is that we are capable of mastering, and ultimately transcending, nature itself.

Like the other foundational texts we've looked at, the *Yoga-sūtra* is written in a compressed and elliptical fashion, though the Yoga master who wrote it has less trouble with conventional grammar than Master Yoda. In fact the author in question shares the name of a famous grammarian, Patañjali, author of the *Great Commentary* on Pāṇini. As if that weren't enough, Patañjali is also said to be the incarnation of a divine serpent named Ananta.[2] We can, however, be confident that the grammarian Patañjali was not the Patañjali who wrote the *Yoga-sūtra;* whether either of them was really a snake god is a question for further research. And the confusion with names doesn't stop here. Like other *sūtra* texts, the *Yoga-sūtra* has an authoritative commentary or *bhāṣya,* which in this case is ascribed to "Vyāsa." This, too, may ring a bell, as it's the name of the bard who supposedly wrote or compiled the *Mahābhārata.* But "Vyāsa" here is probably just a generic name for a commentator. In fact recent philological work by Philipp Maas has revealed that the *Yoga-sūtra* and *Yoga-bhāṣya* were probably both written by one and the same author.[3] Apparently Patañjali followed custom by setting down his Yoga teaching in *sūtra* form, and then immediately provided his own exegesis rather than waiting for other commentators to come along. Maas dates the combined work (which he calls the *Yoga-śāstra*) to between AD 325 and 425, which would be long after the grammarian Patañjali, but right around the time at which Īśvarakṛṣṇa wrote his *Sāṃkhya-kārikā*.

This is not a mere historical coincidence. Yoga has an intimate relationship with Sāṃkhya, to the point that scholars sometimes speak of a combined "Yoga-Sāṃkhya" school. One particular sequence in the *Yoga-sūtra* (2.17–26) reads like a summary of ideas we find at greater length in Īśvarakṛṣṇa. It explains that when the "seer" is conjoined to "that which is seen," suffering is the inevitable result—a clear allusion to the Sāṃkhya idea that suffering can be ended only when we free ourselves from nature or *prakṛti* and identify ourselves with the pure consciousness that is *puruṣa*. Patañjali also invokes the dynamic forces called *guṇas* to explain the evolution of things out of the "unmanifest" principle of *prakṛti* (2.19, 4.13). If we turn from the *sūtra* to the commentary, we see him going even further in the direction of Sāṃkhya, showing how the many elements of its cosmology and psychology could be fitted into the apparently simpler account of the *Yoga-sūtra*. If we assume that the *sūtra* and commentary are really by the same person, then we must conclude that the Sāṃkhya system, in all its complexity, provides the framework for both Yoga texts. The *sūtra* simply leaves out a lot, as would be appropriate given its concise and condensed form, reserving the technical details for the commentary.

Do we even need to bother with the *Yoga-sūtra*, if its philosophical teaching just echoes what we find in the *Sāṃkhya-kārikā*? At the very least, the two texts do differ in purpose and emphasis. It's common to observe that Sāṃkhya offers "theory" where Yoga concentrates on "practice." The contrast isn't quite so neat as that, though. Both Sāṃkhya and Yoga emphasize that our goal is the higher knowledge or insight (*vijñāna, viveka*) that comes when we discriminate between nature and consciousness.[4] But it is true enough that the *Yoga-sūtra* is more practical in its orientation: where Īśvarakṛṣṇa provides a blueprint of the world and the individual person, Patañjali offers a user's manual. This is true to earlier uses of the terms *sāṃkhya* and *yoga*, not least in the *Bhagavad-gītā*, which also treats them as complementary strands of thought. We need the practical advice offered in Yoga, because liberation cannot be achieved just by intellectually understanding the difference between *prakṛti* and *puruṣa*. Freeing oneself from nature takes long practice and steady effort (1.12, 1.14).

The Sanskrit word we're translating as "practice" is *abhyāsa*, which literally means "repetition."[5] Patañjali makes this the focus of the second chapter of his *sūtra*, explaining the three techniques that make up what he calls "action yoga (*kriyā-yoga*)" (2.1). First, we should impose ascetic disciplines (*tapas*) upon ourselves, deliberately undergoing hunger and thirst, and making vows, which might commit us to silence or celibacy. Second, we should repeatedly recite certain words. This is an ancient practice within Vedic culture, which could involve memorized parts of sacred text or even just the single syllable *om* (on the use of such *mantras*, see Chapter 46). Third, we should engage in religious devotion, on which more presently. Together, these practices will help to eliminate the sources of affliction (*kleśas*), which include desires, the fear of death, and a sense of one's own individual self (*asmitā*, sometimes translated "egoity"; 2.2–3). Later on in the second chapter, Patañjali adds a further list, itemizing the eight so-called "limbs" of Yoga (2.29), which you have to say is eight more limbs than you'd expect from a snake god. They include ethical guidelines, control over posture and breath, withdrawing from the senses, and three kinds of meditation. This is the part of the text that corresponds to the ideas we most readily associate with yoga nowadays.

The central insight of this second chapter is a rather ironic one. In keeping with Sāṃkhya theory, we are seeking to wean ourselves away from mental and physical engagement, since it binds us to the world of nature. But we can only desist from such action by undertaking other actions.[6] Hence the term "action yoga." Through discipline and lengthy practice of both mind and body, we can teach the mind and body to be still, to avoid the tumult of "fluctuations" that arise as *prakṛti* is transformed by the *guṇas*. It's important that the stillness being sought here is indeed mental, not only physical. In place of Sāṃkhya's rather complicated analysis of the human mind as consisting of several powers, which together form the so-called "interior organ," Patañjali speaks of one simple mental faculty, the *citta*.[7] And he goes so far as to define Yoga as the cessation (*nirodha*) of activity within this mind (*citta-vṛtii*). Again, the *Yoga-sūtra* is perhaps taking a simpler approach than we find in the *Sāṃkhya-kārikā*, but the texts are in basic agreement.

On another point, though, many scholars have seen a strong contrast. We just mentioned that the third practice recommended by Patañjali is "devotion." Devotion to whom? The answer already comes in the first chapter of the *Yoga-sūtra*, where Patañjali introduces the concept of Īśvara, or God (1.23). He recommends that, instead of allowing ourselves to focus on or contemplate the self, we should instead pursue focus and contemplation (*samādhi*) of God (1.17–18, 1.23). We saw no such theistic component in the *Sāṃkhya-kārikā*: despite his name, Īśvarakṛṣṇa had nothing to say about a deity called Īśvara. Some interpreters have seen this as a fundamental divergence between Sāṃkhya and Yoga. But remember that Sāṃkhya does speak of a divine realm, which suggests that it is at the very least open to the existence of godlike beings. A divine being could simply be a particularly pure version of consciousness, relatively untouched by the turbulence of the natural world. This is, in fact, exactly what we find in the *Yoga-sūtra*. It says that Īśvara is a special sort of *puruṣa* (1.24) who is always liberated from the suffering that comes from attachment to nature.

Why though is it so hard for us to live like God? What prevents someone from reading the *Sāṃkhya-kārikā*, realizing that this Īśvarakṛṣṇa fellow knows what he's talking about, and just deciding on the spot to be liberated by identifying with *puruṣa*? An intellectualist answer might be that it is one thing to understand the teaching, and another to be sincerely convinced by it. But this is not Patañjali's way of seeing things. Instead he believes that our bondage to *prakṛti* is perpetuated by powerful habits (*saṃskāras*), which must be gradually subdued. Suppose you have a strong desire for almond croissants. It's all very well to realize that, so long as you keep wanting to have them, you will have to perform certain activities: paying for each croissant, eating it, immediately starting to wonder when you might get to eat another, worrying that the bakery may be closed next time you're in the mood for one, and so on. Even if you are convinced that this is going to bring you more suffering than pleasure, that will not just make the affection for almond croissants disappear. Your desire is a deep-seated habit or disposition, so you cannot just decide to abandon it. You have to *train* yourself not to want croissants. The training prescribed by Patañjali for such purposes is of course the threefold regimen of "action yoga."

Thus far we may seem to be dealing with a fairly commonsensical idea, about the difficulties of rehabituation. But Patañjali puts a distinctively ancient Indian twist on the process by describing it in terms of *karma* (2.12, 4.6–12). He says that our actions build up so-called "karmic deposits," which will bring fruits either in this or the next life. One implication is that each of us is born already burdened with *karma* from actions in previous lives. All this is more or less familiar from earlier theories of *karma* (see Chapter 6). But there's a puzzle lurking. If action causes *karma*, and *karma* prevents liberation, why does Patañjali recommend further actions as a means for achieving liberation? This sounds like the sort of "fight fire with fire" strategy that just leads to a larger conflagration. But perhaps it is not the action as such that causes *karma* to build up. Rather, it is the immediate fruits of the action we perform.[8] When you eat an almond croissant, it's not the eating as such, but the resulting pleasure that makes you want to have more croissants in the future. The solution, then, is to train oneself to disengage from the results of one's actions. Tailor-made for this purpose are the ascetic practices recommended in the *Yoga-sūtra*, which obviously involve actions that are not intended to yield enjoyable results. Recitation and devotion would also be activities that direct my attention to something other than my own urges and anxieties.

On this reading, Patañjali's advice aligns with the teaching of the *Bhagavad-gītā*. The path to liberation is not complete withdrawal from action, of the sort recommended by those early renouncers who resorted to the radical strategy of standing still until they starved to death. Instead we should seek detachment from the *fruits* of action. If this is right then the practitioner of yoga would still gradually disengage from the fluctuations of mental life, through long and patient practice. But that might not mean disengaging from practical life entirely. Which brings us back to the relationship between Yoga and Sāṃkhya. We described Sāṃkhya as a fundamentally dualist theory, which offers us a choice: either engage with the phenomenal world that evolved from *prakṛti*, or identify yourself with the pure consciousness that is *puruṣa*. At first Yoga seemed to be equally dualist. But what if there were a way to remain mentally aloof from the world of action even while continuing to live fully within that world? In that case the purpose of Yoga would not be to help us *escape* from nature, but to live with it in a way that involves no suffering for oneself or others.

This "anti-dualist" approach to Yoga has been put forth by modern-day interpreter Ian Whicher.[9] He points out that, even in Sāṃkhya, we hear only good things about one of the three *guṇas* that govern cosmic evolution and mental life. Turmoil and despondency are caused by *rajas* and *tamas*, the second and third of the *guṇas*. But the first one, *sattva*, has good connotations. It is "light" and connected to pleasant feelings. Whicher thus suggests that Yoga is a technique for eliminating the states of affliction that are caused by ignorance, desire, and concern for the self, all of them traced to *rajas* and *tamas*. This would leave intact the influences of *sattva*, which lead the person to engage with the world of *prakṛti* in what Whicher calls "a nonconflicting and unselfish manner."[10] However, this proposal hasn't been greeted with universal agreement. Some other scholars think that the purpose of Yoga is to eliminate *all* mental activity, even apparently beneficial activity.[11] After all doesn't Patañjali even *define* Yoga as cessation from all such activity?

The debate turns in part on what Patañjali means when he speaks of "cessation," or in Sanskrit *nirodha*. For Whicher, this does not actually mean eliminating or restraining the activity of the mind and body. He takes it to suggest that the mind remains *unaffected* even as it is involved in action. The adept of Yoga can achieve this so long as she does not confuse her real self with her phenomenal self. The goal is not to be sitting still in a cave or on a mountaintop with a completely empty mind. One can keep living an engaged life so long as one shifts one's perspective on that life, by identifying oneself with consciousness rather than the things of which one is conscious. In support of this Whicher points out that, if the fulfillment of Yoga involved complete disengagement, then it would be hard to explain the fact that Yoga gurus are active in teaching their disciples. This point was raised in earlier periods, when some asked why gurus offered teaching to students, given that they should surely have no desire to do so. One response was that teaching emerges spontaneously, much as we saw with Buddhist compassion, rather than being pursued out of an otherwise unfulfilled desire.

A similar puzzle arises in connection with the divine Īśvara. We are told that he is pure *puruṣa,* living outside of time. Yet Īśvara's very timelessness means that he has always been there, so that he was able to instruct the first adepts of Yoga in the long distant past (1.26).[12] This is a puzzling statement in several ways. How can God be a guru or teacher, and how can a timeless being relate to creatures who are subject to time? Patañjali doesn't say. But the little that he does say indicates that Īśvara, at least, can be simultaneously liberated and involved in a form of selfless action that gives rise to no suffering. It only makes sense that we should aspire to do the same. Another clue in the same direction is found in the commentary (on 1.12), where "Vyāsa"—who as we saw is probably Patañjali himself—speaks about the instruction to eliminate desire and engage in constant practice (*abhyāsa*). The latter is meant to yield a "smooth flow" in the mind. Again, the goal is apparently to have unconflicted, unattached mental activity that remains untouched by fluctuations of any kind. This is significantly different from banishing activity entirely.

It's an alluring picture of the good life. The Yoga adept can, as it were, have her almond croissant and eat it too, as long as she remains unaffected as she does so. But at the very end of the *Yoga-sūtra,* Patañjali certainly sounds like he is recommending total withdrawal from the world of the *guṇas,* as he speaks of achieving *kaivalya,* meaning "aloneness" (4.30–4). He says that at this stage *karma* and change come to an end, that everything in the world of nature has served out its purpose because *puruṣa* has returned to itself. This sounds like more than just a shift in point of view, though it could all just indicate that *puruṣa* is "alone" in the sense that it sees without being attached to what it is seeing.[13] The same ambiguity arises in other passages. Earlier Patañjali has defined different stages of meditative contemplation, or *samādhi.*[14] As we make progress, we may take part in a kind of contemplation that still involves some kind of knowledge (*samprajñata-samādhi*). But ultimately what we want is a pure contemplative state that has no object (*nir-bīja,* 1.51). All karmic burdens have been eliminated and the mind is at peace. Is this because nothing is happening, or because the adept's mind is not changed by what is happening?

25

WHERE THERE'S SMOKE THERE'S FIRE

GAUTAMA'S *NYĀYA-SŪTRA*

These days most philosophers are specialists. They work in metaphysics, ethics, epistemology, the philosophy of mind, or what have you, and would not claim expertise in all these sub-disciplines. In earlier historical periods of European thought, by contrast, philosophers were more likely to be all-rounders. Plato is famous for his political theory and for his metaphysics of Forms, Hume for his critique of causation and his theory of ethical sentiment. Early Indian philosophy, though, seems more to have anticipated our contemporary scene. Given its devotion to scriptural exegesis, it was natural for Mīmāṃsā to focus on questions about language, while Vedānta naturally followed the Upaniṣads in investigating the nature of the self. Likewise, we said that Sāṃkhya and Yoga formed something of a double-act, devoting themselves respectively to theoretical and practical philosophy. The same sort of thing happens with our final pair of post-Vedic schools: Nyāya specializes in logic and epistemology, Vaiśeṣika in metaphysics.

Of course we shouldn't exaggerate here. It's not as if there were ancient Indian philosophy departments with one chair for each of the six schools, with controversies over whether to think about finally hiring a Buddhist. Some figures did have interests spanning the supposed boundaries of the schools. The ultimate example was Vācaspati Miśra, who in the tenth century wrote works within the traditions of Nyāya, Sāṃkhya, Yoga, Mīmāṃsā, and Vedānta and was thus honored with the title "master of all systems." Then, too, we find each school exploring a range of issues rather than sticking relentlessly to its distinctive topic. Nyāya is no exception here, as it has a good deal to say about liberation and rebirth. Still, Nyāya is first and foremost a tradition of logical and epistemological reflection, which grew out of a longer history of thinking about knowledge and its sources. We have already touched on a number of texts that discuss *pramāṇas*, the sources of knowledge. Most recently we saw the medical treatise *Caraka-saṃhitā* listing the *pramāṇas* while explaining how doctors have come to learn about the human body and its treatment (see Chapter 23). Nyāya is going to specialize in expounding the *pramāṇas*, and face up to skeptical attack on the possibility of knowledge, coming especially from the Buddhists.

This intellectual mission is mentioned explicitly in the foundational texts of Nyāya, which as usual consist of a set of canonical *sūtras* followed by a *bhāṣya* commentary, and then further exegetical works. We'll mostly be discussing the *Nyāya-sūtra* itself, which according to latest estimates was written in the first or second century AD, as well as the commentary by Vātsyāyana, written around the year 450.[1] We will also make occasional mention of Uddyotakara, who wrote a further commentary (*vārttika*) on Vātsyāyana in the late sixth century. The foundational *Nyāya-sūtra* is ascribed to a man named Gautama, also known as Akṣapāda. His *sūtras*, or perhaps we should say the *sūtras* that were eventually collected under his name, are divided into five books. In addition to analysis of argument structure and the sources of knowledge, they give advice on the proper way to conduct debates. Occasionally the brief is extended to the kind of metaphysical issues associated more with Vaiśeṣika, like the nature of parts and wholes, the existence of atoms, and universals.

The commentator Vātsyāyana is in no doubt as to what makes Nyāya distinctive, though. He says:

> Nyāya is the examination of things with the help of evidence (*pramāṇa*). An argument based on observation and received belief is called an *anvīkṣā* or reconsideration, and the discipline known as *ānvīkṣikī* or *nyāya* is that which pertains to such arguments. (1.1.1)

We've actually seen that word *ānvīkṣikī* before, though you may not remember it since this was back in Chapter 2. We mentioned there that in his political treatise the *Arthaśāstra*, Kauṭilya mentioned *ānvīkṣikī* as one of four branches of learning. The word means something like "rational investigation," and in Kauṭilya presumably has a rather broad meaning. Now Vātsyāyana is trying to appropriate the term for his own school, applying it specifically to the study of arguments based on evidence.

He makes these remarks in the course of commenting on the opening sentence of the *Nyāya-sūtra*. It lists sixteen items that, according to Gautama, comprise the subject matter of the Nyāya system. The list spans epistemological concepts—starting right off the bat with the term *pramāṇa* itself—and elements of inquiry and debate, like destructive criticism (*vitaṇḍā*) and intentional distortion of the opponent's view (*chala*). Vātsyāyana states that "without the specific mention of these items for study, *ānvīkṣikī* would have been a mere 'study of the self' or spiritual discipline like the Upaniṣads. By its discussion of the topics listed it is shown to have its unique subject matter" (1.1.1). In other words, this list encapsulates what distinguishes the investigative, critical discipline of Nyāya from the philosophies of path and purpose we examined in detail early in this series, and for that matter from the agendas pursued by other Vedic schools. A close examination of this list will thus reveal how the Naiyāyikas conceived of their own intellectual endeavor.

Let's begin with the term that opens the treatise, *pramāṇa*.[2] This refers, roughly speaking, to a means of getting at truth or acquiring knowledge. Gautama's Nyāya recognizes four such *pramāṇas*: perception (*pratyakṣa*), inference (*anumāna*), comparison (*upamāna*), and testimony (*śabda*) (1.1.3). In Gautama's initial list, the word *pramāṇa* is followed by the term *prameya*, which just means whatever one comes to know by using a *pramāṇa*. Thus perception counts as a *pramāṇa*, because it lets me know the objects around me, whereas an object that I actually see or hear would be a *prameya*. In Nyāya, and especially in the commentary by Vātsyāyana, knowledge is regarded as a form of activity. Just as we might say that someone "cuts a tree with an axe," so we can say that someone "sees a tree with her eyes," and in general, someone "knows something by means of some *pramāṇa*." Yet again we're seeing here the influence of the grammatical reflections found in Pāṇini, who made action central to the analysis of sentences, and explained other grammatical elements as contributing factors, like the instrument or purpose of the action.

For Vātsyāyana, the purpose of knowledge is indeed crucially important. He begins his commentary by saying that knowledge is needed in order to secure any desired objective (*artha*). Each of us exerts effort only for the sake of achieving such an objective. Here one might think of an idea we encountered in Mīmāṃsā, that it is a sacrificer's desire that makes a ritual incumbent upon the sacrificer. No desire, no action. Now Vātsyāyana adds: no knowledge, no result! After all, how can you get what you want when you literally don't know what you're doing? Vātsyāyana invokes the point again later on, when he responds to the standard skeptical argument that any means of knowledge must be ratified by some further means of knowledge, leading to a regress (2.1.20). Thus, the skeptic is suggesting, we cannot trust a *pramāṇa* like perception unless some further perception tells us that it is trustworthy. No, replies Vātsyāyana. If this were true then "the activities of practical life" would be impossible, since the only way we ever achieve anything that we want is by knowing how to get it. This applies to mundane goals like wealth and pleasure, and to more exalted goals too. Nyāya competes with the Buddhists not only on the epistemological front, by refuting skeptical arguments like the one just mentioned, but also on what we may, with apologies to Monty Python, call the liberation front. The elimination of suffering, promised by Buddhists and Naiyāyikas alike, is one more objective that can be achieved through knowledge and through knowledge alone.

As this little bit of dialectic reminds us, in Indian philosophy it was never enough to be right; your opponents had to be wrong. Which brings us to the other major interest of Nyāya, the theory of debate. Gautama says there are two kinds: honest debate (*vāda*), whose aim is to ascertain the truth, and tricky debate (*jalpa*), in which the goal is to defeat the opponent at all costs, even if this means resorting to underhanded tactics (1.2.1). A third style of debate (*vitaṇḍā*) is that used by skeptics, who wish to refute the claims of all philosophical doctrines without advancing any positive stance of their own. The master of this third style lived at about the same time that the *Nyāya-sūtra* was given its current form. He was the Buddhist thinker Nāgārjuna, and posed a formidable challenge to the whole project of Nyāya (see Chapters 36–8).

Vātsyāyana dismisses this sort of general skepticism as being incoherent. Merely by rejecting the positive theories of other philosophers, the skeptics are forced to make positive claims of their own, because to deny a proposition is to assert its opposite. If the Buddhists deny that there is an enduring self, this means asserting that there is *no* enduring self, which is itself a philosophical claim. Whether Nāgārjuna can rise to this challenge is something we'll have to decide later. For now, we want to point out a more subtle way that the Naiyāyikas part ways with their skeptical opponents. Given the centrality of the *pramāṇas* to Nyāya thought, you might expect that they would be at pains to defend the legitimacy of these ways of knowing. But this isn't exactly right. Instead, the Nyāya thinkers tend simply to assume that the *pramāṇas* must be reliable. Theirs is a theory of "default trust" in our cognitions.[3] This may sound familiar: it sounds like the "innocent until proven guilty" epistemology of Mīmāṃsā.

The two schools are indeed in basic agreement on this, and Nyāya supplies a further argument that can be used against skeptics who refuse to assume that the *pramāṇas* do indeed provide knowledge. Uddyotakara puts it like this: "false cognitions are imitations of correct cognitions. Therefore you must provide some example of correct cognition." In other words false cognitions, such as those we have in perceptual illusions or dreams, can only be called "false" in contrast to other, true cognitions. Vātsyāyana already provides an example to make the same point. Suppose I see a wooden post from a distance and think it is a person (4.2.34). Obviously in this case perception has gone wrong, so it is not functioning to provide me with knowledge. Yet this very same case also shows that perception does sometimes succeed in giving me knowledge. If I had never correctly perceived a human being, I would not be in a position to perceive a wooden post incorrectly as a person.

So much for the destructive kind of debate practiced by the skeptic, which Uddyotakara denounced as mere "quibbles," even though he took them seriously enough to rise to the defense of Gautama's philosophy.[4] What about the more productive, "honest" sort of debate, which actually seeks truth? This practice forms the basis of the Nyāya method of philosophical inquiry. Such an inquiry, thinks Gautama, is a process by which we move from an initial uncertainty about a given thing, to understanding that it has certain properties. The procedure involves seven essential ingredients: doubt, purpose, observational data, background principles, "five-limbed" argument, hypothetical argument, and final decision. Let's examine each of these in turn.

We begin with the initial doubt (*saṃśaya*) that launches the investigation. It always takes the form of wondering whether a given object has some feature or not. Within this broad category, there are five more specific types of doubt (1.1.23). There is the ordinary sort of doubt when an object is perceived in outline, but its specific character is unclear. We just mentioned an example like this, the wooden post mistaken for a person. Then there is the sort of doubt where the nature of an object is known, but its properties are unknown. We might wonder whether sound, like the noise of something breaking, is a quality of air or a movement in the air.[5] There is also the sort of uncertainty that occurs when two contradictory statements are made concerning the same object, and we are unsure which statement is true. Furthermore there are doubts about whether a thing is real at all, or only an illusion, like the appearance of water in a desert mirage. Finally, we might doubt whether an object that we cannot see is really there, such as the giraffe that may or may not be in the kitchen.

Of course you probably wouldn't worry that you may have a giraffe in the kitchen unless you had a good reason to think, or hope, that this is the case. And rightly so, from Gautama's point of view. He is not encouraging us to engage in idle speculation, or to explore every doubt we can think of, no matter how remote. In a rational inquiry, there should be some purpose for inquiring (*prayojana*) (1.2.24). And this is the second element on Gautama's list. Like knowing, inquiring is an action and always has some goal. In this case it is a goal pursued by more than one person. All this is framed as a method of debate, and for debate to proceed successfully the parties to the dispute need some shared common ground. Hence the next items on the list. The debate must proceed on the basis of certain background principles (*siddhānta*) and also empirical data, the so-called "corroborative instances (*dṛṣṭānta*)," to which either side can appeal. Political disputes are often fruitless because this condition is not satisfied: if two sides disagree about all the facts, they aren't likely to have a useful conversation about how to respond to the facts. Assumptions that aren't shared can also be useful in debate, though. If a disputant produces an argument which contradicts a doctrine of his own school, and this is pointed out by the opponent, then his argument is undermined. Sometimes philosophers offer proofs that only work according to the premises of their own school (1.2.29), which may be useful among allies but will cut no ice in a debate with rival schools. And of course we sometimes grant premises for the sake of argument, simply to facilitate the inquiry.

These are the preconditions for debate; now Gautama sets out the ground rules along which the debate should proceed. For the first time in India, we have here in the *Nyāya-sūtra* a schematic analysis of valid argument patterns. In general, Gautama says, a good argument runs as follows (1.1.32). We know that some object has a first property, because it has some second property that is always found together with the first property (the second property "pervades" the first).[6] The classic example is that where there is smoke, there is fire. So if I see smoke on a mountain I can infer that there is a fire on the mountain. The inference is only a good one if the two properties have the right relation. I can only be confident about the fire if there is really fire *wherever* there is smoke. Gautama formalizes this with a "five-limbed" argument scheme. First, I state the thesis to be proved: there is a fire on the mountain. Second, I cite the reason: it's because I see smoke up there. Third, I invoke a universal rule and give an example to illustrate: where there is smoke, there is fire, just like at home in the kitchen. Fourth and fifth, I apply the universal rule and draw my conclusion: there is smoke on the mountain so there must be fire there.

Now, there are several odd things about this analysis. For one thing, why do I need to mention an example? Why bother pointing out that we've seen fire produce smoke in kitchens, like that time the giraffe forgot to turn the oven off? Giving an example doesn't seem logically necessary. Yet it makes good sense in the context of a debate, since the goal is to convince the other side that the universal rule is a valid one. Another problem is that the last step seems rather superfluous. At the very beginning I already stated the thesis that there is fire, so why repeat this at the end? Again, though, it makes sense in a debating context. It's one thing for me to tell you what I am going to prove or state it as a conjecture, another to state that I have proved it, even if I do so in the same words ("there is fire on the mountain"). Of course, Gautama's procedure can also be used in philosophical contexts. His *Nyāya-sūtra* includes a nice case where we are shown that sound is not eternal (2.2.13–33).[7] The universal rule applied here is that everything that is produced is also eventually destroyed, as for instance a jar (remember, you have to give an example!). Since sound is produced it too must eventually be destroyed. Therefore sound is non-eternal.

This isn't the only argument form described by Gautama, though. One of the most interesting elements of philosophical inquiry in his system is called *tarka*.[8] This means hypothetical or counterfactual reasoning: "if this were true, then that would be true, but that isn't true, so this isn't either." For example: "if there were really a giraffe in the kitchen, it would be making a lot of noise. But I don't hear anything, so there is no giraffe in there." This is a style of reasoning also used by the Mādhyamika Buddhists (who call it a *prasaṅga*). It is useful for philosophers because they can use it to eliminate rival theories. In fact we've already seen it in action earlier in this chapter: if, as the skeptic claimed, there were no valid means of acquiring knowledge, we could never get through everyday life successfully. But we do get through everyday life successfully, so there must be some valid means of acquiring knowledge.[9]

Tarka is such a powerful form of argument that you might think that it too would count as a means of knowing. Yet Nyāya denies that this sort of counterfactual reasoning is a *pramāṇa*. Why?[10] The problem might seem to be that we can only use *tarka* to rule things out. It tells me that there is no giraffe in the kitchen but couldn't tell me that there *is* a giraffe in the kitchen. But that seems wrong. After all, we just used it to establish the positive, and highly significant, thesis that there are valid means of knowing. More likely the problem is that *tarka* doesn't really give us any direct basis for knowing something, or for understanding that it is the case. It just shows us that something must be true, given *other* things we know: I perceive directly that the kitchen is quiet and only indirectly infer that there is no giraffe there. Another problem may have been that *tarka* reasoning requires me to hypothesize something that is not true. If there *were* a giraffe in the kitchen, which there isn't, then it would be making a terrific racket. The Naiyāyikas may have hesitated to allow their precious *pramāṇas* to be tainted by the assumption of a falsehood, even if it is done on the way to proving something true.

26

WHAT YOU SEE IS WHAT YOU GET

NYĀYA ON PERCEPTION

Good philosophers should always define their terms, and the authors of the foundational texts of Nyāya were nothing if not good philosophers. So in his *Nyāya-sūtra* Gautama does pause to explain key terms in his theory, and this feature of the text is highlighted by Vātsyāyana. Like other commentators, he wants to bring out the underlying logic and structure in the *sūtras*, which at first glance may look like nothing more than a list of vaguely connected aphorisms. So he introduces a distinction between three kinds of remarks made by Gautama: "naming" *sūtras*, which introduce a topic or concept for analysis; "defining" *sūtras*, which offer a definition of the concept in question; and "critical" *sūtras*, which examine and evaluate the adequacy of the proposed definition.

Of course, if the Naiyāyikas were *really* good philosophers, they would also tell us what they mean by giving a definition. And they were really good philosophers. So they tell us that a sound definition (*lakṣaṇa*) provides some property that is co-extensive with the concept to be defined. We should steer a middle course between overly narrow and overly wide definitions; showing that the proposed definition suffers from neither flaw is the purpose of the "critical" *sūtras*. Take their favorite example, the cow. We shouldn't define "cow" as "something with a tawny color," because not all cows are tawny—some are black and white. This definition therefore suffers from "under-coverage (*a-vyāpti*)." We shouldn't overreact to this by naming just any property that will include all cows. If we say that a cow is "something having horns," we will commit the opposite error of "over-coverage (*ati-vyāpti*)," since of course other things have horns, like reindeer and the James Brown band. A better definition would be, "something with a dewlap," since all cows and only cows have a dewlap (that's the loose skin that hangs from the cow's neck). Notice that Nyāya is settling for a fairly modest achievement here. The definition does not reveal the essence or nature of cows, but just gives us a reliable way of picking out cows from all other things.

This is also what Gautama seeks to do with his definition of "perception (*pratyakṣa*)." It comes early on in the *Nyāya-sūtra*, and of course in one of the aphorisms that Vātsyāyana designates as a "defining *sūtra*" (1.1.4; the "critical" examination comes only later, at 2.1.21–32). Here it is:

> A perceptual experience is that which is produced from "contact" between sense-faculty and object; is a "non-verbal (*avyapadeśya*)" awareness; does not deviate or err from its object (*avyabhicāra*); and is "definite (*vyavasāyātmaka*)" in character.

You have to say, this is pretty impressive. If you asked your friends over dinner what perception is, they would probably say something like, "you know, seeing stuff." Gautama has clearly put more thought into it, giving us a group of features that must all be satisfied before we can say that an experience counts as perception. He may have had polemical reasons for doing so. Gautama's historical influences are a matter of speculation, but it is reasonably certain that he's responding here to early Buddhist discussions of perception.

Early Buddhists tended to view perception as a kind of direct sensory acquaintance with sensible data, like colors, sounds, and smells. That doesn't sound much more advanced than what your friends came up with at dinner, but—as Buddhist skeptics liked to point out—appearances can be deceiving. The Buddhists gave perception a special place in their worldview. Remember that for them, suffering is caused by attachment to false ideas and constructs of the mind, such as the notion of a permanent self, and belief in essences that belong to everyday objects. Freedom from suffering means letting go of such attachments. This will leave us with nothing but simple perceptions, the remaining residue of mental life. This is why the Buddhist definition stresses the immediacy of our sense-experiences: this is perception untainted by false theoretical postulates. For all its complexity, the Nyāya definition has a different and in a way more humble objective. It just seeks to articulate our ordinary, commonsense notion of what constitutes a perceptual awareness.

With this in mind, let's have a look at the four parts of Gautama's definition. The first is that there must be a direct sensory connection or causal link between the object of perception and the perceiver. This makes good sense in ordinary cases of perception, as when you see a cow in a field. But what about seeing something in a mirror, through binoculars, or through a video camera? We would normally call these cases of perceptual experience. But do they really bring us into contact with the sense object, or only with an image of the object? We might try to save the definition by allowing for indirect contact through images and other representations, to account for the mediation of mirrors, binoculars, and so on. But it seems hard to believe that perceiving a representation of something is the same as perceiving that thing. Do I really see my sister when I look at a picture of her, and do you really hear her when I tell you what she said?

It seems clear then that Gautama has not said enough to explain the sort of "connection" involved in perception. But the commentators rise to the challenge. In his super-commentary on Vātsyāyana, Uddyotakara distinguishes six types of perceptual connection.[1] First of all there is direct conjunction, as between me and a pot when I see it on the stove top. Second, there is perceiving something that inheres in an object, like my seeing the blue color of the pot. Third, there is what inheres in something that inheres, for instance perceiving the universal property of blueness that resides in the pot's blue color. Fourth and fifth, I can also perceive *that* such properties, and *that* such universals, inhere in something. So there is a subtle distinction being made here, between seeing the blue of the pot, which was the second type of perception, and seeing that the property blue or the universal blueness is present in the pot, which is the fifth type. Sixth and finally, there is the connection between an object and its absence, as when I see that there is no pot in the kitchen.

Notice that for Uddyotakara, we perceive not just the objects themselves, but also their qualities, properties, and motions. This is crucial from the Nyāya point of view. Unlike the Buddhists, he wants to insist that blueness is objectively out there in the world, so I should be able to perceive it. Yet universal, abstract blueness cannot make me see blue, or anything else for that matter. For that to happen, blueness must inhere in some particular object, like the pot. My sense faculty is, as Uddyotakara puts it, directly "conjoined" with the object in which the universal inheres. Universals by their very nature are located in particulars, but I cannot see or hear them directly. I have to do so by perceiving the particulars in which they occur.

While this is perhaps controversial, the most surprising and provocative kind of perception mentioned by Uddyotakara is the last one. He claims that we can perceive *absences*.[2] This is part of a broader development within Nyāya. As the school evolves, it becomes increasingly known for its wholesale commitment to the reality of negative entities. Consider the classic cinematic study of not showing up, *Ferris Bueller's Day Off*. When Ferris' teacher sweeps his gaze across a room, he doesn't just see an empty chair where Ferris would normally sit. He sees that Ferris Bueller is not there; that is, he sees the absence of Ferris Bueller. But is this really plausible? If the teacher said, "I see that Ferris isn't here," wouldn't this just be a figure of speech? The later Buddhist Dharmakīrti would say that in such a case, we do not really perceive absence, but rather make an inference from a *lack* of perception (*anupalabdhi-hetu*). The teacher implicitly makes a sort of deduction: he does not perceive Ferris Bueller; if Ferris were here he would be perceived; therefore, Ferris is not here, and is presumably skipping school (again!).

Uddyotakara, however, is convinced that we really do sometimes perceive an absence. In fact absences can inhere in objects, just as colors do: the absence of Ferris is a qualifying property that resides in the chair where he normally sits. Already Gautama proposed an example that could help make this claim more plausible. Suppose I am told to get some cloths from a pile of fabric, and to take the ones that are *not* marked (2.2.8).[3] What I'm looking for is the absence of a mark on the cloth. When I see this absence, I know I should take the cloth. The issue may seem pedantic, yet it brings out a deep disagreement between the Nyāya and Buddhist epistemologies. The Naiyāyikas are determined to resist Buddhist attempts to expose the experienced world as one of conceptual fabrication (*prapañca*). For Nyāya, what you see is (for the most part) what you get: experience really does put the world in view.

Another aspect of this debate concerned the question of whether the senses connect with their objects in the more literal sense of being somehow physically connected to them.[4] Nyāya claims that when I see something my vision "reaches out" to the visible object. True to form, the Buddhists offer a battery of objections to this idea, which are rebutted by the Naiyāyikas. One of the Buddhist objections is that if vision really reached out to things, it would see closer things before seeing things that are further away: you would first be aware that your sight contacts a giraffe silhouetted against the full moon, and only thereafter be aware of seeing the moon. The Nyāya response is that vision does indeed contact more distant things slightly later, but the speed at which this happens is such that we are unaware of the lapse in time. They offer a lovely analogy. When I thrust a knife through a pile of flower petals, I am not aware of cutting through each petal separately, even though the knife must indeed pass through them one after another.

Let's finally move on now to the second clause of Gautama's definition of perception, which tells us that perceptual experience is "non-verbal." This may seem to be a concession to the Buddhists' claim that we should strip away conceptual generalizations from perceptual experience. But in fact the point is just the opposite. Gautama wants to say that, although I can indeed perceive something without classifying it in terms of some concept, I can also deploy concepts to enrich my perceptual experience. In other words it is possible to have a mere sensory connection with an object, without having the capacity to recognize what sort of object is being encountered. Your average ancient Indian would have been entirely unfamiliar with giraffes. So if you put a giraffe in front of an ancient Indian, she would be able to see it but would have no concept or word for what she was seeing (she might think it was a very tall cow, apart from the missing dewlap). The Buddhist account of perception makes it sound as if all perception is like this. Gautama disagrees. For him such unvarnished encounters with the world are not even the typical case. Those of us lucky enough to have familiarity with giraffes can perceive them *as* giraffes, and perceive *that* a given object is a giraffe. Later Naiyāyikas will call the first kind of perceiving "conception-free" (*nirvikalpaka*), and the second one "conception-loaded" (*savikalpaka*).[5] The point of this part of Gautama's definition is thus to admit that conception-free perception is possible, but he certainly does not want to concede to the Buddhist that all perceptual experience is non-verbal or non-conceptual. His understanding of human experience is expansive, whereas the Buddhists' is reductive.

The third clause of the definition is perhaps the most philosophically problematic. Gautama says that perception is "non-deviating." He presumably includes this clause to distinguish genuine perceptual experience from illusions, hallucinations, and other types of perceptual error.[6] A genuine perceptual experience must convey the truth of things. In a sense this is just what we'd expect from Gautama, since he dignifies perception with the status of being a *pramāṇa*, or means of knowing. And how could perception be a means of knowledge if it were sometimes in error? Unfortunately, Gautama's claim seems bizarre. Surely perceptions that are erroneous still count as perceptions? Of course the Nyāya thinkers are aware of the problem, and worry about such cases as taking a coiled piece of rope to be a snake. In this case there is a sensory connection with an object, namely the rope. But we would not want to say that a snake is being perceived, since thankfully there is no snake present. The whole point of perception is to provide us with knowledge of the world, and that is precisely what illusions fail to do. From this Gautama concludes that illusions cannot be counted as instances of genuine perceptual experience.

His stipulation that genuine perception is "non-deviating," in other words that it must convey knowledge, leads later Nyāya thinkers to develop a whole theory of cognitive error.[7] In every perceptual experience, whether veridical or erroneous, there is some thing that is somehow in contact with the senses. In our example this is the rope. Error occurs through the inaccurate application of a property to the thing in question. In this case, one wrongly applies the concept of a snake. Snakes are real, and so is the rope; it's just that there is no snakehood present in the rope. A further advantage of this analysis is that it can explain our ability to "see" that ice is cold, or that a flower is fragrant. Our Nyāya commentators say that in a case like this, I am recalling features that I perceived previously. Once I touched ice and felt that it was cold, and now when I encounter ice I can just see that it has this feature, without having to touch it. This is called "presentation through revived memory (*jñāna-lakṣaṇā-pratyāsatti*)." Such cases can count as legitimate perceptions, with vision drawing on the deliverances of touch or smell by using memory. Of course they can also give rise to illusions, like if one were to see a shard of glass as cold because one mistakes it for ice.

With all this the Naiyāyikas are presupposing the aforementioned distinction between concept-laden and concept-free perception. Our earlier example contrasted seeing a giraffe *as* a giraffe, rather than just as an inexplicable object taking up what we might, if we weren't afraid of frightening the giraffe, describe as the lion's share of our field of vision. Something similar happens in the illusion case. I am seeing the rope as a snake when in fact it doesn't have the property of snakehood, and that difference is enough to undermine my right to say that I'm having a genuine perception. Again, it is in the application of a concept that the possibility of error creeps in. The brute perception of the object itself is always immune to error. On this theory there are no outright misidentifications, in which you think you see one object but actually see another. There are only misdescriptions of the things that you see. This is because you are always at least having a brute, concept-free perception of the object in front of you, whether you take it to be a rope or a snake.

This Nyāya theory has its advantages, but it struggles to explain illusory cases where there is actually no object being perceived. Outright hallucinations would fall under this category, but also less deviant cases like seeing the blue sky. The problem here is not merely that the sky isn't really blue—it's that we aren't seeing the sky at all. The blue we see is just scattered sunlight. For Gautama's theory of perception to work in this case, there would have to be a real external object, the sky, which the viewer contacts with her senses, and onto which she superimposes the concept of blueness. Yet it seems instead that we have a perception without any object that can be the bearer of any property, whether truly or falsely ascribed. Taking a cue from the snake he keeps seeing, the Naiyāyika might try to slither out of this, by saying that the perceiver superimposes the property of blueness onto empty space. In other words, empty space would be the perceptual object. But this does not look terribly plausible.

Finally, let's have a look at the fourth of Gautama's conditions: that perceptual experience must be "of definite character." According to Vātsyāyana, Gautama has in mind here cases in which, although I am in sensory contact with a certain object, I cannot tell what sort of object it is. Consider again the example we discussed in the last chapter, where you see something at a distance and are uncertain whether it is a wooden post or a person. Let's suppose it is in fact a person. Are you then perceiving the person? Gautama says no. Genuine perceptual experiences must leave no room for doubt. The mere possibility that what you are seeing is a wooden post prevents you from having a real perception, and prevents the experience from being a *pramāṇa*. This fits with Gautama's earlier claim that perception may be "nonverbal" or concept-free. That kind of rudimentary perceptual experience is not infected by doubt, since it involves seeing the object out there neither as a person, nor as a wooden post, nor as anything else.[8]

As we saw in our initial look at Nyāya, this is a tradition devoted to the art of debate, as much as to the sources of knowledge. And debate is never far below the surface, even when Gautama is giving us what may look like straightforward definitions. We've seen that his treatment of perception is directed against the Buddhists, in ways brought out and made explicit by the commentators, and at some places in the *Nyāya-sūtra* Gautama engages with opponents more openly. In one passage he considers a (probably) Buddhist argument to the effect that all our perceptual claims are really disguised inferences (2.1.31). When I look at an object, I never see the whole thing but only the part that is facing me; the near surface of the body of a giraffe, say. So when I say that I perceive the giraffe what I really mean is that, having seen the part of the giraffe that is facing me, I infer that there is a whole giraffe. This too may seem like mere pedantry. It's not as if there are front halves of giraffes running around without back halves of giraffes connected to them. Besides, as Gautama points out, the argument seems to concede that I can perceive *something* without making an inference: I can perceive the part of the giraffe that is facing me (2.1.32).

But as with the giraffe, there is more going on here than meets the eye. Remember that Buddhists deny that whole entities exist. There are only collections of parts, a point made in that famous passage from the *Milinda-pañhā*, in which the Buddhist sage Nāgasena argued that a whole chariot is really just a collection of parts (see Chapter 8). With such illustrations the Buddhists are driving toward their conception of persons as mere collections of mental and physical processes, which they call *skandhas*. In this context, when Gautama insists that we do perceive a whole giraffe, he is making a controversial philosophical thesis. And he has the metaphysics to back up that thesis. Just as the universal blueness is present in a giraffe that has fallen into a very large pot of blue paint, so the whole giraffe is "present in," or "inheres in," each of the giraffe's parts. This means that we can perceive wholes in just the same way we perceive universals. We experience blue by perceiving the object that has blueness, and perceive a whole by perceiving whichever part makes itself available to sensation. In this way, Gautama manages to fend off the Buddhist claim that all "perception" of objects involves inference. But this is not to say that Gautama underrates the role of inference in acquiring knowledge. To the contrary, he makes inference another *pramāṇa* alongside perception, and gives us a whole theory of how inferences work. We'll see next that, as with perceptual illusions, he has plenty to say about what is happening when inferences go wrong.

27

STANDARD DEDUCTIONS

NYĀYA ON REASONING

According to the Nyāya school, we can know about the world around us simply by perceiving it. We've just seen Gautama and his commentators offering a spirited defense of perception as a source of knowledge. Our senses tell us about things and their properties, and even about absences. But let's face it, we aren't going to be able to get through life working with nothing but perceptions. Suppose you are an ancient Indian walking through a forest. You hear a distinctive, low growling sound, unmistakably the sort of sound made by a tiger. Fortunately, you are familiar with the right way to handle such a situation: run like hell. But to apply this rule, you have to do more than perceive the sound. You need to make an *inference*. You do not run from the sound, but from the unseen tiger whose presence you infer from the sound. As this example shows, your ability to make inferences is crucial to your survival, just as much as your ability to perceive. Gautama duly lists inference alongside perception as a *pramāṇa*, or source of knowledge.

The close link between these two *pramāṇas* is indicated by the Sanksrit term for inference, which is *anu-māna*, meaning "that which follows after perception." It is inference that allows us to go beyond what is directly perceived to that which we cannot perceive. It may be hidden like the tiger in the trees, or it may be the sort of thing that cannot be perceived at all, like the illness whose presence we infer from the symptoms it causes in the body. We choose the example advisedly. In setting out his theory of inference, Gautama seems to have been influenced by early medical works like the *Caraka-saṃhitā*. Diagnosis is a paradigm case of inference. Cough and fever are signs of pneumonia, which is less dangerous than a tiger but still nothing to sneeze at. In Indian discussions of inference, however, the standard example is one with which we're already familiar: "the mountain has fire because it has smoke." Here, what we perceive is smoke on the distant hillside. From this sign, we can arrive at knowledge of the presence of an unseen fire.

Philosophers who like to show off their knowledge of Latin would call the smoke a *probans* and the fire a *probandum*, meaning respectively "that which offers proof" and "that which is proven." The Nyāya thinkers, who were understandably not so strong on scholastic Latin terminology, called the smoke a *hetu* or *liṅga*, meaning "mark" or "sign." A sign must always be present in the object about which we make an inference, which is called the *pakṣa*: the mountain where smoke is observed, or the trees from which emanate the disconcerting growl. Then there is the thing whose presence we infer from the sign in that object, which is called the *sādhya* or *sādhya-dharma*, for instance the fire on the mountain or the tiger in the trees. As we noted in our previous discussion of the smoke and fire example, Nyāya logicians also gave great weight to the ability to mention an example (*dṛṣṭānta*), such as fire in the kitchen, which also produces smoke. In other words, our inferences should be supported by naming a second case where a similar sign revealed the presence of a similar signified thing. Hence when telling you why you should have that cough checked out, I might explain that I knew a guy with these same symptoms who died of pneumonia.

Of course, the fact that you can give one parallel example doesn't mean that your inference reliably yields knowledge. Suppose you see fire on a mountain and infer that there must be smoke. This wouldn't be an acceptable form of reasoning. True, fire sometimes produces smoke, but we've also seen fiery things that *didn't* produce smoke. So fire is not a dependable sign of smoke. Come to think about it, tiger sounds aren't an absolutely reliable sign of tigers, either. Perhaps someone is hiding in the woods doing an incredibly realistic tiger impression, or playing tiger sounds from a tape recorder (younger readers may want to ask their parents what a "tape recorder" is). Clearly, if the Naiyāyikas are going to convince us that inferences are in some cases unimpeachable sources of knowledge, they owe us a story about which sorts of signs are reliable indicators.

We can piece together just such a story from remarks made by Gautama and his commentator Vātsyāyana (*Nyāya-sūtra* 1.1.5, 1.1.34–5, 1.2.4–9).[1] Gautama thinks that there are three kinds of dependable sign. He calls them *pūrvavat* ("based on what is prior"), *śeṣavat* ("based on a remainder"), and *sāmānyatodṛṣṭa* ("observation of a generality"). The original meaning of these three terms is obscure, and even the earliest commentators were unsure what exactly they meant. Vātsyāyana was so uncertain that he offered two alternative interpretations. His first suggestion is that Gautama means reasoning from cause to effect, from effect to cause, and from a generalization to a particular case. Hence the first type would be like saying it will rain because of the large black cloud; the second would be like deducing that it has been raining because the river is swollen; the third that the sun must be moving at the moment, even though it doesn't look like it, because over a longer period of time it is observed to change position. Despite the rather humble examples, we can credit Vātsyāyana with sketching out an account of scientific inference and prediction. His three types of sign have obvious applications in medicine, and the case of the sun's motion suggests how his ideas might be relevant to a field like astronomy.

But as we say, this is only one of two interpretations offered by Vātsyāyana. His second possible reading would assign Gautama's three technical terms to three entirely different sorts of reasoning. We could take the first term, "based on what is prior," to refer to all sorts of causal inference—so this would include all the sorts of inference canvassed in the previous interpretation. The second term, "based on a remainder," might refer to reasoning by process of elimination. Vātsyāyana's example is "sound is a substance, because it is not a universal, not a quality, not a motion, and so on." Here we envision an exhaustive range of possibilities and then eliminate all but one. We might think of the way doctors use tests to rule out possible diagnoses, in order to settle on one particular kind of bad news. Or we might think of Sherlock Holmes' famous remark that "when you have eliminated the impossible, whatever remains, however improbable, must be the truth." Third and finally, Gautama's idea of "observing a generality" could mean that we can assign a property to something because of the class of things to which it belongs. You might infer that tigers are predators from the fact that they are cats, since all cats are predators. Vātsyāyana gives the example, "Mental states are qualities; qualities have subjects. Therefore, there is a subject of mental states, namely the self." If we still hadn't noticed that this whole discussion of inference is important for philosophical method as well as for medical diagnosis and safe passage through forests, this example should set us straight.

And as we know, the Naiyāyikas are very keen on the idea of giving examples. Elsewhere in the *Nyāya-sūtra* Gautama explains why, saying that there are actually two kinds of example that can serve to motivate an inference. On the one hand there are "positive" examples which turn on a similarity (1.1.34). This would be like the favorite case of smoke indicating fire on a mountainside, which also happens in the kitchen. On the other hand there are "negative" examples, where we allude to a situation where the sign is absent, and the thing signified is also absent (1.1.35). Instead of referring to the kitchen, we might refer to the surface of a lake. Here the reasoning trades on a disanalogy instead of an analogy: "in the case of lake water, neither smoke nor fire are found; so, by disanalogy, the mountain, which does have smoke, should have fire as well." Whether we give a positive or negative example, such reasoning moves straightforwardly from one case to another, from kitchen or lake to mountainside. No appeal is made to any law of nature or universal rule.

While this may seem a bit naive, there is in fact much to be said in favor of such case-based reasoning. The *Nyāya-sūtra* offers numerous illustrations for this pattern of reasoning: seeing ants carrying their eggs, one infers that it will rain; seeing a full and swiftly flowing river, one infers that it has been raining; seeing smoke, one infers the presence of an unseen fire. Of course one might delve deeper and try to understand why certain signs are regularly linked to certain things. We may have observed that ants often carry their eggs around when rain is imminent, but remain mystified as to how ants are able to predict the weather in advance. The same applies to a kind of inference we have encountered before, which uses a sampling procedure. From the salty taste of one drop of sea water we infer that the whole sea is salty; by tasting one grain of rice we infer that all the rice is cooked. Of course we make inferences like these constantly in everyday life. We effortlessly and tacitly assume that there is a commonality between the sample and the rest. This one grain was in the same pan as all the other grains, was heated in the same water for the same amount of time, and so on. Hence, if it is ready to eat so is the rest of the rice.

Since case-based reasoning too may go awry, it is a matter of cardinal importance to be able to distinguish between genuine and bogus cases of resemblance. This is the subject of the whole final book of the *Nyāya-sūtra*, a section that some modern scholars have seen as an independent work rather than as an integral part of the text. Whether or not it was written separately, this last book shows us that Gautama was just as interested in how things can go wrong as he was in how we get things right. Argument based on a false resemblance suffers from the fallacy known as *jāti*: merely apparent commonality between an example and a locus. This would be like that example of inferring the presence of a tiger in the trees, on the grounds that that sound has in the past come from a real tiger, but in the case at hand the sound is coming from a tape recorder.

Gautama in fact identifies no fewer than five sorts of fallacy that undermine arguments and inferences (1.2.4–9). The Sanskrit term for "fallacy" is *hetvābhāsa*, which literally means something that has merely the appearance of being a sign. The importance of fallacies has partially to do with the Nyāya interest in debate: spotting a flaw in an opponent's argument is a sure way to win. As we have seen, though, Gautama is also interested in the dependability of scientific prediction and medical prognosis. Then, too, working out the ways that arguments can go astray is an indirect way of showing what a sound argument is. If you manage to avoid all five kinds of fallacy, you can be sure that you are reasoning correctly. Gautama named his five fallacies the "deviating (*savyabhicāra*)," the "incoherent (*viruddha*)," the "indecisive (*prakaraṇasama*)," the "same predicament (*sādhyasama*)," and the "mistimed (*kālātīta*)," which coincidentally are also the five pitfalls faced by teenagers when they start dating. Let's take them each in turn.[2]

First: the deviating. This fallacy occurs when a sign is present but the inferred property is not. Vātsyāyana's illustration is, "sound is eternal, because it is intangible." The problem here is that we can name other cases of intangible things that are not eternal, such as a mental state like pain.[3] Pain is intangible but thankfully not eternal; it will go away eventually. Turning this around, the implication is that a dependable sign must not "deviate" from the property inferred from the sign. It must be the case that "wherever the sign occurs, so does the signified." Gautama is in effect warning us that it is not enough to provide an analogy. There needs to be a universal rule connecting sign with signified. Only if tiger noises *always* signify tigers can you confidently infer that there is a tiger in the trees, though you might want to run anyway just to be on the safe side. The universal rule (*vyāpti*) was to become a major topic of philosophical inquiry in later Nyāya, with a central contribution coming from the thirteenth-century author Gaṅgeśa in his celebrated *Five Definitions of Vyāpti*.

Second: the incoherent. By this Gautama means that the conclusion of an argument should not contradict other well-established beliefs. Here we are not dealing with a purely formal defect, internal to a single inference. His point is rather that we reason within a larger set of commitments. Even if an inference seems sound, if it clashes with your other firmly held beliefs then it would be rational to doubt your premises. A rather strained example given by the Naiyāyikas runs like this: fire is cold because it is a substance. Their thought here is that this inference is more plausible than it sounds, because all substances other than fire and fiery things are indeed cold. But of course the reasoning is fallacious, because fire is the one exception to the general rule. We can avoid falling into the trap by calling on our wider net of beliefs, which raise a warning flag by telling us that fire is in fact hot, so the argument must have gone wrong.

Third: the indecisive. In the situation envisaged here, two equally strong arguments lead to opposite conclusions. Although neither can be faulted on formal grounds, we should reserve judgment as to whether either one is any good. Consider the rather trivial argument, "sound is eternal, because it is eternal." The argument is formally valid, because it is a tautology and all tautologies are valid, though not very informative. (Compare: "Socrates is mortal, and all mortals are mortal; therefore, Socrates is mortal.") So why is this not a good argument? Because we might equally well reason, "sound is non-eternal, because it is non-eternal." In the absence of any ground for preferring one of these tautologies over the other, neither can be accepted. The point is reminiscent of the skepticism practiced by ancient Greek thinkers like Sextus Empiricus.[4] They tried to induce "suspension of judgment" in their readers by arguing on both sides of a given philosophical issue: if there are persuasive considerations on both sides, the only rational thing to do is withhold assent. But of course Gautama's identification of the indecisive fallacy is not intended to support skepticism. While cautioning us to avoid making inferences in the face of an equally compelling contrary inference, he assumes that this problem will arise only occasionally and not be pervasive to philosophical argumentation.

Fourth: the same predicament. Gautama declares that "a sign that is not distinguished from what is signified is said to have the same predicament (*sādhyasama*) because it [itself] needs to be proved." Once again we can be grateful to Vātsyāyana for making things clear with an example. Consider the argument, "a shadow is a substance, because it moves." This looks like a good inference insofar as movement is something unique to substances. The problem here is that the sign, the proposition that a shadow moves, has not itself been demonstrated. It's no good arguing for a doubtful proposition on the strength of some other doubtful proposition. Rather, we want to resolve the doubtful case by appealing to known facts.[5]

Fifth and finally, and rather enigmatically, we have the mistimed. Commentators could not agree on what Gautama meant here. The basic idea is apparently that sometimes merely formulating a thesis would be enough to show that it cannot be true. In such a case offering a reason in support of the thesis would be unnecessary or pointless, hence "mistimed." The later Naiyāyikas, however, interpret it rather differently. They think of cases where an intended conclusion has already been shown to be false by some other means. Thus argumentation becomes redundant or otiose. But this seems an implausible reading, since that would rather be a case of the incoherent fallacy, where the inference fails to fit with what one is already committed to. (The redundancy was in fact pointed out by the Buddhist philosopher Śāntarakṣita.) Alternatively then, we might think of a thesis that is just obviously false. It's a waste of time to try to reason in favor of a contradictory thesis like "there is a tiger in the trees, but no tiger in the trees," or one that is patently absurd, like "there is a tiger in the trees, but don't worry, he's a vegetarian."

Gautama's discussion of argumentation and its potential failure displays a keen sensitivity to the nature of philosophical activity, and to the demands of science. We have considered his logical teachings in some detail because the Nyāya school is so notable for its analysis of philosophical method and the nature of argument. Even the most determined skeptic would have difficulty denying that this is "philosophy," though from a Western perspective we may be puzzled by the lack of a sharp distinction between the purely rational and the empirical, or if you too prefer to show off with Latin terminology, the a priori and the a posteriori. As we'll see later, though, it was not only Gautama and his followers in the Nyāya school who contributed to logical analysis in the Indian tradition. Nagārjuna, a determined skeptic, subjected the theory of reasoning to a searching critique, and another Buddhist named Dignāga would go on to provide a more precise definition of the "good" inferential sign.

28

THE TRUTH SHALL SET YOU FREE

NYĀYA ON THE MIND

At this point, we have a pretty good understanding of Gautama's epistemology. He insists, in the face of the various skeptical arguments making the rounds in ancient India, that we can indeed have knowledge. We get it through various means of knowing (*pramāṇas*), most fundamentally sense-perception, as well as argumentative inferences, which Gautama and his fellow Naiyāyikas have rigorously analyzed. What isn't as clear, so far, is which things Gautama actually believes we can know. The endless talk of fires on the mountainside might seem relevant, but only if you're a forest ranger, in which case avoiding tigers in trees may also come in handy. The theory will really earn its stripes when we come to philosophical understanding. What do Gautama's vaunted sources of knowledge tell us about the structure of the world around us, and about ourselves? This is not something the Nyāya school simply outsource to their more metaphysically minded colleagues in Sāṃkhya and Vaiṣeśika. Gautama too offers us an enumeration of the things we can know (1.1.9).

But if this is a list of metaphysical categories, it's one that is characteristic of Gautama, whose primary interests are epistemology and liberation. Of the twelve items he names, half of them have to do mostly with psychology and the nature of human beings, the other half with ethics and *karma*. In the first group are the self, the mind, the body, the sense faculties, the objects of the senses, and finally the various sorts of mental states and events. Notice that only one thing on that list lies outside of the human knower, and even it is defined with reference to human knowledge: a catch-all category for things that are available to the senses. Then the second group includes motivation, evil, rebirth, the fruits of action, suffering, and finally the destination toward which Gautama's philosophy finally leads: liberation.

Let's have a closer look at the items on this list, first exploring Gautama's understanding of the human subject, and then turning to the promise of ultimate freedom (if we started with that, you might not bother finishing the chapter). As with his treatment of knowledge, Gautama's discussion of the self, mind, and so on is developed with an eye toward responding to and refuting other schools. The Buddhists serve as one target, since they refuse to accept the reality of an enduring self, and Gautama is also concerned with the sort of reductionism espoused by the Carvaka philosophers (see Chapters 32–3). Against these opponents, Gautama argues for the existence of the ingredients that make up the human, insisting in particular that the self is not to be identified with the "collection of body, sense-faculties, mental processes, and so on," and also that there is a difference between *ātman* and *manas*, which we may translate as "self" and "mind" (though as we'll see, its function is rather more specialized than what we usually understand by the word "mind"). Gautama goes one better than the mind–body dualism of Descartes, proposing that we each have a self in addition to a mind and body.[1]

Or is this going one worse than Descartes? Most philosophers nowadays are pretty skeptical about positing a mind distinct from the body, never mind a further self that is distinct from the mind—and these philosophers are, according to informal surveys, not even Buddhists. So Gautama has a lot of arguing to do if he's going to persuade us or his opponents. Fortunately, arguments are what he does best. Let's begin with his case for positing the self. He contends that the self is needed to serve as the subject of mental states like beliefs and desires, pleasures and pains (*Nyāya-sūtra* 1.1.10; *Nyāya-bhāṣya* 1.1.9). Clearly, if there is a belief or a desire, then there must be someone to do the believing and desiring. When there is pleasure or pain, there must be someone to enjoy the good times and suffer through the bad times. We've seen this argument already. It was Vātsyāyana's illustration of arguments that go from generalities to particular instances, rather than from cause to effect or effect to cause. The Buddhists doubted that the self could be discovered through any kind of causal inference, often repeating the point that the self does not show up when we go in search of it, as if it were one more thing in the world. Anticipating this line of argument, Gautama proposes the self as something more like a theoretical entity, something that is not observed in itself but rather hypothesized to explain the things that we can observe.

This fits into a wider pattern in Nyāya-Vaiśeṣika, whereby the self is often proven without any appeal to ideas of cause and effect. Just like the *Nyāya-sūtra*, the *Vaiśeṣika-sūtra* (1.1.5) mentions that beliefs and pains are qualities. They can hardly be substances in their own right, nor would they fit into any of the other metaphysical categories recognized in Vaiśeṣika, like motions or universals. But if beliefs and desires are qualities, then there must be something to which they belong. Qualities don't float around free on their own, like ontological balloons that have been cut loose. The subject or "substrate" to which mental qualities are tied is, of course, the self. This argument illustrates a second kind of non-causal reasoning we saw being discussed by Nyāya, namely argument by process of elimination: a belief or desire is neither a substance, nor a universal, nor a motion, and so on, and so can only be a quality.

Yet another type of argument, which may have seemed to you rather strange the first time we mentioned it, was the "negative example." You might support the claim that smoke indicates fire by alluding to water in a lake, where both smoke and fire are absent. This same strategy is used in Nyāya for proving the self. Mental events like beliefs and desires are absent in inanimate objects, because a self is also absent, whereas in humans mental qualities and the self are found together, like smoke and fire.[2] It seems then that one reason the Nyāya school was so interested in cataloguing different kinds of argument is that they wanted to give themselves tools for establishing the existence of the self. Hardly surprising, since this school is heir to the earlier Vedic tradition and thus committed to the proposition that we should seek self-knowledge above all else.

Another argument for the self is found in the commentator Vātsyāyana, who pulls together scattered ideas found in Gautama to mount the following proof (*Nyāya-sūtra* 1.1.10, 3.1.1). In addition to serving as the subject for individual mental states, the self also integrates mental states that occur at different times. I might have a desire for an almond croissant, but only because I have experienced croissants in the past. Without a self that endures over time, how could I recognize something I have experienced before, a recognition that allows me to realize that this would be just the thing to have with my coffee? The same sort of argument is used within the Nyāya theory of *karma*. If I am rightly made accountable for my own past actions—for instance the eating of too many croissants—then the person who receives the karmic fruits of the actions must be the same person who performed those actions. Surely this implies that one and the same self is both the agent of the original act and the recipient of reward and punishment?

The argument about recognition trades on the fact that different mental events happen for the same person at different times. But you can also run the argument with multiple events happening at the same time. This may be more effective against the Buddhists, who could always deal with recognition or memory by claiming that sequential events cause one another in a chain, with no enduring self needed to bind them together. So consider a case like this: imagine that you're looking at Jonardon's pet crocodile Gena, who is basking in the mud at the side of the river. He's raised him from birth so he's quite tame, and you can safely pat him on the back. When you do, you're perceiving one and the same object, Gena, through both vision and touch. You could think to yourself, "I touch the crocodile that I see." How could you be doing this if there is no single judge to compare the deliverances of the different senses? Furthermore, since it stands over vision, hearing, touch, and so on, this judge must be distinct from all of them. It is nothing other than your self, which is distinct from sensation (*Nyāya-sūtra* 3.1.1).[3]

So there you have it, or rather, there you have your self. But as we said, Gautama thinks you are more than a body with a self. You also have a mind (*manas*). The *Nyāya-sūtra* assigns two distinct roles to the mind. It is both a kind of internal sense and a faculty of attention. Why do we need to postulate an internal sense in addition to the more familiar external senses that you used to see and touch Gena? Well, you have mental processes that are completely interior, like wondering whether fraternizing with a crocodile is really such a good idea, or having a dream about being attacked by a tiger. You can also have internal awareness of your own mental states, by reflecting on what you are perceiving, desiring, and so on. All of this goes on backstage, as it were, and cannot be observed by anyone else or through your external senses. According to Gautama, this shows that there must be a faculty whose role is to perceive inner happenings. This is the "mind," a faculty of introspection, something like an inner monitor (*Nyāya-sūtra* 1.1.15).

Why can't the self do this job? After all, it is not identical with the senses either, and it is supposedly the subject of mental life. Gautama argues that the mind is very much like a sense faculty, different simply in that its activity is inward rather than outward. The self is the underlying agent and subject of this activity, for which it uses mind as an instrument (3.1.15–17). The argument turns on an observation made in Pāṇini's grammar, namely that an agent of an action is distinct from the instrument with which the action is performed. You don't need to know Sanskrit to get the point; show off again with your Latin, and consider the distinction between nominative and ablative case endings. Sanskrit grammarians mark the contrast by saying that the agent is an "independent" causal factor, whereas the instrument is dependent on the agent. If we say, "Jonardon leads Gena with a leash," clearly Jonardon is not identical with the leash. He is the agent using the leash. The same holds for inner mental states. Your self is the agent that thinks or dreams about a crocodile using the mind, just as it uses the outer senses to see or touch the crocodile.

Some philosophers think that the self has immediate or "transparent" access to the contents of its interior awareness, so that you need no special faculty to discover what you are thinking, believing, desiring, and so on. This would make the activity of thinking about Gena very different from the activity of seeing Gena. In the case of seeing, it's obvious that you are using an instrument, namely your sense faculty, and other conditions also need to be satisfied; for instance, Gena cannot be in total darkness or hiding in the river. By contrast, you might suppose, the self has a privileged and unmediated access to its own thoughts and other internal mental activities. But even though Gautama and other early Nyāya thinkers agree that each person's interior mental life is "private," available to that person alone, they deny that mental activity is transparent to the self.[4] The reason you have privileged access to your thoughts is that your internal monitor can monitor only your own particular mental life. Jonardon can't use his mind to be aware that Peter is thinking of a giraffe, nor can Peter use his mind to be aware that Jonardon is dreaming of crocodiles.

The mind's second function is to be a faculty of attention (1.1.16). Here, at least according to Gautama, we have a striking difference between external sensation and the mind. We were just noticing that the sense faculties can operate simultaneously, as when you see and touch the same thing at the same time. But awareness is not like this. There is a single successive flow of thought that can direct itself to only one object of awareness at a time. So there must be an additional factor in the production of awareness, working something like a switch, selecting one stream of inner experience for the self to appreciate at each moment. This is a remarkable proposal, as it makes Gautama perhaps the first figure in the history of philosophy to formulate what is sometimes called the "bottleneck" or "filter" theory of attention.[5]

But is it really true that the self is able to enjoy experience only sequentially and in a stream, rather than all at once, in a single burst of awareness fed by multiple sources at the same time (3.2.57–9)? Don't we in fact often find that two or more mental events happen at the same time, like remembering a crocodile while thinking of a giraffe? Gautama thinks not. Though we may sometimes *seem* to have multiple, simultaneous cognitions, this is a mere illusion caused by the rapid succession of distinct awareness, just as a flame on a whirling rope looks as if it is a single continuous circle of fire. In some cases apparent simultaneity is due to the existence of ongoing, subconscious processes, as when we understand the meaning of a sentence on hearing its separate words. We hear the words one after the other, but seem to understand the meaning of the whole sentence in a flash. For Gautama this experience is again nothing but an illusion, one that, as you may remember, convinced the grammarian Bhartṛhari that such sudden grasping of a whole is indeed the way that we comprehend language (see Chapter 21).

Gautama's idea of selective awareness faces another problem, though. If I need to use my mind to attend deliberately to my senses, for example by deciding to listen to the sounds around me, how could I ever be aware of something without first consciously choosing to listen? This can't be right. When a tiger leaps unexpectedly out of the jungle at me with a tremendous roar, I certainly have a big problem but the problem isn't that I don't hear the tiger. Rather the sudden, loud noise forces me to attend to it. The objection is noted in the *Nyāya-sūtra* (3.2.32) but not answered satisfactorily. A possible response might be that the mind is constantly engaged in a subconscious process of scanning for potential input from the senses. If so it must be doing this even while we're asleep, otherwise alarm clocks wouldn't work.

Where exactly in this model of the human subject does consciousness reside? The answer is clear: in the self. For the self is the subject of conscious mental states like believing and perceiving. This seems rather strange. Why would anyone deny that the mind can be the conscious subject of mental states? It seems even harder to swallow than I would be for a tiger. But consider that if I already have a conscious self and the mind too is conscious, then I would have two centers of consciousness. My inner life would be split in half, between the mind and the self. Gautama avoids this by insisting that mind as such is not conscious (3.2.38–9). Again, mind is not the agent of thinking but its instrument: it is really an organ of internal awareness, rather than a seat of all mental activity. It is therefore dependent on the agent that uses it, the self, and cannot act independently. The mind directs attention, but this does not amount to full blown consciousness, which can reside only in the *ātman*, the self.

Yet another argument for the same conclusion invokes the doctrine of *karma*. A basic premise of traditional *karma* theory is that we all enjoy or suffer the results of our own actions. Nothing that *I* do can make *you* better or worse off in karmic fruits. But if we supposed that the self and the mind were two independent subjects of consciousness, exactly this would happen: the mind's actions could have moral consequences for the self.[6] This may seem a strange idea, with moral responsibility being shifted between two separate agents within the same person. But of course the point is precisely that the mind cannot *be* a morally responsible agent, and that supposing it to be an agent would lead to precisely this absurd result. Notice that the argument doesn't actually require us to believe in reincarnation or *karma* as such. Anyone who thinks that we do bear moral responsibility for our past actions will want to ensure that moral responsibility belongs to a single agent for each person, not two or more agents within each person.

Gautama, though, certainly does believe in *karma*. This brings us to the final topic we want to look at in his *Nyāya-sūtra*: liberation. The whole Nyāya theory of knowledge, with its *pramāṇas*, *prameyas*, its various accounts of argument, inference, and debating procedure—all this is meant to yield attainment of the "highest good" (*niḥśreyasa*). In the second *sūtra* Gautama explains how this is supposed to happen; how, that is to say, the study of philosophy leads to liberation. It all has to do with the relationship between beliefs and actions. It seems evident that actions stem from beliefs along with desires. If I succeed in the action of patting a crocodile fondly on its spiny back, it's because I have a desire to pat a crocodile and true beliefs about what crocodiles look like, where to find them, and how best to go about patting them on the back (very carefully). But actions are not just successful or unsuccessful—they can also be good or bad. The moral quality of an action, claims Gautama, depends on the desire that gives rise to that action. It is malicious desire (*doṣa*) that causes bad action (*pravṛtti*).

Which is not to say that beliefs are always innocent. They do not only guide actions and help them succeed, but actually give rise to the desires that motivate actions. True beliefs cause benevolent desires, false ones malicious desires. If Peter believes that wealth is worth more than friendship, he might steal Jonardon's pet crocodile to sell on the black market. Having true beliefs is paramount, then, which means we have every reason to seek a proper understanding of Nyāya philosophy. For it teaches us the reliable sources of true belief and the difference between sound arguments and spurious ones. Effectively it is a tool for avoiding false belief. No false beliefs means no wicked desires; no wicked desires means no bad actions; and no bad actions means no punishment through *karma* further down the line.

With this final step Gautama is signaling his acceptance of the traditional idea that every action I perform has a future effect on me: character is destiny. If the action I perform is good, the effect will be "pleasurable" (*sukha*), whereas if the action is wicked, the effect will be "painful" (*duḥkha*), in a broad and all-encompassing sense of these terms. The point is that things will either go well for me, or else badly, and either way I will be reaping what I have sown. Aside from the karmic rewards, truth will also set you free. Gautama defines the "highest good" or "liberation" (*apavarga*) as the absence of suffering, the complete elimination of all forms of distress. There could be many ways of realizing such a state, insofar as there are many forms of life in which pain does not feature. But to reach this happy condition, we must avoid committing bad actions and so avoid bad desires by, again, avoiding false beliefs. In other words we must study the *Nyāya-sūtra* and implement its teachings carefully. For Gautama there is a direct link between our rational aim, which is to believe truth and nothing but the truth, and the moral imperative to do good and avoid evil. For all the technical sophistication of Nyāya logic and epistemology, the teaching of this school is really an answer to the question of how best to live.

29

FINE-GRAINED ANALYSIS

KAṆĀDA'S *VAIŚEṢIKA-SŪTRA*

The ninth-century Muslim philosopher al-Kindī had some strange ideas about music. It's reported that he once temporarily cured a young man of apoplexy by having tunes played on a lute, and in his own writings on music he talks about the way that music can affect the soul. Music also expresses the character of the people who play it. This, al-Kindī says, is why different cultures have different numbers of strings on their instruments. So the Greeks, who invented the theory of four elements, played lutes with four strings. As for the Indians, they made do with a single-stringed instrument, to represent their view that the whole world arises from only one cause.[1] But we know better. If our survey of the Vedic philosophical schools has taught us anything, it is that all Indian thinkers were not singing from the same hymn sheet. True, the Vedānta school did emphasize the derivation of all things from the one *brahman*, or even the identity of things with this source, according to Advaita Vedānta. But ancient India had its fair share of pluralists too. The heroes of metaphysical pluralism were to be found in the partner school of Nyāya, who went by the name of Vaiśeṣika.

Śaṅkara, the founder of Advaita Vedānta, scornfully dismissed the Vaiśeṣikas as "semi-nihilists (*ardhavaināśika*)" because of their failure to ground all things in the true reality of *brahman*.[2] But Vaiśeṣika is actually committed to thoroughgoing realism. Unlike Advaita, it assumes that there is a structured world out there, one that is independent of human conceptions and thought. It is also a world we can understand, in the first instance by offering a classification or division of reality into its various types. This task is undertaken in the founding document of the school, which as you probably don't need us to tell you is called the *Vaiśeṣika-sūtra*. It is thought to have been compiled in about the first century AD, though Vaiśeṣika ideas were certainly in circulation much earlier. Its author is Kaṇāda, also known as Ulūka: "the owl." There are several possible explanations for this nickname. Perhaps it is just based on the name Kaṇāda, which means "grain eater," like an owl—though it may also be interpreted as meaning "atom eater," because Vaiśeṣika is committed to atomism. A more fabulous explanation of the name Ulūka is that the whole Vaiśeṣika system was revealed to Kaṇāda by a god who had assumed the form of an owl.

At least as much as other *sūtras*, the *Vaiśeṣika-sūtra* is difficult to understand, and since no further explanation was forthcoming from divine owls, the tradition usually turned for clarification to Praśastapāda, who lived in the sixth century AD. In a departure from the usual procedure, he did not compose a formal commentary or *bhāṣya* but a freestanding treatise, albeit one clearly inspired by the work of Kaṇāda. It becomes the touchstone for later authors, even more so than the *sūtra* itself, to the point that Wilhelm Halbfass has called Praśastapāda "the most authoritative representative, if not the creator, of the classical Vaiśeṣika."[3] Though Kaṇāda and Praśastapāda are above all known for the metaphysical system articulated in their works, they maintain a keen interest in questions of ethics and liberation. The ethically loaded term *dharma* even appears in the opening sentence of the *Vaiśeṣika-sūtra* (1.1),[4] though here it may well have the more metaphysical meaning found in Buddhism rather than the ethical one we know from Mīmāṃsā. This would go along better with what immediately follows in the text, namely the metaphysical analysis that epitomizes the teaching of the Vaiśeṣika school (1.4).

Our earlier experiences with Sāṃkhya would probably lead us to expect this analysis to come in the form of a list, perhaps with the items on the list subdivided into further lists. If that's what we're anticipating, Kaṇāda doesn't disappoint. The initial analysis itemizes six "categories," some of which are indeed broken down using further lists. Thus the first category of substance is said to have nine types, the second category of quality no fewer than twenty-four types, and so on. A clue to the inspiration of this project is the very word "category," in Sanskrit *padārtha*. The commentators tell us that this term combines the words *pada* and *artha*, or "meaning" and "word." Thus a "category" is a type of thing that can be signified by language. The noun "owl" refers to a substance, the first of Kaṇāda's categories, the adjective "white" to the color of its feathers, which falls under the second category of quality, and so on. Thus the system of categories tells us that the world is structured in such a way as to correspond to our language. Yet again, we see Indian philosophers taking their cue from grammar.

The master list has six items on it. The first three are substance (*dravya*), quality (*guṇa*), and motion (*karma*). As we've just seen, an owl is a substance, and it has qualities such as the color of its feathers; it also has motions, like its swooping down on an unsuspecting mouse. According to Vaiśeṣika, a quality or motion is just as much a particular, individual entity as the owl. The white of this owl belongs only to it, as does the particular swoop it performs to land on the shoulder of its wizard owner. Though the theory is meant to accommodate such familiar examples, the substances in Kaṇāda's first category are not necessarily even observable. Clearly you can perceive an owl, even if its rodent victims never see it coming. But from the Vaiśeṣika point of view there are also substances that are in principle unobservable. In fact these are most fundamental. They include atoms, space, time, and a pervasive substance called *ākāśa*, sometimes translated as "ether."

Observable beings like owls are composed from atoms, which unlike owls are indestructible and eternal. But so are ether and the other, more familiar elements, earth, water, fire, and air: in fact the latter group have their own special atoms, so that there are earth-atoms, water-atoms, and so on. The larger group of five basic elements are called *bhūta*, or "physical substance," by which the Vaiśeṣikas mean that they have sensible qualities. Originally they may have supposed that these five substances are correlated to the five sensible qualities, with each quality residing in one and only one substance. Thus odor would reside in earth, color in fire, and so on. It would be the combination of all five elements that makes a complex substance like an owl perceptible to the full range of our senses. Actually this may even be the reason for positing five basic substances: it would match our five senses. If so, the guiding idea does not seem very plausible. It is hard to believe that, say, earth is invisible unless it is mixed with fire to give it color. But this is neither here nor there because, if that simple version of the story was ever put forth, it has been abandoned by the time of the *Vaiśeṣika-sūtra*. Kaṇāda does draw correlations between the basic physical substances and sensible qualities, but makes these correlations more complex (2.1.1–9, 8.2.5–6).

At any rate, we have as our most basic bodily substances atoms of the basic elements. That is, there will be atoms of earth, of water, and so on. The atoms are too tiny to be perceived, and in fact have a special size simply called *aṇu* ("small"), which indicates that they are as tiny as any existing thing can be. How do we know that bodies are at bottom made of indivisible particles? The standard Vaiśeṣika argument goes like this. It is an empirically established truth that whatever is perceived is composite. Even the smallest perceptible thing, namely a fleck of dust in a sunbeam, must therefore have parts. Since its parts are of course smaller than this smallest perceptible thing, the parts are themselves invisible. But according to Vaiśeṣika, these invisible parts have still further parts. After all, with visible things we observe that parts have parts, as for instance a piece of cloth is made of threads, and threads made up of smaller strands. To be more precise, the invisible particle is a "triad (*tryaṇuka*)" made up of three sub-parts, each of which in turn is a "dyad (*dyaṇuka*)" that has two parts, and these two sub-sub-parts are atoms. So going the other way from small to large: we have pairs of atoms coming together, joining in groups of three pairs to form invisible particles, and then combining to form things we can actually see.

There are a number of questions one might raise here, but we'll just ask the most obvious one. How do we know that the process of division can't go on forever? Let's grant that there are particles too small to see, each made of six tiny bits arranged in three pairs. Still, why not say that those six bits are each divisible into still tinier sub-sub-sub-parts? One answer given by Vaiśeṣika is that if indefinite division were possible, then a mountain and a mustard seed would have the same size, as each would have the same number of constituent parts, namely, an infinite number. An implicit premise here (made explicit by other Vaiśeṣikas) is that the size of a whole is a function of the size, number, and spatial arrangement of its parts. The argument seems to be question begging, for the implicit premise is only true if atomism is already accepted. A non-atomist will say that the size of an object is determined, not by the number of its fundamental parts, but by the spatial boundaries of the continuous "stuff" it is made of.[5]

Elsewhere in the history of philosophy, atomists have been tempted to think that non-atomic substances and their qualities are somehow unreal, since the atoms of which they are made are more fundamental. Hence a statement ascribed to the classical Greek atomist Democritus: "by convention sweet... by convention color, but in reality atoms and void."[6] As we've said, though, Vaiśeṣika has a strong commitment to realism. For Kaṇāda and his successors, the owl, the owl's color, and the atoms of which the owl is made are all real. Later in the tradition, from about the twelfth century onward, this realism was extended even to the *absences* of things, which were added as a seventh category. This is the metaphysical version of the thesis we encountered in Vaiśeṣika's sister school Nyāya, which held that you can perceive an absence, like Ferris Bueller missing behind his desk (see Chapter 26). The later Vaiśeṣikas agreed, and thus included such absences in their metaphysical account of the world.

But we're jumping ahead here, both historically and in our list of categories. So let's turn back to Kaṇāda's original account and find out what categories four, five, and six might be. The fourth item on the list is universals (*sāmānya*; *jāti*). These are the general classes or notions under which substances, qualities, and motions fall. There are not just individual owls like Hedwig, but also the whole species to which Hedwig belongs. This might be the species of "snowy owl," which in turn belongs to the more general class of "owls," with owls in turn belonging to a still more general class of "animals." The chain of universals does not go on indefinitely, though. In Vaiśeṣika "being" is considered to be the highest, most general universal, because everything that there is is a being. There are also universals for the qualities and motions we mentioned before. As we said, Hedwig's white color belongs to her alone, but whiteness is found in many other substances, so whiteness is a general class just like "owl" is.

Next, Kaṇāda (or his source) seems to have asked himself, how is it that an individual owl becomes that individual owl? This was a major issue for thinkers of the European middle ages, raised by such figures as Peter Abelard, Gilbert of Poitiers, and Duns Scotus. The Vaiśeṣika answer is strikingly reminiscent of the one given by Scotus—or rather we should say that Scotus' solution is reminiscent of Vaiśeṣika, since Kaṇāda proposed it more than a millennium earlier.[7] He suggests that there must be some unique "distinguisher (*viśeṣa*)" or principle of individuation for each particular. Actually Kaṇāda's need for something like this in his system probably has to do not so much with owls as with atoms. Even if one snowy owl looks a lot like another, there are ways of telling them apart. One has especially white feathers, the other is especially tired from delivering the post. But one fire atom is liable to be completely indistinguishable from all the others. Its distinguishing principle will explain why it is the individual atom that it is, just as Hedwig is the owl that she is. This is all the more crucial when you consider that owls, and all other bodies, are atomic compounds. So the individuality of these complex bodies will ultimately stand or fall with the individuality of atoms.

The sixth and final entry in Kaṇāda's list of categories is "inherence (*samavāya*)." Again, he seems to be anticipating a problem and solving it before anyone can complain about it; or perhaps someone had in fact complained about it, which prompted the addition of inherence to the list of categories. The problem would be this. On the one hand we have substances, on the other the qualities, motions, universals, and individuating "distinguishers" that belong to the substances. But what connects all these features to the substances that display them? What explains the fact that this particular white color belongs to Hedwig? Simply the fact that it "inheres" in her. This connection of inherence is something real, so it deserves a place on the list of categories. We can also use this concept of inherence to explain why substances have a special place among things. They alone do not inhere in anything else, but rather have other things inhering in them. That is to say, our owl does not belong to anything else the way that the owl's white color belongs to the owl.

Well, actually that isn't quite right. As we'll be seeing, the Vaiśeṣikas are very interested in the question of how wholes relate to the parts of which they are made. At the risk of jumping ahead again—though only by one chapter this time rather than numerous centuries—the reason for this obsession is not far to seek. Kaṇāda and his followers want to refute the Buddhists, who deny the reality and unity of wholes by decomposing them into parts, like the chariot which is nothing more than wheels, axle, and so on. As usual the Vaiśeṣika view on this matter is instead realist, and recognizes wholes as perfectly respectable entities. As we just said, Hedwig is real even if she is made of atoms. Still, there is a difference between an owl and her atoms, insofar as the owl is a composite being, that is, a being made out of parts. In Vaiśeṣika this difference is expressed in terms of inherence. The whole inheres in its parts, much as white color inheres in Hedwig. So if we want to be strictly accurate, we have to say that an owl has both kinds of inherence relations. White color inheres in her, and she inheres in her own parts, which ultimately are the atoms from which she is made. Atoms do not inhere at all, since they do not belong to anything the way a quality or motion would, and they also have no parts.

At this point we may seem to have strayed far afield from the concerns of moral duty and liberation stressed by the other Vedic schools. What could such ethical goals have to do with the metaphysical project embodied in the list of six categories, which seeks, as later Vaiśeṣikas put it, "to enumerate everything in this world that has the character of being"?[8] Plenty, according to Praśastapāda. He insists that knowing the truth about the six categories of being does help lead us to the highest good. It makes perfect sense that Vaiśeṣika joined forces with Nyāya, since both promise that knowledge will lead us to this lofty goal—Nyāya providing an account of what knowledge consists in, and Vaiśeṣika the analysis of the world we grasp when knowledge is achieved. Like the United States, Gautama has a friendly neighbor in the shape of Kaṇāda.

But Nyāya-Vaiśeṣika also has a serious rival, namely the anti-realism of the Buddhists. They too promise to bring us to liberation and the highest good, but by unmasking the unreality of what seems real. For the Buddhist the only effective therapy for human suffering is to undermine the commitment to a world of enduring subjects and objects, because the belief that we and other things are real and endure through time inevitably provokes needs, cravings, and attachments. Some Hindu thinkers, inspired instead of appalled by this Buddhist strategy, also embraced anti-realism. This is arguably the case with Advaita Vedānta thinkers, who remained committed to the authority of the Upaniṣads but thought that these texts pointed toward *brahman*, a single reality hidden behind appearances. For Vaiśeṣika philosophers a better response was to demonstrate that realism is true; for if realism is true, then Buddhist therapy rests on a mistake.

30

THE WHOLE STORY

VAIŚEṢIKA ON COMPLEXITY AND CAUSATION

Perhaps you've sat through a particularly incoherent film, sighed, and said to a friend, "well, that wasn't much more than the sum of its parts." Entertainment should be more than an unconnected series of celebrity cameos or action scenes. A movie like *Chariots of Fire* becomes a classic not only because of a good theme song and some memorable moments, like the opening scene where they run on the beach. It also needs to have a well-structured and coherent narrative, and compelling characters whose development we follow throughout the film. Of course this isn't the only thing people look for in films, as shown by the successful career of Quentin Tarantino. But it shows how deeply we believe that coherence and structure give rise to something new. They produce wholes, which are indeed more than just the sum of their parts.

If this is true of *Chariots of Fire*, it is also true of plain old chariots. They are more than mere heaps of axles, wheels, and carriages, such as you might find lying around at the chariot making factory. It is only once the parts have been put together as an organized assembly, with a certain structure, that they become a chariot. Thanks to this structure a chariot can do things that a heap of chariot parts cannot, such as carry Arjuna into war against his foes on the battlefield of Kurukṣetra. And what goes for the chariot goes for the charioteer. A person is not just a random sequence of individual thoughts and feelings, but an organized unity of cognition and conception who persists over time. That is why a person can say things like "I saw *Chariots of Fire* last night and I still can't get the theme song out of my head." Merely using the word "I" in this way presupposes that experience is not just a sequence of disunited parts or impressions, first the watching of a movie, later remembering that theme song. Rather there is an enduring and united self.

This, at any rate, is the view of the Vaiśeṣika philosopher Kaṇāda. We've seen that he is a defender of metaphysical realism, about substances, their properties, and the universals that apply to these things. He is also a realist about complex things.[1] This means that for him, over and above an aggregate or collection of "parts (*avayava*)," there is a further object called a "whole (*avayavin*)." Wholes include the middle-sized objects of ordinary experience. When you hold this book in your hands, you are holding something that is more than just pages, covers, and spine; when you ride in a chariot, you are borne along by something more than axles, wheels, and carriage. Though he presumably didn't realize he was agreeing with Kaṇāda, the twentieth-century British philosopher Bertrand Russell captured this view nicely when he said that a whole is "a new single term, distinct from each of its parts and from all of them. It is one, not many, and is related to the parts, but has a being distinct from theirs."[2]

The Vaiśeṣika view on wholes thus agrees with both Bertrand Russell and common sense, which sounds like an unbeatable combination. Unfortunately it also faces a formidable opponent: the Buddhist philosophers who took such objects as books and chariots, the objects of everyday experience, to be fabrications or constructions of our minds. The Buddhists offered two distinctive lines of argument for this apparently outlandish claim.[3] First, they suggested that the concepts of things like chariots or books are formed from nothing more than momentary sensory experiences. If this is so then there need be no persisting chariot, only a stream of fleeting impressions. Second, the Buddhists also doubt that there is a single, enduring person who is experiencing these impressions one after another. A person may seem to be a kind of whole made out of parts, but as we know it is a central Buddhist tenet that there is no enduring self, and that giving up belief in the illusion of the self is a step on the road to liberation.

An obvious objection that the Vaiśeṣikas can make to the Buddhists is this. If a chariot is not really a whole, but just a bunch of parts, then what is the difference between the chariot and a random grab bag of unrelated things, like the collection whose members are Gena the crocodile, an old videotape of *Chariots of Fire*, and the moon? There you have three things that, even more obviously than the latest Tarantino effort, *fail* to form a single, coherent whole. On the Buddhist view, though, such a random assortment of objects would be no different than the chariot. Since this seems hard to believe, the Vaiśeṣikas conclude that there is a metaphysical difference between the two cases. The random assortment is not a true whole whereas the chariot (or the chariot driver) is a real thing made up of parts. To this the Buddhists respond that we distinguish the two sorts of case simply as a matter of convention. Human concerns and interests make it more useful to speak of a chariot than of a collection consisting of a crocodile, a videotape, and the moon. But neither whole is more real than the other.

You don't have to be Bertrand Russell to think that, so far, Vaiśeṣika seems to have the better of this debate. The Buddhists insist on banishing familiar objects and persons from the inventory of reality, whereas Vaiśeṣika wants to validate our everyday assumptions. The burden of proof would thus seem to lie with the Buddhists. Realizing this, they offer several arguments for their anti-realist position. For one thing at least *some* of the objects of everyday experience actually are mere sums of parts. A forest is nothing more than a bunch of trees, an army just a bunch of soldiers. Or, consider again the film *Chariots of Fire*. No matter how coherent its narrative, it is actually just a series of images which are shown in rapid succession to produce the illusion of continuity. Furthermore, when shown on a digital screen the movie is just built up out of individual pixels of light that cohere into a single image, much like an impressionist painting seen from a distance. Clearly, some apparently real wholes are nothing more than assemblages of parts, whose unity is a matter of illusion or convention. So don't we have good reason to suspect that this may be true in other cases as well? It seems extravagant to assume that there are ever real wholes, when we know that a mere collection of parts can generate a convincing, yet false, impression that there is such a whole.

Vaiśeṣika is particularly vulnerable to this line of argument, since this school holds that the familiar objects around us, like crocodiles and chariots, are actually collections of atoms. So why not think that the crocodile or the chariot is just an illusion created by the conjunction of the atoms? But as we've already remarked, the Vaiśeṣikas are not the sort of atomists tempted by this reductionist move. They remind us that individual atoms are too small to be perceived. So it cannot be that when I look at a crocodile, I am seeing a vast number of atoms and bringing together my experience of them as one alarmingly large animal. To the contrary, I cannot see the individual atoms at all. This means that the crocodile in front of me must be a real thing over and above the atoms. If the only real things present were atoms, there would be nothing for me to perceive.

Another Buddhist argument focuses on the relation between a supposed whole and the parts of which it is made. Kaṇāda and his Vaiśeṣika followers want to say that a whole "inheres" in its parts; we might more loosely say that it "resides" or "occurs" in them. This book thus resides in its pages and cover. Now the Buddhist tries to force the realist into a dilemma, by asking: does the entire book reside in each page? That seems impossible. If the book is entirely in page 56, it can't also be entirely in page 57, since it would be in two different places at the same time. So the book must reside only partly in each page. But then the whole is actually divided up—into as many bits as it has parts—whereas the realist's idea was to insist that the whole is a unity over and above its parts.

Such considerations forced Vaiśeṣika to clarify their conception of the part–whole relation, and in particular to explain more carefully what is meant by "inherence." Let's first consider the kind of inherence involved when a universal inheres in its particulars. The Vaiśeṣikas are convinced that the universal nature of crocodiles is a real thing, but they are also convinced that its reality depends on there being actual, particular crocodiles like Gena. If we got rid of him and all other crocodiles, there would no longer be a universal. Thus we can say that the universal is "inseparable" from its instances, unlike the transcendent Forms acknowledged by Platonists in ancient Greek philosophy, and more like the kind of immanent universal recognized by their Aristotelian colleagues. The same goes for the inherence relation between a whole and its parts. The chariot is more than just the axle, wheels, and carriage, but could not exist if these parts did not exist.

Yet the case of the whole is not exactly like the case of the universal. The Vaiśeṣikas assume that universals are eternal and uncreated. Though they depend on particular instances to exist, there are always some instances around so that the universals never vanish. This is not true of wholes. A book, a videotape, or, sadly, a crocodile, will all break up and disappear eventually. For this reason Vaiśeṣika recognizes the parts that make up a whole as a special kind of cause, which they call a "substrate (*samavāyin*)." The difference between this and the universal case is that the universal can survive even when its instances do not. The universal nature of crocodile is untroubled by the fact that crocodiles die, as long as other crocodiles are born to replace them. It only needs there to be some relevant instances, and it doesn't matter which ones. A whole by contrast cannot survive without its particular parts surviving. Despite this difference, it still makes sense to think of both universals and wholes as having a relation of "inherence," to their particulars and their parts, respectively. They are both subject to a special kind of causation. Universals depend on their instances, and a whole depends on its parts for its survival, so that the instances are causes of the universal, and the parts causes of the whole.

The Vaiśeṣika idea of inherence is thus a contribution to a long-running debate in India about causation. It has been with us pretty well throughout this entire book. The earliest cosmological speculations in Vedic literature were fundamentally an inquiry into causes. As Bimal Matilal has pointed out, "philosophic activity in India arose out of the cosmogonic speculations of the Vedas and the Upaniṣads. The all-important business of philosophy was to attempt to discover some simple, unitary cause for the origin of this complex universe."[4] The influential tradition of Sanskrit grammar also had causal reflection at its heart. Pāṇini's system of *kārakas* or relations between verb and noun was based on an underlying causal model, in which the verb in a sentence designates an event, and the nouns in the sentence contribute somehow to bringing about that event (as an agent, as an instrument, or what have you). The same idea informed Indian epistemology and its theory of *pramāṇas*, the processes that cause an event of awareness (*pramā*) and knowledge. We saw that in Nyāya epistemology, four such *pramāṇas* are recognized: perception, inference, comparison, and testimony. In each case Nyāya offers an explanation in terms of causation, seeking to answer such questions as "What causes a perceptual experience?" "What are the distinguishing causal factors of true and false perceptual experiences?" and "Under what conditions does knowledge of the premises of an argument cause knowledge of the conclusion?"

So anyone who reads ancient Indian philosophical literature will quickly get accustomed to these sorts of causal accounts. They will also get used to seeing the same examples again and again. Nyāya and Vaiśeṣika philosophers almost invariably illustrate their discussions of causation with one of three examples. One is the case of the ceramic pot. Its causes include, most obviously, the potter, but also the potter's wheel and stick, and far less obviously, such things as the two halves of the pot (which the potter joins together), the contact between each of the pot-halves, and the contact between them and the stick. A second standard example is a cloth made of threads. Among its causes are the threads from which it is woven, the weaver, the shuttle, the loom, and various instances of contact, like the contact between the threads that are woven together so that they touch. Third, we have the example of chopping down a tree. Here the felling of the tree is caused by an axe, by its contact with the tree, by the lumberjack who wields the axe, and so on.

Notice how in these examples parts are included amongst the causes, like the threads in the cloth. Such parts are "substrate" or "inherence" causes (*samavayi-kāraṇa*), as contrasted with "non-substrate" or "non-inherence" causes (*a-samavayi-kāraṇa*), like the weaver or the contact between the threads, and "instrumental" causes (*nimitta-kāraṇa*), like the weaver's shuttle. Notice also that the effect of these causes might be a thing, like a pot or a cloth, but can also be an event, like a tree's being felled. Yet events, too, can have substrates, which in this case would be the tree. Readers familiar with ancient philosophy may be tempted to detect here a parallel with the four types of cause recognized by Aristotle. Doesn't the Vaiśeṣika "substrate cause" sound a lot like the material cause in his philosophy? Perhaps, but it's not quite the same. The parts of an object are not necessarily identical with the material from which it is made—that would be clay for the pot, wood for the chariot, and obscure 1970s martial arts flicks in the case of a Tarantino movie. Also, an immaterial substance can obviously not be an Aristotelian material cause, but the Vaiśeṣikas would admit that it can be a substrate cause. The soul, for instance, is the substrate cause of mental events.[5]

All of this puts Vaiśeṣika in a position to respond to another Buddhist argument against wholes. The Buddhist points out that two distinct objects cannot occupy the same region of space at the same time. You can stuff a cloth inside a pot, but only because the pot is hollow. The two of them can't literally be in the same place. In this sense matter is "impenetrable." But if wholes were real over and above their parts, they would violate this rule. The two halves of the pot, clearly, are in exactly the same place as the whole pot, so the Vaiśeṣika has to admit that there is more than one thing in the same location. To this the Vaiśeṣika can say that the rule about impenetrability needs to be qualified. Though it is true that material objects can't usually occupy the same space, this needn't be true if one inheres in the other as in a substrate. In fact, the whole *has* to be in the same place as its parts, because whenever the parts move, the whole has to move with them.

Another argument against wholes is due to the late sixth-century Buddhist Dharmakīrti. He cites the example of a cloth made from threads of different colors.[6] Suppose some of the threads are blue, and others not. What color then is the whole cloth? It clearly isn't blue, since some of its parts are not blue, nor is it not blue, since some of its parts are blue. But to say that it is both blue and not-blue is a contradiction. So, on closer inspection, there is no color that this multicolored (*citra-rūpa*) cloth can be. This suggests that the cloth as a whole is not real. Dharmakīrti's argument is strikingly similar to one proposed by a contemporary philosopher, David Lewis.[7] He considers a criticism of the idea that things that persist over time are wholes made up of so-called "temporal parts" or "slices." According to this proposal, a cloth would persist over time by having "parts" that exist at different times. But if this were so, Lewis pointed out, then whole objects would have contrary properties. Suppose I dye a white cloth red. Then one and the same cloth is both white before I dye it, and then red after I dye it; if the cloth is one and the same whole thing over time then it has contrary properties.

But of course the Vaiśeṣika philosophers remain determined to weave genuine wholes into the fabric of reality. Yet again they claim that the Buddhist argument can be defeated if we just define our terms more carefully. The Buddhists are trading on the idea that a cloth is either blue or not-blue, and more generally that a given object either has a property or not. But things are not that simple. There are actually two different ways of having a property, which the Vaiśeṣikas call "pervasive" and "non-pervasive." A property occurs "pervasively" if it occurs in every part of an object, like the red in Little Red Riding Hood's cloak. But red can also occur non-pervasively, like red in the plaid tartan of a Scotsman's kilt. The kilt does have *color* pervasively, since every part of it is colored. But it has *particular* colors only non-pervasively, since no one color appears in every part of the kilt. With this distinction in hand, the Buddhist argument is shown to be like the Scotsman's kilt: impressive at first glance, but nothing underneath.

One lesson to be drawn from the example of the multicolored cloth is that wholes may or may not share properties with their parts. It may be tempting to think that wholes must inherit all their features from their parts. Just think again of the sort of inference we've mentioned numerous times, based on sampling: we infer that all the rice is done cooking by tasting a randomly selected grain of rice from the pot. Sometimes, though, wholes lack properties that their parts have. A thread may be entirely blue, yet be part of a cloth that is not entirely blue; a thread weighs very little, but can be part of a heavy tapestry. Likewise a whole can have properties that are lacking in the parts of the whole. The pot is a suitable vessel for making stew, whereas one half of the pot would be quite unsuitable. A chariot can convey Arjuna into battle, once he finally makes up his mind to fight, whereas no axle, wheel, or carriage can do this by itself. And according to the Vaiśeṣikas, the pot, the cloth, and the chariot are all wholes that have the property of visibility, despite being made from invisible atoms.

A curious thing about these disputes is that Kaṇāda and Vātsyāyana apparently just wanted to defend common sense from the Buddhists, yet wound up adopting highly theoretical and speculative ideas. To distinguish between pervasive and non-pervasive properties, or classify the different ways that one thing can inhere in another, does not fly in the face of our intuitive beliefs in the way that Buddhist teachings do. Yet neither are they just part and parcel of our commonsense worldview. Much as Nyāya makes sophisticated proposals about epistemology in order to uphold the reliability of our everyday inferences, so Vaiśeṣika offers a sophisticated metaphysics to defend the reality of everyday things like pots, chariots, and textiles. Under dialectical pressure, the Vaiśeṣikas were provoked into making ever more subtle distinctions and into recognizing new types of real entities, such as inherence and absences. The result is a rather complicated but admirably consistent theory, one that is, appropriately enough, more than the sum of its parts.

31

A DAY IN THE LIFE

THEORIES OF TIME

A historian should never dismiss as unserious ideas that historical figures took seriously. Take astrology: whereas nowadays, horoscopes are usually seen as an amusement included in newspapers along with the comic strips, in former ages astrology was seen as an important branch of knowledge. We now distinguish sharply between astronomy and astrology, the first a science, the second a pseudo-science. But in ancient and medieval societies an expert in one was liable to be expert in the other, with the second century AD scientist Ptolemy leading the way.[1] Astrology is also a remarkable example of the way that ideas travel between cultures. Babylonian astronomical ideas and techniques for time measurement influenced Indian astrologers in the Mauryan period, and Greek astrological writing was translated into Sanskrit in the second century AD. By the fourth and fifth centuries, we even see Indians deploying the Greek theory of epicycles, according to which planets are seated on smaller rotating spheres carried by larger celestial spheres.[2]

Aside from its importance as a marker of cultural exchange, there is also the fact that astrology embodies a particular view of the cosmos and our place in it. It is, among other things, the study of time. This did not escape the fifth century BC author Lagadha, who wrote, "the Vedas went forth for the sake of the sacrifices; the sacrifices were established as proceeding regularly in time. Therefore, he who knows astrology (*jyotiṣa*), this science of time, knows all."[3] Here Lagadha is alluding to the fact that astronomical measurements were used to determine the auspicious moment for certain Vedic rituals. He calls astrology the "science of time" because it is by studying the motions of the stars that the Indians, and for that matter we, divide time: the days and years of our lives are astronomically defined. But the ancient Indian scientists didn't stop with days and years. They envisioned much larger spans of time, the days in the life of God, or *brahmā*.

This brings us to a notorious feature of ancient Indian thought, the cosmic world cycle. You may have heard terms like *kalpa* or *yuga*, and have the vague sense that these are extremely long periods of time with which the Indians measured the age of the universe. *Kalpa*, a word that already appears in the inscriptions of Aśoka with the meaning of "a very long time," came to be the name for one *brahmā* day, which is a very long time indeed. We know that Indian deities needed to be very patient. Just remember Indra waiting 101 years to receive instruction from Prajāpati (see Chapter 5). But that's nothing compared to the patience of *brahmā*. His day lasts as long as the entire cosmic cycle, reckoned as 4.32 billion years, and he lives for 72,000 such days. So if you want to figure out his full life span you're going to need a calculator with an extra wide screen. Each of his days sees a cycle in which the cosmos is first created, then endures, and is finally destroyed.

This idea of a destructive world cycle does not yet appear in the early Vedas, but is thematized in the *Mahābhārata*. One expert on the topic has written that "by the end of the Vedic period and the time of the composition of the *Mahābhārata* the importance of time as a destructive force had reached new heights, and the word *kāla* ['time'] had practically become synonymous with death."[4] Another pessimistic idea, also found in the *Mahābhārata*, is that each world cycle is subdivided into four periods of unequal lengths, characterized by gradual degradation and loss of *dharma*, as manifested for instance in shorter life spans for humans. The four sub-periods or *yugas* are named after four, unequally valuable throws in a game of dice. Depressingly, we're now living in the time corresponding to the least valuable throw, known as the *kāli*, which is why our age is called a *kāliyuga* and our ideal lifespan is a mere 100 years. If you're a nervous type, the next thing you probably want to know is how close we are to the end of the present cycle. Here views varied. Astrologers calculated the most recent "great conjunction" of the stars, from which the *kāliyuga* began, as having occurred relatively recently in 3102 BC. That would give us hundreds of thousands of years until the end of our age. But we also find texts predicting a more imminent cosmic demise, perhaps a reflection of the destabilizing invasion of India by foreign armies in the period between the Mauryan and Gupta empires.[5]

This awe-inspiring conception of cosmic chronology forms the background to such ideas as karmic retribution and reincarnation. One thing's for sure: if you escape just punishment for your misdeeds, it won't be for lack of time. The gods too are subject to time and even live through daily cycles, with cosmic genesis and destruction correlated to dawn and dusk. This might seem to suggest that time is itself a kind of divine principle, or even a principle beyond divinity. But that notion finds full expression only in one unusual passage of the *Artharaveda* (§19.53–4), which has all things including the creator god Prajāpati being originated by time itself.[6] It is not a notion that catches on in Vedic literature. In fact, one of the Upaniṣads explicitly rejects the claim that time is a creative principle.[7] The Vedic philosophical tradition goes further still in this metaphysical demotion of time, by doubting whether it is real at all.

We might expect this in the Vedānta tradition, especially in its Advaita variety, where all things other than *brahman* are exposed as illusions. One of the more interesting treatments of time from a broadly Vedānta point of view does not go quite that far. This is a section of the *Vākyapadīya* (§3.9) written by the grammarian Bhartṛhari. He already introduces time as a topic at the outset of his treatise, explaining that it conditions the appearance of the one *brahman* as many things that are subject to growth and decay. On this reckoning time is not exactly unreal, but a mere instrument or power through which *brahman* makes itself manifest in the form of our multifarious, changing world. Because of this all things in the phenomenal world are bound to time, like birds held captive by strings. Still, from the point of view of *brahman* and of the Vedānta philosopher too, there is no real difference between past, present, and future. As usual in Sanskrit grammar, Bhartṛhari puts the performance of an action at the center of his analysis of time. When we use the three tenses, this is nothing but an attitude we take toward actions: past tense marks actions that have already been performed, present tense actions that are in the midst of being completed, and future tense actions that have not yet been undertaken.[8]

Other thinkers in the Vedic tradition adopt even more skeptical views.[9] Sāṃkhya and Yoga, in particular, claim that time is merely a product of our minds.[10] The *Yoga-sūtra* speaks of a knowledge that arises from our awareness of moments and succession (3.52). This is rather obscure, par for the course with the *Yoga-sūtra*. Fortunately, the accompanying commentary explains that a moment (*kṣaṇa*) is the smallest part of time, just as an atom is the smallest part of matter. We mentally combine them to produce an impression of flowing, continuous time, but time is nothing real out in the world. Most of us see things only from the perspective of the present moment, and thus do not realize that past and future are also real (4.12), even if only present events are "manifest." Similarly, the Sāṃkhya commentators take their cue from a *sūtra* in the *Sāṃkhya-kārikā*, which says that the external senses grasp only the present whereas the mental organ can also grasp past and future (§33). Gauḍapāda explains that the mind can infer past and future events from present perceptions, as with the familiar examples of realizing it must have rained because the river is swollen, or that it will rain because ants are carrying their eggs to safety.

So far it would seem that ancient Indians were impressed by the sheer immensity of time and its role in measuring out the cycles of the world, but not so impressed that they were willing to admit that time is actually real. But let's not be hasty. We haven't yet considered the account of time given by the Vedic school most notable for its realist approach: Vaiśeṣika. Having defended the reality of such controversial items as qualities, universals, and the self, Kaṇāda is not likely to adopt an anti-realist theory of time. His general strategy is already suggested by the way he handles the topic of space (*Vaiśeṣika-sūtra* 5.41–3) which he of course also takes to be real. Space is like the self, in that it cannot be apprehended directly. We need to infer that it exists by observing things that are spatially arranged.

Kaṇāda proceeds on the assumption that relative arrangement is best explained in terms of contact. Suppose you see a young couple walking down the street holding hands. Their relative position is secured by the fact that they are in direct physical contact with one another: the young woman is to the man's left, because he is holding her right hand. But imagine the same couple a few years later, walking down the same street but now with their child in the middle. The mother is again to the left of the father, despite the fact that she isn't in contact with him: she's holding the child's hand, not the father's. What then determines the relative position of the two parents? The answer, according to Kaṇāda, is still contact. Not the contact between the parents, or indirect contact between the parents via their child, but the contact that both parents have with space. Space provides a framework within which the woman can be to the left of the man.

For this answer to make sense, space needs to be the sort of thing that you can indeed contact, which for Kaṇāda means that it needs to be a substance. Not just any substance, but a unique, ubiquitous (*vibhu*), and eternal substance. It is an instrumental cause of every physical effect, with respect to which objects can have two sorts of spatial relation to one another, nearness (*aparatva*) and farness (*paratva*). It's thanks to the reality of space that we can say, for instance, "the mother is to the father's left," or "Germany is to the east of the United Kingdom." Given our earlier discussion of the vast extent of time, we might wonder how big space is. Does it have any limits at all or just extend infinitely in all directions? Kaṇāda's view on this is not entirely clear. Since he introduces space to explain the relations between physical objects, it seems that it would be enough for space to be the same size as the cosmos. That is, after all, where all the physical objects are, so there is no point imagining more empty space beyond the confines of the universe. On the other hand, Kaṇāda says that most bodies are either "long (*dīrgha*)" or "short (*hrasva*)," which only makes sense if the bodies in question have parts that bound them at their edges. But space has no parts and hence no boundary, so how can it have a determinate size? For this very reason some later Vaiśeṣikas conclude that space is limited in extent. Others argue that it has a special dimension, which they call *paramadīrgha* or "maximal length."[11]

Kaṇāda's views on time are very similar to what he says about space. It too is a substance, it too is unique, eternal, and ubiquitous, and an instrumental cause of every effect (*Vaiśeṣika-sūtra* 5.42). Just as space is the basis for relative judgments of position, time is the basis for relative judgments about past, present, and future events. It is thanks to time that we can say things like "he lived in the United Kingdom before he lived in Germany." There is, however, a difference between space and time, according to the Vaiśeṣikas. Whereas what is spatially near or far varies from person to person, what is temporally near or far is the same for all persons. We might say that we are all right now in contact with the same present moment, whereas each of us is in contact with a different region of space.

Unfortunately the notion of a "present moment" turns out to be rather problematic. In the *Nyāya-sūtra*, Gautama mentions an argument against the possibility of present time (2.1.39), which is strikingly reminiscent of a paradox introduced by the Presocratic philosopher Zeno.[12] Imagine an object falling toward the ground. We can divide its path into two parts, the part it has already traversed and the part it has not yet traversed. Together these two parts make up the whole path, measured out by past and future time. So there is no part of the trajectory left that could correspond to the present moment. Rather, that moment could be only an imaginary point that distinguishes elapsed time from the time that has not yet occurred. Gautama replies that the concepts of past and future are relative to the present, not to one another. By this he may mean that, even if the present is only a boundary, it may still be real. After all, how could the present moment divide past from future if it were imaginary? Gautama also points out that if there were no such thing as the present moment, then nothing could be known through our senses, because (as we just found the *Sāṃkhya-kārikā* saying) the external senses grasp things only in the present.

As the example of the falling object shows, philosophical debates about time are inextricably bound up with philosophical debates about motion. Beginning with Praśastapāda, early Vaiśeṣika philosophers took a serious interest in the behavior of projectiles and other moving bodies.[13] There is another striking parallel with Greek thought here, since Praśastapāda's ideas are comparable with the celebrated theory of "impetus" found in a near contemporary, John Philoponus (both lived in the sixth century AD, unless of course time is unreal).[14] According to Praśastapāda, motion is the cause of conjunction and disjunction. It comes in various varieties, each of which is explained by a quality in the bodies that move. "Heaviness (*gurutva*)" causes downward motion, "fluidity (*dravatya*)" causes flowing motion, and so on. The claim that motions are always caused by qualities, not by other motions, is intended to avoid an infinite regress where every motion has to be caused by another, previous motion. Praśastapāda also appeals to qualities to explain why motion continues once it has started. In particular he refers to a quality called *vega*, "impetus" or "speed." This is a tendency or disposition (*saṃskāra*) of the body, comparable to other dispositions like "elasticity (*sthitisthāpaka*)." Impetus explains why falling things continue to fall, elasticity why bodies return to their original shape after being stretched or squeezed.

Praśastapāda further illustrates his idea of impetus by giving two examples: a fruit falling from a tree, and a thrown javelin. Before it falls the fruit is stationary in the branches of a tree. It does have the quality of "weight," but this quality is being counteracted by its contact with the tree via its stem. Then the stem breaks. No longer impeded, the fruit's weight can now make the fruit move to a new position. In light of Kaṇāda's discussion of space we can say that it goes from contacting one part of the substance of space to contacting another part, which is located just below. But the weight only makes the fruit *start* falling. To explain what happens next we need to say that, at the same moment, there is produced in the fruit an "impetus." This causes a further motion downwards, and so on for every subsequent time in the fruit's downward fall. It's the fact that weight initiates motion, but then has no further effect, that encourages us to translate *vega* as "impetus." It should not be confused with the idea of "inertia." The point is not that bodies in motion will simply continue to move unless something impedes them, but that there is an intrinsic quality in the falling fruit, just like the intrinsic quality of elasticity that causes a rubber ball to adopt a spherical form again after being compressed in your hand.

Praśastapāda's second example of the javelin involves something moving despite its weight, whereas the fruit moved because of its weight. The throwing of the javelin upward gives it both an initial motion and an initial impetus. This impetus counteracts the javelin's weight so that it is able to continue traveling upwards. Eventually, the impetus is exhausted by contact with the air, and the javelin's weight takes over and imparts a downwards impetus. At which point the javelin falls towards the ground, now behaving like a particularly long, sharp piece of fruit. So this explains the upward and then downward motion of the javelin. Assuming it is thrown at an angle, it will also move horizontally. Again, once it gets going its continued flight is caused by an "impetus" imparted by the thrower, which will be depleted as a result of contact with the air. Of course, the harder you throw the more impetus you impart to the javelin, which is what determines how far the javelin travels.

Later Vaiśeṣikas try to extend the theory to other sorts of motion, such as the movement of an iron needle toward a magnet, the upward flickering of flames, or the circulation of air. Following Praśastapāda's lead, they assume that in each case there must be some quality which initiates motion. Sadly, none of the qualities we've mentioned so far—weight, fluidity, elasticity—really seem to do the job. So the Vaiśeṣikas resort to something they call *adṛṣṭa*, literally the "unseen," which is postulated to account for movements like these. While this may look more like magical thinking than scientific explanation, we could actually see it as admirably open-minded. Realist as ever, the Vaiśeṣikas assume that there is *some* genuine property in things making them behave the way they do, even if we cannot tell for sure what it is. Empirical investigation of each case may reveal more about these qualities. On the other hand, the "unseen" starts to assume a range of other, more speculative functions in later Vaiśeṣika, for instance by explaining why atoms start to move at the creation of the universe, or to account for our fate in the afterlife. Praśastapāda would probably not have approved.

Despite these developments within the school's doctrine, it seems fair to describe Vaiśeṣika as down-to-earth, or perhaps better, "naturalistic." They offer accounts of the physical world and the place of human beings within it, avoiding appeals to supernatural forces. God is given no significant explanatory role in the system, at least in early Vaiśeṣika. But if you're a fan of naturalism, there is another school that may appeal to you even more. The groups we've examined thus far have defended a wide variety of metaphysical positions, but all of them gave some role to non-physical things, whether it was the gods, *brahman*, or the human self and mind. But next on the agenda is a group of thinkers who shocked their contemporaries by banning all supernatural, non-physical entities from their worldview. This radical stance was defended by the Cārvāka school, who could trace their philosophy to a figure from the time of the Buddha, by the name of Payāsi.

32

THE WOLF'S FOOTPRINT

INDIAN NATURALISM

When you are trying to persuade somebody of something, it's usually a mistake to be too insistent. It makes interlocutors dig in their heels, since it's just human nature to greet confident certainty with stubborn skepticism. Thus it was all but guaranteed that the Brahmanical schools of ancient India would provoke disagreement. By insisting so emphatically on the truth of the Vedas, on their indispensability as we travel the path to wisdom and liberation, these thinkers invited contradiction and criticism. It came above all from the Buddhists and the Jainas, to whom we'll be turning soon. First though, we will look at an even more radical response, a school of thought that used the *sūtra*-and-commentary form of writing that has become so familiar to us from the Brahmanical schools, but in order to reject everything held dear by the philosophers of those schools. This school was equally inimical to the beliefs of Buddhists and Jainas, making them the true outsiders of classical Indian thought, champions of a philosophy and way of life grounded firmly within this world.

Called Cārvāka or Lokāyata, the school took its cue from early materialist ideas already circulating around the time of the Buddha. The key text of the tradition is ascribed to a man named Bṛhaspati and is called (of course) the *Cārvāka-sūtra*. It is unfortunately lost, but can be reconstructed to some extent thanks to quotations found in angry rivals. Evidence of later Cārvāka thinkers, and of verses (*ślokas*) encapsulating the Cārvāka teaching, are also transmitted only indirectly.[1] Indeed, of all the traditions we have examined so far Cārvāka is by far the least well preserved in surviving texts, precisely because of its irreverence. Yet it was still known in India in the sixteenth century, when it was explained to the great Mughal emperor Akbar that the Cārvākas "regard paradise as a state in which man lives as he chooses, free from the control of another, and hell the state in which he lives subject to another's rule . . . They admit only of such disciplines as tend to the promotion of external order, that is, a knowledge of just administration and benevolent government."[2]

The Cārvākas thus disputed the truths of both Vedic ritual practice and the ascetic *śramaṇa* movements, which promised that favorable deeds will be rewarded with good fruits in either this life, in another world, or during a further incarnation in this world. Bṛhaspati dismisses all this, stating bluntly in two consecutive *sūtras* that "religious acts are not to be performed," and that religion's "instructions are not to be relied upon" (A.V.1–2). The Cārvāka verses are even more forthright: "there is no heaven, no final liberation, nor any soul in another world." Nor do the actions of the four castes, orders, and so on, produce any real effect. Bṛhaspati says: "the fire ritual, the three Vedas, the ascetic's three staves, and smearing oneself with ashes, all these are the livelihood of those destitute of knowledge and manliness" (C.1–2). Bṛhaspati is an equal opportunity offender, ridiculing both the Vedic believer and the Buddhist or Jaina ascetic. Other Cārvāka verses likewise take aim at both targets, mocking first the Brahmins: "if beings in heaven are gratified by our offering here, then why not give food down below to those who are standing on the housetop?" and then the *śramaṇa* movements: "the naked one [i.e. Jaina], ascetic [i.e. Buddhist], dimwit, given to practicing physical hardship—who has taught you this way of leading life?" (C.6 and 12).

Bṛhaspati was not the first to make such unpopular statements. Ajita Kesakambala, a rough contemporary of the Buddha, said that "there is no [consequence to] almsgiving, sacrifice or oblation. A good or bad action produces no result."[3] As we'll see in the next chapter, Ajita also held that a human being has no self or soul that can survive bodily death. On the strength of these teachings, Cārvāka expert Ramkrishna Bhattacharya has credited Ajita with being "the originator of materialism in India."[4] In a typical instance of the way that the views of such philosophers have been inaccurately transmitted by their opponents, we are also told that Ajita denied the reality of both this world and the other world. This makes him sound like a radical skeptic or nihilist. But in fact, he probably said only that we are guaranteed no future fruits from our actions, in either this or the next world. In place of the unfounded promises of the Vedas, the Buddha, or Mahāvīra, the advice of Ajita and the later Cārvākas is to look solely to the evident and immediate consequences of what we do.

So what guidelines do these naturalists offer in evaluating the consequences of actions? The reports of their rivals suggest that, having rejected both Vedic and ascetic practices, and given up on any prospect of a life after death, the Cārvāka school could do no better than to embrace crass hedonism. Indeed, the very name "Cārvāka" may relate to the word *cāru*, meaning "pleasant," though an alternative etymology connects it to *carva* or "chew," because the Cārvāka thinker is one who "chews" or destroys the self.[5] An alternate designation of the school, "Lokāyata," suggests the same ethical orientation, since it means "this-worldly." In keeping with this, one of the Cārvāka verses states, "while life remains let a man live happily; nothing is beyond death" (C.7). The Jaina author Hemacandra, a staunch enemy of the Cārvākas, represents their teaching with the following picturesque analogy: "abandoning pleasures in this world and striving for them in the next world is like licking the elbow, leaving what is to be licked in the hand."[6]

But like someone licking up the last drops of a margarita, we should take this with a grain of salt. An instructive comparison may be drawn with the ancient Greek Epicureans, a school that was likewise excoriated for its supposed hedonist excesses. Now, the Epicureans actually were hedonists: they taught that pleasure is the highest good.[7] But they were certainly not in favor of debauched, unrestrained pleasure-seeking, or even the more refined search for enjoyment evoked by the word "epicurean" in modern English. To the contrary, Epicurus held that the highest pleasure consists simply in the absence of pain, and that one can best achieve this by training oneself to have minimal desires. In the case of the Cārvākas, the hedonist interpretation may be even more misleading. Our best collection of the fragments of the *Cārvāka-sūtra* makes no mention of pleasure, and other critics fail to confirm Hemacandra's portrayal of Cārvāka ethics; it is hard to believe that they would have missed such a golden opportunity. In fact, a standard complaint about the Cārvākas is that they have no positive teaching at all, something you would hardly say about a school committed to forthright hedonism.[8] More likely, Cārvāka did not challenge the basic premise of Vedic ritualism, namely that we want concrete rewards for our actions; their criticism was simply that rituals are no way to reap such rewards. If you want fruits, harvest them here and now.

From what we've seen so far, Cārvāka philosophy consisted largely in a forthright rejection of other teachings, but without much in the way of detailed argument. This too is misleading, though. On at least two central topics of Indian philosophy, these materialists made significant contributions. One of them is the theory of the self or soul, and we'll be looking at this below. The other is epistemology, in particular the reliability of inference. We saw that the Nyāya school, among others, recognized inference as a source of knowledge, or *pramāṇa*; you may recall our example of inferring the presence of a tiger in the trees after hearing its growl. Cārvāka adopts a critical response to this theory too, but because of the problematic nature of the evidence on their teaching, it is not clear just how radical that critical response was.

What is certain is that they were happy with the first source of knowledge admitted by the Nyāya school, namely sense-perception. The trickier question is whether they reject the use of inferences based on sense-perception, or accept them under certain circumstances. It's clear that later commentators in the

Cārvāka tradition adopted the latter view. One of these commentators, named Purandara, is reported as saying that the Cārvākas "accept inference, although they object to anyone employing inference beyond the limits of perceptual experience."[9] Some scholars believe that this represents a softening of an original, extreme empiricism put forth by Bṛhaspati in the *Cārvāka-sūtra*, according to which only sense-perception can give us knowledge. They might have made this move to render their school's teaching more competitive with the sophisticated epistemologists of other traditions.

Still, the balance of evidence suggests that Bṛhaspati was already willing to admit the validity of what we might call "everyday" inference.[10] Consider the following passage: "perception indeed is the means of right knowledge. Since the means of right knowledge is to be non-secondary, it is difficult to ascertain an object by means of inference. There is no means of knowledge for determining the other world" (A.III.1–IV.1). One could certainly take this to mean that sensation, and sensation alone, is a *pramāṇa*. And indeed, the Cārvākas were sometimes called *pramāṇaikavādins*, meaning "those who accept only one *pramāṇa*."[11] In the compressed sequence of *sūtras* just quoted, Bṛhaspati even gives us something like an argument for this restriction of knowledge to the realm of perception. It alone is "primary" whereas inference or testimony would be "secondary." If you hear a tiger sound, you can be sure there is a tiger sound, because you are immediately aware of it. But as we noted earlier, inferring on this basis that there is really a tiger, or accepting testimony from someone else, falls below the standard of certainty. Nonetheless, it might be perfectly acceptable to form beliefs in this way. Perhaps you don't particularly mind about being certain. Or perhaps you can use sense-perception to double-check the belief in question. This is what happens in everyday life, as when you believe that eating rice will eliminate hunger because it has done so in the past.[12] You can satisfy any doubt you might have on the score right along with satisfying the hunger, by just eating some rice.

The problem, as Bṛhaspati's remarks suggest, is whether such inferences can be drawn on such topics as the "other world" or the existence of an incorporeal self. These are of course precisely the sorts of inference that Nyāya and other Vedic schools wanted to make—ultimately, their epistemology was in the service of arguing for the self, liberation, and so on—and these are also precisely the inferences that Cārvāka is committed to refuting. Here we are dealing with highly controversial claims, with no possibility of checking the claims using sense-perception. After all, it's not like we can go now to the other world just to see whether it is really there. Extrapolating a bit, we could imagine that Cārvāka would even be happy with the sorts of inference made in scientific explanations of natural phenomena. After all, these explanations are hypotheses that can indeed be checked against empirical evidence. The point is made in the Cārvāka verses, which ask: "who will deny the validity of inference when one infers fire from smoke, and so on? For even ordinary people ascertain what is to be proven by such inferences, though they may not be pestered by the logicians. However, inferences that seek to prove a self, God, an omniscient being, the other world, and so on, are not considered valid by those who know the real nature of things" (C.18–19). To this the verses add the traditional refrain of the commonsense philosopher, namely that everyday people will do just fine making inferences "so long as their mind is not vitiated by cunning logicians" (C.20).

There is a beautiful anecdote that encapsulates the Cārvākas' approach better than we ever could: the parable of the wolf's footprints. Related by several authors, it tells of a married couple, the husband a materialist and the wife a devout believer in Brahmanical teaching (the terms used here are *nāstika* and *āstika*). He is unable to convince her by arguments, and comes up with a different approach. When no one is watching, he uses his fingers to make marks in the dust of a crossroads, mimicking the footprints of a wolf. When the marks are discovered, the local scholars agree that these marks can only be explained by a wolf that has come into the village out of the forest. The husband triumphantly tells his wife to "consider the case of these footprints of the wolf." We're lucky to have this detailed version of the story, since it explains an otherwise incomprehensible Cārvāka verse, which compares the teachings of learned scholars to saying "look at the footprint of the wolf" (B.13).[13]

It may seem that the parable is a caution against using everyday inference. Wolves are not imperceptible, like the other world or an immaterial self, and concluding from apparent wolf footprints that a wolf is about is hardly an example of exotic philosophical reasoning. This impression might be confirmed by the verse just mentioned, which prefaces the remark about the footprint by stating, "man consists of only as much as is within the scope of the senses." But a fourteenth-century author named Somatilaka, who transmits one of the more complete versions of the story, emphasizes the fact that the villagers duped by the husband include the self-styled scholars who solemnly inform the rest of the people that a wolf must be nearby. He says, "these people, knaves in the garb of the pious" deceive normal folk "by somehow convincing them of the infallibility of certain inferences and verbal testimonies . . . enticing them away with the hope of enjoying pleasures to be attained after reaching heaven, and produce blind faith in pious acts."[14] So, at least on this interpretation, the parable is not intended to induce a wide-ranging skepticism about all inference. It is an analogy, meant to cast doubt on the misleading promises made by the "learned men" of the Vedic tradition.

Our puzzle about the scope and nature of the Cārvāka epistemological critique echoes another feature of Hellenistic philosophy, in this case having to do (unsurprisingly) with the Skeptics. Before explaining the parallel, we hasten to say that the Cārvāka school is clearly *not* skeptical, at least not in the way that the ancient Greek Skeptics were. They do accept one authoritative *pramāṇa* or source of knowledge, namely sense-perception.[15] In this respect their epistemology fits better with the aforementioned Epicureans, who likewise grounded all knowledge in sensation. But, just as it is controversial how to take the Cārvāka criticism of inferences that go beyond perception, so it is controversial how to understand the Hellenistic Skeptics' attitude towards belief in general. On one reading, they withheld their endorsement or assent from *all* beliefs; on another reading, they suspended judgment only concerning the more abstruse and technical claims made by the dogmatic schools.[16] On the reading we've been defending, Cārvāka would line up with the second interpretation of the Hellenistic Skeptics: they were happy to accept everyday inferences, but not the more ambitious and contentious inferences made by their Vedic and *śramaṇa* rivals.

Having said this, there is actually a more fundamental difference between Cārvāka and Greek Skepticism, at least in the form defended by the late ancient thinker Sextus Empiricus. As we've just said, his Skepticism manifested as a suspension of judgment, concerning at the very least philosophical doctrines, and maybe all possible topics of belief. But it's abundantly clear from our evidence that Cārvāka did not suspend judgment about the fruits of ritual or the existence of a self independent from the body. They judged all right, and very harshly: they thought all of it was bunk. But on what basis? To say that there is no watertight inference or testimony to establish the truth of these things is far from establishing that they are false. This would be like seeing a mark in the dust that looks like a wolf's footprint, realizing it could in theory have been made by a husband trying to score a point in a marital dispute, and leaping to the conclusion that the mark was definitely *not* made by a wolf. To put the point more abstractly, it seems that for the Cārvākas, if there is no definite proof of something then it should be taken *not* to exist.[17] And that seems like a crass philosophical error.

At least two sorts of response might be made on the Cārvākas' behalf. One is that in the case of something like the other world or the independent self, proof is unavailable *in principle*. This is not like the wolf who may or may not have made a footprint. In that case, we can use sense-perception to track it down and verify its existence. By contrast, another world reached only after death would be completely inaccessible to sense-perception, the source of all our knowledge. And it does make a certain amount of sense to reject belief in things that are in principle unknowable, that are simply beyond our ken, given that there could not possibly be any evidence for them. Sextus Empiricus would still say that this falls short of giving us grounds to *reject* the existence of such things. That would be an example of what he called negative "dogmatism," whereas the truly skeptical response is to refuse to make any judgment one way or another. But the lack of evidence, even of the possibility of evidence, may have been enough for Bṛhaspati, and might be enough for us too.

33

MIND OUT OF MATTER

MATERIALIST THEORIES OF THE SELF

There are basically two ways to get modern-day philosophers interested in the history of philosophy. First, you can point out that ideas from past eras are excitingly different from the ideas and assumptions we have today. As Peter Geach once said, "the usefulness of historical knowledge in philosophy is that the prejudices of our own period may lose their grip on us if we imaginatively enter into another period, when people's prejudices were different."[1] Ancient Indian philosophy offers plenty of material for this sort of approach. How many contemporary philosophers are seriously engaged with the question of acting without desire, the central topic of the *Bhagavad-gītā*, or with the sort of consciousness monism put forward by Advaita Vedānta? But there is also a second, diametrically opposed strategy, which involves pointing out startling anticipations of modern ideas in the historical record. This chapter will explore just such a case: the Cārvāka theory of mind, which is remarkably similar to a position defended by many philosophers nowadays, called "emergentism."[2]

As the name implies, this is a theory according to which the mind "emerges" from the body. This means on the one hand that physical properties, like chemical processes going on in the brain, somehow give rise to mental life—philosophers sometimes speak of the mental "supervening" on the physical. On the other hand, mental life cannot simply be reduced to processes in the body. The mind has its own causal powers, and even the most sophisticated scientific theory wouldn't be able to eliminate talk of the mental and replace it with talk of things happening in the brain or elsewhere in the body. Emergentism forges a middle path, holding that consciousness and other features of the mind are generated by the body, but are not mere impotent by-products, with all the real causation happening strictly at the physical level. Once they emerge, mental phenomena have their own explanatory force. A nice metaphor found in discussions of Cārvāka makes the point beautifully. A spark of flame is produced by rubbing two sticks together, and then the resulting fire can be a genuine cause of heat and burning, with the help of other materials.[3]

Analogously the body's composition gives rise to such things as thoughts and desires, which can then cause further thoughts and desires.

This view of the mind is powerfully opposed to what we have seen in other ancient Indian schools of thought. The strongest contrast would be with the Vedānta tendency to make *brahman,* a mental principle, the cause of all physical phenomena, which may even be seen as unreal. But Sāṃkhya and Nyāya-Vaiśeṣika insisted that humans have some immaterial psychological aspect, and more generally there was a widespread acceptance that the mind or self (if it exists at all) can survive on its own without the body. Widespread though the idea may have been, it came under attack very early in Indian history. We have just met the pioneering materialist Ajita Kesakambala and seen how he rejected Vedic ritual and its fruits, either in this or the next life. In support of this polemic, Ajita claimed that the human person "is but a compound of the four great primary elements." After death the person is dissolved, with earth returning to earth, water to water, and so on.[4]

Another forerunner of the Cārvāka view on mind was a prince called Payāsi. Like Ajita he seems to have lived around the same time as the Buddha himself, and we have a report of his ideas in the Buddhist *Nikāya.*[5] It tells of how Payāsi undertook experiments to show that there is no self separable from the body, experiments that would not pass muster with a modern-day scientific ethics committee. He suggested putting a person in a large, sealed vessel, and then baking the vessel until the person is dead. We then open the jar and, Payāsi instructs, "watch carefully: maybe we can see his soul escaping. But we do not see any soul escaping." If you don't have a jar that big, then just beat the life out of the person and see if a soul departs at the moment of death; or weigh someone before and after killing him to see if anything has escaped. Or if you're feeling sadistic and curious in equal measure, you can peel the person layer by layer, to see if a soul is exposed at the core.[6]

All of this is proposed in a dialogue with Kāśyapa, supposedly a companion of the Buddha. Of course Kāśyapa can hardly insist that the soul is detectable through Payāsi's gruesome experiments. But he denies the relevance of this, arguing that thrashing a person's body to see its soul is like thrashing a trumpet to get at the music it used to make. Like the trumpet that is not being played by a musician, the body without soul is inert. Without "life, heat and consciousness," it is incapable of motion, sense-perception, and thought. Of course as a Buddhist, Kāśyapa has no interest in defending the idea of the self as an enduring, simple entity. His objection is rather a methodological one: whatever doctrine of the self we adopt, we should not suppose that the mental can be investigated using the same approach we take in studying the natural world.

The figure of Payāsi (here "Paesi") is also known from Jaina literature, which again makes him an interlocutor in a dialogue about the soul, in this case with a man named Kesi.[7] Paesi puts it to Kesi that an ant and an elephant should have souls of the same size. Why, then, are the activities performed by an elephant so more impressive than those of the ant? Kesi responds with a metaphor. Imagine a hall in a building with no doors or windows that would let light out. A lamp is then lit in the middle of the hall. It would illuminate the entire hall, but nothing further outside. If one then covers the lamp with a bushel, then only the much smaller space inside of the bushel is illuminated. "In just the same way," says Kesi, "the soul too is reborn in such a body as it is bound to by the karma of its previous existence. It animates it, be it small or big, by innumerous soul units. Therefore, Paesi, you should believe that the soul and the body are different and not identical."

The story of Payāsi demonstrates that naturalism was a strong undercurrent in Indian philosophy from the very beginning. Like its rival schools of thought, it was a "philosophy of path and purpose," but one that recommended living for the here and now rather than in search of transcendental ideals. Ajita and Payāsi dismissed the pretensions of Vedic ritual as a means to satisfying desire and rejected the idea that God exists and can intervene on earth. Their skepticism regarding the soul was thus part and parcel of a more general philosophy, one that could offer a serious challenge to the Vedic tradition, and also to Buddhism and Jainism, once the materialist position was systematized as a proper school of thought. As so often, that meant producing a canonical text in *sūtra* form, hence the *Cārvāka-sūtra* ascribed to Bṛhaspati.

We saw already that Bṛhaspati, and Cārvāka more generally, carried on the early naturalist project with an epistemology that privileged sense-perception over inference and testimony. But at least as much emphasis was placed on the materialist account of mind. Indeed this topic seems to have featured at the very beginning of the *Cārvāka-sūtra*. The latest reconstruction of the text has it starting more or less as follows (1.1–8):

> Next then we will examine the nature of the reals.
> Earth, fire, air and water are the reals.
> Their combination is called the "body," "senses," and "objects."
> Consciousness (*caitanya*) [is formed] out of these [elements].
> As the power to intoxicate [is formed] out of fermenting ingredients.
> A human being (*puruṣa*) is a body qualified by consciousness.
> [Thinking is] from the body alone.
> Because of its presence when there is a body.

This is a stunningly forthright affirmation of naturalism or physicalism. Everything that exists, states Bṛhaspati, is identical to the elements or to some combination of them. Lest we wonder how our complex surroundings could have arisen from such simple ingredients, he adds two further aphorisms (2.1–2):

> The world is varied due to variations in origin (*janma*).
> As the eye in the peacock's tail.

Today's philosophers might instead speak of the "causal history" of different things. Yes, things are complicated, but this is because they arose from a complex process of combination and interaction between simple materials.

As stated in those opening lines, Bṛhaspati's account applies also, or even especially, to the human mind. Tellingly he does not speak of "self (*ātman*)" but only of the generation of the "human being" or "person" (*puruṣa*). He doesn't do his opponents the favor of assuming that there is any such thing as a self that could be independent of body. Instead the whole person, including the power of thought, is made from the four elements. A certain combination of those elements generates mental life. Bṛhaspati compares the emergence of consciousness from matter to the way that the capacity to intoxicate arises from the mixture of the ingredients in an alcoholic beverage. This analogy strongly suggests that the mind that arises from matter would have its own causal powers, as modern-day emergentism requires. Earth or water cannot think on their own, just as hops, barley, and water cannot make you drunk on their own. The trick, as any brewer can tell you, is all in what Bṛhaspati calls the "combination," from which arises a new power to intoxicate.

Unfortunately, what we find here in the *Cārvāka-sūtra* leaves some doubt as to the exact relationship between the mind and its material basis. The problem centers on the use of the noun *bhūtebhyaḥ*, which means "elements" and apparently is in the ablative case.[8] As in Latin, the ablative case in Sanskrit can mean several different things. Bṛhaspati might be saying that the mind is *made from* the elements, that thinking is *because of* the elements, or that thought is *produced out of* them. This, along with the typically concise and compressed mode of expression in the whole string of aphorisms, left commentators with room to offer several different interpretations. One idea was to say that mind is only the manifestation of processes going on at the physical level, with those physical processes carrying all the explanatory weight. On this reading Bṛhaspati was actually identifying the mind with a combination of elements in the body. Our mental life would simply be the way that we register the physical processes caused by the combination of elemental bodies.

While this may seem a disappointingly reductive view of the mind, it would resonate well with some modern-day ideas. In the late nineteenth century T.H. Huxley proposed that mental phenomena could be just a kind of by-product of physical phenomena. He compared the mind to the steam whistle of a locomotive, which has no role in the running of the train, or to the bell of a clock that doesn't help it to keep time.[9] In the same way, the interpretation we have just been discussing makes Bṛhaspati's mind causally inert. Mental life doesn't do anything in its own right, but is just a side effect of the elemental combination. Yet we have already seen good reasons to doubt this reading. Consider again the comparison of mind to the intoxicating beverage: the whole point of that analogy would seem to be that the mind does do something distinctive of its own. Other Cārvākas duly held that the mind is a distinct power which emerges from the combination of material elements, without being identical to it.

There is textual evidence of this disagreement among the Cārvākas. Prabhācandra, a Jaina philosopher from the eleventh century, discusses their views with unprecedented detail, explaining what they meant when they claimed that the mind is a "manifestation" of the underlying bodily composition. He says that a manifestation "puts together well" or "refines" and "perfects" (*saṃskāraka*) what is already there, rather than bringing into being something that was not there before. As such, the manifestation is not a separate thing, over and above the four elements, not a "distinct reality" (*tattvāntara*) in its own right. Prabhācandra also provides an illuminating discussion of various options open to philosophers who want to explain mind in terms of the body. The most radical proposal is the one we have just considered, namely that the mind or self simply *is* the body: there is an identity (*svabhāva*) between the two. But the physicalist need not go this far. She might say that the mind is one of the body's qualities or states. For this idea of "quality" Prabhācandra uses the term *guṇa*, familiar to us from Sāṃkhya. This would align with the idea that mind is like the train whistle, a mere by-product. Finally, and for our money the most plausible as an interpretation of the *Cārvāka-sūtra*, Prabhācandra mentions the option of saying that the self is an effect (*kārya*) of the body. This would be well captured by the aforementioned idea of mind emerging from the elements like a spark which gives rise to flame.

Another insightful opponent of the Cārvāka position was the ninth-century Nyāya philosopher Jayanta, who explained the theory in order to refute it.[10] He confirms Prabhācandra's observation that for Cārvāka, the self is not a separate entity. Befitting a Nyāya thinker, Jayanta focuses on Cārvāka's epistemological arguments against an independent self. We saw in the last chapter that the Cārvākas grounded all human knowledge in perception. In keeping with this they reprised

Payāsi's point that our external senses do not give us access to any self distinct from the body. When was the last time you saw or heard a self? Nor can introspection give us access to the self, since this kind of "internal perception" is always a perception of something like a particular pain or pleasure, rather than of a subject of consciousness. This sounds a bit more controversial but is actually rather convincing given the views Cārvāka is criticizing. Remember how Nyāya carefully distinguished the internal perception enjoyed by the interior mental organ from the role played by the self (see Chapter 26).

If the self cannot be perceived directly, perhaps we could infer or deduce that it exists? Again, we've already seen that Cārvāka doubted the possibility of inferences concerning things beyond the realm of the senses, and Jayanta confirms that here. He also says that Cārvāka rejected arguments that inferred a separate self from its apparent function in our mental lives. We need posit no self in order to explain things like memory or comparing multiple sensory experiences. These are all things the body can do. No better, from the Cārvāka point of view, would be trying to establish the existence of the self by citing authoritative testimony, such as is provided by the ancient scriptures. Of course Cārvāka gives such arguments from authority no credence in any case. But they also point out, according to Jayanta, that one can just as well use the scriptures to support a naturalist view of the mind. They cite a passage stating that the self is "a single mass of cognition (*vijñāna-ghana*)," which has "risen up out of these elements and is dissolved into them."[11]

With such arguments Cārvāka carried on the early naturalism of Ajita Kesakambala and Payāsi, challenging the core commitment of the Vedic schools to an autonomous mind or self that can outlive the body. It might be tempting to associate them with the Buddhists, whose famous "no-self" theory posed a similar challenge to the Brahmanical tradition. But we should not conflate the two movements. Admittedly Bṛhaspati does avoid using the term "self." But the Cārvākas are not, like the Buddhists, questioning the idea that the human mind persists over time. They are fully committed to the reality of such an enduring mind; it's just that they believe it emerges from and depends on the body. So we might say that Cārvāka could agree with the other *sūtra* traditions that we have persisting minds, while disagreeing with them by explaining such mental subjects in a "bottom up" way rather than a "top down" way. Cārvāka is like a mirror image of Vedānta, where the mental arises out of the material world rather than the other way around. Yet this language is slightly misleading (even if "bottoms up" would go nicely with the analogy to alcoholic beverages). If it is right to see Bṛhaspati as an early forerunner of emergentism, then in a sense he does make room for "top down" causation. Once the mind is produced out of material composition, it can exert its own causal influence. Thoughts are not inert, but play a role in our explanations of the world. The point is rather that the thinking subject is not a *fundamental* explanatory principle, as so many Vedic philosophers would have insisted. It is merely an effect of the body.

It's a real shame the Cārvāka theory of mind is not better preserved, that the works of the school are lost and known only indirectly through hostile reports. Bṛhaspati proposed that human beings are physical bodies which can be conscious, that consciousness is something that emerges out of the organization of physical matter, and disappears again when the organization that sustains it is destroyed. His position is thus one that resonates powerfully with those taken by most philosophers of mind nowadays, who likewise tend to see an intimate relationship between mind and body, with the physical somehow giving rise to the mental. But we should not underestimate our first motivation for doing the history of philosophy. If Indian theories of the mind and knowledge often resonate with the theories of today, they can also be interesting because they are so different. We'll see illustrations on both sides of that contrast in the next section of this book, as we turn to the Buddhists and Jainas.

PART III

BUDDHISTS AND JAINAS

34

WE BEG TO DIFFER

THE BUDDHISTS AND JAINAS

We have now seen how a variety of different philosophical systems arose in ancient India, each having a core text comprised of a collection of aphoristic verses or *sūtras*. The great plurality of doctrinal opinions in India is its strength, but also a philosophical problem in its own right. For it is obvious that, even as these systems emerged out of the same Vedic culture, they adopted contradictory positions on pretty well every key issue in philosophy: self, mind, and world, human aspiration and human ability. In this section of the book we will explore two more traditions that offer a response to this problem of philosophical diversity, that is, to the availability of different and opposing standpoints or systems. One response is that of the skeptic, who claims that our inability to reach agreement on philosophical questions shows that no one answer is justified. The other response is that of the syncretist: every position contains at least a grain of truth, so we should accept all philosophical positions, but only in a conditional manner. In India, the first approach was advanced by a school of Buddhism, and most notably by Nāgārjuna, while the second was the preferred option of philosophers within the Jaina tradition. We will see that both ways of rejecting dogmatism led to innovations in epistemology and logic, as our protagonists sought to avoid falling into self-refutation.

Nāgārjuna lived in the second century AD, at a critical time for the development of both Buddhism and Jainism. It was in this period that thinkers of both traditions began writing in Sanskrit, having previously stuck with Pāli in the case of Buddhism and Prakrit in the case of the Jainas. This allowed the *śramaṇa* movements to meet Vedic opponents on their own linguistic ground, even as the Buddhists and Jainas also engaged in debate with one another. Often the story of Buddhist philosophy is described as if it emerged in an intellectual vacuum. But just as we've seen that the Brahmanical schools refined their ideas in response to Buddhist critique, so we need to factor in the broader intellectual context if we want to understand Buddhist or Jaina thought. With our survey of the systems behind us, we are in an especially good position to do this.[1]

We can pick up the story starting after the death of Aśoka, the emperor who worked so hard to promote Buddhist thought. He reigned in the third century BC, approximately at the time that Buddhism underwent the first of its several divisions into rival intellectual theories called *vādas*. They set forth systematic accounts of what they took to be Buddhist doctrine, in seven canonical texts each of which is called an *abhidharma*. For a sense of how things developed, let's consider the central Buddhist tenet that there is no eternal, unchanging self or soul. Though we readily associate the phrase "no-self" with Buddhism, mental reality was in some sense affirmed. This is why, as we just saw, the Buddhists reacted critically to the frank materialism of the Cārvāka forerunner Payāsi. The truth about the self is somewhere in between. We are neither identical to our bodies, as Cārvāka would have it, nor are we souls that lack connection to anything else, a view which is rather similar to the Jaina theory of the self. (Here it seems the Buddha was at least as interested in positioning himself relative to other dissident groups in ancient India, as he was in critiquing the Brahmanical hegemony.) To express his own view, the Buddha offered similes: a person is not like the thread running through a necklace of pearls, but like the flowing of a river or the flickering of a candle flame. In keeping with this last comparison, liberation from bodily existence is described as *nibbāna* or *nirvāṇa*, meaning the blowing out of a flame. Pressing the metaphor a little further, there is a certain sort of fuel which keeps the flame burning, and in the case of a human being that fuel is craving, attachment, and false desire.

The Buddha's ideas about the self were avidly explored in subsequent generations, as we can see from one of the earliest works of philosophical Buddhism. It's one we have mentioned before: a work written in Palī that describes an encounter between the Buddhist monk Nāgasena and King Menander (here called "Milinda"). At one stage Menander asks, "he who is reborn, Nāgasena, is he the same person or another?" Nāgasena replies, "neither the same nor another." Menander asks for an illustration, and Nāgasena offers this: "in the case of a pot of milk which turns to curds, then to butter, then to ghee, it would not be right to say that the ghee, butter and curds were the same as the milk but they have come from that. So neither would it be right to say that they are something else."[2] The rival *vādas* tried to work out the philosophical theory behind such metaphors. We have already made brief mention of one of these groups, the Puggalavāda (see Chapter 8). They were distinguished by their willingness to admit that there is in some sense an enduring person or self that changes over time. Another group, the Sarvāstivāda, rejected this proposal but were themselves reluctant to admit that nothing is real apart from fleeting, momentary *dharmas* that make up an aggregate thing. In part to explain how there can be karmic effects from previous deeds, the Sarvāstivādins proposed that past and future things are real or existent.

In the Abhidharma writings that put forth such interpretations, we see the Buddhists adopting strategies different from those of the Brahmanical schools. Buddhists did not write *sūtra* texts, the compressed and difficult works that stood in obvious need of explanatory commentary. Somewhat confusingly the early Buddhists actually do use the term *sūtra*, or rather its Pāli equivalent *sutta*, but with a quite different meaning: here it refers to the recorded sayings of the Buddha himself as set down in the *Nikāyas*. The various Buddhist schools tried to get under the surface of these explicit teachings, in order to reveal the deep unity of the philosophical truth within. One standard exegetical move was to draw a distinction between those utterances of the Buddha which do express this deep truth, and those whose meaning is in need of "drawing out (*neyārtha*)" in one way or another. This will be a running theme also in later Buddhism. Especially the Mahāyāna Buddhists deploy the notion of "skillful means (*upāya-kauśalya*)," which includes the notion that as an ideal teacher, the Buddha often said things that are not strictly true in order to help his listeners move along the path to liberation.

The Abhidharma teachings had disparate afterlives. While Sarvāstivāda Buddhism became dominant in northern India and central Asia, Theravāda Buddhism developed on the island of Ceylon or Sri Lanka.[3] The most remarkable ancient representative of Theravāda lived in the fifth century AD: Buddhaghosa, author of a definitive unified commentary on both the *Nikāyas* and the canonical Abhidharma treatises (see Chapter 45). His work the *Visuddhimagga* (*Path of Purification*) continues to exercise great influence today in Sri Lanka, Burma, and Thailand, where the Theravāda school is still alive and well. The Sarvāstivāda branch of Abhidharma enjoyed even wider influence. Its key philosopher was Vasubandhu, who lived around AD 400. He wrote a pivotal digest of Abhidharma theory, called the *Abhidharma-kośa*, and also an important analysis of the "five factors (*pañca-skandha*)" which according to the Buddha constitute the psychophysical river that is a human being.

Vasubandhu also features in the next chapter of this history: the spread of Mahāyāna ("Great Vehicle") Buddhism, so called because its proponents wished to distinguish it from what they considered to be less complete or advanced accounts of the Buddha's teaching.[4] Thus they applied the condescending term Hīnayāna ("Lesser Vehicle") to rival Buddhist groups including Theravāda. After starting out as a proponent of Sarvāstivāda, Vasubandhu was apparently persuaded by his brother Asaṅga to switch to the Mahāyāna school (see Chapter 41). Vasubandhu went on to write some of its fundamental texts, and even to write a self-commentary on his own, *Abhidharma-kośa*, now from the Mahāyāna perspective. That was enough to annoy another Ābhidharmika named Saṃghabhadra. He was provoked into writing a rival commentary, which defends Vasubandhu's old view against his new one! Among Vasubandhu's new Mahāyāna works, his *Twenty Verses* and his *Thirty Verses* are works of immense philosophical accomplishment.

Mahāyāna Buddhism had in fact already emerged well before the time of Vasubandhu, sometime around the last century BC or first century AD. Its self-styled superiority to other Buddhist groups turned on its claim to be pursuing a higher ethical goal. Where others might be content to become enlightened and so achieve the status of an *arahat*, the Mahāyānas emphasized the more exalted role of the *bodhisattva*—indeed their school was originally also called the Bodhisattva-yāna. A *bodhisattva* is more than an *arahat* or even a *buddha*, because he goes beyond perfect liberation and wisdom by seeking to bring others to this same state. Thus the Mahāyānas put "other regarding" ethics at the center of their conception of Buddhism.[5] They recognize that great sacrifice and patience will be required to reach the level of a *bodhisattva*; they speak of needing millions of world cycles in order to achieve this. Mahāyāna is also distinguished from other Buddhist schools in terms of the texts it recognizes as authoritative. It considers a number of new *sūtra* texts to be genuine records of things said by the Buddha, despite having become available only centuries after his death. These had been hidden in the meantime, or were posthumously divulged by the Buddha in dreams. More generally Mahāyāna tends to think of "buddha" less as an individual person and more as a functional role. They tell us that the Buddha teaches at all times and adopts many guises to do so, and assert that there has been more than one buddha, indeed "as many as the grains of sand in the Ganges."[6]

Buddhist history would thus seem to be less a single flowing river than a set of branching tributaries. This continues with Mahāyāna Buddhism, which itself subdivided into two main sub-schools. One is Madhyamaka, the philosophy of the "Middle Way," founded by the aforementioned Nāgārjuna (see Chapters 36–8). Nāgārjuna's philosophy was destined to go on to great things in Tibet, China, and Japan, and is in fact the ultimate source of Zen Buddhism.[7] It can be tempting to think of Buddhism as having a first, Indian phase and a later phase where it gradually disappeared from India, even as Buddhist ideas were disseminated throughout the rest of Asia. But actually the waters are a bit muddier than that. We've already seen that Sri Lanka was the home of Theravāda Buddhism from early on, and some of our earliest sources for the various strands of Buddhism, including Madhyamaka, are in Chinese. We have valuable information about Indian Buddhism from two Chinese travelers, Fa-Hsien in the fifth century and Hsüan-Tsang in the seventh century,[8] and also cases where Buddhist works were written in Chinese and translated into Sanskrit.

Nāgārjuna lived around AD 150 to 200, making him a contemporary of Gautama, the author or compiler of the *Nyāya-sūtra*. His two most famous works are the *Mūla-madhyamaka-kārikā* (*Verses on the Middle Way*), and the *Vigraha-vyāvartanī* (*Dispeller of Disputes*), in which he tries to undermine the Nyāya theory of knowledge and answers Nyāya criticisms of his own work. His central thesis—though as we'll see calling it a "thesis" is to some extent problematic—is that all human conceptual schemes and all philosophical systems are "empty" or "null" (*śūnya*). His teaching is therefore also known as the philosophy of emptiness. He is a severe critic of the *pramāṇa* method for conducting rational inquiry, and instead urges the use of reason to expose inconsistencies within the fabric of one's own conceptions (to say nothing of the conceptions of rival philosophers). This all sounds pretty radical. So why does Nāgārjuna call his brand of Buddhism "Madhyamaka," or "Middle Way"? Because it neither embraces the permanence of things, nor does it deny that anything is real. Much as Nāgasena told King Menander that things are neither the same nor different over time, so Nāgārjuna says that things are not simply independently existent or non-existent. Rather, they are real insofar as they depend on other things. To be is to be relative. Don't worry if this sounds mysterious, because we're going to get into it more deeply in the next few chapters (after which it may still sound fairly mysterious, but a Buddhist would advise you not to worry about that either).

The other school of Mahāyāna is Yogācāra, which was first set out by the two brothers Asaṅga and Vasubandhu. It is not so much opposed to Madhyamaka as complementary to it, focusing especially on psychological and spiritual issues. Obviously it is not to be confused with the Yoga branch of Brahmanical thought, though Yogācāra is in fact so named because it places emphasis on spiritual practices (*yoga*) like meditation. Around AD 500, so about a century after Vasubandhu, Yogācāra found its most brilliant exponent in the person of Dignāga. We'll be looking at his ideas in logic and epistemology, as well as the criticism and revision of Dignāga's thought at the hands of Dharmakīrti, who wrote about one further century on, at about AD 600 (see Chapters 42–4). That's about as far as we'll be going in this book, but it should be mentioned that these figures set the agenda for subsequent Buddhist philosophy. Later authors tend to write either commentaries on Dharmakīrti, as in Dharmottara's *Nyāyabinduṭīkā* (*Gloss on the Drop of Logic*), or manuals presenting the main elements of his thought in a more manageable form, as in Mokṣākaragupta's *Tarkabhāṣā* (*The Language of Logic*), written in the eleventh century.

The fairly bewildering multiplication of schools and textual traditions within Buddhism may recall the scholasticism of later Islamic or Latin medieval thought. All the more so given that the social and institutional context for all these developments was not entirely dissimilar. Just as the Latin Christian Church and secular princes of Europe facilitated the rise of the universities, and the *madrasa* system was put in place by Muslim rulers and their viziers, so Buddhism received intermittent but often substantial support from various Indian rulers. Generous laypersons too were willing to do more than just put food in the begging bowls of monks. The lavish gifts of both groups made it possible to build spectacular *stūpas*, or Buddhist shrines; to carve out and decorate whole complexes of caves for monastic life and study; and to found such establishments as the great center of learning at Nālandā, a huge monastery that is frequently described as playing the role of a "university." Before we took you along the forking paths of the history of ancient Buddhism, you might have wondered how Buddhist scholars could have spent decades studying at such a place, given the relative simplicity of the Buddha's original teaching. But when you consider the mass of writings produced by all these different groups and the fact that a competent Buddhist philosopher would furthermore need detailed understanding of the Brahmanical schools for the sake of refuting them, you begin to believe that one or two reincarnations might be needed to explain a truly accomplished thinker like Vasubandhu or Dharmakīrti.

Things are a bit more straightforward with the Jainas. As we have mentioned already (Chapter 11), Jainism too split into two branches, the Śvetāmbara and Digambara, or "white clad" and "sky clad." But fortunately we can ignore this, because the philosophers we'll be discussing would be read and accepted by both sides. The three founding figures of Jaina philosophy are Kundakunda, Umāsvati, and Siddhasena Divākara. They may have lived in the third, fourth, and fifth centuries respectively, but their dates are not known with much accuracy. No less than the Buddhists, the Jainas were deeply knowledgeable about other systems of Indian philosophy. Their descriptions of these other systems tend to be faithful, which can make them a useful source for otherwise lost ideas. They are also sophisticated doxographers. The eighth-century Haribhadra Sūri composed a very useful book called *Compendium of the Six Systems*. This does not refer to the six Brahmanical schools we considered earlier, but rather Buddhism and Jainism plus four Hindu systems. The only thing Haribhadra really regards as beyond the pale is Cārvāka naturalism.[9]

There is a good reason for the Jainas' interest in the ideas of other intellectual traditions, and in this case it was not just a matter of knowing one's enemy. Actually Jainas don't really have enemies. Their philosophy is justly celebrated for its inclusivism, codified in a theory of the "non-onesidedness" (*anekāntavāda*) of reality and in the idea that truth is always approached from a specific point of view (*naya*).[10] The pluralism of Jaina metaphysics is summed up by Kundakunda in the following rather dense remark: "all substances are nondifferent from the substantial viewpoint, but again they are different from the modificational viewpoint, because of the individual modification pervading it for the time being. According to some modification or other it is stated that a substance exists, does not exist, is indescribable, is both or otherwise."[11] We will explain the various elements in this statement below, in particular the idea that there are different metaphysical standpoints (see Chapter 39).

Whereas Kundakunda wrote exclusively in Prakrit, Umāsvati was the first Jaina philosopher to compose philosophical works in Sanskrit. He even calls his great treatise a *sūtra*: the *Tattvārtha-sūtra* (*Sūtra on What There Is*). Almost every Jaina philosopher of any significance would, in the course of the subsequent centuries, write a commentary on this book, using the opportunity to defend their own views and attack those of their foes. So maybe Jainas do have enemies after all? Certainly they were willing to defend their own perspectivalism against its critics. We should bear this in mind as we consider the relation of Jaina epistemology to the other teachings of their tradition. It's often assumed that this epistemology is a kind of intellectual version of *aḥimsā*: just as the Jaina observes strict non-violence in practical matters, so in theoretical matters the Jaina embraces principles of tolerance and harmony. While this interpretation may not be entirely wrongheaded, it seems at least too simple. For the Jainas were just as ready as the Brahmanical thinkers and the Buddhists to engage in that quintessential ancient Indian philosophical practice: debate.

35

IT ALL DEPENDS

NĀGĀRJUNA ON EMPTINESS

Unless you count the Beatles' *White Album*, the Rolling Stones' song "Paint it Black" is rock music's greatest tribute to monochrome. With the opening lyric Mick Jagger means to tell us something about his mental state. But he also tells us something about the way things outside us relate to our mental states. He would *like* the door to be black, either because that would match his mood or because he was hoping to visit the prime minister. Yet it stubbornly insists on being a jolly red. We might say that the door and its properties are independent of us, of our desires and attitudes, and indeed independent of anything else. The door is red in itself, just as it is in itself a door, and our perception and knowledge of the door needs to be true to those independent and intrinsic facts. Well, we might say that, but Nāgārjuna would not. He challenges the assumption that there are such independent, free-standing things and properties. Instead, all things are marked by "dependent origination (*pratītya-samutpāda*)," which means that they are "empty."

This is the core teaching of the Madhyamaka or "Middle Way" Buddhist philosophy. As Nāgārjuna puts it his *Verses on the Middle Way*, "whatever is dependently co-arisen, that is explained to be emptiness. That, being a dependent designation, is itself the middle way" (*MK* 24.18).[1] Nāgārjuna's teaching on emptiness is one of the most intriguing, but also most controversial, developments in ancient Indian thought. It has been seen as mystical and skeptical, as metaphysical and anti-metaphysical, as admirably consistent and deliberately contradictory; it has provoked comparisons to philosophers ranging from the ancient skeptics to Kant, Heidegger, and Wittgenstein. Its historical influence has also been enormous, with Madhyamaka enjoying only limited success in India but flourishing elsewhere in Asia, especially Tibet, where Nāgārjuna is revered as "the second Buddha." His writings are powerfully opposed to the theories of the Vedic schools we have been looking at for much of this book. He argues vociferously with the Nyāya, the Vaiśeṣika, and to some extent the other "systems" we have considered. Apparently he was a contemporary of Gautama, given that there are passages in the latter's

Nyāya-sūtra that look as if they have Nāgārjuna in mind, and conversely, passages where Nāgārjuna seems to be attacking Gautama.[2] Yet Nāgārjuna's principal philosophical opponents are arguably other Buddhists, mainly the Abhidharma school.

In fact, one way of thinking about Nāgārjuna's project is that he takes earlier Buddhist skeptical tendencies further than other Buddhists had been willing to go—indeed about as far as anyone could imagine going. As we know, it was standard fare in Buddhist philosophy to reject the reality of certain entities, especially "selves" but also wholes, the classic example being the chariot that is nothing more than its parts. The Buddha sometimes seemed to admit the existence of such things, as with remarks suggesting that the self can survive into another life and reap the karmic fruits of its actions. But most Buddhists saw this as a concession to conventional modes of thinking, made for the sake of teaching those who have not yet understood the deeper truths of Buddhism. According to that deeper teaching, the doctrine of rebirth requires no enduring self.[3] Nāgārjuna's philosophy makes no such concession. It instead convicts all apparent reality of being "empty (*śūnya*)." We had better be careful to get this idea right, given the warning issued by Nāgārjuna himself: "emptiness wrongly conceived can ruin a slow-witted person. It would be like a mis-held snake or a poorly executed incantation" (*MK* 24.11).

It seems clear that with his notion of emptiness Nāgārjuna is making a contribution to metaphysics. To say that an object is "empty" means denying that it has what he calls *svabhāva*, or "self-nature" (*VV* 1.22).[4] And this in turn means for it to be independent of other things. Consider Mick Jagger standing before the red door. As we said, it would seem that the redness is "intrinsic" to the door. Jagger's viewing the door does not make it red, nor does anything else. It is just red in itself. By contrast, the door has other properties that arise only through a relation, such as the door's being six feet away from a depressed rock star. In his *Verses on the Middle Way*, however, Nāgārjuna works to undermine this contrast between the intrinsic and relative properties of things. He considers a wide range of phenomena—whole and part, cause and effect, sensation and what is sensed, motion and what is moved—and shows that in every case, what may seem to have a fixed essence of its own is in fact relative. When Mick Jagger sees the red door, he depends on the door in order to be someone who sees, and the red door depends on him to be seen as red, or as a door. Sensation is like a child born of two parents (*MK* 3.7).

This constitutes Nāgārjuna's interpretation of the Buddha's famous teaching that everything in the world is "interdependent." He would see rival Buddhist schools as insufficiently committed to this teaching, as insufficiently careful to avoid essentialism. His view can be contrasted to Abhidharma Buddhist theories that invoked so-called *dharmas*, which analyzed all experience as being made up of fleeting, individual processes.[5] Where an Ābhidharmika might say that a *dharma* such as a moment of conscious awareness (*citta*) has the property of "arising," Nāgārjuna would say that this makes no sense. "Arising" cannot have any instrinsic reality, which would allow it to ground the occurrence of the moment of consciousness. The "arising" of that moment of consciousness would itself have to "arise," or be produced, and this would lead to a regress (MK 7.3).[6] More generally, insofar as some Abhidharma Buddhists described *dharmas* as having an independent "self-nature," their theory will fall prey to Nāgārjuna's battery of skeptical arguments.[7] Of course, these same arguments will also destroy a system like that put forward by Vaiśeṣika, which envisions that an independently existing substance (*dravya*) can have intrinsic properties.

What does this theory of emptiness leave standing? Some think the answer is obvious: nothing. A few modern-day scholars and many ancient thinkers have associated Nāgārjuna with "nihilism," the view that nothing is real. But this seems more like a polemical criticism of his teaching than a plausible interpretation. This philosophy styles itself as a "Middle Way," and as Nāgārjuna expert Jan Westerhoff has rightly pointed out, it's hard to imagine a more extreme and less moderate view than nihilism.[8] Instead, Nāgārjuna charts a course between two more extreme positions, eternalism and annihilationism, which were prevalent in Nāgārjuna's own day and perhaps more so in the days of the Buddha. The eternalist is an essentialist, and claims that each object exists independently of any others by having an immutable essence. The annihilationist claims that objects do not exist at all. Nāgārjuna's middle position is that objects do indeed exist, but not by subsisting in themselves. Instead, the nature and subsistence of each thing is determined by that thing's relations to other objects. Thus redness is "empty" not because there is no such thing as red, but because redness always depends on other things—the door that has the red color, for instance.

Here it's worth mentioning that the Sanskrit word for "empty," *śūnya*, has another technical sense in Sanskrit. It was used by the early Indian mathematicians as the name for zero. The point of introducing "zero" in their counting system was to provide a place-marker: in the number 307, the zero in the middle indicates that the tens' place is "empty." It seems unlikely that there is an actual historical connection between this mathematical use of *śūnya* and Nāgārjuna's philosophical use. Yet there is an analogy between the two. As Bimal Matilal has remarked, in Madhyamaka "objects are like zeroes, having a value (a claim to reality) only in relation to something else or to the position it occupies in a complex, and consequently no absolute value."[9]

One might object that redness cannot be like zero. It needs to have some kind of intrinsic essence to secure the meaning of the word. We would refer to this essence every time we use the word "red," whether we apply it to the door or Mick Jagger's gloriously full lips. But Nāgārjuna insists that our words, and also our concepts and philosophical theories, have no independent meaning, any more than objects have independent "metaphysical" properties. The word "redness" does play a role in our language, but there is no discrete thing out in the world to which it refers. To unmask the emptiness of words and concepts, Nāgārjuna uses a style of argument called *prasaṅga*. Basically this means showing that a given concept would imply a contradiction if it had independent reality or essence. It's obvious how this would work in the case of something like a round square. Suppose I say "this round square is round." That obviously involves a contradiction, namely that a square is round. But neither can I deny that a round square is round—if a round square is anything, then it is surely round. The upshot is that the "round circle" is not anything after all. The phrase has no referent and no real meaning, since allowing the reality of a round square would land us in absurdities.

Nāgārjuna is a master at applying this form of argument to apparently innocuous cases, and showing that they too are "empty." A nice example is his treatment of causation (*MK* 1; see also *MK* 7).[10] Nāgārjuna begins by distinguishing between a cause as such (*hetu*) and a mere causal condition (*pratyaya*). A cause as such is that from which something originates, while a causal condition is that whose occurrence is necessary for its existence. This idea of a causal condition has an impeccable Buddhist pedigree, since it appears in the formulation of the Four Noble Truths: there is suffering, suffering has a cause, the removal of the causes of suffering will result in the cessation of suffering, and there is an eightfold Path for removing the causes of suffering. Here the cause of suffering, namely attachment, is what Nāgārjuna calls a "condition," something whose continuing presence is necessary for the continuing existence of its effect. So long as you continue to be attached to things, you will continue to suffer.

This gives us another way to express the meaning of "emptiness." When Nāgārjuna says that all things are empty, he is saying that all things have causal conditions on which they depend. Again, the existence of each thing depends on something else, and nothing is self-sufficient. An opponent might reply that this is obviously false. Once a potter makes a pot, the pot is self-sufficient. In general, the opponent will infer, we can say that many things "originate" from their causes and then have independent existence. Nāgārjuna opens his *Verses on the Middle Way* with a *prasaṅga* attack on this way of thinking, which shows that the notion of "origination" leads to contradictions. He lays out four options for how such origination might come about (*MK* 1.1). First, a thing might originate spontaneously, so that it is self-caused. But this cannot be right, because the thing would have to exist first in order to bring itself into existence, which is absurd. So let's consider a second possibility: each thing is entirely originated by something else, like when a potter makes a pot. But upon reflection we see that the pot's continued existence does not depend on the potter; the potter can die without the pot's vanishing. So something else—for instance the clay from which the pot is made—must be explaining how the pot is continuing to persist.

Fine then, the opponent may say. How about a third option? The thing's existence might be caused by both itself *and* something else. To this option, too, Nāgārjuna says "no" (he is much better at saying "no" than he is at saying "yes"). If this were the case, then one part of the thing would depend on itself while another part of it would depend on something else. Having made this distinction, we can just apply the previous arguments against self-causation and other-causation to these two parts. Now rather exasperated, the opponent may resort to saying that things originate neither out of themselves nor out of others. In an entirely predictable move, Nāgārjuna says "no." This would be tantamount to admitting that the thing is permanent or eternal, rather than being originated, which would be to give up on the whole notion that it was caused in the first place. The upshot is that there is no option according to which the notion of causal origination makes sense. As a concept it fares no better than the round square.

Now, it doesn't necessarily follow from this that Nāgārjuna wants to ban all talk of origination. Though it has been said that he "attempts to shatter any set of concepts designed to give an intelligible account of the everyday world,"[11] he may be happy for us to continue using our concepts in that everyday world. A predominant line of interpretation of Nāgārjuna, beginning with his sixth-century commentator Candrakīrti and carrying on in the later Tibetan tradition, claims that he is trying to show that our concepts are *conventional*, fit for communication and other practical purposes.[12] It is only when these concepts are deployed in philosophical theories, theories about how things "really are in themselves," that the Madhyamaka critique begins to bite. This is why Nāgārjuna is sometimes compared to figures like Wittgenstein. So long as one is using language as it is meant to be used, there is no problem saying that the potter makes the pot. It is only when this making is taken as an aspect of "ultimate reality" or a theory of causation that we run into problems, because we have moved away from the conventional use of the words. This would explain why Nāgārjuna, and the Madhyamaka school of Buddhism in general, put so much weight on a distinction between "two truths." There is the truth as it seems in the conventional world of everyday transaction (*samvṛtti-sat*), and there is truth as things are in reality (*paramārtha-sat*), how things really are in themselves, quite apart from their utility to us. Again, this distinction could be rooted in early interpretations designed to dispel apparent contradictions within the Buddha's own teaching. Here it would be turned to a more ambitious philosophical—or better, anti-philosophical—purpose.

According to the conventionalist reading, Nāgārjuna thinks that we cannot get at things in themselves, either because the very notion of an ultimate reality is incoherent or simply because we do not have the cognitive resources to get at things as they truly are. But a rival interpretation—the one we suggested above—would happily admit that Nāgārjuna has a metaphysical view about ultimate reality. He is saying that reality is always relative. His point then would be that "conventional" concepts and language misrepresent things by treating them as if they were independent and had intrinsic properties; the theory of emptiness would allow us to see things aright by exposing their interdependence. To this we can add yet a third possible way of understanding Nāgārjuna. Perhaps he is just a thoroughgoing skeptic, like his near contemporary Sextus Empiricus. On this reading, Nāgārjuna's arguments are neither negative nor positive but simply dialectical and reactive. His sole aim would be to undermine the concepts and theories of other philosophers, without ever putting forward any philosophical position or theory of his own. This interpretation is supported by Nāgārjuna's famous remark that his teaching involves the "abandonment of all views (*dṛṣṭi*)" (*MK* 27.30, the concluding verse of the book).[13]

A good way of testing these interpretations, and of testing Nāgārjuna as a philosopher, is to ask whether his Madhyamaka teaching collapses into self-refutation. If his position is that all statements are empty of content or reference, then it seems to undermine itself. For if the statement that all statements are empty is itself empty, then it can safely be dismissed. If on the other hand the Middle Way philosophy is not empty, then it is a counterexample to what it itself claims, namely that all philosophical formulations are empty! Nāgārjuna's critics must have pressed this point upon him during his own life, whether Gautama the Naiyāyika or the Abhidharma Buddhists he so vigorously attacked. To answer them Nāgārjuna wrote a second book, winningly entitled *Dispeller of Disputes*, in which he tried to defuse the allegation that Middle Way philosophy is self-defeating. To the accusation that his arguments can achieve nothing if they are "empty," he responds that the chariot too is empty, but it can still carry wood.[14]

What, then, would it mean to say that the emptiness thesis is itself empty? Nāgārjuna's answer seems to be that he in fact has no thesis, no philosophical theory, at least not of the same type as his rival philosophical systems. To explain this he offers two analogies, both meant to show the difference between his "empty" statements and the statements that constitute a philosophical system. First, there is what we might call the silence analogy (*VV* 3.25–6). Nāgārjuna imagines his opponent saying that the doctrine of emptiness is like someone who shouts the command "silence!" In so doing, he only succeeds in making a noise, thus defeating his own purpose. But Nāgārjuna turns the analogy to his own advantage. If there is indeed silence, we cannot announce that there is. The fact that there is silence cannot be said out loud. In the same way, if all the concepts we habitually use to make the world around us intelligible are devoid of meaning and significance, then this is something that cannot itself be announced using those same empty concepts. But although it cannot be announced, this does not mean it isn't true, just as there can be silence even though no one can observe that there is silence without falsifying this very observation.

A second analogy invokes the idea of an "artificial person" (*VV* 23, 27). The Middle Way philosophy is like the action of one artificial person preventing the actions of another, or of a magician doing magic to counter another magician's spell. The point of this analogy is perhaps just that, even though the statement that all theses are empty is itself empty and so cannot state anything, it can still show or reveal that this is the true state of affairs. Nāgārjuna fights empty statements with more empty statements. Certainly these statements do not urge us to make emptiness itself into a kind of metaphysical reality. To claim that the redness of the door is empty is not to say that there is emptiness there instead of redness. It is to correct a mistake about the redness of the door, namely the error of believing that redness has independent existence.[15] Nāgārjuna's Middle Way is not, then, self-refuting. His words imply something that cannot be stated: that the very words he is using are without foundation. This is not just another move in the game of language, but an ironic intervention within it.[16]

36

MOTION DENIED

NĀGĀRJUNA ON CHANGE

It has been helpful in writing this book together that we agree about most things. In particular, we both believe that Indian philosophy is fascinating. We part ways, however, when it comes to the relative merits of giraffes and crocodiles. Jonardon is unfailingly polite on the subject of giraffes, whereas Peter is somewhat more grudging in his admiration of crocodiles. But we each have a clear preference. To settle the matter we recently agreed to organize a race between Gena and Hiawatha. Gena being a crocodile, his legs are on the short side, so we allowed his a head start. Jonardon was confident that despite her fleetness of hoof, Hiawatha could not possibly overtake Gena. Peter assumed that Jonardon must have been reading Zeno of Elea, the ancient Greek thinker who invented a series of paradoxes to challenge the possibility of motion. According to Zeno, Gena's lead cannot be overcome, because Hiawatha would always first need to arrive at the point recently occupied by Gena, by which time Gena would have made further forward progress. It turned out, though, that Jonardon was not thinking of Zeno at all. He'd actually been reading Nāgārjuna.

Nāgārjuna was not the first Indian thinker to deny the possibility of motion. In his great commentary on Pāṇini, the grammarian Patañjali refers to a teaching that motion is not an objectively real thing. It is a mere conceptual construct, used to explain the fact that things arrive at a given place.[1] This same idea is maintained by Nāgārjuna in the second chapter of his *Verses on the Middle Way*. He applies his *prasaṅga* dialectical method to two questions about motion, arguing that they are unanswerable: where are movements located and when do they begin? His aim, as usual, is to show us that our concept of motion is an empty one. And as usual, scholars disagree about the purpose of his arguments. Is Nāgārjuna saying that human cognition is simply not up to the job of conceiving the world correctly, and that we should stop trying? Or that our conventional idea of motion needs to be replaced with some more refined philosophical theory, which avoids postulating intrinsic essences in things? Some help in interpreting him is offered by the

Madhyamaka commentator Candrakīrti, who does much to elaborate Nāgārjuna's discussion. So we will also refer to him, while bearing in mind that his reading is only one possible interpretation of Nāgārjuna's verses.

Our first question is, where are movements located? We can approach this question with the help of those same Sanskrit grammarians.[2] They tell us that verbal roots may refer to either actions, or events, and that actions and events may be "located" either where the agent is, or where the object of the verb is. Thus a verb like "enter" could refer to the event of Jonardon's walking into a racetrack to watch a contest between a giraffe and a crocodile. The event of his entering is located where he is located, namely at the gate. By contrast a verb like "hit" would refer to an action which is located in the thing being hit, such as the gong that Peter strikes to signal the start of the race. Presupposing these grammatical notions, Nāgārjuna says that if we imagine someone traveling, we can say that "the traveler travels [the place that] is being traveled." The verb "travel" marks an event, namely the event of traveling, which is located in the place where the traveling happens, perhaps a spot on a road. In fact, Nāgārjuna proposes, there are two things going on here. The place of traveling is being traveled, and the traveler is traveling (*MK* 2.1).

So far, so common sense. But this is Nāgārjuna, who likes to use common sense as a jumping off point for *prasaṅga* refutations. If we take the path of a motion, such as Gena's rather slow progress along a 100-meter track, then we can divide it into three portions: the part already traversed, the part yet to be traversed, and the part currently being traversed. Which of these portions is the location of the event that is Gena's motion? Obviously not the first or the second, since the place *currently* being traversed cannot be the place that he has already managed to traverse, or the place he has not yet reached. So the motion must be occurring in the place that is just now being moved across. But this too is impossible, thinks Nāgārjuna. Candrakīrti explains the reasoning as follows.[3] Every point on the path of motion is either a point not yet traversed, or a point yet to be traversed, and there is no portion of the path left over to accommodate the current motion. This is reminiscent of a skeptical argument about time we have seen before, in Gautama's *Nyāya-sūtra*: past and future do not currently exist, while the present has no duration, being merely the dividing line between past and future (see Chapter 31).

If you don't find that convincing, here is another argument (*MK* 2.2–6). Consider again the sentences "the place of traveling is being traveled" and "the place of movement is being traversed." Nāgārjuna points out that such sentences are redundant. It is like announcing, "I am where I am" (which, coincidentally, is what Popeye would say if he were a GPS navigation device) or like replying to the question "where was the race held?" by saying "it happened where the race took place." Such statements make no substantive claim at all, any more than does someone who claims to have solved a crime by saying that it was committed by whoever perpetrated the crime. Similar considerations can be brought to bear against "the mover moves." This statement is what philosophers call a tautology. It is guaranteed to be true but at the price of being uninformative, like "the bachelor is unmarried." It is useless to point to Hiawatha as she sprints along a racetrack and remark, "the running Hiawatha is running." On the other hand, if Hiawatha is *not* running, then it is false to point to her and say that she is running (*MK* 2.3).[4] It seems, then, that there is no way to say truly and informatively that she is running.

A way around this might be to suggest that there is some *further* motion (MK 2.6). The thought here seems to be that we can explain Hiawatha's running by positing a second motion that makes her to be running. But if there are two motions, surely there should be two things moving and not only one. Or perhaps not. Mightn't the one giraffe Hiawatha be the subject of numerous actions and motions, as when she simultaneously runs, hears the cheering crowds, and narrows her eyes as she glares ahead at her opponent Gena? Candrakīrti's answer to this objection trades on a subtlety of Sanskrit grammatical theory.[5] We can say numerous things about an axe, such as "the axe is made of metal," "she sees the axe," and "she cuts the tree with the axe." In these three statements one and the same object, the axe, is playing different grammatical roles in relation to a verb. First it is the agent, then the direct object, then the instrument. So these various statements refer to the axe only insofar as it adopts these different roles. To speak of cutting a tree with an axe is to refer to the axe-as-instrument, not the axe-as-object-of-vision.

Likewise, running-Hiawatha is not identical to hearing-Hiawatha or seeing-Hiawatha. Only running-Hiawatha is Hiawatha insofar as she exercises the capacity to run. The same observation can be applied to the place where Hiawatha is running. Insofar as Hiawatha is traversing that place, it is not just a patch of ground but a spot-being-traveled-over. This is an illuminating explanation of Nāgārjuna's compressed argument. The problem is not simply that it is trivial and uninformative to say that the place being traveled over is being traveled over, and that the mover moves. It is also that this uninformative explanation is actually the *only* way to describe what is happening. For it is only the thing insofar as it is moving that moves, only the running Hiawatha who runs.

Notice that this whole line of argument can easily be applied to phenomena other than motion. If Mick Jagger sees a red door and wants it painted black, then he sees the door insofar as it is seen, and wants it painted black only insofar as it is the object of his desire. When Nāgārjuna tackles the subject of motion here toward the beginning of his *Verses on the Middle Way*, he is giving us a first taste of his idea of dependent origination. The motion of running is dependent on, or cannot exist without, running-Hiawatha, and vice versa. The same style of argument is later used to show that an object of vision is "co-originated" with an act of seeing, and the object of desire "co-originated" with a desire. Jan Westerhoff has thus written that the chapter on movement "was not meant to be a specific investigation of the problem of motion and the various structural properties of time and space. Rather it uses the discussion of motion as an example to illustrate an argumentative template which can be used in a variety of different contexts."[6]

Assuming that we have reconstructed Nāgārjuna's argument correctly, we can now ask whether there is any way to escape it. It may seem that the answer is obviously "yes." All we need to do is distinguish between, on the one hand, the various roles that Hiawatha can perform and, on the other hand, Hiawatha herself. The fact that Hiawatha plays different grammatical functions in different statements does not show what Candrakīrti seems to think it does, namely that it is impossible for us to form a notion of Hiawatha in herself. Nor need we deny that one and the same patch of ground on a racetrack could first be the place occupied by Gena and then a few seconds later the place occupied by Hiawatha. But of course this reply presupposes the very idea that Nāgārjuna's Madhyamaka philosophy is devoted to undermining. It presupposes that there are in fact things in themselves, like the substances recognized by Vaiśeṣika, which can take on and then lose various properties and relations. As we saw last time, Nāgārjuna offers a powerful challenge to this way of thinking, namely that *any* way of describing a supposed "substance" will need to invoke some property with which the substance as so described is mutually interdependent. And Sanskrit grammar would seem to agree with him. If you cannot frame a sentence about Hiawatha or a patch of ground without associating it somehow with a certain verb, then you cannot refer to these things without treating them as playing a certain role that is marked by the grammar of a sentence.

A second line of argument offered by Nāgārjuna seems to be more specifically concerned with the nature of motion itself, rather than being just one example of a more general strategy. Here he turns to the other question we mentioned at the outset: "when do motions begin?" Nāgārjuna of course wants to show that any answer to this question is bound to be incoherent (*MK* 2.12–14). Let's consider the very start of the race, when Gena starts to run (well, waddle). As before, we may make a threefold division. There is a period of time at which Gena's waddling has not yet occurred, another period of time when her waddling is taking place, and a third period of time at which she has already finished waddling. In which of these three does her motion begin? Obviously not in the time before she begins her ponderous journey, since at that point she is still waiting to hear the starter's gong. Just as obviously she does not begin moving in the time after she has already moved. But neither does she *begin* to waddle while she is moving, since once she is underway, she must already have started. The implication is that she does not begin to move at all, which means that Hiawatha should have a good chance of catching her—if only she could begin moving herself.

Here we can see why many scholars have sought to compare Nāgārjuna with Zeno.[7] His paradoxes of motion included the argument that an arrow in flight can never reach its target, since at each moment the arrow is as Zeno put it, "against something equal." He probably meant that in a durationless instant of time, the arrow occupies a spatial extension identical in size to the arrow's own size. During a single instant the arrow cannot get from one spatial region to the next. But if this is true at every instant, then it cannot move at all. Thus, as Tom Stoppard observed, Saint Sebastian died of fright.[8] Nāgārjuna's argument is indeed reminiscent of Zeno's. It would license the similar conclusion that all the warriors slain by Arjuna's bow in the *Mahābhārata* likewise died of fright, and it turns on the same problem about the relation between motion and an unextended part of time. Yet Nāgārjuna is not making quite the same point. He is asking about the time at which motion *begins*, and not just any instant at which motion supposedly occurs. Indeed, a closer comparison from Greek philosophy may be Aristotle's worries about whether changes may be said to have a first or last instant.[9]

Furthermore, if we step back and consider the whole battery of arguments offered by Nāgārjuna—especially if we follow the interpretation of Candrakīrti—we see that they are unlike Zeno's in that they are inspired by grammar. We might say that Nāgārjuna focuses not so much on the question whether motion is a coherent concept, as on the question whether language can consistently and informatively *describe* motion. Sentences about motion appear to have the same logical form as sentences describing actions and events. He takes this to mean that the motion, like any action or event, is located at a place and at a time. But motion is precisely a *displacement during a passage of time*, so the attempt to fix just one location or moment for any motion is doomed to failure. We might introduce an artificial way of speaking in order to evade the contradiction, as when physicists designate points of space and time using a coordinate system. Yet this would just be to concede his point that natural languages have no adequate resources for describing motion.

As we've said, Nāgārjuna uses the same style of argument to unmask the emptiness of things other than motion. A comparable discussion concerns cognition, which is a particularly central issue since it is the bone of contention between him and his Nyāya critics. Nāgārjuna again exploits the rules of Sanskrit grammar, which force us to treat verbs of thinking and knowing as acts that "happen to" an agent, just like motion does. In the *Dispeller of Disputes*, Nāgārjuna attempts to undermine the concept of knowledge by attacking the notion of giving a proof (*VV* 31–51). As you might recall, according to Gautama's Nyāya epistemology we are justified in reaching our beliefs on the basis of a "means of knowing" or *pramāṇa*, such as sensation or the faculty of reason. The thing known by such a legitimate means is called a *prameya*. So here we have the "instrument" and "direct object" that go with a verb of knowing. Just as Jonardon restrains Gena by using the instrument of a leash in order that she doesn't bite Hiawatha in anger after losing the race, so Jonardon knows that Gena is dark green by using the instrument of his eyesight. Here Jonardon is the knower, Gena the object known or *prameya*, and Jonardon's vision is the *pramāṇa*, the means by which knowledge is achieved.

Now, like an angered crocodile, Nāgārjuna strikes. We have just said that everything we know is known through some instrument by which knowledge is achieved. But how do we reach knowledge concerning these instruments, in particular the knowledge that they are reliable? If Jonardon is to know that Gena is green by using his eyesight, surely he also needs to know that his eyesight can be trusted. If he appeals to some further instrument of knowing, by which he reassures himself that his vision is indeed functioning properly, then he might still worry about that further instrument. Thus we have an infinite regress, with each *pramāṇa* standing in need of confirmation by a further *pramāṇa*. That at least is Nāgārjuna's basic idea, as we have mentioned previously when looking at strategies of skeptical argumentation (see Chapter 16). But let's look more carefully at the way he mounts his challenge, since it is such a good illustration of his argumentative technique.

As usual Nāgārjuna begins by classifying all possible responses to his own question, which in this case is the question how a *pramāṇa* can be established as reliable. One option is that a source of knowledge may be validated "intrinsically," that is, without any reference to things that are known. There are three ways this might happen. First, a source of knowledge might be validated by another source of knowledge; this is where Nāgārjuna invokes the infinite regress. Second, we might simply insist that sources of knowledge do not require validation. This is, one could argue, the whole point of distinguishing between a *prameya* and a *pramāṇa*. The object needs to be established, but the source or means of knowledge does not. Nāgārjuna rules this out, though, on the basis of our starting assumption that whatever is known must be known through some means. After all, if things can simply be known without assurance from a means of knowledge, why do we need the *pramāṇa* in the first place? Furthermore, what is the basis for distinguishing between the *pramāṇa* that supposedly needs no verification, and the *prameya* that does? Any *pramāṇa*, such as vision, can become a *prameya*. When I am asked to read the optician's chart, this is a test that seeks to establish whether or not my eyesight is functioning well. So there is no general difference in kind between means of knowledge and objects of knowledge.

The final option is that each means of knowledge is self-validating. It establishes itself along with the other objects of knowledge that it makes known. Thus eyesight would have to guarantee its own reliability, even as it makes known visible objects. It would be like a fire that illuminates both itself and other things. To this Nāgārjuna retorts that it is meaningless to say that "fire is illuminated." Fire is the source of light, whereas what is illuminated is what receives light from such a source. To suppose that a *pramāṇa* can make itself known the way it makes other things known is like saying that an axe cuts itself. Again, the argument invokes a grammatical point. If the source of knowledge plays the role of *instrument* for the action of knowing, then it cannot also play the role of the *object* for that action.

So much for the idea that sources of knowledge are validated intrinsically. Might they instead be justified "extrinsically (*parataḥ*)," that is, in relation to the objects of knowledge? This time there are only two alternatives to consider. First, we might suppose that the source of knowledge is actually validated by its own objects. This may sound a bit bizarre, but the idea is actually quite straightforward. He simply means that vision, for example, is validated so long as it represents visible objects the way that they really are. We might say that the source of knowledge is corroborated by its "correspondence" to the things it makes known. But this, says Nāgārjuna, is to assume the very thing at issue, namely that the objects of knowledge are established. But that was precisely the job of the *pramāṇa*, so it cannot be assumed as a basis for confirming the *pramāṇa* itself. The opponent would be committing the logical fallacy called *siddha-sādhana*, "proving what is already proven." This leaves only one further option for the opponent, but it is entirely unpromising. We might suppose that the sources of knowledge and the objects known are mutually interdependent. Actually this sounds pretty congenial to Madhyamaka, but as Nāgārjuna points out it is hopeless as a theory of justification that his opponent would want to adopt, since it is obviously circular.

The result of all this is, apparently, to let us know that nothing can be known. Obviously, this looks like another case where Nāgārjuna may be refuting himself. How can I *know* that *knowledge* is impossible? And how can a complex set of logical arguments be given for the conclusion that no conclusion can ever be established by reason, or by any other means? Nāgārjuna might respond that he is simply using the methods of his opponents against them. If the whole exercise is an internal critique of the justificatory system put forth by philosophers like Gautama, then it can establish the incoherence of that system without implying any commitment to the system on Nāgārjuna's part. This is actually a rather familiar phenomenon. Consider an anti-democratic political movement trying to come to power through a democratic election, a poem about the impossibility of writing poetry, or even phrases like "I can't recommend Buster Keaton silent films highly enough," which one might say precisely to get across with sufficient emphasis how strongly the films are being recommended. It seems then that Nāgārjuna can avoid being bitten by his own snake.

37

NO FOUR WAYS ABOUT IT

NĀGĀRJUNA'S TETRALEMMA

Life is full of yes–no questions. Will you marry me? Is that new movie worth seeing? Do you want fries with that? But sometimes things are more complicated. If you are asked whether the *Godfather* movies are worth seeing, you shouldn't just say "yes" or "no," but "yes and no," because the first two are essential viewing, the third one a disappointment. In other cases, the answer is "neither yes nor no." If you are asked whether the fourth *Godfather* movie is worth seeing, the right answer would be to challenge the question itself: no such film has so far been made. The same is true in philosophy. Frequently philosophers straightforwardly argue for a positive or negative answer to a given question: yes, we do have free will; no, God doesn't exist. But perhaps just as often, they argue for a more nuanced conclusion. We see this in a work of medieval scholastic philosophy like Thomas Aquinas' *Summa theologiae*, where questions are posed and then resolved by means of distinctions: depending on how the question is construed, it is susceptible of different answers. As for saying neither yes nor no, a standard bit of philosophical repertoire nowadays is the identification of "category mistakes." If you're asked whether the soul is located in the brain, you might reply by saying that the very way the question is posed is mistaken, because the soul is immaterial and has no spatial location at all.[1]

Despite the fact that these are standard philosophical moves, the philosophical study of logic has usually contented itself with studying the simpler "yes or no" situation. Indeed a fundamental rule of classical logic, beginning with Aristotle, is the law of the excluded middle. It states that, for any given proposition, either it is true or its negation is.[2] Either *The Godfather* is worth seeing or it is not; there is no third option. You might wonder how Aristotle could have overlooked the two more complex possibilities "yes and no," and "neither yes nor no." After all, Aristotle was himself fond of the "yes and no" answer, and in fact helped inspire Aquinas' use of that tactic. But he could defend the law of the excluded middle by saying that it only applies to meaningful propositions with clearly defined terms. It will hold only so long as we are not making a category mistake, like assuming the soul has spatial location, or speaking too imprecisely, as when we ask about the quality of all *Godfather* movies collectively instead of taking them one by one. This solution involves limiting the range of statements to which our logic is applied. But there is another possibility: we could expand our logic to take in the more nuanced possibilities. This is what we find in Buddhism, and in particular in Nāgārjuna.

In the past couple of chapters we've already seen him using the *prasaṅga* technique to undermine the pretensions of dogmatic philosophical systems. His strategy is to set out an exhaustive and exclusive list of all the logically possible positions concerning some topic, and then to show that each position is untenable. Typically his list of options has four, not two, possibilities. This is his doctrine of the "four alternatives (*catuṣkoṭi*)," usually translated as "tetralemma." Nāgārjuna takes it to be definitive of Buddhist philosophy. He writes, "everything is such as it is, not such as it is, both such as it is and not such as it is, and neither such as it is nor not such as it is. That is the Buddha's teaching" (*MK* 18.8). As Nāgārjuna says here, the tetralemma is not original with him—it appears in earlier reports on the Buddha's teachings—but he does deploy it with unprecedented rigor and relentlessness.

In the formulation we just quoted, Nāgārjuna simply lays out the four options. That isn't the whole method, though. Typically what he does is to give us the options and then refute *all four*. One can easily imagine Aristotle or Aquinas raising a quizzical eyebrow at this. It's one thing to say that a philosophical question can receive no clear "yes or no" answer, because it is insufficiently precise. It's another to rule out "yes," "no," "both," *and* "neither." We find a good example of this in the very opening of the *Verses on the Middle Way*, as if Nāgārjuna is modeling for us how he will be arguing in the entire work. Beginning as he means to go on, Nāgārjuna says, "at nowhere and at no time can entities ever exist by originating out of themselves, from others, from both [themselves and others], or from the lack of causes" (*MK* 1.1; discussed in Chapter 36). Later he applies the tetralemma to his own doctrine of emptiness, writing, "nothing could be asserted to be empty, not empty, both empty and not empty, and neither empty nor not empty. They are asserted only for the purpose of provisional understanding (*prajñapti*)" (*MK* 22.11). He seeks here to avoid self-refutation by refusing to endorse any philosophical thesis that would be on a par with all other philosophical doctrines.

Because the tetralemma is so central to Nāgārjuna's style of philosophy, and because it seems to flout the rules of logic as we know them, many scholars have tried to understand it. In this chapter we will, appropriately enough, discuss four such attempts. The great Polish Indologist Stanisław Schayer was the first to appreciate that the tetralemma presents a worthwhile logical problem.[3] He was a student of Łukasiewicz, the Polish logician who breathed new life into medieval Aristotelian syllogistic logic with the use of modern formal methods. It seems that Schayer wanted to do something similar for Nāgārjuna. He thought the tetralemma could be understood within the framework of classical propositional logic. Thus he took Nāgārjuna's options to be that a given disputed statement is either true, not true, both true and not true, or neither true nor not true:

p
not-p
p and not-p
not-p and not-not-p

But this interpretation is unsatisfactory, and for two reasons. For one thing the third option, that a given proposition is "both true and not true," is a straightforward contradiction. It doesn't represent a genuine alternative at all, so Nāgārjuna would be displaying considerable confusion by bothering to refute this as if it were a meaningful option. (Imagine someone taking trouble to refute the claim that there both is and is not a fourth *Godfather* movie.)

For another thing, on Schayer's reading the fourth option is equivalent to the third. That's because two negations cancel out, something exploited in the first *Godfather* movie by Sonny Corleone when he says that the FBI "don't respect nothing." Thus, to use another example from that film, the admittedly rather strange assertion "Luca Brasi both sleeps with the fishes and does not sleep with the fishes" would be equivalent to "Luca Brasi does not sleep with the fishes and does not *not* sleep with the fishes." Some scholars have nevertheless embraced this reading of Nāgārjuna, and triumphantly declared that Nāgārjuna rejects the law of non-contradiction, sometimes going on to add that this is what distinguishes Eastern philosophy from Western philosophy, adding for good measure that it also proves that Eastern philosophy is essentially mystical in orientation.[4] But this extravagant line of interpretation falls at the first hurdle, given that Nāgārjuna endorses the law of non-contradiction quite explicitly. In the midst of one of his refutations, he says that nobody can "perform an action that is both existent and non-existent, for they are contradictory. Where can existence and non-existence co-exist?" (*MK* 8.7).

Fortunately there are more plausible ways of understanding what Nāgārjuna is up to. One has been suggested by Richard Robinson.[5] He proposed that the tetralemma is not about whether propositions are true or false, but about whether a certain property belongs to a certain class of objects. This would bring the project closer to Aristotle's logic, since he was especially concerned with statements like "all humans are rational": that is, the property of rationality belongs to every member of the class of humans. As evidence Robinson could point to those lines that supposedly summarize the Buddha's teaching: "*everything* is such as it is, not such as it is," and so on (*MK* 18.8). Likewise in the other case we mentioned, where Nāgārjuna says that *everything* is self-caused, or *everything* is caused by another, and so on.

The advantage of this reading is that the third option will no longer be contradictory. Let's see why by using a simple example: having a color. On Robinson's reading, the tetralemma here would go as follows. First, maybe everything is blue. Seems unlikely, but it does make sense. Second, maybe nothing is blue. This too is comprehensible, though it would thwart the traditional advice given to brides about what to wear on their wedding day. Third, everything is blue and not blue. This may still sound contradictory, but it needn't be. It could mean simply that some things are blue and some not. When Billie Holiday asked "Am I Blue?" she was wondering which category she fell into. Fourth and finally, everything is both blue and not blue. This looks more problematic: yet again, it sounds like a straightforward contradiction. But Robinson thinks this too could be a meaningful option. The idea would be that if anything at all existed, it would be both blue and not blue. But we know it is impossible to be both blue and not blue; so on this option we could infer that nothing exists.

Unfortunately this reading does not fit the text very well. Nāgārjuna gives us no warning that the subject of the third statement, the "everything" in "everything is blue and not blue," needs to be split up, and understood as a claim about some things that are blue and some other things that are not blue. Also, the whole basis of Robinson's reading is that the tetralemma deals solely with classes of things, and not individuals. But if that is right, then Nāgārjuna would be unable to apply his favorite argumentative tool to counter one-off claims about particular objects. If I said "Billie Holiday really is blue, just listen to her sing," he would have to shrug his shoulders and agree.

More promising is the interpretation given by K.N. Jayatilleke, a Sri Lankan expert in early Buddhist logic and epistemology.[6] This turns on two insights. First, the oppositions considered by Nāgārjuna might have to do with opposite properties rather than sheer negations, for instance black and white, rather than black and not-black. Second, Nāgārjuna might be exploiting the idea that a part of something can have a property that the whole thing lacks. Jayatilleke gives the following example of a tetralemma: A is east of B, or A is west of B, or A is both east and west of B, or A is neither east nor west of B. Here again the third possibility, "A is both east and west of B," looks contradictory at first glance, but it isn't. Perhaps B is a point and A is an east–west running line that goes through that point (so A could be a line of latitude, and B a city it runs through). Then part of line A would indeed be east of B, and another part west of B—no contradiction arises at all. What about the "neither" alternative? Again, A could be a line and B a point, but this time the whole line is north of the point—as the line of latitude running through Boston is north of New York. That line of latitude is neither east, nor west, of New York.

Very clever, you might say, but isn't Jayatilleke cheating by using these unusual properties of east and west? Not really. We can also apply it in something simpler like the case of color. First, some things are wholly white, like a piece of chalk. Second, other things are wholly non-white, that is to say a wholly different color, like a lump of coal that is wholly black. Third, however much it might frustrate Mick Jagger, not everything is just painted black: some things are white and non-white, like a zebra. Finally, certain things are neither white nor non-white. Why? For a reason we mentioned at the outset of this chapter: it could just be a category mistake to apply the concept of color at all. The line of latitude running through Boston, for instance, is neither white, nor black, nor any other color.

Jayatilleke's reading seems promising, especially since it makes the tetralemma obviously applicable in philosophical contexts. When, at the beginning of his *Verses on the Middle Way*, Nāgārjuna raises the various options about whether things are self-caused or not, his reasoning would go as follows. First, perhaps every object is wholly self-caused and spontaneous (some theologians have thought this about God, for instance). Second, perhaps every object is caused by something else (like a movie which was made by the director, the actors, the crew, and so on). Third, things may be caused both by themselves and by others (like an animal, which is generated by its parents but can then make its own limbs move). Finally, things may be neither self-caused nor caused by another, because causation may just not apply to them (the number four might be like this). All of these are respectable philosophical positions concerning causation. So to show that the concept of "causation" is empty, each of them needs to be refuted, which is exactly what Nāgārjuna does.

But we're not out of the woods yet. Having made sense of the tetralemma itself, we now need to ask how Nāgārjuna could sensibly formulate an exhaustive list of four logical options, and then deny *all* of them. Imagine someone denying that a movie is good, denying that it is bad, denying that parts of it are good and other parts bad, and finally denying that it is a movie for which questions of good and bad fail to arise in any normal sense (perhaps a cult film that is "so bad that it's good"). Bizarre though this may seem, it is exactly what Nāgārjuna does with his *prasaṅga* method, listing all logical possibilities and then rejecting them, even the negative ones. What is Nāgārjuna playing at here? It seems obvious that when he rejects all four options of a tetralemma, the "rejection" involved must be a rather special one.

For help we can turn to a fourth interpretation of Nāgārjuna, which has been put forward by Bimal Matilal and defended subsequently by Jan Westerhoff.[7] They allude to an ancient Indian distinction, originally made in grammatical contexts, between two kinds of negation, called *paryudāsa* and *prasajya*. The first turns one noun into another noun, like adding "in-" to "vertebrate" to get "invertebrate." The second is like the "not" in "I do not say I will come to your house." An important difference is that the negation of a noun still involves a positive assertion, as when I say "the snail is an invertebrate." This is not so when I negate the verb. If I tell you, "I do not say I will come to your house," then perhaps I will come after all—I might just be unwilling to commit myself until I know what movie you'll be showing. The distinction was used elsewhere in ancient Indian philosophy, notably in the Mīmāṃsā theory of ritual. How, they wondered, should we interpret a prohibition on performing a certain ritual act? "Don't slaughter a goat" might mean that you should slaughter a non-goat. Here the noun ("goat") is negated: you should indeed slaughter something, perhaps a cow or a chicken, just not a goat. Or the verb ("slaughter") might be negated: the instruction would tell you to refrain from any sacrificial act at all.

The idea of *prasajya* negation, where you negate the verb, works nicely with the aforementioned phenomenon of category errors. When a dualist says "the mind is not the brain," she is not asserting that it is some other organ in the body (like the heart which is "not the brain"). The mind is no organ at all. Hence it is not the noun "brain" being negated, but the verb "is." And there are other cases that call for *prasajya* negation, without involving category errors. Consider the famous leading question "have you stopped beating your wife?" If a lawyer put this to a married man in a trial, the man would presumably want to challenge the presupposition behind the question. Yet the question is not a category mistake: as a husband he is indeed someone who could engage in domestic abuse, as unfortunately happens all the time. We might take Nāgārjuna to be engaging in this sort of noncommittal negation when he rejects all four options in a tetralemma. Since failing to assert a proposition is different from asserting the opposite, Nāgārjuna can withhold assent from all of the four alternatives. He wants to show that each alternative involves a concept with no purchase on reality.

As he would want us to point out, this has a precedent in the Buddha's own practice. We've mentioned before that the Buddha sometimes fell silent when questions were pressed upon him. Asked whether the world is eternal, he did not answer; nor would he speak when asked if the world is not eternal. Likewise when asked whether the self is identical to the body, or not identical. In one text he is even silent when a series of four questions is posed, questions that have the structure of a tetralemma: he was asked whether an enlightened being survives mortal death, does not survive death, both survives and does not survive, or neither survives nor does not survive. The Buddha's silence in the face of such demands surely does not indicate uncertainty, but a rejection of the very line of questioning. Nāgārjuna's rejection of the four alternatives in a tetralemma likewise wants to dispel our belief in the reality of the thing being talked about in all four options. Consider one last time the opening of the *Verses on the Middle Way*. The first three alternatives laid out there claim that objects have some sort of cause, internal or external or mixed, while the fourth alternative denies that this is so. In refusing to agree to any of these possibilities, Nāgārjuna suggests that the word "cause" does not refer to anything at all. It has no independent reality, no *svabhāva*. When the dogmatic philosopher gives us a choice between self-causation and other-causation, he is making us an offer we can and should refuse.

38

TAKING PERSPECTIVE

THE JAINA THEORY OF STANDPOINTS

"Once there was a merchant's wife who sought a means for restoring the affections of her husband, who had deserted her for another woman. She obtained a spell that was guaranteed to put her husband in such a state that she could lead him about with a string. When she applied the spell, she discovered that this was a literal promise, not a figurative one, as her husband was transformed into a bull. She led him to a pasture to graze... and there overheard Śiva saying that in the shade of that very tree was an herb that would restore her husband to his human form. The woman gathered every plant she could find growing beneath the tree, and forced the bull to eat them all, with the result that he was restored to his human form."[1] This story was supposedly told by the Śvetāmbara Jaina thinker Hemacandra, who lived in the twelfth century. As John Cort explains, the point of the tale is that if we want to attain salvation, we should not embrace only one teaching or tradition. We should embrace them all.

The Jainas are the great syncretists of ancient Indian thought. Rather than defending a single point of view concerning the metaphysics of the soul and its liberation, as the various Vedic schools did, and rather than rejecting all such theories as incoherent, as Buddhists like Nāgārjuna did, the Jainas accept *all* the available points of view. Hemacandra's tale may suggest that the purpose of this is to spread out our bets. Since we cannot know for sure which teaching is the right one we should adopt all teachings at once, trusting that the correct viewpoint is among them. But in fact the Jainas' approach is more sophisticated than that, and amounts to a profound epistemological theory in its own right. The theory is named "the teaching of non-onesidedness (*anekāntavāda*)"; we may also call it the "theory of standpoints." As the name suggests, the Jainas are unwilling to accept particular, or "one-sided (*ekānta*)," answers to philosophical questions. Such an answer merely expresses a limited point of view and will be incapable of grasping the "manifold" nature of things as they really are.

Indeed, to grasp the world aright would be to grasp it from an unlimited number of perspectives. This has been achieved only by the omniscient figures acknowledged in

Jainism, especially Mahāvīra, the last of the so-called "ford-makers," saviors who have shown us the way to liberation. The job of the Jaina philosopher is to come as close as possible to such omniscience by understanding the contribution made by various intellectual traditions, while also realizing that these traditions offer only partial truths. The origins of the theory of standpoints can be traced back to Mahāvīra himself, and his reaction to early Buddhist doctrine. Early Buddhist tradition mentions ten "unanswered (*avyākṛta*)" questions, questions the Buddha refused to resolve.[2] They are:

(1) Is the world eternal?
(2) Is the world not eternal?
(3) Is the world finite?
(4) Is the world not finite?
(5) Is the soul identical with the body?
(6) Is the soul different from the body?
(7) Does the Tathāgata (Buddha) exist after death?
(8) Does he not exist after death?
(9) Does he both exist and not exist after death?
(10) Does he neither exist nor not exist after death?[3]

The Buddha was unwilling to answer these questions on the ground that they were like asking, "where does a flame go after it is extinguished?" For the Buddhist the right response to a question is often to point out that the presuppositions behind the question are faulty.

Mahāvīra responded to these questions very differently. Confronted with the third and fourth of the Buddhists' questions, whether or not the world is finite or not, he did not remain silent, nor did he choose between the two possibilities. Instead he embraced both. The world is finite in size, but infinite in time because it will never end. It is also infinite in properties, because the world has "limitless properties of colour, smell, taste, and touch." Likewise, when asked whether the soul is eternal, he said that in a sense it is and in a sense it is not. It is eternal because, like the world, it never ends. But it is non-eternal because it takes on different forms in the cycle of reincarnation, first living as an animal, then as a human, then as a god.[4] This is a central illustration for the Jaina approach to philosophy. Confronted with Buddhists who say that there is no enduring self at all, and Vedic thinkers who make the self eternal and unchanging, the Jainas argue that both sides are partially right, and thus partially wrong too. The Buddhists are wrong because the self or soul does persist over time, whereas Vedic thinkers are wrong to make it unchanging.

Much as Madhyamaka offered a systematic expansion of themes found in the Buddhist scriptures, so the Jaina theory of standpoints was a generalization of these and other reports about Mahāvīra. It has sometimes been proposed that Jainism underwent a period of commentary on the scriptural texts known as *āgamas*, with a more philosophical or "logical" approach emerging thereafter. But in fact things are messier. The two genres overlapped chronologically, and issues of exegesis animated Jaina philosophical literature, much as we saw in the Brahmanical schools.[5] As usual, questions of chronology are also bedeviled by the uncertainty about the dates of key figures, notably Umāsvati, whose *Sūtra on What Is* (*Tattvārthādhigamasūtra*) was the first to set out Jaina thought in the Sanskrit language.[6] He probably wrote in the late fourth century, but this is uncertain.[7] Other important early Jaina philosophers include Kundakunda, who probably lived before Umāsvati, and Siddhasena Divākara, around AD 700.

It was above all these three thinkers who developed the theory of standpoints as an expression of Mahāvīra's method. Or perhaps we should say that Mahāvīra himself did not have so much a special philosophical method as a special kind of insight. The Jainas observe a fundamental distinction between "indirect" and "direct" ways of knowing, using here the standard term for a means of knowledge, *pramāṇa* (§1.6).[8] Most of us have to make do with the "indirect" access provided by perception and the scriptural tradition, whereas Mahāvīra enjoyed "direct" omniscience. This is why he was able to see things from all points of view, whereas normal humans can grasp things only from a limited number of perspectives. Worse still is to have a limited perspective without realizing that it is limited. This is the situation of the Jainas' rivals from other traditions, both Vedic and Buddhist, who fetishize a single standpoint as the only valid view on things.

Though there are in fact an infinity of ways to look at anything, Umāsvati breaks the possible perspectives down into seven types of standpoint, or *naya* (§1.32–5). These are as follows: (1) the non-distinguished (*naigama*), (2) the general (*saṃgraha*), (3) the practical (*vyavahāra*), (4) the "straight-thread" (*ṛjusūtra*), (5) the verbal (*śabda*), (6) the subtle (*samabhirūḍha*), and (7) the "thus-happened" (*evambhūta*). Standardly the first three were said to involve affirming substance (*dravyāstika*), while the remaining have to do with the modifications or predicates of substance (*paryāyāstika*). Here we can already detect an echo of Mahāvīra's remarks on the soul, which first took the perspective that the soul endures as a substance does, then the perspective that it changes over time. That contrast between the substance point of view and the modification point of view is fundamental to Jainism (§5.29–31).[9] Kundakunda already affirms that substance (*dravya*), both sentient (*jīva*) and non-sentient (*ajīva*), is that which undergoes and endures through all change. Substance can thus be seen from two perspectives, depending on whether we want to emphasize the endurance or the change. If we contrast, on the one hand, Vedic approaches to metaphysics—especially Advaita Vedānta which makes the single, unchanging *brahman* the only true reality—and, on the other hand, the Buddhist rejection of the very notion of an enduring, independent substance as incoherent, we may begin to see the Jaina point of view. Which is precisely to convict those other schools of being nothing but points of view, "one-sided" because they manage only a partial perspective on things.

Clearly though, Umāsvati has something more complicated in mind. He gives us seven different kinds of standpoint, not only two that emphasize substance and modification. So let's work through them, beginning with the three that involve a commitment to enduring substances.[10] First, the "non-distinguished." It gets us off to a tricky start, since this is the least clear of the seven *nayas*, and was even omitted in the overview of the theory given by Siddhasena. It seems almost to be the standpoint of refusing to take any particular standpoint, for instance by thinking of a thing without bothering to distinguish whether it is a substance or a property. It may seem strange to call this a particular "perspective" on things. But it could reflect the approach of someone who is concerned merely to catalogue what there is, without worrying about what different kinds of thing there are. Somewhat puzzling, too, is that the Jainas ascribe this approach to the Nyāya-Vaiśeṣika philosophers. Presumably their thinking is that these two schools depicted properties as if they were objects in their own right, hence failing to distinguish between substance and property. The Jainas do not exactly say that this is illegitimate. To the contrary, all the viewpoints are legitimate; it is just that no one of them has a monopoly on validity.

The second of Umāsvati's standpoints is "the general."[11] This standpoint involves attending only to the broadest commonalities between things, and ignoring the specific properties which distinguish one thing from another. We might for example note that everything shares the property of being an existent. When adopted dogmatically, and not as just one possible standpoint, this attitude leads to monism in metaphysics: Advaita Vedānta is unsurprisingly fingered as the leading culprit. The third standpoint is "the practical," and is the complement of the previous one. Here we instead stress the special distinguishing features of things, and the way they can be classified under a variety of headings. It is from this point of view that a philosopher would say that every existent is either a substance or a property. Some Jainas like to place the Cārvāka "materialists" into this camp, probably because they classify both the material body and the spiritual self as substances rather than properties, and thus come to assume that they are the same kind of entity.

Fourth up is the standpoint of the "straight-thread," an approach that pays attention only to what is presently perceived, like the pleasure or pain one is feeling right now. Those who take this to be the uniquely correct standpoint wind up reducing enduring substances and persons to the ephemeral deliverances of the senses. Of course it is the Buddhists, or at least some of them, who are accused of making this mistake. Notice that in explaining these first four standpoints, the Jaina writers supply us with a kind of survey of Indian metaphysics. This is why (as mentioned in Chapter 35) the Jainas are often useful as a source of information about non-Jaina thinkers. Hence we were able to turn to the Jaina thinker Prabhācandra for information about the otherwise obscure tradition of Cārvāka philosophy.

Notice also that these other schools are not just being named—they are also being shamed, exposed as one-sided. It is sometimes thought that the theory of standpoints is a kind of abstract embodiment of the Jaina commitment to non-violence (*ahiṃsā*).[12] The thought here would be that disagreeing with people is a form of conflict, a kind of intellectual "violence." To avoid such aggression, the Jainas find a way of agreeing with everyone by adopting their theory of non-onesidedness. But this is to overlook that the Jainas do not simply congratulate the other schools on being partially right. If anything, they stress that the other schools are partially wrong. The Jainas, no less than their rivals, emphasize that knowledge leads to liberation. But their understanding of knowledge requires the liberated person to see things from a variety of viewpoints, whereas a Brahmanical or Buddhist thinker manages to adopt just one standpoint. The Jainas have no hesitation in asserting that such one-sided philosophical theories are "false," precisely insofar as they are one-sided. Nor do they seem to think that engaging in disagreement or debate with such benighted philosophers would violate their vow of non-violence. Hence the story of a Jaina who held forth in a public dispute against a Buddhist at such great length that his opponent finally died from exhaustion.[13]

But let's get back to our sevenfold list of standpoints. The three we have not yet discussed show the Jainas joining in that most typical of ancient Indian philosophical pursuits: analyzing language. This is already clear from the name of the fifth standpoint, the "verbal." Here we take grammar as a guide to reality, for example by inferring from the use of past, present, and future verbs that the subjects of these verbs are different from one another. According to this standpoint, if you say "the mountain existed" and then "the mountain will exist," you are referring to two different mountains. This may seem rather odd, but it's a kind of "perspective" we saw very recently, in Madhyamika philosophy. Nāgārjuna, at least according to his commentator Candrakīrti, thought that we should be able to distinguish the axe that is seen from the axe that is used for chopping, with this distinction being marked by grammatical case: one axe is the object of an action, the second an instrument. Here again, the Jainas seem to be right in thinking that it's a perspective that could be useful so long as it is not applied indiscriminately, in a one-sided way. It's quite plausible to say that the grammatical contrast between subject and predicate may often correspond to a real metaphysical contrast between a thing and its property. But it would not do to infer real distinctions *wherever* we have grammatical distinctions. A German who did this would be led by the grammatical gender of German nouns to think that doors are female, houses neuter, and tables masculine.

The next item in the group of linguistic standpoints is "the subtle." Which is slightly alarming, since what has come so far is already pretty subtle, but in fact the point made here is quite straightforward. From this perspective we distinguish different words that refer to the same thing, words that have different etymologies. The example given is the lord of the gods. He is called both "Indra," which comes from the verb "to rain," and "Śakra," derived from the verb "to be able." Though both names pick out the same god, they differ in meaning because of their derivation. This is a striking point, because—leaving aside the focus on etymology—it anticipates the contrast between sense and reference made by the German logician Gottlob Frege. His illustration was that "morning star" and "evening star" both refer to Venus but are different in meaning, as is clear from the fact that someone might not know that the last heavenly body seen in the morning is in fact the same object as the first one seen at night.

The final standpoint is called the "thus-happened." Here we note that many words have "functional" senses: they refer to objects on the basis of a capacity or function which the object can perform, like "cook" or "swimmer." From this perspective, we should use such terms only when the object is actually performing its function, and not at other times. If we name objects after the capacities and powers they possess, we refer to them only insofar as they are actually exercising the capacity. Thus we would call someone a swimmer only when she is actually swimming. This standpoint seems to be a linguistic version of the earlier "straight-thread" standpoint, which reduces everything to what is currently present to us. Adopting the "thus-happened" standpoint dogmatically would lead to the fallacy of refusing to admit that the swimmer is a swimmer when she is sleeping. Again, we saw an idea like this in Nāgārjuna and Candrakīrti, who argued that the "running giraffe" is distinct from the "seeing giraffe" because of the different actions they are performing.

Let's conclude by seeing how these standpoints were used in practice. A nice example is found in Siddhasena, who uses them to deal with the aforementioned problem of substance.[14] Leaving aside the first, "non-determined" standpoint, he begins with the "general" perspective that sees all substance as one; as we said, this would be the approach of Advaita monism. The "practical" standpoint distinguishes substance into different types, which is the attitude of the pluralists among other Vedic schools. Since the "straight-thread" standpoint ignores everything but present reality, it yields a theory of constant flux such as we find in Buddhists. Grammarians cannot see past the "verbal" perspective (here one might think of Bhartṛhari) while other language enthusiasts use the "subtle" standpoint to classify substances through the etymology of the names of those substances. And we've just seen how the "thus-happened" standpoint would involve reducing the substance to its currently performed action. Broadly speaking, only the "general" and "practical" standpoints can do justice to the stability and independence of substances, while the remaining ones capture something about the modifications undergone by substances. Again, to adopt a one-sided standpoint is to get things partially right; but to adopt it narrowly and exclusively is to get things wrong.

It seems clear from all this that the Jainas must have a rather idiosyncratic view of truth. They are not skeptics, who insist that truth is inaccessible or simply suspend judgment about whether we ever have it. Rather, they seem to be relativists, in the special sense of thinking that truth is always relative to a point of view or a context in which the truth is uttered or believed. Unlike most modern-day relativists, though, they think that ultimate truth is possible: this is the truth attained by embracing an infinity of valid viewpoints all at once. The Jaina philosophers realized that they were not going to be able to make this theory work within the logical system of the Nyāya school, and of course Nāgārjuna's destructive use of the tetralemma would hardly suit their non-onesided aims. Instead, the Jainas developed a remarkable logical theory with seven kinds of predication.

39

WELL QUALIFIED

THE JAINAS ON TRUTH

When you're evaluating a philosophical theory, there are a few tests you should always carry out. Does the theory preserve our intuitions? If not, does it give us sufficient reason to prefer this new theory to our previously held beliefs? Does the theory fall prey to counterexamples or leave unexplained exceptions? And here is one more test that should never be omitted: can the theory survive being applied to itself? We saw that Nāgārjuna had to deal with this problem. His work *Dispeller of Disputes* tries to respond to the criticism that the arguments in favor of his emptiness theory can safely be dismissed, since Nāgārjuna himself must admit that those very arguments are empty. It might seem that the Jaina theory of standpoints we have just examined is also vulnerable to this line of attack. They say that various philosophical theories are true only from a certain perspective. But is this assertion itself only the expression of a certain standpoint?

The Jainas can readily answer this objection. Take as an example their approach to the metaphysics of universals. Adopting their theory of *nayas* or standpoints, they say that there is a perspective on things that affirms their sharing a universal character, and another perspective on things that emphasizes the reality of individual particulars. From the first standpoint, a realist about universals argues that all pots share pot-ness in common. From the second viewpoint, a skeptic about universals will say that only each individual pot is real. Now the Jaina says that both standpoints are, in a sense, correct, because both capture something about reality. In doing so, the Jaina is adopting a third standpoint: the one from which both the universal and the particular way of looking at things have contributed something to our understanding.[1] Though this third standpoint may likewise be somehow partial, there is also the prospect of a most comprehensive, "omniscient" point of view that incorporates *all* standpoints. This is the point of view of someone like the "ford-maker" Mahāvīra. It is the only adequate standpoint, because of the complexity of things in the world. As Siddhasena puts it, "since a thing has a manifold character, it is [fully] comprehended [only] by the omniscient. But a thing becomes the subject matter of a *naya*, when it is conceived from one particular standpoint."[2] We normal humans are not omniscient, yet we can make progress by understanding how each philosophical theory contributes a merely partial truth.

Unfortunately there is another, even simpler test that the Jainas are in danger of failing. Does their theory not involve self-contradiction? Again, we saw this threat looming in the case of Nāgārjuna, whose tetralemma argument form has seemed to some to involve entertaining contradictory propositions. We resisted that interpretation when looking at Nāgārjuna (Chapter 38), and want to resist it again in the case of the Jainas. Admittedly, you can see why they might be accused of contradicting themselves. As philosophical pluralists, the Jainas reply to pairs of questions like "is the world infinite?" and "is the world finite?" with a qualified "yes" in both cases: both express a partial truth about the world. Many commentators on the Jaina system, both past (Śaṅkara, Śāntarakṣita) and present,[3] have felt that the Jaina attempt to reconcile opposite philosophical positions does involve a challenge to the notion of contradiction, that it "tolerates" inconsistency. How else could they reach agreement with philosophical schools whose theories are antithetical, finding something true in both the Buddhist no-self theory and the Advaita theory that all things are really a single self, namely *brahman*?

No less than Nāgārjuna, the Jainas are alive to the threat, and seek to show how they can strive for impartiality or "non-onesideness" without lapsing into self-contradiction. Their answer centers on a single Sanskrit word, *syāt*. It is derived from an optative form of the verb "to be," and means "perhaps" or "possibly." In this context its meaning is better expressed as "in a sense," "conditionally," or even "arguably." We can use the term *syāt* to capture the Jaina refusal to make categorical assertions, and instead to answer philosophical questions from one or another perspective or within the framework of a certain metaphysical stance (*naya*). Thus, rather than asserting without qualification that the world is eternal, they say only "conditionally, the world is infinite," which means "from a certain standpoint, the universe is infinite." We could compare this to the use of words like "possibly" and "necessarily," which modern-day philosophers and logicians call "modal operators" because these words indicate the way in which a statement is true. If I say, "possibly, the universe is infinite," I am indicating that something *might* be true, whereas if I preface the same remark with "necessarily," I am indicating something that *must* be true. In either case, I am modifying the assertion that the universe is infinite.

To this the Jainas add a list of seven types of statement or modes of predication (the *saptabhaṅgī*), each of which is to be qualified by the word *syāt*. This is comparable to Nāgārjuna's tetralemma, though the Jainas go three better than him by offering seven alternatives where he had only four. Just as we traced the tetralemma back to the Buddha's refusal to answer questions, so we can discover the origins of this remarkable and unprecedented theory in reports about Mahāvīra. Rather than falling silent when confronted with philosophical questions like "is the world infinite?" and "is the world finite?" Mahāvīra said yes to both, but with a conditional "yes" and not an absolute "yes." Furthermore he was asked whether a question might have no expressible answer at all. Here is where the Buddha might finally have said "yes," given that his silence was a rebuke to the question as it had been posed. Mahāvīra likewise admits that the right answer may be inexpressible, but even this admission is conditional, an expression of a certain standpoint.

One Jaina philosopher, the eleventh-century Vādi Devasūri, explains the theory with particular clarity:

> The sevenfold predicate theory consists in the use of seven modes of assertion, each preceded by "conditionally" (*syāt*), [all] concerning a single object and its particular properties, composed of attributions and denials, either simultaneously or successively, and without contradiction. They are as follows:
>
> (1) Conditionally, [some object] exists (*syād asty eva*). The first predicate pertains to an attribution.
> (2) Conditionally, it does not exist (*syān nāsty eva*). The second predicate pertains to a denial.
> (3) Conditionally, it exists; conditionally, it doesn't exist (*syād asty eva syān nāsty eva*). The third predicate pertains to successive attribution and denial.
> (4) Conditionally, it is "non-assertible" (*syād avakyavyam eva*). The fourth predicate pertains to a simultaneous attribution and denial.
> (5) Conditionally, it exists; conditionally it is non-assertible (*syād asty eva syād avaktavyam eva*). The fifth predicate pertains to an attribution and a simultaneous attribution and denial.
> (6) Conditionally, it doesn't exist; conditionally it is non-assertible (*syān nāsty eva syād avaktavyam eva*). The sixth predicate pertains to a denial and a simultaneous attribution and denial.
> (7) Conditionally, it exists; conditionally it doesn't exist; conditionally it is non-assertible (*syād asty eva syān nāsty eva syād avaktavyam eva*). The seventh predicate pertains to a successive attribution and denial and a simultaneous attribution and denial.[4]

Nāgārjuna's tetralemma distinguished four possibilites: yes, no, both, and neither. We had a difficult time figuring out how he could get away with this, and are going to have to work even harder now to get our heads around the Jaina sevenfold theory of predication.

One difference is that for Jainas, there are three basic answers, not just "yes" and "no," but also a third option that they label as the "non-assertible" or "inexpressible" (*avaktavya*). We'll say something shortly about what this means, but for the moment let's just focus on how it gets us up to seven options. Obviously we have three simple modes: (1) something is the case, (2) something is not the case, (4) something is inexpressible. The example given is that something exists, for instance (1) "there is a pot," (2) "there is no pot," (4) "it is inexpressible whether there is a pot." But one could extend the theory to handle statements about things other than existence, like (1) "the pot is blue," (2) "the pot is not blue," (4) "it is inexpressible whether the pot is blue."[5] Next, the Jainas combine these three simple cases to form new, more complex options. The statement "a pot exists" could be (3) both true and false, (5) true yet inexpressible, (6) false yet inexpressible, or finally all three, (7) true, false, *and* inexpressible. This gets us up to seven options all told, three simple cases and four compound cases.

Remember, though, that all seven cases are prefaced by *syāt*, "conditionally." So even the simple option, where something is said to be the case, isn't so simple after all. We can say "conditionally, there is a pot" or "conditionally, the universe is infinite," just in case there is a standpoint according to which these things are the case. This is compatible with the same things being false from another point of view. As we saw in the last chapter, insofar as the universe has no temporal ending it is infinite, yet it is not infinite in size so that there is also a standpoint from which it is finite. Similarly, from the point of view that focuses on stable, enduring substances, there is a pot. Yet from the perspective that focuses only on momentary sensory experiences, there is no pot, only ephemeral experiences of color, shape, and hardness. This contrast can also be brought out with more banal examples. If the pot is in Munich but not in New York, then from the point of view of someone in Munich it is true to say "there is a pot" (meaning "there is a pot present here") but not from the point of view of someone in New York.

This is relatively straightforward. But things get trickier when we contemplate the option of saying (3) that something is both true *and* false. This sounds dangerously close to being a standpoint adopted by people who are happy to contradict themselves. Yet Vādi Devasūri prefaced the entire account by saying that the seven options do *not* involve self-contradiction.[6] We can see why this might be if we notice another feature of Vādi Devasūri's explanation. He says the mixed predicate "true-and-false" involves the *successive* attribution and denial of a property. So this would just be the standpoint of someone—like a Jaina philosopher—who first notes a perspective from which a claim is true, and then adds that there is another perspective from which the same claim is false. This is quite sensible and could be illustrated by the Jaina's saying something like, "our Vaiśeṣika colleagues believe the pot exists, but the Buddhists deny it, and both have a point." The sevenfold list of predications is intended to explain how the theory of standpoints works, but really we need to invoke that theory to explain why the sevenfold list does not involve intentional inconsistency.

We're not out of the woods yet. We still need to consider the most puzzling of the three basic options, where the answer is neither "yes" nor "no," but (4) "inexpressible." Here Vādi Devasūri does seem to court contradiction, because he says that "inexpressible" means the simultaneous attribution and denial of a property. The natural way to read this is that there is a standpoint from which both a statement and its denial can be endorsed at the same time. So we are back after all to the standpoint of those who contradict themselves or indulge in paradox.[7] Then again, as we already pointed out, Vādi Devasūri promises that the sevenfold predications involve no contradiction. So he was under the impression that one can assert a statement to be inexpressible without falling into inconsistency. What is going on here?

Several explanations have been given. One rather simple explanation is that we cannot say both "yes" and "no" to a question *at the same time*, because no one can assert two contradictory ideas at once. Hence the key Jaina insight that both answers are right, but from different points of view, is "inexpressible" simply because of the limitations of normal language.[8] This fits well with the way that Vādi Devasūri explains the inexpressible, namely that it has to do with "*simultaneous* attribution and denial." But we find a different understanding in the tenth-century Jaina philosopher Prabhācandra. We've met him before as a source for Cārvāka thought, but he is a brilliant philosopher in his own right, born in 980 (the same year as Avicenna, and similarly full of brilliant observations and arguments, including a thought experiment very similar to Avicenna's "flying man"). He wrestles with the problem of what makes the seven alternatives in the Jaina catalogue of predication actually distinct from one another, while also comprehensive in the sense that no option is left out.

When he comes to explain what it means to say that an answer to a question is "inexpressible," he does not say that it involves simultaneous assertion and denial, but instead ties it to the idea of neutrality. It means that from the standpoint one occupies, one cannot endorse a certain claim, nor can one deny it.[9] The point could be a very simple one. There are standpoints from which one can make neither an affirmation nor a denial simply because of a lack of information. If I am in New York and haven't been in Munich recently, I might just shrug when asked whether there is a pot in Munich. Or, here's a more interesting possibility. Let's step back for a moment and think again about what it means to assert something from a certain standpoint. It means adopting a perspective from which certain claims are ratified and others undermined. Consider an example the Jainas could not have contemplated, namely modern physics. From the standpoint of today's physicist, claims about the existence of subatomic particles are affirmed, while claims about the existence of the four elements from ancient Greek philosophy are denied. But regarding some propositions, a standpoint may be simply neutral or indifferent. Physics neither grounds nor undermines claims about morality. We can't work out whether it is wrong to steal, or solve the moral dilemmas which so perplexed the protagonists of the *Mahābhārata*, by studying modern physics. We might thus say that such propositions are neither affirmed nor denied from inside that standpoint; it could be in this sense that the answer is "inexpressible."

Notice that if this is right, it is different from the Buddhist idea that one should sometimes refuse to answer questions. A Buddhist would vehemently resist the notion that Buddhism is nothing but one more standpoint, which may not provide the resources to answer a given question, the way that physics lacks the resources to answer questions about morality. The Buddhist standpoint claims to be the whole truth and nothing but the truth, so if it fails to provide an answer to a question, then the question is to blame. It must be somehow ill-formed or proceed on the basis of faulty assumptions, like the reality of wholes or enduring selves. This explains why Nāgārjuna's strategy was to expose the incoherence in other philosophical views, whereas the Jaina strategy is to expose their dogmatic insistence on being the only truth, when in fact there is more to truth than the other schools claim. Thus the Jainas hold that there are indeed ways to answer the questions the Buddha was asked, and point to scriptures in which Mahāvīra did answer them. It is just that the right answer requires us to take up a standpoint other than the Buddhist one, indeed several different complementary standpoints.

We have been insisting on the coherence of Jaina epistemology and on its commitment to the possibility of attaining a true standpoint on things. This isn't just because it annoys us when people deny the principle of non-contradiction (actually, it kind of annoys us and kind of doesn't). It's also because we want to do justice to the fact that Jainism, like its rivals, is a philosophy in aid of a soteriology. No less than other ancient Indian thinkers, the Jainas hold out the prospect of liberation and claim that liberation is achieved through knowledge. This is also why they are ready and willing to say that other schools have got things wrong. The partial perspective of a Buddhist or a Vedic thinker is not genuinely liberating, because it captures only a fragment of the holistic and comprehensive grasp of things that is nothing other than omniscience.

40

CHANGE OF MIND

VASUBANDHU AND YOGĀCĀRA BUDDHISM

One of the many inspired details in George Orwell's novel *1984* is a sinister repurposing of the phrase "big brother." The totalitarian rulers of that dystopian society are playing on the fact that big brothers are objects of both love and admiration. If you have a big brother yourself, you know what we mean: even if you fought with him occasionally, you probably also looked up to your older brother, hoping to benefit from his protection, as well as his greater experience and know-how. Perhaps this explains something about the intellectual career of Vasubandhu, a Buddhist thinker who lived around AD 400. According to legend he was converted to the Mahāyāna branch of Buddhism through the good offices of his own older half-brother, Asaṅga. Prior to that Vasubandhu had been a controversialist within the Abhidharma branch of Buddhism, attacking rival Ābhidharmikas for their views about past and future reality. Once brought around to the Mahāyāna way of seeing things, Vasubandhu joined Asaṅga as a co-founder of one branch within Mahāyāna, which is known as Yogācāra.[1] It is often seen as offering a kind of "idealist" version of Buddhism, rejecting even the minimal concessions to extramental reality made by the Abhidharma Buddhists.

Thus the career of this one man Vasubandhu ties together numerous strands of the ancient Buddhist tradition. The welter of schools and sub-schools can be confusing, especially since some of them have more than one name. Yogācāra is also known as Vijñānavāda, or "the teaching of consciousness," for reasons that will become clear below. We did explain the various branches in Chapter 35, but it might be helpful to go over them again now to set the stage for the emergence of Yogācāra. And it might be even more helpful if we concentrate on one central philosophical question that was debated between the schools: how do we account for the apparent continuity of things in the world, whether these are inanimate objects, animate beings, or our own selves? Everyday common sense would give a straightforward answer. These things seem to be continuously real because they are real. Suppose you see your brother reading a book. The book in your brother's hand, your brother, and you yourself, are all substances that persist through time. We can also interact with one another, like when you look over your brother's shoulder to see what he's reading and ask why he hasn't chosen a book about something more interesting, like the history of philosophy. Such causal interactions can also take place across time, as when you remember the next day what he was reading.

The Buddhists, of course, reject this commonsensical view. Belief in the enduring self is indelibly linked to suffering, so we must give it up if we are to achieve liberation. More generally, according to an Abhidharma teaching, continuous substances have only apparent reality. What is really real are atomic qualities that exist only momentarily, the so-called *dharmas*.[2] When we seem to see a book or a brother stably existing from one moment to another, we are putting together fleeting elements into a whole, one that has only conventional reality, like the famous chariot that is no more than the sum of its parts. Yet we still need to explain the causal relations between apparent things. This is especially problematic in the case of causation across time. When your only conventionally real brother tosses his conventionally real book onto the conventionally real table and it makes a loud noise, how do the elemental features that you register as his body and its throwing motion produce the noise one second later?

In his early career, Vasubandhu is out to refute a group of Buddhists who gave a surprising answer to that question. To ensure maximum confusion this school also goes by two names; we'll refer to it as Sarvāstivāda, but they are also known as Vaibhāṣika. Like other Ābhidharmikas, the Sarvāstivādins deny the persistent reality of objects, which are nothing but fictitious combinations of momentary *dharmas*. However, for them all the *dharmas* are indeed real—whether they are past, present, or future. This ensures that causation across time is possible: if it were non-existent and unreal, a *dharma* that is now past could not give rise to a present *dharma*. And here is where we come to the early phase of Vasubandhu's career. He studied Sarvāstivāda and wrote a treatise explaining its doctrines in a set of verses. But then he subjected these same teachings to a thorough critique, in the form of a commentary on these very verses (the *Abhidharmakośabhāṣya*).[3]

Vasubandhu calls his own version of the Abhidharma theory "Sautrāntika," meaning that it follows the Buddhist *sūtras*.[4] Like modern-day philosophers who give themselves the more self-explanatory title of "presentists," Vasubandhu wants to insist that only present things are real. That may seem a refreshing concession to common sense in the midst of this intra-Buddhist debate. But Vasubandhu is not merely relying on common sense; he has arguments on his side. From his point of view the Sarvāstivāda theory sounds, ironically, like a form of eternalism. After all, for them past, present, and future things are all permanently real—hardly a suitable doctrine for Buddhists. Besides, if all these things are real, then why are only some of them present to us, and currently "active"? Unless we can explain this, we can't account for the fact that you can only read this book about the history of philosophy that is presently in your hands, and not a book that still lies in the future or has itself been lost to history.

The Sarvāstivādin may repeat that past things *do* have an effect presently. There are memories of previous events, and the conventionally real book tossed aside a second ago makes a sound only now when it lands on the apparent table. But Vasubandhu is able to explain how past things can continue having their effects even once they stop existing (which, since they are all instantaneous, they always do immediately). There is a causal continuum from one *dharma* to the next, so that the motion of throwing the book causes further motion of the book through the air, the chain culminating with a bang when the book lands. Or to take a case that interests him more, past actions may cause present karmic fruits indirectly, through an unbroken chain of momentary *dharmas*. Vasubandhu compares this to the way that a seed that no longer exists has given rise to a sprout, then a mature plant, and finally the flower we see presently.[5] The same analysis applies to the apparent "self" that initiated the previous action and now reaps its karmic reward or punishment. The elements we falsely take to constitute the self are part of a chain of causal influence passing from one second to the next, like a flame being passed from one candle to another.

So to sum up, according to the traditional story Vasubandhu wrote this defense of Sautrāntika Abhidharma Buddhism, attacking Sarvāstivāda Abhidharma Buddhism, before he came over to Māhāyana Buddhism under the influence of his brother Asaṅga. (If you're still having trouble keeping up, don't worry: all these people and schools were merely conventional realities anyway.) Once convinced by Asaṅga to convert, Vasubandhu wrote a series of powerfully argumentative works attacking the Abhidharma approach as a whole.[6] Now, this is not our first contact with Māhāyana. That branch of Buddhist thought includes the Madhyamaka philosophy so ably, if perplexingly, represented by Nāgārjuna. And in fact, Asaṅga and Vasubandhu may have seen themselves as defending something like Nāgārjuna's position, to the extent that he had a position.[7] The brothers' approach is prefigured in a text called the *Sūtra of Profound Secrets* (*Saṃdhinirmocana-sūtra*), which offers what it calls a "third turning" of the wheel of Buddhist doctrine.[8] It claims to bring together the teachings of the first two wheels, namely Abhidharma and Mahāyāna.

On the other hand, this latest version of Vasubandhu shares with Nāgārjuna a frankly critical approach to the *dharma* theory of Abhidharma. He does to these *dharmas* what Abhidharma had done to everyday objects. Just as they rejected books and brothers as figments of the mind, now Vasubandhu suggests that even the momentary, elemental *dharmas* are mental constructions. This may seem a radical shift from his earlier, Sautrāntika position. But it actually retains something of that doctrine. Before, Vasubandhu was insisting that past and future things are unreal. Only the present phenomena of the world outside us and of mental life exist. Now he realizes that he can do without the external phenomena, while retaining the internal or mental phenomena. Things outside us are merely apparent, comparable to the hair-like images seen by somebody who has an eye disease (161). Since everything is a construction of the mind, mental reality is the only reality there is.

How does Vasubandhu justify this breathtaking move? We might see him as applying a principle of philosophical economy, one that had been used already by other Buddhists. If we can explain our experiences without recognizing something as real, then we should eliminate it from our metaphysics. The Ābhidharmikas had already eliminated chariots, books, and brothers; the early Vasubandhu had shown that we can do without past and future reality; now the later Vasubandhu contends that we don't need present external reality either. So he feels able to argue for his own position mostly by responding to possible objections, which try to force him to accept that something is externally existent. His hypothetical opponent complains that if external things were unreal, they could have no effect on us. To this Vasubandhu rejoins that people are affected by unreal things in dreams and hallucinations, or images they see in the afterlife when in hell (162).

The point of this is not that "life is but a dream." Dreaming is in fact a distinctive mental state, as is being in a faint (172). So Vasubandhu does not need to appeal to the idea that we cannot tell whether or not we are awake. Rather his point is to show that our mental experiences can arise without any real external stimulus. His approach is not skeptical, but reductionist: he wants to show that mental events are caused, and in fact can only be caused, by other mental events (106–7). An external *dharma* could never be the thing I am perceiving right now, because the *dharma* is only momentary, and would have to cease existing by the time I have registered my awareness of it (171). Instead there is a stream of mental experience, which Vasubandhu calls *citta*, *manas*, or *vijñāna*, more or less interchangeable words that refer to the mind or consciousness (71, 161). Hence the alternative name for Yogācāra mentioned earlier: his *vāda* or teaching is the *vijñānavāda*, "the teaching of consciousness," or the doctrine of "mind-only" or "consciousness-only" (*cittamātra*).

Vasubandhu still holds on to his earlier idea of a chain of causality, though now the chain consists only of mental events. Everything about our current mental life is the result of previous mental events. A past event may take time to make itself felt in current awareness. Using another botanical metaphor, and a rather beautiful one, he compares this to the way that dye may be absorbed through the stem of a growing flower and eventually color the petals as they unfold (116). At a more technical level, he invokes the so-called "storehouse consciousness (*ālaya-vijñāna*)" (72, 113, 215, 291), something that had already been proposed in the *Sūtra of Profound Secrets*. The idea here is that mental events are like currents coming to the surface of a stream (186) or—again the gardening metaphor—like seeds planted earlier that are coming finally to fruit. These metaphors represent the way we can direct our attention to impressions received in past moments of awareness. Consider a childhood memory, like the time your big brother defended you from a bully in the school playground. Though this heroic act has not been continuously remembered over the years since it first occurred, the memory of it remains "in storage" and available as possible content for consciousness. Vasubandhu is sensitive to the fact that this idea of a storehouse consciousness is not found in Buddhist scriptures. He shrugs this off: plenty of what was written about the Buddha has been lost and perhaps some of what has gone missing included a reference to this doctrine (115).

Any doubts about Vasubandhu's Buddhist motivation should in any case be dispelled by his frequent references to liberation from suffering. The reductionist metaphysics of Buddhism had always aimed at the elimination of suffering. Suffering comes from attachment, and if we can forsake belief in the reality of things, we should be able to wean ourselves off of attachment to them, though that change in perspective will also require extensive spiritual training and not just the ability to follow Buddhist arguments to their conclusion. These features of Buddhism are alive and well in Yogācāra, whose name in fact comes from its emphasis on spiritual practices (*yoga*) of meditation and mindfulness (248). Vasubandhu puts a name to the attitude that gives rise to attachment: "duality" (211). We suffer because we contrast ourselves as subjects to the objects of perception and desire. In reality this contrast is an illusion. Common sense is wrong to suppose that there is a world of persisting objects outside us, and Abhidharma Buddhism does not go far enough in dispelling this mistake, since it still accepts that there are external objects of awareness, namely the *dharmas*. Yogācāra takes a further step, or rather, two further steps. First, for Vasubandhu the objects of the mind are internal to the mind—they are themselves part of mental life. Then comes the still more challenging step of giving up on even a mental version of the contrast between subject and object. The correct, "non-dual" attitude is one in which the mind no longer treats anything as an object of its awareness. It's such a fundamental undermining of everything we take ourselves to know about reality that Vasubandhu calls his teaching of non-duality a "revolution at the basis" (189).

Thus the revolution of this third wheel of Buddhist teaching has, appropriately enough, three stages. Vasubandhu explains them as follows:

> What is it that appears?
> A construction of the non-existent.
> How is it that it appears?
> Through dualities.
> What is its non-existence?
> A state of non-duality.[9]

He refers here to his teaching concerning three kinds of "independent nature," or *svabhāva* (see also 213).[10] The first kind of independent nature is entirely fictive: it is "fabricated" or "constructed" (*paraikalpita*) by the mind. These would be the natures of the apparent things in our external environment. Vasubandhu compares them to an elephant conjured out of wooden props by a magician's sleight of hand (294). The second type of nature is called "interdependent (*paratantra*)": the subject and object of awareness that depend upon one another, for example an act of sight and that which is seen. Third and finally, there is awareness that has given up duality and become "perfected" or "fulfilled" (*pariniṣpanna*): even the mind is not an object for itself (295). At this stage one is finally liberated from suffering by being liberated from illusion.

It's significant that Vasubandhu's three stages are set out using the familiar word *svabhāva*, which we just translated as "independent nature." We saw this word in Nāgārjuna, who targeted the very notion in his own critique. This brings us back to the question of where Yogācāra sits in the history of Buddhism. It is grouped together with Nāgārjuna's "Middle Way" or Madhyamaka school, under the broader heading of Māhāyana Buddhism. And Yogācāra seems to have much in common with Madhyamaka.[11] Yogācāra, too, styles itself as a "middle way," and for the same reason mentioned by Nāgārjuna: it tries to steer between the extremes of nihilism and eternalism (or reification), of banning all things as non-existent, on the one hand, and taking all things to have stable and independent reality, on the other hand. Furthermore, both Māhāyana traditions express their middle way as an acknowledgement of the "emptiness" of things. This was the upshot of Nāgārjuna's skeptical attack on such notions as substance, motion, and perception. It is also the upshot of the Yogācāra critique of subject–object duality in consciousness. As Asaṅga puts it, "the non-existence of duality is indeed the existence of non-existence; this is the definition of emptiness."[12]

Nonetheless, the subsequent tradition would see disagreement and even harsh polemic developing between the two schools. A sixth-century Madhyamaka thinker, Bhāviveka, argues that Yogācāra manages to fall into *both* extremes on either side of the correct middle way. Whereas Madhyamaka recognizes the legitimacy of conventional attitudes toward reality, Yogācāra rejects conventional belief entirely, which according to Bhāviveka is a form of nihilism. Yet Yogācāra is also reificationist, because it accepts the genuine reality of some phenomena, namely those that occur in the mind. Like a sharpened pencil or a soccer team that has just managed a hard-earned draw, Bhāviveka has a good point. Vasubandhu certainly does aim to expose the fictionality of everyday objects, so that conventional reality would seem to be completely undermined in his Yogācāra philosophy. And even if the "mental forms" of Yogācāra are empty, they do constitute a reality that is mental. Nāgārjuna would presumably not hesitate to attack this mental version of reality as itself empty.

Let's conclude with a few words on yet another name that has been given to Yogācāra, in this case by modern scholars: "idealism." Vasubandhu makes reality exclusively mental, constituted by nothing but presently occurrent mental events that are caused by earlier mental events. In this light Yogācāra certainly seems to merit the name of "idealism." We might even take it to be one of the earliest forms of idealism to appear in the whole history of philosophy. But in a sense calling Vasubandhu an idealist may underestimate his radicalism. Remember that the third, "perfected" nature in his system is not just one in which we realize that all the objects of our mental activity are themselves mental. It is one in which there is no duality between the mind and its objects at all. It is not easy, perhaps not even possible, to say what lies beyond mental activity that is structured "dualistically." But whatever this reality might be, it does not seem to consist of ideas. If Vasubandhu is an idealist, then his idealism is only the last step but one on the path to enlightenment.[13]

41

WHO'S PULLING YOUR STRINGS?

BUDDHAGHOSA ON NO-SELF AND AUTONOMY

Nobody likes to be pushed around. We like to think that when we do things, it's because we chose to do them, and that we could have chosen otherwise. If I speed up while walking, it's because I've decided to go faster; if I look down as I go it's because I want to watch my step. And if, without moving at all, I consciously think about a problem or task—even one I'd prefer not to be thinking about—isn't this, too, something that I am doing myself? It seems natural, even inevitable, to think of this in terms of *control*. It's like a flying drone whose movements are controlled from the ground by a pilot, except that here the thing doing the controlling and the thing being controlled are both inside one person. Self-control is just a more intimate version of the causal relationship involved in remote control. For the Buddhist philosopher Buddhaghosa, however, this would be a huge mistake. He thinks that the whole point of the Buddha's refusal to acknowledge the self, to allow that there is anything that can be called "I," is precisely a denial of the "controller self." This is a new perspective within the tradition. Earlier Buddhists had understood the theory of "no-self" to say that the person is just a stream or heap of individual experiences and feelings. Buddhaghosa instead insists that the doctrine of "no-self" has to do with our capacity for agency.

Although he was born in fifth-century India, and by all accounts had a thorough education in the various Indian philosophical systems, Buddhaghosa decided that the true Buddhist teachings were best preserved in the island of Sri Lanka.[1] There the teachings were still recorded and studied in the actual language of the Buddha, Pāli, rather than the language of elite discourse, Sanskrit. So Buddhaghosa traveled to the great monastic university of Anurādhapūra, and there embarked on an enormously thorough study of the various parts of the Buddhist canon, both the *Nikāya* and Abhidharma treatises. He studied all the various commentaries that had been written over centuries by a series of talented Sinhala philosophers. So impressed were the monks that they charged Buddhaghosa with the task of writing definitive explanations that would organize and order the teachings. With a team of assistants and apprentices, he did just that, in a monumental project of textual production. For good measure he also composed an independent treatise, called the *Path of Purification (Visuddhimagga)*, which would both present the doctrine in a systematic fashion and serve as a training manual for aspirants on the Buddhist path.[2]

It would seem then that Buddhaghosa was a pretty willful and motivated individual. Yet when it came to describing what it means to be willful and motivated, he had no truck with the idea that each of us is or has a self, an origin of willed directives. A deeply entrenched model of the self encourages us to think of it along the lines of a charioteer who controls his horses from the chariot's platform. Buddhaghosa finds in this picture of human agency only metaphysical magic. Time and again he rejects the idea that there is something inside which controls each of our bodily movements or the psychological processes that go on within us. "The self of the sectarians (*titthiyānaṃ attā*)," he likes to say, "just does not exist" (*Dispeller* 77).[3] The best way to counter the hold a metaphor has on the imagination is to replace it with another one. To combat the analogy of the charioteer, he compares the human being to a mechanical doll whose limbs, torso, and head are held together by strings: "Just as a mechanical doll (*dāru-yanta*) is empty (*suñña*), soulless (*nijjiva*), and undirected (*nirīhaka*), and while it walks and stands merely through the combination of strings and wood, yet it seems as if it had direction and occupation (*savyāpāra*); so too, this minded body (*nāma-rūpa*) is empty, soulless and undirected, and while it walks and stands merely through the combination of the two together, yet it seems as if it had direction and occupation" (*Path* §18.31).

Buddhaghosa is living dangerously here, deploying a metaphor that can easily work against him. If we are just marionettes, surely there must be someone else pulling our strings? Who could that "someone" be other than a god, a being with its hands on the control units of each and every one of us? That is in fact exactly a picture of human agency which was encouraged by Kṛṣṇa as depicted in the *Bhagavad-gītā*. "O Arjuna," Kṛṣṇa states, "the Lord resides in the heart-area of all beings, making every being revolve through His magical power [as if they were] mounted on a machine (*yantrārūḍhāni*)" (*Gītā* §18.61). The later commentator Madhūsudana Sarasvatī would identify the machine in question as our friend the marionette. What Kṛṣṇa meant to say, he explains, is that the Lord is "just like a magician who causes completely non-independent wooden human forms to revolve, seated on a machine, and so on, moved by a rope."[4]

But it can't possibly be Buddhaghosa's view that human beings, or "minded bodies" (*nāma-rūpa*) as the Buddhists prefer to call us, are automata whose movements are controlled from the outside.[5] Not just because he doesn't believe in the existence of a divine agency, though he certainly doesn't. Nor only because in the

Nikāya the Buddha himself is reported as saying that there is what he calls "self-doing" (*atta-kāro*) in the performance of the actions of stepping forward or back.[6] More fundamentally, it is central to the Buddhist understanding of ethics that the moral value of an action is constrained by the intention (*cetanā*) with which that action is performed. If actions are merely the result of some divine puppet master, then nobody should be praised or blamed on the basis of their intentions, as these would have no causal role in what they do. So in introducing the risky metaphor of the marionette, Buddhaghosa simply wants to push back against the insidious grip of the alternative charioteer metaphor, which leads us into thinking that there must be some inner controller. If Buddhaghosa lived today, perhaps he would be tempted to compare humans to those self-driving cars that we are promised will soon populate our streets. Like a self-driving car, the human being is a complex mechanism in which there are a variety of instruments. Some have the job of detecting what is in the environment, some monitor the functioning of the mechanism itself, still others search for objectives or destinations and calculate the best ways of achieving them. But there is no driver in the car directing all these functions.

Buddhaghosa develops his alternative metaphor by arguing that all consciousness is already active, that each and every conscious mental state is an expression of agency. He does this by turning a more ancient Buddhist description of the mind on its head. In that older description, the flow of mental life was compared to a rope made out of many interwoven strands.[7] One strand is the series of sensory encounters or perceptions one has had and is having; another strand is a series of feelings and affective reactions; another strand is made up of habits and dispositions; still another includes our concepts. All these are woven together with a final strand made up of the physical states of the human body. Together they produce a human being, a rope stretched across time. Within this complex there appear moments of intention and choice, which provide the whole "rope" with agency and direction. Since this picture was drawn by Buddhists it gives no place to a unitary inner self. But it still suggests that control emanates from discrete elements within the person, namely the volitions that are woven into that person.

Instead, Buddhaghosa insists that control and activity are built into every single moment of conscious experience. Our awareness is built up out of many activities, which together produce the mindedness that belongs to the human being. Buddhaghosa recalls the simile used in the *Sāṃkhya-kārikā*: an odd couple consisting of someone who is blind but can walk, and a sighted but lame person sitting on that first person's shoulders (see Chapter 22). His point is that each deliberate action, such as moving in a certain direction, is the joint product of several capacities working together. Conscious awareness itself is no passive response to the environment, but the activity of the mind's "bending" itself onto the world. There is an interplay between mind and body, and between minded body and worldly environment. Buddhaghosa identifies a number of different kinds of activities that make up human experience (*Path* §18.8). There is awareness, which brings us "into touch" with our environment, in a way we are not when we are asleep. We are also able to "reach out" or direct attention to specific objects, which is what gives thought an object, a goal, or an orientation. Once something comes to our specific attention, we can evaluate it, either by judging it as worth pursuing or avoiding, or by classifying it under a certain category. For Buddhaghosa being minded is being attentive, as we direct ourselves toward certain things and not others. Attention is like a window frame: it sets a boundary to what we see, though we can also focus on certain features of the things perceived through that frame. So experience is not a matter of passively being affected, but of engaging with the environment. Nor is this active engagement the job of just one part or power of the mind, the one that is "in charge." We need no self to serve as a source of motivation, intention, evaluation, or awareness, controlling things from the top down. All these features were already present in the various components of mental activity, built into it from the ground up.[8]

As so often in philosophy, Buddhaghosa's account seems to work better for some examples than for others. What he is saying sounds pretty convincing if you think about reading a book. You decide to read up on Buddhism, go to the library, find a relevant volume, sit down and attend to a given sentence on a given page. You are living the life of the mind, and it is a life full of activity. But aren't there other cases where our mental life seems to be passive, at the mercy of the world outside? A loud noise may force itself upon your attention, as when a car backfires just outside the library, making you look up from your engrossing book. Pain would be another example. Perhaps you are on a meditative walk through the forest, and then step on a thorn. If active attention is involved here, it would seem to come in only secondarily. It certainly seems as though you involuntarily become aware of noise or pain, and only then actively direct your attention toward it, thinking "what was that noise?" or "boy, that hurt!"

But Buddhaghosa denies this. He thinks that the mind already must be actively involved if we are to become aware of the distracting noise or stabbing pain. In support of this he offers three vivid analogies.[9] In the first, we are asked to imagine a man asleep under a mango tree, who is woken up by the sound of a falling mango. The man grabs the mango, gives it a squeeze, smells it, and finally eats it. The second analogy is to a king contentedly sitting inside his palace. There is a knock at the palace gate: a villager has come bearing a gift. The doorkeeper is deaf and doesn't hear the knock, but the king's attendant does and instructs the doorkeeper to open the gate, thereby permitting the gift to reach the king. The third analogy likens the unperturbed mind to a spider happily nestled in the center of its web. An insect comes into contact with the web, sending vibrations through to the center. On detecting these vibrations the spider shoots off toward its prey, ready to suck out the insect's juices.

What each of these similes is meant to illustrate is that there is quite a lot of mental activity going on "backstage," as it were, with various functions cooperating to bring something to our attention. The man sees the mango, then touches, smells, and tastes it, but only because he heard it first. This represents the fact that awareness often requires coordination between the different senses. Similarly the villager could not just walk into the palace, because an instruction needs to be sent to open the gates, which can happen only once the king's attendant has heard the knocking and instructed the doors to be opened. In this analogy, consciousness is compared with the king's receiving and enjoying the gift, and sophisticated mental activity has unfolded in the background of conscious awareness. In the third simile, it looks as if the web is exploited twice: first to transmit the quiver from the insect's impact along the web to the spider, and again to transport the spider out to where the insect is. What this case suggests, then, is that a single sense modality can do double duty, first to sound a subliminal alert that a certain stimulus is present, and second to reach out to that stimulus in conscious awareness.

All this helps Buddhaghosa to a major revision of ancient Buddhist theory. In both Vedic and Buddhist thought it was frequently held that there are six sense faculties, not five. As well as the familiar senses of sight, taste, touch, smell, and hearing, there is the "mind," or perhaps better "inner sense," whose job is to perceive cognitive activity. Now, every sense faculty has its own special domain of objects, as sight for instance is tasked with seeing colors. So if the mind is a sixth faculty, there must be inner "mental objects" (*dhammārammaṇa*) for it to grasp. Earlier Buddhists also thought that each distinct sense faculty has its own physical basis, like the eye in the case of vision. Extending this also to the mind, they assumed that there must be a physical basis for the sixth sense, called the "heart-base" (*hadaya-vatthu*).[10] It's a memorable term, evoking as it does the headquarters of a group of militant cardiologists, but Buddhaghosa is nonetheless going to offer a wholesale revision of the theory.

In keeping with his sophisticated and nuanced approach to mental activity, he argues that the word "mind" cannot be reduced to an additional sense faculty.[11] Rather, it refers to a range of different kinds of function associated with sensory perception, in fact four types in all. The first role of mind is like that of the king's attendant in the story about the gift from the villager. Mental activity is required to get the senses to orient themselves toward something, as when you turn back from a loud noise to focus on your book again, which is analogous to the attendant's command that the palace doors be opened. Such orientation need not be connected only to vision, of course. You could stop watching television to listen to what your spouse is saying, for example (we do not recommend the reverse procedure). Or, you could notice the sound of a falling mango. When it plays this role the mind is not a distinct, sixth kind of perception but spans across all five senses, being embedded in their normal functioning. The same goes for the remaining functions Buddhaghosa assigns to the mind, which are three stages in the sequence of sensory perception. First, there is the basic receiving of a sensory stimulus into perception, which as yet involves no attempts to classify or, if you will, "describe" what is being sensed. (Here we may be reminded of Dignāga's idea of perceptions (see Chapter 42) that have not yet received the constructions placed on them at the level of concepts.) Second, there is the stage of classification: this thing I am seeing is a mango. And there's one further role for mind to play. Buddhaghosa's third stage of perception looks rather like the modern psychologist's notion of working memory. The mind can, as he says, "run across (*javana*)" the processed perceptions from the various senses, putting them in order so that we can have a unified awareness in consciousness. In this last capacity, Buddhaghosa's mind is more like a "workspace" than an inner sixth sense.

This is a formidably sophisticated account concerning the workings of the mind. Given the proliferation of distinctions, the compelling analogies and examples, and the fierce critique of rival views, you might get the impression that Buddhaghosa wouldn't be out of place in a modern-day analytic philosophy department. Indeed, he would no doubt hold his own just fine in such an environment. Yet as so often in the Indian tradition, his technical theories were advanced with an eye on questions about how to live, and how to be liberated. We mentioned at the outset that some account of motivation was needed in order to preserve our intuitions concerning moral praise and blame. And there is a further important ethical implication of Buddhaghosa's philosophy of mind. His account could have emerged through reflection on the workings of his own mind, but we can direct our notice to other people, just as well as library books or mangos. For Buddhaghosa those other people have no selves, of course, but that does not make them unworthy of our attention. To the contrary. Each human is a unique complex of mental and bodily activities, with its own internal interactions and characteristics. According to Buddhaghosa, coming to understand this should lead to the development of empathy, where one conscious creature focuses its attention on another and becomes aware of that other's particular traits and states of mind. This is something we do suggest trying at home, and in fact in society at large. What is a flourishing community apart from humans empathizing with one another, quite literally keeping each other "in mind" as they symbiotically interact with a common environment? This aspect of Buddhaghosa's thought, along with his philosophy as a whole, was dispersed widely throughout the world of Theravāda Buddhism, not just in Sri Lanka but across much of South and Southeast Asia. His views have thus helped to shape ideas about human nature and human community in a vast sector of the global population.

42

UNDER CONSTRUCTION

DIGNĀGA ON PERCEPTION AND LANGUAGE

Jack and Jill went up the hill. Their original plan was to fetch a pail of water, but these were idle and lazy children, so instead they wound up lying on their backs, looking up at the clouds. They fell to arguing about one particular cloud, which in Jill's opinion looked like a crocodile, whereas Jack felt it was a dead ringer for a giraffe. A third child named Liza wandered past, having more conscientiously fetched some water. She resolved the dispute by pointing out that the cloud was simply a cloud. The animals that Jack and Jill were seeing were the work of their imaginations. Or as it was phrased by Liza, the giraffe and crocodile were being "superimposed" on the cloud. Actually, she added, even the concept of "cloud" is something we superimpose on our perception. "So what is it that we are perceiving?" asked Jill. "Only something fluffy and white?" "No," replied Liza, "actually the object of our perception is ineffable, and such general concepts as fluffiness and whiteness are themselves mental constructions." With that she departed. A smiling Jack said, watching her go, "dear Liza has been reading Dignāga, I guess. And there's a hole in her bucket."

Liza's enthusiasm for Dignāga was well-placed. One of the most original thinkers in the whole history of Indian philosophy, he put forward ideas that transformed Buddhist thought. Philosophers who came after him grappled with his ideas and with the reworking of those ideas achieved by his great follower Dharmakīrti. Even their opponents subtly changed their systems so as to incorporate within them the approaches and distinctions they introduced. Dignāga's greatest work is the *Collected Verses on the Sources of Knowledge* (*Pramāṇa-samuccaya*), for which he wrote an accompanying prose explanation, probably at the same time.[1] He wrote two short treatises as well, the *Study of the Wheel of Reasons* (*Hetucakraḍamaru*), a novel and innovative analysis of fallacious argumentation, and the *Investigation of the Percept* (*Ālambana-parīkṣa*),[2] a work of just eight verses that offers a radical rethink of Buddhist ideas about perception. We'll start our look at Dignāga by telling you about this little treatise.

Common sense would tell you that we use perception to grasp ordinary objects in our environment, like clouds, giraffes, and crocodiles. Philosophers are rarely willing to leave common sense alone, though. At the very least they want to come up with a fancy name. So they call this straightforward understanding of perception "direct realism." In the Indian tradition direct realism was upheld by the Nyāya school (see Chapter 26). Admittedly, they were led to making some strange claims too—that we can also perceive universals and absences—but in general their point was that common sense is right. We do perceive whole objects and not only, for example, the nearest surface of an object, or mere flashes of color, wafting scents, and momentary noises. Other philosophers prefer to revise common sense. Dignāga was one of them, which is hardly surprising given that he was a Buddhist. But he goes so far as to criticize earlier Buddhist theories as insufficiently skeptical. Here he's following in the footsteps of Vasubandhu, who may have been his teacher,[3] and further developing the Yogācāra approach to perception.

In his *Investigation of the Percept*, Dignāga argues with great force that the immediate objects of perception cannot be "external" things, not even the fleeting *dharmas* recognized in Abhidharma Buddhism. His argument goes like this. Suppose we are perceiving some object out there—the Buddhists call it the "foundation," "ground," or "objective support" (*ālambana*) of the perceptual experience. Dignāga says that this supposed "foundation" would have to be the cause of the experience. For me to see a giraffe, the giraffe must cause my visual perception. But this clearly isn't enough. If a mad scientist causes me to have a visual perception of a giraffe, then the mad scientist is the cause of the perception but I am not seeing the scientist. In addition, my perception must match up with the thing being perceived. As Dignāga puts it, my experience should have the same "form (*ākāra*)" as that thing. After all, how could I be perceiving a giraffe if the thing I claim to be perceiving has the shape of a crocodile?

Unlike Liza's bucket, this seems to be pretty watertight as an account of what is needed for perception to occur. Dignāga is going to draw a surprising result from it, though, by showing that external things cannot satisfy his two demands.[4] Sautrāntika Buddhists held that clouds, giraffes, and crocodiles are made of atoms, and atoms do seem to be the sort of thing that can cause perception, so they would tick the first box: the atoms that make up a cloud do cause me to see the cloud. Yet I am not seeing the atoms. Atoms are not perceptible, and even if they can be observed under special conditions, it is not atoms I see when my gaze falls upon a cloud; what I see is a cloud. So here the second requirement is not satisfied. The atoms, the objects that cause the perception, do not match the perception in form. Perhaps someone will say that we don't see individual atoms, but rather a conglomerate of them, like the collection of atoms that makes up a crocodile. That should fix the problem, because the conglomeration does have the form that matches the perception of a crocodile. Sadly, the conglomeration is nothing over and above the atoms, so it cannot be a distinct cause of my perception, and the first condition is not satisfied. An analogous case would be your perception of a forest. From a distance you see just the conglomerate, the wood and not the trees. Yet we know that it is the trees that cause your perception, because in reality there are only trees to do the causing.

Dignāga considers a third way that external things could cause perception. Perhaps it is not the atoms themselves, or a conglomerate of them, but some power or "shape" in the atoms. By virtue of this power they can make you perceive, as it might be, a crocodile or a cloud. To stay with the meteorological theme, consider what happens when you see a rainbow. There is no real arc of color there. Rather, the rainbow is composed of droplets of water, each of which is helping produce in you a vision of a rainbow. This is a rather promising idea, but Dignāga gives it short shrift. He points out that if the feature that causes the perception belongs to the atoms intrinsically, then the same atoms should still cause the same perception when rearranged. But when the airborne particles shift you no longer see a rainbow. Which is to say nothing of the more radical recombination of atoms that ensues when a crocodile eats and digests a giraffe, with the giraffe's atoms going to make up the crocodile's body. It's not as if crocodiles who feast on giraffe meat start to look more and more like giraffes. Dignāga concludes from all this that what we take to be ordinary objects of perception are really only the products of the human mind. What we in fact perceive are "knowable interior forms." These internal forms both cause our experience and provide it with content, something nothing outside us can do.

For a more elaborate and somewhat different account of perception we can turn to Dignāga's mature treatise, the *Collected Verses on the Sources of Knowledge*. He opens the first chapter by distinguishing between two ways of apprehending the world, which he labels "perception (*pratyakṣa*)" and "inference (*anumāna*)"; an alternative translation might be "experience" and "reasoning." This by the way is not original with him. Already Vasubandhu's brother Asaṅga had defined three sources of knowledge, namely perception, inference, and testimony,[5] so Dignāga is just taking over this list and dropping the third item (for more on this, see Chapter 43). The two remaining kinds of cognition, perception and inference, correspond respectively to the individual and the general, or as philosophers would say with their fancy names, to "particulars (*sva-lakṣaṇa*)"[6] and universals "(*sāmānya-lakṣaṇa*)." Again, this may at first sound like common sense. There is, on the one hand, the particular white cloud;

on the other, the general or universal feature of whiteness that appears in this cloud, in that cloud, in an alarming number of the hairs on your head, and so on.

Dignāga, however, insists that universals do not exist in nature, but only in our minds. They are mere concepts, and everything real is a singular or individual item. Indeed, he takes it to be a straightforward contradiction that *one* universal could be in *multiple* instances, like the single *whiteness* in many clouds.[7] So certainly we cannot perceive universals. As for what we *can* perceive, you might expect this to be for example one individual cloud, or perhaps the individual white color of a given cloud. But even to say this is to deploy the very universal concepts that are mere fantasies of the human mind, like "white" and "cloud." Instead, Dignāga claims, the objects of perception are "inexpressible" or "ineffable" (*avyapadeśa*). Perhaps the closest we could come to imagining what he has in mind would be something like a perceived flash of color, or better, an entirely unclassified flash of visual awareness—although, bearing in mind the critique of external objects we just discussed, such a flash of awareness is indeed something in the mind, and not an external object. It is a particular, indefinable, and momentary object of experience within our mental life.

So that's perception. What about inference? Even though the universals are mental constructs—or perhaps we should say, precisely because they are mental constructs—we are able to think about the relationship between concepts like color, whiteness, cloud, and giraffe. Thus we could think that white things are colored, that some clouds look like giraffes, that giraffes are not white, and so on. This kind of thinking enables us to organize concepts into hierarchies, like genera and species in the logic of Aristotle. The concept of giraffe falls under that of animal, the concept of white under that of color, and so on.[8] As we'll see shortly this is going to play an important role in Dignāga's theory of language. For now, though, we've learned that human thought is largely a matter of exploring the relationship between mentally constructed concepts. What lies under these constructions is not external objects, whether atoms or everyday things, but particular perceptions. Notice that Dignāga is not a radical skeptic who disavows all possibility of knowledge. To the contrary, he thinks we have immediate knowledge through perception, a direct and undistorted sensory acquaintance not contaminated by the fantasies of human imagination. To ensure this he even stipulates that perception can never be in error, and therefore complains about the Nyāya definition of perception as "cognition that arises from sense objects and is unerring and inexpressible." The definition is not so much wrong as redundant: all true cognition is perception, and it is always unerring and inexpressible.[9]

Of course this fits nicely with Dignāga's argument that what we see is internal, not external. It is only when you are perceiving an external thing that the possibility of error arises, like when you see a rope and think it is a snake. For it is in these cases that there can be a mismatch between the object and the way it is perceived. Mistakes occur when concepts, which are necessarily general, are superimposed onto the data of perceptual experience, which is necessarily particular and unique. It follows that pure, unconceptualized perception is invariably error-free. Of course Dignāga also thinks that if we were to see a rope and correctly classify it under the concept "rope," that too would involve mental construction and not just immediate perception. This is not to say, though, that Dignāga is denying the reality of the rope, or the reality of something or other out in the world. Instead he simply brackets the question of whether there are any external things. As we saw, they cannot be the objects of perception, in the sense of both causing the perception and matching it in form. So the knowledge we have through perception neither vindicates the existence of external things nor indicates that they do not exist.[10] Perception is entirely internal to the perceiver.

On both these points, Dignāga's great follower Dharmakīrti is going to offer a different opinion. He does reject the reality of external things, adopting an explicitly idealist theory where Dignāga's might more accurately be called "phenomenalist," if we wanted to give it another fancy name. As for error, Dharmakīrti makes a subtle but crucial change by insisting that accurate perception must be not merely "free from conceptual structure" but also free from illusion. Remember that for Dignāga, *all* perceptual experience is free from illusion. Dharmakīrti instead thinks that there can be unconceptualized but still erroneous perceptual experience. He mentions three examples. If I suffer from jaundice, he claims, I see objects with a yellow color that they do not actually have. The yellowness is a product of a defect in my vision and has nothing to do with the object. But this is not a case of conceptual construction, since defects of vision can affect even those who lack concepts, like small children and animals. Similarly, when I watch someone whirling a torch on the end of a piece of rope, all I see is a continuous circle of light. That too, thinks Dharmakīrti, is a case of perceptual error that does not involve the misapplication of concepts. It is simply because human vision cannot distinguish the torch at each place on its circular trajectory.

Dharmakīrti's third case is one we have all experienced, when the vehicle we are in begins to move but it looks to us as if we are stationary and the world around is moving. Dharmakīrti's example involves a boat, but the modern reader may more readily think of sitting in a train when there is another train on the adjacent platform. When your train moves off, it looks as if the other train has started to move in the opposite direction. Again, Dharmakīrti claims, this sort of perceptual error cannot be assimilated to any conceptual mishap; it's purely visual. So

Dharmakīrti revises Dignāga's concept of perception with the extra clause. Unfortunately this means that he can no longer locate all error at the conceptual level. The elegance and explanatory power of Dignāga's theory has been compromised, albeit in the quest for truth.

The sort of nominalism espoused by Dignāga is confronted with an obvious objection. Language is full of references to universals, so if there are no universals, then how does language latch on to the world? He takes up this challenge with his customary brilliance. Before Dignāga, philosophers had given extensive thought to the meaning of words. Take that most Indian of examples, the word "cow." None of us has difficulty understanding its meaning, despite the various ways it can be used. In a sentence like "the cow is standing" or "bring me the cow," it appears to stand for a particular object, an individual cow. But in a sentence like "a cow is an animal" or "a cow is shorter than a giraffe," it seems to stand for something else, perhaps a generic cow or the class of all particular cows. Again, in statements like "he is playing with cows" (said of a child playing with toys) or "this is a cow" (said while pointing to a picture), it seems to stand for anything which has the shape or structure (*ākṛti*) of a cow. The great Nyāya thinker Gautama concluded from such examples that the meaning of the term "cow" is a composite of all three stand-ins. It takes within its significance the individual cow, the cow-shape, and the universal cow-hood. Commenting on Gautama, Vātsyāyana seems to interpret him as meaning that "cow" is systematically ambiguous: the word takes different meanings in different uses. It seems odd, though, to say that a word as simple as "cow" is systematically ambiguous in its various uses, and, moreover, there is clearly something common to the different uses. The later Naiyāyikas Uddyotakara and Jayanta give the *sūtra* a different and more compelling reading, therefore. They try to find something that can serve as the common meaning in each and every use of the word. Their idea is that an utterance of "cow" refers to an individual cow only insofar as it is a possessor of the feature cow-hood. In other words the word "cow" has a deep logical form, meaning something like "that thing, being a cow," a complex comprising a demonstrative indicating a particular ("that thing") and a predicate attributing a property ("being a cow"). So a sentence like "the cow is white" is true so long as the thing being picked out by the sentence is both a cow and is white, while "a cow is an animal" means something like "whatever thing is picked out as possessing cow-hood is a thing that possesses animality."

Dignāga replaces this complicated story with a simple and powerful analysis of words.[11] His theory of the meaning of terms, given in the fifth chapter of his *Collected Verses*, draws on the hierarchical account of concepts we looked at earlier. Concepts are organized by relations of containment and exclusion. Thus the concept color "contains" the concept white, because anything that is white is also colored, while the concept white "excludes" the concept blue, meaning that nothing is both white and blue. What does this tell us about the meaning of words like "white" and "color"? The old answer was that the conceptual hierarchy corresponds to the hierarchy of things in nature. The world itself is organized in a certain way and our conceptual classifications are not invented but reflect that organization. As for individual words, they refer to things on the basis of the universals instantiated by those things. That thing up there is a cloud because it is an instance of cloud-ness, not cow-ness.

Dignāga has a different idea altogether. In what has come to be called the theory of exclusion (*apoha*), he proposes that words do not need to correspond to anything external; their meaning is determined merely by their location in the conceptual hierarchy. It's a bit like the way groups of people form identity by excluding outsiders. Someone might struggle to say what exactly it means to be British or American, while being all too ready to exclude other people from being "properly" British or American because they have the wrong religion, skin color, or accent. For Dignāga this same sort of mechanism explains the meaning of everyday words. What exactly is a cloud? It is, if you'll pardon the expression, a rather nebulous idea, difficult to define in positive terms. There are many different shapes and colors of cloud, clouds can be made up of either water or other vaporized substances, and so on. Dignāga would simply say that "cloud" gets its meaning from its relation to other terms. The concept of cloud "excludes" concepts such as giraffe, because even if there are giraffe-shaped clouds, no cloud is really a giraffe. Exclusion can also be used to explain compound expressions like "white cloud." The difference between saying "white cloud" and merely saying "cloud" is that the first excludes more things than the second: the phrase "white cloud" excludes both things that are not clouds and things that are not white, whereas the word "cloud" excludes only things that are not clouds.

A major advantage of Dignāga's *apoha* theory is that it shows how he can do without real universals.[12] When we apply the term "cow" we are not saying that it instantiates some general feature found in the world. We are just discriminating a thing from what is dissimilar to it, in this case, from whatever is not a cow. Universals are, in short, concealed double-negations. To say that something is a cow is to say that it is not a non-cow. This is how language works, positioning concepts relative to one another. You might object that language doesn't *always* work that way. What about proper names, like "Bessie," "Gena," and "Hiawatha"? Here Dignāga's answer would be that we never apply such names to individual objects of perception. As we've seen, he thinks those cannot be expressed in language at all. The proper name of a certain cow, crocodile, or giraffe actually refers to a combination of many individual perceptions. So the name "Bessie" or concept of Bessie is just as much a conceptual construction as a universal like "cow." And this exemplifies another advantage of Dignāga's theory of language: it meshes beautifully with his account of perception. His idea is that we never get a concept so fine-grained that it excludes everything except a single particular. Particulars are inexpressible in words and can only be directly perceived, while concepts and the words that express them (even proper names) always work at the level of mental construction. We move internally within that conceptual world when we observe that whatever is a cow is not a giraffe, even though both are animals, or that if something is a white cloud then it is a cloud. It is these movements that constitute the work of inference and reason.

43

FOLLOW THE EVIDENCE

DIGNĀGA'S LOGIC

Have you ever been asked to serve on a jury? It's an unusually high stakes case of applied epistemology, where you must decide whether to let yourself be persuaded by evidence. Often that evidence takes the form of testimony. Perhaps someone has been accused of arson and a witness claims to have seen them set the fire. If the witness is being truthful, then she knows that the defendant is guilty: she watched him set the fire with her own eyes. Can she now transfer that knowledge to you through a convincing account of what she saw? The philosophers of the Nyāya school would have said yes. For them, testimony (*śabda*) is one of the fundamental sources of knowledge, and is thus designated as a *pramāṇa* (see Chapter 27). But as a juror, you may be in doubt about the witness' credibility. And as a philosopher, you may doubt whether testimony is really a source of knowledge. If so, you might call as your own witness Dignāga.

We mentioned in Chapter 42 that he acknowledges only two means of acquiring knowledge, namely perception and inference. He refuses to dignify "testimony (*śabda*)," the assertions of authoritative persons, with the title of *pramāṇa*.[1] This is not because he thinks that testimony never gives us knowledge, but because when it does do so, an inference is required. To get knowledge from that witness in the arson case, you would have to combine her testimony about the setting of the fire with the knowledge that she is reliable. From these two pieces of information you may infer that the defendant is guilty. This might sound like pedantic bookkeeping, a way of getting the number of *pramāṇas* down from three to two. But it is actually a case of a Buddhist not wanting to keep the books venerated in the Brahmanical tradition. Prosecuting the case against the vaunted testimony of Vedic texts, Dignāga insists that they can provide no independent source of knowledge.

Though his position here responds most directly to the Nyāya school, it also makes a vivid contrast with the epistemology of Mīmāṃsā. Testimony is not innocent until proven guilty, as they claimed, but needs to be evaluated on each occasion as to its reliability. Dignāga is to this extent a "rationalist," in the sense that he thinks every claim to knowledge must be based on evidence directly available to the individual knower. Knowledge by testimony is no counterexample to this rule, because it is up to each of us to judge the credibility of the testimony and, only if it passes muster, to infer that the claims set out in the testimony are true. But this is not the only kind of inference Dignāga recognizes. As we've seen, he thinks we use direct perception to grasp unique particulars. Reflection at the general or universal level—such as the judgment that smoke billows from houses that have been set on fire—is imposed onto such perceptual experience, an act of human construction. It is at this level that we have inferences. "Ah," you might think, "this house is billowing with smoke. When houses do that, that means they are on fire. So this house is evidently on fire. Good thing it isn't mine."

Dignāga calls this kind of reflection "inferring to oneself (*svārthānumāna*)," which is thus basically his term for reasoning. He contrasts it to "inferring for others (*parārthānumāna*)," which is what you do when you are trying to convince someone else of something as opposed to deciding whether to be convinced yourself.[2] If inferring to oneself is reasoning, then inferring for others is demonstration: producing an explicit argument, as I might do if I calmly explained to you that your house is on fire, because there is smoke billowing out of it (calmly, because it's your house, not mine). Here we have one of Dignāga's signal achievements as a philosopher. He is the first Indian thinker to distinguish the rules of *reasoning*, which effectively means determining which arguments are formally valid, from the rules of *debate*, which have to do with persuading other people of things.

Another fundamental achievement is that in his *Collected Verses on the Sources of Knowledge*, Dignāga explains to us the difference between good and bad inferences—whether these are involved in inferring to oneself, that is, the distinction between reasoning well or badly, or for others, the difference between debating fairly or unfairly. Thus far Dignāga's Yogācāra Buddhism has been an obvious background to his epistemology. We just mentioned the critique of Vedic tradition implied by his demotion of knowledge by testimony to a form of inference, and his claim that general concepts are human constructions gives him a place in the Buddhists' own tradition of philosophical skepticism. It would seem, though, that when he comes to offer a theory of inference, he is trying to remain neutral. Philosophers of various schools might adopt his account, and in fact this is exactly what happened. Dignāga's analysis was assimilated by a wide range of later thinkers, including even the Nyāya school from Uddyotakara onwards.

In honor of this one instance where the Naiyāyikas and Buddhists got on with one another like a house on fire, let's shift from the arson case to the classic Nyāya example of smoke that reveals the presence of fire on a mountain. According to

Dignāga, any inference can be rendered in a form like the following: "this mountain has fire, because it has smoke." First a proposition is stated—the mountain has fire—then a reason is given, in this case smoke. Note that this is the reverse of the deductive pattern we often find in European logicians, starting with Aristotle, where one or more premises are given and then a conclusion is drawn: "the mountain has smoke; therefore, it has fire." In another contrast with Aristotle, in Dignāga the reason that is given is not really explanatory. Instead, the smoke reveals the presence of fire, or allows us to predict that the mountain has fire, but there is no talk of answering the question of *why* there is a fire. Still, Dignāga would agree with Aristotle that the proposition to be proved is something we do not yet know, and that it is not something that can be immediately determined by perception. Aristotle gives the memorable example that if you were standing on the moon, you could just see the cause of an eclipse and would not need to seek an explanation for it.[3]

The inference patterns Dignāga studies all have the same structure. There is always an object which is the "locus" or "basis" (*pakṣa*) of the inference, which in our example is the mountain. Our inference will seek to show that the locus possesses a certain property (*sādhya*), such as the property of having fire. We establish this by citing a *hetu*, meaning another property possessed by the locus, that is, evidence or a reason for inferring the property we are interested in, so in this case the property of having smoke. Thus every inference has the form, "the locus has an inferred property because it has an evidential property," or if you prefer that in Sanskrit, "the *pakṣa* (the mountain) has a *hetu* (smoke) so it must have the *sādhya* (fire)." Now, there are many inferences which do have this form but are not good inferences. You shouldn't infer that the mountain is covered in grass because it is green, since there are many green things other than grass. The mountain might be covered with moss, green paint, or be the site of a St Patrick's Day parade. So being green cannot serve as good evidence for the presence of grass. The evidential property (being green) and the inferred property (being covered in grass) are not connected in the right way.

Dignāga's goal in his theory of inference is to say what this "right way" is, to define the relation between *pakṣa*, *sādhya*, and *hetu*. This is just to ask, when is evidence sufficient to convince us that one property always comes together with another?[4] Dignāga's answer is that the evidence must satisfy a certain set of three conditions. This is his celebrated *trairūpya* theory, the theory of the triple-conditioned sign.[5] The first condition is that the evidential property must indeed occur in the locus of the inference. This is basically obvious. I cannot use smoke as my evidence that a mountain is on fire unless there is indeed smoke on the mountain. The other two conditions are less obvious and involve a bit more terminology. Dignāga introduces the notions of a "homologue (*sapakṣa*)" and a "heterologue (*vipakṣa*)," or we might say in plainer English, a "similar case" and a "dissimilar case." Dignāga defines them as follows. A "similar case" is any other object, apart from the locus, that has the inferred property. In our example this would be something else that is on fire. A "dissimilar case" is some other object which lacks the inferred property, that is, something that is not on fire.

Dignāga is effectively describing a method of investigation here. If you want to know whether a given thing has a given property, then notice some second property it has and look to see whether other things with that second property have the first property you're interested in. In our example the second property is the smoke, so let's consider something *similar*: a smoky kitchen. Lo and behold, there is fire there too. Smoke is looking like good evidence for fire. Next let's consider something *dissimilar*, something that lacks the second property. No arsonist has been round to your house, so happily it lacks smoke, and the absence of smoke billowing from your house coincides with your house's not being on fire. This confirms that smoke really does correlate with fire, so that the presence of smoke on the mountain would seem to be a convincing sign of fire there.

All this is summed up in Dignāga's second and third conditions. The second condition is that the evidential property must come together with the inferred property in at least one similar case, like the smoky kitchen where fire is also found. The third condition is that in every known dissimilar case where the evidential property is absent, so is the inferred property, like your smoke-free house that is not on fire. We might call these the "positive example" condition and the "no counterexample" condition. Taking them together, we can conclude that whatever has the evidential property must have the inferred property. If every locus of smoke is also a locus of fire, then we can soundly infer from the presence of smoke in a particular place to the presence of fire there. Notice that Dignāga is being true to his promise that inferences always operate at a general level, involving universal concepts. Good inferences are the ones where some general rule or law connects the evidential and inferred properties, so that we can say "whatever is like this is like that," or "whatever is X is Y." Dignāga calls such a connection a relation of "pervasion (*vyāpti*)," something that will be a topic of huge importance in later centuries. Gaṅgeśa in the fourteenth century will review more than a dozen accounts of pervasion that emerged in the generations after Dignāga.

We said earlier that inference as Dignāga analyzes it does not have the form of a deduction, with premises leading to a conclusion. That might seem to be a superficial point, a mere matter of presentation. After all, couldn't we rephrase what he is saying as a pure deduction? We could begin with the premise "the mountain has smoke," add the further premise, "whatever has smoke has fire," and then conclude, "therefore the mountain has fire." Well, not quite. For one thing Dignāga is primarily interested in inference as a means of acquiring knowledge. He tries to articulate the conditions under which the result of an inference is a "rationally acceptable" or justified belief. So he is not interested only in the *form* of the argument, like a logician who simply wants to point out the validity of the argument pattern "this is an X, every X is a Y, therefore this is a Y." Dignāga is more demanding than that. He thinks that a good inference is not only valid, but also sound: it must have *true* premises. In fact he goes further still. Not only must the argument pattern be valid and have true premises, but the premises must be *known* to be true. Only if this is so can we say that the reasoner knows the conclusion to be true, so only then do we have an inference that meets Dignāga's specifications.

And in keeping with this focus on what the reasoner actually knows, Dignāga actually doesn't quite lay down a condition of the form "every X is Y." In this respect his demand is weaker: the reasoner must satisfy herself that "every known X is known to be Y." She doesn't need to be able to say that all smoky things, past, present, and future have been, are, and will be on fire. If she can state confidently that every time she has experienced something to be smoky, it has been on fire, then by Dignāga's lights she is in a position to infer fire from smoke when she sees it on the mountain. The lack of exceptions proves the rule. This shows again that Dignāga is not really interested in pure deductions. What he is describing comes closer to the notion of induction, where we look to our previous experience to justify the inferences we make about the present and future.

To that extent Dignāga's *trairūpya* may seem familiar and even rather straightforward. But there are a couple of details in his formulation that may give us pause. One is the relationship between the second condition, about finding a similar case, and the third, about excluding counterexamples. The worry is that these two may be redundant.[6] Saying that anything that has smoke has fire would seem to be equivalent to saying that anything that lacks smoke lacks fire. So why does Dignāga give these as two distinct criteria, rather than as one criterion that can be formulated either positively or negatively? Perhaps it is because the second criterion requires us to find at least one actual similar case. All the third criterion tells us to do is verify that where smoke is absent fire is absent too. This wouldn't guarantee that there are really any cases apart from the locus we started from—namely the mountain—that have both smoke and fire. What the second criterion adds, then, is a positive basis for induction.

Another, more subtle, problem is that Dignāga always tells us to look at things *other than the locus* when we are checking similar and dissimilar cases. That makes perfect sense with a one-off topic of inquiry like the smoke billowing from this particular mountain or that particular house. We just need to look at other things that are and are not smoky. But consider the inference "odd numbers are divisible by two, because they are integers." If we exclude the class of odd numbers from our search because it is the locus, then we will have to look at other integers to test the inference. And every remaining integer is indeed divisible by two; but that obviously doesn't make the inference a good one. (Here being an integer is the "evidential property" and being divisible by two is the "inferred property.") So this would count as a good piece of inference according to Dignāga's conditions. This unwelcome result was pointed out by Jaina philosophers, who criticized him for it and tried to repair the problem.

Criticism and modification of the theory also emerged within the Buddhist tradition. By far the most influential figure here was his commentator Dharmakīrti, so influential in fact that his writings seem to have replaced Dignāga's among readers of Sanskrit. For this reason Dignāga's *Collected Verses* and the comments he added to it until very recently had to be read in Tibetan translation, until evidence of the Sanskrit original was uncovered. Dharmakīrti's own works (principally the *Pramāṇa-vārttika*, the *Nyāya-bindu*, and the *Hetu-bindu*),[7] became the basis for later Buddhist epistemology, which tended to come in the form of commentaries on Dharmakīrti (such as Dharmottara's *Nyāya-bindu-ṭīkā*) or manuals presenting the main elements of Dharmakīrti's thought in a more manageable form. Dharmakīrti had two main complaints about Dignāga's discussion of inference: an imprecision in the formulation of the triple-condition, and Dignāga's failure properly to address the problem of induction.

The first complaint goes back to what we were just saying about cases where the locus we are interested in is a class rather than a single item. When Dignāga says in his first condition that the evidential property must be present, this is ambiguous. Suppose a policeman, while testifying in a trial, were to say that arsonists love candles. This could mean that *all* arsonists, in his experience, love candles, or merely that they tend to love them, or even just that the policeman has come across candle-loving arsonists now and again. Hence Dharmakīrti's complaint. If our locus is a class then stating that the evidential property is present in the locus could mean that it belongs to every member of the class or only to some members. Dignāga's formulation of the second and third conditions is similarly ambiguous. Do I have to examine *all* potentially similar and dissimilar cases to see if the evidential property really does pervade the inferred property, or only find a few examples? This bears on the question we mentioned earlier, as to whether the second and third conditions are equivalent. If it is sufficient to find just one similar case, but we have to conduct an exhaustive search for counterexamples, then the two conditions are clearly not the same. But if the examination of both similar and dissimilar cases is to be exhaustive, then they amount to one and the same investigation. After all, making sure that every time smoke appears, fire is present, means verifying that when smoke does not appear fire is not present.

Dharmakīrti solved these problems by reformulating the three conditions.[8] He introduces a Sanskrit restrictive particle, *eva*, which means "only," "exactly," or "really." His new conditions are now as follows. The first, called the "locus condition (*pakṣa-dharmatā*)," now states that the evidential property is observed to be present *exactly* in the locus (*pakṣe sattvam eva niścitam*). The second and third, which he calls the "agreement" and "disagreement" conditions (*anvaya* and *vyatireka*), say that this evidential property is observed *only* in similar cases (*sapakṣe eva sattvam niścitam*) and is *really* absent from dissimilar cases (*vipakṣe asattvam eva niścitam*). The restrictive particle clears up the ambiguity in each case. It indicates that the evidential property is present in the *whole* locus, that it is present in *some* similar cases though not necessarily all of them, and that it is absent from *all* dissimilar cases. On this updated version of the theory it is really the last condition that does the work. "Pervasion" of one property by another means that the evidential property is absent from whatever *lacks* the inferred property, for instance that smoke is absent from whatever lacks fire. This is much stronger than the second condition, which simply tells us to find at least one similar case, like the smoky kitchen where fire is also present.

As for Dharmarkīrti's second worry, it strikes at the heart of inductive reasoning. The problem arises whether we try to justify an inference positively by finding similar cases (things with both smoke and fire), or negatively, by finding cases where both properties are lacking (what is not smoking has no fire). How can we support a universal generalization having seen only a limited number of examples? The ninety-nine smoky things I have seen thus far involved fire, but what about the hundredth, or thousandth, or millionth? Dharmakīrti's solution is to go beyond the mere observation of properties that always come together, or "pervade" one another, and demand a link that explains why the properties come together. To do this he identifies different kinds of reason that could link properties. The first type is a reason that links cause and effect (*kārya-hetu*). This is the kind of case we've been talking about the whole time: because smoke is an effect of fire, it never appears without fire also being present. Or two properties might both be effects of a shared cause. The generalization "night follows day" is true, not because day causes night, but because day and night are both caused by the rotation of the earth. An example cited by some Buddhists is the inference of lemon color from lemon taste, when both are products of the same cause, the lemon itself.

A second kind of link is what Dharmakīrti calls a "natural reason (*svabhāva-hetu*)." To illustrate, he says that being a *śiṃśapā* tree is a reason for being a tree. Obviously, being a *śiṃśapā* tree, or for that matter a lemon tree, is not a *cause* for being a tree; but neither is the relation between these two properties accidental. In the term *svabhāva-hetu* you'll recognize the word *svabhāva*, meaning the essence or nature of a thing, which was the target of Nagārjuna's critical philosophy. So what Dharmakīrti is saying is that the nature of *śiṃśapā* tree includes or implies the nature of tree. Puzzlingly he says that such inferences are based on the relation of identity (*tādātmya*), as opposed to causality (*tadutpatti*). He might mean that the *śiṃśapā* tree and the tree are the same thing, whereas cause and effect are always distinct. Or maybe he means that the tree actually has only one property, which is being described in a more and a less precise way, as we might say that someone has the property of "being tall" and of "being six foot three inches," where these two properties are really identical.

Finally, there is the "reason based on non-observation (*anupalabdhi-hetu*)," which we came across earlier when looking at the Nyāya claim that we can perceive absences (see Chapter 26). It is the pattern of reasoning exemplified by such inferences as "there is no pot here, because it is not observed." Such inferences rest on the truth of a counterfactual claim: if there *were* a pot here it *would* be observed, assuming normal lighting conditions, properly working sense faculties, and so on. As with the first two kinds of reason, this third kind of reason based on non-observation shows not just that two properties do in fact come together in our experience, but that they *must* come together. A good inference requires some real link or tie between the properties. Nothing has the taste of lemon without the scent of lemon, because both are caused by lemons; nothing can be a lemon tree without being a tree; when you don't find that life has given you lemons, you can't make lemonade. This is Dharmakīrti's solution to the problem of induction. A genuine link between properties explains why we have always seen the properties together, and gives us a guarantee that they will continue to come together in the future.

44

DOORS OF PERCEPTION

DIGNĀGA ON CONSCIOUSNESS

Let's get back to Mick Jagger, who is still where we left him (in Chapter 35): seeing a red door. It's still not painted black, as he wanted, but that should be no surprise to Mick since he has told us himself that you can't always get what you want. Now here's a question about the experience he is having. In addition to seeing the red door, is Mick Jagger aware that he is seeing a red door? You might think that we can't tell for sure. Obviously we are sometimes aware that we are having a given experience, as when reflecting on how much we are enjoying a piece of music. It may seem, though, that some experiences come without self-awareness of that kind. Indeed, it may even seem that if you enjoy a piece of music enough, you may become so immersed in it that you are no longer aware of yourself listening to it. Or at the other end of the spectrum, you may be hearing music playing in the background—as at a loud coffee shop—without being aware of hearing it. Someone might need to bring it to your attention, at which point you may realize in retrospect that a Rolling Stones song has been playing since you sat down.

Plausible though these examples may seem, Dignāga would reject the lesson we just drew from them. For him there is no perception without self-awareness. And when he speaks of "self-awareness" (*svasaṃvitti* or *svasaṃvedana*), he has in mind an awareness that is built into the very perception itself. It is just part of seeing a red door to be aware of seeing a red door, and under no circumstances can you be oblivious of seeing it while seeing it. With these controversial claims, Dignāga was rejecting a leading theory of how self-awareness works, which we find in the Nyāya school. For Nyāya one reason to postulate a faculty of "mind (*manas*)" in the first place is to explain the phenomenon of self-awareness. Mick Jagger's vision would do nothing more than to perceive the red door, and his mind would need to get involved in order to give him awareness of this perception.

This is an example of what we might call a "reflective" theory of self-awareness, because according to Nyāya the perceiver has to reflect mentally on their perception to become aware of it. The mind is thereby performing a specific function, called "inner apperception (*anuvyavasāya*)." It is up to Mick Jagger's mind to perceive that he is seeing, much as his seeing perceives the door. On this view, awareness is what philosophers call a "second order" phenomenon, like a belief about a belief (as when I believe that Mick's belief that the door is red is a correct judgment on his part) or a desire about a desire (as when Mick wishes he could stop wanting everything to be painted black). Dignāga does not think that awareness is like that. As we'll see shortly, he certainly thinks that we can engage in second order reflection on our perceptions. But this is not what awareness is, for him. He instead adopts what we might call a "reflexive" view, according to which awareness of perceiving is built into the perception itself, already at the first order level.[1]

Whether you think that awareness is reflective or reflexive—or as the Indian philosophers put it, whether it involves "other-illumination (*paraprakāśa*)" or "self-illumination (*svaprakāśa*)"—you can still think that some perceptions occur without awareness. This seems especially likely on the reflective view. If I need to engage in second order reflection on my perceptions to be aware of them, then it stands to reason that I only do that some of the time. The Nyāya could say that the person in the coffee shop is prompted to such an act of reflection when they are made aware that they have already been hearing the Rolling Stones without noticing it. Even on the reflexive view, though, one could imagine that we sometimes have perceptions with built-in awareness, and sometimes have perceptions that lack awareness. Thus the person in the coffee shop might first have perception of music without awareness, then an aware perception once it is called to their attention.

Dignāga, however, insists that awareness is reflexive and that it is *always* present. Why? It has something to do with his theory of perception. As we've seen, Dignāga is a phenomenalist (Chapter 42). He does not think that we immediately perceive external objects in the world around us, but at best grasp them indirectly by means of what he calls "knowable interior forms," representations that are internal to the perceiver. His idea then is that awareness of such a representation is part of what it is to perceive. As he states in his *Collected Verses on the Means of Knowing* (§1.9–11), every thought or experience has two aspects, "objective" and "subjective." It's easy to understand why cognition needs an objective aspect: it is just in the nature of thought that it is directed toward some object or other. Even dreams and imaginings have some object or "content," as a dream of a red door is of the door and not anything else. We should remember, though, that for Dignāga, this content is not going to be an *external* object, like a real red door. A thought or perception is directed to an internal representation and he seems to leave it open whether there is some thing outside in the world to which that representation corresponds.

It's not so easy to say what the "subjective" aspect of cognition might be. It may be helpful to think about it as the *way* that the content, like the red door, presents itself to us. An analogy here could be photographs and paintings. A photograph of a face has the face as its "object" but it also has its own qualities, like brightness, sharpness, and contrast, factors that depend on the way the photograph was taken. When you look at a photograph and say that it is overexposed or underdeveloped, you're paying attention to features of the photograph itself, and may be ignoring what the photograph shows. The same is true of paintings: there are many different frescoes of the Buddha, and what makes one "serene," another "typically Burmese," and so on, are the subjective qualities of the individual paintings.

To prove that perception does have such a built-in, subjective aspect, Dignāga points to the very phenomenon that Nyāya made responsible for awareness: second order reflection. When I think that I am enjoying a piece of music, or for that matter tell myself in a dream that I am only dreaming, I am attending to an experience of which I must *already* have been aware. If the first order perception had only its objective content, this would be impossible. Consider again Mick Jagger seeing the red door. If this perception contains nothing but its object, namely the door, then when Mick reflected on it he could only be reflecting on the door. But in fact Mick can reflect on the fact that he is seeing the door, attending to his own subjective role in the perception. This could include reflection on the way that the door looks: if he's in London and it's foggy, he might think to himself that he's seeing the door but only through a haze, or that in such poor lighting conditions the door almost looks orange. The analogy to paintings and photographs is again helpful here. A painting of a painting is not the same as a duplicate of the original, and taking a photograph of a photograph is not the same as ordering a second set of prints. The second order images record the way the first images represented their objects: if the first photo was an overexposed image of a face, then the object of the second photo is an overexposed photograph, and not just the face.

You might think that someone who believes that all cognition has built-in awareness could simply invite his readers to introspect and see that he's right. After all, if you are always aware of having perceptions when you have them, then you ought to know about it. Dignāga does not, however, rest his case on our everyday experience, perhaps because the awareness he is speaking of may often be tacit, in the sense that it rarely comes to our active attention. Consider that you spend your waking day being conscious without explicitly thinking about the fact that you are conscious. Perhaps Dignāga's self-awareness is like that. So to make his case, Dignāga offers a complex argument (*Collected Verses* §1.11–12), which like other aspects of his work would be taken up and further developed by later Buddhists from Dharmakīrti onwards.

He points to the phenomenon of memory. Suppose Mick Jagger goes home and cheers up, now thinking that the door's red shade was actually quite lovely. When he looks back on his earlier experience he does not, Dignāga suggests, simply remember a red door. He remembers *perceiving* the red door while standing in front of it. Again this is very plausible. You will remember that the Buddhist king, Aśoka, erected inscriptions around his empire with ethical teachings on them, but unless you are remarkably old you won't remember actually seeing the inscriptions erected. Dignāga's double aspect theory of cognition explains this. When you "remember" an event you didn't experience yourself, you are recalling only objective content: you have a belief that the event did occur. When you remember experiencing an event, you are recalling the subjective awareness you had of that event.

Compelling though this is, it may seem to cut no ice against Dignāga's opponent, who thinks that awareness arises through a second order reflection on cognition. This opponent might simply say that when we remember an event, we are remembering two things, the content of an original experience alongside a second order reflection directed toward that experience. Thus Mick Jagger would remember the red door, and furthermore remember reflecting on the fact that he was seeing a red door. Against this, Dignāga offers a regress argument.[2] How will Mick Jagger remember reflecting on the experience he was having? He will need to have been aware of this very reflective act, too, if he is to remember it. But Dignāga's opponent doesn't think that cognitions have built-in awareness. So when Mick thinks to himself, "ah, here I am, seeing a door," his second order thought will need a further, third order thought if it is to come to his attention, along the lines of, "ah, here I am, noticing that I am seeing a door." Obviously the same argument can be applied at this stage and then again, indefinitely. Since, according to the opponent, a cognition is determined entirely by its objective content and not by subjective awareness, the higher order thoughts will never get awareness into the picture. We might say that they will never include a first-person perspective. We will have only seeing a red door, thinking of seeing a red door, thinking of thinking about seeing a red door, and so on.

This is a fairly powerful argument, but it may achieve less than Dignāga needs it to. Remember, he needs to show us not just that some cognitions include subjective awareness, but that they *all* do. And his regress argument simply doesn't show this. The opponent who believes in reflective awareness could stop the regress at any stage by saying that we have reached a cognition that is, unlike simple perception, self-aware.[3] Imagine being in a coffee shop, unaware that you are hearing music, and then having the music brought to your attention. Isn't it reasonable to suppose that in the very act of reflecting on your previously oblivious perception, you are aware that you are reflecting on it? "Ah yes," you might think, "isn't that 'Sympathy for the Devil' I hear, and hasn't it been playing for several minutes already?" We might say that your own mental life has been brought to your attention. And this is what you would remember if you look back on this event in the future. In short, the opponent could plausibly say that awareness is built into the second order reflection, but not into the first order perception.

The same problem seems to apply to Dharmakīrti's presentation of the argument.[4] He adds a new idea to what we find in Dignāga, namely that the original perception itself is somehow in doubt. The perceiver cannot be reassured that the perception is really grasping a given object without being aware that this is so. As Dharmakīrti puts it, awareness would "establish" the perception. If we now add a second order reflection, like Mick Jagger's thinking, "here I am seeing a door," then this second order reflection seems to stand in need of similar ratification. As Birgit Kellner has pointed out, Dharmakīrti may here be depending on the assumption that one thing cannot make another thing known unless it is itself known. Which is all well and good, but it invites the same response we just made to Dignāga. Perhaps the second order reflection includes awareness and is in that sense "self-ratifying," even though first order perception is not.

In defense of Dignāga and Dharmakīrti, we should note that this response involves making a significant concession to them, namely that at least *some* cognitions are reflexively self-aware. If the regress argument is aimed at someone who insists that cognition never has a subjective aspect and so always requires higher order reflection if it is to be noticed, then the regress argument works just fine. One might add that to make this response, we should really explain why some cognitions have self-awareness while others do not. Why is Mick not actively aware of seeing the door, but then aware when he reflects that he sees the door? Dignāga's view has no such problem, since it makes awareness just a part of what it is to be perceiving or cognizing something. As Dharmakīrti puts it, "Someone who does not perceive the awareness of something is not aware of anything at all."

One reason Dignāga's discussion of awareness was so influential is that it could be accepted within several different strands of Buddhism. Dharmakīrti takes the theory in an idealist direction by denying that there are any external objects at all. As we've said, Dignāga seems to have been saying merely that the immediate objects of our perceptions are representations internal to our minds, and that we are always aware of the perceptions we have of these internal representations. Awareness, we might say, is what gives us access to the internal objects of perception.[5] This is compatible with saying that the mental representations do represent things out there in the world. Dharmakīrti, though, seems to have felt that if we are only aware of internal representations, then there remains no role for the external objects to play. This yields the full flowering of Yogācāra Buddhist idealism, which was to be so influential in Tibet.[6] Yet the basic principle established by Dignāga could also be accepted by the Sautrāntika tradition, which does accept the reality of external things.[7] This principle is that we only grasp things as we are representing them, from a first-person perspective. Whether or not we grasp real objects, our grasp is never "objective" in the sense that we are always grasping things in a certain way, as a photographic portrait only presents one particular view of a face.

However one frames Dignāga's theory, it may seem strange that it should have developed within Buddhism, of all traditions. Buddhists reject the real existence of the self, so why would they want to put so much emphasis on self-awareness? Isn't the "person" involved in having a "first-person" perspective precisely the self?[8] This is what Nyāya philosophers like Uddyotakara thought: that the phenomenon of introspective self-awareness establishes the reality of the self. Proponents of the self would also have been quick to point to memory, precisely the phenomenon at the center of Dignāga's proof, as confirmation of their own position that the self must remain identical over time. Indeed, some non-Buddhist philosophers who came after Dignāga borrowed his idea of a reflexive understanding of the conscious mind and transformed it into a theory of self, claiming that the self just consists in reflexive self-consciousness.

But of course, in denying the self the Buddhists never meant to deny that we have a mental life. There are no selves, but there are flowing streams of reflexively self-aware moments of consciousness. Such a flowing stream may include memories of past moments and anticipations of future moments. The mistake is to allow ourselves thoughts of the form "I am happy" or "I am in pain," implying that we can draw a firm boundary around just one stream of subjectivity, saying that this and this alone is "me." It's like trying to keep track of individual waves in the sea, thinking that there is a good answer to the question "is this another wave or the same wave as before?"—a nice example of the sort of question that would have been greeted with silence by the Buddha.

PART IV

BEYOND ANCIENT INDIA

45

IN GOOD TASTE

THE AESTHETICS OF *RASA*

Horror movies are a rather puzzling form of entertainment. Lots of people don't enjoy them at all, and those who do enjoy them might be hard pressed to explain why. After all, in everyday life you wouldn't thrill to the sight of innocent teenagers being chased by an axe-wielding psychopath. Why, then, do horror movie fans like watching it happen on a screen? You might respond that they know it isn't real. But this only makes it more puzzling. Why should unreal danger provoke any emotional response at all? The same questions could be raised about other genres, such as the romantic comedy. We know that Jennifer Aniston and that handsome actor whose name escapes us at the moment aren't really falling in love, yet we are swept away by their flirtation and growing intimacy. How do fictional representations manage to solicit such emotions in us, like fear and romantic yearning, yet without generating exactly the same emotional responses we would have if we were really being pursued by an axe-wielding psychopath, or by Jennifer Aniston?

These questions were central to ancient Indian writings devoted to aesthetics. The key text of this tradition is entitled *Nāṭya-śāstra (Treatise on Drama)*, and ascribed to an author named Bharata.[1] Probably compiled in the early centuries AD, the *Nāṭya-śāstra* is a very lengthy work. It offers detailed instructions on theatrical performance, covering everything from the construction of the theater space to the gestures of the actors and the metrical features of the texts they recite. Because dramatic performances involved poetry and also music, Bharata has much to say about these arts. So later theorists on the aesthetics of literature and music draw from him; for music there was another early work called the *Dattilam*, roughly contemporaneous with the *Nāṭya-śāstra*.[2]

Unlike the modern-day horror movie, ancient Indian dramas were not out to surprise you with their plot twists. The audience would typically have been familiar with the plots of the stories they were going to see. While there was some variation from performance to performance, the real theatrical art lay in the effective, and affecting, presentation of those stories. The key idea in Bharata's explanation of the desired result is *rasa*, an aesthetic response elicited by the drama.[3] Though *rasa* is intimately associated with emotion, it is not just the same thing as an emotion. Rather, it *derives* from emotion (97). Originally, an emotion or feeling (*bhāva*) was felt by the poet who authored the piece. It is then represented (*bhāvayan*) by actors through good dramatic technique; thus erotic love, for instance, is conveyed by sidelong glances and gestures that the skilled actor must learn to master (99).

The poet may play with a wide range of emotions, provoking some of them only in passing to create briefer aesthetic effects. But the most important are the eight "emotional dispositions (*sthāyibhāvas*)" around which a whole drama can be built, reactions we are apt to feel when stimulated in the right way. Bharata says that mere "transitory" emotional effects (*vyabhicāra*) serve to heighten these eight emotions, like attendants surrounding a monarch (101). Corresponding to the dispositions are eight kinds of *rasa*:

Emotional dispositions	***Rasas***
Erotic love (*rasi*)	Erotic (*śṛṅgāra*)
Mirth (*hāsya*)	The comic (*hāsya*)
Sorrow (*śoka*)	The pathetic (*karuṇa*)
Anger (*krodha*)	The furious (*raudra*)
Energy (*utsāha*)	The heroic (*vīra*)
Fear (*bhaya*)	The terrible (*bhayānaka*)
Disgust (*jugupsā*)	The odious (*bībhatsa*)
Astonishment (*vismaya*)	The marvelous (*adbhuta*).[4]

Bharata compares these *rasas* to the overall "taste" of a mixed beverage (96–7), alluding to the basic meaning of *rasa* which is the "savor" or "nutritive juice" in food. We encounter it with that meaning in ancient Indian medical works, in fact.

To see how this may work, consider a horror movie like Alfred Hitchcock's *Psycho*. Bharata's analysis would be that all the aspects of the film, from the disturbing music to the smallest details of Anthony Perkins' uncanny performance as the motel owner, are designed to evoke a continuous feeling of dread or fear in the viewer. Moments evoking disgust or surprise (like the famous reveal of the motel owner's mother) would only serve to build up that core feeling so as to achieve the *rasa* of "the terrible," which is the goal of the entire piece. Hitchcock would have this in mind in his construction of even more innocuous scenes, not only in the more famous moments of violence in the film—even if these are indeed, in every sense of the word, well executed. Of course ancient Indian dramas did not center on murderous motel owners. Even when aiming to provoke the *rasa* of the terrible, they sought to impart moral instruction, and thus played a social function not usually associated with Hollywood horror films.[5]

It is a matter of consummate artistry to produce *rasa*. In light of the word's literal meaning, we might compare it to the skilled chef who uses just the right balance of ingredients to get the right overall savor for the dish. As the later aesthetician Kuntaka puts it, "only when its natural charm is imparted by the beauty coruscating with the innate artistry of the poet and enlivened by the full complement of aesthetic elements can even a fully proper *rasa* convey its deepest beauty to the reader, who is transported by the play of the fantastic and whose heart then overflows with *rasa* the way a moonstone is liquefied by moonbeams" (167). But even when the dramatic conception and acting are top notch, the *rasa* will result only for an audience member who is equally proficient. Extending the analogy between *rasa* and the savor of food and drink, Bharata says that the skilled audience member is like the connoisseur, with a fine appreciation of drama that is, so to speak, in the best possible taste (97). His commentators say that the goal of the audience is to achieve "sympathy of the heart" with the actors on stage, so as fully to experience the emotion that can give rise to *rasa*.

The commentators do not, however, agree as to whether this is the only legitimate goal of drama, or of poetry more generally.[6] Some authors suggest that *rasa* could be a mere "ornament" of a literary performance, as in a poem whose main purpose is flattery (149). The ninth-century Kashmiri literary theorist Ānandavardhana uses this idea to explain why a piece might evoke two rival emotions, for instance sadness and erotic longing, which would seem to impede the production of a single overall *rasa*. Only when a single *rasa* predominates is it the ultimate aim of the poem as a whole. Others argue that *rasa* can never be a mere ornament (163), and that all poetry worthy of the name must have *rasa* as its main purpose and ultimate result.

Attention is also given to the various factors that may impede the successful production of *rasa*. There is a long discussion of this in another aesthetician, a critic of Ānandavardhana named Mahimabhaṭṭa.[7] He complains, for instance, about poets who use redundant expressions, giving the example "[he who] cuts the necks of his evil enemies with the extremely fierce blow of the front end of the drawn, sharpened sword held in [his] hand." As Mahimabhaṭṭa remarks, why not just say "[he who] cuts the necks of enemies with a sword"? Another potential flaw is the use of puns that don't quite work. The pun, or perhaps better "double-meaning," was almost as important an element in Sanskrit literature as in this book series. This device, called *śleṣa*, could exploit ambiguous meanings of words or even of whole sentences, and might be used to reveal the complexity of a literary character.[8] So it wasn't a matter of getting cheap laughs, like our play on the word "executed" a few paragraphs ago.

The idea of *rasa* appears not only in commentaries on the *Nāṭya-śāstra* and works on Indian poetics, but also in treatises on music.[9] The ancient music theorists don't discuss specific compositions, such as you could write down in sheet music, but focus instead on melody types called *jātis*, which were associated with certain moods and emotions.[10] One early theorist, named Mataṅga, gives us a nice example of the way that ideas from literary theorists penetrated into discussions of music. He borrowed the poetic concept of "suggestion (*dhvani*)," the idea that an aesthetic performance could evoke or express something without alluding to it explicitly. And if you think about this, it makes a lot of sense. If you are trying to make the audience appreciate sadness, it is downright counterproductive to have a character say something like "I'm sad now." Or just think of how you may be taken out of the story of a movie if the director selects a song for the soundtrack whose lyrics too obviously refer to the desired emotional effect.

The Indian literary aestheticians were aware of this. It was especially the aforementioned Ānandavardhana who devloped the idea of "suggestion" to explain how *rasa* can be evoked by poetry.[11] In so doing, he appropriated a term found in the grammatical tradition: Bhartṛhari had said that uttered sounds are *dhvani* and make manifest linguistic meaning (*sphoṭa*). Taking inspiration from this idea, Ānandavardhana argues that *dhvani* is a special function performed by poetic language. The poet's art avoids explicit reference to the emotion he wants to produce, and instead implicitly "suggests" that emotion to the listener, thus eliciting the desired *rasa*. He gives the following example: "wander confidently, monk; the dog [that frightened you] has been killed by a lion." His point may be this: the literal meaning is that the frightening dog is gone. And this literal meaning still stands, even when we correctly see the point of the verse, which is that the monk should be more frightened than ever—now it is a lion and not a dog that is on the loose. That is the "suggestion" or unstated meaning.[12] Another example would be saying that a village is on the River Ganges, which conveys its full significance only to someone who knows that this makes the village a holy place.

For Ānandavardhana suggestion is distinct from the function played by words when they have their straightforward meaning, and neither is it an example of metaphorical language. After all, he argues, poetic language can retain its normal meaning while evoking *rasa*, whereas the normal meaning has to be given up when we turn to metaphorical or other kinds of nonliteral interpretation. His example is that when we do say that a village is on the River Ganges, we don't imagine a floating village. Instead we transfer the meaning of the word "on," and understand that the village is arrayed on the bank of the river rather than the river itself. By contrast, poetic suggestion leaves meaning straightforwardly intact. It is something additional that is conveyed by the language only implicitly, which as Ānandavardhana says "shines above the parts [of the poem] like a woman's charm."[13] It is crucial that the poet can express himself in this indirect way, since as we just said it would ruin the effect if the poet tried to convey *rasa* directly.

Ānandavardhana adds that the meaning conveyed by the poem, at least for the skilled audience member (*sahṛdaya*), is the same as the one originally experienced by the poet. He recalls a story about a poet by the name of Vālmīki, the supposed author of the great epic *Rāmāyaṇa* (148). While bathing, he witnessed a hunter killing one of a pair of birds and heard the mate's plaintive cry. Vālmīki himself cried out in a spontaneous verse (*śloka*), which came from divine inspiration. This fits with older ideas about the poet as a kind of religious intermediary, like the so-called "seers" who passed down the Vedas. It was thought that poets benefitted from a special, unbidden inspiration or illumination (*pratibhā*), and that they are distinguished from others who enjoy visions simply because the poets actually set down the visions in words.[14] In an echo of such religious associations, Ānandavardhana explains that the poet may choose any primary meaning he likes in his quest to evoke *rasa* by means of suggestion. "In the boundless world of literature," he says, "the author is sole creator god: the whole universe takes on whatever form he wills" (157). The resulting poem becomes a means of conveying to the listener the *rasa* originally felt by the poet in his moment of inspiration—to taste what he tasted, as it were.

According to Ānandavardhana *rasa* is really an effect of language, like the meaning of the words (thus it is called an *artha*, or "meaning"). But for one of his most important commentators, the tenth-century author Abhinavagupta, the *rasa* experienced and conveyed by the poet is an emotion that is universal in character.[15] He would say that in the story of Vālmīki, the dead bird and its mourning mate are simply the occasion that inspires the poet to experience the generalized feeling of sorrow.[16] Likewise, the audience member who experiences *rasa* is not having the relevant emotion in its everyday sense. As we said before, you are not yourself in love with the characters in a romantic comedy, nor are you afraid for your own safety while watching *Psycho*. You experience feelings of romance and of fear, yet these feelings are not directed at any particular object.

This may remind us of ideas about detachment and liberation we've seen elsewhere in Indian philosophy. And it seems to have reminded Abhinavagupta of the same thing. By this period, the eight canonical types of *rasa* found in Bharata have been joined by a ninth one, called "tranquillity (*śānta*)." For Ānandavardhana this is the *rasa* intended by no less a work than the *Mahābhārata*, which like any good poem has as its sole aim and motif the production of an emotional response or *rasa*. Abhinavagupta links the *rasa* of tranquillity to philosophical notions of liberation:

"this enjoyment [of *rasa*] is like the bliss that comes from realizing [one's identity] with the highest *brahman*, for it consists of repose in the bliss which is the true nature of one's own self."[17]

What about the emotional involvement and experience of the performers who actually portray characters in a theatrical drama? This was a much discussed issue in Indian aesthetics, and for good reason. Consider again Anthony Perkins in *Psycho*. We know that he is not really a murderer, only an actor playing one, yet we emotionally respond to his performance with fear and revulsion. How does Perkins provoke this response without actually having murder in his heart? Bharata already mentioned that the actor's role is somehow to express a particular psychological state without actually being in the very same state as the character being portrayed (102). Later commentators tried to understand the phenomenon in greater depth. One idea was that the actor simply imitates the character at the surface level, by means of gesture and so on, which invites the audience to make an "inference" about the intended emotion. The actor's sidelong glance signifies that he is in love, and we as skilled viewers can interpret it as such, even though we are aware that he is just acting. As one text rather nicely puts it, we as the audience think that the actor is the character, but not that the actor is *really* the character (138).

But this attempt to explain dramatic portrayal as a kind of imitation met with opposition.[18] One complaint was that the inference being made would in fact be fallacious. Consider yet again the example of inferring from smoke that there is fire on the mountain. The inference is a bad one if it is not really smoke that we see but something that merely looks like smoke, such as low-hanging mist (274). Likewise, if the sidelong glance is only an empty imitation of how a lover would look then it would be mistaken to infer that a feeling of love is present. Besides, the actor is not merely an empty vessel, who is quite literally going through the motions. He has his own psychological states which must somehow be connected to the aesthetic effect. Some authors thus took the contrary approach, saying that the actor identifies himself *completely* with the character being portrayed (130–1). Thus the emotion felt by the character would be recreated on stage. But this idea, too, met with skepticism. How would the actor be able to continue performing while in the throes of the powerful emotions he is representing?

In the eleventh century, the aforementioned Mahimabhaṭṭa made a rather convincing proposal that avoids such problems (170–1). Referring us back to Bharata's statement in the *Nāṭya-śāstra* that *rasa* is "manifested" because of the "aesthetic features" of a theatrical performance, he pointed out that such aesthetic features simply do not exist in everyday life. You see an actor on stage as a *representation* of the character, and not as the character who is truly undergoing the events in the drama.

As Mahimabhaṭṭa puts it, "since aesthetic elements are factitious, whereas cause and effect are real, the former pertaining to literature and the others to the world, the former differ from the latter in both their natures and their objects." When we see a terrorized victim in a horror movie, we do not make an erroneous inference from this "fake" representation to a real feeling of fear, like someone inferring real fire from fake smoke. Rather, we experience it as a properly aesthetic representation, and the inference we make is to a properly aesthetic emotion, which is precisely the "savoring of *rasa*."[19]

We ourselves can infer something from this whole debate: that the ideas of the philosophical schools were not confined only to those schools. The wider intelligentsia of Indian society were aware of them, and found ways to apply them in new and surprising contexts. Much as the terminology and conceptual apparatus of the Sanskrit grammarians was appropriated by the philosophers, these literary thinkers and aestheticians appropriated philosophical terms and concepts. Discussion of *rasa* took its initial cue from Bharata, and was sustained for an extraordinarily long time; we have followed the story for the better part of a millennium, and could have gone further still. As that discussion developed, it became increasingly sophisticated in philosophical terms. The later authors continued to take the *Nāṭya-śāstra* as their touchstone text, but connected it to ideals of detachment and liberation, and notions originally explored within philosophy of language. Whatever we make of their judgments concerning aesthetics, these literary scholars were right about one thing: the richness and fruitfulness of the theories put forth by the Vedic schools.[20]

46

LEARN BY DOING

TANTRA

In this book we've had the chance to dispel quite a few misconceptions about ancient Indian culture: that it offered only mysticism or religion but no philosophy; that Yoga is just a kind of gymnastic exercise; that the physical world is real (if you ask Advaita Vedāntins) or alternatively, that anything but the physical world is real (if you ask the Cārvākas). But the word from ancient India most apt to provoke inaccurate associations is "Tantra." In Western countries the first, and probably last, idea people have about Tantra is that it has something to do with sex. In India itself, Tantra is nowadays often equated with black magic. Nor has more detailed historical knowledge about Tantric rituals and beliefs prevented it from being the object of disdain and mockery. A pioneering Indian scholar of classical Tantra in the twentieth century explained the rationale for studying it as follows: "someone should take up the study comprising the diagnosis, aetiology, pathology and prognosis of the disease so that more capable men may take up its treatment and eradication in the future."[1]

It would, however, be more helpful to think of Tantra as a tradition akin to Yoga, in which philosophical ideas were put into practice. A wide range of rituals could enable the Tantric practitioner to achieve liberation from suffering and oneness with the absolute, not to mention performing such feats as seeing objects that are buried underground, flying, and turning invisible. Again, the connection to magic may remind us of Yoga. And like Yoga, Tantra has appeared in many guises in different periods.[2] Its literature spans the divides between the Hindu, Buddhist, and Jaina traditions, and there were numerous varieties and schools even just of Hindu Tantra in the classical period. We're going to focus especially on Tantra in the context of Buddhism and on the religious tradition called Śaivism, that is, the worship of the god Śiva. Within that tradition we'll especially be discussing the "non-dual" strand of Śaivite Tantra represented by Abhinavagupta, who lived around the year 1000. (He just figured prominently in our look at the Indian aesthetic theory of *rasa* in Chapter 45.)

The more central aspects of Tantra are shared by both of these schools and other groups besides. At the risk of disappointing you, we must report that a fascination with ritualistic, spiritualized sex is not really one of them. We do have writings on this topic, including by Abhinava. But sexual practices were not the primary focus of classical Tantra. As we'll see below, even when such practices are discussed there is more (or from a prurient point of view, less) going on than meets the eye. To quote a leading French scholar of Tantra, André Padoux, Abhinavagupta is "not to be confused with the Marquis de Sade."[3] Instead, Tantra is characterized especially by its openness to participants of all classes, often both men and women, and by a range of concrete ritual practices. These include meditation, breath control, repetitive chants called *mantras*, the use of *maṇḍalas*, and the initiation (*dīkṣā*) of the practitioner by a guru who will serve as a spiritual guide.[4] If none of that sounds particularly philosophical, this is because it is only a list of the external practices that manifest and assist in the practitioner's attempt to achieve wisdom and liberation.

Chronologically speaking, Tantric practices go back deep into the ancient past. The Upaniṣads already discuss the ritual formulas called *mantras*, including the central example of *oṃ*.[5] Thus the *Chāndogya Upaniṣad* instructs us, "one should venerate the high chant as this syllable, for one begins the high chant with *oṃ* . . . a man who utters this syllable with that knowledge enters this very syllable, the sound that is immortal and free from fear. As the gods become immortal by entering it, so will he" (§1.4). The same Upaniṣad also describes initiation with a guru (§4.4), and you will remember from our look at these early texts how much stress they placed on the notion of breath. However, the first texts that one can classify as Tantric in the full sense emerge around the fifth to seventh centuries AD, and especially within a strand of Hindu belief that worshipped Śiva. It would seem that the various Tantric practices, like the recitation of *mantras*, were then borrowed from Śaivism by Buddhists.

The Buddhist Tantric texts are rather sensitive on this point and propose an alternative history, ascribing to the Buddha the premonition that the rituals he originally prescribed would later be adopted by other schools.[6] Meanwhile, a legend circulated among Brahmanical authors that Śaivism was the result of a curse designed to punish those who stopped learning the Vedas properly.[7] Clearly, Tantra was being diagnosed as a kind of illness long before the twentieth century. Even as its rituals were adopted across the spectrum of Indian belief systems, writers from across that spectrum dismissed the same rituals as preposterous. No less a thinker than Vasubandhu, whom we saw initiating Yogācāra Buddhism, held that *mantras* are meaningless gibberish. And when you look at the *mantras* you may feel that he had a point. Some of them do indeed consist of apparent nonsense syllables, each of which is called a "seed (*bīja*)." In other cases one repeats a meaningful yet mysterious phrase over and over, like *haṃsaḥ so 'haṃ* meaning "I am that divine *haṃsa* bird."[8] Typical of this *mantra* is that it is a (near) palindrome, a common structure in the many formulas that circulated in Tantra—tradition had it that there are 70 million of them. One standard practice was to begin and end a *mantra* with *oṃ* or some other utterance, effectively "enveloping" the rest of the formula. Breath itself is said to be a kind of *mantra*, as one breathes in and out thousands of times over a single day.

The symmetrical structure of these *mantras*, the way they mimic the outward and inward movement of breath, is a clue to their underlying philosophical rationale, the theory that underlies this particular ritual form and is considered the key to its success. We are told that recitation of *mantras* without knowledge is like casting seed (*bīja*) upon barren stone.[9] That is why initiation with a guru is needed: he shares the *mantra* with the practitioner and reveals its meaning.[10] We are not gurus and this book is no substitute for an initiation rite, but we can still tell you something about the meaning of *mantras* in general terms. As suggested by the palindromic structure, *mantras* evoke the cyclical production of things, in the first instance the outgoing and subsequent return of the entire universe (here we might think back to our discussion of world cycles in Chapter 31). Robert Yelle has thus written, "the belief in the efficacy of mantras is reinforced by their imitation of the natural order."[11] They should be seen not as gibberish, like baby talk or birdsong, but rather as poetic language that symbolizes the world and even the very origin of the world.

A culmination of this way of thinking about *mantra* comes with Kashmir Śaivism and especially the work of Abhinavagupta. As so often an important further source would be a commentary on his work, in this case by the thirteenth-century exegete Jayaratha. Though their extensive writings do not seem to have had much impact on actual religious practice in Kashmir,[12] they do offer something of a high-water mark for philosophical reflection about Tantra. Among other things, Abhinavagupta sets out a sophisticated theory about the production of language in which the generation of words represents or is even identical with the generation of the entire universe. To understand his views on this we will need first to say something about his cosmology and the principles from which his universe is generated.

Or we should rather say "principle," in the singular. Śaivism had long before Abhinavagupta had monotheistic tendencies, indeed among the first Indian belief systems whose elite practitioners envision a single divine principle.[13] The principle or god was of course Śiva, who is identified as a pure, ineffable consciousness which experiences permanent bliss. Abhinavagupta says that attempting to grasp it is like trying to step on the shadow of your own hat while wearing it.[14] Thus far the theory sounds a bit like Advaita Vedānta, and this strand of Śaivism is likewise called "non-dual" in distinction from the Siddhānta variety. The Siddhānta Śaivites acknowledged the reality of the physical world but regretted it deeply, seeing their religious rites as a means for escaping the suffering of this world. For Abhinavagupta and other non-dual Śaivites, the point is instead to free ourselves of the ignorance that makes us think we are distinct from the divinity that is Śiva, who can also be called spirit (*cit*), consciousness (*caitanya*), self (*ātman*), and so on.[15]

While it would not be inaccurate to label this as a kind of monism, it is a kind of monism that is compatible with a complex cosmology. According to Abhinavagupta, the universe as we experience it arises because of a "vibration" of self-awareness (*vimarśa*), which expresses itself in a threefold way as consciousness, will or desire, and cognition. This can occur only because Śiva, a male god, is one with the female god Śakti who represents energy. As the punning motto of the non-dual Śaivites has it, "without Śakti, Śiva would be a corpse (*śava*)." Thanks to the self-directed activity brought by Śakti, consciousness does not remain inert but goes forth to show itself as our multifarious empirical world. Yet all the things we see in this world are in truth one with the divine. The goal of the more intellectually minded Tantric practitioner is to realize his or her own identity with God by engaging in rituals that represent, or again in some sense are just identical with, the process of the unfolding of all things from Śiva-Śakti.

Which brings us back to our *mantras* and the question of language. Śiva is also called the "supreme word," a source of all language but as yet without articulation or expression. This supreme word begins to manifest itself as the aforementioned initial "vibration" of creative energy and self-awareness. As Jayaratha puts it in his commentary on Abhinavagupta, when the supreme word "wishes to appear externally, yet without producing the multiplicity associated with the process of what expresses and what is expressed, since the light of pure consciousness still prevails there, she is called the Seeing or the Visionary and she is a form of the subject who sees."[16] We might think of this as a moment when a thought is entertained mentally all at once without yet spelling it out in words, and in fact Abhinavagupta compares it to the "flash of understanding" posited by the grammarian Bhartṛhari, in which a sentence's meaning is grasped in a single moment (see Chapter 21). At a further stage articulated language is rehearsed mentally before being spoken aloud and thus fully expressed. Following Bhartṛhari, Abhinavagupta claims that there must be such a stage in the production of language, since otherwise children would never be able to learn to speak, nor would mutes be able to comprehend the words of others.[17]

Language is given forth from the human speaker in stages, emerging slowly from the body through its centers of energy, the famous *cakras*. Within each person the origin is at the base of the spine, where power is "coiled" like a snake. "Coiled" translates the name of the goddess Kuṇḍalinī, who is also responsible for the evolution of the phonemes from the simpler, unspoken primordial word at the level of self-awareness. One text says that Kuṇḍalinī "is made of will, cognition, and action, effulgent, endowed with the properties of created things . . . she creates the garland of letters divided into forty-two, ranging from *a* to *sa*, and divides into fifty the garland of the fifty phonemes, and with these phonemes she brings forth in succession [the gods] and the other [things]."[18] This alludes to a frequent yogic practice of breath control, the recitation of a chain of letters whose sequence expresses the unfolding of the cosmos.

So what we have here is a rich fusion of cosmology with philosophy of mind and language. It is important that, as we keep hinting, the production of the world is not merely symbolized by the production of language but actually *is* linguistic, the universe being "pervaded (*vyāpta*) by sound."[19] So cosmic evolution can be mapped on to the Sanskrit alphabet which constitutes words. Those three initial moments in Śiva's emergence into self-awareness—consciousness, will, and cognition—are connected to the three short vowels *a*, *i*, and *u*. Vowels are associated with Śiva as the male principle while consonants are the female analogue, an idea that is sometimes set forth even more concretely: vowels are like the male seed, consonants like the womb. Thus we can think of a single syllable like *oṃ*, or really any combination of vowel and consonant, as representing the two aspects of the first principle, the mating and hence unity of Śiva and Śakti. Perhaps this would have been Abhinava's explanation of another passage in the ancient *Chāndogya Upaniṣad*: "as the leaves of a book are bored through by a pin, so all words are bored through by *oṃ*" (§2.23).[20]

This gets us finally to the theme of sexual union and reproduction. As we've said this theme plays a far more minor role in Tantric literature than you might have expected. Sexual rituals are in fact only one aspect of a more general strand within Tantra called "Kaula," in which a variety of shocking practices were endorsed. These ranged from sexual activities like adultery, incest, and group sex, to the consumption of oft-forbidden things like wine and meat and even the drinking and eating of urine and excrement. In a passage that conveys Kaula Tantricism's apparent goal of being as scandalous as possible, we read the following advice about liberation: "inserting his organ into his mother's womb, pressing his sister's breasts, placing his foot upon his guru's head, [the practitioner] will be reborn no more."[21] It did not take long for some Tantric authors to insist that such advice is to be glossed as symbolic and allegorical. In this case incest with the mother may mean the mind's awareness of the base of the body, the pressing of the sister's breasts a focus on the heart and throat, and the foot upon the guru's head meditation on the brain.

Such allegorical explanations notwithstanding, it is unsurprisingly a much-discussed question to what extent the shocking "left-handed" practices were actually carried out. No doubt it varied widely. Some presumably took the advice literally and others symbolically, while still others thought that both levels of meaning were relevant.[22] Bearing out the possibility of merely symbolic interpretation, some works spell out the true meaning of "coded" terminology, sometimes called "twilight language (*saṃdhyā-bhāṣā*)."[23] Either way there is general agreement across Tantra that we can achieve spiritual aims through the body, correcting what might have been seen as an unwarranted asceticism within both Hinduism and the *śramana* traditions. One sign of this is that Tantra did not demand renunciation. Unlike a Buddhist or Jaina monk, a Tantric practitioner could remain a "householder." Another sign is that many Tantric texts display the frank ambition to achieve worldly advantages, hence the talk of performing magical feats like invisibility, of using Tantra to gain victory in battle, or even to do alchemy.[24]

Then, too, even when sex and other rituals were practiced concretely, just as one would genuinely recite *mantras* thousands of times and not just talk idly about doing it, the aims were not crassly material ones. Thus the sexual act would be a way of realizing one's identity with the union between male and female in the principle of Śiva-Śakti, and would involve practiced control and often the avoidance of climax. As one scholar has written, the sublimation and focus on self-mastery mean that "What is occurring psychologically and physiologically in those practices bears very little resemblance to sex as we generally understand it, since Buddhist Tantric assumptions and aims are virtually indistinguishable from those of traditions more readily recognized as 'ascetic'."[25] It may seem paradoxical that such lofty spiritual aims should be pursued through a focus on bodily powers and experiences. But as Abhinavagupta says, "the body should be seen as full of all the paths… composed of all the divinities, and thus must be made an object of contemplation, of adoration, and of the rites of fulfillment."[26]

This is perhaps the key philosophical idea of Tantra. Especially in its non-dual Śaivite version, Tantra privileges pure consciousness as a first principle of all things, taking the empirical and bodily realm to be the outward manifestation of that principle. We are told to focus on and engage in worldly activities that are structurally identical to the workings of self-directed consciousness and its production of all things, notably the production of language in the form of *mantras*. Thereby we can remove the otherwise impermeable veil that screens us from realizing our identity with the absolute. It is no wonder that in due course, when Islam came to India, Tantra was seen as congenial to Sufism. We might draw a further parallel to mysticism in medieval Christianity or Kabbalah within Judaism. The latter offers particularly strong resonances in the form of an alphabetical cosmology, with the ten letters or *sefirot* structuring a derivation of all things from an ineffable divine principle, the deployment of erotic language, and in "prophetic" Kabbalah even the chanting of apparently meaningless syllables.[27]

In none of these cases are we dealing with an "irrationalism" that competes with rational philosophical thought, but rather with attempts to show how philosophical ideas could be put into practice. It has been said that "While the master logicians like Dignāga or Dharmakīrti were devising hair-splitting arguments to interpret the world as a void entity, Tantric ideas captured the heart of Buddhism through the backdoor."[28] In fact, though, the Tantric authors, both Buddhist and Hindu, had their own philosophical theories and hair-splitting distinctions. It's just that this was not enough, in their view. We must marry abstract understanding to practical action, recognizing that everyday things, even supposedly vulgar and despised things, reflect and instantiate the structures of primordial reality. Sometimes, you need to learn by doing.[29]

47

LOOKING EAST

INDIAN INFLUENCE ON GREEK THOUGHT

If you make it a habit to give public lectures on ancient philosophy, you are almost guaranteed to be asked at some point whether Greek thought was influenced by ancient Indian culture. In fact this might be the single most common question posed by general audiences who are confronted with ideas from ancient Greece or ancient India. Which is perfectly understandable. What could be more intriguing than the possibility that Plato, Aristotle, or Plotinus might have been influenced by ideas found in the Upaniṣads, in early Buddhism, or in Vedānta? Taking the possibility seriously threatens to undermine the very contrast between "Eastern" and "Western" philosophy, which is fine by us since it's a contrast that deserves to be questioned for other reasons anyway.

More problematic is the usually unspoken suggestion that, if Indian thought really did influence Greek thought, that would secure India a rightful place in the history of philosophy. If this book has been even halfway successful, you should by now be convinced that Indian thought amply deserves such a place in its own right. A similar problem arises with philosophy in the Islamic world. Thinkers like Avicenna and Averroes have often attracted attention primarily because they influenced Latin Christendom, rather than being treated as worthy objects of study in their own right. Meanwhile the vast number of Muslim philosophers who lived after the twelfth century have been omitted from most histories of philosophy because they came too late for the Arabic–Latin translation movement and were thus unknown in Europe.[1] So as we delve into the question of influence let's bear in mind that the real importance of Indian philosophy is its intrinsic fascination, not the impact it may or may not have had on another culture. We might add that even if we were going to justify an interest in Indian philosophy on the basis of its influence on other cultures, we'd do better to stress its massive importance for the history of philosophy in China and other parts of Asia, which on any reckoning dwarfs the impact it may have had on ancient or even modern European thought.

Now that we've gotten that off our chests, let's turn to the obvious first question. Was there any contact and cultural exchange between the ancient Greek and ancient Indian cultures at all? To which the answer can only be a resounding "yes." Trade routes between Europe and India were open well before the emergence of Presocratic philosophy, and already in classical antiquity there are scattered literary testimonies to that trade: the Hippocratic corpus refers to pepper, Sophocles to Indian gold, Xenophon to Indian hunting dogs.[2] During this period the Persian Empire would have offered a meeting place for Greek and Indian culture. Apparently the army Xerxes led against the Greeks included Indian soldiers, and Greek and Indian scholars would also have met at the Persian court. Nonetheless, during classical antiquity, the time of the Presocratics, Plato, and Aristotle, knowledge of India would have been rather limited and indirect. The most valuable information was contained in ethnographic writings about India that are now unfortunately lost, notably by the fabulously named Skylax who in the sixth century BC participated in a military expedition to India led by the Persian king Darius. Herodotus also mentions that expedition and draws information about India from another ethnographer named Hecataeus.

But in our story the key moment comes right around the time of Aristotle, with the conquests of Alexander the Great. When he reached Bactria and India in about 330 BC he brought Greek culture with him, founding Hellenistic cities and creating the conditions for a more profound engagement with Indian society. That engagement is most palpable in the work of Megasthenes, an ambassador to the Mauryan court from Seleukos, the Hellenistic king who succeeded Alexander in the eastern lands that had been conquered. He dealt with the mighty Indian emperor Candragupta and may have visited the great city of Pāṭaliputra. He was thus able to describe Indian culture as a direct witness, even if he did so using the tropes of Greek ethnography and made some perplexingly basic errors, as when he denied the existence of slavery in ancient India. Sadly Megasthenes' work is also lost except in the form of quotations found in later authors, notably the historian Strabo. Thanks to him we know that Megasthenes was aware of the *śramaṇa* ascetic movements in India. He even contrasted two kinds of renouncers, those who stayed in the city to work as healers and those who withdrew to the forest.

All this makes it eminently plausible to suppose that Indian philosophical ideas could have reached Greek intellectuals, and anyone who reads around a bit in both traditions will come upon plenty of striking parallels. Someone who has done more than just a bit of reading around is Thomas McEvilly, whose massive book *The Shape of Ancient Greek Thought* detects echoes of Indian ideas in pretty much every ancient Greek philosopher, from the Presocratics down to the late ancient Neoplatonists.[3]

To give you just a sample: he points out that there are matching lists of fundamental elements (air, earth, fire, and water) in both cultures. He finds both Heraclitus and the *Viṣṇu Purāṇa* saying that divine forces are at play like a child. He notes that the *Ṛg-veda* (at 10.129) makes ocean the source of all things, as Thales made water his primary principle, while the Upaniṣads identify air as primary in agreement with Anaximenes. As many others have done he points out that the Pythagorean doctrines of vegetarianism and reincarnation sound rather Indian, and that the monist trend in Brahmanical thought that culminates in Advaita Vedānta has an echo in Parmenides. The *Chāndogya Upaniṣad*, too, sounds rather like Parmenides when it denies that anything can come to be from nothing. As for later ancient philosophy, McEvilly remarks that it is "hard to identify any significant difference between either the methods or the stated purposes of Pyrrhonist and Madhyamika dialectic," thus suggesting a strong parallel between ancient skepticism and Buddhism.[4] He also compares the philosophically motivated rituals of Tantra to theurgy in Neoplatonists like Iamblichus.

McEvilly is largely content to make us aware of such echoes without wedding himself to any one explanation for them. He admits that, alongside more or less direct influence from India, there are two other possibilities. One is of course coincidence. We have here two massive bodies of philosophical writing. Imagine that we went through the many thousands of pages of ancient Pāli and Sanksrit philosophy and found no passages at all that reminded us of anything in the equally voluminous remains of Greek philosophy. That would be truly extraordinary, especially since philosophical reflection is presumably bound to give rise to certain fundamental ideas like atomism in physics, skepticism in epistemology, or monism in metaphysics. So a skeptic could see McEvilly's impressive resume of resonances as nothing more than a collection of similar ideas that were reached independently.

A further possibility, which McEvilly seems to find attractive, is that there are deeper roots to both Greek and Indian philosophy. There are shared mythic tendencies also found in Near Eastern and Egyptian religion and philosophy, which suggests cultural connections from before historical records began. That might explain such parallels as the urge to trace all things back to one physical element, like water or air. Of course, this is unsatisfyingly vague and not really sufficient to account for more exact parallels, resonances so strong that one almost can't help suspecting a direct textual appropriation. It has to be said that McEvilly does not offer many parallels of that sort. One of them, which he considers to be something close to genuine "proof" of real cultural exchange, is a testimony of Heraclitus in which he is said to have explained night and day in light of two "exhalations," one bright and one dark.[5] This same idea is found in the *Chāndogya*

Upaniṣad and *Great Forest Upaniṣad*. Even in cases that are not quite so striking and specific, McEvilly finds it hard to believe that we just have two traditions independently reaching the same conclusions. Realizing that some readers may think the list of basic elements found in both Greece and India is somehow obvious, he points out that in China they had a different list, namely water, fire, wood, metal, and earth. (We might add that in 1970s disco culture, they got the list down to three: Earth, Wind, and Fire.)

To make up our mind whether there really was significant historical influence, it may help to think a bit harder about how the influence could have occurred. Despite the context of cultural exchange sketched above there were formidable obstacles in the way of a serious engagement between Greek and Indian intellectuals. Most obviously, the two civilizations were separated by thousands of miles. It is not so obvious that complex philosophical ideas could travel all that way along with pepper and other luxury goods. To this we can add the problem of linguistic barriers. If we consider cases of profound cultural exchange in the history of philosophy, we see that they have typically involved a deliberate effort to translate writing from one language into another, as when rich Muslims commissioned Arabic versions of Greek science in the eighth and ninth centuries AD, or when the Latin Christians translated from Arabic and Greek in the twelfth century. Nothing like that happened here. There was no Sanskrit–Greek translation movement, indeed not a single case of a philosophical work from India being translated into Greek or Latin in antiquity. Furthermore, we should bear in mind that the ancient Indian elite excluded almost all other Indians from their intellectual activities, never mind foreigners, who were frequently regarded with deep distrust. It may be more plausible to imagine that the less exclusivist *śramaṇa* philosophers, like Buddhists, Jainas, and Ājīvikas, were open to sharing their ideas with outsiders. If ideas did manage to fight their way past all these obstacles, it's easy to imagine that they would have been greatly oversimplified and perhaps distorted in the process of transmission.

So if skeptical, or just cautious, historians are going to be persuaded that there was profound and direct engagement between any Greek philosopher and Indian thought, they will probably want to hear of an intrepid traveler, which in practice means a Greek who finds his way to India since it seems that no Indian thinker went to Europe.[6] They will need to be shown not just evocative parallels, but historical evidence that the thinker in question was genuinely inspired by Indian ideas. And given the points just made about exclusivity, they should perhaps expect that the relevant ideas on the Indian side would not be Brahmanical but would more likely stem from a *śramaṇa* group.

Step forward Pyrrho of Elis. He was the putative founder of Hellenistic Skepticism and the namesake of the radical Pyrrhonian form of Skepticism adopted by the second century AD author Sextus Empiricus.[7] Excitingly, we are told in a detailed account of his life from antiquity, written by Diogenes Laertius, that Pyrrho accompanied Alexander's military expedition to India.[8] There he met with "naked sophists," presumably meaning ascetic philosophers. Such figures are said elsewhere to have been encountered by Alexander's entourage near Taxila. Diogenes tells us that it was a direct result of this meeting with the Indian sages that Pyrrho adopted his signature policy of "suspending judgment" because our beliefs are only a matter of custom, whereas in themselves things are no more one thing than another. On the strength of this evidence, scholars like Everard Flintoff and more recently Christopher Beckwith have argued that Pyrrho's introduction of skepticism to Greek philosophy was a more or less direct borrowing from early Indian skepticism.[9]

Whereas Flintoff is happy to leave open the question of which ascetic, skeptically inclined movement Pyrrho may have encountered, Beckwith has written an entire book arguing that the stories about Pyrrho constitute a crucial piece of evidence for the nature of early Buddhism. This hypothesis is particularly attractive because Pyrrho is renowned for having achieved what the Greeks called *ataraxia*, freedom from disturbance. He was impervious to physical and mental pain, just as the liberated Buddhist is free from all suffering. Moreover, Pyrrho reached the state of *ataraxia* precisely by adopting the skeptical attitude of suspending judgment about all things. He and his followers used an array of arguments and techniques to puncture the pretensions of "dogmatists" who had positive philosophical doctrines. Among them was an argument form that looks strikingly like the tetralemma, the fourfold menu of options used so effectively by Nāgārjuna. The argument form is found in early reports about the Buddha himself, and then also in a testimony about Pyrrho and in numerous passages in the works of Sextus. That's pretty striking, even if arguments of the same form are found already in Plato and Aristotle.[10]

There is one small problem here, though: Buddhists are very far from being Pyrrhonian skeptics. As we know, the Buddha certainly dealt with some philosophical questions by refusing to answer them, but this was typically because the questions made presuppositions or used concepts that he considered misleading, for example by assuming the existence of the self. Indeed, that most signature commitment of Buddhism—the doctrine of no-self—would be regarded as a negative dogmatic belief by any self-respecting (or no-self-respecting) Pyrrhonian skeptic, who would suspend judgment about whether or not there is a self. Likewise each of the famous Four Noble Truths is a straightforward assertion, and a Pyrrhonian skeptic would demur from endorsing any of them.[11] Beckwith rather cheats by trying to persuade us that the Buddha adopted a universally skeptical posture like that of Pyrrho. For instance, he suggests that when Pyrrho said that all things are *adiaphora*, meaning "undifferentiated" or "not distinct," he meant the same thing expressed by the Buddha with the word *anatta*, which indicates a lack of self or independent reality.[12] In fact the two notions are very different. Pyrrho was suggesting that we can never judge that anything is more one thing than another, for instance that an action is more good than bad, whereas the Buddha was rejecting a specific metaphysical thesis. So far from suspending judgment about the reality of the *ātman*, he was forthrightly denying it. Whatever skeptical consequences followed from that, they were not supposed to undermine key positive doctrines of Buddhism, notably the Four Noble Truths.

If we jump ahead to consider the contemporary followers of Pyrrho and the Buddha, namely Sextus and Nāgārjuna, both of whom lived in the second century AD, we can reach a similar conclusion. Nāgārjuna's dialectical subtlety and skill in undermining the arguments of rivals is certainly comparable to that of Sextus. But Sextus would unhesitatingly classify Nāgārjuna as a dogmatist, not a true skeptic, because Nāgārjuna was committed to the principle that all things are empty and "dependently arising." As we saw, it is a matter of great dispute what he meant by that, but whatever he meant we can be sure that Sextus would want to suspend judgment about whether all things are empty. There are, he would no doubt say, good arguments on both sides of the debate between the upholders of *svabhāva* and the adherents of emptiness. The upshot of all this is not, of course, that we can rule out influence from Buddhism on Pyrrho. A likelier conclusion is one that will satisfy neither the skeptic nor the enthusiast concerning Indian influence on Greek thought. Pyrrho may have encountered and been inspired by Indian philosophers while on campaign with Alexander's army. But unsurprisingly, given the cultural and linguistic barriers involved, he failed to understand what those philosophers were saying, or at best borrowed from them very selectively.

Let's now move several centuries ahead to another, even more influential Greek thinker who has often been associated with Indian thought: Plotinus, the third century AD founder of Neoplatonism.[13] As with Pyrrho we have good evidence for his interest in Indian thought and of travel to the east. Plotinus' student, editor, and biographer Porphyry tells us that in AD 242, Plotinus joined the military expedition of the emperor Gordian III precisely in hopes of learning something about the philosophy of the Persians and Indians. Unfortunately this expedition was an abortive one, so it can't really be used as evidence that Plotinus had the sort of encounter he was apparently hoping for. As for internal textual evidence from Plotinus' own writings, he never mentions India or its intellectual traditions, but

Porphyry does. His work on vegetarianism has a reasonably well-informed section on Indian cultural practices. Augustine tells us that in another work, which is now lost, Porphyry set out to compare Neoplatonic philosophy with the "practices and teachings of the Indians."[14]

Apparently, then, Plotinus had both the motive and the means for accessing Indian ideas, even if in only a rather indirect way. Are there signs of its influence in his thought? Positive answers to this question have drawn comparisons between his Neoplatonism and Vedānta, especially of the Advaita variety. This is problematic chronologically speaking, given that Śaṅkara lived about a half millennium later than Plotinus did. Still, we might suppose that Plotinus was picking up on some of the same Indian ideas that would later inspire the emergence of Advaita Vedānta, notably the concept of *brahman* in the Upaniṣads. In apparent agreement with that strand of the tradition, Plotinus identifies the paradigmatic source of being as a single universal mind, and encourages us to realize our unity with that source. He makes the physical universe nothing but an image or outward manifestation of intellect, which is the seat of knowledge and, we might venture to say, consciousness or selfhood. In addition, Plotinus carries forward some of the themes from earlier Greek thought that may remind us of India, such as a belief in reincarnation.

The main argument against Indian inspiration is that Plotinus could, and to be honest quite evidently did, develop all of these ideas through an engagement with earlier Platonism.[15] His universal mind is also the realm of Platonic Forms and is not really a new idea so much as a modification of theories that had been put forward in "Middle" Platonism, the tradition of reflection on Plato's dialogues that unfolded in the generations prior to Plotinus. Indeed some of Plotinus' contemporaries accused him of simply stealing his entire system from a Middle Platonist named Numenius—surely an exaggeration but one with a grain of truth. There's a methodological conundrum here. Should we only accept claims of intercultural influence when developments in a given tradition cannot be explained as a development within that tradition?[16] That may seem unduly demanding. In the present instance, there is nothing to prevent us from supposing that Plotinus was inspired both by his own Platonist predecessors *and* by Indian ideas, especially if he saw them as reaching agreement.

The comparison between Plotinus and Vedānta, or the Upaniṣadic idea of *brahman*, is complicated by the fact that Plotinus posits a higher principle above the universal mind, which is explicitly *not* a mind but a pure unity that does not think about anything, even itself. Besides which, if we wanted to locate a "self" or "seat of consciousness" in Plotinus, we might more plausibly associate it with the individual soul than the universal mind.[17] As with Pyrrho, it would seem that initially striking parallels start to look less exact when we consider the details of the philosophical views in question. Then again, that is perhaps just what we should expect. In a situation where access to Indian thought was bound to be very imperfect, why expect perfect parallels? In this spirit, even scholars who are open to the relevance of Indian philosophy for Plotinus have reached somewhat half-hearted conclusions. Thus McEvilly writes that though it was "virtually certain" that Plotinus had some contact with Indian ideas, that contact probably didn't amount to much, and that the similarities may be due to the longer-standing presence of Indian themes in Greek thought.[18] Another recent assessment remarks more generally that "if we gather together all Greco-Roman views on Indian philosophers, we may think that more information (if not sources) was available to them, though probably in a very general and distorted way."[19]

Such moderate conclusions are salutary given that this question of Indian influence on Greek thought often evokes such strong feelings. Many would like to believe that such influence was not just real, but deeply significant. Others, not least scholars of Greek philosophy who would rather not be required to go learn all about Indian philosophy, are equally determined to exclude the possibility entirely. In fact, we should almost certainly admit that ideas did filter into the ancient European world from ancient Indian culture. But in stark contrast to the tremendous and determinative impact of Greek ideas on the Islamic world and of works from the Islamic world on Latin Christendom, the Indian contribution to ancient Greek thought was intermittent and rather incidental. Rarely, if ever, did it take the form of a detailed and well-informed engagement with Indian philosophy on the part of Greek or Roman intellectuals. For that sort of engagement, we will need to wait for later moments of cultural exchange.

48

THE BUDDHA AND I

INDIAN INFLUENCE ON ISLAMIC AND EUROPEAN THOUGHT

This business of noticing parallels between ancient Indian thought and ancient Greek thought is not a distinctively modern development. It was already a feature of an ambitious intellectual project launched by the medieval scientist al-Bīrūnī. His treatise on India, completed in the year 1030, was aimed at an Arabic-speaking readership who would thereby be equipped for encounters with Indian culture.[1] Al-Bīrūnī's approach is a comparative one. As promised at the outset of the work (7), he systematically juxtaposes the ideas of the Indians to those of Greek philosophy and science. In some cases he even points to the same parallels between Indian and Greek philosophy noted by contemporary historians, such as the transmigration of souls (56). Indeed al-Bīrūnī identifies a belief in reincarnation as the distinctive "characteristic of the Indian creed (*ʿalam al-niḥlat al-hindiyya*)" (50), like the Trinity in Christianity or the observance of the Sabbath among Jews.

The reason al-Bīrūnī could presume familiarity with Greek ideas on the part of his readers is that a prodigious Greek–Arabic translation movement had made those ideas available before his time, back in the eighth to tenth centuries AD.[2] At around the same time some Indian texts were also translated, with efforts focusing on scientific works. There were Arabic versions of medical works like the *Suśruta*, and in the middle of the eighth century an astronomical handbook called in Arabic *Sindhind* was produced at the behest of the caliph al-Manṣūr. In general, Indian astronomy and astrology were an important source for these disciplines in the Islamic world.[3] Beyond the sciences there was also the *Kalīla wa-Dimna*, a literary work based on a Persian translation of an Indian book of fables about animals, called the *Pañcatantra*.

Readers of Arabic could especially thank one family for making Indian culture available to them: the Barmakids. Several of this clan were influential in the caliphate of the late eighth century, and they hailed from Tokharistan in Bactria, the only area that had fallen under Arab rule where Buddhism and Sanskrit literature were still actively studied. With this background, the wealthy and powerful Barmakids took an active interest in the science of India. We are told that they "summoned Indian medical scientists and philosophers" and dispatched a fact-finding mission to India itself. A document on Indian culture written for one of the Barmakids is lost, but the tenth-century bibliophile Ibn al-Nadīm claims to have seen a copy written out by no less a personage than al-Kindī, the first Muslim thinker to make explicit use of Greek philosophical sources.[4] The same Ibn al-Nadīm knows of the Buddhists in Transoxiana. He calls them the *shamaniyya*, a term that goes back to the Indian word for the renouncer movements, *śramaṇa*, and appears elsewhere in Arabic literature. Particularly intriguing are reports about a debate between the early eighth-century theologian Jahm Ibn Ṣafwān and a group of Buddhists (here *samaniyya*), who argued that his belief in the God of Islam could not be substantiated on the basis of empirical evidence.[5] So at a very early stage—a full century before al-Kindī, who is usually recognized as initiating philosophy in the Islamic world—there was at least fleeting awareness of Indian ideas about the sources of knowledge (*pramāṇas*).

Thus al-Bīrūnī was not the first Muslim intellectual to engage with India. Still, he went far beyond what had been achieved up to his time. This was possible because he was attached to the court of Maḥmūd of Ghazna, a warlord who made destructive incursions into India; al-Bīrūnī is frank about the enmity that Indians bore towards Muslims as a result (22). He was able to work together with scholars who were, presumably under considerable duress, brought to the court of Maḥmūd. The result was a kind of small-scale translation movement between Sanskrit and Arabic. With the help of his Indian advisors al-Bīrūnī prepared translations of Patañjali's *Yoga-sūtra*[6] and the *Sāṃkhya-kārikā*. He was also aware of and used Gauḍapāda's commentary on the latter text. In addition al-Bīrūnī had access to an Arabic version of the *Bhagavad-gītā*, which to judge by his quotations often diverged from the version known to us. Furthermore al-Bīrūnī and his collaborators translated in the other direction from Arabic into Sanskrit, producing versions of works by Euclid, Ptolemy, and al-Bīrūnī himself. Sadly these are now lost.

The upshot is that his treatise on India is a remarkably well-informed document, which includes extensive quotation from Sanskrit sources. Al-Bīrūnī relates these sources not just to elements of Greek thought, but also to Christianity, Judaism, and Manicheanism. Islam is implicitly given a special status by being exempted from this comparative project, but he does point out the affinity between Indian philosophy and Sufism. What al-Bīrūnī does not do so well is to convey any sense of the diversity of Indian thought. He sees the ideas of the Indian elite as being a single body of doctrine, which he frequently contrasts to vulgar popular beliefs in India, about which he is openly disdainful. But at least he's an equal opportunity elitist. When explaining that the Indian elite worship God alone whereas Indian commoners often indulge in idolatry (113), he adds that ancient Greeks were also idolators (123) and that the everyday Muslim would no doubt venerate images of the Prophet or Mecca if given half a chance.

As that passage indicates al-Bīrūnī is impressed by the tendencies towards monotheism in Indian philosophy. The first thing he tells us about the religion of the Indians sounds pretty much like a statement of Islamic monotheism: for them God is eternal, free, omnipotent, and resembled by none of His creatures (27).[7] Apparently taking Patañjali as a key for understanding the other Sanskrit sources on which he draws, he presents Indian thought as a single, harmonious teaching intended to liberate the soul from ignorance and from attachment to matter, so as to attain union with God (53, 81). This may remind us of Vedānta, yet that is a tradition that goes unmentioned by al-Bīrūnī. He does discuss monism as a point of similarity between Indian and Greek thought (33–4), but his focus is on the soul's relationship to a single, all powerful God, something we achieve by detaching our actions from desire as instructed in the *Bhagavad-gītā* (29). Al-Bīrūnī's tendency to lump all these ideas together into a single system, and to see them as echoing the ideas of other cultures, sets the tone for subsequent engagements with Indian thought.

In the Islamic world it would be a while before there was another engagement along these lines. In the twelfth century the theologian and philosopher al-Shahrastānī wrote an important survey of religious doctrines and did discuss India, but his treatment is disappointingly sketchy and does not seem to draw on al-Bīrūnī. Better informed is the historian Rashīd al-Dīn, who wrote around 1300 and had the advantage of new information supplied by a Buddhist scholar.[8] Just a bit earlier, the twelfth-century Illuminationist philosopher Suhrawardī insisted that his own teachings were in accordance with the sages of India. There was also some interest in the mystical traditions of India. Knowledge of Yogic meditation practices was disseminated through translations of a work called *The Pool of Nectar* (*Amṛtakunda*). A study of the Islamic reception of this work has, however, concluded that it provided only "a very narrow window onto the world of Indian religions, and one that to many readers was hardly distinguishable from the standard occult and mystical practices found in Islamicate society."[9] It would really be the Islamic invasions of India that created the conditions for renewing al-Bīrūnī's project. His observation that Sufism seems a good match for Indian religious belief was borne out by the success of Islamic mysticism in the subcontinent. This syncretic trend would come to a climax in the work of Dārā Shikūh, a prince who lived in the seventeenth century during the time of Islamic domination in India.[10] He translated some of the Upaniṣads into Persian and wrote a treatise called *Confluence of the Oceans*, the title a reference to the agreement between Indian and Islamic culture, with the latter understood primarily in terms of philosophical Sufism.

By this time information about Indian culture and philosophy was finding its way to Europe as well. The results were not always edifying.[11] Dārā Shikūh's younger contemporary John Locke mocked the conception of a mysterious underlying substance put forward by some of "our European philosophers" by comparing it to the fanciful proposal of a "poor Indian philosopher who imagined that the earth wanted some thing to bear it up," and suggested that the earth rests upon an elephant which is further supported by a tortoise. Another great name of European thought rose to the defense of India, though. Gottfried Wilhelm Leibniz chastised Locke, writing that "this [Indian] conception of substance, for all its apparent thinness, is less empty and sterile than it is thought to be. Several consequences arise from it; these are of the greatest importance to philosophy, to which they can give an entirely new face."[12]

Obviously these remarks do not suggest a deep knowledge of Indian intellectual history, but increasingly there were opportunities to learn more. Alison Gopnik has raised the intriguing possibility that David Hume may have been acquainted with Buddhist philosophy.[13] When he was writing the first and most significant statement of his philosophy, the *Treatise of Human Nature,* Hume was in residence at the Jesuit academy La Flèche. Here he could have encountered a much older man named Charles Dolu, who had been on a trip to Siam in the 1680s. Dolu was in turn acquainted with Ippolito Desideri, who had done missionary work in Tibet. Both Desideri and Dolu were well informed about Buddhism, with Desideri even writing a treatise about what he called a "false and peculiar religion observed in Tibet." Sounding a bit like al-Bīrūnī, he stated that people should know more about this religion in order to "contest" it, and highlighted what he called its "Pythagoreanism," presumably meaning its commitment to reincarnation. Gopnik summarizes her findings better than we could: "in 1735 Hume, apparently rusticating in the peace of a small town in France, was only one remove away from the ideas of philosophers thousands of miles and a cultural gulf away in Siam and Tibet."[14]

Perhaps, then, it is no coincidence that some of Hume's proposals, including his empiricism and skepticism about the self, are strikingly reminiscent of Buddhism. To this we can add that Hume's *Treatise* was most certainly influenced by Nicolas Malebranche and Pierre Bayle, who in turn knew something of Chinese philosophy. Malebranche even wrote a work in 1708 called *Conversation between a Christian Philosopher and Chinese Philosopher,* while Bayle's *Historical and Critical Dictionary,* published five years earlier, offers a description of "Chinese" philosophy that consists basically in a presentation of the Buddha's life and thought. Again, a skeptical attitude toward the soul comes to the fore here, giving us another conduit for the Buddhist doctrine of no-self into European culture.

Yet another source for Indian ideas was the well-traveled François Bernier, who had been to India and served as court physician for none other than the aforementioned Mughal prince Dārā Shikūh. Bernier tells of how he exchanged ideas with one of the court intellectuals who helped Dārā Shikūh translate the Upaniṣads. Writing from the Persian city of Shīrāz in 1667, Bernier said, "Do not be surprised if without knowledge of Sanskrit I am going to tell you many things taken from books in that language," for he had benefitted from a three-year collaboration with this "*paṇḍit*." The two had philosophical debates facilitated by Bernier's own translations of Gassendi and Descartes into Persian.[15] Again, we can forge a link to Hume here. Bernier made known the Indian metaphor comparing God to a spider who extends "filaments" out from itself and then withdraws them: in the same way the divine creation will ultimately be undone as all things collapse back into God. In his *Dialogues Concerning Natural Religion*, Hume refers to this analogy and ascribes it to "brahmins." He is, however, dismissive of the idea, saying that it is a "species of cosmogony, which appears to us ridiculous; because a spider is a little contemptible animal, whose operations we are never likely to take for a model of the whole universe."[16]

As we move forward into the nineteenth century, we finally see Europeans catching up with al-Bīrūnī by making Indology a serious intellectual enterprise. A key figure here was Henry T. Colebrooke, who translated mathematical and philosophical works from India into English. There's another tantalizing connection here, this time between Colebrooke and the philosopher John Stuart Mill. You'd expect Mill to know quite a lot about India, given that his father James Mill was an administrator in the East India Company and author of the colonial manifesto *A History of British India*. Yet the younger Mill's philosophical works fail to make any explicit use of Indian philosophy. He would, however, probably have known about a lecture given by Colebrooke in 1827, which explained the materialist theory of mind put forward by the Cārvāka school. As we proposed in Chapter 33, this theory is comparable to emergentism in the philosophy of mind, a theory that is sometimes traced back to Mill. He sounds rather like a follower of Bṛhaspati, founder of the Cārvāka system, when he writes in his *System of Logic* that "All organised bodies are composed of parts, similar to those composing inorganic nature, and which have even themselves existed in an inorganic state . . . the phenomena of life result from the juxtaposition of those parts in a certain manner."[17]

Meanwhile, Indology was also emerging in Germany, especially with the Schlegel brothers.[18] Friedrich Schlegel learned both Persian and Sanskrit and published a work called *On the Language and Wisdom of the Indians*, while his brother August Wilhelm Schlegel took up the first German chair of Indology in Bonn in 1818. We can trace the impact of the Indologists in a figure such as G.W.F. Hegel, who was aware of Colebrook's essays on Indian thought, published in the *Transactions of the Royal Asiatic Society* in 1824, and who also reviewed August Wilhelm Schlegel's work on the *Bhagavad-gītā*. This put Hegel in a position to evaluate the philosophical contribution of India—or at least it gave Hegel the impression that he was in such a position. For him the Indians had reached only a rather primitive stage in the development of "spirit (*Geist*)." They had a completely abstract notion of substance as a single, underlying principle, which they identified with an equally abstract and empty subject-hood. Again we see Indian philosophy being reduced to a monolithic teaching, with all emphasis being placed upon the monist strand within Brahmanical thought. Hegel's overall assessment manages to combine extravagant praise with casual dismissal: "In the formation of the Oriental world, we do find philosophizing too, indeed the most profound philosophizing...but insofar as it remains the most profound, it remains also abstract...For us the real philosophy begins only in Greece."[19]

A more positive assessment of the Indian tradition can be found in Arthur Schopenhauer, who on occasion went so far as to describe himself as a Buddhist.[20] He was also tremendously impressed by material from the Upaniṣads, which he read in an 1801 Latin translation based on the Persian translation of (you guessed it) Dārā Shikūh. Schopenhauer said of this text, "it is the most profitable and sublime reading that is possible in the world; it has been the consolation of my life and will be that of my death."[21] It's not so easy to say whether Schopenhauer's admiration for Indian thought went together with actual influence on his own thought. He was quite explicit in claiming agreement with Buddhism, along with the medieval mystical author Meister Eckhart.[22] In a passage not entirely free of Hegel's mixture of praise and condescension, he wrote, "the Buddha, Eckhart and I all teach essentially the same, Eckhart within the bounds of his Christian mythology. In Buddhism, these ideas are not encumbered by any such mythology, and are thus simple and clear, to the extent that a religion can be clear. Complete clarity lies with me."[23] However, Schopenhauer also insisted that when he began his great work *The World as Will and Representation*, he was as yet unacquainted with Buddhist philosophy, or at least with those aspects of it that resonated with his own system.

It's telling that, his appreciative mindset notwithstanding, Schopenhauer was still prone to lump Indian traditions together as if they all converged on a single philosophical doctrine. Our own tour through those traditions has revealed the stark opposition between, say, the Vedānta monism of consciousness and Buddhist skepticism regarding the self. But Schopenhauer saw little if any difference between union with the Upaniṣadic *brahman* and the Buddhists' state of liberation, achieved through abandonment of desire and "will." For Schopenhauer *brahman* was simply the "will" of his own philosophy, a self or subject that can see things "as a whole" *sub specie aeternitatis*, or "from an eternal point of view." It's an idea that would later be taken over by Wittgenstein, who writes in his *Tractatus logico-philosophicus* (§6.45), "The view of the world *sub specie aeternitatis* is the view of it as a—limited—whole. The feeling of the world as a limited whole is the mystical feeling."

In our view, this does not really do justice to the Indian sources on which Schopenhauer was drawing. As you may recall from our presentation of the Upaniṣads, we take its exploration of *brahman* to concern the phenomenology of consciousness. It is the underlying subject of thought and perception, not a principle of agency or willing.[24] This is not atypical of the European reception of Indian thought. By the time of Schopenhauer vastly more was known about Indian philosophy than the Greeks could have known in antiquity. The translations from Sanskrit that we were missing in Hellenic culture were now available, and scholars like Colebrooke and the Schlegel brothers were making India the object of sustained and careful philological attention. Yet with such figures as Hume, Hegel, and Schopenhauer, we still see Europeans being influenced as much by what they assumed Indian philosophy should be saying, as by what it really said.

There would, of course, be much more to say about the engagement between Europe and ancient India. Here we have only touched on a few of the more famous names, and we have not taken our story into the twentieth century, when two holders of the Spalding Professorship at Oxford, Sarvepalli Radhakrishnan and Bimal Krishna Matilal, worked hard at convincing British philosophers to pay attention to the riches of India. Radhakrishnan's attempt to display India's rich tradition of philosophical idealism was unfortunately mistimed. By then the short-lived school of British Idealism had already begun to fall into disregard. Matilal had greater success in introducing his Oxford colleagues to a rich vein of Indian epistemology. Peter Strawson, Derek Parfit, and Michael Dummett have all paid tribute both to Matilal's own philosophical brilliance and to the importance of the Indian ideas he brought to their attention (in the case of Parfit, the Buddhist analysis of persons, and for Strawson, the descriptive metaphysics of Nyāya and Vaiśeṣika). Now, in the twenty-first century, there is really no excuse for philosophers to imagine along with Hegel that "real philosophy" began only with the Greeks.

49

WHAT HAPPENED NEXT

INDIAN PHILOSOPHY AFTER DIGNĀGA

In this book our goal has been a modest one: to introduce you to what is a vast philosophical tradition of antiquity. Thus we have had to skip over many barely known figures and movements, and even with the ones we have managed to include, we can hardly claim to have done them full justice. We began with texts older than the Presocratics of ancient Greek thought and worked our way forward as far as Dignāga and his contemporaries around AD 600. Initially, philosophy appeared above all as a reflection on the way one lives one's life. Doing philosophy was the way to reach some final desirable end state, *mokṣa* or *nirvāṇa*, a release from all-too-human suffering. These "philosophies of path and purpose" included the ancient wisdom of the Vedas and the Upaniṣads, poetic visions of the unity of humanity, ritual, and cosmos. Under this heading we also considered the original teachings of the Buddha and Mahāvīra. We counted the vast epic, the *Mahābhārata*, which contains within it the *Bhagavad-gītā*, as another thread woven into the rope of thought through time that was early Indian philosophy. Sticking with the weaving theme, we then turned our attention to what we called the "Age of the Sūtra" (remember, *sūtra* actually means "thread"). The philosophical texts from this period were highly compressed and aphoristic in nature, hence extremely hard to figure out without the aid of an interpretive gloss. Thus we also met the great commentators who are really responsible for bringing systematicity into the Indian debate, and for the evolution of the "schools" of Nyāya, Vaiśeṣika, Sāṃkhya, Yoga, Mīmāṃsā, Vedānta, and Cārvāka.

Buddhist and Jaina philosophers were not to be left out. Their switch to Sanskrit fundamentally transformed philosophy in India until the end of the first millennium. One of the keenest and most fascinating Buddhist philosophers in this period was Nāgārjuna, whose formidable assault on the metaphysical notion of *svabhāva* or "self-nature" inspired the formation of a branch of Buddhist philosophy known as Madhyamaka, the "Middle Way" philosophy. Another was Vasubandhu, who both standardized Abhidharma in Sanskrit and laid the foundations for another new school of Buddhism, Yogācāra. We looked also at the early philosophers of Jainism, including Umāsvati, and their perspectival approach to epistemology. After picking our way through all this early history of Indian philosophy, we finally got on to Dignāga, a philosophical genius of the highest order, who should make it onto even the most selective list of greatest philosophers in history. His work was decisive in shaping the next period of Indian philosophy, a cosmopolitan "age of dialogue" in Sanskrit that lasted until the collapse of Buddhism in India.

We are not alone in seeing Dignāga as the inaugural figure in an entirely new epoch in Indian philosophy, although scholars have different opinions as to the reasons for his extraordinary influence. Of course we have put the emphasis on his theoretical innovations and his invention of new philosophical methods, including new ways of defining terms and new formalizations of sound argumentation. But others have noted that he also invented a new way of writing philosophy. Lawrence McCrea says that Dignāga "initiated a sudden, widespread and radical transformation in the reading, citational, and discursive practices of Sanskrit philosophers, a transformation perhaps even more dramatic in its effects than Dignāga's specifically philosophical contributions... He makes the systematic investigation of and response to the texts of rival philosophical traditions a basic organizing principle of his own work."[1] These new ways of arguing and writing about philosophy were immediately taken up by a large sector of the philosophical community and rapidly became the hallmark of philosophical activity in a broad Sanskrit cosmopolis that was to endure for centuries and whose geographical borders spread well beyond the subcontinent.

We have occasionally glimpsed further ahead, for instance when discussing the ideas of Abhinavagupta who lived into the eleventh century (he appeared in our discussions of aesthetics and Tantra in Chapter 46). Furthermore we have picked out topics and themes for particular attention, such as non-violence, the role women played in the early history of Indian philosophy, animals, *karma*, and time. In effect we have covered the first millennium and a half of Indian philosophy, which isn't too bad for single volume. If anything, things really picked up speed in the next millennium and a half, between Dignāga and the present day. A huge amount of philosophy happened on the Indian subcontinent in that time. Perhaps we will return to treat it properly in a future installment of this book series. For now, we will round off this book with the briefest of hints as to the history of philosophy in India from Dignāga onwards.

It is something of an irony that, despite his enormous impact, the works of Dignāga in Sanskrit were lost for a long time. The reason for this is that he was blessed, or possibly cursed, in having an extremely brilliant successor, Dharmakīrti.

As we've seen, it was Dharmakīrti's work that provided the canon for later authors, widely disseminated, commented on, and attacked even as Dignāga's own writings faded into the background. For at least three centuries, most serious philosophy in India took Dharmakīrti as its principal point of reference in one way or another. As the various schools developed, with him as their foil, they achieved great progress in articulating their core beliefs and providing them with arguments of a higher caliber than had been necessary before. Many important figures come from Kashmir, including Śaiva thinkers like Utpaladeva and the aforementioned Abhinavagupta, as well as the major Nyāya philosopher Jayanta Bhaṭṭa.

We saw that skepticism played an important role in Indian thought from an early period—it may even have helped to trigger ancient Greek skepticism—and that continued to be the case in later times. In the ninth century Jayarāśi described himself as a lion who had come to upturn every philosophical cart, but matters really came to a head with a revolutionary critique of the fundamentals of *pramāṇa* epistemology provided by Śrīharṣa. His twelfth-century philosophical classic, *Amassed Morsels of Refutation* (*Khaṇḍanakhaṇḍakhādya*), is a brilliant destructive analysis of the definition-mongering philosophical activities of past generations of thinkers. Śrīharṣa attempted to demonstrate that a philosophical method based on the search for definitions is misguided, indeed incoherent. He developed a rival method, a method of refutation, to expose as vacuous the way of doing philosophy pursued so influentially by Dignāga. This new method required Śrīharṣa to reconstruct the best *possible* version of any definition, not merely the best one anyone had actually formulated. His ability to articulate philosophical positions with greater insight, accuracy, and acuity than their own proponents is nothing short of astonishing.

Various other sorts of philosophical critique also gathered momentum. One came from new developments in Mīmāṃsa philosophical theory about the nature of inquiry, still pursued within the traditional framework of defending the legitimacy and authority of Vedic knowledge. To suppose that the Vedas are authoritative is to accept as unquestionable the truth of the beliefs we take from them; if the Veda teaches something then there is no need to engage in verification. This led Brahmanical thinkers to reflect on methodology and the nature of knowledge, as they contested the notion that truth must be the outcome of discovery and confirmation. Another sort of critique came in the form of a growing challenge to the metaphysics of commonsense. A series of increasingly sophisticated Advaita philosophers sought to undermine the assumption that appearance is trustworthy, and in particular that there is a world populated by everyday objects that are grasped by many distinct knowers.

In the fourteenth century, and in response to all these different pressures, we would highlight another philosopher who transformed his philosophical landscape: Gaṅgeśa. He wrote only a single book, one that styles itself as the "jewel that fulfills the wish for truth" (*Tattvacintāmaṇi*). His new conceptual methodologies, his response to the general skepticism of Śrīharṣa and the more specific challenges to inquiry from Mīmāṃsā and Advaita, rapidly gained currency throughout the Sanskrit world. Indeed, use of this new method, which was called Navya-Nyāya ("the New Nyāya"), spread to all intellectual disciplines. It was to prove especially influential in the field of jurisprudence. The heart of Gaṅgeśa's new method was a meticulous technique for the disambiguation of terms and assertions, so that an opponent's thesis could be carefully separated into a variety of possible readings, each of which could then be individually refuted.

The sixteenth and seventeenth centuries were an extraordinary period for philosophy in India. This was partly, but only partly, the result of new encounters with Persian culture. Exposure to new paradigms of thinking led Sanskrit philosophers to innovate self-consciously, to think with the old structures but not defer to them. An astonishingly large number of works in Sanskrit exists from this period. In the writings of those philosophers who followed the revolutionary Navya-Nyāya thinker Raghunātha Śiromaṇi, from about the middle of the sixteenth century until the middle of the eighteenth, there is a metamorphosis in epistemology, metaphysics, semantics, and philosophical logic. The works of these philosophers, many of whom lived in Raghunātha's hometown of Navadvīpa in Bengal, are full of phrases indicative of a newly open and exploratory attitude, phrases like "this should be considered further," or "this needs to be reflected on." It was not new exegesis of the ancient texts that drove this work but inquiry into the problems themselves, along with a sense of engaging in an ongoing project. A second group of philosophers, this time based in Vārāṇasī (Benares), and again profoundly influenced by Raghunātha, sought to use his work in reinterpretations of ancient metaphysics, sometimes with the support of the Islamic rulers of Mughal India. At the same time, and in opposition to Raghunātha's band of new reasoners while also co-opting his methods, the works of thinkers like Madhusūdana Sarasvatī, Appayya Dīkṣita and Nīlakaṇṭha Caturdhara brought a distinctive renewal to Advaita Vedānta.

In tandem with these developments in Sanskrit literature, Muslim philosophers were producing important and innovative philosophy in parallel centers of Islamic learning. Three important Islamic trends in India emerge during the seventeenth and eighteenth centuries. As we mentioned in the last chapter, there was the bilingual project of Dārā Shikūh and others who translated philosophy from Sanskrit into

Persian. Then there was the Sufi philosophy of Muḥibballāh Ilāhābādī, a prolific author in Persian and Arabic and defender of the Andalusian mystic Ibn ʿArabī. Finally there was debate between Avicennan thinkers, such as the influential philosopher Maḥmūd Jawnpūrī, and Illuminationists. Meanwhile, Muḥibballāh al-Bihārī's *Sullam al-ʿulūm* is a milestone seventeenth-century Indian textbook in Arabo-Islamic logic.[2] Unfortunately, we still have only the most rudimentary understanding of the nature of intersections between Sanskrit, Persian, and Arabic philosophical scholarship in early modern India. Nor at present do we have much insight into the dynamics of philosophical activity in Indian vernacular languages in the period.

We next move to the era of British colonial occupation which, for all its depredations, was not quite the total disaster for indigenous philosophy in India that one might expect. One effect it did have was to foreground new philosophical priorities, especially the need to respond to an incompatibility at the heart of the colonial project. On the one hand were the pretensions of European claims concerning the values of liberty, tolerance, equality, and secularism. On the other hand were the multiple and manifest illiberalities, intolerances, and inequalities of colonial rule, which began first during a period of exploitative governance by the East India Company from the Battle of Plassey in 1757 until the failed Independence War in 1857, and then under direct colonial rule by the British Crown until independence was finally won in 1947. Brilliant Indian thinkers like Gandhi, Nehru, Ambedkar, and Tagore, now often writing in English, made political and social philosophy the center of philosophical activity in India, whereas in earlier times it had been mind, language, epistemology, and metaphysics. Meanwhile, other philosophers reflected deeply on the nature of the subject, its freedom, agency, and identity, in a concerted effort to formulate the philosophical grounds of an intellectual decolonization. In the struggle for freedom from political and intellectual servitude the whole of India's philosophical past became an immense resource. In particular its perceived spirit of negotiated pluralism and non-coercive cosmopolitanism were made central to the design of a post-independence nation.

Philosophy has continued to progress in India from the 1950s to the present day. Though sometimes struggling to find a voice inside universities first established in the Victorian era, and understandably taking a backseat to the more urgent task of rebuilding the Indian economy after the ravages of extractive colonial governance, there are positive signs that as India enters a new period of economic prosperity, philosophy will again assume its traditional place at the very heart of Indian society and culture. And thanks both to new perspectives from the South Asian diaspora, as well as to a new generation of philosophers in the West who have a more global and cosmopolitan view of the discipline than their predecessors, the study of Indian philosophy in universities around the world is enjoying a period of unprecedented growth. Should this make us expect that insights from Indian thought will be brought into philosophy as it is taught and researched outside India? Of course our hope is that this book and other efforts to familiarize a broad audience with this tradition will give philosophers a push in that direction.

In that spirit, we'll conclude by noting a few areas where the Indian contribution seems both distinctive and promising from a contemporary point of view. Let's begin with the famous Indian ethic of non-violence toward animals.[3] As you may recall from Chapter 14, the rationale given against harming animals was very different from what we usually hear today from partisans of animal welfare, including philosophers who concern themselves with this issue. If you consider a prominent figure in today's philosophical discussion like Peter Singer, you find utilitarian principles being used to argue for better treatment of animals. It is because animals can suffer and get something positive out of life that we should avoid harming them. Other animal ethicists take a rights-based approach, arguing that animals have just as much claim to liberty and welfare as we do. Taken sufficiently seriously, a position like this could justify complete animal "liberation," not in the Buddhist or Jaina sense of that term, but meaning the abolition of all use of animals for human purposes.

By contrast the ancient Indian commitment to non-violence was a holistic way of life, with avoidance of animal suffering as only one of its many consequences or aspects. To live in accordance with *ahiṃsā* is to take a certain attitude toward all living things, including plants, to oneself, and even toward inanimate objects. Kicking a stone in anger could be a violation of this ethic, even though the stone has no rights or ability to suffer. As the *Mahābhārata* puts it, "*ahiṃsā* is the *dharma*. It is the highest purification. It is also the highest truth from which all *dharma* proceeds" (§13.125). It would be interesting to see whether a modern-day philosopher could revive this Indian teaching, putting the avoidance of violence at the center of an ethical theory rather than trying to extract non-violence out of some other core notion like the evil of suffering or the acknowledgement of rights. The relatively recent revival of Aristotelian ethics, which has a similar holism and commitment to virtue as a way of life, could perhaps offer a framework or at least an analogy for this project.

In metaphysics we've seen a number of theories that are fascinating and important for a global history of philosophy, but not so likely to appeal to the average philosopher of today. The prospects for a comeback of Sāṃkhya category theory with its lists of different types of entities, or of Vedānta monism, seem rather remote. But the metaphysical theory (if it is right to call it a "theory") of another author might be a more plausible source of inspiration. The author we have in mind is Nāgārjuna. His patterns of reasoning have already been compared to non-classical logic, and his ideas about emptiness and dependent origination might also be worth revisiting. Let's assume for the sake of argument that we were right in our interpretation of him (after all, it's our book): we argued that to say things are "empty" is to claim that they have no fixed *intrinsic* essence or nature. Rather, the being of things would be purely relational. This, it seems, could be an exciting idea for a modern-day metaphysician. Rather than thinking of the world as being made up of discrete objects that then bear relations to one another, what if we took the relations as the fundamental building blocks? At the very least some philosophers today are ready to admit that relations are "ineliminable" from our view of the world, in other words that we cannot just translate all talk of relations into non-relational properties. And some would say that a relational view of things may fit with modern physics better than a view based around intrinsic natures.[4] Nāgārjuna could be a formidable ally to philosophers who are already inclined to think that way.

Then there's epistemology, which as we've seen was one of the most abiding concerns of the ancient Indian philosophers. Here we have seen both constructive contributions to the theory of knowledge, in the form of developments of the theory of *pramāṇas,* and also rich skeptical traditions. We referred to Śrīharṣa earlier, and his critique of epistemology seems indeed to be attracting the attention of contemporary epistemologists. Something similar is true of Sanskrit work in the philosophy of language, especially its highly developed accounts of metaphor and literary significance. Yet perhaps the area where there has been most activity in the direction of a cross-cultural philosophy has been in the philosophy of mind. Indian theories of mind have fed into contemporary progress in the area of cognitive science and in new philosophical understandings of consciousness, attention, and self-representation. The celebrated Oxford philosopher Michael Dummett thought that philosophy of mind was the area in philosophy which would profit most from collaboration between philosophers working in divergent traditions.

We conclude on an emphatic note by saying that classical Indian thought has everything a historian of philosophy could want. It is a tradition rich with interpretive challenges, full of subtle texts that respond to one another and are often intriguing in their literary form. It has been historically influential, to some extent on European ideas but above all in cultures across Asia. It addressed core questions in every area of philosophy, advancing novel ideas in many if not all of these areas, including ideas that could be taken up by contemporary thinkers. This may not mean that everyone with a serious interest in philosophy has an *obligation* to learn something about Indian philosophy, but it does mean that any philosopher can benefit greatly from doing so. There is no better illustration of the rewards to be had from pursuing the history of philosophy without any gaps.

NOTES

Preface

1. African oral traditions will be covered in a future volume of this book series, now being written in collaboration with Chike Jeffers.
2. For the question of just how independent the two traditions were, see Chapters 47 and 48 in this volume.
3. For other introductory overviews of Indian thought, see the first part of the "further reading" section offered at the end of this book. That reading list also provides a short bibliography for each general topic covered in the volume. For primary texts in translation and secondary literature dealing with more specific issues, please see the notes to each chapter.

Chapter 1

1. P. Olivelle (trans.), *Upaniṣads* (Oxford: 1996), §2.4.5.
2. Our thanks to Chike Jeffers for suggesting this way of putting the contrast.
3. This section is translated in D. Sarma, *Classical Indian Philosophy: A Reader* (New York: 2011), 42–8.
4. See P. Hadot, *What is Ancient Philosophy?* (Cambridge, MA: 2002).
5. Book 12, Part 1, Chapters 154–7. James Fitzgerald (trans.), *The Mahābhārata, Volume 7* (Chicago: 2004), 570–6.
6. Fitzgerald, *The Mahābhārata*, 572.

Chapter 2

1. For the challenges of offering such a division, see E. Franco (ed.), *Periodization and Historiography of Indian Philosophy* (Vienna: 2013).
2. We here pass over the complicated question of the relation between modern-day Hinduism and these classical sources. See on this R. Thapar, "Imagined Religious Communities? Ancient History and the Modern Search for a Hindu Identity," *Modern Asian Studies* 23 (1989), 209–31.
3. H. Bechert (ed.), *The Dating of the Historical Buddha* (Göttingen: 1991).
4. For subsequent developments not covered in detail in the present volume, see Chapter 49.
5. For instance R. King, *Indian Philosophy: An Introduction to Hindu and Buddhist Thought* (Washington, DC: 1999), 44.
6. Admittedly the term *darśana* was used by the eighth-century Jaina doxographer Haribhadra, and others following him, to refer to a perspective or doctrine. See also on this terminology W. Halbfass, "*Darśana, Ānvīkṣikī*, Philosophy," in his *India and Europe: An Essay in Understanding* (Albany: 1988), 263–86.

7. For an English translation, see P. Olivelle, *King, Governance and Law in Ancient India: Kauṭilya's Arthaśastra* (Oxford: 2013). The relevance of the passage has also been noted in J. Ganeri's introduction to the *Oxford Handbook of Indian Philosophy* (Oxford: 2017), 9–10.

Chapter 3

1. For a summary of the current thinking, see G. Flood, *An Introduction to Hinduism* (Cambridge: 1996), 30–5. See also E. Bryant, *The Quest for the Origins of Vedic Culture: The Indo-Aryan Migration Debate* (Oxford: 2003).
2. R. Thapar, *The Penguin History of Early India from the Origins to* AD 1300 (London: 2002), 110.
3. S. Jamison and J. Brereton (trans.), *The Rigveda: The Earliest Religious Poetry of India* (Oxford: 2014), §1.162.
4. All translations of the Upaniṣads are taken from P. Olivelle (trans.), *Upaniṣads* (Oxford: 1996).
5. 1.164, Jamison and Brereton (trans.).
6. See also *Mahābhārata* §11.3, *Great Forest Upaniṣad* §4.4.
7. Thapar, *Penguin History*, 176.

Chapter 4

1. See further L. Patton, "Veda and Upaniṣad," in S. Mittal and G. Thursby (eds), *The Hindu World* (London: 2004), 37–51. All translations are drawn from P. Olivelle (trans.), *Upaniṣads* (Oxford: 1996).
2. On dating the various texts, see H. Nakamura, *A History of Early Vedānta Philosophy* (Delhi: 1983), part 1, 10–47.
3. On the idea of secrecy, see B. Black, "The Rhetoric of Secrecy in the Upaniṣads," in S. Lindquist (ed.), *Essays in Honor of Patrick Olivelle* (Florence: 2011), 101–25.
4. J. Brereton, "The Upaniṣads," in W.T. de Bary and I. Bloom (eds), *Approaches to the Asian Classics* (New York: 1990), 115–35, at 118.
5. Wittgenstein's remark that "the spirit of the snake, of the lion, is *your* spirit. For it is only from yourself that you are acquainted with spirit at all" (*Notebooks 1914–1916* (New York: 1961), trans. G.E.M. Anscombe, 85e) has been claimed by some to reveal an echo of this Upaniṣadic thought.
6. On the models of God as potter, magician, and spider, see B.K. Matilal, *Logical and Ethical Issues: An Essay on Indian Philosophy of Religion* (Calcutta: 2004), 43–6. For more on Hume and Indian thought, see this volume, Chapter 48.

Chapter 5

1. On this, see J. Frazier, "Natural Theology in Eastern Religions," in R. Manning (ed.), *The Oxford Handbook of Natural Theology* (Oxford: 2013), 166–81.
2. B.K. Matilal, *Ethics and Epics* (Delhi: 2002; reprinted 2015), 171.
3. For an overview, see S. Jamison and J. Brereton (trans.), *The Rigveda: The Earliest Religious Poetry of India* (Oxford: 2014), 35–53.
4. Cf. *Kena Upaniṣad* 1.1: "By whom impelled, by whom compelled, does the mind soar forth? By whom enjoined does the breath, march on as the first? By whom is this speech impelled, with which people speak? And who is the god that joins the sight and hearing?"
5. This chapter is based in part on the discussion of the Upaniṣads in J. Ganeri, *The Concealed Art of the Soul: Theories of Self and Practices of Truth in Indian Ethics and Epistemology* (Oxford: 2007).

Chapter 6

1. See J. Bronkhorst, *Karma* (Hawaii: 2011), 10–13.
2. See further P. Balcerowicz, *Early Asceticism in India: Ājīvikism and Jainism* (London: 2016).
3. For the former view, see H.W. Tull, *The Vedic Origins of Karma: Cosmos as Man in Ancient Indian Myth and Ritual* (Albany: 1989), and for the latter, J. Bronkhorst, *Greater Magadha: Studies in the Culture of Early India* (Leiden: 2007), summarized briefly in Bronkhorst, *Karma*, ch. 2.
4. W. Doniger O'Flaherty (ed.), *Karma and Rebirth in Classical Indian Traditions* (Berkeley: 1980), xvi–xvii.
5. *The Long Discourses of the Buddha*, M. Walshe trans. (Somerville, MA: 1987), 95. This is also the source for the following quote concerning the Cārvākas (96).
6. Matilal, *Ethics and Epics*, 414.
7. See further Chapter 12 in this volume and C. Framarin, "Good and Bad Desires: Implications of the Dialogue between Kṛṣṇa and Arjuna," *International Journal of Hindu Studies* 11 (2007), 147–70. For the work, see J.A.B. van Buitenen, *The Bhagavadgītā in the Mahābhārata: Text and Translation* (Chicago: 1981) or R.C. Zaehner, *The Bhagavadgītā, with a Commentary Based on the Original Sources* (Oxford: 1969). Translations are from the Zaehner edition.
8. This chapter is based in part on the discussion of *karma* in J. Ganeri, *The Concealed Art of the Soul: Theories of Self and Practices of Truth in Indian Ethics and Epistemology* (Oxford: 2007).

Chapter 7

1. F. Staal, "Ritual, Grammar and the Origins of Science in India," *Journal of Indian Philosophy* 10 (1982), 3–35, at 11.
2. For a summary, see R.N. Sharma, *The Aṣṭādhyāyī of Pāṇini, vol. 1: Introduction to the Aṣṭādhyāyī as a Grammatical Device* (New Delhi: 2002), 1–2.
3. Cited in F. Staal, "The Concept of Metalanguage and its Indian Background," *Journal of Indian Philosophy* 3 (1975), 315–54, at 329.
4. For Buddhists too, religious concerns play a background role in the investigation of language, which is seen as necessary for liberation and yet as an obstacle to achieving it. See R. Tzohar, *A Yogācāra Buddhist Theory of Metaphor* (Oxford: 2018).
5. Sharma, *The Aṣṭādhyāyī of Pāṇini*, 42.
6. On the importance of action in his grammar, see G. Cardona, "Pāṇini's *Kārakas*: Agency, Animation and Identity," *Journal of Indian Philosophy* 2 (1974), 231–306, and 244 for the absence of grammatical subject.
7. Quoted at Cardona, "Pāṇini's *Kārakas*," 246.
8. B.K. Matilal, "The *kāraka* Theory," in his *The Word and the World: India's Contribution to the Study of Language* (Delhi: 1990), ch. 5.
9. Staal, "Ritual, Grammar," 27.
10. Sharma, *The Aṣṭādhyāyī of Pāṇini*, 43.
11. For the following, see Sharma, *The Aṣṭādhyāyī of Pāṇini*, 144–5; Cardona, "Pāṇini's *Kārakas*," 238–9.
12. For this, see P. Kiparsky, *Some Theoretical Problems in Pāṇini's Grammar* (Poona: 1982), 26–9, criticized by Sharma, *The Aṣṭādhyāyī of Pāṇini*, 57–9.
13. Sharma, *The Aṣṭādhyāyī of Pāṇini*, 43.
14. Sharma, *The Aṣṭādhyāyī of Pāṇini*, 10.
15. Staal, "The Concept of Metalanguage," 331.

16. Or at least these have been credited to him: see Staal, "Ritual, Grammar," 23–4.
17. Our thanks to Malgorzata Wielinska-Soltwedel for advice on this chapter.

Chapter 8

1. For a summary of the biographical material, see the first part of H.H. Penner, *Rediscovering the Buddha: Legends of the Buddha and Their Interpretation* (Oxford: 2009).
2. This material is presented in P.E. Karetzky, *The Life of the Buddha: Ancient Scriptural and Pictorial Traditions* (Lanham: 1992). It should be noted that in this and the next chapter, we are really describing Buddha as he appears in these various sources and not necessarily making claims about the historical Buddha himself.
3. For a discussion of the vocabulary of desire in early Buddhist thought, see D. Webster, *The Philosophy of Desire in the Buddhist Pāli Canon* (London: 2005), ch. 3.
4. B. Bodhi (trans.), *The Connected Discourses of the Buddha* (Somerville, MA: 2000), 1844.
5. Bodhi, *Connected Discourses*, 543.
6. See the discussion at Webster, *The Philosophy of Desire*, 131–40.
7. B. Matthews, *Craving and Salvation: A Study in Buddhist Soteriology* (Ontario: 1983), 81, cited at Webster, *The Philosophy of Desire*, 132.
8. B. Ñāṇamoli and B. Bodhi (trans.), *The Middle Length Discourses of the Buddha* (Somerville, MA: 1995), 1097–1101.
9. For an English version, see I.B. Horner (trans.), *Milinda's Questions* (Oxford: 1996). The passage in question, which is at §2.1, is discussed by A.D. Carpenter, *Indian Buddhist Philosophy* (Durham: 2014), 35–47.
10. Buddhaghosa, *The Path of Purification*, B. Ñāṇamoli (trans.) (Kandy: 1991), 613. On this passage, see S. Radhakrishnan and C.A. Moore, *A Sourcebook in Indian Philosophy* (Princeton: 1957), 284.
11. The example is not casually chosen: in ancient Greek elements were called *stoicheia*, which also means "letters." For a text exploiting the example, see Plato's *Theaetetus* 203a–208b. Plato also gives the example of a wagon made up of parts (207a), which is highly reminscent of Nāgasena's chariot.
12. Ñāṇamoli and Bodhi, *Middle Length Discourses*, 229.
13. *Connected Discourses*, 957–8. See further J.P. McDermott, "Karma and Rebirth in Early Buddhism," in W. Doniger O'Flaherty (ed.), *Karma and Rebirth in Classical Indian Traditions* (Berkeley: 1980), 165–92; the dog analogy is cited at 174.
14. Buddhaghosa, *The Path to Purification*, 531. He says here explicitly that causation replaces identity.
15. On this view, see L. Priestly, *Pudgalavāda Buddhism: The Reality of the Indeterminate Self* (Toronto: 1999).
16. M. Walshe (trans.), *The Long Discourses of the Buddha* (Boston: 1995), 95.
17. Ñāṇamoli and Bodhi, *Middle Length Discourses*, 427.

Chapter 9

1. B. Ñāṇamoli and B. Bodhi (trans.), *The Middle Length Discourses of the Buddha* (Somerville, MA: 1995), 228–9.
2. Ñāṇamoli and Bodhi, *Middle Length Discourses*, 500.
3. K.N. Jayatilleke, *Early Buddhist Theory of Knowledge* (London: 1963), 359.
4. Quoted from B. Watson (trans.), *The Lotus Sūtra* (New York: 1993), 58.

5. See also J. Schroeder, "Truth, Deception, and Skillful Means in the *Lotus Sūtra*," *Journal of Indian Philosophy* 21.1 (2011), 35–52.
6. A. von Staël-Holstein (ed.), *The Kāśyapa-parivarta: A Mahāyānasūtra of the Ratnakūṭa Class* (Peking: 1926), 95–7.
7. Ñāṇamoli and Bodhi, *Middle Length Discourses*, 227.
8. I.B. Horner (trans.), *Milinda's Questions* (Oxford: 1996), 204.
9. On the ethical dimension of Buddhism, see D. Keown, *The Nature of Buddhist Ethics* (Basingstoke: 1992); P. Harvey, *An Introduction to Buddhist Ethics: Foundations, Values, and Issues* (Cambridge: 2000).
10. As suggested by Harvey, *An Introduction to Buddhist Ethics*, 43.
11. This chapter is based partially on the discussion of the nature of the Buddha's teaching in J. Ganeri, *The Concealed Art of the Soul: Theories of Self and Practices of Truth in Indian Ethics and Epistemology* (Oxford: 2007).

Chapter 10

1. For an English translation, see P. Olivelle, *King, Governance and Law in Ancient India: Kauṭilya's Arthaśastra* (Oxford: 2013). Cited in the main text by section number.
2. J.S. Strong, *The Legend of King Aśoka* (Princeton: 1983), 38, quoting Weber's *The Religion of India*, trans. H.H. Gerth and D. Martindale (New York: 1958), 213. On Indian political thought, see, however, H. Scharfe, *The State in Indian Tradition* (Leiden: 1989).
3. Olivelle, *King, Governance and Law*, 14.
4. See the introduction to Olivelle, *King, Governance and Law*, and on the questions of dating and authenticity also A.A. Vigasin and A.M. Samozvantsev, *Society, State and Law in Ancient India* (New Delhi: 1985), 1–27 and R. Choudhary, *Kautilya's Political Ideas and Institutions* (Varanasi: 1971), 27–45.
5. Vigasin and Samozvantsev, *Society, State and Law*, 35.
6. Translated by P. Olivelle, *Manu's Code of Law* (Oxford: 2005). For further texts, see P. Olivelle, *Dharmasūtras: The Law Codes of Āpastamba, Gautama, Baudhāyana, and Vasiṣṭha* (Delhi: 2000). For a thorough exploration of this literature, see P. Olivelle and D. Davis Jr. (eds), *Hindu Law: A New History of Dharmaśāstra* (Oxford: 2018). Note that works in the *Dharmaśastra* genre continue to be written for many centuries and are not only an ancient phenomenon.
7. On the topic in general, see K.M. Agrawai, *Kauṭilya on Crime and Punishment* (Almora: 1990).
8. Choudhary, *Kautilya's Political Ideas*, 8; Vigasin and Samozvantsev, *Society, State and Law*, 37–8. On the Cārvāka school, see further Chapters 32–3 in this volume.
9. M.V. Krishna Rao, *Studies in Kautilya* (Delhi: 1958) admits the superficial similarity, but argues that Kauṭilya is more comparable to his near contemporary Aristotle.
10. For this and the wider historical context, see R. Thapar, *Aśoka and the Decline of the Mauryas* (Oxford: 1961), which also contains an English translation of Aśoka's edicts (250–66). For an alternative translation, see N.A. Nikam and R. McKeon (trans.), *The Edicts of Asoka* (Chicago: 1966).
11. Choudhary, *Kautilya's Political Ideas*, 47 and 90. On Megasthenes, see Chapter 47 in this volume.
12. On these stories, especially the central text known as the *Aśokāvadāna*, see J.S. Strong, *The Legend of King Aśoka* (Princeton: 1983).
13. Strong, *The Legend of King Aśoka*, 117.

14. Strong, *The Legend of King Aśoka*, 81.
15. Thapar, *Aśoka and the Decline of the Mauryas*, 26–7.
16. A point made by Thapar, *Aśoka and the Decline of the Mauryas*, 156.

Chapter 11

1. On this, see S. Jamison, *Sacrificed Wife, Sacrificer's Wife: Women, Ritual, and Hospitality in Ancient India* (Oxford: 2011).
2. *Śatapatha Brāhmaṇa* 5.2.1, translation from P. Olivelle. "Amṛtā: Women and Indian Technologies of Immortality," *Journal of Indian Philosophy* 25 (1997), 427–49, at 431; see also 432 for the following idea of the son as a mirror image.
3. W. Doniger O'Flaherty (ed.), *Karma and Rebirth in Classical Indian Traditions* (Berkeley: 1980), 29.
4. Cited by B. Black, *The Character of the Self in Ancient India: Priests, Kings, and Women in the Early Upaniṣads* (Albany: 2007), 141.
5. For this, see Black, *Priests, Kings and Women*, 136–9.
6. As pointed out by J. Bronkhorst, *Karma* (Hawaii: 2011), 44–5, who cites the *Aitareya Brahmana*: "by means of a son have fathers always crossed over the deep darkness, since he was born as their self from their self . . . Wish for a son, O Brahmins."
7. For the idea that women have a specific *dharma*, see J.L. Fitzgerald, "Dharma and its Translation in the Mahābhārata," *Journal of Indian Philosophy* 32 (2004), 671–85, at 679.
8. P. Adamson, *Philosophy in the Hellenistic and Roman Worlds* (Oxford: 2015), ch. 45.
9. See P.S. Jaini, *Gender and Salvation: Jaina Debates on the Spiritual Liberation of Women* (Berkeley: 1991); D.Y. Paul, *Women in Buddhism: Images of the Feminine in the Mahāyana Tradition* (Berkeley: 1985).
10. For all this, see K.R. Blackstone, *Women in the Footsteps of the Buddha: Struggle for Liberation in the Therīgāthā* (Delhi: 1998), 38. We draw on this book in the following discussion of the *Therīgāthā*.
11. Quoted at Blackstone, *Women in the Footsteps*, 44.
12. C. Hallisey (trans.), *Therīgāthā: Poems of the First Buddhist Women* (Cambridge, MA: 2015).
13. Blackstone, *Women in the Footsteps*, 30–1.
14. On this episode, see E.B. Findly, "Gārgī at the King's Court: Women and Philosophic Innovation in Ancient India," in Y.Y. Haddad and E.B. Findly (eds), *Women, Religion and Social Change* (Albany: 1985), 27–58; S.E. Lindquist, "Gender at Janaka's Court: Women in the Bṛhadāraṇyaka Upaniṣad Reconsidered," *Journal of Indian Philosophy* 36 (2008), 405–26; Black, *Priests, Kings and Women*, ch. 4.
15. Also emphasized by Olivelle, "Amṛtā: Women and Indian Technologies," 440.
16. On her, see N. Falk, "Draupadī and the *Dharma*," in R.M. Gross (ed.), *Beyond Androcentrism: New Essays on Women and Religion* (Missoula: 1977); S.J.M. Sutherland, "Sītā and Draupadī: Aggressive Behavior and Female Role-Models in the Sanskrit Epics," *Journal of the American Oriental Society* 109 (1989), 63–79; B. Black, "Draupadī in the *Mahābhārata*," *Religion Compass* 7 (2013), 169–78.
17. As argued by B. Black, "Eavesdropping on the Epic: Female Listeners in the *Mahābhārata*," in S. Brodbeck and B. Black (eds), *Gender and Narrative in the Mahābhārata* (London: 2007), 53–78.
18. Translated in J. Fitzgerald, "Nun Befuddles King, Shows *Karmayoga* Does Not Work: Sulabhā's Refutation of King Janaka at MBh 12.308," *Journal of Indian Philosophy* 30 (2002), 641–77. Cited by section number from this translation. See further R. Vanita,

"The Self is Not Gendered: Sulabha's Debate with King Janaka," *NWSA Journal* 15 (2003), 76–93.

19. Black, *Priests, Kings and Women*, 146.
20. As pointed out by Lindquist, "Gender at Janaka's Court," 419.

Chapter 12

1. For a consideration of the dilemma, comparing the Kantian treatment to that in the epic, see B.K. Matilal, "Moral Dilemmas and Religious Dogmas," and "Moral Dilemmas: Insights from Indian Epics," both in his *Epics and Ethics* (Oxford: 2002), 3–13 and 19–35. See further B.K. Matilal (ed.), *Moral Dilemmas in the Mahābhārata* (Delhi: 1989). We follow Matilal by focusing on the issue of moral dilemmas in this chapter, which returns to themes also discussed in J. Ganeri, *The Concealed Art of the Soul: Theories of Self and Practices of Truth in Indian Ethics and Epistemology* (Oxford: 2007).
2. For a partial English translation with summary of the untranslated sections, see J.D. Smith (trans.), *The Mahābhārata* (London: 2009). Complete translations in multiple volumes are in progress by J.A.B. van Buitenen et al. (trans.), *The Mahābhārata* (Chicago: 1973–) and P. Wilmot et al. (trans.), *The Clay Sanskrit Library: Mahābhārata* (2009–). We cite by book and section number and quote from the Smith version.
3. The multiple framing is emphasized by A. Hiltebeitel, "Not Without Subtales: Telling Laws and Truths in the Sanskrit Epics," *Journal of Indian Philosophy* 33 (2005), 455–511, at 461, which is also the basis for the following observations.
4. W. Halbfass, *India and Europe: An Essay in Philosophical Understanding* (Delhi: 1988), 310; compare our remarks in Chapter 1 about using *darśana* as an equivalent of "philosophy." On the early meaning of the term, see A. Hiltebeitel, *Dharma: Its Early History in Law, Religion, and Narrative* (Oxford: 2011); A. Bowles, *Dharma, Disorder and the Political in Ancient India: The Āpaddharmaparvan of the Mahābhārata* (Leiden: 2007); and *Journal of Indian Philosophy* 32 (2004), a special issue devoted to *dharma*, with further discussion in P. Hacker, "*Dharma* in Hinduism," *Journal of Indian Philosophy* 34 (2006), 479–96.
5. Hacker, "*Dharma* in Hinduism," 492.
6. P. Horsch, trans. J.L. Whitaker, "From Creation Myth to World Law: The Early History of Dharma," *Journal of Indian Philosophy* 32 (2004), 423–48, at 424–8.
7. P. Olivelle, "The Semantic History of Dharma: The Middle and Late Vedic Periods," *Journal of Indian Philosophy* 32 (2004), 491–511, at 495–6.
8. This "empirical" approach is emphasized by Hacker, "*Dharma* in Hinduism," but the adequacy of this as a general account is questioned by A. Wezler, "Dharma in the Veda and the Dharmaśāstras," *Journal of Indian Philosophy* 32 (2004), 629–54.
9. Olivelle, "The Semantic History."
10. For the idea that an Aśokan ideal of *dharma* may be reflected in the *Mahābhārata*, and even embodied by the character of Yudhiṣṭhira, see Bowles, *Dharma, Disorder and the Political in Ancient India*, 128, with further references.
11. Halbfass, *India and Europe*, 313.
12. *Āpastamba Dharmasūtra* §1.20, in P. Olivelle, *Dharmasūtras: The Law Codes of Āpastamba, Gautama, Baudhāyana, and Vasiṣṭha* (Delhi: 2000).
13. On the difficulties of understanding this passage, see the discussion in Ganeri, *The Concealed Art of the Soul*, 82–5.
14. D. Gitomer, "King Duryodhana: The *Mahābhārata* Discourse of Sinning and Virtue in Epic and Drama," *Journal of the American Oriental Society* 112 (1992), 222–32, at 231.

15. Matilal, "Kṛṣṇa: In Defence of a Devious Divinity," *Epics and Ethics*, 91–108, at 105.
16. For this term, see J.L. Fitzgerald, "Dharma and its Translation in the Mahābhārata," *Journal of Indian Philosophy* 32 (2004), 671–85, at 678.

Chapter 13

1. Reported by A. Chaudhuri, "Diary," in *London Review of Books*, Dec. 17, 2015.
2. For the reception of the work, see C.A. Robinson, *Interpretations of the Bhagavad-Gītā and Images of the Hindu Tradition: The Song of the Lord* (London: 2006), and for scholarly approaches, A. Malinar, *The Bhagavadgītā: Doctrines and Contexts* (Cambridge: 2007), ch. 1, with interpretations inspired by National Socialism discussed at 25.
3. J.A.B. van Buitenen, *The Bhagavadgītā in the Mahābhārata: Text and Translation* (Chicago: 1981), from which we quote below. Citations are to chapter number followed by page numbers from this translation.
4. B.K. Matilal, "Moral Dilemmas and Religious Dogmas," in his *Epics and Ethics* (Oxford: 2002), 3–13, at 7. See also his "Kṛṣṇa: In Defence of a Devious Divinity," in A. Sharma (ed.), *Essays on the Mahābhārata* (Leiden: 1991), 401–21.
5. See Malinar, *The Bhagavadgītā: Doctrines and Contexts*, 68, for the idea that non-attachment is already foreshadowed by the *kṣatriya* ethic of fighting regardless of outcome. For in-depth discussions of agency in the *Gītā*, see R.A. Berg, "Theories of Action in the *Bhagavad-Gītā*," in A. Sharma (ed.), *New Essays in the Bhagavadgītā: Philosophical, Methodological and Cultural Approaches* (New Delhi: 1987), 36–50; S. Brodbeck, "Calling Kṛṣṇa's Bluff: Non-Attached Action in the *Bhagavadgītā*," *Journal of Indian Philosophy* 32 (2004), 81–103; D. C. Mathur, "The Concept of Action in the *Bhagavadgītā*," *Philosophy and Phenomenological Research* 35 (1974), 34–45; G. Teschner, "Anxiety, Anger and the Concept of Agency and Action in the *Bhagavadgītā*," *Asian Philosophy* 2 (1992), 61–77. For discussions of the implicit normative ethics in the *Gītā*, see C. Framarin, "Good and Bad Desires: Implications of the Dialogue between Kṛṣṇa and Arjuna," *International Journal of Hindu Studies* 11 (2007), 147–70; J. Anderson, "Sen and the *Bhagavad Gītā*: Lessons for a Theory of Justice," *Asian Philosophy* 22 (2012), 63–74; S. Sreekumar, "An Analysis of Consequentialism and Deontology in the Normative Ethics of the *Bhagavadgītā*," *Journal of Indian Philosophy* 40 (2012), 277–315.
6. For this parallel, see Malinar, *The Bhagavadgītā: Doctrines and Contexts*, 15, and J.B. Long, "Karma and Rebirth in the Dhamaśāstras," in W. Doniger O'Flaherty (ed.), *Karma and Rebirth in Classical Indian Traditions* (Berkeley: 1980), 61–89.
7. P. Hill, *Fate, Predestination and Human Action in the Mahābhārata: A Study in the History of Ideas* (New Delhi: 2001); J.F. Woods, *Destiny and Human Initiative in the Mahābhārata* (Albany: 2001).
8. Brodbeck, "Calling Kṛṣṇa's Bluff," 92.
9. Indeed some have made precisely this suggestion. For references, see Malinar, *The Bhagavadgītā: Doctrines and Contexts*, 31.
10. On this text and anticipations of its teaching in the *Gītā* and other earlier works, see G.J. Larson, *Classical Sāṃkhya: An Interpretation of its History and Meaning* (Delhi: 1979).
11. But, as with most aspects of the *Gītā*, the extent of its opposition to Buddhism is controversial. See K.N. Upadhyaya, *Early Buddhism and the Bhagavadgītā* (Delhi: 1971).
12. Larson, *Classical Sāṃkhya*, 108–12, who refers to the twelfth book especially.
13. S. Pollock, "The Divine King of the Indian Epic," *Journal of the American Oriental Society* 104 (1984), 505–28.

14. See D. Gitomer, "King Duryodhana: The *Mahābhārata* Dicourse of Sinning and Virtue in Epic and Drama," *Journal of the American Oriental Society* 112 (1992), 222–32, at 224.

Chapter 14

1. For these exceptions, see *Philosophy in the Hellenistic and Roman Worlds*, ch. 33, and for further exceptions in the Islamic world, P. Adamson, "The Ethical Treatment of Animals," in R.C. Taylor and L.X. López-Farjeat (eds), *Routledge Companion to Islamic Philosophy* (London: 2015), 371–82. For a survey of philosophical attitudes from antiquity down to the present day, see P. Adamson and G.F. Edwards (eds), *Animals: A History* (New York: 2018). The latter volume includes a chapter on animals in Indian philosophy by Amber Carpenter.
2. See, in general, C. Chapple (ed.), *Nonviolence to Animals, Earth, and Self in Asian Traditions* (Albany: 1993); T. Sethia (ed.), *Ahiṃsā, Anekānta and Jainism* (Delhi: 2004); U. Tähtinen, *Ahiṃsā: Non-Violence in Indian Tradition* (London: 1976).
3. On this, see L. Alsdorf, *Beiträge zur Geschichte von Vegetarismus und Rinderverehrung in Indien* (Wiesbaden: 1962); L. Schmithausen, "A Note on the Origin of *Ahiṃsā*," in R. Tsuchida and A. Wezler (eds), *Harānandalaharī: Volume in Honour of Professor Minoru Hara on his Seventieth Birthday* (Reinbek: 2000), 253–82.
4. As observed by Schmithausen, "A Note on the Origin of *Ahiṃsā*," 275.
5. *Saṃyuttanikāya* V.353.29, quotation from Schmithausen, "A Note on the Origin of *Ahiṃsā*," 272. See also B. Bodhi (trans.), *The Connected Discourses of the Buddha* (Somerville, MA: 2000), 1797.
6. I.M. Ghosh, *Ahiṃsā: Buddhist and Gandhian* (Delhi: 1989), 47; Alsdorf, *Beiträge zur Geschichte von Vegetarismus*, 33–4.
7. R.J. Zydenbos, "Jainism as the Religion of Non-Violence," in J.E.M. Houben and K.R. van Kooij (eds), *Violence Denied: Violence, Non-Violence and the Rationalization of Violence in South Asian Cultural History* (Leiden: 1999), 185–210; and for Jainism in general, P.S. Jaini, *The Jaina Path of Purification* (New Delhi: 1998) and P. Dundas, *The Jains* (London: 2002).
8. T.G. Kaghatgi, "The Doctrine of Karma in Jaina Philosophy," *Philosophy East and West* 15 (1965), 229–42.
9. Zydenbos, "Jainism as the Religion of Non-Violence," 187.
10. Recounted in P.S. Jaini, "Ahiṃsā and 'Just War' in Jainism," in T. Sethia (ed.), *Ahiṃsā, Anekānta and Jainism* (Delhi: 2004), 47–61, at 49. For an overview of Jaina ascetic practices, see J.E. Cort, "Singing the Glory of Asceticism: Devotion of Asceticism in Jainism," *Journal of the American Academy of Religion* 70 (2002), 719–42.
11. P.S. Jaini, "Fear of Food? Jaina Attitudes on Eating," in R. Smet and K. Watanabe (eds), *Jain Studies in Honour of Jozef Deleu* (Tokyo: 1993), 339–53, at 342.
12. Mentioned in, e.g., Dundas, *The Jains*, 15; Zydenbos, "Jainism as the Religion of Non-Violence," 199.
13. P. Dundas, "The Non-Violence of Violence: Jain Perspectives on Warfare, Asceticism and Worship," in J.R. Hinnells and R. King (eds), *Religion and Violence in South Asia: Theory and Practice* (London: 2007), 41–61. Dundas (at 43) cites an apposite passage from the *Sūtrakṛtānga Sūtra*, concerning Jaina renouncers: "such heroes are free from passion, they destroy anger and fear, they don't kill creatures." For the topic, see also Jaini, "Ahiṃsā and 'Just War' in Jainism."
14. Alsdorf, *Beiträge zur Geschichte von Vegetarismus*, 6–7.

15. K.E. Ulrich, "Food Fights: Buddhist, Hindu, and Jain Dietary Polemics in South India," *History of Religions* 46 (2007), 228–61, at 239.
16. On this, see A. Malinar, *The Bhagavadgītā: Doctrines and Contexts* (Cambridge: 2007), 5–6.
17. Ulrich, "Food Fights," 255.
18. Our thanks to Shalini Sinha and Peter Flugel for advice on this chapter.

Chapter 15

1. A classic example being F.M. Müller, *Six Systems of Indian Philosophy* (London: 1899).
2. For this issue, see D.N. Lorenzen, "Who Invented Hinduism?" *Comparative Studies in Society and History* 41 (1999), 630–59; E. Bryant, *The Indo-Aryan Controversy: Evidence and Inference in Indian History* (London: 2005); A. Nicholson, *Unifying Hinduism: Philosophy and Identity in Indian Intellectual History* (New York: 2013). Thanks to Elisa Freschi's advice on this and other points raised in this chapter.
3. A. Thaukur (ed.), *Nyāya-bhāṣya* (Delhi: 1997), 27 (trans. Ganeri).
4. For this comparison and more discussion of the nature and purpose of commentary in the Indian tradition, see J. Ganeri, "Sanskrit Philosophical Commentary," *Journal of the Indian Council of Philosophical Research* 25 (2008), 107–27. On the idea of a cumulative tradition that builds through commentary, see also E. Deutsch, "Knowledge and the Tradition Text in Indian Philosophy," in G.J. Larson and E. Deutsch (eds), *Interpreting Across Boundaries: New Essays in Comparative Philosophy* (Princeton: 1988), 165–73.
5. R. Thapar, *The Penguin History of Early India from the Origins to AD 1300* (London, 2002), 228.
6. Trans. Kielhorn, cited by Thapar, *The Penguin History*, 224.
7. J. Bronkhorst, *Karma* (Hawaii: 2011), 79.
8. J. Bronkhorst, "The Peacock's Egg: Bhartṛhari on Language and Reality," *Philosophy East and West* 51 (2001), 474–91, at 475.
9. So conscientious are the authors that they sometimes "improve" their opponents' views so as to make them more difficult to refute, which can make it difficult to reconstruct those views if they are otherwise lost. This is pointed out by R. Bhattacharya, *Studies on the Cārvāka/Lokāyata* (London: 2011), 73.

Chapter 16

1. In the case of the *Vaiśeṣika-sūtra* we likewise read, "Now, then, we will explain *dharma* (*athāto dharmaṃ vyākhāsyāmaḥ*)"; note that here *dharma* means the real nature of things, and is not a reference to duty, a usage we also encounter in Buddhist Abhidharma.
2. E. Fauwallner (ed.), *Materialen zur altesten Erkenntnislehre der Karmamīmāṃsā* (Vienna: 1968), 14–15.
3. K.S. Sastri (ed.), *The Ślokavārttika of Kumārila* (Trivandrum: 1983), 57.
4. For more on this connection, see A. Carpenter and J. Ganeri, "Can You Seek the Answer to This Question? Meno in India," *Australasian Journal of Philosophy* 88 (2010), 571–94, on which the following paragraphs are based.
5. N. Sastri and V. Sastri Pansikar (eds), *The Brahmasūtrabhāṣya* (Bombay: 1971), 79–81.
6. Sastri and Pansikar, *The Brahmasūtrabhāṣya*, 81.
7. 10.129.6–7. S. Jamison and J. Brereton (trans.), *The Rigveda* (Oxford: 2015), 1609.
8. 2.1–2. P. Olivelle (trans.), *Upaniṣads* (Oxford: 1996), 228.
9. *Mahābhārata* §12.180.49. A. Wynne (trans.), *Mahābhārata, Book 12: Peace; Volume 3: The Book of Liberation* (New York: 2009), 83.

10. M. Walshe (trans.), *The Long Discourses of the Buddha* (Somerville, MA: 1987), 97.
11. K. Bhattacharya (trans.), *The Dialectical Method of Nāgārjuna* (Delhi: 1986), 115. *Dispeller of Disputes, Vigraha–vyāvartanī* 31–2.
12. On him, see E. Franco, *Perception, Knowledge and Disbelief: A Study of Jayarāśi's Scepticism* (Delhi: 1994) and P. Balcerowicz, "Jayarāśi Against the Philosophers," in J. Ganeri (ed.), *The Oxford Handbook of Indian Philosophy* (Oxford: 2017), 403–19.
13. *The Lion Who Upsets the Systems, Tattvopaplasiṃha*, 1.2, E. Solomon (trans.), *Jayarāśi Bhaṭṭa's Tattvopaplavasiṃha* (Delhi: 2010), 3 (modified).
14. Solomon, *Jayarāśi Bhaṭṭa's Tattvopaplavasiṃha*, 2.
15. See J. Ganeri, *Philosophy in Classical India*, 160–1, citing Śrīharṣa, *Khaṇḍana-khaṇḍa-khādya* (*Amassed Morsels of Refutation*), 1.29.
16. Appropriately enough, this isn't in fact certain. For the debate as to whether the ancient skeptic in fact lives "without belief," see M.F. Burnyeat and M. Frede (eds), *The Original Sceptics* (Indianapolis: 1997).
17. A recent study of the skepticism in the three authors we have been discussing, emphasizing the idea that there is a skepticism about philosophy itself, is E. Mills, *Three Pillars of Skepticism in Classical India* (Lanham: 2018).

Chapter 17

1. As contrasted to the law books concerning *dharma*, like the *Manu-smṛti*; these were collectively called *smṛti*, "what is remembered."
2. As argued in J. Ganeri, "The Ritual Roots of Moral Reason: Lessons from Mīmāṃsā," in K. Schilbrack (ed.), *Thinking Through Rituals: Philosophical Perspectives* (London: 2004), 207–33; see also J. Ganeri, *Identity as Reasoned Choice* (London: 2012), ch. 5.
3. See further N.S. Juhankar, "The Mīmāṃsā Concept of *Dharma*," *Journal of Indian Philosophy* 10 (1982), 51–60.
4. Sanskrit text in M. Nyayaratna (ed.), *Mīmāṃsā-sūtra with Śabara's Bhāṣya* (Calcutta: 1863–77). English versions: M.L. Sandal (trans.) *The Mīmāṃsā-sūtra of Jaimini* (Allahabad: 1925); G. Jhā (trans.), *The Pūrva-Mīmāṃsā Sūtras of Jaimini* (Delhi: 1979). We quote from Sandal's translation, with modifications.
5. For a defense of the claim that the two *sūtras* were originally intended to form a single, united work, see A. Parpola, "On the Formation of the Mīmāṃsā and the Problems Concerning Jaimini," Part I, *Wiener Zeitschrift für die Kunde Südasiens* 25 (1981), 145–77 and Part II, *Wiener Zeitschrift für die Kunde Südasiens* 38 (1994), 293–308. J. Bronkhorst, "*Mīmāṃsāsūtra* and *Brahmasūtra*," *Journal of Indian Philosophy* 42 (2014), 463–9, argues against the idea.
6. J.-M. Verpoorten, *Mīmāṃsā Literature* (Wiesbaden: 1987), 5.
7. L. McCrea, "The Transformations of Mīmāṃsā in the Larger Context of Indian Philosophical Discourse," in E. Franco (ed.), *Periodization and Historiography of Indian Philosophy* (Vienna: 2013), 127–43, argues that the innovations of Kumārila and Prabhākara are driven by the need to respond to the Buddhist thinker Dignāga.
8. With caution: F.X. Clooney, *Thinking Ritually: Rediscovering the Pūrva Mīmāṃsā of Jaimini* (Vienna: 1990) accepts that Śabara's interpretation is vital as an aid to understanding the text, but warns against assuming that Śabara's position is always the same as Jaimini's.
9. See E. Freschi, "Action, Desire and Subjectivity in Prābhākara Mīmāṃsā," in I. Kuznetsova, J. Ganeri, and C. Ram-Prasad (eds), *Hindu and Buddhist Ideas in Dialogue: Self and No-Self, Dialogues in South Asian Traditions* (Farnham: 2012), 147–64, and "Did

Mīmāṃsā Authors Formulate a Theory of Action?" in N. Mirnig, P.-D. Szántó, and M. Williams (eds), *Puṣpikā: Tracing Ancient India Through Texts and Traditions* (Oxford: 2013), 151–72.

10. Actually, we recommend white wine, followed by broth, stirred slowly into the rice; finish with freshly grated parmesan cheese. Buon appetito!
11. V. Das, "Language of Sacrifice," *Man* 18 (1983), 445–62, at 449.
12. Clooney, *Thinking Ritually*, 161. See also F.X. Clooney, "Why the Veda Has No Author: Language as Ritual in Early Mīmāṃsā and Post-Modern Theology," *Journal of the American Academy of Religion* 55 (1987), 659–84, at 666.
13. As argued by Clooney, *Thinking Ritually*, 206–15.
14. Our thanks to Elisa Freschi for advice on the chapters on Mīmāṃsā.

Chapter 18

1. See P. Adamson, *Philosophy in the Islamic World: A History of Philosophy Without Any Gaps, Volume* 3 (Oxford: 2016), ch. 56.
2. We take this apt phrase from J. Taber, "What Did Kumārila Bhaṭṭa Mean by *Svataḥ Prāmāṇya?*" *Journal of the American Oriental Society* 112 (1992), 204–21, at 221.
3. J.-M. Verpoorten, *Mīmāṃsā Literature* (Wiesbaden: 1987), 8.
4. For this, see Taber, "What Did Kumārila Bhaṭṭa Mean by *Svataḥ Prāmāṇya?*" The two interpretations of Kumārila that follow are discussed by Taber, and go back to Umbekabhaṭṭa and Pārthasārathi.
5. Quotation from Taber, "What Did Kumārila Bhaṭṭa Mean by *Svataḥ Prāmāṇya?*" 215.
6. On this, see F.X. Clooney, "Why the Veda Has No Author: Language as Ritual in Early Mīmāṃsā and Post-Modern Theology," *Journal of the American Academy of Religion* 55 (1987), 659–84.
7. This complaint is made by Taber, "What Did Kumārila Bhaṭṭa Mean by *Svataḥ Prāmāṇya?*" 217.
8. This is even recognized in Mīmāṃsā as a distinct *pramāṇa*, called *abhāva*: absence of evidence is evidence of absence. Unsurprisingly, other schools did not agree with this rather bold principle.
9. J. Taber, "The Mīmāṃsā Theory of Self-Recognition," *Philosophy East and West* 40 (1990), 35–57.
10. You can tell a lot about a culture by the meaning it assigns to the syllable *go*: for ancient Indians, it meant "cow"; in Japan, it means a board game of almost infinite complexity and subtlety; for Americans, it's where you start when you are trying to build a monopoly.
11. O. Gächter, *Hermeneutics and Language in Pūrva Mīmāṃsā* (Delhi: 1983), 61, and P.M. Scharf, *The Denotation of Generic Terms in Ancient Indian Philosophy: Grammar, Nyāya and Mīmāṃsā* (Philadelphia: 1996), 201, for the universality of words and Śabara's use of the "cow" example.
12. This takes place through a process of "inclusion" and "exclusion," as if children are confirming hypotheses about what various words might mean. See H.S. Prasad, "The Context Principle of Meaning in Prabhākara Mīmāṃsā," *Philosophy East and West* 44 (1994), 317–46, at 319.
13. For a detailed discussion of this, see L. McCrea, "The Hierarchical Organization of Language in Mīmāṃsā Interpretive Theory," *Journal of Indian Philosophy* 28 (2000), 429–59.

14. On this, see M. Siderits, "The Prabhākara Mīmāṃsā Theory of Related Designation," in B.K. Matilal and J.L. Shaw (eds), *Analytic Philosophy in Comparative Perspective* (Dordrecht: 1985), 253–97; B.K. Matilal and P.K. Sen, "The Context Principle and Some Indian Controversies over Meaning," *Mind* 97 (1988), 73–97; J.A. Taber, "The Theory of the Sentence in Pūrva Mīmāṃsā and Western Philosophy," *Journal of Indian Philosophy* 17 (1989), 407–30; Prasad, "The Context Principle of Meaning."
15. Gächter, *Hermeneutics and Language*, 80.
16. V. Das, "Language of Sacrifice," *Man* 18 (1983), 445–62, at 454.
17. See also F.X. Clooney, "Pragmatism and Anti-Essentialism in the Construction of Dharma in *Mīmāṃsā Sūtras* 7.1.1–12," *Journal of Indian Philosophy* 32 (2004), 751–68, at 754, and Gächter, *Hermeneutics and Language*, 29–30; Scharf, *The Denotation of Generic Terms*, 203.
18. See G.P. Bhatt, *The Basic Ways of Knowing: An In-Depth Study of Kumārila's Contribution to Indian Epistemology* (Delhi: 1989), 154–5, 159–60, 182.

Chapter 19

1. For the historical evolution, see H. Nakamura, *A History of Early Vedānta Philosophy* (Delhi: 1983), with the dating of the *Vedānta-sūtra* given at 434–5. For a translation, see S. Radhakrishnan (trans.), *The Brahma Sūtra* (London: 1960) or G. Thibaut (trans.), *The Vedānta Sūtras of Bādarāyaṇa with the Commentary by Śaṅkara* (New York: 1962). We cite the *sūtra* by section number.
2. If you liked the many names of the *Sūtra*, you'll love the various alternative explanations for the name Vedānta, listed at Nakamura, *A History of Early Vedānta Philosophy*, 94–6.
3. F.X. Clooney, "Binding the Text: Vedānta as Philosophy and Commentary," in J.R. Timm (ed.), *Texts in Context: Traditional Hermeneutics in South Asia* (Albany: 1991), 47–68, at 49.
4. Here we agree with Clooney, "Binding the Text," who calls Vedānta "an exegesis *of* texts and a philosophy responsive *to* texts" (48), against the sort of reading expressed by e.g. Nakamura, *A History of Early Vedānta Philosophy*, 475: "the scriptures even had the power to make people abandon philosophical thought."
5. As noted in Chapter 17, a study of the relation between the two texts can be found in J. Bronkhorst, "*Mīmāṃsāsūtra* and *Brahmasūtra*," *Journal of Indian Philosophy* 42 (2014), 463–9. See also A. Parpola, "On the Formation of the Mīmāṃsā and the Problems Concerning Jaimini," *Wiener Zeitschrift für die Kunde Südasiens* 38 (1994), 293–308.
6. Note that in later texts the author is also called (rather generically) Vyāsa.
7. See Nakamura, *A History of Early Vedānta Philosophy*, 369–408. He sees Kāśakṛtsna as particularly close to the idea of "non-difference" that appears in Bādarāyaṇa and then becomes fundamental for Śaṅkara (372).

Chapter 20

1. *Great Forest Upaniṣad* §2.5, *Chāndogya Upaniṣad* §6.8, and *Muṇḍaka Upaniṣad* §2.2, translations from P. Olivelle (trans.), *The Early Upaniṣads* (New York: 1998). All three passages are cited in §1.1.4 of Śaṅkara's commentary on the *Vedānta-sūtra*, for which see V.H. Date (trans.), *Vedānta Explained: Śaṁkara's Commentary on the Brahma-sūtras* (Bombay: 1954). Abbreviated in this chapter as *Bhāṣya*.
2. H. Nakamura, *A History of Early Vedānta Philosophy*, part 1 (Delhi: 1983), 48–67 discusses the dating issue in depth and decides that Śaṅkara should be placed already in the first half of the century.

3. Cited from J. Lipner, "The Perils of Periodization, or How to Finesse History with Reference to Vedānta," in E. Franco (ed.), *Periodization and Historiography of Indian Philosophy* (Vienna: 2013), 145–69, at 155. For the commentary on the *Gītā*, see S. Gambhirananda (trans.), *Bhagavadgītā with the Commentary of Śaṅkarācārya* (Calcutta: 1984).
4. S. Mayeda, *Śaṅkara's Upadeśasāhasrī* (Tokyo: 1973), translated in E. Deutsch and J.A.B. van Buitenen, *A Source Book of Advaita Vedānta* (Honolulu: 1971), 124–50. Abbreviated in this chapter as *Upad*. The authorship of this text is disputed, but not its reliability as a synopsis of Advaita.
5. B.N.K. Sharma, *History of the Dvaita School of Vedānta and its Literature* (Delhi: 1981).
6. On whom, see D.H.H. Ingalls, "Bhāskara the Vedāntin," *Philosophy East and West* 17 (1967), 61–9.
7. For the importance of this, see D.H.H. Ingalls, "Saṁkara's Arguments against the Buddhists," *Philosophy East and West* 3 (1954), 291–306.
8. T.M.P. Mahedavan, *Gauḍapāda: A Study in Early Advaita* (Madras: 1952); Deutsch and van Buitenen, *Source Book*, 119–21.
9. N. Isayeva, *Shankara and Indian Philosophy* (Albany: 1993), 49.
10. For a discussion of the place of action and responsibility in Śaṅkara, see F.X. Clooney, "Evil, Divine Omnipotence, and Human Freedom: Vedānta's Theology of Karma," *Journal of Religion* 69 (1989), 53–48.
11. For the history of this aspect of Advaita, see S. Timalsina, *Consciousness in Indian Philosophy: The Advaita Doctrine of Awareness Only* (London: 2009).
12. See W. Fasching, "On the Advaitic Identification of Self and Consciousness," in I. Kuznetsova, J. Ganeri, and C. Ram-Prasad (eds), *Hindu and Buddhist Ideas in Dialogue: Self and No-Self* (London: 2012), 165–80.
13. For what follows, see Ingalls, "Saṁkara's Arguments against the Buddhists," and F. Whaling, "Śaṅkara and Buddhism," *Journal of Indian Philosophy* 7 (1979), 1–42.
14. Isayeva, *Shankara and Indian Philosophy*, 81.
15. See further B. Carr, "Śaṅkara on Memory and the Continuity of the Self," *Religious Studies* 36 (2000), 419–34.
16. Ingalls, "Saṁkara's Arguments against the Buddhists," 303–4.
17. Nakamura, *A History*, 114.
18. Whaling, "Śaṅkara and Buddhism," 24.

Chapter 21

1. All citations in the main text are section numbers from Bhartṛhari's *Vākyapadīya*, available in English translation in multiple volumes by K.A.S. Iyer. For this claim about grammar, see also J. Bronkhorst, "Studies on Bhartṛhari 7: Grammar as the Door to Liberation," *Annals of the Bhandarkar Oriental Research Institute* 76 (1995), 97–106.
2. For the history of grammatical works, see H. Sharfe, *A History of Indian Literature, vol. V.2: Grammatical Literature* (Wiesbaden: 1977); J. Bronkhorst, "On the History of Pāṇinian Grammar in the Early Centuries Following Patañjali," *Journal of Indian Philosophy* 11 (1983), 357–412; H.G. Coward and K.K. Raja (eds), *Encyclopedia of Indian Philosophies, Vol. V: The Philosophy of the Grammarians* (Delhi: 1990).
3. This is doubted by J. Bronkhorst, "Études sur Bhartṛhari 1: L'auteur et la date de la Vṛtti," *Bulletin d'Études Indiennes* 6 (1988), 105–43.
4. Bronkhorst, "Grammar as the Door to Liberation," 98.

5. For his position relative to Vedānta, see J. Bronkhorst, "Studies on Bhartṛhari 9: Bhartṛhari and his Vedic Tradition," in M. Chaturvedi (ed.), *Bhartṛhari: Language, Thought and Reality* (Delhi: 2009), 99–117.
6. N. Isayeva, *From Early Vedānta to Kashmir Shaivism* (Albany: 1995), 95–6.
7. A. Akamatsu, "*Pratibhā* and the Meaning of the Sentence in Bhartṛhari's *Vākyapadīya*," *Asiatische Studien* 47 (1993), 37–43.
8. For discussion, see Isayeva, *From Early Vedānta*, 85; B.M. Matilal, *Epistemology, Logic, and Grammar in Indian Philosophical Analysis* (New Delhi: 2005), 9–10.
9. As discussed at length in J. Bronkhorst, *Language and Reality: On an Episode in Indian Thought*, trans. M.S. Allen and R. Raghunathan (Leiden: 2011).
10. For the following two readings, see, respectively, R. Herzberger, *Bhartṛhari and the Buddhists: An Essay in the Development of Fifth and Sixth Century Indian Thought* (Dordrecht: 1986) and J. Bronkhorst, "Studies on Bhartṛhari 3: Bhartṛhari on Sphoṭa and Universals," *Asiatische Studien* 45 (1991), 5–18.
11. For this question, see A. Aklujkar, "The Word is the World: Nondualism in Indian Philosophy of Language," *Philosophy East and West* 51 (2001), 452–73, especially 462–3. Aklujar concludes that for Bhartṛhari, dualism does break down upon achieving liberation.
12. J. Bronkhorst, "The Peacock's Egg: Bhartṛhari on Language and Reality," *Philosophy East and West* 51 (2001), 474–91, and Isayeva, *From Early Vedānta*, 103–4.
13. Isayeva, *From Early Vedānta*, 82–3.
14. Bronkhorst, "Grammar as the Door to Liberation," 102.
15. Herzberger, *Bhartṛhari and the Buddhists*, 54.

Chapter 22

1. For lists, see G.J. Larson and R.S. Bhattacharya (eds), *Encyclopedia of Indian Philosophies, Vol. IV: Sāṃkhya, a Dualist Tradition in Indian Philosophy* (Delhi: 1987), 49, 53, and 56–9.
2. There are numerous translations available, for instance T.G. Mainkar (trans.), *The Sāṃkhyakārikā of Īśvarakṛṣṇa with the Commentary of Gauḍapāda* (Poona: 1972); a full translation is also included in S. Radhakrishnan and C.A. Moore, *A Sourcebook in Indian Philosophy* (Princeton: 1957). Cited in the main text by section number.
3. Citations from G.J. Larson, *Classical Sāṃkhya: An Interpretation of its History and Meaning* (Delhi: 1979), 116, 122.
4. A point made by D. Krishna, "Is Īśvara Kṛṣṇa's *Sāṃkhya Kārikā* Really Sāṃkhya?" *Philosophy East and West* 18 (1968), 194–204.
5. We take this phrase from K.B. Ramakrishna Rao, "The Guṇas of Prakṛti According to the Sāṃkhya Philosophy," *Philosophy East and West* 13 (1963), 61–71, at 63.
6. As explored in J.A.B. van Buitenen, "Studies in Sāṃkhya (II)," *Journal of the American Oriental Society* 77 (1957), 15–25.
7. This double aspect of the *guṇas* is emphasized by Larson, *Classical Sāṃkhya*, 163–4.
8. *Mahābhārata* §12.294.32, cited from Larson, *Classical Sāṃkhya*, 119.
9. For the possible pre-history of this concept, see J.A.B. van Buitenen, "Studies in Sāṃkhya (III)," *Journal of the American Oriental Society* 77 (1957), 88–107.
10. As noticed by Larson, *Classical Sāṃkhya*, 76.
11. We here summarize the argument of J. Bronkhorst, "The Qualities of Sāṃkhya," *Wiener Zeitschrift für die Kunde Südasiens* 38 (1994), 309–22.
12. For more on this issue, see R.J. Parrot, "The Problem of Sāṃkhya *Tattvas*," *Journal of Indian Philosophy* 14 (1986), 55–77 and the critical response by M. Hulin, "Reinterpreting *Ahaṃkāra*

as a Possible Way of Solving the Riddle of Sāṃkhya Metaphysics," *Asiatische Studien* 53 (1999), 713–22.

13. Larson and Bhattacharya, *Sāṃkhya*, 121.
14. B.D. Burke, "Transcendence in Classical Sāṃkhya," *Philosophy East and West* 38 (1988), 19–29, at 22.

Chapter 23

1. On them, see J. Filliozat, *The Classical Doctrine of Indian Medicine* (Delhi: 1964), 86–9.
2. For passages in translation from both works, see Dominik Wujastyk, *The Roots of Āyurveda* (New Delhi: 1998). Cited in the main text by page number. A third ancient treatise, the *Bhela-saṃhitā*, is retained only in one, incomplete manuscript.
3. Dagmar Wujastyk, *Well-Mannered Medicine: Medical Ethics and Etiquette in Classical Ayurveda* (Oxford: 2012), 113.
4. On this tension, see M.G. Weiss, "*Caraka Saṃhitā* on the Doctrine of Karma," in W. Doniger O'Flaherty (ed.), *Karma and Rebirth in Classical Indian Traditions* (Berkeley: 1980), 90–115.
5. See Weiss, "*Caraka Saṃhitā* on the Doctrine of Karma," 99. For more on the combination of medical theory with traditional ideas like demons, see Filliozat, *The Classical Doctrine*, 97.
6. See Wujastyk, *Well-Mannered Medicine*, 40.
7. H. Scharfe, "The Doctrine of the Three Humors in Traditional Indian Medicine and the Alleged Antiquity of Tamil Siddha Medicine," *Journal of the American Oriental Society* 119 (1999), 609–29, at 620.
8. K. Zysk, "The Science of Respiration and the Doctrine of the Bodily Winds in Ancient India," *Journal of the American Oriental Society* 113 (1993), 198–213.
9. Thus Wujastyk, *The Roots of Āyurveda*, 115–16, talks of a "two plus one" humoral theory.
10. For a detailed argument to this effect, see Scharfe, "The Doctrine of the Three Humors." See also G.J. Meulenbeld, "The Characteristics of a Doṣa," *Journal of the European Āyurvedic Society* 2 (1992), 1–5.
11. See P. Adamson, *Philosophy in the Hellenistic and Roman Worlds: A History of Philosophy Without Any Gaps, Volume 2* (Oxford: 2015), ch. 19.
12. Wujastyk, *Well-Mannered Medicine*, 118.
13. See Dominik Wujastyk, "Medicine and *Dharma*," *Journal of Indian Philosophy* 32 (2004), 831–42, at 833, and Wujastyk, *Well-Mannered Medicine*, 133–4.
14. Wujastyk, *Well-Mannered Medicine*, 55, 177.
15. On this, see Filliozat, *The Classical Doctrine*, 2–16.
16. On the topic, see further K. Zysk, *Religious Healing in the Veda* (Philadelphia: 1985).
17. This is the thesis of K. Zysk, *Asceticism and Healing in Ancient India: Medicine in the Buddhist Monastery* (New York: 1991), whose argument we summarize in what follows.
18. Dominik Wujastyk, "The Path to Liberation through Yogic Mindfulness in Early Āyurveda," in D.G. White (ed.), *Yoga in Practice* (Princeton: 2012), 31–42, at 32. The passage is also mentioned by Zysk, *Asceticism and Healing*, 30.
19. Zysk, *Asceticism and Healing*, 34, quoting *Dīgha-nikāya* §22.4–5.
20. Zysk, *Asceticism and Healing*, 37 and 88.
21. The classic study of this question is Filliozat, *The Classical Doctrine*; see further this volume, Chapter 47.

Chapter 24

1. There are many translations into English. Some recent ones include G.J. Larson and R.S. Bhattacharya, *Yoga: India's Philosophy of Meditation* (Delhi: 2008); C. Chapple, *Yoga and the Luminous* (Albany: 2008); E.F. Bryant, *The Yoga Sūtras of Patañjali* (New York: 2009); D. Raveh, *Exploring the Yogasūtra: Philosophy and Translation* (London: 2012). An older translation is also reprinted in S. Radhakrishnan and C.A. Moore, *A Sourcebook in Indian Philosophy* (Princeton: 1957). We cite the text by chapter and *sūtra* number.
2. Another ancient tradition claims that "Caraka," author of the medical text discussed in the previous chapter, was also Patañjali. See J. Filliozat, *The Classical Doctrine of Indian Medicine* (Delhi: 1964), 22.
3. P.A. Maas (ed.), *Sāmadhipāda: The First Chapter of the Pātañjalayogaśāstra for the First Time Critically Edited* (Aachen: 2006). For earlier studies of the question, see T.S. Rukmani, "The Problem of the Authorship of the *Yogasūtrabhāṣyavivaraṇa*," *Journal of Indian Philosophy* 20 (1992), 419–23; J. Bronkhorst, "Patañjali and the Yoga Sūtras," *Studien zur Indologie und Iranistik* 10 (1985), 191–212. Maas' conclusions shed doubt on earlier attempts to detect doctrinal differences between the *sūtra* and *bhāṣya*, for instance C.K. Chapple, "Reading Patañjali without Vyāsa: A Critique of Four *Yoga Sūtra* Passages," *Journal of the American Academy of Religion* 62 (1994), 85–105.
4. M. Burley, *Classical Sāṃkhya and Yoga: An Indian Metaphysics of Experience* (London: 2007), 45, criticizes interpreters who imply that this shared goal is somehow rationalist in Sāṃkhya yet mystical in Yoga.
5. On the concept, see D. Carpenter, "Practice Makes Perfect: The Role of Practice (*abhyāsa*) in Pātañjala Yoga," in I. Whicher and D. Carpenter (eds), *Yoga: The Indian Tradition* (London: 2003), 25–50, the title of which we borrowed for this chapter.
6. This point is made well by Carpenter, "Practice Makes Perfect," 35.
7. As noted by G.J. Larson, "Classical Yoga as Neo-Sāṃkhya: A Chapter in the History of Indian Philosophy," *Asiatische Studien* 53 (1999), 723–32, at 728.
8. Here we summarize the analysis given by C. Framarin, "Habit and Karmic Result in the *Yogaśāstra*," in J. Ganeri (ed.), *The Oxford Handbook of Indian Philosophy* (Oxford: 2017), 133–51.
9. I. Whicher, "Yoga and Freedom: A Reconsideration of Patañjali's Classical Yoga," *Philosophy East and West* 48 (1998), 272–322; *The Integrity of the Yoga Darśana: A Reconsideration of Classical Yoga* (Delhi: 2000); and "The Integration of Spirit (*Puruṣa*) and Matter (*Prakṛti*) in the *Yoga Sūtra*," in I. Whicher and D. Carpenter (eds), *Yoga: The Indian Tradition* (London: 2003), 51–69. In the latter volume, the piece by L.W. Pflueger follows a more dualist reading.
10. Whicher, "Classical Sāṃkhya, Yoga," 786.
11. M.S.A. Ferraz, "Some Remarks on the *Yogasūtra*," *Philosophy East and West* 59 (2009), 249–62, at 254.
12. On this passage, see also Burley, *Classical Sāṃkhya and Yoga*, 50.
13. This is of course Whicher's interpretation: "Yoga and Freedom," 278.
14. T.S. Rukmani, "*Dharmamegha-Samādhi* in the Yogasūtras of Patañjali: A Critique," *Philosophy East and West* 57 (2007), 131–9.

Chapter 25

1. Citations to Vātsyāyana and the *Nyāya-sūtra* itself are to book, section, and chapter numbers. See the translation in M. Gangopadhyaya, *Gautama's Nyāyasūtra with Vātsyāyana's Commentary* (Calcutta: 1982).

2. For discussion, see S. Phillips, *Epistemology in Classical India: The Knowledge Sources of the Nyāya School* (London: 2012), ch. 2.
3. Here we borrow the formulation of M. Dasti, "Parasitism and Disjunctivism in Nyāya Epistemology," *Philosophy East and West* 62 (2012), 1–15, at 8, and 4 for the following quotation from Uddyotakara.
4. B.K. Matilal, *A History of Indian Literature: Nyāya-Vaiśeṣika* (Wiesbaden: 1977), 85. Here he is thinking of Dignāga, on whom see further in this volume, Chapters 42–4.
5. For this distinction as a response to the paradox of inquiry, see Chapter 16.
6. On this, see V.A. Van Bijlert, *Epistemology and Spiritual Authority: The Development of Epistemology and Logic in the Old Nyāya and the Buddhist School of Epistemology* (Vienna: 1989), 11–12.
7. This example is formalized using the five-limbed syllogism by Van Bijlert, *Epistemology and Spiritual Authority*, 29.
8. On this, see S. Bagchi, *Inductive Reasoning: A Study of Tarka and its Role in Indian Logic* (Calcultta: 1953); K.H. Potter, *Encyclopedia of Indian Philosophies, vol. 2: Nyāya-Vaiśeṣika* (Delhi: 1977), 206–7; V.K. Bharadwaja, "A Theory of Tarka Sentences," *Philosophy and Phenomenological Research* 41 (1981), 532–46; and L. Davis, "*Tarka* in the Nyāya Theory of Inference," *Journal of Indian Philosophy* 9 (1981), 105–20.
9. See Phillips, *Epistemology in Classical India*, 21.
10. For discussion, see Davis, "*Tarka* in the Nyāya Theory," 112–15.

Chapter 26

1. A. Thakur (ed.), *Nyāyavārttika* (Delhi: 1997), 28–9.
2. See S. Phillips, *Epistemology in Classical India: The Knowledge Sources of the Nyāya School* (London: 2012), 47–8. For a related issue in logic, see J.L. Shaw, "The Nyāya on Cognition and Negation," *Journal of Indian Philosophy* 8 (1980), 279–302.
3. See also the discussion of this case in Vātsyāyana's prologue to his commentary; the relevant *sūtra* with commentary is translated at B.K. Matilal, *A History of Indian Literature: Nyāya-Vaśeṣika* (Wiesbaden: 1977), 83–4.
4. For translation of relevant passages and discussion, see C.F. Oliver, "Perception in Early Nyāya: *Nyāyabhāṣya* and *Nyāyavārttika* on *Nyāyasūtra* 1,1,4," *Journal of Indian Philosophy* 6 (1978), 243–66, at 251–5. For the mechanism of vision, see *Nyāya-sūtra* 3.1.33–51.
5. On this, see Phillips, *Epistemology in Classical India*, 35–8.
6. See V.A. Van Bijlert, *Epistemology and Spiritual Authority: The Development of Epistemology and Logic in the Old Nyāya and the Buddhist School of Epistemology* (Vienna: 1989), 7.
7. See B.K. Matilal, *Perception* (Oxford: 1986), 201–8; B.K. Matilal, "A Realist View of Perception," in *Mind, Language and World* (Delhi: 2002), 182–200; A. Vaidya, "Nyāya Perceptual Theory: Disjunctivism or Anti-Individualism?" *Philosophy East and West* 63 (2013), 562–85.
8. Later commentators feel a tension within Gautama's definition, so they reinterpret the demand as referring to a distinct variety of "conception-loaded" or propositional perception, such as seeing something *as* a giraffe, as opposed to merely seeing it with no concept imposed.

Chapter 27

1. See also the summaries in V.A. Van Bijlert, *Epistemology and Spiritual Authority: The Development of Epistemology and Logic in the Old Nyāya and the Buddhist School of Epistemology*

(Vienna: 1989), 10–14, and S. Phillips, *Epistemology in Classical India: The Knowledge Sources of the Nyāya School* (London: 2012), ch. 4.

2. For more on fallacies, see N. Bandopadhyay, *The Concept of Logical Fallacies* (Calcutta: 1977); A.B. Keith, *Indian Logic and Atomism* (New Delhi: 1977), 131–57; P.P. Gokhale, *Inference and Fallacies Discussed in Ancient Indian Logic* (Delhi: 1992).
3. Actually, before giving this good example of a problematic parallel, Vātsyāyana first cites a tangible but eternal entity, namely an atom. Unfortunately, this looks logically irrelevant: how things are with tangible objects says nothing about how things are with the intangibles. He may be thinking that if a property P (tangible) is compatible with property Q (eternal), it cannot be that the property not-P (intangible) is a sure sign of Q. But this rule would need further justification.
4. See P. Adamson, *Philosophy in the Hellenistic and Roman Worlds: A History of Philosophy Without Any Gaps, Volume 2* (Oxford: 2015), ch. 18.
5. The fallacy known to the Latin West as *petitio principii*, the fault of "begging the question," where one takes as a premise the very fact one is trying to prove, is a special case of the indecisive fallacy.

Chapter 28

1. For Nyāya as a form of dualism, see K.K. Chakrabarti, *Classical Indian Philosophy of Mind: The Nyāya Dualist Tradition* (Albany: 1999).
2. K.K. Chakrabarti and C. Chakrabarti, "Towards Dualism: The Nyāya-Vaiśeṣika Way," *Philosophy East and West* 41 (1991), 477–91, at 480. They also note that Uddyotakara gives an "elimination" argument to show that mental qualities cannot reside in bodily elements, in space, etc., and so must reside in a self since it is the only remaining candidate.
3. J. Tuske, "Being in Two Minds: The Divided Mind in the *Nyaya-sūtras*," *Asian Philosophy* 9 (1999), 229–38, at 234. See also W. Halbfass, *On Being and What There Is: Classical Vaiśeṣika and the History of Indian Ontology* (Albany: 1992), 104. For a strikingly similar argument, see Plato, *Theaetetus* 185c–e.
4. For privacy of mental events, see Chakrabarti and Chakrabarti, "Towards Dualism," 482; K.H. Potter, *Encyclopedia of Indian Philosophies, Vol. 2: Nyāya-Vaiśeṣika* (Delhi: 1977), 96. For the denial of transparency, see Tuske, "Being in Two Minds," 235.
5. A classic study for this idea in contemporary psychology is D.E. Broadbent, *Perception and Communication* (Oxford: 1958).
6. Vātsyāyana uses a very similar line of reasoning against the Buddhist reduction of a person to a stream of consciousness (*Nyāya-bhāṣya* 3.2.39).

Chapter 29

1. P. Adamson, *Al-Kindī* (New York: 2007), 173.
2. W. Halbfass, *On Being and What There Is: Classical Vaiśeṣika and the History of Indian Ontology* (Delhi: 1992), 81.
3. Halbfass, *On Being*, 149.
4. A translation can be found in A. Thakur, *Origin and Development of the Vaiśeṣika System* (Delhi: 2003). For another version, along with Praśastapāda's *Padārthadharmasaṃgraha*, see N. Sinha (trans.), *The Vaiśeṣika Sūtras of Kaṇāda* (Allahabad: 1923).
5. In fact precisely the same argument was given in Islamic theology, and refuted with this same answer by Averroes (who ascribes to the atomist the example of an elephant and

an ant, rather than a mountain and a mustard seed). See I.Y. Najjar (trans.), *Faith and Reason in Islam: Averroes' Exposition of Religious Arguments* (Oxford: 2001), 22.

6. On this, see P. Adamson, *Classical Philosophy: A History of Philosophy Without Any Gaps, Volume 1* (Oxford: 2014), ch. 8.
7. For Scotus' view, see P. Adamson, *Medieval Philosophy: A History of Philosophy Without Any Gaps, Volume 4* (Oxford: 2019), ch. 51.
8. Halbfass, *On Being*, 69.

Chapter 30

1. On this topic, see U. Mishra, *The Conception of Matter According to Nyāya-Vaiśeṣika* (Allahabad: 1936); S. Bhaduri, *Studies in Nyāya-Vaiśeṣika Metaphysics* (Poona: 1975), ch. 1; K.H. Potter, *Encyclopedia of Indian Philosophies, Vol. 2: Nyāya-Vaiśeṣika* (Delhi: 1977), 74–9; B.K. Matilal, *Epistemology, Logic, and Grammar in Indian Philosophical Analysis* (Oxford: 2006), ch. 2.
2. B. Russell, *The Principles of Mathematics* (Cambridge: 1903), Vol. 1, 141.
3. J. Westerhoff, *The Golden Age of Indian Buddhist Philosophy* (Oxford: 2018), 73–83, 231–5.
4. B.K. Matilal, *Logic, Language and Reality* (Delhi: 1985), 287.
5. As noted by B.K. Matilal, "Causality in the Nyāya-Vaiśeṣika School," *Philosophy East and West* 25 (1975), 41–8, at 42.
6. See on this, P.K. Sen, "The Nyāya-Vaiśeṣika Theory of Variegated Colour (*citrarūpa*): Some Vexed Problems," in *Epistemology, Logic and Ontology after Matilal* (Shimla: 1996), 151–72.
7. D. Lewis, *On the Plurality of Worlds* (Oxford: 1986), 201–3.

Chapter 31

1. See P. Adamson, *Philosophy in the Hellenistic and Roman Worlds: A History of Philosophy Without Any Gaps, Volume 2* (Oxford: 2015), ch. 28.
2. For all this, see D. Pingree, "Astronomy and Astrology in India and Iran," *Isis* 54 (1963), 229–46.
3. Cited by D. Pingree, "The Purāṇas and Jyotiḥśāstra: Astronomy," *Journal of the American Oriental Society* 110 (1990), 274–80, at 278.
4. L. González-Reimann, "Time in the *Mahābhārata* and the Time of the *Mahābhārata*," in S. Pollock (ed.), *Epic and Argument in Sanskrit Literary History* (New Delhi: 2010), 66; for a more detailed study, see his *The Mahābhārata and the Yugas: India's Great Epic Poem and the Hindu System of World Ages* (New York: 2002). A useful overview of the topic in general is L. González-Reimann, "Cosmic Cycles, Cosmology, and Cosmography," in K.A. Jacobsen, H. Basu, and A. Malinar (eds), *Brill's Encyclopedia of Hinduism* (Leiden: 2009), 411–28.
5. As J. Bronkhorst has emphasized in an unpublished paper, "Cyclical Time in India."
6. González-Reimann, "Cosmic Cycles," 413.
7. H. Coward, "Time (*Kāla*) in Bhartṛhari's *Vākypadīya*," *Journal of Indian Philosophy* 10 (1982), 277–87, at 277. We also draw on this study for the following discussion of time in Bhartṛhari.
8. See further G. Cardona, "A Path Still Taken: Some Early Indian Arguments Concerning Time," *Journal of the American Oriental Society* 111 (1991), 445–64 for discussions of time in Sanskrit grammarians, including Bhartṛhari.
9. For surveys of Indian philosophy of time, see S. Schayer, *Contributions to the Problem of Time in Indian Philosophy* (Kraków: 1938); K.K. Mandal, *A Comparative Study of the Concepts*

of Space and Time in Indian Thought (Varanasi: 1968); A. Malinar, *Time in India: Concepts and Practices* (New Delhi: 2007).

10. K.K. Klostermaier, "Time in Patañjali's Yogasūtra," *Philosophy East and West* 34 (1981), 205–10; H.S. Prasad, "Time and Change in Sāṃkhya-Yoga," *Journal of Indian Philosophy* 12 (1984), 35–49.
11. See S. Bhaduri, *Studies in Nyāya-Vaiśeṣika Metaphysics* (Poona: 1947), 214–25.
12. His "arrow" paradox, discussed in P. Adamson, *Classical Philosophy: A History of Philosophy Without Any Gaps, Volume 1* (Oxford: 2014), ch. 7.
13. S. Sen (1966), "The Impetus Theory of the Vaiśeṣika," *Indian Journal for the History of Science* 1, 34–45; B. Subbarayappa, "An Estimate of the Vaiśeṣika Sūtra in the History of Science," *Indian Journal for the History of Science* 2 (1968), 24–34.
14. See P. Adamson, *Philosophy in the Hellenistic and Roman Worlds: A History of Philosophy Without Any Gaps, Volume 2* (Oxford: 2015), ch. 38.

Chapter 32

1. The *sūtras*, key remarks by commentators, and verses are cited from R. Bhattacharya, "Cārvāka Fragments: A New Collection," *Journal of Indian Philosophy* 30 (2002), 597–640, reprinted in R. Bhattacharya, *Studies on the Cārvāka/Lokāyata* (London: 2011).
2. Quoted from H. Blochmann (ed.), *The Aīn-i Akbarī* (Calcutta: 1873–1907), Vol. 3, 217. By sheer chance the same thought was put forward by the early 1970s soul group the Undisputed Truth, who sang, "you make your own heaven and hell right here on earth."
3. Bhattacharya, *Studies on the Cārvāka*, 28, 45.
4. Bhattacharya, *Studies on the Cārvāka*, 29, and 45–9 for the following problem about the reality of this world.
5. Bhattacharya, *Studies on the Cārvāka*, 165–6.
6. Bhattacharya, *Studies on the Cārvāka*, 168.
7. See P. Adamson, *Philosophy in the Hellenistic and Roman Worlds: A History of Philosophy Without Any Gaps, Volume 2* (Oxford: 2015), ch. 5.
8. This tension is pointed out by Bhattacharya, *Studies on the Cārvāka*, 106, 154.
9. J.M. Koller, "Skepticism in Early Indian Thought," *Philosophy East and West* 27 (1977), 155–64, at 156.
10. Here we follow P. Gokhale, "The Cārvāka Theory of *Pramāṇas*: A Restatement," *Philosophy East and West* 43 (1993), 675–82, whose view is consonant with that of Bhattacharya, *Studies on the Cārvāka*, 58, 61, 150; R. Bhattacharya, "What the Cārvākas Originally Meant: More on the Commentators on the *Cārvākasūtra*," *Journal of Indian Philosophy* 38 (2010), 529–42.
11. Bhattacharya, *Studies on the Cārvāka*, 157.
12. For this example, see Bhattacharya, *Studies on the Cārvāka*, 58.
13. It also appears in the *Mahābhārata*. For details and texts, see Bhattacharya, *Studies on the Cārvāka*, 175–84.
14. Translation taken from Bhattacharya, *Studies on the Cārvāka*, 178.
15. As noted by D. Chatterjee, "Skepticism and Indian Philosophy," *Philosophy East and West* 27 (1977), 195–209, at 198.
16. For details, see Adamson, *Philosophy in the Hellenistic and Roman Worlds*, ch. 18.
17. This point is made by Koller, "Skepticism," 156.

Chapter 33

1. P. Geach, *Mental Acts: Their Content and their Objects* (London: 1957), 117.
2. This parallel is explored in J. Ganeri, "Emergentisms, Ancient and Modern," *Mind* 120 (2011), 671–703. On emergentism in modern-day philosophy, see e.g. P. Clayton and P. Davies (eds), *The Re-Emergence of Emergence* (Oxford: 2006); M. Bedau and P. Humphreys (eds), *Emergence: Contemporary Readings in Philosophy and Science* (Cambridge, MA: 2008); C. Macdonald and G. Macdonald (eds), *Emergence in Mind* (Oxford: 2010).
3. See Ganeri, "Emergentisms," 689–89 and 697.
4. R. Bhattacharya, *Studies on the Cārvāka/Lokāyata* (London: 2011), 28.
5. See M.O. Walshe, *The Long Discourses of the Buddha: A Translation of the Dīgha Nikāya* (Boston: 1995), 351–68.
6. Compare *Chāndogya Upaniṣad* §6.12.1–2, with a much less alarming description of a banyan fruit being dissected in search of its inner essence.
7. Translated in W. Bollée, *The Story of Paesi (Paesi-kahāṇayaṃ): Soul and Body in Ancient India. A Dialogue on Materialism* (Wiesbaden: 2002), with the following exchange at 147.
8. The same declension *bhūtebhyaḥ* can also stand for the dative case, in which case it would mean something like "for the elements" instead of "from them." This possibility was exploited by the commentator Bhaṭṭa Udbhaṭṭa to give the *sūtra* an entirely different meaning.
9. T.H. Huxley, "On the Hypothesis that Animals are Automata, and its History," *The Fortnightly Review* 16 (1874), 555–80. We take the reference from William Robinson's article on "Epiphenomalism" in the online *Stanford Encyclopedia of Philosophy.*
10. For more detailed discussion, see J. Ganeri, *The Self* (Oxford: 2012), 112–26.
11. *Great Forest Upaniṣad* §2.4.12, at Olivelle, *Upaniṣads*, 29.

Chapter 34

1. For recent surveys of ancient Buddhist thought, see A. Carpenter, *Indian Buddhist Philosophy* (Durham: 2014); J. Westerhoff, *The Golden Age of Indian Buddhist Philosophy* (Oxford: 2018).
2. B. Pesala, *The Debate of King Milinda: An Abridgement of the Milinda Pañha* (Delhi: 1998), §2.1.
3. On this group, see Y. Karunadasa, *The Theravāda Abhidhamma: Its Inquiry Into the Nature of Conditioned Reality* (Hong Kong: 2010).
4. For a useful overview of the emergence and doctrines of the Mahāyāna, see P. Harvey, *An Introduction to Buddhism: Teachings, History and Practices* (Cambridge: 2013), chs 4–6.
5. Har Dayal, *The Bodhisattva Doctrine in Buddhist Sanskrit Literature* (London: 1932); D. Keown, *The Nature of Buddhist Ethics* (London: 1992).
6. E. Conze, *Buddhism: A Short History* (Oxford: 2008), 30; Harvey, *Introduction*, 162.
7. Madhyamaka itself is seen as later subdividing into the Prāsaṅga and Svātantrika branches, which roughly speaking are distinguished by whether or not they advance theses of their own (Svātantrika) or produce only destructive arguments and accept a conventional understanding of reality without further analysis (Prāsaṅga). For the distinction, see M. Siderits, *Studies in Buddhist Philosophy* (Oxford: 2016), 31–3.
8. For the latter, see T. Watters, *On Yuan Chwang's Travels in India*, 2 vols (London: 1904–5).
9. In addition to those just mentioned, important later Jaina philosophers include Akalaṅka (eighth century), Vidyānandin (*c.*940), Hemacandra (1089–1172), and Vādideva Sūri (twelfth century).

10. P. Balcerowicz (ed.), *Jaina Epistemology in Historical and Comparative Perspective* (Stuttgart: 2000).
11. *Pravacanasāra* §2.22–3. See J. Soni, "*Dravya, guṇa* and *paryāya* in Jaina Thought," *Journal of Indian Philosophy* 19 (1991), 75–88, at 78.

Chapter 35

1. This translation is taken from J.L. Garfield, "Dependent Arising and the Emptiness of Emptiness: Why Did Nāgārjuna Start with Causation?" *Philosophy East and West* 44 (1994), 219–50. Translations of the entire work include S. Katsura and M. Siderits, *Nāgārjuna's Middle Way: Mūla-madhyamaka-kārikā* (Somerville, MA: 2013) and, from its Tibetan version, J.L. Garfield, *The Fundamental Wisdom of the Middle Way: Nāgārjuna's Mūlamadhyamakakārikā* (New York: 1995). We also cite below from *Dispeller of Disputes* (*Vigraha-vyāvartanī*); see K. Bhattacharya, E.H. Johnston, and A. Kunst, *The Dialectical Method of Nāgārjuna: Vigrahavyāvartanī* (Delhi: 1986), and more recently, J. Westerhoff, *The Dispeller of Disputes: Nāgārjuna's Vigrahavyāvartanī* (Oxford: 2010). We refer to the two works by chapter and verse number, with the abbreviations *MK* and *VV*.
2. On the difficult issue of when and where he lived, see I. Mabbett, "The Problem of the Historical Nāgārjuna Revisited," *Journal of the American Oriental Society* 118 (1998), 332–46.
3. For this as a source of the contrast between the real and the merely conventional, see M. Siderits, *Studies in Buddhist Philosophy* (Oxford: 2016), 25.
4. See J. Westerhoff, *Nāgārjuna's Madhyamaka: A Philosophical Introduction* (Oxford: 2009), 19; J. Garfield, *Engaging Buddhism: Why It Matters to Philosophy* (Oxford: 2015), 61–71.
5. See P. Williams, "On the Abhidharma Ontology," *Journal of Indian Philosophy* 9 (1981), 227–57.
6. R.H. Robinson, "Did Nāgārjuna Really Refute All Philosophical Views?" *Philosophy East and West* 22 (1972), 325–31, at 330.
7. Siderits, *Studies in Buddhist Philosophy*, 39, 94–5. E. Chinn, "Nāgārjuna's Fundamental Doctrine of Pratītyasamutpāda," *Philosophy East and West* 51 (2001), 54–72, at 62, sees a particular target in Sarvāstivāda Buddhism, since this school gives the *dharmas* enduring, unchanging essences. See also Westerhoff, *Nāgārjuna's Madhyamaka*, 24.
8. J. Westerhoff, "On the Nihilist Interpretation of Madhyamaka," *Journal of Indian Philosophy* 44 (2016), 337–76, at 338.
9. B.K. Matilal, *Epistemology, Logic and Grammar in Indian Philosophical Analysis* (The Hague: 1971), 152. See also D.S. Ruegg, 'Mathematical and Linguistic Models in Indian Thought: The Case of Zero and *Śūnyatā*," in D.S. Ruegg, *The Buddhist Philosophy of the Middle: Essays on Indian and Tibetan Madhyamaka* (Boston: 2010).
10. On this part of *MK*, see Garfield, "Dependent Arising," and ch. 2.3 of Siderits, *Studies in Buddhist Philosophy*.
11. From the introduction to M. Sprung (trans.), *Lucid Exposition of the Middle Way* (Abingdon: 2008), 5.
12. This line of interpretation is represented by J.L. Garfield, e.g. in the commentary on his translation of *MK*, in Garfield, "Dependent Arising," and in J.L. Garfield and G. Priest, "Nāgārjuna and the Limits of Thought," *Philosophy East and West* 53 (2003), 1–21, which alludes to the precedent of Candrakīrti's conventionalist reading at 5.
13. For a reading emphasizing this absence of doctrine, see G. Ferraro, "Grasping Snakes and Touching Elephants: A Rejoinder to Garfield and Siderits," *Journal of Indian Philosophy* 42 (2014), 451–62.

14. Westerhoff, "On the Nihilist Interpretation," 339.
15. Westerhoff, *Nāgārjuna's Madhyamaka*, 45.
16. Our thanks to Rafal Stepien for helpful comments on this and the following chapters.

Chapter 36

1. *Mahābhāṣya* §3.2.123; see S. Bhaduri, *Studies in Nyāya-Vaiśeṣika Metaphysics* (Poona: 1947), 140; G. Cardona, "A Path Still Taken: Some Early Indian Arguments Concerning Time," *Journal of the American Oriental Society* 111 (1991), 445–64; D. Arnold, "The Deceptive Simplicity of Nagarjuna's Arguments against Motion: Another Look at *Mūlamadhyamakakārikā* Chapter 2," *Journal of Indian Philosophy* 40 (2012), 553–91.
2. The grammatical basis of Nāgārjuna's arguments has been examined in several studies by K. Bhattacharya. See "Nāgārjuna's Arguments against Motion: Their Grammatical Basis," in G. Bhattacharya et al. (eds), *A Corpus of Indian Studies: Essays in Honour of Professor Gaurinath Sastri* (Calcutta: 1980), 85–95; "The Grammatical Basis of Nāgārjuna's Arguments: Some Further Considerations," *Indologica Taurinensia* 8–9 (1980–1), 35–43.
3. M. Sprung, *Lucid Exposition of the Middle Way: The Essential Chapters from the Prasannapadā of Candrakīrti* (Boulder: 1979), 93.
4. See also Candrakīrti's discussion at Sprung, *Lucid Exposition*, 98–9.
5. At Sprung, *Lucid Exposition*, 97. See on this J. Westerhoff, "Nāgārjuna's Arguments on Motion Revisited," *Journal of Indian Philosophy* 36 (2008), 455–79, 467.
6. Westerhoff, "Nāgārjuna's Arguments on Motion," 463.
7. See M. Siderits and J.D. O'Brien, "Zeno and Nāgārjuna on Motion," *Philosophy East and West* 26 (1976), 281–99; I.W. Mabbett, "Nāgārjuna and Zeno on Motion," *Philosophy East and West* 34 (1984), 401–20; B. Galloway, "Notes on Nāgārjuna and Zeno on Motion," *Journal of the International Association of Buddhist Studies* 10 (1987), 81–7.
8. A line from his play *Jumpers*.
9. See R. Sorabji and N. Kretzmann, "Aristotle on the Instant of Change," *Proceedings of the Aristotelian Society, Supplementary Volumes* 50 (1976), 69–89 and 91–114.

Chapter 37

1. Our example is chosen with a sense of irony, because the concept of the "category error" or "type error" was advanced by Gilbert Ryle in his critique of Cartesian conceptions of the mind, in *The Concept of Mind* (London: 1949).
2. This should not be confused with the closely related principle of bivalence, which states that every meaningful assertion is either true or false.
3. S. Schayer, "Altindische Antizipationen der Aussagenlogik," *Bulletin de l'Académie Polonaise* 1–6 (1933), 90–6.
4. L. Stafford Betty, "Nāgārjuna's Masterpiece: Logical, Mystical, Both, or Neither?" *Philosophy East and West* 33 (1983), 123–38.
5. R. Robinson, "Some Logical Aspects of Nāgārjuna's System," *Philosophy East and West* 6 (1957), 291–308.
6. K.N. Jayatilleke, "The Logic of Four Alternatives," *Philosophy East and West* 17 (1967), 69–83.
7. B.K. Matilal, *Perception* (Oxford: 1986), 65–8. J. Westerhoff, *Nāgārjuna's Madhyamaka: A Philosophical Introduction* (Oxford: 2009), ch. 4. For use of the same concepts to offer a somewhat different interpretation, see B.K. Matilal, *Epistemology, Logic, and Grammar in Indian Philosophical Analysis* (The Hague: 1971), 162–5.

Chapter 38

1. We borrow this telling of the story, lightly simplified, from J. Cort, "'Intellectual *Ahiṃsā*' Revisited: Jain Tolerance and Intolerance of Others," *Philosophy East and West* 50 (2000), 324–47, at 340.
2. For these questions and the Buddha's silence as background to Jainism, see B.K. Matilal, *The Central Philosophy of Jainism* (Ahmedabad: 1977), 12.
3. Notice that the last four questions fit the pattern of the tetralemma explained in the last chapter.
4. For these examples, see Matilal, *Central Philosophy*, 19–21.
5. For this, see A. Clavel, "Śvetāmbaras and Digambaras: A Differentiated Periodization?" in E. Franco (ed.), *Periodization and Historiography of Indian Philosophy* (Vienna: 2013), 275–306.
6. Translated in N. Tatia (trans.), *Tattvārtha Sūtra: That Which Is* (London: 1994). Cited in the rest of this chapter by section number.
7. This is the date accepted by Piotr Balcerowicz, but see also S. Ohira, *A Study of Tattvārthasūtra with Bhāṣya* (Ahmedabad: 1982), who prefers a somewhat later date.
8. J. Soni, "Basic Jaina Epistemology," *Philosophy East and West* 50 (2000), 367–77.
9. See J. Soni, "*Dravya, Guṇa* and *Paryāya* in Jaina Thought," *Journal of Indian Philosophy* 19 (1991), 75–88.
10. For a useful analysis, see P. Balcerowicz, "The Logical Structure of the *Naya* Method of the Jainas," *Journal of Indian Philosophy* 29 (2001), 379–403.
11. Unfortunately, considerations of dating make it unlikely that this is a tribute to Buster Keaton's greatest film.
12. For instance Matilal, *Central Philosophy*, 6. The following critique of this idea follows Cort, "'Intellectual *Ahiṃsā*' Revisited."
13. Cort, "'Intellectual *Ahiṃsā*' Revisited," 336.
14. See Matilal, *Central Philosophy*, 33–4.

Chapter 39

1. As pointed out in J. Ganeri, "Jaina Logic and the Philosophical Basis of Pluralism," *History and Philosophy of Logic* 23 (2002), 267–81, at 279.
2. Quoted from J.M. Koller, "Syādvāda as the Epistemological Key to the Jaina Middle Way Metaphysics of Anekāntavāda," *Philosophy East and West* 50 (2000), 400–7, at 401.
3. For instance, F. Bharucha and R.V. Kamat, "Syādvāda Theory of Jainism in Terms of Deviant Logic," *Indian Philosophical Quarterly* 9 (1984), 181–7, B.K. Matilal, "*Anekānta*: Both Yes and No?" *Journal of Indian Council of Philosophical Research* 8 (1991), 1–12.
4. Quoted from Ganeri, "Jaina Logic," 269.
5. As pointed out by P. Jain, "Saptabhaṅgī – the Jaina Theory of Sevenfold Predication: A Logical Analysis," *Philosophy East and West* 50 (2000), 385–99, at 387. Piotr Balcerowicz argues that the sevenfold theory has predications in mind, so that the seven options are possible answers to the question of whether a certain property belongs to a certain subject. See his "Do Attempts to Formalise the *Syād-vāda* Make Sense?" in P. Flügel and O. Qvarnström (eds), *Jaina Scriptures and Philosophy* (London: 2015), 181–248.
6. As Balcerowicz, "Do Attempts to Formalise," notes, this insistence that no self-contradiction is involved can be found in other Jainas as well, like Hemacandra.
7. As noted by B.K. Matilal, *The Character of Logic in India* (Albany: 1998), 137.

8. This is the interpretation of Balcerowicz, "Do Attempts to Formalise." It is not to be confused with the reading of Jain, "Saptabhaṅgī," who argues that there is actually a point of view from which something both does and does not exist, though this standpoint involves no contradiction: "the canceling of predicates leaves nothing to be said" (396).
9. Ganeri, "Jaina Logic," and Balcerowicz, "Do Attempts to Formalise," understand the key sentence in different ways. On Balcerowicz's interpretation the remark agrees with what we have seen in Vādi Devasūri, namely that inexpressibility derives from the impossibility of asserting and denying simultaneously: "because it is completely impossible to express these two when emphasised in such a way [sc. simultaneously], one wants to demonstrate with this [fourth sentence] still another property, 'inexpressibility'." In what follows we retain the basic interpretive line taken in Ganeri, "Jaina Logic."

Chapter 40

1. We here pass over the controversy, triggered by E. Frauwallner, *On the Date of the Buddhist Master of the Law Vasubandhu* (Rome: 1951), as to whether the works ascribed to Vasubandhu may have been authored by multiple authors. For the single author view, see P. Skilling, "Vasubandhu and the *Vyākhyāyukti* Literature," *Journal of the International Association of Buddhist Studies* 23 (2000), 297–350. See also P.S. Jaini, "On the Theory of the Two Vasubandhus," *Bulletin of the School of Oriental and African Studies* 21 (1958), 48–53.
2. For further background, see A. Von Rospatt, *The Buddhist Doctrine of Momentariness: A Survey of the Origins and Early Phase of this Doctrine up to Vasubandhu* (Stuttgart: 1995).
3. For a detailed account of this polemic, see ch. 2 of J.C. Gold, *Paving the Great Way: Vasubandhu's Unifying Buddhist Philosophy* (New York: 2015).
4. See further R. Kritzer, "Sautrāntika in the *Abhidharmakośabhāṣya*," *Journal of the International Association of Buddhist Studies* 26 (2003), 331–84.
5. Gold, *Paving the Great Way*, 54, and 62 for the following candle analogy.
6. Several of these are translated in S. Anacker (trans.), *Seven Works of Vasubandhu: The Buddhist Psychological Doctor* (Delhi: 1984), cited by page number in the main text of this chapter.
7. R. King, "Early Yogācāra and its Relationship with the Madhyamaka School," *Philosophy East and West* 44 (1994), 659–83.
8. Translated in J. Powers (trans.), *Wisdom of the Buddha: The Samdhinirmocana Mahāyāna Sūtra* (Berkeley: 1995).
9. Anacker, *Seven Works*, 291, translation slightly abbreviated.
10. See F. Tola and C. Dragonetti, "The *Trisvabhāvakārikā* of Vasubandhu," *Journal of Indian Philosophy* 11 (1983), 225–66.
11. For this question, see J.L. Garfield and J. Westerhoff (eds), *Madhyamaka and Yogācāra: Allies or Rivals?* (Oxford: 2015). The following draws on several papers in this collection, especially Thakchöe's contribution. See also G. Nagao, *Madhyamaka and Yogācāra: A Study of Māhāyana Philosophies* (Albany: 1991).
12. Quoted from King, "Early Yogācāra," 666.
13. See Siderits in Garfield and Westerhoff, *Madhyamaka and Yogācāra*, 113.

Chapter 41

1. For stories about his biography, see B.C. Law, *The Life and Word of Buddhaghosa* (Calcutta: 1923).

2. B. Ñāṇamoli (trans.), *The Path of Purification: Visuddhimagga by Bhadantācariya Buddhaghosa* (Kandy: 1991), cited in the main text as *Path*.
3. B. Ñāṇamoli (trans.), *The Dispeller of Delusion* (*Sammohavinodanī*), revised by L.S. Cousins et al., 2 vols (Oxford: 1996), cited in the main text as *Dispeller*.
4. Swami Gambhirananda (trans.), *Madhūsudana's Gūdhārtha-dīpikā* (Calcutta: 1998), 982.
5. See J. Ganeri, *Attention, Not Self* (Oxford: 2017), 76–81.
6. B. Bodhi, *The Numerical Discourses of the Buddha* (Somerville, MA: 2012), 901.
7. See S. Collins, *Selfless Persons* (Cambridge: 1990); P. Harvey, *The Selfless Mind: Personality, Consciousness and Nirvāṇa in Early Buddhism* (London: 1995); M. Siderits, *Personal Identity and Buddhist Philosophy* (London: 2003); J. Duerlinger, *Indian Buddhist Theories of Persons* (London: 2003). For Buddhaghosa's view, see M. Heim, *The Forerunner of All Things: Buddhaghosa on Mind, Intention, and Agency* (New York: 2014); J. Ganeri, *Attention, Not Self* (Oxford: 2017).
8. For general discussion of Buddhist approaches to agency and intentionality, see the essays in R. Repetti (ed.), *Buddhist Perspectives on Free Will: Agentless Agency* (London: 2017), and J. Davis (ed.), *A Mirror is for Reflection: Understanding Buddhist Ethics* (Oxford: 2017).
9. *Atthasālinī (The Fount of Meaning)*, ed. E. Muller (London: 1897), 271–2, 279–80.
10. See Y. Karunadasa, *The Theravāda Abhidhamma* (Hong Kong: 2010), 79–80.
11. *Atthasālinī*, ed. E. Muller, 280–1.

Chapter 42

1. For partial translations, see M. Hattori, *Dignāga on Perception: Being the Pratyakṣapariccheda of Dignāga's Pramāṇasamuccaya from the Sanskrit Fragments and the Tibetan Versions* (Cambridge, MA: 1968) and R. Hayes, *Dignāga on the Interpretation of Signs* (Dordrecht: 1988). For the simultaneous composition of the verses and commentary, see B. Kellner, "Self-Awareness (*svasaṃvedana*) in Dignāga's *Pramāṇasamuccaya* and *-vṛtti*: A Close Reading," *Journal of Indian Philosophy* 38 (2010), 203–31, at 207.
2. Translated in N.A. Shastri, *Ālambanaparīkṣā and Vṛtti by Diṅnāga with the Commentary of Dharmapāla* (Madras: 1942); F. Tola and C. Dragonetti, "Dignāga's *Ālambanaparīkṣā*," *Journal of Indian Philosophy* 10 (1982), 105–34. The Tibetan commentaries are also translated, along with critical discussion by several authors, in D. Duckworth, M. Eckel, J. Garfield, and S. Thakcho (eds), *Dignāga's Investigation of the Percept: A Philosophical Legacy in India and Tibet* (Oxford: 2016).
3. On this question, see Hattori, *Dignāga on Perception*, 3.
4. For other accounts of the argument, see R. Hayes, *Dignāga on the Interpretation of Signs* (Dordrecht: 1988), 133 and following; J. Chu, "On Dignāga's Theory of the Object of Cognition as Presented in *PS(V)* 1," *Journal of the International Association of Buddhist Studies* 29 (2006/8), 211–53.
5. R.K. Payne, "The Theory of Meaning in Buddhist Logicians: The Historical and Intellectual Context of *Apoha*," *Journal of Indian Philosophy* 15 (1987), 261–84, at 266.
6. On this terminology, see D. Arnold, "Candrakīrti on Dignāga on *Svalakṣaṇas*," *Journal of the International Association of Buddhist Studies* 26 (2003), 139–74.
7. Hayes, *Dignāga on the Interpretation of Signs*, 183.
8. The hierarchical structure of inference has been stressed by S. Katsura, for instance in "Dignāga and Dharmakīrti on *Apoha*," in E. Steinkellner (ed.), *Studies in the Buddhist Epistemological Tradition* (Vienna: 1991), 129–46.
9. Hayes, *Dignāga on the Interpretation of Signs*, 139.

10. S.H. Phillips, "Dharmakīrti on Sensation and Casual Efficiency," *Journal of Indian Philosophy* 15 (1987), 231–59, at 236; see also A. Wayman, "Yogācāra and the Buddhist Logicians," *Buddhist Studies* 2 (1979), 65–78, at 70.
11. See H. Masaaki, "*Apoha* and *Pratibhā*," in M. Nagatomi et al. (eds), *Sanskrit and Indian Studies: Essays in Honour of Daniel H. H. Ingalls* (Dordrecht: 1980), 61–74; Payne, "Theory of Meaning"; and D. Sharma, "Buddhist Theory of Meaning (*Apoha*) and Negative Statements," *Philosophy East and West* 18 (1968), 3–10.
12. See Hayes, *Dignāga on the Interpretation of Signs*, 184–5; Payne, "The Theory of Meaning," 272; Sharma, "Buddhist Theory of Meaning," 5–6.

Chapter 43

1. See the text at R. Hayes, *Dignāga on the Interpretation of Signs* (Dordrecht: 1988), 238.
2. On this contrast, see V.A. van Bijlert, *Epistemology and Spiritual Authority* (Vienna: 1989), 73, 81; J. Westerhoff, *The Golden Age of Indian Buddhist Philosophy* (Oxford: 2018), 227.
3. *Posterior Analytics* 2.2.
4. Note that this is indeed a logic about the interrelation between properties and not, in the first instance at least, propositions, as noted by Hayes, *Dignāga on the Interpretation of Signs*, 154.
5. For the text, see Hayes, *Dignāga on the Interpretation of Signs*, 239, with discussion at 145–54. For discussion of the *trairūpya* theory, see B. Gillon, "Logic in Classical Indian Philosophy," *The Stanford Encyclopedia of Philosophy*, ed. E. Zalta (online; Fall 2016 edition); B. Matilal, *The Character of Logic in India* (Albany: 1998), J. Ganeri, "Indian Logic," in D. Gabbay and J. Woods (eds), *Handbook of the History of Logic*, Vol. 1 (Amsterdam: 2004).
6. B.K. Matilal, *The Character of Logic in India* (Albany: 1998), 92.
7. For translations of Dharmakīrti, see T. Stcherbatsky, "A Short Treatise of Logic by Dharmakīrti with its Commentary by Dharmottara," in *Buddhist Logic*, Vol. 2 (New York: 1962), 1–253; P. Gokhale, *Vādanyāya of Dharmakīrti: The Logic of Debate* (Delhi: 1993); G.C. Pande, *Nyāyabindu* (Sarnath: 1996). On him, see also G. Dreyfus, *Recognizing Reality: Dharmakīrti's Philosophy and its Tibetan Interpretations* (Albany: 1997); J. Dunne, *Foundations of Dharmakīrti's Philosophy* (Somerville, MA: 2004).
8. For a good overview of Dharmakīrti's innovation, and indeed of Indian logic generally, see Gillon, "Logic in Classical Indian Philosophy."

Chapter 44

1. For the contrast between the two approaches, see M. MacKenzie, "The Illumination of Consciousness: Approaches to Self-Awareness in the Indian and Western Traditions," *Philosophy East and West* 57 (2007), 40–62.
2. See B. Kellner, "Infinite Regress Arguments (*anavasthā*) in Connection with Self-Awareness (*svasaṃvedana*): A Closer Look at Dignāga and Dharmakīrti," *Journal of Indian Philosophy* 39 (2011), 411–26.
3. For this weakness in the argument, see J. Ganeri, "Self-Intimation, Memory and Personal Identity," *Journal of Indian Philosophy* 27 (1999), 469–83, at 481; K.C. Lo, "On the Argument of Infinite Regress in Proving Self-Awareness," *Journal of Indian Philosophy* 46 (2018), 553–76.
4. For which see Kellner, "Infinite Regress Arguments," 420.

5. In speaking of "access" we follow B. Kellner, "Self-Awareness (*svasaṃvedana*) in Dignāga's *Pramāṇasamuccaya* and *-vṛtti*: A Close Reading," *Journal of Indian Philosophy* 38 (2010), 203–31, at 227.
6. G. Dreyfus, *Recognizing Reality: Dharmakīrti's Philosophy and its Tibetan Interpretations* (Albany: 1997).
7. D. Arnold, "Self-Awareness (*svasaṃvitti*) and Related Doctrines of Buddhists Following Dignāga: Philosophical Characterizations of Some of the Main Issues," *Journal of Indian Philosophy* 38 (2010), 323–78, at 327.
8. For discussion of this problem, see M. MacKenzie, "Self-Awareness Without a Self: Buddhism and the Reflexivity of Awareness," *Asian Philosophy* 18 (2008), 245–66; C.K. Fink, "The 'Scent' of a Self: Buddhism and the First-Person Perspective," *Asian Philosophy* 22 (2012), 289–306.

Chapter 45

1. Selections in translation in S. Pollock (trans.), *A Rasa Reader: Classical Indian Aesthetics* (New York: 2016); page references throughout the chapter refer to this volume. There is a complete translation in M. Ghosh (trans.), *Nāṭyaśāstra of Bharata* (Varanasi: 1950–67). See further, e.g. P. Kale, *The Theatric Universe: A Study of the Natyasastra* (Bombay: 1974) and S. Nair (ed.), *The Natyasastra and the Body in Performance* (Jefferson, NC: 2015).
2. For early writings on music, see L. Rowell, *Music and Musical Thought in Early India* (Chicago: 1992); J. Katz (ed.), *The Traditional Indian Theory and Practice of Music and Dance* (Leiden: 1992); J. Katz, "Music and Aesthetics: An Early Indian Perspective," *Early Music* 24 (1996), 407–20.
3. On this concept, see e.g. K.C. Bhattacharya, "The Concept of *Rasa*," in his *Studies in Philosophy*, Vol. 1 (Calcutta: 1956), K.C. Pandey, "A Bird's-Eye View of Indian Aesthetics," *Journal of Aesthetics and Art Criticism* 24 (1965), 59–73; P. Patnaik, *Rasa in Aesthetics* (New Delhi: 2004); S.L. Schwarz, *Rasa: Performing the Divine in India* (New York: 2004); K.M. Higgins, "An Alchemy of Emotions: *Rasa* and Aesthetic Breakthroughs," *Journal of Aesthetics and Art Criticism* 65 (2007), 43–54.
4. We reproduce the translation of the lists from Higgins, "An Alchemy of Emotions," 45.
5. On the moral function of Indian drama, see S. Pollock, "The Social Aesthetic and Sanskrit Literary Theory," *Journal of Indian Philosophy* 29 (2001), 197–229.
6. See J.L. Masson, "Philosophy and Literary Criticism in Ancient India," *Journal of Indian Philosophy* 1 (1971), 167–80.
7. L. McCrea, "Mahimabhaṭṭa's Analysis of Poetic Flaws," *Journal of the American Oriental Society* 124 (2004), 77–94.
8. See Y. Bronner, *Extreme Poetry: The South Asian Movement of Simultaneous Narration* (New York: 2010).
9. A.A. Bake, "The Aesthetics of Indian Music," *British Journal of Aesthetics* 4 (1964), 47–57.
10. Katz, "Music and Aesthetics," 409, 415–16.
11. See A. Amaladass, *Philosophical Implications of Dhvani: Experience of Symbol Language in Indian Aesthetics* (Vienna: 1984), on which we draw in what follows.
12. For the example and its purpose, see L. McCrea, "'Resonance' and its Reverberations: Two Cultures in Indian Epistemology of Aesthetic Meaning," in A. Chakrabarti (ed.), *The Bloomsbury Research Handbook of Indian Aesthetics and the Philosophy of Art* (London: 2016), 25–41, at 26–8.
13. Amaladass, *Philosophical Implications*, 83 and 134.

14. E. Christie, "Indian Philosophers on Poetic Imagination (*Pratibhā*)," *Journal of Indian Philosophy* 7 (1979), 153–207.
15. On the relation between the two, see K. Kunjunni Raja, "Ānandavardhana and Abhinavagupta: A Contrastive Study," *Adyar Library Bulletin* 47 (1983), 15–24.
16. On this idea, see A. Chakrabarti, "Play, Pleasure, Pain: Ownerless Emotions in *Rasa* Aesthetics," in K. Vatsyayan and D.P. Chattopadhyay (eds), *Aesthetic Theories and Forms in Indian Tradition* (New Delhi: 2008), 189–202.
17. Cited by S.L. Schwarz, *Rasa: Performing the Divine in India* (New York: 2004), 17.
18. P. Dave-Mukheriji, "Who is Afraid of Mimesis? Contesting the Common Sense of Indian Aesthetics through the Theory of 'Mimesis' or Anukaraṇa Vāda," in Chakrabarti (ed.), *The Bloomsbury Research Handbook*, 71–92.
19. For his defense of the relevance of inference, see McCrea, "'Resonance' and its Reverberations," 33.
20. We are grateful to Malcolm Keating for his advice on this chapter.

Chapter 46

1. From the preface of B.T. Bhattacharyya, *An Introduction to Buddhist Esotericism* (Oxford: 1932), quoted by N.N. Bhattacharyya, *History of the Tantric Religion* (New Delhi: 1999), 41–2.
2. For a discussion of the connections between Tantra and Yoga, see M. Eliade, *Yoga: Immortality and Freedom* (New York: 1958), ch. 6.
3. A. Padoux, *Vāc: The Concept of the Word in Selected Hindu Tantras*, trans. J. Gontier (Albany: 1990), 48 n.40. For an account giving more prominence to sexual aspects of the tradition, see D.G. White, *Kiss of the Yoginī: "Tantric Sex" in its South Asian Contexts* (Chicago: 2003).
4. This list is adapted from C.D. Wallis, *Tantra Illuminated: The Philosophy, History, and Practice of a Timeless Tradition* (San Rafael, CA: 2013), a useful popular guide to Tantra especially in the non-dual Śaivite tradition.
5. The term *mantra* could originally mean any part of a Vedic text. On the term, see further J. Gonda, "The Indian Mantra," *Oriens* 16 (1963), 244–97.
6. A. Sanderson, "The Śaiva Age: The Rise and Dominance of Śaivism during the Early Medieval Period," in S. Einoo (ed.), *Genesis and Development of Tantrism* (Tokyo: 2009), 41–350, at 130.
7. Bhattacharyya, *History of the Tantric Religion*, 46–7.
8. See R. Yelle, *Explaining Mantras: Ritual, Rhetoric, and the Dream of a Natural Language in Hindu Tantra* (London: 2003), 11 and 28. On the topic, see also H.A. Alper, *Understanding Mantras* (Albany: 1989).
9. Yelle, *Explaining Mantras*, 24; see also Padoux, *Vāc*, 384.
10. See A. Bharati, *The Tantric Tradition* (New York: 1975), ch. 7.
11. Yelle, *Explaining Mantras*, 23.
12. A. Sanderson, "The Śaiva Literature," *Journal of Indological Studies* 24–5 (2012–13), 1–113, at 53.
13. For dualist and monistic tendencies in Śaivism, see Sanderson, "The Śaiva Age."
14. P.E. Muller-Ortega, *The Triadic Heart of Śiva: Kaula Tantricism of Abhinavagupta in the Non-Dual Shaivism of Kashmir* (Albany: 1989), 89.
15. Muller-Ortega, *The Triadic Heart of Śiva*, 85.
16. Quoted in Padoux, *Vāc*, 170; 187 and 212 n.109 for the following points about Bhartṛhari and the learning of language among children.

17. See further R. Torella, "From Adversary to the Main Ally: The Place of Bhartṛhari in the Kashmirian Śaiva Advaita," in A. Aklujkar and M. Kaul (eds), *Linguistic Traditions of Kashmir* (Delhi: 2008), 508–24.
18. Padoux, *Vāc*, 133.
19. Padoux, *Vāc*, 131.
20. Yelle, *Explaining Mantras*, 5.
21. Quoted in Bharati, *Tantric Tradition*, 171.
22. Bhattacharyya, *History of the Tantric Religion*, 82, mentions a text from around AD 1000 which takes the third combined view.
23. G.R. Elder, "Problems of Language in Buddhist Tantra," *History of Religions* 15 (1975), 321–50, reprinted in P. Williams (ed.), *Buddhism: Critical Concepts in Religious Studies*, Vol. 6: *Tantric Buddhism* (London: 2005); Bharati, *The Tantric Tradition*, ch. 6.
24. Sanderson, "The Śaiva Literature," 73.
25. R.R. Jackson, "Ambiguous Sexuality: Imagery and Interpretation in Tantric Buddhism," *Religion* 22 (1992), 85–100, at 155 in the reprinted version in Williams, *Buddhism: Critical Concepts*. For the idea of Kashmir Śaivite Tantra as an ascetic movement, see also G. Flood, *The Ascetic Self: Subjectivity, Memory and Tradition* (Cambridge: 2004), ch. 4.
26. Quoted at Muller-Ortega, *The Triadic Heart of Śiva*, 59–60.
27. See P. Adamson, *Philosophy in the Islamic World: A History of Philosophy Without Any Gaps, Volume 3* (Oxford: 2016), ch. 39.
28. Bhattacharyya, *History of the Tantric Religion*, 214.
29. Our thanks to Robert Yelle and Eva-Maria Glasbrenner for their help with this chapter.

Chapter 47

1. As detailed in P. Adamson, *Philosophy in the Islamic World: A History of Philosophy Without Any Gaps, Volume 3* (Oxford: 2016).
2. K. Karttunen, *India in Early Greek Literature* (Helsinki: 1989), 57, 86–7. We also draw on this book in what follows.
3. T. McEvilley, *The Shape of Ancient Thought* (New York: 2002).
4. McEvilley, *The Shape of Ancient Thought*, 484.
5. McEvilley, *The Shape of Ancient Thought*, 43.
6. On the possibility of the western spread of Buddhism, see, however, E. Seldeslachts, "Greece: The Final Frontier?" in A. Heirman et al. (eds), *The Spread of Buddhism* (Leiden: 2007), 131–66.
7. See on them, P. Adamson, *Philosophy in the Hellenistic and Roman Worlds: A History of Philosophy Without Any Gaps, Volume 2* (Oxford: 2015), chs 15 and 18.
8. *Lives of the Philosophers* 9.61. It should be noted that the atomist Democritus is also claimed to have been a bold traveler and to have gone to Egypt, Persia, Ethiopia, and India.
9. E. Flintoff, "Pyrrho and India," *Phronesis* 25 (1980), 88–108; C.I. Beckwith, *Greek Buddha: Pyrrho's Encounter with Early Buddhism in Central Asia* (Princeton: 2015).
10. Beckwith, *Greek Buddha*, 40.
11. As admitted in passing by Flintoff, "Pyrrho and India," 94.
12. Beckwith, *Greek Buddha*, 26, 35, 51.
13. On him, see Adamson, *Philosophy in the Hellenistic and Roman Worlds*, chs 29–32. For the question of Indian influence on Neoplatonism, see J.F. Staal, *Advaita and Neoplatonism: A Critical Study in Comparative Philosophy* (Madras: 1961); R.B. Harris (ed.), *Neoplatonism and Indian Thought* (Albany: 1982); P.M. Gregorios (ed.), *Neoplatonism and Indian Philosophy*

(Albany: 2002); J. Lacrosse, "Plotinus, Porphyry and India: A Re-Examination," in P. Vassilopoulou (ed.), *Late Antique Epistemology: Other Ways to Truth* (New York: 2009), 103–13.

14. For references, see Lacrosse, "Plotinus, Porphyry and India," 106.
15. For the skeptical view, see, for instance, A.H. Armstrong, "Plotinus and India," *The Classical Quarterly* 30 (1936), 22–8, responding to the positive proposal of E. Bréhier, *The Philosophy of Plotinus*, trans. J. Thomas (Chicago: 1958). See also A.M. Wolters, "A Survey of Modern Scholarly Opinion on Plotinus and Indian Thought," in Harris, *Neoplatonism and Indian Thought*, 293–308.
16. A problem noted by D.H. Sick, "When Socrates Met the Buddha: Greek and Indian Dialectic in Hellenistic Bactria and India," *Journal of the Royal Asiatic Society* 17 (2007), 253–78, at 256.
17. See G. Aubry, *Plotin: Traité 53 (I,1)* (Paris: 2004) and P. Remes, *Plotinus on Self: The Philosophy of the "We"* (Cambridge: 2007).
18. McEvilley, *The Shape of Ancient Thought*, 550; see also 581 ("most of what he used was already present in the Greek tradition, though it may have come over from India at an earlier date").
19. Lacrosse, "Plotinus, Porphyry and India," 110.

Chapter 48

1. Cited in the text by page number from E.C. Sachau (trans.), *Alberuni's India*, 2 vols (London: 1910).
2. On this, see P. Adamson, *Philosophy in the Islamic World: A History of Philosophy Without Any Gaps, Volume 3* (Oxford: 2016), ch. 3.
3. See D. Pingree, *Pathways into the Study of Ancient Sciences: Selected Essays*, ed. I. Pingree and J.M. Steele (Philadelphia: 2014).
4. K. van Bladel, "The Bactrian Background of the Barmakids," in A. Akasoy, C. Burnett, and R. Yoeli-Tlalim (eds), *Islam and Tibet: Interactions along the Musk Routes* (Farnham: 2011), 43–88, at 75.
5. D. Xiuyuan, "The Presence of Buddhist Thought in Kalām Literature," *Philosophy East and West*, forthcoming. See also S. Pines, "A Study of the Impact of Indian, Mainly Buddhist, Thought on Some Aspects of Kalām Doctrines," *Jerusalem Studies in Arabic and Islam* 17 (1994), 182–203.
6. S. Pines and T. Gelblum, "Al-Bīrūnī's Arabic Version of Patañjali's *Yogasūtra*," *Bulletin of SOAS* 29 (1966), 302–25; 40 (1977), 522–49; 46 (1983), 258–304; 52 (1989), 265–305.
7. On this passage, see M. Kozah, *The Birth of Indology as an Islamic Science* (Leiden: 2015), 41–3.
8. For details, see W. Halbfass, *India and Europe: An Essay in Philosophical Understanding* (Albany: 1988), 29.
9. C.W. Ernst, "The Islamization of Yoga in the *Amrtakunda* Translations," *Journal of the Royal Asiatic Society* 13 (2003), 199–226, at 203.
10. Discussed in Adamson, *Philosophy in the Islamic World*, ch. 56.
11. For more details and references for what follows, see J. Ganeri, *Identity as Reasoned Choice: A South Asian Perspective on the Reach and Resources of Public and Practical Reason in Shaping Individual Identities* (London: 2012), 214ff.
12. G.W.F. Leibniz, *New Essays on the Human Understanding*, trans. P. Remnant and J. Bennett (Cambridge: 1981), 218.

13. A. Gopnik, "Could David Hume have Known about Buddhism? Charles Francois Dolu, the Royal College of La Flèche, and the Global Jesuit Intellectual Network," *Hume Studies* 35 (2009), 5–28.
14. Gopnik, "Could David Hume have Known about Buddhism?" 22.
15. "Letter to Monsieur Chapelain, Despatched from Chiras in Persia, the 4th October 1667," in F. Bernier, *Voyage dans les Etats du Grand Mogul*, ed. F. Bhattacharya (Paris: 1981); see also I. Brock (trans.), *Travels in the Mogul Empire AD 1656–1668* (London: 1834), 323–5.
16. D. Hume, *Dialogues Concerning Natural Religion* (London: 1990), 90–1.
17. Book III, ch. 6, §1.
18. In what follows we draw on Halbfass, *India and Europe*, chs 5–7.
19. Quoted from Halbfass, *India and Europe*, 97–8.
20. In addition to the discussion found in Halbfass, see P. Abelsen, "Schopenhauer and Buddhism," *Philosophy East and West* 43 (1993), 255–78 and M. Nicholls, "The Influences of Eastern Thought on Schopenhauer's Doctrine of The Thing-In-Itself," in C. Janaway (ed.), *The Cambridge Companion to Schopenhauer* (Cambridge: 1999), 171–212.
21. A. Schopenhauer, *Parerga and Paralipomena*, trans. E.F.J. Payne, 2 vols (Oxford: 1974), vol. 2, 397.
22. On whom, see P. Adamson, *Medieval Philosophy: A History of Philosophy Without Any Gaps, Volume 4* (Oxford: 2019), ch. 68.
23. Quoted from Halbfass, *India and Europe*, 114.
24. For a contrast between Schopenhauer and the genuine teachings of Buddhism, see also Abelsen, "Schopenhauer and Buddhism."

Chapter 49

1. L. McCrea, "The Transformations of Mīmāṃsā in the Larger Context of Indian Philosophical Discourse," in E. Franco (ed.), *Periodization and Historiography of Indian Philosophy* (Vienna: 2013), 127–43, at 129–30.
2. For more on figures in the Islamic tradition within India, see P. Adamson, *Philosophy in the Islamic World: A History of Philosophy Without Any Gaps, Volume 3* (Oxford: 2016), ch. 56.
3. See further A. Carpenter, "Illuminating Community: Animals in Classical Indian Thought," in P. Adamson and G.F. Edwards (eds), *Animals: A History* (New York: 2018), 63–85.
4. See the papers collected in A. Marmodoro and D. Yates (eds), *The Metaphysics of Relations* (Oxford: 2016).

FURTHER READING

Further reading is suggested here for each of the main sections of the book, followed by recommendations for the topics of specific chapters. References on more specific topics and for primary literature in translation can be found in notes to the chapters of this volume.

General Overviews

C. Bartley, *An Introduction to Indian Philosophy* (London: 2015).
S.N. Dasgupta, *A History of Indian Philosophy* (Cambridge: 1922–55).
E. Franco (ed.), *Periodization and Historiography of Indian Philosophy* (Vienna: 2013).
J. Ganeri (ed.), *Indian Logic: A Reader* (Richmond: 2000).
J. Ganeri, *Philosophy in Classical India* (London: 2001).
J. Ganeri, *The Concealed Art of the Soul: Theories of Self and Practices of Truth in Indian Ethics and Epistemology* (Oxford: 2007).
J. Ganeri (ed.), *Indian Philosophy* [a four-volume set]. Routledge Critical Concepts in Philosophy (London: 2016).
J. Ganeri (ed.), *Oxford Handbook of Indian Philosophy* (Oxford: 2017).
W. Halbfass, *Tradition and Reflection: Explorations in Indian Thought* (Albany: 1991).
S. Hamilton, *Indian Philosophy: A Very Short Introduction* (Oxford: 2001).
R. King, *Indian Philosophy: An Introduction to Hindu and Buddhist Thought* (Washington, DC: 1999).
D. Krishna, *Indian Philosophy: A Counter-Perspective* (Oxford, 1992).
B.K. Matilal, *Perception: An Essay on Classical Indian Theories of Knowledge* (Oxford: 1986).
B.K. Matilal, *Ethics and Epics* (Delhi: 2002; reprinted 2015).
B.K. Matilal, *Mind, Language, and World* (Delhi: 2002; reprinted 2015).
B.K. Matilal, *Logical and Ethical Issues* (New Delhi: 2004).
J.N. Mohanty, *Reason and Tradition in Indian Thought* (Oxford: 1998).
J.N. Mohanty, *Classical Indian Philosophy* (London: 2000).
K. Potter (ed.), *Encyclopedia of Indian Philosophies* (Princeton: 1977–).
S. Radhakrishnan and C.A. Moore, *A Sourcebook in Indian Philosophy* (Princeton: 1957).
D. Sharma, *Classical Indian Philosophy: A Reader* (New York: 2011).
N. Smart, *Doctrine and Argument in Indian Philosophy* (London: 1964).

Origins

F. Edgerton, *The Beginnings of Indian Philosophy: Selections from the Rg Veda, Atharva Veda, Upanisads, and Mahabharata* (London: 1965).
R. Gethin, *The Foundations of Buddhism* (Oxford: 1998).
K.N. Jayatilleke, *Early Buddhist Theory of Knowledge* (London: 1963).
B.K. Matilal, *Epics and Ethics* (Oxford: 2002).
W.D. O'Flaherty (ed.), *Karma and Rebirth in Classical Indian Traditions* (Berkeley: 1980).
B. Smith, *Reflections on Resemblance, Ritual and Religion* (New York: 1989).

The Upaniṣads

B. Black, *The Character of the Self in Ancient India: Priests, Kings, and Women in the Early Upaniṣads* (Albany: 2007).
B. Black, "The Rhetoric of Secrecy in the Upaniṣads," in S.E. Lindquist (ed.), *Religion and Identity in South Asia and Beyond* (Florence: 2011), 101–25.
B. Black, "The Upaniṣads," on the *Internet Encyclopedia of Philosophy*, https://www.iep.utm.edu/upanisad/.
J. Brereton, "The Upaniṣads," in W.T. de Bary and I. Bloom (eds), *Approaches to the Asian Classics* (New York: 1990), 115–35.
S. Cohen, *Text and Authority in the Older Upaniṣads* (Leiden: 2008).
S. Cohen (ed.), *The Upaniṣads: A Complete Guide* (London: 2017).
D.C. Mathur, "The Concept of Self in the Upanishads: An Alternative Interpretation," *Philosophy and Phenomenological Research* 32 (1972), 390–6.
P. Olivelle, *Upaniṣads: A New Translation* (Oxford: 2008).

Sanskrit Grammar

G. Cardona, "Some Principles of Pāṇini's Grammar," *Journal of Indian Philosophy* 1 (1970), 40–74.
G. Cardona, "Pāṇini's *Kārakas*: Agency, Animation and Identity," *Journal of Indian Philosophy* 2 (1974), 231–306.
M. Keating, *Language, Meaning and Use in Indian Philosophy* (London: 2019).
P. Kiparsky, *Some Theoretical Problems in Pāṇini's Grammar* (Poona: 1982).
B. Matilal, *The Word and the World: India's Contribution to the Study of Language* (Delhi: 1991).
H. Sharfe, *A History of Indian Literature, Vol. V.2: Grammatical Literature* (Wiesbaden: 1977).
R.N. Sharma, *The Aṣṭādhyāyī of Pāṇini, Vol. 1: Introduction to the Aṣṭādhyāyī as a Grammatical Device* (New Delhi: 2002).
F. Staal, "Euclid and Pāṇini," *Philosophy East and West* 15 (1965), 99–116.
F. Staal, "Ritual, Grammar and the Origins of Science in India," *Journal of Indian Philosophy* 10 (1982), 3–35.
R. Tzohar, *A Yogācāra Buddhist Theory of Metaphor* (Oxford: 2017).

Early Buddhism

R. Gethin, *The Foundations of Buddhism* (Oxford: 1998).
R. Gombrich, *What the Buddha Thought* (London: 2009).
C. Gowans, *Philosophy of the Buddha* (London: 2003).
S. Hamilton, *Early Buddhism: A New Approach. The I of the Beholder* (London: 2000).
P. Harvey, *An Introduction to Buddhist Ethics: Foundations, Values, and Issues* (Cambridge: 2000).
D. Keown, *The Nature of Buddhist Ethics* (Basingstoke: 1992).
M. Siderits, *Buddhism as Philosophy: An Introduction* (Farnham: 2007).
D. Webster, *The Philosophy of Desire in the Buddhist Pāli Canon* (London: 2005).

Ancient Indian Political Thought

R. Choudhary, *Kauṭilya's Political Ideas and Institutions* (Varanasi: 1971).
J. Gonda, *Ancient Indian Kingship from the Religious Point of View* (Leiden: 1966).
P. Olivelle (ed.), *Aśoka in History and Historical Memory* (Delhi: 2009).

P. Olivelle, *King, Governance and Law in Ancient India: Kauṭilya's Arthaśāstra* (Oxford: 2013).
R. Thapar, *Aśoka and the Decline of the Mauryas* (Oxford: 1961).
A.A. Vigasin and A.M. Samozvantsev, *Society, State and Law in Ancient India* (New Delhi: 1985).

Women in Ancient India

B. Black, "Draupadī in the *Mahābhārata*," *Religion Compass* 7 (2013), 169–78.
K.R. Blackstone, *Women in the Footsteps of the Buddha: Struggle for Liberation in the Therīgāthā* (Delhi: 1998).
S. Brodbeck and B. Black (eds), *Gender and Narrative in the Mahābhārata* (London: 2007).
J. Fitzgerald, "Nun Befuddles King, Shows *Karmayoga* Does Not Work: Sulabhā's Refutation of King Janaka at MBh 12.308," *Journal of Indian Philosophy* 30 (2002), 641–77.
S.E. Lindquist, "Gender at Janaka's Court: Women in the Bṛhadāraṇyaka Upaniṣad Reconsidered," *Journal of Indian Philosophy* 36 (2008), 405–26.
P. Olivelle. "Amṛtā: Women and Indian Technologies of Immortality," *Journal of Indian Philosophy* 25 (1997), 427–49.
R. Vanita, "The Self is Not Gendered: Sulabha's Debate with King Janaka," *NWSA Journal* 15 (2003), 76–93.

The *Mahābhārata* and *Bhagavad-gītā*

J. Brockington, *The Sanskrit Epics* (Leiden: 1998).
A. Chakrabarti and S. Bandhopadhyay (eds), *Mahābhārata Now: Narration, Aesthetics, Ethics* (Routledge: 2014).
C. Framarin, "Good and Bad Desires: Implications of the Dialogue between Kṛṣṇa and Arjuna," *International Journal of Hindu Studies* 11(2) (2007): 147–70.
D. Gitomer, "King Duryodhana: The *Mahābhārata* Discourse of Sinning and Virtue in the Epic and Drama," *Journal of the American Oriental Society* 112 (1992), 222–32.
A. Hiltebeitel, *The Ritual of Battle: Kṛṣṇa in the Mahābhārata* (Albany: 1990).
A. Hiltebeitel, *Rethinking the Mahābhārata: A Reader's Guide to the Education of the Dharma King* (Chicago: 2001).
A. Malinar, *The Bhagavadgītā: Doctrines and Contexts* (Cambridge: 2007).
B.K. Matilal (ed.), *Moral Dilemmas in the Mahābhārata* (Delhi: 1989).
R.N. Minor, *Bhagavad-Gītā: An Exegetical Commentary* (Delhi: 1982).
P. Olivelle, "The Conception of God in the *Bhagavadgītā*," *International Philosophical Quarterly* 4 (1964), 514–40.
C.A. Robinson, *Interpretations of the Bhagavad-Gītā and Images of Hindu Tradition* (London: 2005).
A. Sharma (ed.), *New Essays in the Bhagavadgītā: Philosophical, Methodological and Cultural Approaches* (New Delhi: 1987).
S. Sreekumar, "An Analysis of Consequentialism and Deontology in the Normative Ethics of the *Bhagavadgītā*," *Journal of Indian Philosophy* 40 (2012), 277–315.

Non-Violence

C. Chapple, *Nonviolence to Animals, Earth, and Self in Asian Traditions* (Albany: 1993).
J.R. Hinnells and R. King (eds), *Religion and Violence in South Asia: Theory and Practice* (London: 2007).

J.E.M. Houben and K.R. van Kooij (eds), *Violence Denied: Violence, Non-Violence and the Rationalization of Violence in South Asian Cultural History* (Leiden: 1999).
T. Sethia (ed.), *Ahiṃsā, Anekānta and Jainism* (Delhi: 2004).
U. Tähtinen, *Ahiṃsā: Non-Violence in Indian Tradition* (London: 1976).

The Age of the Sūtra

C. Bartley, *An Introduction to Indian Philosophy* (London: 2011).
J. Bronkhorst, *Language and Reality: On an Episode in Indian Thought*, trans. M.S. Allen and R. Raghunathan (Leiden: 2011).
J. Gonda (ed.), *A History of Indian Literature* (Wiesbaden: 1975–).
D. Krishna (ed.), *Discussion and Debate in Indian Philosophy: Issues in Vedānta, Mīmāṃsā and Nyāya* (New Delhi: 2004).
K.H. Potter (ed.), *Encyclopedia of Indian Philosophies* (Princeton: 1977–).

Skepticism

A. Carpenter and J. Ganeri, "Can You Seek the Answer to this Question? Meno in India," *Australasian Journal of Philosophy* 88 (2009), 571–94.
G. Dreyfus and J. Garfield, "Madhyamaka and Classical Greek Skepticism," in The Cowherds, *Moonshadows: Conventional Truth in Buddhist Philosophy* (Oxford: 2010), 115–30.
E. Franco, *Perception, Knowledge and Disbelief: A Study of Jayarāśi's Scepticism* (Delhi: 1994).
B.K. Matilal, *Perception: An Essay on Classical Indian Theories of Knowledge* (Oxford: 1986).
E. Mills, *Three Pillars of Skepticism in Classical India* (Lanham, 2018).

Mīmāṃsā

G.P. Bhatt, *The Basic Ways of Knowing: An In-Depth Study of Kumārila's Contribution to Indian Epistemology* (Delhi: 1989).
F.X. Clooney, "Why the Veda Has No Author: Language as Ritual in Early Mīmāṃsā and Post-Modern Theology," *Journal of the American Academy of Religion* 55 (1987), 659–84.
F.X. Clooney, *Thinking Ritually: Rediscovering the Pūrva Mīmāṃsā of Jaimini* (Vienna: 1990).
O. Gächter, *Hermeneutics and Language in Pūrva Mīmāṃsā* (Delhi: 1983).
J. Ganeri, "The Ritual Roots of Moral Reason: Lessons from Mīmāṃsā," in K. Schilbrack (ed.), *Thinking Through Rituals: Philosophical Perspectives* (London: 2004), 207–33.
G. Jha, *The Prābhākara School of Pūrva Mīmāṃsā* (Delhi: 1978).
N.S. Juhankar, "The Mīmāṃsā Concept of Dharma," *Journal of Indian Philosophy* 10 (1982), 51–60.
L. McCrea, "The Hierarchical Organization of Language in Mīmāṃsā Interpretive Theory," *Journal of Indian Philosophy* 28 (2000), 429–59.
J.A. Taber, "The Theory of the Sentence in Pūrva Mīmāṃsā and Western Philosophy," *Journal of Indian Philosophy* 17 (1989), 407–30.
J. Taber, *A Hindu Critique of Buddhist Epistemology: Kumārila on Perception* (London: 2005).

Vedānta

F.X. Clooney, "Binding the Text: Vedānta as Philosophy and Commentary," in J.R. Timm (ed.), *Texts in Context: Traditional Hermeneutics in South Asia* (Albany: 1991), 47–68.
P. Deussen, *The System of the Vedānta*, trans. C. Johnston (New York: 1973).

N. Isayeva, *Shankara and Indian Philosophy* (Albany: 1993).
H. Nakamura, *A History of Early Vedānta Philosophy*, parts 1–2 (Delhi: 1983, 2004).
A. Rambachan, *The Advaita Worldview: God, World and Humanity* (Albany: 2006).
J.G. Suthren Hirst, *Śaṁkara's Advaita Vedānta: A Way of Teaching* (London: 2005).
S. Timalsina, *Consciousness in Indian Philosophy: The Advaita Doctrine of "Awareness Only"* (London: 2009).

Bhartṛhari

J. Bronkhorst, "Studies on Bhartṛhari 3: Bhartṛhari on *Sphoṭa* and Universals," *Asiatische Studien* 45 (1991), 5–18.
J. Bronkhorst, "The Peacock's Egg: Bhartṛhari on Language and Reality," *Philosophy East and West* 51 (2001), 474–91.
M. Chaturvedi (ed.), *Bhartṛhari: Language, Thought and Reality* (Delhi: 2009).
R. Herzberger, *Bhartṛhari and the Buddhists: An Essay in the Development of Fifth and Sixth Century Indian Thought* (Dordrecht: 1986).
J. Houben, *The Sambandha-samuddeśa and Bhartṛhari's Philosophy of Language* (Groningen: 1995).

Ayurvedic Medicine

J. Filliozat, *The Classical Doctrine of Indian Medicine* (Delhi: 1964).
J. Jolly, *Indian Medicine*, trans. C.G. Kashikar (New Delhi: 1977).
G.J. Larson, "Āyurveda and the Hindu Philosophical Systems," in T.P. Kasulis et al. (eds), *Self as Body in Asian Theory and Practice* (Albany: 1993), 103–21.
G.J. Meulenbeld, *A History of Indian Medical Literature*, 5 vols (Groningen: 1999–2002).
G.J. Meulenbeld and Dominik Wujastyk (eds), *Studies on Indian Medical History* (Delhi: 2001), 39–55.
Dagmar Wujastyk, *Well-Mannered Medicine: Medical Ethics and Etiquette in Classical Ayurveda* (Oxford: 2012).
Dominik Wujastyk, "Medicine and *Dharma*," *Journal of Indian Philosophy* 32 (2004), 831–42.
K. Zysk, *Asceticism and Healing in Ancient India: Medicine in the Buddhist Monastery* (New York: 1991).

Sāṃkhya

J. Bronkhorst, "The Qualities of Sāṃkhya," *Wiener Zeitschrift für die Kunde Südasiens* 38 (1994), 309–22.
M. Burley, *Classical Sāṃkhya and Yoga: An Indian Metaphysics of Experience* (London: 2007).
P. Chakravarti, *Origin and Development of the Sāṃkhya System of Thought* (New Delhi: 1975).
E. Frauwallner, "Die Erkenntnislehre des Klassischen Sāṃkhya-Systems," *Wiener Zeitschrift für die Kunde Süd- und Ostasiens* 2 (1958), 84–139.
G.J. Larson, *Classical Sāṃkhya: An Interpretation of its History and Meaning* (Delhi: 1979).
A. Sen Gupta, *Classical Sāṃkhya: A Critical Study* (New Delhi: 1982).
J.A.B. van Buitenen, "Studies in Sāṃkhya (I) (II) and (III)," *Journal of the American Oriental Society* 76 (1956), 153–7; 77 (1957), 15–25; and 77 (1957), 88–107.
S.G.M. Weerasinghe, *The Sāṅkhya Philosophy: A Critical Evaluation of its Origins and Development* (Delhi: 1993).

Yoga

M. Eliade, *Yoga: Immortality and Freedom* (Princeton: 1970).

M.S.A. Ferraz, "Some Remarks on the *Yogasūtra*," *Philosophy East and West* 59 (2009), 249–62.

K.A. Jacobsen (ed.), *Theory and Practice of Yoga: Essays in Honour of Gerald James Larson* (Delhi: 2008).

P. Maas, "Valid Knowledge and Belief in Classical Sāmkhya Yoga," in P. Balcerowicz (ed.), *Logic and Belief in Indian Philosophy* (Delhi: 2010), 383–92.

I. Whicher, *The Integrity of the Yoga Darśana: A Reconsideration of Classical Yoga* (Delhi: 2000).

I. Whicher and D. Carpenter (eds), *Yoga: The Indian Tradition* (London: 2003).

Nyāya

S. Bhattacharyya, *Development of Nyāya Philosophy and its Social Context* (Delhi: 2004).

M. Gangopadhyaya, *Indian Logic in its Sources* (Delhi: 1984).

P. Gokhale, *Inference and Fallacies Discussed in Ancient Indian Logic* (Delhi: 1992).

B.K. Matilal, *Nyāya-Vaiśeṣika* (Wiesbaden: 1977).

B.K. Matilal, *The Character of Logic in India* (Albany: 1998).

S. Phillips, *Epistemology in Classical India: The Knowledge Sources of the Nyāya School* (London: 2012).

K. Potter, *The Tradition of Nyāya-Vaiśeṣika up to Gaṅgeśa*, Encyclopedia of Indian Philosophies, Vol. 2 (Princeton: 1978).

E. Solomon, *Indian Dialectics*, 2 vols (Ahmedabad: 1976).

V.A. Van Bijlert, *Epistemology and Spiritual Authority: The Development of Epistemology and Logic in the Old Nyāya and the Buddhist School of Epistemology* (Vienna: 1989).

Vaiśeṣika

S. Bhaduri, *Studies in Nyāya-Vaiśeṣika Metaphysics* (Poona: 1975).

M. Gangopadhyaya, *Indian Atomism: History and Sources* (Atlantic Highlands: 1981).

W. Halbfass, *On Being and What There is: Classical Vaiśeṣika and the History of Indian Ontology* (Delhi: 1992).

U. Mishra, *The Conception of Matter According to Nyāya-Vaiśeṣika* (Allahabad: 1936).

S.H. Phillips, *Classical Indian Metaphysics* (Chicago: 1995).

A. Thakur, *Origin and Development of the Vaiśeṣika System* (Delhi: 2003).

Theories of Time

H. Coward, "Time (*Kāla*) in Bhartṛhari's *Vākypadīya*," *Journal of Indian Philosophy* 10 (1982), 277–87.

R. Gombrich, "Ancient Indian Cosmology," in C. Blacker and M. Loewe (eds), *Ancient Cosmologies* (London: 1975), 110–42.

L. González-Reimann, "Cosmic Cycles, Cosmology, and Cosmography," in K.A. Jacobsen, H. Basu, and A. Malinar (eds), *Brill's Encyclopedia of Hinduism* (Leiden: 2009), 411–28.

A. Malinar, *Time in India: Concepts and Practices* (New Delhi: 2007).

H.S. Prasad, "Time and Change in Sāṃkhya-Yoga," *Journal of Indian Philosophy* 12 (1984), 35–49.

Cārvāka

R. Bhattacharya, "Cārvāka Fragments: A New Collection," *Journal of Indian Philosophy* 30 (2002), 597–640.

R. Bhattacharya, "What the Cārvākas Originally Meant: More on the Commentators on the *Cārvākasūtra*," *Journal of Indian Philosophy* 38 (2010), 529–42.

R. Bhattacharya, *Studies on the Cārvāka/Lokāyata* (London: 2011).

D. Chattopadhyaya, *Lokāyata: A Study in Ancient Indian Materialism* (New Delhi: 1973).

D. Chattopadhyaya, *Defence of Materialism in Ancient India* (New Delhi: 1989).

J. Ganeri, "Emergentisms, Ancient and Modern," *Mind* 120 (2011), 671–703.

P. Gokhale, "The Cārvāka Theory of *Pramāṇas*: A Restatement," *Philosophy East and West* 43 (1993), 675–82.

K.K. Mittal, *Materialism in Indian Thought* (New Delhi: 1974).

D. Riepe, *The Naturalistic Tradition in Indian Thought* (Seattle: 1961).

Buddhism

S.C. Berkwitz, *South Asian Buddhism: A Survey* (London: 2010).

A.D. Carpenter, *Indian Buddhist Philosophy* (Durham: 2014).

E. Conze, *Buddhist Thought in India* (Ann Arbor: 1967).

E. Conze, *Buddhism: A Short History* (Oxford: 2008).

W. Edelglass and J.L. Garfield (eds), *Buddhist Philosophy: Essential Readings* (Oxford: 2009).

P. Harvey, *An Introduction to Buddhism: Teachings, History and Practices* (Cambridge: 2013).

A. Hirakawa, *A History of Indian Buddhism*, trans. P. Groner (Honolulu: 1990).

M. Siderits, *Studies in Buddhist Philosophy* (Oxford: 2016).

E. Steinkellner (ed.), *Studies in the Buddhist Epistemological Tradition* (Vienna: 1991).

J. Westerhoff, *The Golden Age of Indian Buddhist Philosophy* (Oxford: 2018).

P. Williams and A. Tribe, *Buddhist Thought: A Complete Introduction to the Indian Tradition* (London: 2000).

Nāgārjuna

C.W. Huntington, *The Emptiness of Emptiness: An Introduction to Early Indian Madhyamaka* (Honolulu: 1989).

R. Robinson, "Did Nāgārjuna Really Refute All Philosophical Views?" *Philosophy East and West* 22 (1972), 325–31.

T. Tillemans, "Philosophical Quietism in Nāgārjuna and Early Madhyamaka," in J. Ganeri (ed.), *The Oxford Handbook of Indian Philosophy* (Oxford: 2017), 110–32.

J. Walser, *Nāgārjuna in Context: Mahāyāna Buddhism and Early Indian Culture* (New York: 2005).

J. Westerhoff, "Nāgārjuna's Arguments on Motion Revisited," *Journal of Indian Philosophy* 36 (2008), 455–79.

J. Westerhoff, *Nāgārjuna's Madhyamaka: A Philosophical Introduction* (Oxford: 2009).

J. Westerhoff, "On the Nihilist Interpretation of Madhyamaka," *Journal of Indian Philosophy* 44 (2016), 337–76.

T.E. Wood, *Nāgārjunian Disputations* (Honolulu: 1994).

Jainism

L.A. Babb, *Understanding Jainism* (Edinburgh: 2015).
P. Balcerowicz, *Essays in Jaina Philosophy and Religion* (Delhi: 2003).
P. Balcerowicz, *Early Asceticism in India: Ājīvikism and Jainism* (London: 2016).
P. Dundas, *The Jains* (London: 2002).
K.W. Folkert, *Scripture and Community: Collected Essays on the Jains* (Atlanta: 1993).
J.L. Jaini, *Outlines of Jainism* (Cambridge: 2013).
P.S. Jaini, *The Jaina Path of Purification* (New Delhi: 1998).
B.K. Matilal, *The Central Philosophy of Jainism* (Ahmedabad: 1977).

Jaina Epistemology

P. Balcerowicz, "Do Attempts to Formalise the *Syād-vāda* Make Sense?" in P. Flügel and O. Qvarnström (eds), *Jaina Scriptures and Philosophy* (London: 2015), 181–248.
J. Cort, "'Intellectual *Ahiṃsā*' Revisited: Jain Tolerance and Intolerance of Others," *Philosophy East and West* 50 (2000), 324–47.
J. Ganeri, "Jaina Logic and the Philosophical Basis of Pluralism," *History and Philosophy of Logic* 23 (2002), 267–81.
M.-H. Gorisse, "The Taste of the Mango: A Jaina-Buddhist Controversy on Evidence," *International Journal of Jaina Studies* 11 (2015), 1–19.
J.M. Koller, "*Syādvāda* as the Epistemological Key to the Jaina Middle Way Metaphysics of *Anekāntavāda*," *Philosophy East and West* 50 (2000), 400–7.
Y. J. Padmarajiah, *Jaina Theories of Reality and Knowledge* (Bombay: 1963).
J. Soni, "Basic Jaina Epistemology," *Philosophy East and West* 50 (2000), 367–77.
F. Van Den Bossche, "Jain Relativism: An Attempt at Understanding," in R. Smet and K. Watanabe (eds), *Jain Studies in Honour of Jozef Deleu* (Tokyo: 1993), 457–74.

Vasubandhu and Yogācāra Buddhism

H. Buescher, *The Inception of Yogācāra-Vijñānavāda* (Vienna: 2008).
J. Duerlinger, *Indian Buddhist Theories of Persons: Vasubandhu's Refutation of the Theory of a Self* (London: 2003).
J.L. Garfield and J. Westerhoff (eds), *Madhyamaka and Yogācāra: Allies or Rivals?* (Oxford: 2015).
J.C. Gold, *Paving the Great Way: Vasubandhu's Unifying Buddhist Philosophy* (New York: 2015).
I. Harris, *The Continuity of Madhyamaka and Yogācāra in Indian Mahāyāna Buddhism* (Leiden: 1991).
R. King, "Early Yogācāra and its Relationship with the Madhyamaka School," *Philosophy East and West* 44 (1994), 659–83.
T.E. Wood, *Mind Only: A Philosophical and Doctrinal Analysis of Vijñānavāda* (Honolulu: 1991).

Buddhaghosa

J. Ganeri, *Attention, Not Self* (Oxford: 2017).
P. Harvey, *The Selfless Mind: Personality, Consciousness and Nirvāṇa in Early Buddhism* (London: 1995).
M. Heim, *The Forerunner of All Things: Buddhaghosa on Mind, Intention, and Agency* (New York: 2014).
Y. Karunadasa, *The Theravāda Abhidhamma: Its Inquiry into the Nature of Conditioned Reality* (Hong Kong: 2010).
R. Repetti (ed.), *Buddhist Perspectives on Free Will: Agentless Agency* (London: 2017).

Dignāga

D. Arnold, "Candrakīrti on Dignāga on *Svalakṣaṇas*," *Journal of the International Association of Buddhist Studies* 26 (2003), 139–74.

M. Hattori, *Dignāga on Perception* (Cambridge, MA: 1968).

R. Hayes, *Dignāga on the Interpretation of Signs* (Dordrecht: 1988).

S. Katsura, "The *Apoha* Theory of Dignāga," *International Journal of Buddhist Studies* 2 (1979), 493–89.

S. Katsura, "Dignāga on *Trairūpya*," *Journal of Indian and Buddhist Studies* 32 (1983), 15–21.

B. Kellner, "Self-Awareness and Infinite Regress," *Journal of Indian Philosophy* 39 (2011), 411–26.

H. Masaaki, "*Apoha* and *Pratibhā*," in M. Nagatomi et al. (eds), *Sanskrit and Indian Studies: Essays in Honour of Daniel H. H. Ingalls* (Dordrecht: 1980), 61–74.

B.K. Matilal, "Buddhist Logic and Epistemology," in B.K. Matilal and R.D. Evans (eds), *Buddhist Logic and Epistemology: Studies in the Buddhist Analysis of Inference and Language* (Dordrecht: 1982), 1–30; reprinted in his *The Character of Logic in India* (Albany: 1998).

R.K. Payne, "The Theory of Meaning in Buddhist Logicians: The Historical and Intellectual Context of *Apoha*," *Journal of Indian Philosophy* 15 (1987), 261–84.

Aesthetics of *Rasa*

A. Amaladass, *Philosophical Implications of Dhvani: Experience of Symbol Language in Indian Aesthetics* (Vienna: 1984).

A. Chakrabarti (ed.), *The Bloomsbury Research Handbook of Indian Aesthetics and the Philosophy of Art* (London: 2016).

E. Gerow, *Indian Poetics* (Wiesbaden: 1977).

K.M. Higgins, "An Alchemy of Emotions: *Rasa* and Aesthetic Breakthroughs," *Journal of Aesthetics and Art Criticism* 65 (2007), 43–54.

S. Pollock, *A Rasa Reader: Classical Indian Aesthetics* (Columbia: 2016).

S.L. Schwarz, *Rasa: Performing the Divine in India* (New York: 2004).

Tantra

M. Basu, *Fundamentals of the Philosophy of Tantras* (Calcutta: 1986).

A. Bharati, *The Tantric Tradition* (New York: 1975).

N.N. Bhattacharyya, *History of the Tantric Religion* (New Delhi: 1999).

K. Mishra, *Kashmir Śaivism: The Central Philosophy of Tantrism* (Cambridge, MA: 1993).

P.E. Muller-Ortega, *The Triadic Heart of Śiva: Kaula Tantricism of Abhinavagupta in the Non-Dual Shaivism of Kashmir* (Albany: 1989).

A. Padoux, *Vāc: The Concept of the Word in Selected Hindu Tantras*, trans. J. Gontier (Albany: 1990).

C.D. Wallis, *Tantra Illuminated: The Philosophy, History, and Practice of a Timeless Tradition* (San Rafael, CA: 2013).

R. Yelle, *Explaining Mantras: Ritual, Rhetoric, and the Dream of a Natural Language in Hindu Tantra* (London: 2003).

Influence of India on Europe

P. Abelsen, "Schopenhauer and Buddhism," *Philosophy East and West* 43 (1993), 255–78.

C.I. Beckwith, *Greek Buddha: Pyrrho's Encounter with Early Buddhism in Central Asia* (Princeton: 2015).

G.P. Conger, "Did India Influence Early Greek Philosophy?" *Philosophy East and West* 2 (1952), 102–28.

E. Flintoff, "Pyrrho and India," *Phronesis* 25 (1980), 88–108.

A. Gopnik, "Could David Hume have Known about Buddhism? Charles Francois Dolu, the Royal College of La Flèche, and the Global Jesuit Intellectual Network," *Hume Studies* 35 (2009), 5–28.

P.M. Gregorios (ed.), *Neoplatonism and Indian Philosophy* (Albany: 2002).

W. Halbfass, *India and Europe: An Essay in Philosophical Understanding* (Albany: 1988).

R.B. Harris (ed.), *Neoplatonism and Indian Philosophy* (Albany: 1982).

K. Karttunen, *India in Early Greek Literature* (Helsinki: 1989).

A.L. Macfie (ed.), *Eastern Influences on Western Philosophy: A Reader* (Edinburgh: 2003).

T. McEvilley, *The Shape of Ancient Thought* (New York: 2002).

INDEX

Numbers in **bold** refer to whole-chapter discussions.

vegetarianism 91–6, 327, 331
"Vyāsa" 74, 77, 107, 162, 167

wholes 53–4, 169, 181, 198, 200, 201–7, 239, 242, 272–5, 288, 301
Wittgenstein, Ludwig 48, 238, 242, 339, 350
women 38, 67, **70–6**, 87, 121, 341

Xenophon 326

Yājñavalkya 23–4, 27–8, 32–4, 37, 73–4, 76, 130, 132
Yoga, school of 12, 15, 89, 101, 103, 105, 108, 110, 128, 149, 168, 318, 340
Yogācāra 235, 273, 276–9, 288, 296, 308, 319, 341

Zeno of Elea 212, 245, 249
zero 240